Routledge International Handbook of Heterosexualities Studies

While a majority of people identify as "heterosexual" if asked about their sexual identity, what does that really mean? How did identifying as "straight" arise, particularly in relation to identifying as "queer," "lesbian," and "gay"? How are individuals socialized to view themselves and others as straight, even when many people are sexually fluid? How do institutions like government bodies, the educational system, and the family reinforce heterosexuality? This collection introduces the field of Critical Heterosexualities Studies and key lines of inquiry within the field.

Like Masculinity Studies and Whiteness Studies, Heterosexualities Studies critically examines the dominant category and identity group in order to illuminate the taken-for-granted assumptions that surround heterosexual identities. This critical perspective questions the idea that heterosexuality is natural, normal, and biologically driven. A recurring question throughout this Handbook is: what does it mean to say that there are multiple forms of heterosexuality? The answer is provided by cases showing how straightness varies between men and women but also across different racial groups, social classes, and one's status as trans or cisgender.

Organized around key themes of inquiry including heterosexualities across the life course, straight identities and their intersections, the power of straightness in state politics, and the changing meaning of heterosexualities in the context of sexual fluidity, this collection provides readers with an introduction to Critical Heterosexualities Studies through important theoretical statements, key historical studies, and current empirical research. Featuring both classic works and original essays written expressly for this volume, this collection provides a state-of-the-art overview of this exciting new field in sexualities studies.

James Joseph Dean is Professor of Sociology at Sonoma State University in Northern California. He is the author of *Straights: Heterosexuality in Post-Closeted Culture* (2014). Dean's work has appeared in *Contexts*, *Sexualities*, *The Sociological Quarterly*, and *Sociology Compass*, among others. His research interests include LGBTQ studies, Critical Heterosexualities Studies, and transgender studies.

Nancy L. Fischer is Associate Professor and Chair of the Sociology Department at Augsburg University in Minneapolis. Nancy is a co-editor of the anthology *Introducing the New Sexuality Studies* (along with Steven Seidman). She also edited a special issue on contemporary heterosexuality studies for the journal *The Sociological Quarterly*. She is a former chair and secretary of the American Sociological Association's Section on Sexualities. A sociologist with broad interests, she has written about incest, sexual morality, urban sustainability, and the social meaning of second-hand and vintage clothing.

Routledge International Handbooks

Routledge Handbook of Identity Studies, 2e
Edited by Anthony Elliott

Routledge International Handbook of Poverty
Edited by Bent Greve

Routledge International Handbook of New Digital Practices in Galleries, Libraries, Archives, Museums and Heritage Sites
Edited by Hannah Lewi, Wally Smith, Dirk vom Lehn and Steven Cooke

Routledge International Handbook of Human Trafficking
A Multi-Disciplinary and Applied Approach
Edited by Rochelle L. Dalla and Donna Sabella

The Routledge Handbook of Comparative Rural Policy
Edited by Matteo Vittuari, John Devlin, Marco Pagani and Thomas Johnson

Routledge International Handbook of Masculinity Studies
Edited by Lucas Gottzén, Ulf Mellström and Tamara Shefer

Routledge Handbook of European Welfare Systems, 2e
Edited by Sonja Blum, Johanna Kuhlmann and Klaus Schubert

Routledge International Handbook of Heterosexualities Studies
Edited by James Joseph Dean and Nancy L. Fischer

Routledge Handbook of Contemporary European Social Movements
Protest in Turbulent Times
Edited by Cristina Flesher Fominaya and Ramón A. Feenstra

For more information about this series, please visit: www.routledge.com/Routledge-International-Handbooks/book-series/RIHAND

Routledge International Handbook of Heterosexualities Studies

Edited by James Joseph Dean and Nancy L. Fischer

Routledge
Taylor & Francis Group
LONDON AND NEW YORK

First published 2020 by Routledge

2 Park Square, Milton Park, Abingdon, Oxon OX14 4RN
605 Third Avenue, New York, NY 10017

Routledge is an imprint of the Taylor & Francis Group, an informa business

First issued in paperback 2021

British Library Cataloguing-in-Publication Data
A catalogue record for this book is available from the British Library

Library of Congress Cataloging-in-Publication Data
Names: Dean, James Joseph, editor. | Fischer, Nancy L. (Nancy Linnay), editor.
Title: Routledge international handbook of heterosexualities studies / edited by James Joseph Dean and Nancy L. Fischer.
Description: Abingdon, Oxon ; New York, NY : Routledge, 2020. | Series: Routledge international handbooks | Includes bibliographical references and index. |
Identifiers: LCCN 2019031583 (print) | LCCN 2019031584 (ebook) | ISBN 9781138340305 (hardback) | ISBN 9780429440731 (ebook)
Subjects: LCSH: Heterosexuality. | Sex.
Classification: LCC HQ72.8 .R68 2020 (print) | LCC HQ72.8 (ebook) | DDC 306.76/4—dc23
LC record available at https://lccn.loc.gov/2019031583
LC ebook record available at https://lccn.loc.gov/2019031584

ISBN: 978-1-138-34030-5 (hbk)
ISBN: 978-1-03-217844-8 (pbk)
DOI: 10.4324/9780429440731

Typeset in Bembo
by Apex CoVantage, LLC

MIX
Paper from responsible sources
FSC www.fsc.org FSC™ C013985

Printed in the United Kingdom
by Henry Ling Limited

Contents

Tables

Contributors

Eric Anderson is Professor of Sport, Masculinities, and Sexualities at the University of Winchester, England. He holds degrees in health, psychology, and sociology and has published 17 books and 70 peer-reviewed articles. His research is regularly featured in international television, print, and digital media. He is a leading expert in several disciplines and he is the architect of Inclusive Masculinity Theory, which was generated from his research showing that decreased and still decreasing homophobia leads to a softening of heterosexual masculinities. This permits young straight men to kiss, cuddle, and maintain bromances with other males, while also leading to semi-sexual behaviors between men and the increased recognition of bisexuality.

Tristan Bridges is Assistant Professor of Sociology at the University of California, Santa Barbara. His research and teaching interests surround politics and performances of masculinities. Having undertaken multiple ethnographic projects with bodybuilders, fathers' rights activists, pro-feminist men, bar regulars, and more, his work speaks to transformations in contemporary expressions of masculinity. He has published in *Gender & Society, Body & Society* in addition to other venues.

Joshua R. Brown is Associate Professor of German and Linguistics at the University of Wisconsin, Eau Claire.

Judith Butler is Maxine Elliot Professor in the Department of Comparative Literature and the Program of Critical Theory at the University of California, Berkeley. She is the author of several books: *Gender Trouble: Feminism and the Subversion of Identity* (1990), *Bodies That Matter: On the Discursive Limits of "Sex"* (1993), *The Psychic Life of Power: Theories in Subjection* (1997), *Excitable Speech* (1997), *Antigone's Claim: Kinship Between Life and Death* (2000), *Precarious Life: Powers of Violence and Mourning* (2004), and *Undoing Gender* (2004). Her books have been translated into more than 20 languages.

Margot Canaday is Associate Professor of History at Princeton University. Her first book, *The Straight State: Sexuality and Citizenship in Twentieth Century America* (Princeton, 2009), won the Organization of American Historians' Ellis Hawley Prize, the American Political Science Association's Gladys M. Kammerer Award (co-winner), the American Studies Association's Lora Romero Prize, the American Society for Legal History's Cromwell Book Prize, the Committee on LGBT History's John Boswell Prize, and the Lambda Literary Award for LGBT Studies.

Laura M. Carpenter is Associate Professor of Sociology at Vanderbilt University and author of *Virginity Lost: An Intimate Portrait of First Sexual Experiences.*

Héctor Carrillo is Professor of Sociology and Gender and Sexuality Studies at Northwestern University. He is the author of two books: *The Night is Young: Sexuality in Mexico in the Time of AIDS* (University of Chicago Press, 2002) and *Pathways of Desire: The Sexual Migration of Mexican Gay Men* (University of Chicago Press, 2017). His current research investigates the sexualities of straight-identified men who are sexually interested in both women and men, as part of a larger project on the paradoxes of sexual identity as a social construction.

Patricia Hill Collins is Professor of Sociology at the University of Maryland and a social theorist whose research and scholarship have examined issues of race, gender, social class, sexuality, and/or nation. Her first book, *Black Feminist Thought: Knowledge, Consciousness, and the Politics of Empowerment* (Routledge), published in 1990, with a revised tenth anniversary edition published in 2000, won the Jessie Bernard Award of the American Sociological Association (ASA) for significant scholarship in gender, and the C. Wright Mills Award of the Society for the Study of Social Problems. Her second book, *Race, Class, and Gender: An Anthology* (8th edition, 2013), edited with Margaret Andersen, is widely used in undergraduate classrooms in over 200 colleges and universities. *Black Sexual Politics: African Americans, Gender, and the New Racism* (Routledge, 2004) received the ASA's 2007 Distinguished Publication Award.

Carissa M. Froyum is an associate professor of sociology at the University of Northern Iowa. She is co-editor of *Inside Social Life* (Oxford) and *Creating and Contesting Inequalities* (Oxford) and former deputy editor of *The Journal of Contemporary Ethnography*. Her work on how identities and emotions reproduce inequality appears in *Qualitative Sociology*, *Ethnic and Racial Studies*, *Sociological Studies of Children and Youth*, and *Symbolic Interaction*.

Patrick R. Grzanka, PhD, is Associate Professor of Psychology and Chair of the Interdisciplinary Program in Women, Gender, and Sexuality at the University of Tennessee. His research on complex inequalities at the nexus of race, gender, and sexualities has been funded by the National Science Foundation and published in a wide range of academic journals, including *Journal of Counseling Psychology*, *Sexualities*, *WSQ: Women's Studies Quarterly*, *Sexuality Research and Social Policy*, and *American Journal of Bioethics*. He is the 2018 recipient of the Michele Alexander Early Career Award from the Society for the Psychological Study of Social Issues. His first book, *Intersectionality: Foundations and Frontiers* (Routledge, 2019) is now in its second edition, and he is working on a new book (under contract with Cambridge University Press) that traces scientific, legal, and cultural debates about the etiology of sexuality orientation and their implications for civil rights and social justice.

Melanie Heath is an associate professor in the Department of Sociology at McMaster University. Her teaching and research interests include gender, sexualities, family, politics, culture, and the law. She is the author of *One Marriage Under God* (New York University Press, 2012).

Jenny Hockey is Emeritus Professor of Sociology at Sheffield University, UK. Her published work on gender includes articles in *Sociological Review*, *Gender Place and Culture*, *Sociological Research Online*, *Journal of Gender Studies*, and *Gender, Work and Organisation*. She is currently publishing work on masculinities, grounded in an ESRC-funded research project on masculinities in transition.

Amanda Hoffman received a Master's degree in Sexuality Studies from San Francisco State University where she studied the experiences of heterosexual-identified men seeking sex with men. Following graduation, she became the project director for Project Teal.

Chrys Ingraham is Professor of Sociology at SUNY Purchase. She is an active scholar in areas of social inequality – gender, race, class, accessibility – social organizations, conflict, and social change. Her most notable accomplishments are in the areas of critical heterosexual studies – weddings – and materialist feminism. Her key contribution is in feminist theory with concepts such as the heterosexual imaginary and heterogender and her groundbreaking study, *White Weddings: Romancing Heterosexuality in Popular Culture*. Her most recent research focuses on the recent emergence of consciousness communities as a new effort toward social change.

Rachel Kalish is Visiting Assistant Professor at SUNY Old Westbury, USA.

Emily W. Kane is Professor of Sociology at Bates College. She is the author of two books, one on how parents reproduce and resist gendered childhoods (*The Gender Trap*, published in 2012 by NYU Press) and the other a textbook on gender and sexuality in childhood (*Rethinking Gender and Sexuality in Childhood*, published in 2013 by Continuum Publishing).

Jonathan Ned Katz is an independent scholar, historian, and political activist who focuses on lesbian, gay, bisexual, transgender, and heterosexual American history. He is the author of many books, including *Gay American History* and *Love Stories: Sex Between Men Before Homosexuality*.

Michael Kimmel is the SUNY Distinguished Professor of Sociology and Gender Studies at Stony Brook University. His books include *Changing Men* (1987), *Men Confront Pornography* (1990), *Men's Lives* (9th edition, 2012), *Against the Tide: Profeminist Men in the United States, 1776–1990* (1992), *The Politics of Manhood* (1996), *Manhood: A Cultural History* (1996), and *The Gendered Society* (5th edition, 2013), and the best-seller *Guyland* (2008).

Celia Kitzinger is Honorary Professor in the School of Law and Politics at Cardiff University, Wales.

Mark McCormack, PhD, is a sociologist at Durham University. His research examines how social trends of gender and sexuality influence the sexual lives and gendered behaviors of young people in the United Kingdom and United States. He has published widely on these topics, including in *Archives of Sexual Behavior*, *British Journal of Sociology*, and *Sociology*. His first book, *The Declining Significance of Homophobia*, is published with Oxford University Press, and *The Changing Dynamics of Bisexual Men's Lives* is published with Springer.

Karin A. Martin is Professor of Sociology at the University of Michigan, Ann Arbor. She received her PhD at the University of California, Berkeley. She conducts research on the intersections of gender, sexuality, and childhood and adolescence. She is the author of *Puberty, Sexuality, and the Self: Boys and Girls at Adolescence* (Routledge, 1996).

Angela Meah is a Research Associate at Sheffield University, UK. Her research interests include families, gender, agency, feminist epistemologies, and the co-construction of knowledge.

Marcia Oliver is Associate Professor of Law and Society at Wilfrid Laurier University, Canada.

Kendall Ota is a graduate student in the Sociology Department at the University of California, Santa Barbara.

C.J. Pascoe researches young people, gender, sexuality, masculinity, and new media. Her book *Dude, You're a Fag: Masculinity and Sexuality in High School* won the American Educational Research Association's Book of the Year award in 2008. This book examines the relationship of masculinity, sexuality, and homophobia among high school students. Her articles have appeared in *Sexualities, Body & Society, QED: A Journal in Gay and Lesbian Worldmaking*, and *American Behavioral Scientist.* At present, she is working on a book for the University of California Press entitled *Just a Teenager in Love: Gender, Romance and New Media* that examines young people's cultures of love and romance. She currently teaches in the department of sociology at the University of Oregon.

Janelle M. Pham is Assistant Professor of Sociology at Oglethorpe University.

Emma Renold is Professor in Childhood Studies at the School of Social Sciences, Cardiff University, Wales, and the author of *Girls, Boys and Junior Sexualities* (Routledge, 2005) and *Children, Sexuality and the Sexualisation of Culture* (Palgrave, 2015).

Adrienne Cecile Rich (1929–2012) was for decades among the most influential writers of the feminist movement and one of the best-known American public intellectuals. She wrote two dozen volumes of poetry and more than a half-dozen of prose. Her constellation of honors includes two National Book Awards, a MacArthur Foundation "genius" grant, and a Medal for Distinguished Contribution to American Letters by the National Book Foundation. Rich's volumes of poetry include *The Dream of a Common Language, A Wild Patience Has Taken Me This Far, An Atlas of the Difficult World, The School Among the Ruins*, and *Telephone Ringing in the Labyrinth.* Her prose includes the essay collections *On Lies, Secrets, and Silence*; *Blood, Bread, and Poetry*; an influential essay, "Compulsory Heterosexuality and Lesbian Existence," and the nonfiction book *Of Woman Born*, which examines the institution of motherhood as a socio-historic construct. In 2010, she was honored with The Griffin Trust for Excellence in Poetry's Lifetime Recognition Award.

Victoria Robinson is Senior Lecturer in Sociology at the University of Sheffield, UK. She is co-editor, with Diane Richardson, of *Introducing Gender and Women's Studies: Feminist Theory and Practice* and author of *Everyday Masculinities and Extreme Sport: Male Identity and Rock Climbing.*

Leila J. Rupp is Distinguished Professor of Feminist Studies and Associate Dean of Social Sciences at the University of California, Santa Barbara. Rupp's books include *Sapphistries: A Global History of Love Between Women* (2009); *Drag Queens at the 801 Cabaret* (2003), co-authored with Verta Taylor; *A Desired Past: A Short History of Same-Sex Sexuality in America* (1999); *Worlds of Women: The Making of an International Women's Movement* (1997); *Survival in the Doldrums: The American Women's Rights Movement, 1945 to the 1960s* (1987), with Verta Taylor; and *Mobilizing Women for War: German and American Propaganda, 1939–1945* (1978).

Kristen Schilt is Associate Professor of Sociology and Director of the Center for the Study of Gender and Sexuality at the University of Chicago. Her research interests center on sociology of gender and sexualities, the sociology of culture, and the sociology of work and occupations. A central focus of her work is finding new ways to make visible the taken-for-granted cultural assumptions about gender and sexuality that serve to naturalize and reproduce social inequality. She recently published *Other, Please Specify: Queer Methods in Sociology* (University of California Press, 2018).

Steven Seidman has written widely in the areas of gender, sexuality, queer studies, and American culture. His books include *Romantic Longings: Love in America 1830–1980*, *Embattled Eros: Sexual Politics and Ethics in Contemporary America*, and *Beyond the Closet: The Transformation of Gay and Lesbian Life*. He is currently a psychoanalyst in private practice in New York City, USA.

Tony Silva is a postdoctoral fellow at Northwestern University. His research and teaching interests include inequality, gender, sexuality, rural sociology, qualitative and quantitative methods, public health, and race/ethnicity. His published papers appear in *Social Forces*, *Sociological Perspectives*, *Sexuality Research and Social Policy*, *Gender & Society*, and *Sexualities*.

Verta Taylor is Professor of Sociology and Affiliated Professor of Feminist Studies. Her research focuses on social movements, gender, and sexuality. Her books include *Drag Queens at the 801 Cabaret* (with Leila J. Rupp), winner of the 2005 outstanding book award from the American Sociological Association's (ASA) Sex and Gender section, and *Survival in the Doldrums: The American Women's Rights Movement, 1945 to the 1960s* (with Leila J. Rupp) that received an outstanding book award from the Collective Behavior and Social Movements section of the American Sociological Association.

Laurel Westbrook is Associate Professor of Sociology at Grand Valley State University. Westbrook's research and teaching interests include gender, sexuality, violence, transgender studies, social movements, the media, methods, and poststructuralist theory. Westbrook's work has been published in *Contexts*, *Gender & Society*, and *Socius*, among others.

Introduction

Thinking straightness

An introduction to Critical Heterosexualities Studies

James Joseph Dean and Nancy L. Fischer

This is an interesting cultural moment in which to critically examine heterosexuality. Picture two different scenes that one might encounter in a given day in contemporary western societies. The first scene is set in a university classroom, where one mixed race student who uses they/them pronouns is talking about what it means to identify as pansexual and refers to their current partner as their "girlfriend." In the same small-group discussion is another white student who uses she/her pronouns, identifies as transgender, enacts a rather masculine self-presentation and talks about her "boyfriend" and what they will do this weekend. A few hours later in a hotel bar, a second scene unfolds between three straight, white, middle-class men in their early 30s who are catching up over drinks. Two of them are single, while the third talks about how his love life has changed since his girlfriend became his wife, and the couple now has two small children. He wistfully recalls the days when his partnership was filled with more sexual desire, which has diminished since the birth of their children. His tone has the air of inevitability about the trajectory his life has taken, from the fun sexy times with his girlfriend to the adult responsibility of married couplehood with two children.

Conventional heterosexual nuclear families comprising two married biological parents and their children – like that of the wistful father in the bar – are not the statistical family norm in America, even if they are still the culturally sanctioned ideal family (Essig 2019; Stacey 2012). Nostalgic images of conventional nuclear heterosexual families have been increasingly challenged by today's shifting gender and techno-social dynamics. We are witnessing changing norms in heterosexual arrangements like online dating and hooking up (Kalish and Kimmel 2011; Wade 2018), the increase in single-person households (Klinenberg 2014), and the decoupling of gender identity from sexual identity. Straightness and its identity forms are bending into new arrangements, identity conceptions, and more flexible social statuses that build upon, morph, and attempt to supplant older, traditional patriarchal gender-normative arrangements. In return, those who hold traditional patriarchal beliefs about gender and heterosexuality continue to try to use their positions of political and institutional power to make heterosexuality "compulsory" and try to erase and/or demean new gender and sexual identities and relationships. At this cultural moment of both progressive change and reactionary politics, heterosexual identities, practices, and institutions are ripe for social analyses, theoretical explanations, and historical contextualization.

Critical Sexuality Studies

Heterosexualities Studies is a subfield of a larger critical turn in sexualities scholarship known as Critical Sexuality Studies (Plummer 2012), or as Critical Gender/Sexuality Studies (Beasley and Brook 2014). The "Critical" in Critical Sexuality Studies denotes the field's *critique* of commonly held beliefs that sexuality (i.e. *heterosexuality*) is natural and that our sexual desires, sexual conduct and practices, and sexual identities emanate from biological sources in some universal, ahistorical way (Plummer 2012). Feminists refer to this set of essentialist assumptions that biological sex = gender identity = heterosexual identity as the Sex/Gender/Sexuality System (Westbrook 2016). Scholars who contribute to Critical Sexuality Studies instead argue that sexuality develops from the specific social and cultural contexts in which we find ourselves (Simon and Gagnon 1974).

Critical Sexuality Studies is interdisciplinary and has a variety of other subfields under its umbrella including Lesbian, Gay and Bisexual Studies, Queer Studies, Black Queer Studies, Transgender Studies, Women's Studies, and Masculinity Studies. Most critical inquiries into gender, sexuality, and society focus on the social dynamics that create and maintain oppression toward a marginalized group and ask questions such as "What does it mean to be queer in a heteronormative world?" "What does it mean to be transgender in a cisgender world, or to identify as a woman in a man's world?"

In contrast, Heterosexualities Studies, like Masculinity Studies, turns its primary gaze onto the *dominant* category of heterosexuality as both an institution and an identity, the social practices that maintain heterosexual dominance, the patterns of behavior that typically characterize heterosexuality, as well as the variety of ways of expressing heterosexuality. By making heterosexualities visible, the field exposes heterosexualities as a particular standpoint, a specific set of interests, and a form of privilege that is often unmarked, unseen, taken-for-granted, and mundane.

Like its umbrella field Critical Sexuality Studies, Critical Heterosexualities Studies is an interdisciplinary subfield that traverses and draws from the social sciences, the humanities and arts, and the physical and life sciences. Critical Heterosexualities Studies has important contributions to make to, and implications for, the interdisciplinary field of Critical Sexualities Studies, as well as for a range of disciplinary subject areas. In the vein of other interdisciplinary fields like Queer or Masculinities Studies, Critical Heterosexualities Studies provides accounts of the social differences that create hierarchies between heterosexualities and homosexualities as well as the hierarchies within heterosexualities.

Challenging essentialism: the social construction of heterosexualities

Heterosexualities Studies involves viewing heterosexuality as socially constructed (rather than natural) and examines the ways that heterosexuality is used to invoke and reinforce particular gendered, sexual power relations between men and women, and between heterosexuals and queer folk (Fischer 2013). The social construction of heterosexualities means analytically focusing on how heterosexuality is a principle of social organization in society and culture, based on a logic of difference.

Historically speaking, the terms "heterosexual" and "homosexual" were invented in 1868, according to the *Oxford English Dictionary Supplement*, though the initial meaning of heterosexual first described a form of perversion rather than the presumed norm (Katz 1996). Katz (1996, p. 10) notes that the "terms heterosexual and homosexual apparently came into common use only in the first quarter of this [twentieth] century and before that time, if words are clues to concepts, people did not conceive of a social universe polarized into heterosexuals and homosexuals." Over time, European sexologists, physicians, and other scientists sought to distinguish homosexuality and homosexuals from a changing group that they referred to as "normal," "unafflicted," and, eventually, "heterosexual" (Terry 1999). Indeed, the notion of a sexual *identity* was new to American culture in the nineteenth century, when people understood themselves through a social organization based on a gender principle primarily arranged through the institutions of marriage and family. In the early twentieth century, sexual *identity* was a new form of selfhood, where erotic life became a defining part of one's self and a new form of difference distinguishing one from others (Duggan 2000). "Heterosexual identity" names an individual's sense of self and the collective grouping he or she identifies with on its basis.

In this history, we can see how the social construction of heterosexual identities developed through its relationship to homosexual identities. Thus, heterosexuality was and is defined against homosexuality. However, by being defined against homosexuality, heterosexuality is dependent upon the existence of homosexuality for its meaning (Fuss 1991). The birth of the heterosexual/homosexual binary in western culture, then, became imbricated with other key categories of modern western culture, such as disclosure/secrecy, public/private, masculine/feminine, majority/minority, and natural/artificial (Sedgwick 1990).

Critical Heterosexualities Studies challenges the essentialist, taken-for-granted assumption that heterosexuality is a natural, biological, or even a genetic phenomenon. Although we do not deny the biological aspects of heterosexuality, we contest the idea that the social aspects of heterosexuality are built upon an immutable, objective biological foundation. We view the biological and social as intertwined and mutually shaping one another. For example, medical science describes reproduction as akin to a complicated social process that gives social meanings to seemingly every aspect of its development from the gestation of sperm and egg to pregnancy, breastfeeding, and so on (Almeling 2011; Martin 1991; Stearns 2013). Likewise, in terms of heterosexuality as an identity, *heterosexual identity* is not reducible to the reproduction of the human species; nor is it simply an extension of one's sexed body, whether understood as based on genitalia, chromosomes, or hormonal differences. Heterosexual identity is also not reducible to one's gender identity. In other words, embodying gender-conforming behaviors and thus being viewed as a "masculine" man or a "feminine" woman does not make one heterosexual. This is a culturally dominant ideology that falsely equates the embodiment of traditional gender displays of women and men with heterosexuality. And, finally, heterosexual identity is not reducible to sexual intercourse between a man and a woman, as what counts as "sex" is ambiguous in the first place (Carpenter 2001; Christina 1992); and moreover, sexual *behaviors* do not necessarily include the adoption of a specific *identity*.

The bodies and acts associated with heterosexuality and heterosexual identities are routinely socially transformed into norms, values, socialization practices, gender dynamics, identities, relationships, legal statuses, institutional rules and practices, means of social organization, and culture. Through these social transformations, heterosexuality is made to *seem* natural and inevitable, experienced by many individuals as a trajectory to adulthood and social respectability, as the scene of the father in the bar seems to convey: "First comes love, then comes marriage, then comes a baby in a baby carriage."

Studying heterosexualities

In academic discussions, the term "heterosexuality" encompasses a variety of meanings. Depending on the author, heterosexuality "can denote a mode of erotic attraction, and/or a cultural norm, and/or an institution involving wider social relations between women and men, and/or a set of practices" (Jackson and Scott 2010, p. 82). Heterosexualities generally, but not necessarily, align with sexual behaviors and desires oriented to another – as opposed to the same – gender.

In this volume, we view heterosexuality and heteronormativity as major principles of social organization across local contexts, societies, and the global world. The field of Critical Heterosexualities treks the slippery slopes between binary pairings: straight versus queer, straight *behavior* versus straight *identity*, and unconscious versus conscious enactments of straightness. Heterosexualities Studies questions the hierarchical boundaries drawn between heterosexuals and non-heterosexuals including those who identify as queer, gay, lesbian, bisexual, sexually fluid, pansexual, demi-sexual, asexual, and so on. In uncovering these analytical framings, the field turns a critical eye to the normative status, unearned privilege, and assumed dynamics that enforce, animate, and obfuscate the operation of heterosexualities.

Heteronormativity subordinates queer identities, and it also normalizes and circumscribes the recognition of the multiple forms of heterosexualities and the hierarchies that exist between them. Heteronormativity produces differences, conflicts, and hierarchies among heterosexualities at the level of identity, culture, and politics. A heteronormative model of identity is linked to monogamy and procreation within couple relations and views sexuality as a private matter. It also occupies a hierarchical position over non-monogamous, non-married, non-procreative, non-white, and non-private sexual practices in the lives of these *other* straight men and women (as well as queer folk), since they fail to meet the normative ideal of heterosexuality (Richardson 1996; Rubin 2011; Seidman 2009). Put another way, cisgender, white, middle- and upper-class, married couples are far more privileged through social policies and in cultural representations than heterosexuals whose gender identity, race or ethnicity, class standing, and marital status are just outside of "the charmed circle" that denotes western sexual ideals (Essig 2019; Rubin 2011). In this sense, scholars should think of "normative heterosexualities" in the plural, recognizing the multiplicity of hierarchies among heterosexualities in its normative construction.

The importance of Critical Heterosexualities Studies as an emerging subfield is paradoxically both obvious and subtle. On the obvious side, it is important to study heterosexuality because it continues to be normative, bolstered by state and institutional supports. The state's certification of a heterosexual partnership through marriage laws is the most obvious example of state support for heterosexuality (Ingraham 2008). Even with the incorporation of marriage equality for queer partners, states in the USA still communicate their implicit approval for heterosexual couples over queer ones (Heath 2012). According to Margot Canaday (2009), US immigration policy, welfare policy, and military policy were all explicitly implemented in ways that made heterosexual relationships key to citizenship, while legally regulating those who were suspected of harboring same-sex attractions. Similarly, the Ugandan state's policies have been influenced by US Christian groups to pass laws which potentially punish homosexuality with death and institute a belief system that erases pre-colonial Ugandan sexual mores, which were not hostile to same-sex behavior (Oliver 2016). A similar line of research focuses on how heterosexuality was part of empire-building projects. For example, Patil (2018) theorizes how Judith Butler's concept of the heterosexual matrix can be historicized within colonial and imperial histories. Stoler (2002) documented the role of heterosexual sex and intimate relations with native Indonesian women who were concubines for Dutch settler men in their colonization of the archipelago during the nineteenth and twentieth centuries. Other work on post-colonial India by Puri (1999) used in-depth interviews with middle- and upper-class Indian women, who were both single and married, to explore how they incorporated English to talk about their heterosexual sexual desires, justify premarital sex, and use pornography with their partners. These English terms, however, took on different meanings in their usage and mixing with Hindi.

On the subtle side, heterosexualities are choices, psychological compromise formations, social identities and arrangements subject to historical change, contextual variation, and social location. For example, Eva Illouz (2013) describes how, in the early 1800s, decisions about whom to marry were once based on a suitor's good "character" and record of keeping promises, while beauty and sexual desirability were considered superficial reasons for partner selection. Today, good looks, sexual attractiveness, and hopes for a lifelong exciting sexual life are often viewed as crucial for prospective heterosexual long-term partners (Green 2013; Illouz 2013).

Heterosexualities and gender identities

Critical Heterosexualities Studies takes the dynamics of sexual-gender normativity, heteronormativity, and the hetero/homo binary as the foci of study and points of analytical departure. A key area of scholarship within the field examines how the construct of heterosexuality underpins notions of "opposite" sexes, gender differences, the dominant positions of men, the subordinate positions of women, and the marginalization of transgender and other non-conforming gender identities (Butler 1990). Much of the empirical work on the links between heterosexuality and gender dynamics focus on child socialization. While many straight parents might regard heterosexuality as a path of *natural* sexual development, they engage in a great deal of socialization to try to assure that their children will grow up to be heterosexual and follow traditional gender roles (Kane 2012; Kitzinger 2005; Martin 2009). Parents may communicate their hetero expectations by joking with children about their future marriages and children, or about them being attracted to a differently-gendered child (Kane 2012; Martin 2009). Children get the message and from a young age may talk about having a boyfriend or girlfriend and convey distinct ideas of what it means to be a girl versus a boy that reflect heteronormative assumptions (Renold 2000). Moreover, the media as a social institution is heavily invested in pushing what Laurie Essig (2019) refers to as "Love, Inc.," an ideology of white heterosexual romance, white weddings, and romance-based capitalist consumerism that drive us to distraction. Chrys Ingraham (2008) refers to this happily-ever-after set of ideals associated with heterosexual romance and weddings as the "heterosexual imaginery."

Thus, we examine heterosexuality in relationship to gender, specifically in terms of heterosexual femininities and heterosexual masculinities. By *heterosexual femininities* and *heterosexual masculinities*, we mean configurations of sexual-gender practices and discourses that refer to the identity categories "heterosexuals," "women," and "men" and are organized in relation to the structures of sexual and gender orders (Connell and Messerschmidt 2005). There are also queer and transgender heterosexualities, which this collection acknowledges, though our emphasis here is on the gender-sexual normative variations. We focus upon heteronormative gender identities in order to describe and analyze the major power hierarchy that structures heterosexual gendered lives and marginalizes queer lives, social arrangements, and discourses.

Heterosexual femininities

A key area of scholarship within the field examines how the construction of heterosexual femininities are situated within power relations that intersect with other identity statuses such as race and class. But instead of establishing hierarchies among groups of heterosexual women, these power relations enact forms of marginalization that malign, stigmatize, and pollute other non-normative heterosexual femininities. The particular ways that gender differences are constructed among heterosexual women depend upon both race and class. For example, some straight, white, middle- and upper-class women perform femininity in non-threatening ways such as being the willing helpmates of men, and they are generally associated with sexual respectability. Straight working-class women, in contrast, may instead be more sexually vulnerable to sexual coercion and assault because their sexual respectability is often suspect (Armstrong and Hamilton 2015; Tolman 2009). In terms of race, African American women are often stereotyped as hypersexual, outspoken, and, therefore, less "feminine" and in need of men's protection (Collins 2006). Asian and Asian American women are characterized as being particularly submissive and hyperfeminine (Nemoto 2009), while performing heterosexual femininity for Latinx women often emphasizes filial piety and varies by ethnic group within this pan-ethnic category (Garcia 2012).

The idea of women and men as "opposite sexes" who must live out very different gender dynamics – with men's proper location in the public sphere of labor outside the home and women's proper location as reigning over the domestic sphere of housework and childcare – emerged during the Industrial Revolution. Middle- and upper-class white families who were able to manage raising a family on just one adult or "breadwinner" salary (for working-class families and for families of color, every single family member including children may have worked in early industrial factories or in domestic service) embodied this idealized norm. The *first-wave* feminists from this time period, who were mostly middle- and upper-class white women, fought a violent battle to win women's suffrage. They sometimes questioned heterosexual institutions like marriage and monogamy, and even explored social experiments like free love societies (D'Emilio and Freedman 2012), but they did not necessarily question the institution of heterosexuality itself.

Second-wave feminists like Monique Wittig, Catherine MacKinnon, and Adrienne Rich, however, did question heterosexuality as both a discourse and an institution. Wittig (1992) theorized how heterosexuality discursively operates to constitute the categories "women" and "men." She contended that from a semiotic standpoint the very category "woman" is a heterosexual construct which derives its meaning in relation to the category "man," and that what we think of as "women" are really *heterosexual* women. Heterosexuality discourses that are embedded in television, porn, advertising, literature, and other cultural products clearly position women as subordinate to men (Wittig 1992). Catherine MacKinnon (1997) similarly argued that patriarchal culture is so infused with a version of eroticism that reflects the standpoint of the heterosexual male gaze that it is impossible for women to authentically desire or consent to heterosexual intercourse.

Adrienne Rich (1994 [1980]) perhaps most famously theorized the power of heterosexuality as a political institution that women had no choice but to participate in for their own survival. "Women have married," Rich (1994 [1980], p. 24) explains,

> because it was necessary, in order to survive economically, in order to have children who would not suffer economic deprivation or social ostracism, in order to remain respectable, in order to do what was expected of women . . . because heterosexual romance has been represented as the great female adventure, duty, and fulfillment.

Rich's conception of compulsory heterosexuality highlights how male domination works to make heterosexuality obligatory for women in different ways than for men, due to women's different structural positions in social institutions, particularly in normative roles as wives in marriages and mothers in families. Rich maintains that the norms, relations, and institutions that organize women's lives as wives and mothers, as well their historical economic dependence on husbands and fathers, enforce the norm of heterosexuality on women in qualitatively distinct ways compared to men. Compulsory heterosexuality makes salient the connections between systems of masculine and heterosexual domination and the oppressive processes that women are forced into, and subordinated through, that help make sense of how women systematically face unwanted sexual advances from men at work, on the street, or even in their own homes as wives. Moreover, heterosexuality is a structural norm and system of power that creates hierarchies that differentially value, reward, and enfranchise heterosexuals over non-heterosexuals. Rich elucidates how the gender and sexual orders work together in support of compulsory heterosexuality.

In summary, second-wave feminist scholars tended to describe heterosexual femininity as passive, dependent, dominated, and sexually objectified. They described heterosexuality as hegemonically operating as a default; the heterosexual woman lacks agency and is a "cultural dupe" who has been socialized within hetero-patriarchy to want what is wanted of her. For a heterosexual woman to be "sexual" she must be titillating for the male gaze. She must find arousal in what pleases straight men rather than discover and cultivate her own desires and pleasures. Straight women in a patriarchal culture are instrumental for men's sexual pleasure, yet necessary for the reproduction of children, the unpaid labor of raising children, and caring for the home. Her role is to selflessly serve men and her children. Critics of second-wave feminist theorists' characterizations of straight women remarked that such accounts were totalizing and gave no acknowledgment of straight women's pleasure, happiness, sense of agency, or resistance to hetero-patriarchal norms (Jackson 1999; Richardson 1996; Smart 1996; Wilkinson and Kitzinger 1993).

Scholars have since taken a more nuanced approach to explaining straight women's challenges in finding sexual pleasure, personal happiness, and fulfillment. For example, Tolman (2009) found that most of the teen girls she interviewed experienced themselves as sexual *objects*, without a sense of their own sexual desire and agency, rather than as sexual *subjects*, an observation that backs up the second-wave feminist characterizations of straight women. And yet in the same study she also interviewed girls who had developed a confident sense of themselves as sexual beings who had a right to have their own desires and needs fulfilled.

In a similar vein, Armstrong, England, and Fogarty (2012) found an "orgasm gap" between men and women participating in college campus "hook-up culture," where women were unlikely to experience orgasm in these brief sexual encounters. In contrast to hook-ups, they found that straight women were more likely to experience sexual enjoyment and orgasm in "relationship sex" with men they knew well. Similarly, Gavey, McPhillips, and Braun (1999) observed that despite the risks associated with sexual intercourse, straight women valued the act of intercourse because heterosexuality discourse makes intercourse the defining feature of straight sexual activity, an act that is seen as "natural," "normal," and "intimate," as well as "easy and non-intimate," which suggests that straight women engage in intercourse for multiple reasons other than pure sexual pleasure. The emphasis on the "coital imperative" of intercourse as the defining sexual activity of straight relationships continues across the life course. Loe (2006) and Sandberg (2016) both discuss how post-menopausal women look forward to an expanded sexual repertoire with their male partners to include more foreplay and cuddling as straight partners age, only to find that the use of the drug Viagra serves to re-center sexual intimacy on intercourse. Yet, even for older generations, straight women experience more of a sense of agency than second-wave feminists theorized. Hockey, Meah, and Robinson (2010) examined how an older woman navigated institutionalized heterosexuality throughout her lifetime, experiencing both pleasure and challenges, as well as moments of conformity and resistance. Nonetheless, according to psychologist Paul Dolan straight women in long-term relationships report less lifetime happiness (and shorter life expectancy) than their counterparts who remained single; in fact, single women who have never married or who have no children were the happiest subgroup in a US longitudinal study (Cain 2019).

In navigating institutionalized heterosexuality, straight women may be rewarded for doing gender in ways that reinforce their subordinate position in a patriarchal society, for example by focusing their efforts on being sexually appealing to men rather than developing an agentic sense of their own sexual selfhood. The compromises heterosexual women forge in the name of emotional, financial, and psychological security are what Deniz Kandiyoti (1988) refers to as "patriarchal bargains." In a sense, patriarchal bargains are a key component of normative straight femininity. Sociologist Raewyn Connell (1987) argues that women enact "emphasized femininity" by generally being supplicants to men, particularly in the workplace, as well as by establishing their roles as wives and mothers as central to their sense of selves. Emphasized femininity, she states (1987, p. 187), is "the display of sociability rather than technical competence, fragility in mating scenes, compliance with men's desire for titillation and ego-stroking in office relationships, acceptance of marriage and childcare as a response to labor-market discrimination against women." Similarly, sociologist Mimi Schippers refers to this type of straight feminine performance as "hegemonic femininity." She states (2007, p. 94) that hegemonic femininity "consists of the characteristics defined as womanly that establish and legitimate a hierarchical and complementary relationship to hegemonic masculinity, and that, by doing so guarantee the dominant position of men and the subordination of women."

If the predominant form of normative hetero-femininity represents subtly reinforcing women's second-class citizen status by compromising with the hetero-patriarchal social structure, what about those heterosexual women who resist normative femininity, while still defining themselves as heterosexual?

Some straight women experiment with same-gender relationships and still call themselves heterosexual, or deploy new terms like "heteroflexible." The idea that heterosexuality is compulsory – that one must identify as 100 percent straight – is changing (Seidman 2009). Morgan and Thompson (2011) found in a survey of straight women that 67 percent had at some time questioned their heterosexual orientation. However, Diamond (2005) notes that in film and other media, terms like "heteroflexible" and same-gender sexual experimentation are represented in ways that ultimately reinforce the centrality of heterosexuality through characters that experiment with same-gender intimacy only to decide in the end that they are "authentically" heterosexual.

Sexual fluidity among women across their life course – as well as taking place in their lives during a specific context or event, such as in college or through participation in feminist conscious-raising groups (Diamond 2009; Rupp 2009; Stein 1997) – has been a prominent theme in Critical Sexualities Studies. Diamond's (2009) research on sexual fluidity amongst "lesbian" women showed that sexual identities can change over a lifetime and shift from "lesbian" or "queer" to "straight" to "bisexual" or "sexually fluid" (the women she interviewed thought of themselves as lesbian at the start of the study). Rupp, Taylor, and Pham (Chapter 22 of this volume) found that on a large college campus, the phenomenon of "straight girls kissing" at parties is often performed by heterosexual women for the male gaze, although such acts may also lead to broader explorations with same-gender sexual behavior and identities. Rupp, Taylor, and Pham (Chapter 22) also document how young women may embrace queer and sexually fluid identities to avoid reinforcing transphobia. Likewise, amongst student populations, there is an increase of people who were designated female at birth (DFAB) identifying with non-binary gender identities.

However, not all straight women are so open to their queer peers. Hamilton (2007), Armstrong and Hamilton (2015), and Froyum (2007) found that heterosexual young people will socially ostracize or put down their queer women peers in order to bolster their own heterosexual privilege. In this vein, we should think of homophobia as a gender strategy for performing one's straight femininity or masculinity. A gender strategy is defined by the actions one takes to negotiate the cultural norms of gender, given the current ideological conditions one faces (Hamilton 2007; Hochschild and Machung 2012 [1989]). Dean (2014) explores this idea of homophobia (and anti-homophobia) as a gender strategy that straight women enact to perform their sexual-gender identity status in post-closeted contexts.

What this body of research indicates about heterosexual femininities is that straight women are differently positioned in terms of how they are stereotyped by white patriarchal culture, though generally they are constructed as the opposites and subordinates of straight men. Straight women are socialized to regard themselves as sexual objects rather than cultivate their own sexual subjectivities, and in order to navigate a hetero-patriarchal culture they often make compromises – or patriarchal bargains – in terms of participating in a society that sexually objectifies them, and values straight men's sexual pleasure first. College-educated straight women in particular are exploring new gender and sexual identities that go beyond the gender binary (both in terms of self-definition and in terms of the possibilities of who they may be attracted to), and even older generations of straight women have negotiated a heterosexual life in ways that have given them a sense of agency and sexual pleasure.

Heterosexual masculinities

Heterosexualities also continue to be axiomatic in the construction of dominant masculinities and the ability to claim power, status, and authority over others (Connell 1987; Kimmel 2005; Silva 2018). For example, if second-wave feminists viewed straight women as socialized to be subordinate, passive sexual objects who lacked opportunities to express their own sexual agency, then straight men were the opposite – dominating, aggressive, sexually controlling, and they used women for their personal pleasure. Connell developed the concept of *hegemonic masculinity* to theorize the superordinate form of masculinity that men must negotiate in enacting their gender practices; a concept which captures and expands upon the domineering characterization of straight men by earlier feminists (1987, 1995). The subordination of women and the repudiation of practices associated with femininity continue to be central to conceptions of hegemonic masculinity (Connell and Messerschmidt 2005; Schippers 2007). Moreover, masculinity scholars (Carrigan, Connell, and Lee 2002; Whitehead and Barrett 2001) conceptualize masculinity as multiple and hierarchical. For instance, the masculine practices of straight men of color as well as straight working-class men on one hand are marginalized for their less-valued racial and class statuses, yet on the other hand they are valued for their "hypermasculine" performances of gender and sexual normativity.

In addition to the repudiation of the feminine, straight men have also tended to invoke homophobic practices to subordinate gay masculinities as effeminate (Hennen 2008). Thus, hegemonic masculinity tends to be straight masculinity. Demetriou (2001) argues that hegemonic masculinity exhibits both "external hegemony" with men's institutional dominance over women and "internal hegemony," where one group of men dominates all other men (particularly over gay men). There has been much scholarly discussion and debate over the relational links between practices of straight masculinities and the expression of homophobia. Kimmel (2005, 2008) argues that "homophobia, men's fear of other men, is the animating condition of dominant definition of [heterosexual] masculinity in America, [and] the reigning definition of masculinity is a defensive effort to prevent being emasculated" (2005, p. 39). In this view, homophobia can be understood as both a gender *and* sexual identity strategy that solves the problem of identifying oneself as both normatively masculine and heterosexual by deriding LGBTQ individuals.

This line of theorizing masculinity and homophobia can run the risk of binding masculinity to the social construction of heterosexuality so tightly that the two concepts collapse into one another, with masculinity serving as a proxy for heterosexuality. This conflation is understandable, since many straight men aim to be conventionally, even exaggeratedly, masculine in their identity performances as a way to project a straight status. For example, there has been considerable research on straight men who seek sexual encounters with other straight men, but still identify as straight. For example, Ward's (2015) work on white straight-identified men who display homophobic and misogynistic attitudes while soliciting sex with other "str8 dudes" illustrates this tendency. Based on research from the "Casual Encounters" personal ad section of the website Craigslist (which no longer hosts personal ads due to legal liabilities), Ward (2008, 2015) finds a subculture of straight-identified white men who generally seek others like themselves for anonymous sexual encounters. The ads read like pornographic scenes. These men have specific erotically scripted requests for the encounter, from hanging out and watching porn while jerking off in front of each other, to wanting to give another man oral sex and taking a Polaroid of the encounter, to sometimes just seeing what happens in the moment (2008, p. 420). Not surprisingly, this subcultural group of men who seek "dude sex" distanced themselves from the "Men Seeking Men" section of the website where many of the ads placed were composed by openly gay men seeking sex with other men (2008, p. 418).

Building on Ward's work on men who have sex with men (MSM) and who are straight-identified, Silva (2018) describes an older rural group of men who have regular same-sex partners but still identify as straight and desire to remain married to their wives. He calls this practice "bud-sex" as it captures the secretive, nonromantic, but ongoing sexual encounters these white straight-identified men have with their buddies, who are also generally white, married men like themselves. They view themselves and their partners as normatively masculine and disparage gay men. Carrillo and Hoffman (2017) interviewed 100 white, straight men who were married or in stable relationships with women, but who also sought male sexual partners online. Carrillo and Hoffman (2017, p. 90) conclude that "in the process of maintaining identities as straight men, they change the definition of heterosexuality, in effect turning it into a considerably elastic category that is perceived as fully compatible with having and enacting same-sex desires."

While straight men who have sex with men may invoke homophobia to distance themselves from gay identity, the available performances of straight masculinity are expanding with a growing set of *non-homophobic* and *anti-homophobic* dynamics and discourses in how straight masculinity is performed (Dean 2014). For example, the concept of *hybrid masculinities* has reinvigorated debate on whether contemporary straight masculinities enforce, reconfigure, or challenge the sexual and gender inequality associated with hegemonic masculinity that uniformly subordinates homosexualities beneath normative heterosexualities (Anderson 2009; Bridges and Pascoe 2014; Dean 2014; McCormack 2012). Bridges and Pascoe define hybrid masculinities as "the selective incorporation of elements of identity typically associated with various marginalized and subordinated masculinities and – at times – femininities into privileged men's gender performances and identities" (2014, p. 246). The hybrid masculinity concept has emerged out of a social context of newfound LGBTQ inclusion and visibility in many western societies (Seidman 2002; Walters 2001, 2014; Weeks 2007). Some argue that this new context of gay acceptance has led some white straight men to "hybridize," appropriating "gay elements and practices" into their changing configuration of masculinity (Demetriou 2001, p. 348).

Yet the performance of hybrid masculinities among young, white, straight men can still enact new, more subtle forms of homophobia. Gay aesthetics, Bridges argues, are part of hybrid masculinity and can reinforce homophobia in new, more complicated ways than previous studies of homophobia (Pascoe 2007; Plummer 1999). Bridges (2014) explains that hybrid masculinity among straight men involves the incorporation of gay aesthetic practices that range from their personal tastes to specific comportment behaviors to adopting a feminist ideology. Regarding taste, for example, these straight men essentialize gay male culture, associating it with wine, not beer, having a neat and clean house, not a messy one (pp. 69–71). As they do this, some men reclaim straight status and privilege by saying "no homo" in order to distance themselves from actual gay men while still embracing "gay" aesthetics (Brown 2011).

However, the empirical evidence used to illustrate this argument shows that hybrid masculinity practices can also *challenge* homophobia. Some straight men non-defensively incorporate gay aesthetics of being stylish or engaging in acts of kindness as positive even though they are stereotyped as gay for embodying them (Bridges 2014, p. 67). One distinction to draw, then, is that many, if not all, of these straight men aim to reclaim straight status and its accompanying heterosexual privilege, but some of them do this without invoking homophobic practices that enforce sexual prejudice and inequality. However, as straight allies to LGBTQ+ people, they may still center their allyship activities on their own personal psychological needs rather than the needs of the queer community (see Grzanka, Chapter 27 of this volume). In sum, the conceptual value of hybrid masculinities underscores the persistence of homophobias in a post-closeted cultural landscape, where LGBTQ individuals and representations of them are variably integrated into social life, media, and legal policies.

Other scholars explore inclusive masculinity and straight men's sexual flexibility; the thesis of this work is that pro-gay discourses or anti-homophobias are on the rise among a younger generation of heterosexual men (e.g. Adams 2011; Anderson 2009; McCormack 2012). For example, McCormack (2012) researched the decline of homophobia among straight boys in high school in England where he found that straight teenage boys intellectualized their support for gay equality, generally avoided using homophobic language, and were friends with openly gay students (2012, pp. 73–84). Likewise, Anderson's (2005, 2009) research found that white, heterosexual male college cheerleaders often become less homophobic when they befriend gay men on their teams. Anderson also observes gay-friendly attitudes among a college fraternity that recruits gay members (2009, pp. 121–123).

Male sexual flexibility has only recently become a theme in the changing social dynamics between straight and gay men and their cultural discourses (Anderson 2009; Savin-Williams 2017). According to Anderson and Robinson (2016), straight men do not tend to change identity labels based on their same-sex sexual encounters as do women. Therefore, they consider straight men who have physical and sexual intimacy with men as "sexually flexible" rather than "sexually fluid." In their work together for this volume, Anderson and McCormack show that same-sex kissing among straight college men may be less about sexual fluidity and more about a decrease in the stigmatizing of same-sex sexualities broadly. The physically tactile relationships between straight high school boys neither raised suspicion of these boys as gay nor led to homophobic derision from their student peers (McCormack 2012, pp. 79–82), nor did same-sex kissing among some college men lead to homophobic retribution by peers at the university level (Anderson, Adams, and Rivers 2010). We should note that although this research on straight men's inclusivity and sexual flexibility indicates a pattern of decreasing homophobia accompanying the increasing visibility of gays and lesbians, it does not capture the regional variability found in the United States in places like the Bible Belt (see Barton 2012; Gray 2009), nor does it recognize the subtle forms of homophobia that persist among seemingly progressive straight men as documented by Bridges (2014) and Dean (2014, pp. 111–123) and more conservative Millennials (Risman 2018).

Straight masculinities occupy a paradoxical status in many western societies today. On one hand, there are formations that challenge and contest sexual and gender inequalities in everyday life and support more inclusive legal, policy, and institutional developments. On the other hand, straight men continue to deploy homophobias and sexisms to maintain masculine and heterosexual privilege, recoup status, and preserve their position in hierarchies of dominance. The empirical studies evidence this paradoxical claim in how they illustrate competing claims in their attempts to define the contemporary landscape of straight masculinities as challenging inequalities or reinforcing them in new ways. Although we view each study as having merit and purchase for advancing our understandings of straight masculinities, we underscore that these studies taken as a whole highlight more of a micro social interactional focus among specific groups, institutions, and cultural discourses. The empirical research in the field tends to lack a macro assessment of the status of straightness at the level of law and other social institutions.

The kaleidoscope of straight masculinities in contemporary western societies today evidences homophobic, non-homophobic, and anti-homophobic discourses and cultures. Of course, age, race, and generation, among other factors, shape and change these dynamics but they do not mean the total absence of homophobia. Still, the preponderance of non- and anti-homophobic practices, discourses, and cultures is a clear and emerging pattern.

Transgender heterosexualities

Heterosexuality as an institution has also been quite visible in the history of transgender identities. Normative heterosexuality played a central role in the medical transitions of transsexual individuals throughout the twentieth century (Stryker 2006). Historically, the adoption of a *heterosexual* identity status (with the presumed goal of being heterosexually coupled and married) was part of the set of medical requirements for being an acceptable candidate for sex reassignment surgery for transsexual individuals (Meyerowitz 2002). Before the 1980s, "sex reassignment surgery" – now referred to as gender affirmative surgeries – came with several criteria that doctors used to evaluate candidates. For example, viable candidates for Male to Female (MtF) surgeries were to have only had sex with men or not had sex at all rather than a history of sex with women. After surgery, doctors viewed "successful" MtF patients as those who were socially recognized as non-transsexual, heterosexually orientated women. The emphasis by doctors on their patients' exclusive attraction to men prior to surgery was meant to assure a heterosexual identity post-surgery. The requirement that surgery help an individual achieve an adult heterosexual identity and relationship has also been reflected in how the medical establishment has treated intersex patients (Preves 2003).

With heterosexual marriage as the end goal, doctors affirmed the normativity of heterosexuality in the lives of transsexuals chosen for surgical procedures (Meyerowitz 2002, pp. 225–226). This changed, however, in the 1980s, when university hospitals stopped performing these surgeries. Due to the mounting criticisms of research that documented the surgeries to be often unsuccessful, painful, and damaging or destroying of sexual response, university gender identity clinics closed. Instead, private for-profit medical practices took their place (Denny 2006).

During this same period, the term transgender was coined and started to gain wider currency after Leslie Feinberg (2013) used the term in her pamphlet "Transgender liberation: a movement whose time has come" in 1992. Later, writer and activist Sandy Stone (1992) argued in her post-transsexual manifesto for transsexual individuals to come out as transsexual and to not aim to be seen as non-transsexual individuals (Stryker 2006). Stone's manifesto for coming out overlapped with the new identity politics of the term transgender. Transgender identity politics shifted the emphasis from medicalized transitions as the basis and the fulcrum of the identity to one that focused on gender non-conforming expression as its defining axiom (Westbrook 2016). In doing so, transgender identity as an umbrella category brought together a diverse range of groups that included any and all individuals who had moved away from the sex they were assigned at birth. This included Male to Female (MtF) and Female to Male (FtM) transsexuals, transvestites, cross-dressers, butch lesbians, drag queens and kings, along with other gender non-conforming individuals who chose to embrace the term (Stryker 2006, 2008).

Examining the role of normative heterosexuality in enforcing a gender binary that makes only males who identify as men and females who identify as women as worthy of respect, recognition, and rights, Kristin Schilt and Laurel Westbrook's research (2009) on transgender men shows that they face exposure and stigma by workplace colleagues when they would like to date prospective cisgender women who are informally told by other coworkers that these transgender men lack penises and thus are not "really men." More disturbingly, Schilt and Westbrook describe how transgender women face a disproportionate risk of violence and murder from cisgender heterosexual men when they are in sexual situations with cisgender men who become aware of, anxious about, or angered by the transgender women's trans identity status. Such men use violence and murder as the punishment for the idea that transgender women have deceived them by not being female-born women.

As recognition of trans, non-binary, and gender non-conforming people grows, heteronormativity continues to be a central factor in framing transphobic policies around women's public restrooms that view trans women as "really men" dressed up as women who might assault girls and women. In contrast, transgender men's use of men's restrooms is not made a focus in these cases. This backlash suggests that transgender bathroom battles are based in a gender panic, specifically a penis panic, revolving around the genitals of transgender women who use women's restrooms (Cavanagh 2010; Grant, Mottet, and Tannis 2011; Schilt and Westbrook 2015).

Other research finds that while straight identity statuses are embraced by some transgender individuals (see Doorduin and van Berlo 2014; Pfeffer 2017), their most common sexual orientation labels are queer and pansexual (Kuper, Nussbaum, and Mustanski 2011). Pfeffer (2017), for example, in her study of cisgender women in relationships with transgender men, found that many of the women identified as queer and thought of their relationships as queer as well. However, in public spaces many of these cisgender female–transgender male couples would play along with individuals' recognition of them as a heterosexual couple. At times playing along was due to safety concerns. However, it also was the case that their transgender male partners wished to be viewed as a heterosexual couple in public because their identities as men were affirmed and validated when others saw them as heterosexual (Pfeffer 2017, pp. 35–54).

Normative heterosexuality shapes trans lives in a myriad number of ways. At times, trans individuals aim to resist the comfort of its normative privileges while in other contexts the safety, validation, and legitimacy it provides is embraced. Trans heterosexualities challenge normative constructions of heterosexual identity as based in cisgender notions of gender expression as matching the sex one was assigned at birth. This, then, shows the elasticity of the category of heterosexuality and its expansion beyond normative cisgender enactments.

Overall, the rich body of scholarship around gender and sexuality illustrates how heteronormativity fundamentally underpins western cultural ideas about gender, including gender displays, roles, expression, and performances. Even those individuals whose visibility and activism challenge essentialist, biologically based notions of sex and gender are still regulated by the norms of heterosexuality, whether by the medical establishment or by the state.

The future of Heterosexuality and Critical Heterosexualities Studies

In their history of American sexual politics, *Intimate Matters* (2012), historians John D'Emilio and Estelle Freedman caution against viewing the history of sexuality as a linear, non-stop march toward greater sexual progressiveness. For every development that opens the door to more sexual and gender openness and tolerance, reactionary sexual politics may be just around the corner. For example, feminist and LGBTQ+ gains have often been swiftly followed by backlash

(Faludi 2006). Straight sexual power relations are front and center in today's cultural climate. Movements to end sexual harassment and sexual coercion have been calling attention to sexual harassment and double standards in the workplace, as well as tired (hetero)sexual tropes of men pursuing and women enjoying being pursued. At the same time our culture questions a "boys will be boys" mentality toward sexual coercion and harassment of women, some states in the USA have adopted the most restrictive abortion laws in history that severely limit women's reproductive rights. And while many educational institutions seek to become more welcoming to their students' rapidly changing gender and sexual identities, laws banning transgender individuals from using particular bathrooms or joining the American military persist. These polarized developments illustrate that institutionalized heterosexuality is in crisis, as younger generations push the boundaries of heteronormativity and gender conformity, and older generations (who disproportionately still hold positions of power) attempt to re-trench gender conformity and hetero-patriarchy.

And yet, at the same time that it seems apparent that heterosexuality is in crisis at the political level, there is also a sense of a lack of a crisis within some cultural discourses of heterosexuality. The banality of a normative form of heterosexuality – exemplified in the straight men's bar-room discussion of dating, marriage, and children at the beginning of this chapter – illustrates how heterosexuality and its accompanying privileges still exist within a "charmed circle" of sexualities where monogamy, marriage, and heterosexuality remain a presumed, mostly unchallenged set of culturally sanctioned norms (Rubin 2011). In the meantime, new sexual formations from polyamory to asexuality to trans heterosexualities have complicated the cultural landscape of heterosexualities and non-heterosexualities in the decades since Rubin (2011) wrote her 1984 essay.

Generationally speaking, western culture has witnessed a great deal of change on the sexuality front. In the 1960s and 1970s, Baby Boomers in the gay liberationist and feminist movements identified heterosexuality as a source of oppression, yet today, other Baby Boomers are highly invested in hegemonic masculinity, exemplified by both older men and women from that generation who have criticized the progressive #MeToo Movement as "taking the fun out of office romance." Gen X has exhibited a great deal of acceptance and facility with conducting transactions online, including dating. The Millennial generation has tended to be accepting of queer rights and some members have brought new relationship forms into the public eye, such as non-monogamous, polyamorous relationships and new sexual categories of sexual behavior like "pansexual" and "heteroflexible," among others. Further, Millennials and Generation Z members are known for pushing gender and sexuality categories even further, bringing non-binary gender identities and the use of non-binary pronouns onto the public scene, as well as new sexual identity categories like asexual, demi-sexual, and a-romantic. These new gender and sexuality identity categories fundamentally challenge any essentialist, universalistic notions of heterosexuality. Moreover, the ways that heterosexual identities are performed have changed in the face of queer visibility. The future of heterosexualities is very much contingent on how these different generations' sexual politics play out in the long-term. The future of Critical Heterosexualities Studies is unknowable from the present, and is ultimately contingent on the sexual-political-generational battles that are currently unfolding.

References

Adams, A., 2011. "Josh wears pink cleats": inclusive masculinity on the soccer field. *Journal of Homosexuality*, 58 (5), 579–596.

Almeling, R., 2011. *Sex cells: the medical market for eggs and sperm*. University of California Press.

Anderson, E., 2005. Orthodox and inclusive masculinity: competing masculinities among heterosexual men in a feminized terrain. *Sociological Perspectives*, 48 (3), 337–355.

Anderson, E., 2009. *Inclusive masculinity: the changing nature of masculinities.* Routledge.

Anderson, E. and Robinson, S., 2016. Men's sexual flexibility. In: *Introducing the new sexuality studies.* Routledge, pp. 250–259.

Anderson, E., Adams, A., and Rivers, I., 2010. "I kiss them because I love them": the emergence of heterosexual men kissing in British institutes of education. *Archives of Sexual Behavior*, 41 (2), 421–430.

Armstrong, E.A. and Hamilton, L.T., 2015. *Paying for the party: how college maintains inequality.* Harvard University Press.

Armstrong, E.A., England, P., and Fogarty, A.C.K., 2012. Accounting for women's orgasm and sexual enjoyment in college hookups and relationships. *American Sociological Review*, 77 (3), 435–462.

Barton, B.C., 2012. *Pray the gay away: the extraordinary lives of bible belt gays.* New York University Press.

Beasley, C. and Brook, H., 2014. *Heterosexuality in theory and practice.* Routledge.

Bridges, T., 2014. A very "gay" straight? *Gender & Society*, 28 (1), 58–82.

Bridges, T. and Pascoe, C.J., 2014. Hybrid masculinities: new directions in the sociology of men and masculinities. *Sociology Compass*, 8 (3), 246–258.

Brown, J.R., 2011. No homo. *Journal of Homosexuality*, 58 (3), 299–314.

Butler, J., 1990. *Gender trouble: feminism and the subversion of identity.* Routledge.

Cain, S., 2019. Women are happier without children or a spouse, happiness expert says [online]. *Guardian.* Available from: www.theguardian.com/lifeandstyle/2019/may/25/women-happier-without-children-or-a-spouse-happiness-expert.

Canaday, M., 2009. *The straight state: sexuality and citizenship in twentieth-century America.* Princeton University Press.

Carpenter, L.M., 2001. The ambiguity of "having sex": the subjective experience of virginity loss in the United States. *Journal of Sex Research*, 38 (2), 127–139.

Carrigan, T., Connell, R.W., and Lee, J., 2002. Toward a new sociology of masculinity. In: *The masculinity studies reader.* Blackwell, pp. 99–118.

Carrillo, H. and Hoffman, A., 2017. "Straight with a pinch of bi": the construction of heterosexuality as an elastic category among adult US men. *Sexualities*, 21 (1–2), 90–108.

Cavanagh, S.L., 2010. *Queering bathrooms: gender, sexuality, and the hygienic imagination.* University of Toronto Press.

Christina, G., 1992. Are we having sex yet or what? In: *The erotic impulse: honoring the sensual self.* Tarcher, pp. 24–29.

Collins, P.H., 2006. *Black sexual politics: African Americans, gender, and the new racism.* Routledge.

Connell, R.W., 1987. *Gender and power.* Polity.

Connell, R.W., 1995. *Masculinities.* University of California Press.

Connell, R.W. and Messerschmidt, J.W., 2005. Hegemonic masculinity. *Gender & Society*, 19 (6), 829–859.

D'Emilio, J. and Freedman, E.B., 2012. *Intimate matters: a history of sexuality in America.* University of Chicago Press.

Dean, J.J., 2014. *Straights: heterosexuality in post-closeted culture.* New York University Press.

Demetriou, D.Z., 2001. Connell's concept of hegemonic masculinity: a critique. *Theory and Society*, 30 (3), 337–361.

Denny, D., 2006. Transgender communities of the United States in the late twentieth century. In: *Transgender rights.* University of Minnesota Press, pp. 171–191.

Diamond, L.M., 2005. "I'm straight, but I kissed a girl": the trouble with American media representations of female-female sexuality. *Feminism & Psychology*, 15 (1), 104–110.

Diamond, L.M., 2009. *Sexual fluidity: understanding women's love and desire.* Harvard University Press.

Doorduin, T. and van Berlo, W., 2014. Trans people's experience of sexuality in the Netherlands: a pilot study. *Journal of Homosexuality*, 61 (5), 654–672.

Duggan, L., 2000. *Sapphic slashers: sex, violence, and American modernity.* Duke University Press.

Essig, L., 2019. *Love, inc.: dating apps, the big white wedding and chasing the happily neverafter.* University of California Press.

Faludi, S., 2006. *Backlash: the undeclared war against American women.* Three Rivers Press.

Feinberg, L., 2013. *Transgender liberation: a movement whose time has come.* Trans Oral History Project.

Fischer, N.L., 2013. Seeing "straight," contemporary critical heterosexuality studies and sociology: an introduction. *The Sociological Quarterly*, 54 (4), 501–510.

Froyum, C.M., 2007. At least I'm not gay: heterosexual identity making among poor black teens. *Sexualities*, 10 (5), 603–622.

Fuss, D., 1991. *Inside/out: lesbian theories, gay theories.* Routledge.

Garcia, L., 2012. *Respect yourself, protect yourself: Latina girls and sexual identity.* New York University Press.
Gavey, N., McPhillips, K., and Braun, V., 1999. Interruptus coitus: heterosexuals accounting for intercourse. *Sexualities*, 2 (1), 35–68.
Grant, J., Mottet, L., and Tannis, J., 2011. *Injustice at every turn: a report of the National Transgender Discrimination Survey.* National Center for Transgender Equality.
Gray, M.L., 2009. *Out in the country: youth, media, and queer visibility in rural America.* New York University Press.
Green, A.I., 2013. *Sexual fields: towards a sociology of collective sexual life.* University of Chicago Press.
Hamilton, L., 2007. Trading on heterosexuality. *Gender & Society*, 21 (2), 145–172.
Heath, M., 2012. *One marriage under God: the campaign to promote marriage in America.* New York University Press.
Hennen, P., 2008. *Fairies, bears, and leathermen: men in community queering the masculine.* University of Chicago Press.
Hochschild, A.R. and Machung, A., 2012 [1989]. *The second shift: working families and the revolution at home.* Penguin Books.
Hockey, J., Meah, A., and Robinson, V., 2010. A heterosexual life: older women and agency within marriage and the family. *Journal of Gender Studies*, 13 (3), 227–238.
Illouz, E., 2013. *Why love hurts: a sociological explanation.* Wiley.
Ingraham, C., 2008. *White weddings: romancing heterosexuality in popular culture.* Routledge.
Jackson, S., 1999. *Heterosexuality in question.* Sage Publications.
Jackson, S. and Scott, S., 2010. *Theorising sexuality.* Open University Press.
Kalish, R. and Kimmel, M., 2011. Hooking up: hot hetero sex or the new numb normative? *Australian Feminist Studies*, 26 (67), 137–151.
Kandiyoti, D., 1988. Bargaining with patriarchy. *Gender & Society*, 2 (3), 274–290.
Kane, E.W., 2012. *The gender trap: parents and the pitfalls of raising boys and girls.* New York University Press.
Katz, J.N., 1996. *The invention of heterosexuality.* University of Chicago Press.
Kimmel, M.S., 2005. *The gender of desire: essays on male sexuality.* State University of New York Press.
Kimmel, M.S., 2008. *Guyland: the perilous world where boys become men.* Harper.
Kitzinger, C., 2005. "Speaking as a heterosexual": (how) does sexuality matter for talk-in-interaction? *Research on Language & Social Interaction*, 38 (3), 221–265.
Klinenberg, E., 2014. *Going solo: the extraordinary rise and surprising appeal of living alone.* Duckworth.
Kuper, L.E., Nussbaum, R., and Mustanski, B., 2011. Exploring the diversity of gender and sexual orientation identities in an online sample of transgender individuals. *Journal of Sex Research*, 49 (2–3), 244–254.
Loe, M., 2006. *The rise of Viagra: how the little blue pill changed sex in America.* New York University Press.
McCormack, M., 2012. *The declining significance of homophobia: how teenage boys are redefining masculinity and heterosexuality.* Oxford University Press.
MacKinnon, C., 1997. Sexuality. In: *The second wave: a reader in feminist theory.* Routledge, pp. 158–180.
Martin, E., 1991. The egg and the sperm: how science has constructed a romance based on stereotypical male-female roles. *Signs: Journal of Women in Culture and Society*, 16 (3), 485–501.
Martin, K.A., 2009. Normalizing heterosexuality: mothers' assumptions, talk, and strategies with young children. *American Sociological Review*, 74 (2), 190–207.
Meyerowitz, J.J., 2002. *How sex changed: a history of transsexuality in the United States.* Harvard University Press.
Morgan, E.M. and Thompson, E.M., 2011. Processes of sexual orientation questioning among heterosexual women. *Journal of Sex Research*, 48 (1), 16–28.
Nemoto, K., 2009. *Racing romance: love, power, and desire among Asian American/white couples.* Rutgers University Press.
Oliver, M., 2016. Uganda's anti-homosexuality bill: reflections from a transnational frame. In: *Introducing the new sexuality studies*, third edition. Routledge, pp. 625–635.
Pascoe, C.J., 2007. *Dude, you're a fag: masculinity and sexuality in high school.* University of California Press.
Patil, V., 2018. The heterosexual matrix as imperial effect. *Sociological Theory*, 36 (1), 1–26.
Pfeffer, C.A., 2017. *Queering families: the postmodern partnerships of cisgender women and transgender men.* Oxford University Press.
Plummer, D., 1999. *One of the boys: masculinity, homophobia and modern manhood.* Harrington Park.
Plummer, K., 2012. Critical sexualities studies. In: *The Wiley-Blackwell companion to sociology.* Wiley-Blackwell, pp. 243–269.
Preves, S.E., 2003. *Intersex and identity: the contested self.* Rutgers University Press.

Puri, J., 1999. *Women, body, and desire in post-colonial India.* Routledge.
Renold, E., 2000. Coming out: gender, (hetero)sexuality and the primary school. *Gender and Education*, 12 (3), 309–326.
Rich, A., 1994 [1980]. Compulsory heterosexuality and lesbian existence. *Signs: Journal of Women in Culture and Society*, 5 (4), 631–660.
Richardson, D., 1996. *Theorising heterosexuality: telling it straight.* Open University Press.
Risman, B.J., 2018. *Where the millennials will take us: a new generation wrestles with the gender structure.* Oxford University Press.
Rubin, G.S., 2011. *Deviations: a Gayle Rubin reader.* Duke University Press.
Rupp, L.J., 2009. *Sapphistries: a global history of love between women.* New York University Press.
Sandberg, L., 2016. Inventions of hetero-sex in later life: beyond dysfunction and the coital imperative. In: *Introducing the new sexuality studies.* Routledge, pp. 304–312.
Savin-Williams, R., 2017. *Mostly straight: sexuality fluidity among men.* Harvard University Press.
Schilt, K. and Westbrook, L., 2009. Doing gender, doing heteronormativity. *Gender & Society*, 23 (4), 440–464.
Schilt, K. and Westbrook, L., 2015. Bathroom battlegrounds and penis panics. *Contexts*, 14 (3), 26–31.
Schippers, M., 2007. Recovering the feminine other: masculinity, femininity, and gender hegemony. *Theory and Society*, 36 (1), 85–102.
Sedgwick, E.K., 1990. *Epistemology of the closet.* University of California Press.
Seidman, S., 2002. *Beyond the closet: the transformation of gay and lesbian life.* Routledge.
Seidman, S., 2009. Critique of compulsory heterosexuality. *Sexuality Research and Social Policy*, 6 (1), 18–28.
Silva, T., 2018. "Helpin' a buddy out": perceptions of identity and behavior among rural straight men that have sex with each other. *Sexualities*, 21 (1–2), 68–89.
Simon, W. and Gagnon, J., 1974. *Sexual conduct: the social sources of human sexuality.* Hutchinson.
Smart, C., 1996. Collusion, collaboration and confession: on moving beyond the heterosexuality debate. In: *Theorising heterosexuality: telling it straight.* Open University Press, pp. 161–177.
Stacey, J., 2012. *Unhitched: love, marriage, and family values from West Hollywood to Western China.* New York University Press.
Stearns, C.A., 2013. The embodied practices of breastfeeding: implications for research and policy. *Journal of Women, Politics & Policy*, 34 (4), 359–370.
Stein, A., 1997. *Sex and sensibility: stories of a lesbian generation.* University of California Press.
Stoler, L., 2002. *Carnal knowledge and imperial power.* University of California Press.
Stone, S., 1992. The empire strikes back: a post transsexual manifesto. *Camera Obscura: Feminism, Culture, and Media Studies*, 10 (2), 150–176.
Stryker, S., 2006. (De)subjugated knowledges: an introduction to transgender studies. In: *The transgender studies reader.* Routledge, pp. 1–17.
Stryker, S., 2008. *Transgender history: the roots of today's revolution.* Seal Press.
Terry, J., 1999. *An American obsession: science, medicine, and homosexuality in modern society.* University of Chicago Press.
Tolman, D.L., 2009. *Dilemmas of desire: teenage girls talk about sexuality.* Harvard University Press.
Wade, L., 2018. *American hookup: the new culture of sex on campus.* W.W. Norton & Company.
Walters, S.D., 2001. *All the rage: the story of gay visibility in America.* University of Chicago Press.
Walters, S.D., 2014. *The tolerance trap: how God, genes, and good intentions are sabotaging gay equality.* New York University Press.
Ward, J., 2008. Dude-sex: white masculinities and authentic heterosexuality among dudes who have sex with dudes. *Sexualities*, 11 (4), 414–434.
Ward, J., 2015. *Not gay sex between straight white men.* New York University Press.
Weeks, J., 2007. *The world we have won: the remaking of erotic and intimate life.* Routledge.
Westbrook, L., 2016. Transforming the sex/gender/sexuality system: the construction of trans categories in the United States. In: *Introducing the new sexuality studies.* Routledge, pp. 33–42.
Whitehead, S. and Barrett, F., 2001. The sociology of masculinity. In: *The masculinities reader.* Blackwell, pp. 1–26.
Wilkinson, S. and Kitzinger, C., 1993. *Heterosexuality: a feminism & psychology reader.* Sage.
Wittig, M., 1992. *The straight mind and other essays.* Harvester Wheatsheaf.

Part I

Origins, histories, theories

1

Compulsory heterosexuality and lesbian existence*

Adrienne Cecile Rich

Foreword

I want to say a little about the way "Compulsory Heterosexuality" was originally conceived and the context in which we are now living. It was written in part to challenge the erasure of lesbian existence from so much of scholarly feminist literature, an erasure which I felt (and feel) to be not just anti-lesbian, but anti-feminist in its consequences, and to distort the experience of heterosexual women as well. It was not written to widen divisions but to encourage heterosexual feminists to examine heterosexuality as a political institution which disempowers women—and to change it. I also hoped that other lesbians would feel the depth and breadth of woman identification and woman bonding that has run like a continuous though stifled theme through the heterosexual experience, and that this would become increasingly a politically activating impulse, not simply a validation of personal lives. I wanted the essay to suggest new kinds of criticism, to incite new questions in classrooms and academic journals, and to sketch, at least, some bridge over the gap between *lesbian* and *feminist*. I wanted, at the very least, for feminists to find it less possible to read, write, or teach from a perspective of unexamined heterocentricity.

Within the three years since I wrote "Compulsory Heterosexuality"—with this energy of hope and desire—the pressures to conform in a society increasingly conservative in mood have become more intense. The New Right's messages to women have been, precisely, that we are the emotional and sexual property of men, and that the autonomy and equality of women threaten the family, religion, and state. The institutions by which women have traditionally been controlled—patriarchal motherhood, economic exploitation, the nuclear family, compulsory heterosexuality—are being strengthened by legislation, religious fiat, media imagery, and efforts at censorship. In a worsening economy, the single mother trying to support her children confronts the feminization of poverty which Joyce Miller of the National Coalition of Labor Union Women has named one of the major issues of the 1980s. The lesbian, unless in disguise, faces discrimination in hiring and harassment and violence in the street. Even within feminist-inspired institutions such as battered-women's shelters and Women's Studies programs, open lesbians are fired and others warned to stay in the closet. The retreat into sameness—assimilation for those who can manage it—is the most passive and debilitating of responses to political repression, economic insecurity, and a renewed open season on difference.

I want to note that documentation of male violence against women—within the home especially—has been accumulating rapidly in this period (see pages 34–35, 42, note 9). At the same time, in the realm of literature which depicts woman bonding and woman identification as essential for female survival, a steady stream of writing and criticism has been coming from women of color in general and lesbians of color in particular—the latter group being even more profoundly erased in academic feminist scholarship by the double bias of racism and homophobia.[1]

There has recently been an intensified debate on female sexuality among feminists and lesbians, with lines often furiously and bitterly drawn, with *sadomasochism* and *pornography* as key words which are variously defined according to who is talking. The depth of women's rage and fear regarding sexuality and its relation to power and pain is real, even when the dialogue sounds simplistic, self-righteous, or like parallel monologues.

Because of all these developments, there are parts of this essay that I would word differently, qualify, or expand if I were writing it today. But I continue to think that heterosexual feminists will draw political strength for change from taking a critical stance toward the ideology which *demands* heterosexuality, and that lesbians cannot assume that we are untouched by that ideology and the institutions founded upon it. There is nothing about such a critique that requires us to think of ourselves as victims, as having been brainwashed or totally powerless. Coercion and compulsion are among the conditions in which women have learned to recognize our strength. Resistance is a major theme in this essay and in the study of women's lives, if we know what we are looking for.

I

Biologically men have only one innate orientation—a sexual one that draws them to women,—while women have two innate orientations, sexual toward men and reproductive toward their young.[2]

> *I was a woman terribly vulnerable, critical, using femaleness as a sort of standard or yardstick to measure and discard men. Yes—something like that. I was an Anna who invited defeat from men without ever being conscious of it. (But I am conscious of it. And being conscious of it means I shall leave it all behind me and become—but what?) I was stuck fast in an emotion common to women of our time, that can turn them bitter, or Lesbian, or solitary. Yes, that Anna during that time was . . .*

[Another blank line across the page:][3]

The bias of compulsory heterosexuality, through which lesbian experience is perceived on a scale ranging from deviant to abhorrent or simply rendered invisible, could be illustrated from many texts other than the two just preceding. The assumption made by Rossi, that women are "innately" sexually oriented only toward men, and that made by Lessing, that the lesbian is simply acting out of her bitterness toward men, are by no means theirs alone; these assumptions are widely current in literature and in the social sciences.

I am concerned here with two other matters as well: first, how and why women's choice of women as passionate comrades, life partners, coworkers, lovers, community has been crushed, invalidated, forced into hiding and disguise; and second, the virtual or total neglect of lesbian existence in a wide range of writings, including feminist scholarship. Obviously there is a connection here. I believe that much feminist theory and criticism is stranded on this shoal.

My organizing impulse is the belief that it is not enough for feminist thought that specifically lesbian texts exist. Any theory or cultural/political creation that treats lesbian existence as a marginal or less "natural" phenomenon, as mere "sexual preference," or as the mirror image of either heterosexual or male homosexual relations is profoundly weakened thereby, whatever its other contributions. Feminist theory can no longer afford merely to voice a toleration of "lesbianism" as an "alternative life style" or make token allusion to lesbians. A feminist critique of compulsory heterosexual orientation for women is long overdue. In this exploratory paper, I shall try to show why.

I will begin by way of examples, briefly discussing four books that have appeared in the last few years, written from different viewpoints and political orientations, but all presenting themselves, and favorably reviewed, as feminist.[4] All take as a basic assumption that the social relations of the sexes are disordered and extremely problematic, if not disabling, for women; all seek paths toward change. I have learned more from some of these books than from others, but on this I am clear: each one might have been more accurate, more powerful, more truly a force for change had the author dealt with lesbian existence as a reality and as a source of knowledge and power available to women, or with the institution of heterosexuality itself as a beachhead of male dominance.[5] In none of them is the question ever raised as to whether, in a different context or other things being equal, women would *choose* heterosexual coupling and marriage; heterosexuality is presumed the "sexual preference" of "most women," either implicitly or explicitly. In none of these books, which concern themselves with mothering, sex roles, relationships, and societal prescriptions for women, is compulsory heterosexuality ever examined as an institution powerfully affecting these, or the idea of "preference" or "innate orientation" even indirectly questioned.

In *For Her Own Good: 150 Years of the Experts' Advice to Women* by Barbara Ehrenreich and Deirdre English, the authors' superb pamphlets *Witches, Midwives and Nurses: A History of Women Healers* and *Complaints and Disorders: The Sexual Politics of Sickness* are developed into a provocative and complex study. Their thesis in this book is that the advice given to American women by male health professionals, particularly in the areas of marital sex, maternity, and child care, has echoed the dictates of the economic marketplace and the role capitalism has needed women to play in production and/or reproduction. Women have become the consumer victims of various cures, therapies, and normative judgements in different periods (including the prescription to middle-class women to embody and preserve the sacredness of the home—the "scientific" romanticization of the home itself). None of the "experts'" advice has been either particularly scientific or women-oriented; it has reflected male needs, male fantasies about women, and male interest in controlling women—particularly in the realms of sexuality and motherhood—fused with the requirements of industrial capitalism. So much of this book is so devastatingly informative and is written with such lucid feminist wit, that I kept waiting as I read for the basic proscription against lesbianism to be examined. It never was.

This can hardly be for lack of information. Jonathan Katz's *Gay American History*[6] tells us that as early as 1656 the New Haven Colony prescribed the death penalty for lesbians. Katz provides many suggestive and informative documents on the "treatment" (or torture) of lesbians by the medical profession in the nineteenth and twentieth centuries. Recent work by the historian

Nancy Sahli documents the crackdown on intense female friendships among college women at the turn of the present century.[7] The ironic title *For Her Own Good* might have referred first and foremost to the economic imperative to heterosexuality and marriage and to the sanctions imposed against single women and widows—both of whom have been and still are viewed as deviant. Yet, in this often enlightening Marxist-feminist overview of male prescriptions for female sanity and health, the economics of prescriptive heterosexuality go unexamined.[8]

Of the three psychoanalytically based books, one, Jean Baker Miller's *Toward a New Psychology of Women*, is written as if lesbians simply do not exist, even as marginal beings. Given Miller's title, I find this astonishing. However, the favorable book reviews the book has received in feminist journals, including *Signs* and *Spokeswoman*, suggest that Miller's heterocentric assumptions are widely shared. In *The Mermaid and the Minotaur: Sexual Arrangements and the Human Malaise*, Dorothy Dinnerstein makes an impassioned argument for the sharing of parenting between women and men and for an end to what she perceives as the male/female symbiosis of "gender arrangements," which she feels are leading the species further and further into violence and self-extinction. Apart from other problems that I have with this book (including her silence on the institutional and random terrorism men have practiced on women—and children—throughout history,[9] and her obsession with psychology to the neglect of economic and other material realities that help to create psychological reality), I find Dinnerstein's view of the relations between women and men as "a collaboration to keep history mad" utterly ahistorical. She means by this a collaboration to perpetuate social relations which are hostile, exploitative, and destructive to life itself. She sees women and men as equal partners in the making of "sexual arrangements," seemingly unaware of the repeated struggles of women to resist oppression (their own and that of others) and to change their condition. She ignores, specifically, the history of women who—as witches, *femmes seules*, marriage resisters, spinsters, autonomous widows, and/or lesbians—have managed on varying levels *not* to collaborate. It is this history, precisely, from which feminists have so much to learn and on which there is overall such blanketing silence. Dinnerstein acknowledges at the end of her book that "female separatism," though "on a large scale and in the long run widely impractical," has something to teach us: "Separate, women could in principle set out to learn from scratch—undeflected by the opportunities to evade this task that men's presence has so far offered—what intact self-creative humanness is."[10] Phrases like "intact self-creative humanness" obscure the question of what the many forms of female separatism have actually been addressing. The fact is that women in every culture and throughout history *have* undertaken the task of independent, nonheterosexual, woman-connected existence, to the extent made possible by their context, often in the belief that they were the "only ones" ever to have done so. They have undertaken it even though few women have been in an economic position to resist marriage altogether, and even though attacks against unmarried women have ranged from aspersion and mockery to deliberate gynocide, including the burning and torturing of millions of widows and spinsters during the witch persecutions of the fifteenth, sixteenth, and seventeenth centuries in Europe.

Nancy Chodorow does come close to the edge of an acknowledgement of lesbian existence. Like Dinnerstein, Chodorow believes that the fact that women, and women only, are responsible for child care in the sexual division of labor has led to an entire social organization of gender inequality, and that men as well as women must become primary carers for children if that inequality is to change. In the process of examining, from a psychoanalytic perspective, how mothering by women affects the psychological development of girl and boy children, she offers documentation that men are "emotionally secondary" in women's lives, that "women have a richer, ongoing inner world to fall back on . . . men do not become as emotionally important to women as women do to men."[11] This would carry into the late twentieth century

Smith-Rosenberg's findings about eighteenth- and nineteenth-century women's emotional focus on women. "Emotionally important" can, of course, refer to anger as well as to love, or to that intense mixture of the two often found in women's relationships with women—one aspect of what I have come to call the "double life of women" (see below). Chodorow concludes that because many women have women as mothers, "the mother remains a primary internal object [*sic*] to the girl, so that heterosexual relationships are on the model of the nonexclusive, second relationship for her, whereas for the boy they re-create an exclusive, primary relationship." According to Chodorow, women "have learned to deny the limitations of masculine lovers for both psychological and practical reasons."[12]

But the practical reasons (like witch burnings, male control of law, theology, and science, or economic nonviability within the sexual division of labor) are glossed over. Chodorow's account barely glances at the constraints and sanctions which historically have enforced or ensured the coupling of women with men and obstructed or penalized women's coupling or allying in independent groups with other women. She dismisses lesbian existence with the comment that "lesbian relationships do tend to re-create mother-daughter emotions and connections, but most women are heterosexual" (implied: more mature, having developed beyond the mother-daughter connection?). She then adds: "This heterosexual preference and taboos on homosexuality, in addition to objective economic dependence on men, make the option of primary sexual bonds with other women unlikely—though more prevalent in recent years."[13] The significance of that qualification seems irresistible, but Chodorow does not explore it further. Is she saying that lesbian existence has become more *visible* in recent years (in certain groups), that economic and other pressures have changed (under capitalism, socialism, or both), and that consequently more women are rejecting the heterosexual "choice"? She argues that women want children because their heterosexual relationships lack richness and intensity, that in having a child a women seeks to re-create her own intense relationship with her mother. It seems to me that on the basis of her own findings, Chodorow leads us implicitly to conclude that heterosexuality is *not* a "preference" for women, that, for one thing, it fragments the erotic from the emotional in a way that women find impoverishing and painful. Yet her book participates in mandating it. Neglecting the covert socializations and the overt forces which have channelled women into marriage and heterosexual romance, pressures ranging from the selling of daughters to the silences of literature to the images of the television screen, she, like Dinnerstein, is stuck with trying to reform a man-made institution—compulsory heterosexuality—as if, despite profound emotional impulses and complementarities drawing women toward women, there is a mystical/biological heterosexual inclination, a "preference" or "choice" which draws women toward men.

Moreover, it is understood that this "preference" does not need to be explained unless through the tortuous theory of the female Oedipus complex or the necessity for species reproduction. It is lesbian sexuality which (usually, and incorrectly, "included" under male homosexuality) is seen as requiring explanation. This assumption of female heterosexuality seems to me in itself remarkable: it is an enormous assumption to have glided so silently into the foundations of our thought. The extension of this assumption is the frequently heard assertion that in a world of genuine equality, where men are nonoppressive and nurturing, everyone would be bisexual. Such a notion blurs and sentimentalizes the actualities within which women have experienced sexuality; it is a liberal leap across the tasks and struggles of here and now, the continuing process of sexual definition which will generate its own possibilities and choices. (It also assumes that women who have chosen women have done so simply because men are oppressive and emotionally unavailable, which still fails to account for women who continue to pursue relationships with oppressive and/or emotionally unsatisfying men.) I am suggesting that heterosexuality, like motherhood, needs to be recognized and studied as a *political institution*—even, or especially, by those individuals who feel they are, in their personal experience, the precursors of a new social relation between the sexes.

II

If women are the earliest sources of emotional caring and physical nurture for both female and male children, it would seem logical, from a feminist perspective at least, to pose the following questions: whether the search for love and tenderness in both sexes does not originally lead toward women *why in fact women would ever redirect that search*; why species survival, the means of impregnation, and emotional/erotic relationships should ever have become so rigidly identified with each other; and why such violent strictures should be found necessary to enforce women's total emotional, erotic loyalty and subservience to men. I doubt that enough feminist scholars and theorists have taken the pains to acknowledge the societal forces which wrench women's emotional and erotic energies away from themselves and other women from woman-identified values. These forcers, as I shall try to show, range from literal physical enslavement to disguising and distorting of possible options.

I do not assume that mothering by women is a "sufficient cause" of lesbian existence. But the issue of mothering by women has been much in the air of late, usually accompanied by the view that increased parenting by men would minimize antagonism between the sexes and equalize the sexual imbalance of power of males over females. These discussions are carried on without reference to compulsory heterosexuality as a phenomenon, let alone as an ideology. I do not wish to psychologize here, but rather to identify sources of male power. I believe large numbers of men could, in fact, undertake child care on a large scale without radically altering the balance of male power in a male-identified society.

In her essay "The Origin of the Family," Kathleen Gough lists eight characteristics of male power in archaic and contemporary societies which I would like to use as a framework: "men's ability to deny women sexuality or to force it upon them; to command or exploit their labor to control their produce; to control or rob them of their children; to confine them physically and prevent their movement; to use them as objects in male transactions; to cramp their creativeness; or to withhold from them large areas of the society's knowledge and cultural attainments."[14] (Gough does not perceive these power characteristics as specifically enforcing heterosexuality, only as producing sexual inequality.) Below, Gough's words appear in italics; the elaboration of each of her categories, in brackets, is my own.

Characteristics of male power include *the power of men*

1 *to deny women* [their own] *sexuality*—[by means of clitoridectomy and infibulation; chastity belts; punishment, including death, for female adultery; punishment, including death, for lesbian sexuality; psychoanalytic denial of the clitoris; strictures against masturbation; denial of maternal and post menopausal sensuality; unnecessary hysterectomy; pseudolesbian images in the media and literature; closing of archives and destruction of documents relating to lesbian existence]
2 *or to force it* [male sexuality] *upon them*—[by means of rape (including marital rape) and wife beating; father-daughter, brother-sister incest; the socialization of women to feel that male sexual "drive" amounts to a right;[15] idealization of heterosexual romance in art, literature, the media, advertising, etc.; child marriage; arranged marriage; prostitution; the harem; psychoanalytic doctrines of frigidity and vaginal orgasm; pornographic depictions of women responding pleasurably to sexual violence and humiliation (a subliminal message being that sadistic heterosexuality is more "normal" than sensuality between women)]

3 *to command or exploit their labor to control their produce*—[by means of the institutions of marriage and motherhood as unpaid productions; the horizontal segregation of women in paid employment; the decoy of the upwardly mobile token woman; male control of abortion, contraception, sterilization, and childbirth; pimping; female infanticide, which robs mothers of daughters and contributes to generalized devaluation of women]

4 *to control or rob them of their children*—[by means of father right and "legal kidnapping";[16] enforced sterilization; systematized infanticide; seizure of children from lesbian mothers by the courts; the malpractice of male obstetrics; use of the mother as the "token torturer"[17] in genital mutilation or in binding the daughter's feet (or mind) to fit her for marriage]

5 *to confine them physically and prevent their movement*—[by means of rape as terrorism, keeping women off the streets; purdah; foot binding; atrophying of women's athletic capabilities; high heels and "feminine" dress codes in fashion; the veil; sexual harassment on the streets; horizontal segregation of women in employment; prescriptions for "full-time" mothering at home; enforced economic dependence of wives]

6 *to use them as objects in male transactions*—[use of women as "gifts"; bride price; pimping; arranged marriage; use of women as entertainers to facilitate male deals—e.g., wife-hostess, cocktail waitress required to dress for male sexual titillation, call girls, "bunnies," geisha, *kisaeng* prostitutes, secretaries]

7 *to cramp their creativeness*—[witch persecutions as campaigns against midwives and female healers, and as pogrom against independent, "unassimilated" women;[18] definition of male pursuits as more valuable than female within any culture, so that cultural values become the embodiment of male subjectivity; restriction of female self-fulfilment to marriage and motherhood; sexual exploitation of women by male artists and teachers; the social and economic disruption of women's creative aspirations;[19] erasure of female tradition][20]

8 *to withhold from them large areas of the society's knowledge and cultural attainments*—[by means of noneducation of females; the "Great Silence" regarding women and particularly lesbian existence in history and culture; [21] sex-role tracking which deflects women from science, technology, and other "masculine" pursuits; male social/professional bonding which excludes women; discrimination against women in the professions]

These are some of the methods by which male power is manifested and maintained. Looking at the schema, what surely impresses itself is the fact that we are confronting not a simple maintenance of inequality and property possession, but a pervasive cluster of forces, ranging from physical brutality to control of consciousness, which suggests that an enormous potential counterforce is having to be restrained.

Some of the forms by which male power manifests itself are more easily recognizable as enforcing heterosexuality on women than are others. Yet each one I have listed adds to the cluster of forces within which women have been convinced that marriage and sexual orientation toward men are inevitable—even if unsatisfying or oppressive—components of their lives. The chastity belt; child marriage; erasure of lesbian existence (except as exotic and perverse) in art, literature, film; idealization of heterosexual romance and marriage—these are some fairly obvious forms of compulsion, the first two exemplifying physical force, the second two control of consciousness. While clitoridectomy has been assailed by feminists as a form of woman torture,[22] Kathleen Barry first pointed out that it is not simply a way of turning the young girl into a "marriageable" woman through brutal surgery. It intends that women in the intimate proximity of polygamous marriage will not form sexual relationships with each other, that—from a male, genital-fetishist perspective—female erotic connections, even in a sex-segregated situation, will be literally excised.[23]

The function of pornography as an influence on consciousness is a major public issue of our time, when a multibillion-dollar industry has the power to disseminate increasingly sadistic, women-degrading visual images. But even so-called soft-core pornography and advertising depict women as objects of sexual appetite devoid of emotional context, without individual meaning or personality—essentially as a sexual commodity to be consumed by males. (So-called lesbian pornography, created for the male voyeuristic eye, is equally devoid of emotional context or individual personality.) The most pernicious message relayed by pornography is that women are natural sexual prey to men and love it, that sexuality and violence are congruent, and that for women sex is essentially masochistic, humiliation pleasurable, physical abuse erotic. But along with this message comes another, not always recognized: that enforced submission and the use of cruelty, if played out in heterosexual pairing, is sexually "normal," while sensuality between women, including erotic mutuality and respect, is "queer," "sick," and either pornographic in itself or not very exciting compared with the sexuality of whips and bondage.[24] Pornography does not simply create a climate in which sex and violence are interchangeable; *it widens the range of behavior considered acceptable from men in heterosexual intercourse*—behavior which reiteratively strips women of their autonomy, dignity, and sexual potential, including the potential of loving and being loved by women in mutuality and integrity.

In her brilliant study *Sexual Harassment of Working Women: A Case of Sex Discrimination*, Catherine A. MacKinnon delineates the intersection of compulsory heterosexuality and economics. Under capitalism, women are horizontally segregated by gender and occupy a structurally inferior position in the workplace. This is hardly news, but MacKinnon raises the question why, even if capitalism "requires some collection of individuals to occupy low-status, low-paying positions . . . such persons must be biologically female," and goes on to point out that "the fact that male employers often do not hire qualified women, *even when they could pay them less than men* suggests that more than the profit motive is implicated" [emphasis added].[25] She cites a wealth of material documenting the fact that women are not only segregated in low-paying service jobs (as secretaries, domestics, nurses, typists, telephone operators, child-care workers, waitresses), but that "sexualization of the woman" is part of the job. Central and intrinsic to the economic realities of women's lives is the requirement that women will "market sexual attractiveness to men, who tend to hold the economic power and position to enforce their predilections." And MacKinnon documents that "sexual harassment perpetuates the interlocked structure by which women have been kept sexually in thrall to men at the bottom of the labor market. Two forces of American society converge: men's control over women's sexuality and capital's control over employees' work lives."[26] Thus, women in the workplace are at the mercy of sex as power in a vicious circle. Economically disadvantaged, women—whether waitresses or professors—endure sexual harassment to keep their jobs and learn to behave in a complaisantly and ingratiatingly heterosexual manner because they discover this is their true qualification for employment, whatever the job description. And, MacKinnon notes, the woman who too decisively resists sexual overtures in the workplace is accused of being "dried up" and sexless, or lesbian. This raises a specific difference between the experiences of lesbians and homosexual men. A lesbian, closeted on her job because of heterosexual prejudice, is not simply forced into denying the truth of her outside relationships or private life. Her job depends on her pretending to be not merely heterosexual, but a heterosexual *woman* in terms of dressing and playing the feminine, deferential role required of "real" women.

MacKinnon raises radical questions as to the qualitative differences between sexual harassment, rape, and ordinary heterosexual intercourse. ("As one accused rapist put it, he hadn't used 'any more force than is usual for males during the preliminaries.'") She criticizes Susan Brownmiller[27] for separating rape from the mainstream of daily life and for her unexamined premise that "rape is violence, intercourse is sexuality," removing rape from the sexual sphere altogether. More crucially she argues that "taking rape from the realm of 'the sexual,' placing it in the realm of 'the violent,' allows one to be against it without raising any questions about the extent to which the institution of heterosexuality has defined force as a normal part of 'the preliminaries.'"[28] "Never is it asked whether, under conditions of male supremacy, the notion of 'consent' has any meaning."[29]

The fact is that the workplace, among other social institutions, is a place where women have learned to accept male violation of their psychic and physical boundaries as the price of survival; where women have been educated—no less than by romantic literature or by pornography—to perceive themselves as sexual prey. A woman seeking to escape such casual violations along with economic disadvantage may well turn to marriage as a form of hope-for protection, while bringing into marriage neither social nor economic power, thus entering that institution also from a disadvantaged position. MacKinnon finally asks:

> What if inequality is built into the social conceptions of male and female sexuality, of masculinity and femininity, of sexiness and heterosexual attractiveness? Incidents of sexual harassment suggest that male sexual desire itself may be aroused by female vulnerability. . . . Men feel they can take advantage, so they want to, so they do. Examination of sexual harassment, precisely because the episodes appear commonplace, forces one to confront the fact that sexual intercourse normally occurs between economic (as well as physical) unequals . . . the apparent legal requirement that violations of women's sexuality appear out of the ordinary before they will be punished helps prevent women from defining the ordinary conditions of their own consent.[30]

Given the nature and extent of heterosexual pressures—the daily "eroticization of women's subordination," as MacKinnon phrases it[31]—I question the more or less psychoanalytic perspective (suggested by such writers as Karen Horney, H.R. Hayes, Wolfgang Lederer, and, most recently, Dorothy Dinnerstein) that the male need to control women sexually results from some primal male "fear of women" and of women's sexual insatiability. It seems more probable that men really fear not that they will have women's sexual appetites forced on them or that women want to smother and devour them, but that women could be indifferent to them altogether, that men could be allowed sexual and emotional—therefore economic—access to women *only* on women's terms, otherwise being left on the periphery of the matrix.

The means of assuring male sexual access to women have recently received searching investigation by Kathleen Barry.[32] She documents extensive and appalling evidence for the existence, on a very large scale, of international female slavery, the institution once known as "white slavery" but which in fact has involved, and at this very moment involves, women of every race and class. In the theoretical analysis derived from her research, Barry makes the connection between all enforced conditions under which women live subject to men: prostitution, marital rape, father-daughter and brother-sister incest, wife beating, pornography, bride price, the selling of daughters, purdah, and genital mutilation. She sees the rape paradigm—where the victim of sexual assault is held responsible for her own victimization—as leading to the rationalization and acceptance of other forms of enslavement where the woman is presumed to have "chosen" her fate, to embrace it passively, or to have courted it perversely through rash or unchaste behavior. On the contrary, Barry maintains, "female sexual slavery is present in ALL situations where women or girls cannot change the conditions of their existence; where regardless of how they got into those conditions, e.g., social pressure, economic hardship, misplaced trust or the longing for affection, they cannot get out; and where they are subject to sexual violence and exploitation."[33] She provides a spectrum of concrete examples, not only as to the existence of a widespread international traffic in women, but also as to how this operates—whether in the form of a "Minnesota pipeline" funnelling blond, blue-eyed Midwestern runaways to Times Square, or the purchasing of young women out of rural poverty in Latin America or Southeast Asia, or the providing of *maisons d'abattage* for migrant workers in the eighteenth arrondissement of Paris. Instead of "blaming the victim" or trying to diagnose her presumed pathology, Barry turns her floodlight on the pathology of sex colonization itself, the ideology of "cultural sadism" represented by the pornography industry and by the overall identification of women primarily as "sexual beings whose responsibility is the sexual service of men."[34]

Barry delineates what she names a "sexual domination perspective" through whose lens sexual abuse and terrorism of women by men has been rendered almost invisible by treating it as natural and inevitable. From its point of view, women are expendable as long as the sexual and emotional needs of the male can be satisfied. To replace this perspective of domination with a universal standard of basic freedom for women from gender-specific violence, from constraints on movement, and from male right of sexual and emotional access is the political purpose of her book. Like Mary Daly in *Gyn/Ecology*, Barry rejects structuralist and other cultural-relativist rationalizations for sexual torture and anti-woman violence. In her opening chapter, she asks of her readers that they refuse all handy escapes into ignorance and denial. "The only way we can come out of hiding, break through our paralyzing defenses, is to know it all—the full extent of sexual violence and domination of women. . . . In *knowing*, in facing directly, we can learn to chart our course out of this oppression, by envisioning and creating a world which will preclude sexual slavery."[35]

"Until we name the practice, give conceptual definition and form to it, illustrate its life over time and in space, those who are its most obvious victims will also not be able to name it or define their experience."

But women are all, in different ways and to different degrees, its victims; and part of the problem with naming and conceptualizing female sexual slavery is, as Barry clearly sees, compulsory heterosexuality.[36] Compulsory heterosexuality simplifies the task of procurer and pimp in worldwide prostitution rings and "eros centers," while in the privacy of the home, it leads the daughter to "accept" incest/rape by her father, the mother to deny that it is happening, the battered wife to stay on with an abusive husband. "Befriending or love" is a major tactic of the procurer, whose job it is to turn the runaway or the confused young girl over to the pimp for seasoning. The ideology of heterosexual romance, beamed at her from childhood out of fairy tales, television, films, advertising, popular songs, wedding pageantry, is a tool ready to the procurer's hand and one which he does not hesitate to use, as Barry documents. Early female indoctrination in "love" as an emotion may be largely a Western concept; but a more universal ideology concerns the primacy and controllability of the male sexual drive. This is one of many insights offered by Barry's work:

> As sexual power is learned by adolescent boys through the social experience of their sex drive, so do girls learn that the locus of sexual power is male. Given the importance placed on the male sex drive in the socialization of girls as well as boys, early adolescence is probably the first significant phase of male identification in a girl's life and development. . . . As a young girl becomes aware of her own increasing sexual feelings . . . she turns away from her heretofore primary relationships with girlfriends. As they become secondary to her, recede in importance in her life, her own identity also assumes a secondary role and she grows into male identification.[37]

We still need to ask why some women never, even temporarily, turn away from "heretofore primary relationships" with other females. And why does male identification—the casting of one's social, political, and intellectual allegiances with men—exist among lifelong sexual lesbians? Barry's hypothesis throws us among new questions, but it clarifies the diversity of forms in which compulsory heterosexuality presents itself. In the mystique of the overpowering, all-conquering male sex drive, the penis-with-a-life-of-its own, is rooted the law of male sex right to women, which justifies prostitution as a universal cultural assumption on the one hand, while defending sexual slavery within the family on the basis of "family privacy and cultural uniqueness" on the other.[38] The adolescent male sex drive, which, as both young women and men are taught, once triggered cannot take responsibility for itself or take no for an answer, becomes, according to Barry, the norm and rationale for adult male sexual behavior: a condition of *arrested sexual development*. Women learn to accept as natural the inevitability of this "drive" because they receive it as dogma. Hence, marital rape; hence, the Japanese wife resignedly packing her husband's suitcase for a weekend in the *kisaeng* brothels of Taiwan; hence, the psychological as well as economic imbalance of power between husband and wife, male employer and female worker, father and daughter, male professor and female student.

The effect of male identification means

> internalizing the values of the colonizer and actively participating in carrying out the colonization of one's self and one's sex. . . . Male identification is the act whereby women place men above women, including themselves, in credibility, status, and importance in most situations, regardless of the comparative quality the women may bring to the situation. . . . Interaction with women is seen as a lesser form of relating on every level.[39]

What deserves further exploration is the doublethink many women engage in and from which no woman is permanently and utterly free: However woman-to-woman relationships, female support networks, a female and feminist value system are relied on and cherished, indoctrination in male credibility and status can still create synapses in thought, denials of feeling, wishful thinking, a profound sexual and intellectual confusion.[40] I quote here from a letter I received the day I was writing this passage: "I have had very bad relationships with men—I am now in the midst of a very painful separation. I am trying to find my strength through women—without my friends, I could not survive." How many times a day do women speak words like these or think them or write them, and how often does the synapse reassert itself?

Barry summarizes her findings:

> Considering the arrested sexual development that is understood to be normal in the male population, and considering the numbers of men who are pimps, procurers, members of slavery gangs, corrupt officials participating in this traffic, owners, operators, employees of brothels and lodging and entertainment facilities, pornography purveyors, associated with prostitution, wife beaters, child molesters, incest perpetrators, johns (tricks) and rapists, one cannot but be momentarily stunned by the enormous male population engaging in female sexual slavery. The huge number of men engaged in these practices should be cause for declaration of an international emergency, a crisis in sexual violence. But what should be cause for alarm is instead accepted as normal sexual intercourse.[41]

Susan Cavin, in a rich and provocative, if highly speculative, dissertation, suggests that patriarchy becomes possible when the original female band, which includes children but ejects adolescent males, becomes invaded and outnumbered by males; that not patriarchal marriage, but the rape of the mother by the son, becomes the first act of male domination. The entering wedge, or leverage, which allows this to happen is not just a simple change in sex ratios; it is also the mother-child bond, manipulated by adolescent males in order to remain within the matrix past the age of exclusion. Maternal affection is used to establish male right of sexual access, which, however, must ever after be held by force (or through control of consciousness) since the original deep adult bonding is that of woman for woman.[42] I find this hypothesis extremely suggestive, since one form of false consciousness which serves compulsory heterosexuality is the maintenance of a mother-son relationship between women and men, including the demand that women provide maternal solace, nonjudgmental nurturing, and compassion for their harassers, rapists, and batterers (as well as for men who passively vampirize them).

But whatever its origins, when we look hard and clearly at the extent and elaboration of measures designed to keep women within a male sexual purlieu, it becomes an inescapable question whether the issue feminists have to address is not simple "gender inequality" nor the domination of culture by males nor mere "taboos against homosexuality," but the enforcement of heterosexuality for women as a means of assuring male right of physical, economic, and emotional access.[43] One of the many means of enforcement is, of course, the rendering invisible of the lesbian possibility, an engulfed continent which rises fragmentally into view from time to time only to become submerged again. Feminist research and theory that contribute to lesbian invisibility or marginality are actually working against the liberation and empowerment of women as a group.[44]

The assumption that "most women are innately heterosexual" stands as a theoretical and political stumbling block for feminism. It remains a tenable assumption partly because lesbian existence has been written out of history or catalogued under disease, partly because it has been treated as exceptional rather than intrinsic, partly because to acknowledge that for women heterosexuality may not be a "preference" at all but something that has had to be imposed, managed, organized, propagandized, and maintained by force is an immense step to take if you consider yourself freely and "innately" heterosexual. Yet the failure to examine heterosexuality as an institution is like failing to admit that the economic system called capitalism or the caste system of racism is maintained by a variety of forces, including both physical violence and false consciousness. To take the step of questioning heterosexuality as a "preference" or "choice" for women—and to do the intellectual and emotional work that follows—will call for a special quality of courage in heterosexually identified feminists, but I think the rewards will be great: a freeing-up of thinking, the exploring of new paths, the shattering of another great silence, new clarity in personal relationships.

III

I have chosen to use the term *lesbian existence* and *lesbian continuum* because the word *lesbianism* has a clinical and limiting ring. *Lesbian existence* suggests both the fact of the historical presence of lesbians and our continuing creation of the meaning of that existence. I mean the term *lesbian continuum* to include a range—through each woman's life and throughout history—of women-identified experience, not simply the fact that a woman has had or consciously desired genital sexual experience with another woman. If we expand it to embrace many more forms of primary intensity between and among women, including the sharing of a rich inner life, the bonding against male tyranny, the giving and receiving of practical and political support, if we can also hear it in such associations as *marriage resistance* and the "haggard" behavior identified in Mary

Daly (obsolete meanings: "intractable," "willful," "wanton," and "unchaste," "a woman reluctant to yield to wooing"),[45] we begin to grasp breadths of female history and psychology which have lain out of reach as a consequence of limited, mostly clinical, definitions of *lesbianism*.

Lesbian existence comprises both the breaking of a taboo and the rejection of a compulsory way of life. It is also a direct or indirect attack on male right of access to women. But it is more than these, although we may first begin to perceive it as a form of naysaying to patriarchy, an act of resistance. It has, of course, included isolation, self-hatred, breakdown, alcoholism, suicide, and intrawoman violence; we romanticize at our peril what it means to love and act against the grain, and under heavy penalties; and lesbian existence has been lived (unlike, say, Jewish or Catholic existence) without access to any knowledge of a tradition, a continuity, a social underpinning. The destruction of records and memorabilia and letters documenting the realities of lesbian existence must be taken very seriously as a means of keeping heterosexuality compulsory for women, since what has been kept from our knowledge is joy, sensuality, courage, and community, as well as guilt, self-betrayal, and pain.[46]

Lesbians have historically been deprived of a political existence through "inclusion" as female versions of male homosexuality. To equate lesbian existence with male homosexuality because each is stigmatized is to erase female reality once again. Part of the history of lesbian existence is, obviously, to be found where lesbians, lacking a coherent female community, have shared a kind of social life and common cause with homosexual men. But there are differences: women's lack of economic and cultural privilege relative to men; qualitative differences in female and male relationships—for example, the patterns of anonymous sex among male homosexuals, and the pronounced ageism in male homosexual standards of sexual attractiveness. I perceive the lesbian experience as being, like motherhood, a profoundly *female* experience, with particular oppressions, meanings, and potentialities we cannot comprehend as long as we simply bracket it with other sexually stigmatized existences. Just as the term *parenting* serves to conceal the particular and significant reality of being a parent who is actually a mother, the term *gay* may serve the purpose of blurring the very outlines we need to discern, which are of crucial value for feminism and for the freedom of women as a group.[47]

As the term *lesbian* has been held to limiting, clinical associations in its patriarchal definition, female friendship and comradeship have been set apart from the erotic, thus limiting the erotic itself. But as we deepen and broaden the range of what we define as lesbian existence, as we delineate a lesbian continuum, we begin to discover the erotic in female terms: as that which is unconfined to any single part of the body or solely to the body itself; as an energy not only diffuse but, as Audre Lorde has described it, omnipresent in "the sharing of joy, whether physical, emotional, psychic," and in the sharing of work; as the empowering joy which "makes us less willing to accept powerlessness, or those other supplied states of being which are not native to me, such as resignation, despair, self-effacement, depression, self-denial."[48] In another context, writing of women and work, I quoted the autobiographical passage in which the poet H.D. described how her friend Bryher supported her in persisting with the visionary experience which was to shape her mature work:

> I knew that this experience, this writing-on-the-wall before me, could not be shared with anyone except the girl who stood so bravely there beside me. This girl said without hesitation, "Go on." It was she really who had the detachment and integrity of the Pythoness of Delphi. But it was I, battered and dissociated . . . who was seeing the pictures, and who was reading the writing or granted the inner vision. Or perhaps, in some sense, we were "seeing" it together, for without her, admittedly, I could not have gone on.[49]

If we consider the possibility that all women—from the infant suckling at her mother's breast, to the grown woman experiencing orgasmic sensations while suckling her own child, perhaps recalling her mother's milk smell in her own, to two women like Virginia Woolf's Chloe and Olivia, who share a laboratory,[50] to the woman dying at ninety, touched and handled by women—exist on a lesbian continuum, we can see ourselves as moving in and out of this continuum, whether we identify ourselves as lesbian or not.

We can then connect aspects of woman identification as diverse as the impudent, intimate girl friendships of eight or nine year olds and the banding together of those women of the twelfth and fifteenth centuries known as the Beguines who "shared houses, rented to one another, bequeathed houses to their room-mates . . . in cheap subdivided houses in the artisans' area of town," who "practiced Christian virtue on their own, dressing and living simply and not associating with men," who earned their livings as spinsters, bakers, nurses, or ran schools for young girls, and who managed—until the Church forced them to disperse—to live independent both of marriage and of conventual restrictions.[51] It allows us to connect these women with the more celebrated "Lesbians" of the women's school around Sappho of the seventh century B.C., with the secret sororities and economic networks reported among African women, and with the Chinese marriage-resistance sisterhoods—communties of women who refused marriage or who, if married, often refused to consummate their marriages and soon left their husbands, the only women in China who were not footbound and who, Agnes Smedley tells us, welcomed the births of daughters and organzied successful women's strikes in the silk mills.[52] It allows us to connect and compare disparate individual instances of marriage resistance: for example, the strategies available to Emily Dickinson, a nineteenth-century white woman genius, with the strategies available to Zora Neale Hurston, a twentieth-century Black woman genius. Dickinson never married, had tenuous intellectual friendships with men, lived self-convented in her genteel father's house in Amherst, and wrote a lifetime of passionate letters to her sister-in-law Sue Gilbert and a smaller group of such letters to her friend Kate Scott Anthon. Hurston married twice but soon left each husband, scrambled her way from Florida to Harlem to Columbia University to Haiti and finally back to Florida, moved in and out of white patronage and poverty, professional success, and failure; her survival relationships were all with women, beginning with her mother. Both of these women in their vastly different circumstances were marriage resisters, committed to their own work and selfhood, and were later characterized as "apolitical." Both were drawn to men of intellectual quality; for both of them women provided the ongoing fascination and sustenance of life.

If we think of heterosexuality as *the* natural emotional and sensual inclination for women, lives as these are seen as deviant, as pathological, or as emotionally and sensually deprived. Or, in more recent and permissive jargon, they are banalized as "life styles." And the work of such women, whether merely the daily work of individual or collective survival and resistance or the work of the writer, the activist, the reformer, the anthropologist, or the artist—the work of self-creation—is undervalued, or seen as the bitter fruit of "penis envy" or the sublimation of repressed eroticism or the meaningless rant of a "man-hater." But when we turn the lens of vision and consider the degree to which and the methods whereby heterosexual "preference" has actually been imposed on women, not only can we understand differently the meaning of individual lives and work, but we can begin to recognize a central fact of women's history: that women have always resisted male tyranny. A feminism of action, often though not always without a theory, has constantly re-emerged in every culture and in every period. We can then begin to study women's struggle against powerlessness, women's radical rebellion, not just in male-defined "concrete revolutionary situations"[53] but in all the situations male ideologies have not perceived as revolutionary—for example, the refusal of some women to produce children, aided at great risk by other women;[54] the refusal to produce a higher standard of living and leisure for men (Leghorn and Parker show how both are part of women's unacknowledged, unpaid, and ununionized economic contribution). We can no longer have patience with Dinnerstein's view that women have simply collaborated with men in the "sexual arrangements" of history. We begin to observe behavior, both in history and in individual biography, that has hitherto been invisible or misnamed, behavior which often constitutes, given the limits of the counterforce exerted in a given time and place, radical rebellion. And we can connect these rebellions and the necessity for them with the physical passion of woman for woman which is central to lesbian existence: the erotic sensuality which has been, precisely, the most violently erased fact of female experience.

Heterosexuality has been both forcibly and subliminally imposed on women. Yet everywhere women have resisted it, often at the cost of physical torture, imprisonment, psychosurgery, social ostracism, and extreme poverty. "Compulsory heterosexuality" was named as one of the "crimes against women" by the Brussels International Tribunal on Crimes against Women in 1976. Two pieces of testimony from two very different cultures reflect the degree to which persecution of lesbians is a global practice here and now. A report from Norway relates:

> A lesbian in Oslo was in a heterosexual marriage that didn't work, so she started taking tranquillizers and ended up at the health sanatorium for treatment and rehabilitation. . . . The moment she said in family group therapy that she believed she was a lesbian, the doctor told her she was not. He knew from "looking into her eyes," he said. She had the eyes of a woman who wanted sexual intercourse with her husband. So she was subjected to so-called "couch therapy." She was put into a comfortably heated room, naked, on a bed, and for an hour her husband was to . . . try to excite her sexually. . . . The ideal was that the touching was always to end with sexual intercourse. She felt stronger and stronger aversion. She threw up and sometimes ran out of the room to avoid this "treatment." The more strongly she asserted that she was a lesbian, the more violent the forced heterosexual intercourse became. This treatment went on for about six months. She escaped from the hospital, but she was brought back. Again she escaped. She has not been there since. In the end she realized that she had been subjected to forcible rape for six months.

And from Mozambique:

> I am condemned to a life of exile because I will not deny that I am a lesbian, that my primary commitments are, and will always be to other women. In the new Mozambique, lesbianism is considered a left-over from colonialism and decadent Western civilization. Lesbians are sent to rehabilitation camps to learn through self-criticism the correct line about themselves. . . . If I am forced to denounce my own love for women, if I therefore denounce myself, I could go back to Mozambique and join forces in the exciting and hard struggle of rebuilding a nation, including the struggle for the emancipation of Mozambiquan women. As it is, I either risk the rehabilitation camps, or remain in exile.[55]

Nor can it be assumed that women like those in Carroll Smith-Rosenberg's study, who married, stayed married, yet dwelt in a profoundly female emotional and passional world, "preferred" or "chose" heterosexuality. Women have married because it was necessary, in order to survive economically, in order to have children who would not suffer economic deprivation or social ostracism, in order to remain respectable, in order to do what was expected of women, because coming out of "abnormal" childhoods they wanted to feel "normal" and because heterosexual romance has been represented as the great female adventure, duty, and fulfillment. We may faithfully or ambivalently have obeyed the institution, but our feelings—and our sensuality—have not been tamed or contained within it. There is no statistical documentation of the numbers of lesbians who have remained in heterosexual marriages for most of their lives. But in a letter to the early lesbian publication *The Ladder*, the playwright Lorraine Hansberry had this to say:

> I suspect that that problem of the married woman who would prefer emotional-physical relationships with other women is proportionally much higher than a similar statistic for men. (A statistic surely no one will ever really have.) This because of the estate of women being what it is, how could we ever begin to guess the numbers of women who are not prepared to risk a life alien to what they have been taught all their lives to believe was their "natural" destiny—AND—their only expectation for ECONOMIC security. It seems to be that this is why the question has an immensity that it does not have for male homosexuals. . . . A woman of strength and honesty may, if she chooses, sever her marriage and marry a new male mate and society will be upset that the divorce rate is rising so—but there are few places in the United States, in any event, where she will be anything remotely akin to an "outcast." Obviously this is not true for a woman who would end her marriage to take up life with another woman.[56]

This *double life*—this apparent acquiescence to an institution founded on male interest and prerogative—has been characteristic of female experience: in motherhood and in many kinds of heterosexual behavior, including the rituals of courtship; the pretense of asexuality by the nineteenth-century wife; the simulation of orgasm by the prostitute, the courtesan, the twentieth-century "sexually liberated" woman.

Meridel LeSueur's documentary novel of the depression, *The Girl*, is arresting as a study of female double life. The protagonist, a waitress in a St. Paul working-class speakeasy, feels herself passionately attracted to the young man Butch, but her survival relationships are with Clara, an older waitress and prostitute, with Belle, whose husband owns the bar, and with Amelia, a union activist. For Clara and Belle and the unnamed protagonist, sex with men is in one sense an escape from the bedrock misery of daily life, a flare of intensity in the gray, relentless, often brutal web of day-to-day existence:

> It was like having a magnet pulling me. It was exciting and powerful and frightening. He was after me too and when he found me I would run, or be petrified, just standing in front of him like a zany. And he told me not to be wandering with Clara to the Marigold where we danced with strangers. He said he would knock the shit out of me. Which made me shake and tremble, but it was better than being a husk full of suffering and not knowing why.[57]

Throughout the novel the theme of double life emerges; Belle reminisces about her marriage to bootlegger Hoinck:

> You know, when I had that black eye and said I hit it on the cupboard, well he did it the bastard, and then he says don't tell anybody. . . . He's nuts, that's what he is, nuts, and I don't see why I live with him, why I put up with him a minute on this earth. But listen kid, she said, I'm telling you something. She looked at me and her face was wonderful. She said, Jesus Christ, Goddam him I love him that's why I'm hooked like this all my life, Goddam him I love him.[58]

After the protagonist has her first sex with Butch, her women friends care for her bleeding, give her whiskey, and compare notes.

> My luck, the first time and I got into trouble. He gave me a little money and I come to St. Paul where for ten bucks they'd stick a huge vet's needle into you and you start it and then you were on your own. . . . I never had no child. I've just had Hoinck to mother, and a hell of a child he is.[59]
>
> Later they made me go back to Clara's room to lie down. . . . Clara lay down beside me and put her arms around me and wanted me to tell her about it but she wanted to tell about herself. She said she started it when she was twelve with a bunch of boys in an old shed. She said nobody had paid any attention to her before and she became very popular. . . . They like it so much, she said, why shouldn't you give it to them and get presents and attention? I never cared anything for it and neither did my mama. But it's the only thing you got that's valuable.[60]

Sex is thus equated with attention from the male, who is charismatic though brutal, infantile, or unreliable. Yet it is the women who make life endurable for each other, give physical affection without causing pain, share, advise, and stick by each other. *(I am trying to find my strength through women—without my friends, I could not survive.)* LeSueur's *The Girl* parallels Toni Morrison's remarkable *Sula*, another revelation of female double life:

> Nel was the one person who had wanted nothing from her, who had accepted all aspects of her. . . . Nel was one of the reasons Sula had drifted back to Medallion. . . . The men . . . had merged into one large personality: the same language of love, the same entertainments of love, the same cooling of love. Whenever she introduced her private thoughts into their rubbings and goings, they hooded their eyes. They taught her nothing but love tricks, shared nothing but worry, gave nothing but money. She had been looking all along for a friend, and it took her a while to discover that a lover was not a comrade and could never be—for a woman.

But Sula's last thought at the second of her death is "Wait'll I tell Nel." And after Sula's death, Nel looks back on her own life:

> "All that time, all that time, I thought I was missing Jude." And the loss pressed down on her chest and came up into her throat. "We was girls together," she said as though explaining something. "O Lord, Sula," she cried, "Girl, girl, girlgirlgirl!" It was a fine cry—loud and long—but it had no bottom and it had no top, just circles and circles of sorrow.[61]

The Girl and *Sula* are both novels which examine what I am calling the lesbian continuum, in contrast to the shallow or sensational "lesbian scenes" in recent commercial fiction.[62] Each shows us woman identification untarnished (till the end of LeSueur's novel) by romanticism; each depicts the competition of heterosexual compulsion for women's attention, the diffusion and frustration of female bonding that might, in a more conscious form, reintegrate love and power.

IV

Woman identification is a source of energy, a potential springhead of female power, curtailed and contained under the institution of heterosexuality. The denial of reality and invisibility to women's passion for women, women's choice of women as allies, life companions, and community, the forcing of such relationships into dissimulation and their disintegration under intense pressure have meant an incalculable loss to the power of all women *to change the social relations of the sexes, to liberate ourselves and each other.* The lie of compulsory female heterosexuality today afflicts not just feminist scholarship, but every profession, every reference work, every curriculum, every organizing attempt, every relationship or conversation over which it hovers. It creates, specifically, a profound falseness, hypocrisy, and hysteria in the heterosexual dialogue, for every heterosexual relationship is lived in the queasy strobe light of that lie. However we choose to identify ourselves, however we find ourselves labeled, it flickers across and distorts our lives.[63]

The lie keeps numberless women psychologically trapped, trying to fit mind, spirit, and sexuality into a prescribed script because they cannot look beyond the parameters of the acceptable. It pulls on the energy of such women even as it drains the energy of "closeted" lesbians—the energy exhausted in the double life. The lesbian trapped in the "closet," the woman imprisoned in prescriptive ideas of the "normal" share the pain of blocked options, broken connections, lost access to self-definition freely and powerfully assumed.

The lie is many-layered. In Western tradition, one layer—the romantic—asserts that women are inevitably, even if rashly and tragically, drawn to men; that even when that attraction is suicidal (e.g., *Tristan and Isolde*, Kate Chopin's *The Awakening*), it is still an organic imperative. In the tradition of the social sciences it asserts that primary love between the sexes is "normal"; that women *need* men as social and economic protectors, for adult sexuality, and for psychological completion; that the heterosexually constituted family is the basic social unit; that women who do not attach their primary intensity to men must be, in functional terms, condemned to an even more devastating outsiderhood than their outsiderhood as women. Small wonder that lesbians are reported to be a more hidden population than male homosexuals. The Black lesbian-feminist critic Lorraine Bethel, writing on Zora Neale Hurston, remarks that for a Black woman—already twice an outsider—to choose to assume still another "hated identity" is problematic indeed. Yet the lesbian continuum has been a life line for Black women both in Africa and the United States.

> Black women have a long tradition of bonding together . . . in a Black/women's community that has been a source of vital survival information, psychic and emotional support for us. We have a distinct Black women-identified folk culture based on our experiences as Black women in this society; symbols, language and modes of expression that are specific to the realities of our lives. . . . Because Black women were rarely among those Blacks and females who gained access to literary and other acknowledged forms of artistic expression, this Black female bonding and Black woman-identification has often been hidden and unrecorded except in the individual lives of Black women through our own memories of our particular Black female tradition.[64]

Another layer of the lie is the frequently encountered implication that women turn to women out of hatred for men. Profound scepticism, caution, and righteous paranoia about men may indeed be part of any healthy woman's response to the misogyny of male-dominated culture, to the forms assumed by "normal" male sexuality, and to *the failure even of "sensitive" or "political" men to perceive or find these troubling.* Lesbian existence is also represented as mere refuge from male abuses, rather than as an electric and empowering charge between women. One of the most frequently quoted literary passages on lesbian relationship is that in which Colette's Renée, in *The Vagabond*, describes "the melancholy and touching image of two weak creatures who have perhaps found shelter in each other's arms, there to sleep and weep, safe from man who is often cruel, and there to taste *better than any pleasure, the bitter happiness of feeling themselves akin, frail and forgotten* [emphasis added]."[65] Colette is often considered a lesbian writer. Her popular reputation has, I think, much to do with the fact that she writes about lesbian existence as if for a male audience; her earliest "lesbian" novels, the Claudine series, were written under compulsion for her husband and published under both their names. At all events, expect for her writings on her mother, Colette is a less reliable source on the lesbian continuum than I would think, Charlotte Brontë, who understood that while women may, indeed must, be one another's allies, mentors, and comforters in the female struggle for survival, there is quite extraneous delight in each other's company and attraction to each others' minds and character, which attend a recognition of each others' strengths.

By the same token, we can say that there is a *nascent* feminist political content in the act of choosing a woman lover or life partner in the face of institutionalized heterosexuality.[66] But for lesbian existence to realize this political content in an ultimately liberating form, the erotic choice must deepen and expand into conscious woman identification—into lesbian feminism.

The work that lies ahead, of unearthing and describing what I call here "lesbian existence," is potentially liberating for all women. It is work that must assuredly move beyond the limits of white and middle-class Western Women's Studies to examine women's lives, work, and groupings within every racial, ethnic, and political structure. There are differences, moreover, between "lesbian existence" and the "lesbian continuum," differences we can discern even in the movement of our own lives. The lesbian continuum, I suggest, needs delineation in light of the "double life" of women, not lonely women self-described as heterosexual but also of self-described lesbians. We need a far more exhaustive account of the forms the double life has assumed. Historians need to ask at every point how heterosexuality as institution has been organized and maintained through the female wage scale, the enforcement of middle-class women's "leisure." The glamorization of the so-called sexual liberation, the withholding of education from women, the imagery of "high art" and popular culture, the mystification of the "personal" sphere, and much else. We need an economics which comprehends the institution of heterosexuality, with its doubled workload for women and its sexual divisions of labor, as the most idealized of economic relations.

The question inevitably will arise: Are we then to condemn all heterosexual relationships, including those which are least oppressive? I believe this question, though often heartfelt, is the wrong question here. We have been stalled in a maze of false dichotomies which prevents our apprehending the institution as a whole: "good" versus "bad" marriages; "marriage for love" versus arranged marriage; "liberated" sex versus prostitution; heterosexual intercourse versus rape; *Liebeschmerz* versus humiliation and dependency. Within the institution exist, of course, qualitative differences of experience; but the absence of choice remains the great unacknowledged reality, and in the absence of choice, women will remain dependent upon the chance or luck of particular relationships and will have no collective power to determine the meaning and place of sexuality in their lives. As we address the institution itself, moreover, we begin to perceive a history of female resistance which has never fully understood itself because it has been so fragmented, miscalled, erased. It will require a courageous grasp of the politics and economics, as well as the cultural propaganda, of heterosexuality to carry us beyond individual cases or diversified group situations into the complex kind of overview needed to undo the power men everywhere wield over women, power which has become a model for every other form of exploitation and illegitimate control.

Afterword

In 1980, Ann Snitow, Christine Stansell, and Sharon Thompson, three Marxist-feminist activists and scholars, sent out a call for papers for an anthology on the politics of sexuality. Having just finished writing "Compulsory Heterosexuality" for *Signs*, I sent them that manuscript and asked them to consider it. Their anthology, *Powers of Desire*, was published by the Monthly Review Press New Feminist Library in 1983 and included my paper. During the intervening period, the four of us were in correspondence, but I was able to take only limited advantage of this dialogue due to ill health and resulting surgery. With their permission, I reprint here excerpts from that correspondence as a way of indicating that my essay should be read as one contribution to a long exploration in progress, not as my own "last word" on sexual politics. I also refer interested readers to *Powers of Desire* itself.

Dear Adrienne,

. . . In one of our first letters, we told you that we were finding parameters of left-wing/ feminist sexual discourse to be far broader than we imagined. Since then, we have perceived what we believe to be a crisis in the feminist movement about sex, an intensifying debate (although not always an explicit one), and a questioning of assumptions once taken for granted. While we fear the link between sex and violence, as do Women Against Pornography, we wish we better understood its sources in ourselves as well as in men. In the Reagan era, we can hardly afford to romanticize any old norm of a virtuous and moral sexuality.

In your piece, you are asking the question, what would women choose in a world where patriarchy and capitalism did *not* rule? We agree with you that heterosexuality is an institution created between these grind stones, but we don't conclude, therefore, that it is entirely a male creation. You only allow for female historical agency insofar as women exist on the lesbian continuum while we would argue that women's history, like men's history, is created out of a dialectic of necessity and choice.

All three of us (hence one lesbian, two heterosexual women) had questions about your use of the term "false consciousness" for women's heterosexuality. In general, we think the false-consciousness model can blind us to the necessities and desires that comprise the lives of the oppressed. It can also lead to the too easy denial of others' experience when that experience is different from our own. We posit, rather, a complex social model in which all erotic life is a continuum, one which therefore includes relations with men.

Which brings us to this metaphor of the continuum. We know you are a poet, not an historian, and we look forward to reading your metaphors all our lives—and standing straighter as feminists, as women, for having read them. But the metaphor of the lesbian continuum is open to all kinds of misunderstandings, and these sometimes have odd political effects. For example, Sharon reports that at a recent meeting around the abortion-rights struggle, the notion of continuum arose in the discussion several times and underwent divisive transformation. Overall, the notion that two ways of being existed on the same continuum was interpreted to mean that those two ways were the *same*. The sense of range and gradation that your description evokes disappeared. Lesbianism and female friendship became exactly the same thing. Similarly, heterosexuality and rape became the same. In one of several versions the continuum that evolved, a slope was added, like so:

Lesbianism

Sex with men, no penetration

Sex with men, penetration

Rape

This sloped continuum brought its proponents to the following conclusion: An appropriate, workable abortion-rights strategy is to inform all women that heterosexual penetration is rape, whatever their subjective experience to the contrary. All women will immediately recognize the truth of this and opt for the alternative of nonpenetration. The abortion-right struggle will thus be simplified into a struggle against coercive sex and its consequences (since no enlightened woman would voluntary undergo penetration unless her object was procreation—a peculiarly Catholic-sounding view.)

The proponents of this strategy were young women who have worked hard in the abortion-rights movement for the past two or more years. They are inexperienced but they are dedicated. For this reason, we take their reading of your work seriously. We don't think, however, that it comes solely, or even at all, from the work itself. As likely a source is the tendency to dichotomize that has plagued the women's movement. The source of that tendency is harder to trace.

In that regard, the hints in "Compulsory" about the double life of women intrigue us. You define the double life as "the apparent acquiescence to an institution founded on male interest and prerogative." But that definition doesn't really explain your other references—to, for instance, the "intense mixture" of love and anger in lesbian relationships and to the peril of romanticizing what it means "to love and act against the grain." We think these comments raise extremely important issues for feminists right now; the problem of division and anger among us needs airing and analysis. Is this, by any chance, the theme of a piece you have in the works?

. . . We would still love it if we could have a meeting with you in the next few months. Any chance? . . . Greetings and support from us—in all your undertakings.

We send love,
Sharon, Chris, and Ann

New York City
April 19, 1981

Dear Ann, Chris, and Sharon,

. . . It's good to be back in touch with you, you who have been so unfailingly patient, generous, and persistent. Above all, it's important to me that you know that ill health, not a withdrawal because of political differences, delayed my writing back to you. . . .

"False consciousness" can, I agree, be used as a term of dismissal for any thinking we don't like or adhere to. But, as I try to illustrate in some detail, there is a real, identifiable system of heterosexual propaganda, of defining women as existing for the sexual use of men, which goes beyond "sex role" or "gender" stereotyping or "sexist imagery" to include a vast number of verbal and nonverbal messages. And this I call "control of consciousness." The possibility of a woman who does not exist sexually for men—the lesbian possibility—is buried, erased, occluded, distorted, misnamed, and driven underground. The feminist books—Chodorow, Dinnerstein, Ehrenreich and English, and others—which I discuss at the beginning of my essay contribute to this invalidation and erasure, and as such are part of the problem.

My essay is founded on the belief that we all think from within the limits of certain solipsisms—usually linked with privilege, racial, cultural, and economic as well as sexual—which present themselves as "the universal," "the way things are," "all women," etc., etc. I wrote it equally out of the belief that in becoming conscious of our solipsisms we have certain kinds of choices, that we can and must re-educate ourselves. I never have maintained that heterosexual feminists are walking about in a state of "brainwashed" false consciousness. Nor have such phrases as "sleeping with the enemy" seemed to me either profound or useful. *Homophobia* is too diffuse a term and does not go very far in helping us identify and talk about the sexual solipsism of heterosexual feminism. In this paper I was trying to ask heterosexual feminists to examine their experience of heterosexuality critically and antagonistically, to critique the institution of which they are a part, to struggle with the norm and its implications for women's freedom, to become more open to the considerable resources offered by the lesbian-feminist perspective, to refuse to settle for the personal privilege and solution of individual "good relationship" within the institution of heterosexuality.

As regards "female historical agency," I wanted, precisely, to suggest that the victim model is insufficient; that there *is* a history of female agency and choice which has actually challenged aspects of male supremacy; that, like male supremacy, these can be found in many different cultures. . . . It's not that I think all female agency has been solely and avowedly lesbian. But by erasing lesbian existence from female history, from theory, from literary criticism . . . from feminist approaches to economic structure, ideas about "the family," etc., an enormous amount of female agency is kept unavailable, hence unusable. I wanted to demonstrate that the kind of obliteration continues to be acceptable in seriously regarded feminist texts. What surprised me in the responses to my essay, including your notes, is how almost every aspect of it has been considered, except this—to me—central one. I was taking a position which was neither lesbian/separatist in the sense of dismissing heterosexual women nor a "gay civil rights" plea for . . . openness to lesbianism as an "option" or an "alternate life style." I was urging that lesbian *existence* has been an unrecognized and unaffirmed claiming by women of their sexuality, thus a pattern of resistance, thus also a kind of borderline position from which to analyze and challenge the relationship of heterosexuality to male supremacy. And that lesbian existence, when recognized, demands a conscious restructuring of feminist analysis and criticism, not just a token reference or two.

I certainly agree with you that the term *lesbian continuum* can be misused. It was, in the example you report of the abortion-rights meeting, though I would think anyone who had read my work from *Of Woman Born* onward would know that my position on abortion and sterilization abuse is more complicated than that. My own problem with the phrase is that it can be, is, used by women who have not yet begun to examine the privileges and solipsisms of heterosexuality, as a safe way to describe their felt connections with women, without having to share in the risks and threats of lesbian existence. What I had thought to delineate rather complexly as a continuum has begun to sound more like "life-style shopping." *Lesbian continuum*—the phrase—came from a desire to allow for the greatest possible variation of female-identified experience, while paying a different kind of respect to *lesbian existence*—the traces and knowledge of women who have made their primary erotic and emotional choices for women. If I were writing the paper today, I would still want to make this distinction, but would put more caveats around *lesbian continuum*. I fully agree with you that Smith-Rosenberg's "female world" is not a social ideal, enclosed as it is within prescriptive middle-class heterosexuality and marriage.

My own essay could have been stronger had it drawn on more of the literature by Black women toward which Toni Morrison's *Sula* inevitably pointed me. In reading a great deal more of Black women's fiction I began to perceive a different set of valences from those found in white women's fiction for the most part: a different quest for the woman hero, a different relationship both to sexuality with men and to female loyalty and bonding. . . .

You comment briefly on your reactions to some of the radical-feminist works I cited in my first footnote.[67] I am myself critical of some of them even as I found them vitally useful. What most of them share is a taking seriously of misogyny—of organized, institutionalized, normalized hostility and violence against women. I feel no "hierarchy of oppressions" is needed in order for us to take misogyny as seriously as we take racism, anti-Semitism, imperialism. To take misogyny seriously needn't mean that we perceive women merely as victims, without responsibilities or choices; it does mean recognizing the "necessity" in that "dialectic of necessity and choice"—identifying, describing, refusing to turn aside our eyes. I think that some of the apparent reductiveness, or even obsessiveness, of some white radical-feminist theory derives from racial and/or class solipsism, but also from the immense effort of trying to render women hating visible amid so much denial. . . .

Finally, as to poetry and history: I want both in my life; I need to see through both. If metaphor can be misconstrued, history can also lead to misconstrual when it obliterates acts of resistance or rebellion, wipes out transformational models, or sentimentalizes power relationships. I know you know this. I believe we are all trying to think and write out of our best consciences, our most open consciousness. I expect that quality in this book which you are editing, and look forward with anticipation to the thinking—and the actions—toward which it may take us.

In sisterhood,
Adrienne

Montague, Massachusetts
November 1981

Notes

1 See for example, Paula Gunn Allen, *The Sacred Hoop: Recovering the Feminine in American Indian Traditions* (Boston: Beacon, 1986); Beth Brant, ed., *A Gathering of Spirit: Writing and Art by North American Indian Women* (Montpelier, Vt.: Sinister Wisdom Books, 1984); Gloria Anzaldúa and Cherríe Moraga, eds., *This Bridge Called My Back: Writings by Radical Women of Color* (Watertown, Mass.: Persephone, 1981; distributed by Kitchen Table/Women of Color Press, Albany, N.Y.); J.R. Roberts, *Black Lesbians: An Annotated Bibliography* (Tallahassee, Fla.: Naiad, 1981); Barbara Smith, ed., *Home Girls: A Black Feminist Anthology* (Albany, N.Y.: Kitchen Table/Women of Color Press, 1984). As Lorraine Bethel and Barbara Smith pointed out in *Conditions 5: The Black Women's Issue* (1980), a great deal of fiction by Black women depicts primary relationships between women. I would like to cite here the work of Ama Ata Aidoo, Toni Cade Bambara, Buchi Emecheta, Bessie Head, Zora Neale Hurston, Alice Walker. Donna Allegra, Red Jordan Arobateau, Audre Lorde, Ann Allen Shockley, among others, write directly as Black lesbians. For fiction by other lesbians of color, see Elly Bulkin, ed., *Lesbian Fiction: An Anthology* (Watertown, Mass.; Persephone, 1981).

See also, for accounts of contemporary Jewish-lesbian existence, Evelyn Torton Beck, ed., *Nice Jewish Girls: A Lesbian Anthology* (Watertown, Mass.; Persephone, 1982; distributed by Crossing Press, Trumansburg, N.Y. 14886); Alice Bloch, *Lifetime Guarantee* (Watertown, Mass.; Persephone, 1982); and Melanie Kaye-Kantrowitz and Irena Klepfisz, eds., *The Tribe of Dina: A Jewish Women's Anthology* (Montpelier, Vt.: Sinister Wisdom Books, 1986).

The earliest formulation that I know of heterosexuality as an institution was in the lesbian-feminist paper *The Furies*, founded in 1971. For a collection of articles from that paper, see Nancy Myron and Charlotte Bunch, eds., *Lesbianism and the Women's Movement* (Oakland, Calif.: Diana Press, 1975; distributed by Crossing Press, Trumansburg, N.Y. 14886).

2 Alice Rossi, "Children and Work in the Lives of Women," paper delivered at the University of Arizona, Tucson, February 1976.

3 Doris Lessing, *The Golden Notebook*, 1962 (New York: Bantam, 1977), p.480.

4 Nancy Chodorow, *The Reproduction of Mothering* (Berkeley: University of California Press, 1978); Dorothy Dinnerstein, *The Mermaid and the Minotaur: Sexual Arrangements and the Human Malaise* (New York: Harper & Row, 1976); Barbara Ehrenreich and Deirdre English, *For Her Own Good: 150 Years of the Experts' Advice to Women* (Garden City, N.Y.: Doubleday, Anchor, 1978); Jean Baker Miller, *Toward a New Psychology of Women* (Boston: Beacon, 1976).

5 I could have chosen many other serious and influential recent books, including anthologies, which would illustrate the same point: e.g. *Our Bodies, Ourselves*, the Boston Women's Health Book Collective's best seller (New York: Simon and Schuster, 1976), which devotes a separate (and inadequate) chapter to lesbians, but whose message is that heterosexuality is most women's life preference; Berenice Carroll, ed., *Liberating Women's History: Theoretical and Critical Essays* (Urbana: University of Illinois Press, 1976), which does not include even a token essay on the lesbian presence in history, though an essay by Linda Gordon, Persis Hunt, et. al. notes the use by male historians of "sexual deviance" as a category to discredit and dismiss Anna Howard Shaw, Jane Addams, and other feminists ("Historical Phallacies: Sexism in American Historical Writing"); and Renate Bridenthal and Claudia Koonz, eds., *Becoming Visible: Women in European History* (Boston: Houghton Mifflin, 1977), which contains three mentions of male heterosexuality but no materials that I have been able to locate on lesbians. Gerda Lerner, ed., *The Female Experience: An American Documentary* (Indianapolis: Bobbs-Merrill, 1977), contains an abridgement of two lesbian-feminist-position papers from the contemporary movement but no other documentation of lesbian existence. Lerner does note in her preface, however, how the charge of deviance has been used to fragment women and discourage women's resistance. Linda Gordon, in *Woman's Body, Woman's Right: A Social History of Birth Control in America* (New York: Viking, Grossman, 1976), notes accurately that "it is not that feminism has produced more lesbians. There have always been many lesbians, despite the high levels of repression; and most lesbians experience their sexual preference as innate" (p. 410).

[A.R., 1986: I am glad to update the first annotation in this footnote. *"The New" Our Bodies, Ourselves* (New York: Simon and Schuster, 1984) contains an expanded chapter on "Loving Women: Lesbian Life and Relationships" and furthermore emphasizes *choices* for women throughout—in terms of sexuality, health care, family, politics, etc.]

6 Jonathan Katz, ed., *Gay American History: Lesbians and Gay Men in the U.S.A.* (New York: Thomas Y. Crowell, 1976).

7 Nancy Sahli, "Smashing Women's Relationships before the Fall," *Chysalis: A Magazine of Women's Culture* 8 (1979): 17–27.

8 This is a book which I have publicly endorsed. I would still do so, though with the above caveat. It is only since beginning to write this article that I fully appreciated how enormous is the unasked question in Ehrenreich and English's book.

9 See, for example, Kathleen Barry, *Female Sexual Slavery* (Englewood Cliffs, N.J.: Prentice-Hall, 1979); Mary Daly, *Gyn/Ecology: The Metaethics of Radical Feminism* (Boston: Beacon, 1978); Susan Griffin, *Woman and Nature: The Roaring inside Her* (New York: Harper & Row, 1978); Diana Russell and Nicole van de Ven, eds., *Proceedings of the International Tribunal of Crimes against Women* (Millbrae, Calif.: Les Femmes, 1976); and Susan Brownmiller, *Against Our Will: Men, Women, and Rape* (New York: Simon and Schuster, 1975); *Aegis: Magazine on Ending Violence against Women* (Feminist Alliance against Rape, P.O. Box 21033, Washington, D.C. 20009).

[A.R., 1986: Work on both incest and on woman battering has appeared in the 1980s which I did not cite in the essay. See Florence Rush, *The Best-kept Secret* (New York: McGraw-Hill, 1980); Louise Armstrong, *Kiss Daddy Goodnight: A Speakout on Incest* (New York: Pocket Books, 1979); Sandra Butler, *Conspiracy of Silence: The Trauma of Incest* (San Francisco: New Glide, 1978); F. Delacoste and F. Newman, eds., *Fight Back!: Feminist Resistance to Male Violence* (Minneapolis: Cleis Press, 1981); Judy Freespirit, *Daddy's Girl: An Incest Survivor's Story* (Langlois, Ore.: Diaspora Distribution, 1982); Judith Herman, *Father-Daughter Incest* (Cambridge, Mass.: Harvard University Press, 1981); Toni McNaron and Yarrow Morgan, eds., *Voices in the Night: Women Speaking about Incest* (Minneapolis: Cleis Press, 1982); and Betsy Warrior's richly informative, multipurpose compilation of essays, statistics, listings, and facts, the *Battered Women's Directory* (formerly entitled *Working on Wife Abuse*), 8th ed. (Cambridge, Mass.: 1982).

10 Dinnerstein, p. 272.

11 Chodorow, pp. 197–198.

12 *Ibid.*, p.198–199.

13 *Ibid.*, p. 200.

14 Kathleen Gough, "The Origin of the Family," in *Toward an Anthropology of Women*, ed. Rayna [Rapp] Reiter (New York: Monthly Review Press, 1975), pp. 69–70.

15 Barry, pp. 216–219.

16 Anna Demeter, *Legal Kidnapping* (Boston: Beacon, 1977), pp. xx, 126–128.

17 Daly, pp. 139–141, 163–165.

18 Barbara Ehrenreich and Deirdre English, *Witches, Midwives and Nurses: A History of Women Healers* (Old Westbury, N.Y.: Feminist Press, 1973); Andrea Dworkin, *Women Hating* (New York: Dutton, 1974), pp. 118–154; Daly, pp. 178–222.

19 See Virginia Woolf, *A Room of One's Own* (London: Hogarth, 1929), and *id.*, *Three Guineas* (New York: Harcourt Brace, [1938] 1966); Tillie Olsen, *Silences* (Boston: Delacorte, 1978); Michelle Cliff, "The Resonance of Interruption," *Chrysalis: A Magazine of Women's Culture* 8 (1979): 29–37.

20 Mary Daly, *Beyond God the Father* (Boston: Beacon, 1973), pp. 347–351; Olsen, pp. 22–46.

21 Daly, *Beyond God the Father*, p. 93.

22 Fran P. Hosken, "The Violence of Power: Genital Mutilation of Females," *Heresies: A Feminist Journal of Art and Politics* 6 (1979): 28–35; Russell and van de Ven, pp. 194–195.

[A.R., 1986: See especially "Circumcision of Girls," in Nawal El Saadawi, *The Hidden Face of Eve: Women in the Arab World* (Boston: Beacon, 1982), pp. 33–43.]

23 Barry, pp. 163–164.

24 The issue of "lesbian sadomasochism" needs to be examined in terms of dominant cultures' teachings about the relation of sex and violence. I believe this to be another example of the "double life" of women.

25 Catherine A. MacKinnon, *Sexual Harassment of Working Women: A Case of Sex Discrimination* (New Haven, Conn.: Yale University Press, 1979), pp. 15–16.

26 *Ibid.*, p. 174.

27 Brownmiller, *op. cit.*

28 MacKinnon, p. 219. Susan Schecter writes: "The push for heterosexual union at whatever cost is so intense that . . . it has become a cultural force of its own that creates battering. The ideology of romantic love and its jealous possession of the partner as property provides the masquerade for what can become severe abuse" (*Aegis: Magazine on Ending Violence against Women* [July-August 1979]: 50–51).

29 MacKinnon, p. 298

30 *Ibid.*, p. 220.

31 *Ibid.*, p. 221.

32 Barry, *op. cit.*

[A.R., 1986: See also Kathleen Barry, Charlotte Bunch, and Shirley Castley, eds., *International Feminism: Networking against Female Sexual Slavery* (New York: International Women's Tribune Center, 1984).]

33 Barry, p. 33.

34 *Ibid.*, p. 103.

35 *Ibid.*, p. 5.

36 *Ibid.*, p. 100.

[A.R., 1986: This statement has been taken as claiming that "all women are victims" purely and simply, or that "all heterosexuality equals sexual slavery." I would say, rather, that all women are affected, though differently, by dehumanizing attitudes and practices directed at women as a group.]

37 *Ibid.*, p. 218.

38 *Ibid.*, p. 140.

39 *Ibid.*, p. 172.

40 Elsewhere I have suggested that male identification has been a powerful source of white women's racism and that it has often been women already seen as "disloyal" to male codes and systems who have actively battled against it (Adrienne Rich, "Disloyal to Civilization: Feminism, Racism, Gynephobia," in *On Lies, Secrets, and Silence: Selected Prose, 1966–1978* [New York: W. W. Norton, 1979]).

41 Barry, p. 220.

42 Susan Cavin, "Lesbian Origins" (Ph.D. diss., Rutgers University, 1978), unpublished, ch. 6.

[A.R., 1986: This dissertation was recently published as *Lesbian Origins* (San Francisco: Ism Press, 1986).]

43 For my perception of heterosexuality as an economic institution I am indebted to Lisa Leghorn and Katherine Parker, who allowed me to read the unpublished manuscript of their book *Woman's Worth: Sexual Economics and the World of Women* (London and Boston: Routledge & Kegan Paul, 1981).

44 I would suggest that lesbian existence has been most recognized and tolerated where it has resembled a "deviant" version of heterosexuality—e.g., where lesbians have, like Stein and Toklas, played heterosexual roles (or seemed to in public) and have been chiefly identified with male culture. See also Claude E. Schaeffer, "The Kuterai Female Berdache: Courier, Guide, Prophetess and Warrior," *Ethnohistory* 12, no. 3 (Summer 1965): 193–236. (Berdache: "an individual of definite physiological sex [m. or f.] who assumes the role and status of the opposite sex and who is viewed by the community as being of one sex physiologically but as having assumed the role and status of the opposite sex" [Schaeffer, p. 231].)

Lesbian existence has also been relegated to an upper-class phenomenon, an elite decadence (as in the fascination with Paris salon lesbians such as Renée Vivien and Natalie Clifford Barney), to the obscuring of such "common women" as Judy Grahn depicts in her *The Work of a Common Woman* (Oakland, Calif.: Diana Press, 1978). *True to Life Adventure Stories* (Oakland, Calif.: Diana Press, 1978).

45 Daly, *Gyn/Ecology*, p.15.

46 "In a hostile world in which women are not supposed to survive except in relation with and in service to men, entire communities of women were simply erased. History tends to bury what it seeks to reject" (Blanche W. Cook, "'Women Alone Stir My Imagination': Lesbianism and the Cultural Tradition," *Signs: Journal of Women in Culture and Society* 4, no. 4 [Summer 1979]: 719–720). The Lesbian Herstory Archives in New York City is one attempt to preserve contemporary documents on lesbian existence—a project of enormous value and meaning, working against the continuing censorship and obliteration of relationships, networks, communities in other archives and elsewhere in the culture.

47 [A.R., 1986: The shared historical and spiritual "crossover" functions of lesbians and gay men in cultures past and present are traced by Judy Grahn in *Another Mother Tongue: Gay Words, Gay Worlds* (Boston: Beacon, 1984.) I now think we have much to learn both from the uniquely female aspects of lesbian existence and from the complex "gay" identity we share with gay men.]

48 Audre Lorde, "Uses of the Erotic: The Erotic as Power," in *Sister Outsider* (Trumansburg, N.Y.: Crossing Press, 1984).

49 Adrienne Rich, "Conditions for Work: The Common World of Women" in *On Lies, Secrets, and Silence*, p. 209; H.D., *Tribute to Freud* (Oxford: Carcanet, 1971), pp. 50–54.

50 Woolf, *A Room of One's Own*, p. 126.

51 Gracia Clark, "The Beguines: A Mediaeval Women's Community," *Quest: A Feminist Quarterly* 1, no. 4 (1975): 73–80.

52 See Denise Paulmé, ed., *Women of Tropical Africa* (Berkeley: University of California Press, 1963), pp. 7, 266–267. Some of these sororities are described as "a kind of defensive syndicate against the male element," their aims being "to offer concerted resistance to an oppressive patriarchate," "independence in relation to ones' husband with regard to motherhood, mutual aid, satisfaction of personal revenge." See also Audre Lorde, "Scratching the Surface: Some Notes on Barriers to Women and Loving," in *Sister Outsider*, pp. 45–52; Marjorie Topley, "Marriage Resistance in Rural Kwangtung," in *Women in Chinese Society*, ed. M. Wolf and R. Witke (Stanford, Calif.: Stanford University Press, 1978), pp. 67–89; Agnes Smedley, *Portraits of Chinese Women in Revolution*, ed. J. MacKinnon and S. MacKinnon (Old Westbury, N.Y.: Feminist Press, 1976), pp. 103–110.

53 See Rosalind Petchesky, "Dissolving the Hyphen: A Report on Marxist-Feminist Groups 1–5," in *Capitalist Patriarchy and the Case for Socialist Feminism*, ed. Zillah Eisenstein (New York: Monthly Review Press, 1979), p. 387.

54 [A.R., 1986: See Angela Davis, *Women, Race and Class* (New York: Random House, 1981), p. 102; Orlando Patterson, *Slavery and Social Death: A Comparative Study* (Cambridge: Harvard University Press, 1982), p. 133.]

55 Russell and van de Ven, pp. 42–43, 56–57.

56 I am indebted to Jonathan Katz's *Gay American History* (*op. cit.*) for bringing to my attention Hansberry's letters to *The Ladder* and to Barbara Grier for supplying me with copies of relevant pages from *The Ladder*, quoted here by permission of Barbara Grier. See also the reprinted series of *The Ladder*, ed. Jonathan Katz *et al.* (New York: Arno, 1975), and Deirdre Carmody, "Letters by Eleanor Roosevelt Detail Friendship with Lorena Hickok," *New York Times* (October 21, 1979).

57 Meridel LeSueur, *The Girl* (Cambridge, Mass: West End Press, 1978), pp. 10–11. LeSueur describes, in an afterword, how this book was drawn from the writings and oral narration of women in the Workers Alliance who met as a writers' group during the depression.

58 *Ibid.*, p. 20.

59 *Ibid.*, pp. 53–54.

60 *Ibid.*, p. 55.

61 Toni Morrison, *Sula* (New York: Bantam, 1973), pp. 103–104, 149. I am indebted to Lorraine Bethel's essay "'This is a Conscious Pain': Zora Neale Hurston and the Black Female Literary Tradition," in *All the Women Are White, All the Blacks Are Men, but Some of Us are Brave: Black Women's Studies*, ed. Gloria T. Hull, Patricia Bell Scott, and Barbara Smith (Old Westbury, N.Y.: Feminist Press, 1982).

62 See Maureen Brady and Judith McDaniel, "Lesbians in the Mainstream: The Image of Lesbians in Recent Commercial Fiction," *Conditions 6* (1979): 82–105.

63 See Russell and van de Ven, p. 40: "Few heterosexual women realize their lack of free choice about their sexuality, and few realize how and why compulsory heterosexuality is also a crime against them."

64 Bethel, "'This Infinity of Conscious Pain,'" *op. cit.*

65 Dinnerstein, the most recent writer to quote this passage, adds ominously: "But what has to be added to her account is that these 'women enlaced, are sheltering each other not just from what men want to do to them, but also from what they want to do to each other" (Dinnerstein, p. 103). The fact is, however, that woman-to-woman violence is a minute grain in the universe of male-against-female violence perpetuated and rationalized in every social institution.

66 Conversation with Blanche W. Cook, New York City, March 1979.

67 See note 9, above, 30–31.

2

Bodily inscriptions, performative subversions

Judith Butler

> "Garbo 'got in drag' whenever she took some heavy glamour part, whenever she melted in or out of a man's arms, whenever she simply let that heavenly-flexed neck . . . bear the weight of her thrown-back head. . . . How resplendent seems the art of acting! It is all *impersonation*, whether the sex underneath is true or not."
>
> —Parker Tyler, "The Garbo Image," quoted in Esther Newton, *Mother Camp*

Categories of true sex, discrete gender, and specific sexuality have constituted the stable point of reference for a great deal of feminist theory and politics. These constructs of identity serve as the points of epistemic departure from which theory emerges and politics itself is shaped. In the case of feminism, politics is ostensibly shaped to express the interests, the perspectives, of "women." But is there a political shape to "women," as it were, that precedes and prefigures the political elaboration of their interests and epistemic point of view? How is that identity shaped, and is it a political shaping that takes the very morphology and boundary of the sexed body as the ground, surface, or site of cultural inscription? What circumscribes that site as "the female body"? Is "the body" or "the sexed body" the firm foundation on which gender and systems of compulsory sexuality operate? Or is "the body" itself shaped by political forces with strategic interests in keeping that body bounded and constituted by the markers of sex?

The sex/gender distinction and the category of sex itself appear to presuppose a generalization of "the body" that preexists the acquisition of its sexed significance. This "body" often appears to be a passive medium that is signified by an inscription from a cultural source figured as "external" to that body. Any theory of the culturally constructed body, however, ought to question "the body" as a construct of suspect generality when it is figured as passive and prior to discourse. There are Christian and Cartesian precedents to such views which, prior to the emergence of vitalistic biologies in the nineteenth century, understand "the body" as so much inert matter, signifying nothing or, more specifically, signifying a profane void, the fallen state: deception, sin, the premonitional metaphorics of hell and the eternal feminine. There are many occasions in both Sartre's and Beauvoir's work where "the body" is figured as a mute facticity, anticipating some meaning that can be attributed only by a transcendent consciousness, understood in Cartesian terms as radically immaterial. But what establishes this dualism for us? What separates off "the body" as indifferent to signification, and signification itself as the act of a radically disembodied consciousness or, rather, the act that radically disembodies that consciousness? To what extent is that Cartesian dualism presupposed in phenomenology adapted to the structuralist frame in which mind/body is redescribed as culture/nature? With respect to gender discourse, to what extent do these problematic dualisms still operate within the very descriptions that are supposed to lead us out of that binarism and its implicit hierarchy? How are the contours of the body clearly marked as the taken-for-granted ground or surface upon which gender significations are inscribed, a mere facticity devoid of value, prior to significance?

Wittig suggests that a culturally specific epistemic *a priori* establishes the naturalness of "sex." But by what enigmatic means has "the body" been accepted as a *prima facie* given that admits of no genealogy? Even within Foucault's essay on the very theme of genealogy, the body is figured as a surface and the scene of a cultural inscription: "the body is the inscribed surface of events."[1] The task of genealogy, he claims, is "to expose a body totally imprinted by history." His sentence continues, however, by referring to the goal of "history"—here clearly understood on the model of Freud's "civilization"—as the "destruction of the body" (148). Forces and impulses with multiple directionalities are precisely that which history both destroys and preserves through the *entstehung* (historical event) of inscription. As "a volume in perpetual disintegration" (148), the body is always under siege, suffering destruction by the very terms of history. And history is the creation of values and meanings by a signifying practice that requires the subjection of the body. This corporeal destruction is necessary to produce the speaking subject and its significations. This is a body, described through the language of surface and force, weakened through a "single drama" of domination, inscription, and creation (150). This is not the *modus vivendi* of one kind of history rather than another, but is, for Foucault, "history" (148) in its essential and repressive gesture.

Although Foucault writes, "Nothing in man [*sic*]—not even his body—is sufficiently stable to serve as the basis for self-recognition or for understanding other men [*sic*]" (153), he nevertheless points to the constancy of cultural inscription as a "single drama" that acts on the body. If the creation of values, that historical mode of signification, requires the destruction of the body, much as the instrument of torture in Kafka's *In the Penal Colony* destroys the body on which it writes, then there must be a body prior to that inscription, stable and self-identical, subject to that sacrificial destruction. In a sense, for Foucault, as for Nietzsche, cultural values emerge as the result of an inscription on the body, understood as a medium, indeed, a blank page; in order for this inscription to signify, however, that medium must itself be destroyed—that is, fully transvaluated into a sublimated domain of values. Within the metaphorics of this notion of cultural values is the figure of history as a relentless writing instrument, and the body as the medium which must be destroyed and transfigured in order for "culture" to emerge.

By maintaining a body prior to its cultural inscription, Foucault appears to assume a materiality prior to signification and form. Because this distinction operates as essential to the task of genealogy as he defines it, the distinction itself is precluded as an object of genealogical investigation. Occasionally in his analysis of Herculine, Foucault subscribes to a prediscursive multiplicity of bodily forces that break through the surface of the body to disrupt the regulating practices of cultural coherence imposed upon that body by a power regime, understood as a vicissitude of "history." If the presumption of some kind of precategorial source of disruption is refused, is it still possible to give a genealogical account of the demarcation of the body as such as a signifying practice? This demarcation is not initiated by a reified history or by a subject. This marking is the result of a diffuse and active structuring of the social field. This signifying practice effects a social space for and of the body within certain regulatory grids of intelligibility.

Mary Douglas' *Purity and Danger* suggests that the very contours of "the body" are established through markings that seek to establish specific codes of cultural coherence. Any discourse that establishes the boundaries of the body serves the purpose of instating and naturalizing certain taboos regarding the appropriate limits, postures, and modes of exchange that define what it is that constitutes bodies:

> ideas about separating, purifying, demarcating and punishing transgressions have as their main function to impose system on an inherently untidy experience. It is only by exaggerating the difference between within and without, above and below, male and female, with and against, that a semblance of order is created.[2]

Although Douglas clearly subscribes to a structuralist distinction between an inherently unruly nature and an order imposed by cultural means, the "untidiness" to which she refers can be redescribed as a region of *cultural* unruliness and disorder. Assuming the inevitably binary structure of the nature/culture distinction, Douglas cannot point toward an alternative configuration of culture in which such distinctions become malleable or proliferate beyond the binary frame. Her analysis, however, provides a possible point of departure for understanding the relationship by which social taboos institute and maintain the boundaries of the body as such. Her analysis suggests that what constitutes the limit of the body is never merely material, but that the surface, the skin, is systemically signified by taboos and anticipated transgressions; indeed, the boundaries of the body become, within her analysis, the limits of the social *per se*. A poststructuralist appropriation of her view might well understand the boundaries of the body as the limits of the socially *hegemonic*. In a variety of cultures, she maintains, there are

> pollution powers which inhere in the structure of ideas itself and which punish a symbolic breaking of that which should be joined or joining of that which should be separate. It follows from this that pollution is a type of danger which is not likely to occur except where the lines of structure, cosmic or social, are clearly defined.
>
> A polluting person is always in the wrong. He [*sic*] has developed some wrong condition or simply crossed over some line which should not have been crossed and this displacement unleashes danger for someone.[3]

In a sense, Simon Watney has identified the contemporary construction of "the polluting person" as the person with AIDS in his *Policing Desire: AIDS, Pornography, and the Media*.[4] Not only is the illness figured as the "gay disease," but throughout the media's hysterical and homophobic response to the illness there is a tactical construction of a continuity between the polluted status of the homosexual by virtue of the boundary-trespass that *is* homosexuality and the disease as a specific modality of homosexual pollution. That the disease is transmitted through the exchange of bodily fluids suggests within the sensationalist graphics of homophobic signifying systems the dangers that permeable bodily boundaries present to the social order as such. Douglas remarks that "the body is a model that can stand for any bounded system. Its boundaries can represent any boundaries which are threatened or precarious."[5] And she asks a question which one might have expected to read in Foucault: "Why should bodily margins be thought to be specifically invested with power and danger?"[6]

Douglas suggests that all social systems are vulnerable at their margins, and that all margins are accordingly considered dangerous. If the body is synecdochal for the social system *per se* or a site in which open systems converge, then any kind of unregulated permeability constitutes a site of pollution and endangerment. Since anal and oral sex among men clearly establishes certain kinds of bodily permeabilities unsanctioned by the hegemonic order, male homosexuality would, within such a hegemonic point of view, constitute a site of danger and pollution, prior to and regardless of the cultural presence of AIDS. Similarly, the "polluted" status of lesbians, regardless of their low-risk status with respect to AIDS, brings into relief the dangers of their bodily exchanges. Significantly, being "outside" the hegemonic order does not signify being "in" a state of filthy and untidy nature. Paradoxically, homosexuality is almost always conceived within the homophobic signifying economy as *both* uncivilized and unnatural.

The construction of stable bodily contours relies upon fixed sites of corporeal permeability and impermeability. Those sexual practices in both homosexual and heterosexual contexts that open surfaces and orifices to erotic signification or close down others effectively reinscribe the boundaries of the body along new cultural lines. Anal sex among men is an example, as is the radical re-membering of the body in Wittig's *The Lesbian Body.* Douglas alludes to "a kind of sex pollution which expresses a desire to keep the body (physical and social) intact,"[7] suggesting that the naturalized notion of "the" body is itself a consequence of taboos that render that body discrete by virtue of its stable boundaries. Further, the rites of passage that govern various bodily orifices presuppose a heterosexual construction of gendered exchange, positions, and erotic possibilities. The deregulation of such exchanges accordingly disrupts the very boundaries that determine what it is to be a body at all. Indeed, the critical inquiry that traces the regulatory practices within which bodily contours are constructed constitutes precisely the genealogy of "the body" in its discreteness that might further radicalize Foucault's theory.[8]

Significantly, Kristeva's discussion of abjection in *The Powers of Horror* begins to suggest the uses of this structuralist notion of a boundary-constituting taboo for the purposes of constructing a discrete subject through exclusion.[9] The "abject" designates that which has been expelled from the body, discharged as excrement, literally rendered "Other." This appears as an expulsion of alien elements, but the alien is effectively established through this expulsion. The construction of the "not-me" as the abject establishes the boundaries of the body which are also the first contours of the subject. Kristeva writes:

> *nausea* makes me balk at that milk cream, separates me from the mother and father who proffer it. "I" want none of that element, sign of their desire; "I" do not want to listen, "I" do not assimilate it, "I" expel it. But since the food is not an "other" for "me," who am only in their desire, I expel *myself,* I spit *myself* out, I abject *myself* within the same motion through which "I" claim to establish myself.[10]

The boundary of the body as well as the distinction between internal and external is established through the ejection and transvaluation of something originally part of identity into a defiling otherness. As Iris Young has suggested in her use of Kristeva to understand sexism, homophobia, and racism, the repudiation of bodies for their sex, sexuality, and/or color is an "expulsion" followed by a "repulsion" that founds and consolidates culturally hegemonic identities along sex/race/sexuality axes of differentiation.[11] Young's appropriation of Kristeva shows how the operation of repulsion can consolidate "identities" founded on the instituting of the "Other" or a set of Others through exclusion and domination. What constitutes through division the "inner" and "outer" worlds of the subject is a border and boundary tenuously maintained for the purposes of social regulation and control. The boundary between the inner and outer is confounded by those excremental passages in which the inner effectively becomes outer, and this excreting function becomes, as it were, the model by which other forms of identity-differentiation are accomplished. In effect, this is the mode by which Others become shit. For inner and outer worlds to remain utterly distinct, the entire surface of the body would have to achieve an impossible impermeability. This sealing of its surfaces would constitute the seamless boundary of the subject; but this enclosure would invariably be exploded by precisely that excremental filth that it fears.

Regardless of the compelling metaphors of the spatial distinctions of inner and outer, they remain linguistic terms that facilitate and articulate a set of fantasies, feared and desired. "Inner" and "outer" make sense only with reference to a mediating boundary that strives for stability. And this stability, this coherence, is determined in large part by cultural orders that sanction the subject and compel its differentiation from the abject. Hence, "inner" and "outer" constitute a binary distinction that stabilizes and consolidates the coherent subject. When that subject is challenged, the meaning and necessity of the terms are subject to displacement. If the "inner world" no longer designates a topos, then the internal fixity of the self and, indeed, the internal locale of gender identity, become similarly suspect. The critical question is not *how* did that identity become *internalized?* as if internalization were a process or a mechanism that might be descriptively reconstructed. Rather, the question is: From what strategic position in public discourse and for what reasons has the trope of interiority and the disjunctive binary of inner/outer taken hold? In what language is "inner space" figured? What kind of figuration is it, and through what figure of the body is it signified? How does a body figure on its surface the very invisibility of its hidden depth?

From interiority to gender performatives

In *Discipline and Punish* Foucault challenges the language of internalization as it operates in the service of the disciplinary regime of the subjection and subjectivation of criminals.[12] Although Foucault objected to what he understood to be the psychoanalytic belief in the "inner" truth of sex in *The History of Sexuality,* he turns to a criticism of the doctrine of internalization for separate purposes in the context of his history of criminology. In a sense, *Discipline and Punish* can be read as Foucault's effort to rewrite Nietzsche's doctrine of internalization in *On the Genealogy of Morals* on the model of *inscription*. In the context of prisoners, Foucault writes, the strategy has been not to enforce a repression of their desires, but to compel their bodies to signify the prohibitive law as their very essence, style, and necessity. That law is not literally internalized, but incorporated, with the consequence that bodies are produced which signify that law on and through the body; there the law is manifest as the essence of their selves, the meaning of their soul, their conscience, the law of their desire. In effect, the law is at once fully manifest and fully latent, for it never appears as external to the bodies it subjects and subjectivates. Foucault writes:

> It would be wrong to say that the soul is an illusion, or an ideological effect. On the contrary, it exists, it has a reality, it is produced permanently *around, on, within,* the body by the functioning of a power that is exercised on those that are punished (my emphasis).[13]

The figure of the interior soul understood as "within" the body is signified through its inscription *on* the body, even though its primary mode of signification is through its very absence, its potent invisibility. The effect of a structuring inner space is produced through the signification of a body as a vital and sacred enclosure. The soul is precisely what the body lacks; hence, the body presents itself as a signifying lack. That lack which *is* the body signifies the soul as that which cannot show. In this sense, then, the soul is a surface signification that contests and displaces the inner/outer distinction itself, a figure of interior psychic space inscribed *on* the body as a social signification that perpetually renounces itself as such. In Foucault's terms, the soul is not imprisoned by or within the body, as some Christian imagery would suggest, but "the soul is the prison of the body."[14]

The redescription of intrapsychic processes in terms of the surface politics of the body implies a corollary redescription of gender as the disciplinary production of the figures of fantasy through the play of presence and absence on the body's surface, the construction of the gendered body through a series of exclusions and denials, signifying absences. But what determines the manifest and latent text of the body politic? What is the prohibitive law that generates the corporeal stylization of gender, the fantasied and fantastic figuration of the body? We have already considered the incest taboo and the prior taboo against homosexuality as the generative moments of gender identity, the prohibitions that produce identity along the culturally intelligible grids of an idealized and compulsory heterosexuality. That disciplinary production of gender effects a false stabilization of gender in the interests of the heterosexual construction and regulation of sexuality within the reproductive domain. The construction of coherence conceals the gender discontinuities that run rampant within heterosexual, bisexual, and gay and lesbian contexts in which gender does not necessarily follow from sex, and desire, or sexuality generally, does not seem to follow from gender—indeed, where none of these dimensions of significant corporeality express or reflect one another. When the disorganization and disaggregation of the field of bodies disrupt the regulatory fiction of heterosexual coherence, it seems that the expressive model loses its descriptive force. That regulatory ideal is then exposed as a norm and a fiction that disguises itself as a developmental law regulating the sexual field that it purports to describe.

According to the understanding of identification as an enacted fantasy or incorporation, however, it is clear that coherence is desired, wished for, idealized, and that this idealization is an effect of a corporeal signification. In other words, acts, gestures, and desire produce the effect of an internal core or substance, but produce this *on the surface* of the body, through the play of signifying absences that suggest, but never reveal, the organizing principle of identity as a cause. Such acts, gestures, enactments, generally construed, are *performative* in the sense that the essence or identity that they otherwise purport to express are *fabrications* manufactured and sustained through corporeal signs and other discursive means. That the gendered body is performative suggests that it has no ontological status apart from the various acts which constitute its reality. This also suggests that if that reality is fabricated as an interior essence, that very interiority is an effect and function of a decidedly public and social discourse, the public regulation of fantasy through the surface politics of the body, the gender border control that differentiates inner from outer, and so institutes the "integrity" of the subject. In other words, acts and gestures, articulated and enacted desires create the illusion of an interior and organizing gender core, an illusion discursively maintained for the purposes of the regulation of sexuality within the obligatory frame of reproductive heterosexuality. If the "cause" of desire, gesture, and act can be localized within the "self" of the actor, then the political regulations and disciplinary practices which produce that ostensibly coherent gender are effectively displaced from view. The displacement of a political and discursive origin of gender identity onto a psychological "core" precludes an analysis of the political constitution of the gendered subject and its fabricated notions about the ineffable interiority of its sex or of its true identity.

If the inner truth of gender is a fabrication and if a true gender is a fantasy instituted and inscribed on the surface of bodies, then it seems that genders can be neither true nor false, but are only produced as the truth effects of a discourse of primary and stable identity. In *Mother Camp: Female Impersonators in America,* anthropologist Esther Newton suggests that the structure of impersonation reveals one of the key fabricating mechanisms through which the social construction of gender takes place.[15] I would suggest as well that drag fully subverts the distinction between inner and outer psychic space and effectively mocks both the expressive model of gender and the notion of a true gender identity. Newton writes:

> At its most complex, [drag] is a double inversion that says, "appearance is an illusion." Drag says [Newton's curious personification] "my 'outside' appearance is feminine, but my essence 'inside' [the body] is masculine." At the same time it symbolizes the opposite inversion; "my appearance 'outside' [my body, my gender] is masculine but my essence 'inside' [myself] is feminine."[16]

Both claims to truth contradict one another and so displace the entire enactment of gender significations from the discourse of truth and falsity.

The notion of an original or primary gender identity is often parodied within the cultural practices of drag, cross-dressing, and the sexual stylization of butch/femme identities. Within feminist theory, such parodic identities have been understood to be either degrading to women, in the case of drag and cross-dressing, or an uncritical appropriation of sex-role stereotyping from within the practice of heterosexuality, especially in the case of butch/femme lesbian identities. But the relation between the "imitation" and the "original" is, I think, more complicated than that critique generally allows. Moreover, it gives us a clue to the way in which the relationship between primary identification—that is, the original meanings accorded to gender—and subsequent gender experience might be reframed. The performance of drag plays upon the distinction between the anatomy of the performer and the gender that is being performed. But we are actually in the presence of three contingent dimensions of significant corporeality: anatomical sex, gender identity, and gender performance. If the anatomy of the performer is already distinct from the gender of the performer, and both of those are distinct from the gender of the performance, then the performance suggests a dissonance not only between sex and performance, but sex and gender, and gender and performance. As much as drag creates a unified picture of "woman" (what its critics often oppose), it also reveals the distinctness of those aspects of gendered experience which are falsely naturalized as a unity through the regulatory fiction of heterosexual coherence. *In imitating gender, drag implicitly reveals the imitative structure of gender itself—as well as its contingency.* Indeed, part of the pleasure, the giddiness of the performance is in the recognition of a radical contingency in the relation between sex and gender in the face of cultural configurations of causal unities that are regularly assumed to be natural and necessary. In the place of the law of heterosexual coherence, we see sex and gender denaturalized by means of a performance which avows their distinctness and dramatizes the cultural mechanism of their fabricated unity.

The notion of gender parody defended here does not assume that there is an original which such parodic identities imitate. Indeed, the parody is *of* the very notion of an original; just as the psychoanalytic notion of gender identification is constituted by a fantasy of a fantasy, the transfiguration of an Other who is always already a "figure" in that double sense, so gender parody reveals that the original identity after which gender fashions itself is an imitation without an origin. To be more precise, it is a production which, in effect—that is, in its effect—postures as an imitation. This perpetual displacement constitutes a fluidity of identities that suggests an openness to resignification and recontextualization; parodic proliferation deprives hegemonic culture and its critics of the claim to naturalized or essentialist gender identities. Although the gender meanings taken up in these parodic styles are clearly part of hegemonic, misogynist culture, they are nevertheless denaturalized and mobilized through their parodic recontextualization. As imitations which effectively displace the meaning of the original, they imitate the myth of originality itself. In the place of an original identification which serves as a determining cause, gender identity might be reconceived as a personal/cultural history of received meanings subject to a set of imitative practices which refer laterally to other imitations and which, jointly, construct the illusion of a primary and interior gendered self or parody the mechanism of that construction.

According to Fredric Jameson's "Postmodernism and Consumer Society," the imitation that mocks the notion of an original is characteristic of pastiche rather than parody:

> Pastiche is, like parody, the imitation of a peculiar or unique style, the wearing of a stylistic mask, speech in a dead language: but it is a neutral practice of mimicry, without parody's ulterior motive, without the satirical impulse, without laughter, without that still latent feeling that there exists something *normal* compared to which what is being imitated is rather comic. Pastiche is blank parody, parody that has lost it humor.[17]

The loss of the sense of "the normal," however, can be its own occasion for laughter, especially when "the normal," "the original" is revealed to be a copy, and an inevitably failed one, an ideal that no one *can* embody. In this sense, laughter emerges in the realization that all along the original was derived.

Parody by itself is not subversive, and there must be a way to understand what makes certain kinds of parodic repetitions effectively disruptive, truly troubling, and which repetitions become domesticated and recirculated as instruments of cultural hegemony. A typology of actions would clearly not suffice, for parodic displacement, indeed, parodic laughter, depends on a context and reception in which subversive confusions can be fostered. What performance where will invert the inner/outer distinction and compel a radical rethinking of the psychological presuppositions of gender identity and sexuality? What performance where will compel a reconsideration of the *place* and stability of the masculine and the feminine? And what kind of gender performance will enact and reveal the performativity of gender itself in a way that destabilizes the naturalized categories of identity and desire?

If the body is not a "being," but a variable boundary, a surface whose permeability is politically regulated, a signifying practice within a cultural field of gender hierarchy and compulsory heterosexuality, then what language is left for understanding this corporeal enactment, gender, that constitutes its "interior" signification on its surface? Sartre would perhaps have called this act "a style of being," Foucault, "a stylistics of existence." And in my earlier reading of Beauvoir, I suggest that gendered bodies are so many "styles of the flesh." These styles all never fully self-styled, for styles have a history, and those histories condition and limit the possibilities. Consider gender, for instance, as *a corporeal style*, an "act," as it were, which is both intentional and performative, where "*performative*" suggests a dramatic and contingent construction of meaning.

Wittig understands gender as the workings of "sex," where "sex" is an obligatory injunction for the body to become a cultural sign, to materialize itself in obedience to a historically delimited possibility, and to do this, not once or twice, but as a sustained and repeated corporeal project. The notion of a "project," however, suggests the originating force of a radical will, and because gender is a project which has cultural survival as its end, the term *strategy* better suggests the situation of duress under which gender performance always and variously occurs. Hence, as a strategy of survival within compulsory systems, gender is a performance with clearly punitive consequences. Discrete genders are part of what "humanizes" individuals within contemporary culture; indeed, we regularly punish those who fail to do their gender right. Because there is neither an "essence" that gender expresses or externalizes nor an objective ideal to which gender aspires, and because gender is not a fact, the various acts of gender create the idea of gender, and without those acts, there would be no gender at all. Gender is, thus, a construction that regularly conceals its genesis; the tacit collective agreement to perform, produce, and sustain discrete and polar genders as cultural fictions is obscured by the credibility of those productions—and the punishments that attend not agreeing to believe in them; the construction "compels" our belief in its necessity and naturalness. The historical possibilities materialized through various corporeal styles are nothing other than those punitively regulated cultural fictions alternately embodied and deflected under duress.

Consider that a sedimentation of gender norms produces the peculiar phenomenon of a "natural sex" or a "real woman" or any number of prevalent and compelling social fictions, and that this is a sedimentation that over time has produced a set of corporeal styles which, in reified form, appear as the natural configuration of bodies into sexes existing in a binary relation to one another. If these styles are enacted, and if they produce the coherent gendered subjects who pose as their originators, what kind of performance might reveal this ostensible "cause" to be an "effect"?

In what senses, then, is gender an act? As in other ritual social dramas, the action of gender requires a performance that is *repeated*. This repetition is at once a reenactment and reexperiencing of a set of meanings already socially established; and it is the mundane and ritualized form of their legitimation.[18] Although there are individual bodies that enact these significations by becoming stylized into gendered modes, this "action" is a public action. There are temporal and collective dimensions to these actions, and their public character is not inconsequential; indeed, the performance is effected with the strategic aim of maintaining gender within its binary frame—an aim that cannot be attributed to a subject, but, rather, must be understood to found and consolidate the subject.

Gender ought not to be construed as a stable identity or locus of agency from which various acts follow; rather, gender is an identity tenuously constituted in time, instituted in an exterior space through a *stylized repetition of acts.* The effect of gender is produced through the stylization of the body and, hence, must be understood as the mundane way in which bodily gestures, movements, and styles of various kinds constitute the illusion of an abiding gendered self. This formulation moves the conception of gender off the ground of a substantial model of identity to one that requires a conception of gender as a constituted *social temporality.* Significantly, if gender is instituted through acts which are internally discontinuous, then the *appearance of substance* is precisely that, a constructed identity, a performative accomplishment which the mundane social audience, including the actors themselves, come to believe and to perform in the mode of belief. Gender is also a norm that can never be fully internalized; "the internal" is a surface signification, and gender norms are finally phantasmatic, impossible to embody. If the ground of gender identity is the stylized repetition of acts through time and not a seemingly seamless identity, then the spatial metaphor of a "ground" will be displaced and revealed as a stylized configuration, indeed, a gendered corporealization of time. The abiding gendered self will then be shown to be structured by repeated acts that seek to approximate the ideal of a substantial ground of identity, but which, in their occasional *dis*continuity, reveal the temporal and contingent groundlessness of this "ground." The possibilities of gender transformation are to be found precisely in the arbitrary relation between such acts, in the possibility of a failure to repeat, a de-formity, or a parodic repetition that exposes the phantasmatic effect of abiding identity as a politically tenuous construction.

If gender attributes, however, are not expressive but performative, then these attributes effectively constitute the identity they are said to express or reveal. The distinction between expression and performativeness is crucial. If gender attributes and acts, the various ways in which a body shows or produces its cultural signification, are performative, then there is no preexisting identity by which an act or attribute might be measured; there would be no true or false, real or distorted acts of gender, and the postulation of a true gender identity would be revealed as a regulatory fiction. That gender reality is created through sustained social performances means that the very notions of an essential sex and a true or abiding masculinity or femininity are also constituted as part of the strategy that conceals gender's performative character and the performative possibilities for proliferating gender configurations outside the restricting frames of masculinist domination and compulsory heterosexuality.

Genders can be neither true nor false, neither real nor apparent, neither original nor derived. As credible bearers of those attributes, however, genders can also be rendered thoroughly and radically *incredible.*

Notes

1 Michel Foucault, "Nietzsche, Genealogy, History," in *Language, Counter-Memory, Practice: Selected Essays and Interviews by Michel Foucault,* trans. Donald F. Bouchard and Sherry Simon, ed. Donald F. Bouchard (Ithaca: Cornell University Press, 1977), p. 148. References in the text are to this essay.
2 Mary Douglas, *Purity and Danger* (London, Boston, and Henley: Routledge and Kegan Paul, 1969), p. 4.
3 Ibid., p. 113.
4 Simon Watney, *Policing Desire: AIDS, Pornography, and the Media* (Minneapolis: University of Minnesota Press, 1988).
5 Douglas, *Purity and Danger,* p. 115.
6 Ibid., p. 121.
7 Ibid., p. 140.
8 Foucault's essay "A Preface to Transgression" (in *Language, Counter-Memory, Practice)* does provide an interesting juxtaposition with Douglas' notion of body boundaries constituted by incest taboos. Originally written in honor of Georges Bataille, this essay explores in part the metaphorical "dirt" of transgressive pleasures and the association of the forbidden orifice with the dirt-covered tomb. See pp. 46–48.
9 Kristeva discusses Mary Douglas' work in a short section of *The Powers of Horror: An Essay on Abjection,* trans. Leon Roudiez (New York: Columbia University Press, 1982), originally published as *Pouvoirs de l'horreur* (Paris: Éditions de Seuil, 1980). Assimilating Douglas' insights to her own reformulation of Lacan, Kristeva writes, "Defilement is what is jettisoned from the *symbolic system.* It is what escapes that social rationality, that logical order on which a social aggregate is based, which then becomes differentiated from a temporary agglomeration of individuals and, in short, constitutes a *classification system* or *a structure*" (p. 65).
10 Ibid., p. 3.
11 Iris Marion Young, "Abjection and Oppression: Unconscious Dynamics of Racism, Sexism, and Homophobia," paper presented at the Society of Phenomenology and Existential Philosophy Meetings, Northwestern University, 1988. The paper will be published in the proceedings of the 1988 meetings by the State University of New York Press. It will also be included as part of a larger chapter in her forthcoming *The Politics of Difference.*
12 Parts of the following discussion were published in two different contexts, in my "Gender Trouble, Feminist Theory, and Psychoanalytic Discourse," in *Feminism/Postmodernism,* ed. Linda J. Nicholson (New York: Routledge, 1989) and "Performative Acts and Gender Constitution: An Essay in Phenomenology and Feminist Theory," *Theatre Journal,* Vol. 20, No. 3, Winter 1988.
13 Michel Foucault, *Discipline and Punish: the Birth of the Prison,* trans. Alan Sheridan (New York: Vintage, 1979), p. 29.
14 Ibid., p. 30.
15 See the chapter "Role Models" in Esther Newton, *Mother Camp: Female Impersonators in America* (Chicago: University of Chicago Press, 1972).
16 Ibid., p. 103.
17 Fredric Jameson, "Postmodernism and Consumer Society," in *The Anti-Aesthetic: Essays on Postmodern Culture,* ed. Hal Foster (Port Townsend, WA.: Bay Press, 1983), p. 114.
18 See Victor Turner, *Dramas, Fields and Metaphors* (Ithaca: Cornell University Press, 1974). See also Clifford Geertz, "Blurred Genres: The Refiguration of Thought," in *Local Knowledge, Further Essays in Interpretive Anthropology* (New York: Basic Books, 1983).

3
The invention of heterosexuality*

Jonathan Ned Katz†

Heterosexuality is old as procreation, ancient as the lust of Eve and Adam. That first lady and gentleman, we assume, perceived themselves, behaved, and felt just like today's heterosexuals. We suppose that heterosexuality is unchanging, universal, essential: ahistorical.

Contrary to that common sense conjecture, the concept of heterosexuality is only one particular historical way of perceiving, categorizing, and imagining the social relations of the sexes. Not ancient at all, the idea of heterosexuality is a modern invention, dating to the late nineteenth century. The heterosexual belief, with its metaphysical claim to eternity, has a particular, pivotal place in the social universe of the late nineteenth and twentieth centuries that it did not inhabit earlier. This essay traces the historical process by which the heterosexual idea was created as ahistorical and taken-for-granted.

The first part of this essay focuses on the history of heterosexuality (and a complementary homosexuality) as words and ideas—as ideology recorded in a variety of sources, medical journals and books, works on sexual theory, sexual and gender advice literature, sexual surveys, dictionaries, a play, a movie, a Broadway show song, fiction, and *The New York Times.*‡ Advancing beyond heterosexuality as idea, the last part of this essay argues that the rise of the hetero notion is associated with the development of a historically-specific heterosexual identity, role, psychology, behavior, and institution. Since heterosexuality didn't exist, it had to be invented.

Considering the popularity of the heterosexual idea, one imagines that tracing the notion's history would have tempted many eager scholar-beavers. The importance of analyzing the dominant term of the dominant sexual ideology seems obvious. But heterosexuality has been the

* "The Invention of Heterosexuality", *Socialist Review,* 20 (Janu-March 1990. 7–34. Copyright© 1990 by Jonathan Ned Katz. Used with permission.

† ©1990 by Jonathan Ned Katz. I'm grateful to Lisa Duggan, Judith Levine, Sharon Thompson, Carole S. Vance, and Jeffrey Weeks for comments on a recent version of this manuscript, and to Manfred Herzer and his editor, John DeCecco, for sharing, prepublication, Herzer's most recent research on Kertbeny. I'm also indebted to John Gagnon, Philip Greven, and Catharine R. Stimpson for bravely supporting my (unsuccessful) attempts to fund research for a full-length study of heterosexual history.

‡ Research in *The Times,* though of course only one inconclusive record, does provide a single, continuous source on the changing historical definitions of heterosexuality for the diverse national and international culture of the middle class.

idea whose time has not come. The role of the universal heterosexual hypothesis as prop to the dominant mode of sexual organization has determined its not-so-benign scholarly neglect.

By not studying the heterosexual idea in history, analysts of sex, gay and straight, have continued to privilege the "normal" and "natural" at the expense of the "abnormal" and "unnatural." Such privileging of the norm accedes to its domination, protecting it from questions. By making the normal the object of a thoroughgoing historical study we simultaneously pursue a pure truth and a sex-radical and subversive goal: we upset basic preconceptions. We discover that the heterosexual, the normal, and the natural have a history of changing definitions. Studying the history of the term challenges its power.

Contrary to our usual assumption, past Americans and other peoples named, perceived, and socially organized the bodies, lusts, and intercourse of the sexes in ways radically different from the way we do. If we care to understand this vast past sexual diversity, we need to stop promiscuously projecting our own hetero and homo arrangement. Though lip-service is often paid to the distorting, ethnocentric effect of such conceptual imperialism, the category heterosexuality continues to be applied uncritically as a universal analytical tool. Recognizing the time-bound and culturally-specific character of the heterosexual category can help us begin to work toward a thoroughly historical view of sex.

This historical approach to the analysis of heterosexuality builds on and extends recent work by feminists on the making of womanhood and manhood, and recent work by gay and lesbian liberationists on the historical construction of homosexuality.[1] Contrary to ivory tower supposition, work on the social construction of sex did not start with Michel Foucault. But writers on homosexual history have ironically perpetuated a traditional error of the anti-homosexualists: the exclusive focus on homosexuality. While that sex-love has been subjected to intense historical questioning, heterosexuality has been allowed to go its merry way untouched by basic doubt as to its own timelessness. Historical study of heterosexuality is needed to complete the historical study of its dialectical counterpart, homosexuality.

Though this article contests the universality of a heterosexual identity, experience, and behavior, the legitimacy of that identification, emotion, and activity are certainly not in question. The social construction of heterosexuality and homosexuality implies nothing at all about their reality, profundity, and importance. The value of any eros is independent of its origin.

This is an exploratory first pass at an historically-specific heterosexual history—a call for a complete rethinking and total historicization of heterosexuality, and for new research based on that radical reviewing. So, come with me on a journey into the sexual past to observe and ponder the invention of heterosexuality.

Before heterosexuality: early Victorian True Love, 1820–1860

In the early nineteenth century United States, from about 1820 to 1860, the heterosexual did not exist. Middle-class white Americans idealized a True Womanhood, True Manhood, and True Love, all characterized by "purity"—the freedom from sensuality.[2] Presented mainly in literary and religious texts, this True Love was a fine romance with no lascivious kisses. This ideal contrasts strikingly with late-nineteenth and twentieth century American incitements to a hetero sex.*

* Some historians have recently told us to revise our idea of sexless Victorians: their experience and even their ideology, it is said, were more erotic than we previously thought. Despite the revisionists, I argue that "purity" was indeed the dominant early Victorian, white, middle-class standard. For the debate on Victorian sexuality see John D'Emilio and Estelle Freedman, *Intimate Matters: A History of Sexuality in America* (New York: Harper & Row, 1988), p. xii.

Early Victorian True Love was only realized within the mode of proper procreation, marriage, the legal organization for producing a new set of correctly gendered women and men. Proper womanhood, manhood, and progeny—not a normal male-female eros—was the main product of this mode of engendering and of human reproduction.

The actors in this sexual economy were identified as manly men and womanly women and as procreators, not specifically as erotic beings or heterosexuals. Eros did not constitute the core of a heterosexual identity that inhered, democratically, in both men and women. True Women were defined by their distance from lust. True Men, though thought to live closer to carnality, and in less control of it, aspired to the same freedom from concupiscence.

Legitimate natural desire was for procreation and a proper manhood or womanhood; no heteroerotic desire was thought to be directed exclusively and naturally toward the other sex; lust in men was roving. The human body was thought of as a means towards procreation and production; penis and vagina were instruments of reproduction, not of pleasure. Human energy, thought of as a closed and severely limited system, was to be used in producing children and in work, not wasted in libidinous pleasures.

The location of all this engendering and procreative labor was the sacred sanctum of early Victorian True Love, the home of the True Woman and True Man—a temple of purity threatened from within by the monster masturbator, an archetypal early Victorian cult figure of illicit lust. The home of True Love was a castle far removed from the erotic exotic ghetto inhabited most notoriously then by the prostitute, another archetypal Victorian erotic monster. Between 1820 and 1860, only rarely was reference made to those other illicit erotic figures, the "sodomite" and "sapphist"—terms with no antonyms. State sodomy laws defined a particular, obscure act, referred to in a limited legalese, not a criminal, medical, or psychological type of person.[3] Because the social organization of gender was dominant, not the mode of pleasure, the term "invert" was one of the early medical names for deviants from True Womanhood and True Manhood.[4] "Invert," stressing gender rather than erotic deviation, was one of those terms that did not take in the hetero- and homoeroticized twentieth century.

Because early Victorian True Love was not lust-linked, sex-reformers of the late Victorian era and early twentieth century began to refer to a new, hyphenated "sex-love." Their coinage was designed specifically to distinguish the new heteroerotic amour from the old lust-free True Love.

Late Victorian sex-love: 1860–1892

Heterosexuality and "homosexuality" did not appear out of the blue in the 1890s. These two eroticisms were in the making from the 1860s on. In late Victorian America and in Germany, from about 1860 to 1892, our modern idea of an eroticized universe began to develop, and the experience of a heterolust began to be widely documented and named. Playing a pioneering role in the titling and theorizing of sexual normalcy we may be surprised to find the early theorists and defenders of man-man love.

At the start of this era, one eloquent, embattled exponent of the new male-female lustiness was Walt Whitman, whose third edition of *Leaves of Grass*, published in 1860, first included a section, "Children of Adam," frankly evoking the sexual-procreational intercourse of men and women. As a pioneering heterosex radical, Whitman broke with the Victorian idea that women's passion for motherhood included no eros. Whitman's women participated lustily and equally with men in the act of conceiving robust babies. Another of Whitman's new sections, "Calamus," vividly detailed acts of erotic communion between men. Whitman named and evoked hot "amative" relations between men and women, and sizzling "adhesive" intimacies between men.[5] In the perspective of heterosexual history, Whitman's titling of these amative and adhesive intimacies was as an attempt to position male-female and male-male eroticisms together as a natural, "healthy" division of human erotic responses. Though now perhaps better known as man-lover, Whitman was also the trailblazer of a previously silent and vilified male-female lust.[6]

At about the same time, in 1863, in Germany, another pioneer defender of man-man love, Karl Heinrich Ulrichs, was also producing new sexual names to defend the love of the man who loved men, the "Urning," for the True Man. (His theory later included "women with a masculine love-drive": women who loved women.) The Urning's sex-love for a True Man, Ulrichs argued, was as natural as the "Dioning-love" of True Man and True Woman. In Ulrichs' eroticized update of the early Victorian True Man prototype, the real man possessed a male body and the male's sex-love for women. The Urning, as a Non-True Man (the True Man's opposite, but not a pervert), possessed a male body and the female's sex-love for a male. The Victorian concept of the "true," applied to women, men, and love, linked sex-biology with sex-psychology, so that feelings were thought of as female or male in exactly the same sense as penis or clitoris: anatomy equalled psychology. The True Love of True Man and Woman was a physical appurtenance like the other private parts.[7]

A few years later in Germany, in a letter of May 6, 1868 to Ulrichs, another early sodomy-law reformer, Karl Maria Kertbeny, is first known to have *privately* used two new terms coined by him: "heterosexuality" and "homosexuality"—the debut of the modern lingo! Kertbeny's "Heterosexualität" referred to a strong lust drive toward "opposite sex" intercourse (associated with numbers of morally reprehensible acts). It had the same sense as another of his new terms, "Normalsexualität." Kertbeny's term homosexual was first used *publicly* in an 1869 appeal for sodomy-law reform. His term heterosexual was first used publicly in Germany, in 1880, in a defense of homosexuality published as the work of "Dr. M".[8] Kertbeny's coinage of the term heterosexual in the service of homosexual emancipation is considering the term's later use—one of sex history's grand ironies.

Heterosexual next made its public appearance in 1889, in the fourth German edition of Dr. Richard Krafft-Ebing's *Psychopathia Sexualis*, where it was distinguished from homosexual.[9] The homosexual emancipationist's word homosexual was appropriated by Krafft-Ebing and other late Victorian German medical men (and later, by American doctors) as these Dr. Frankensteins' way of naming, condemning, and asserting their own right to regulate a group of homoerotic creatures just then emerging into sight in the bars, dance halls, and streets of their countries' larger cities.

But naming and specifying the sex deviant simultaneously delimited a sex norm—the new heterosexuality. The medical moralists' interest in a few powerless perverts would help to ensure the conformity of the majority to a new sex ethic, one that was congruent with the pursuit of consumer happiness and capitalist profit.

In the late nineteenth-century United States, several social factors converged to cause the eroticizing of consciousness, behavior, emotion, and identity that became typical of the twentieth-century Western middle class. The transformation of the family from producer to consumer unit resulted in a change in family members' relation to their own bodies; from being an instrument primarily of work, the human body was integrated into a new economy, and began more commonly to be perceived as a means of consumption and pleasure. Historical work has recently begun on how the biological human body is differently integrated into changing modes of production, procreation, engendering, and pleasure so as to alter radically the identity, activity, and experience of that body.[10]

The growth of a consumer economy also fostered a new pleasure ethic. This imperative challenged the early Victorian work ethic, finally helping to usher in a major transformation of values. While the early Victorian work ethic had touted the value of economic production, that era's procreation ethic had extolled the virtues of human reproduction. In contrast, the late Victorian economic ethic hawked the pleasures of consuming, while its sex ethic praised an erotic pleasure principle for men and even for women.

In the late nineteenth century, the erotic became the raw material for a new consumer culture. Newspapers, books, plays, and films touching on sex, "normal" and "abnormal," became available for a price. Restaurants, bars, and baths opened, catering to sexual consumers with cash. Late Victorian entrepreneurs of desire incited the proliferation of a new eroticism, a commoditized culture of pleasure.

In these same years, the rise in power and prestige of medical doctors allowed these upwardly mobile professionals to prescribe a healthy new sexuality. Medical men, in the name of science, defined a new ideal of male-female relationships that included, in women as well as men, an essential, necessary, normal eroticism. Doctors, who had earlier named and judged the sex-enjoying woman a "nymphomaniac," now began to label women's *lack* of sexual pleasure a mental disturbance, speaking critically, for example, of female "frigidity" and "anesthesia."*

By the 1880s, the rise of doctors as a professional group fostered the rise of a new medical model of Normal Love, replete with sexuality. The new Normal Woman and Man were endowed with a healthy libido. The new theory of Normal Love was the modern medical alternative to the old Cult of True Love. The doctors prescribed a new sexual ethic as if it were a morally neutral, medical description of health. The creation of the new Normal Sexual had its counterpart in the invention of the late Victorian Sexual Pervert. The attention paid the sexual abnormal created a need to name the sexual normal, the better to distinguish the average him and her from the deviant it.

Heterosexuality: the first years, 1892–1900

In the periodization of heterosexuality American history suggested here, the years 1892 to 1900 represent "The First Years" of the heterosexual epoch, eight key years in which the idea of the heterosexual and homosexual were initially and tentatively formulated by US doctors. The earliest-known American use of the word "heterosexual" occurs in a medical journal article by Dr. James G. Kiernan of Chicago, read before the city's medical society on March 7, 1892 and published that May—portentous dates in sexual history.[11] But Dr. Kiernan's heterosexuals were definitely not exemplars of normality. Heterosexuals, said Kiernan, were defined by a mental condition, "psychical hermaphroditism." Its symptoms were "inclinations to both sexes." These heterodox sexuals also betrayed inclinations "to abnormal methods of gratification," that is, techniques to insure pleasure without procreation. Dr. Kiernan's heterogeneous sexuals did demonstrate "traces of the normal sexual appetite" (a touch of procreative desire). Kiernan's normal sexuals were implicitly defined by a monolithic other-sex inclination and procreative aim. Significantly, they still lacked a name.

Dr. Kiernan's article of 1892 also included one of the earliest known uses of the word homosexual in American English. Kiernan defined "Pure homosexuals" as persons whose "general mental state is that of the opposite sex." Kiernan thus defined homosexuals by their deviance from a gender norm. His heterosexuals displayed a double deviance from both gender and procreative norms.

* This reference to females reminds us that the invention of heterosexuality had vastly different impacts on the histories of women and men. It also differed in its impact on lesbians and heterosexual women, homosexual and heterosexual men, the middle class and working class, and on different religious, racial, national, and geographic groups.

Though Kiernan used the new words heterosexual and homosexual, an old procreative standard and a new gender norm coexisted uneasily in his thought. His word heterosexual defined a mixed person and compound urge, abnormal because they wantonly included procreative and non-procreative objectives, as well as same-sex and different-sex attractions.

That same year, 1892, Dr. Krafft-Ebing's influential *Psychopathia Sexualis* was first translated and published in the United States.[12] But Kiernan and Krafft-Ebing by no means agreed on the definition of the heterosexual. In Krafft-Ebing's book, "hetero-sexual" was used unambiguously in the modern sense to refer to an erotic feeling for a different sex. "Homo-sexual" refered unambiguously to an erotic feeling for a "same sex." In Krafft-Ebing's volume, unlike Kiernan's article, heterosexual and homosexual were clearly distinguished from a third category, a "psychosexual hermaphroditism," defined by impulses toward both sexes.

Krafft-Ebing hypothesized an inborn "sexual instinct" for relations with the "opposite sex," the inherent "purpose" of which was to foster procreation. Krafft-Ebing's erotic drive was still a reproductive instinct. But the doctor's clear focus on a different-sex versus same-sex sexuality constituted a historic, epochal move from an absolute procreative standard of normality toward a new norm. His definition of heterosexuality as other-sex attraction provided the basis for a revolutionary, modern break with a centuries-old procreative standard.

It is difficult to overstress the importance of that new way of categorizing. The German's mode of labeling was radical in referring to the biological sex, masculinity or femininity, and the pleasure of actors (along with the procreant purpose of acts). Krafft-Ebing's heterosexual offered the modern world a new norm that came to dominate our idea of the sexual universe, helping to change it from a mode of human reproduction and engendering to a mode of pleasure. The heterosexual category provided the basis for a move from a production-oriented, procreative imperative to a consumerist pleasure principle—an institutionalized pursuit of happiness.

Despite the clarity of Krafft-Ebing's heterosexual/homosexual distinction, Dr. Kiernan was not the only American medical writer to have difficulty understanding the hetero/homo pair as a normal/pervert duo. Perceived as ambivalent procreator, the heterosexual did not at first exemplify the quintessence of the normal. In 1893, for example, Dr. Charles Hughes assured his fellow medical men that, by medical treatment (hypnosis and sometimes surgery!), the mind and feelings could be "turned back into normal channels, the homo and hetero sexual changed into beings of natural erotic inclination, with normal impulsions."[13] The hetero, as person of mixed, procreative and nonprocreative, disposition, still stood with the nonprocreative homo as abnormal characters in the late nineteenth-century pantheon of sexual perverts.

But Krafft-Ebing's clear hetero/homo opposition began to catch on—although at first only in medical journals. By 1895, for example, one of these late Victorian purveyors of explicit sex published a translation from the French of an article by Marc-André Raffalovich. Here, as in Krafft-Ebing's work, the terms heterosexual and homosexual referred consistently to different-sex/same-sex eroticisms—two, symmetrical, polarized erotic desires, mental states, and persons—the present dominant usage.[14] As late as 1901, however, *Dorland's Medical Dictionary,* published in Philadelphia, still defined "Heterosexuality" as "Abnormal or perverted appetite toward the opposite sex."[15]

Only gradually did doctors agree that heterosexual referred to a normal, "other-sex" eros. This new standard-model heterosex provided the pivotal term for the modern regularization of eros that paralleled similar attempts to standardize masculinity and femininity, intelligence, and manufacturing.[16] The idea of heterosexuality as the master sex from which all others deviated was (like the idea of the master race) deeply authoritarian. The doctors' normalization of a sex that was hetero proclaimed a new heterosexual separatism—an erotic apartheid that forcefully segregated the sex normals from the sex perverts. The new, strict boundaries made the emerging erotic world less polymorphous—safer for sex normals. However, the idea of such creatures as heterosexuals and homosexuals emerged from the narrow world of medicine to become a commonly accepted notion only in the early twentieth century. In 1901, in the comprehensive *Oxford English Dictionary,* "heterosexual" and "homosexual" had not yet made it.

The distribution of the heterosexual mystique: 1900–1930

In the early years of this heterosexual century the tentative hetero hypothesis was stabilized, fixed, and widely distributed as the ruling sexual orthodoxy: The Heterosexual Mystique. Starting among pleasure-affirming urban working-class youths, southern blacks, and Greenwich-Village bohemians as defensive subculture, heterosex soon triumphed as dominant culture.[17]

In its earliest version, the twentieth-century heterosexual imperative usually continued to associate heterosexuality with a supposed human "need," "drive," or "instinct" for propagation, a procreant urge linked inexorably with carnal lust as it had not been earlier. In the early twentieth century, the falling birth rate, rising divorce rate, and "war of the sexes" of the middle class were matters of increasing public concern. Giving vent to heteroerotic emotions was thus praised as enhancing baby-making capacity, marital intimacy, and family stability. (Only many years later, in the mid-1960s, would heteroeroticism be distinguished completely, in practice and theory, from procreativity and male-female pleasure sex justified in its own name.)

The first part of the new sex norm—hetero—referred to a basic gender divergence. The "oppositeness" of the sexes was alleged to be the basis for a universal, normal, erotic attraction between males and females. The stress on the sexes' "oppositeness," which harked back to the early nineteenth century, by no means simply registered biological differences of females and males. The early twentieth-century focus on physiological and gender dimorphism reflected the deep anxieties of men about the shifting work, social roles, and power of men over women, and about the ideals of womanhood and manhood. That gender anxiety is documented, for example, in 1897, in *The New York Times*' publication of the Reverend Charles Parkhurst's diatribe against female "andromaniacs," the preacher's derogatory, scientific-sounding name for women who tried to "minimize distinctions by which manhood and womanhood are differentiated."[18] The stress on gender difference was a conservative response to the changing social-sexual division of activity and feeling which gave rise to the independent "New Woman" of the 1880s and eroticized "Flapper" of the 1920s.

The second part of the new hetero norm referred positively to sexuality. That novel upbeat focus on the hedonistic possibilities of male-female conjunctions also reflected a social transformation—a revaluing of pleasure and procreation, consumption and work in commercial, capitalist society. The democratic attribution of a normal lust to human females (as well as males) served to authorize women's enjoyment of their own bodies and began to undermine the early Victorian idea of the pure True Woman—a sex-affirmative action still part of women's struggle. The twentieth-century Erotic Woman also undercut nineteenth-century feminist assertion of women's moral superiority, cast suspicions of lust on women's passionate romantic friendships with women, and asserted the presence of a menacing female monster, "the lesbian."[19]

A major medical manufacturer of the heterosexual mystique was Dr. Havelock Ellis, whose multi-volume *Studies in the Psychology of Sex* began to be published in Philadelphia in 1901. The other early, major hetero-mystique maker was Dr. Sigmund Freud, whose *Three Contributions to the Sexual Theory* was first published in New York in 1910.[20]

In this work, Freud presented heterosex as a familial imposition upon an originally roving eros. Freud's 1910 version of the normal developmental process involved fantasies of incest and parent and sibling murder—high melodrama, to say the least. Despite its deeply troubled origins, heterosexuality was finally defined by Freud's arbitrary, authoritarian assertion as "maturity." Homosex was similarly defined as the "fixated," "immature" resolution of the same family sex play. In the name of Freud and popular psychology, heterosexuality would be proclaimed throughout the land as, simply, perfection.

In conscious opposition to Freud, Ellis claimed that heterosexuality and homosexuality were inborn; he nervously rejected the idea that the species might depend for its continued reproduction on such an open-ended intrafamily war and fallible developmental process as that proposed by Freud. Despite their argument over the physiological versus family origins of heterosex, both doctors were major publicists of the different-sex erotic among a "progressive" public.

From about 1900 on through the 1920s, a mixed bag of novelists, playwrights, sex educators, and profit-seeking publishers and play producers struggled to establish the legal right to discuss and distribute a new commodity, the explicit (for its time) heterosexual drama, novel, and advice book. The writers included James Branch Cabell, Theodore Dreiser, F. Scott Fitzgerald, Elinor Glyn, James Joyce, D.H. Lawrence, and sex educators like Mary Ware Dennett.[21]

In the perspective of heterosexual history, this early twentieth century struggle for the more explicit depiction of an "opposite-sex" eros appears in a curious new light. Ironically, we find sex-conservatives, the social-purity advocates of censorship and repression, fighting against the depiction not just of sexual perversity but also of the new normal heterosexuality. That a more open depiction of normal sex had to be defended against forces of propriety confirms the claim that heterosexuality's predecessor, Victorian True Love, had included no legitimate eros.

Before 1930 in the United States, heterosexuality was still fighting an uphill battle. As late as 1929, a federal court in Brooklyn found Mary Ware Dennett, author of a 21-page sex education pamphlet for young people, guilty of mailing this obscene essay. Dennett's pamphlet criticized other sex-education materials for not including a "frank, unashamed declaration that the climax of sex emotion is an unsurpassed joy, something which rightly belongs to every normal human being" *after* they fell in love and married. If it seemed "distasteful" that the sex organs were "so near . . . our 'sewerage system,'" Dennett assured America's youth that this offensive positioning of parts was probably protective ("At any rate, there they are, and our duty is . . . to take mighty good care of them."). The word heterosexual did not appear.[22]

The heterosexual steps out: 1930–1945

In 1930, in *The New York Times,* heterosexuality first became a love that dared to speak its name. On April 30th of that year, the word "heterosexual" is first known to have appeared in *The New York Times Book Review.* There, a critic described the subject of André Gide's *The Immoralist* proceeding "from a heterosexual liaison to a homosexual one." The ability to slip between sexual categories was referred to casually as a rather unremarkable aspect of human possibility. This is also the first known reference by *The Times* to the new hetero/homo duo.[23]

The following month the second reference to the hetero/homo dyad appeared in *The New York Times Book Review,* in a comment on Floyd Dell's *Love in the Machine Age.* This work revealed a prominent antipuritan of the 1930s using the dire threat of homosexuality as his rationale for greater heterosexual freedom. *The Times* quoted Dell's warning that current abnormal social conditions kept the young dependent on their parents, causing "infantilism, prostitution and homosexuality." Also quoted was Dell's attack on the "inculcation of purity" that "breeds distrust of the opposite sex." Young people, Dell said, should be "permitted to develop normally to heterosexual adulthood." "But," *The Times* reviewer emphasized, "such a state already exists, here and now." And so it did. Heterosexuality, a new gender-sex category, had been distributed from the narrow, rarified realm of a few doctors to become a nationally, even internationally cited aspect of middle-class life.[24]

In 1933, in an English novel published in the United States, the colloquial abbreviation "hetero" is first known to have made its published appearance. In Eileen A. Robertson's *Ordinary Families* a character declared: "The odd thing about me is that . . . I should be so purely 'hetero' in spite of lack of opportunity." Quote marks around that 'hetero' suggest the newness of the colloquialism. But the slang usage suggests that people were now on quite familiar terms with the hetero on both sides of the Atlantic.[25]

By December 1940, when the risque musical *Pal Joey* opened on Broadway, a song titled "Zip" satirized the striptease artist Gypsy Rose Lee, who was quoted: "I don't like a deep contralto, Or a man whose voice is alto, Zip, I'm a heterosexual." That lyric registered the historically new, self-conscious, public proclamation of a heterosexual identity.[26]

Heterosexual hegemony: 1945–1965

The "cult of domesticity" following World War II—the reassociation of women with the home, motherhood, and child-care; men with fatherhood and wage work outside the home—was a period in which the predominance of the hetero norm went almost unchallenged, an era of heterosexual hegemony. This was an age in which conservative mental-health professionals reasserted the old link between heterosexuality and procreation. In contrast, sex-liberals of the day strove, ultimately with success, to expand the heterosexual ideal to include within the boundaries of normality a wider-than-ever range of nonprocreative, premarital, and extra-marital behaviors. But sex-liberal reform actually helped to extend and secure the dominance of the heterosexual idea, as we shall see when we get to Kinsey.

The post-war sex-conservative tendency was illustrated in 1947, in Ferdinand Lundberg and Dr. Marnia Farnham's book, *Modern Woman: The Lost Sex*. Improper masculinity and femininity was exemplified, the authors decreed, by "engagement in heterosexual relations . . . with the complete intent to see to it that they do not eventuate in reproduction."[27] Their procreatively defined heterosex was one expression of a post-war ideology of fecundity that, internalized and enacted dutifully by a large part of the population, gave rise to the postwar baby boom.

The idea of the feminine female and masculine male as prolific breeders was also reflected in the stress, specific to the late 1940s, on the homosexual as sad symbol of "sterility"—that particular loaded term appears incessantly in comments on homosex dating to the fecund forties.

In 1948, in *The New York Times Book Review,* sex liberalism was in ascendancy. Dr. Howard A. Rusk declared that Alfred Kinsey's just published report on *Sexual Behavior in the Human Male* had found "wide variations in sex concepts and behavior." This raised the question: "What is 'normal' and 'abnormal'?" In particular, the report had found that "homosexual experience is much more common than previously thought," and "there is often a mixture of both homo and hetero experience."[28]

Kinsey's counting of orgasms indeed stressed the wide range of behaviors and feelings that fell within the boundaries of a quantitative, statistically accounted heterosexuality. Kinsey's liberal reform of the hetero/homo dualism widened the narrow, old hetero category to accord better with the varieties of social experience. He thereby contradicted the older idea of a monolithic, qualitatively defined, natural procreative act, experience, and person.[29]

Though Kinsey explicitly questioned "whether the terms 'normal' and 'abnormal' belong in a scientific vocabulary," his counting of climaxes was generally understood to define normal sex as majority sex. This quantified norm constituted a final, society-wide break with the old qualitatively-defined reproductive standard. Though conceived of as purely scientific, the statistical definition of the normal as the-sex-most-people-are-having substituted a new, quantitative moral standard for the old, qualitative sex ethic—another triumph for the spirit of capitalism.

Kinsey also explicitly contested the idea of an absolute, either/or antithesis between hetero and homo persons. He denied that human beings "represent two discrete populations, heterosexual and homosexual." The world, he ordered, "is not to be divided into sheep and goats." The hetero/homo division was not nature's doing: "Only the human mind invents categories and tries to force facts into separated pigeonholes. The living world is a continuum."[30]

With a wave of the taxonomist's hand, Kinsey dismissed the social and historical division of people into heteros and homos. His denial of heterosexual and homosexual personhood rejected the social reality and profound subjective force of a historically constructed tradition which, since 1892 in the United States, had cut the sexual population in two and helped to establish the social reality of a heterosexual and homosexual identity.

On the one hand, the social construction of homosexual persons has led to the development of a powerful gay liberation identity politics based on an ethnic group model. This has freed generations of women and men from a deep, painful, socially induced sense of shame, and helped to bring about a society-wide liberalization of attitudes and responses to homosexuals.[31] On the other hand, contesting the notion of homosexual and heterosexual persons was one early, partial resistance to the limits of the hetero/homo construction. Gore Vidal, rebel son of Kinsey, has for years been joyfully proclaiming:

> there is no such thing as a homosexual or a heterosexual person. There are only homo- or heterosexual acts. Most people are a mixture of impulses if not practices, and what anyone does with a willing partner is of no social or cosmic significance.
>
> So why all the fuss? In order for a ruling class to rule, there must be arbitrary prohibitions. Of all prohibitions, sexual taboo is the most useful because sex involves everyone. . . . we have allowed our governors to divide the population into two teams. One team is good, godly, straight; the other is evil, sick, vicious.[32]

Though Vidal's analysis of our "wacky division" is persuasive, we may now go one step further and question not only the division into hetero and homo persons but the hetero/homo division itself.

Kinsey popularized the idea of a "continuum" of activity and feeling between hetero and homo poles. His liberal reform of the hetero/homo dualism did widen the narrow, old hetero category to accord with social experience, suggesting there were degrees of heterosexual and homosexual behavior and experience. But that famous continuum of erotic acts and feelings reaffirmed the idea of a sexuality divided between the hetero and homo. Kinsey's hetero/homo rating scale, from zero to six, sounded neat, quantitative, and ever-so scientific; his influential sex-liberalism thus upheld and consolidated the hetero/homo polarity, giving it new life and legitimacy.

In 1953, in *The New York Times,* anthropologist Clyde Kluckhohn reviewed the new Kinsey report on women. The word heterosexual appeared once. Kluckhohn complained that the report did *not* treat the "frequency of rectal heterosexual coitus"—no doubt the first overt mention of hetero sodomy in the decorous *Times.* This historic sodomitical occasion illustrates how the Kinsey reports and responses to them expanded the discussion of heterosex to include a wider range of variations than the "respectable" media had previously admitted.[33]

That era's liberalization of the heterosexual ideal is also illustrated by the play *Tea and Sympathy,* reviewed in *The Times* in 1953; the "story of a schoolboy falsely suspected of homosexuality." But the false homo was a true hetero. Though our hero was gentle, quiet, shy, intellectual, and nonconforming, the playwright finally certified him as straight. (As usual, it turned out the villain had homo tendencies.) More about heterosexuality than homosexuality, the play decried the era's narrow, loutish genderism, advocating the expansion of heterosex to include young men lacking in the brutish manly virtues.[34] The progressive expansion of heterosexuality to include a wider range of gender-appropriate behaviors and feelings served to strengthen the dominance of the hetero ideal, the rule of the hetero/homo dualism.

Heterosexuality questioned: 1965–1982

By the late 1960s, anti-establishment counterculturalists, fledgling feminists, and homosexual-rights activists had begun to produce an unprecedented critique of sexual repression in general, of women's sexual repression in particular, of marriage and the family—and of some forms of heterosexuality. This critique even found its way into *The New York Times.*

In March 1968, in the theater section of that paper, freelancer Rosalyn Regelson cited a scene from a satirical review brought to New York by a San Francisco troup:

> a heterosexual man wanders inadvertently into a homosexual bar. Before he realizes his mistake, he becomes involved with an aggressive queen who orders a drink for him. Being a broadminded liberal and trying to play it cool until he can back out of the situation gracefully, he asks, "How do you like being a ah homosexual?" To which the queen drawls drily, "How do you like being ah whatever it is you are?"

Regelson continued:

> The Two Cultures in confrontation. The middle-class liberal, challenged today on many fronts, finds his last remaining fixed value, his heterosexuality, called into question. The theater . . . recalls the strategies he uses in dealing with this ultimate threat to his world view.[35]

Just a few weeks later in March 1968, *Times* critic Clive Barnes reviewed Paddy Chayefsky's new play, *The Latent Heterosexual.* In this play, a middle-aged and extremely effeminate writer discovered that "his homosexuality was . . . merely a cover-up for his fears of impotence." The play, said the ever-earnest Barnes, "makes a serious point."[36] In the perspective of heterosexual history, Chayefsky's holding out hope of hetero happiness for even the most unlikely homosexual queen is a document of heterosexuality on the defensive. Chayefsky's portrayal of latent heterosexuality triumphing against all odds was nervous propaganda for a norm increasingly challenged by feminists, counterculturalists, homosexualists, and those advanced other-sex lovers aware of something radically wrong in the house of heterosex.

The new hetero defensiveness was illustrated again six months later in *The New York Times,* in a classic document of heterosexual history. In September 1968, Judy Klemesrud's interview with Cliff Gorman, who played "The Definitive Screaming Queen" in *The Boys in the Band,* was headlined "You Don't Have To Be One To Play One." Klemesrud satirically skewered the macho excess of Gorman's nervous assertion of heterosexuality.[37]

The nasty subtext of Klemesrud's humor suggested that the actor did protest too much; his uneasy heterosex, she implied, revealed a hint of the homo. But whatever private psychodramas were performed on the stage of this particular male's mind, the exquisite anguish of the actor, desperate to dissociate himself from a homosexual role, was just an extreme example of many men's new need to publicly proclaim their heterosexuality to define themselves to the world as *not* one of those perverts now more openly portrayed in the media. The coming out of the homo provoked the coming out of the het.*

Klemesrud began: Gorman's "Flitting and floating and fluttering" as Emory, "the pansy interior decorator," was "not exactly the kind of part you'd imagine for a nice Jewish boy from Jamaica, Queens." But Gorman had taken the part, and *Boys in the Band* had become a "smash hit." Gorman had recently signed for television to play a rapist. Gorman was quoted: "What can be more heterosexual than that?"

"With a can of Schlitz in his hand," said Klemesrud, Gorman "rapped" with the reporter about what everyone's asking him these days: "How can a straight guy like you play a fag in a gay play?"

> "It's simple—I needed the money," he says in his very butch real-life voice. "I really don't give a damn what people think. . . . There's no question in my mind of my gender. And there's no question in my wife's mind. . . . I'm buying my own beer now. . . . If I was playing a psychopath that doesn't mean I'm psychopathic."
>
> His incredibly beautiful wife, Gayle, tiptoes across the room and pours Cliffs beer into a glass. . . .
>
> Cliff is still seething. "People think it's so amazing that a guy can play a homosexual in such a flamboyant way and still be straight. I guess we publicize the point because it's a selling point and makes everybody want to come and see the show. . . ."
>
> Cliff unties his bandanna, flings it on the coffee table and strolls across the room to flip on a recording of the only kind of music that really moves him—country and western. Then he pops open his second Schlitz. "They told me they called a lot of gay actors, but nobody wanted to do Emory. I guess a real homosexual might be too inhibited. . . . I didn't do anything special to prepare for [the part], although the walk took a lot of practice. . . . But I already knew how to lisp because I'd been telling gay jokes since I was a kid."

After making it as an actor, said Gorman, "I want to have four kids and a stereo and a boat and move to Baja California, and fish and skin dive and all that wholesome stuff." Printed with this *Times* interview was a large photograph of Gorman, his arms clasped tightly around his wife, both sad-eyed and clinging—a classic image in the historical iconography of heterosexuality, a documentation of heterosex haunted by the specter of homosex.

The haunting of heterosex continued. By the early 1970s, militant homosexuals and feminists were explicitly criticizing some institutional forms of heterosexuality. A "heterosexual dictatorship," enforcing that single erotic standard, had been named by Christopher Isherwood.[38] "Compulsory heterosexuality" was named in 1976 as one of the crimes against women by the Brussels Tribunal on Crimes Against Women.[39] In the winter of 1977–1978, in a gay movement periodical, I reviewed Mary P. Ryan's *Womanhood in America,* and said:

> Throughout her book Ryan applies a simple conceptual innovation. This is to casually refer to "heterosexual relations" and "heterosexual women," rather than the usual "sexual

* Examples are legion of men's need to defensively assert their heterosexuality. For example, on April 16, 1989, Bruce Weber, an editor of *The New York Times Magazine,* writes an "About Men" column on "My Best Friend's Girlfriend." He begins by confessing his fear that the new live-in female lover of his male friend will disrupt the men's long-standing intimacy—then immediately identifies his sexual orientation: "We are the oldest two heterosexual men I know who have never lived with a woman." On March 16, 1989, the single front-page headline of *New York Newsday* proclaimed: "Koch: 'I'm Heterosexual'".

> relations" and "women." Ryan thus refuses to take for granted as natural and universal the specifically heterosexual character of the history being studied. The existence of such a particular thing as heterosexual history, along with homosexual history, has not yet been generally recognized, its implications analyzed. Ryan furthers such analysis.

The naming of "heterosexual history" was a step toward theorizing it.[40]

In 1979, Lillian Faderman coined the term "heterocentric" to condemn a world-view that made homosexuals (especially lesbians) invisible.[41] And in the summer of 1980, *Signs,* the feminist scholarly journal, published Adrienne Rich's "Compulsory Heterosexuality and Lesbian Existence." Taking off from earlier discussions among feminists in the movement press, Rich's was the first "respectable" work to so explicitly question the implicit assumption of heterosexuality. Rich's essay was important in beginning to legitimize the serious study of heterosexuality as social and political institution.[42]

In 1982, ninety years after the US invention of heterosexuality, *The New York Times* was regularly sending out distress signals about a heterosexuality in crisis criticized from within and without its own ranks.

In August 1982, novelist Margaret Atwood reviewed Marge Piercy's poems, calling them the

> product of a mind rooted firmly in time and place and engaging itself with the central dilemmas of its situation. How, for instance, is a heterosexual feminist to respond to (a) men as they are and (b) more extreme feminists who want her to divest herself of them?[43]

Lesbian feminists' questioning of heterosexuality had received serious recognition in *The Times.*

In October 1982, in John Osborne's review of Noel Coward's *Diaries,* we learned that Coward "challenged heterosexuality as a failure of style." Coward's aesthetic critique (the resistance tactic of the old-time cultured queen) has roots reaching back to Oscar Wilde.[44] And in the last month of 1982, *The Times* described *Tootsie* as a film about "the crucial importance of friendship as a prerequisite to love between a man and a woman." *Tootsie*'s writer-producer was quoted: "Isn't it a sad comment on heterosexual relationships that it's so rare to see a man and a woman who are best friends?" Ninety years after heterosexuality's American debut, its crisis had become a cliche. That year, its crisis was so acute an embattled California psychologist felt compelled to publish the world's first book *In Defense of Heterosexuality.*[45,*]

Several years before herpes and AIDS became focal points for the anxiety of heterosexuals, their sex-love had begun to lose its old certainty, its unquestioned status. Masters and Johnson's *Crisis: Heterosexual Behavior in the Age of AIDS* in fact named an emergency predating AIDS.[46] Yet the media response to AIDS has created a major, unremarked, quantitative increase in references to heterosexuality and a historic, qualitative change in the public perception of heterosexuals as one of the endangered erotic species.

Heterosexual history: out of the shadows

Our brief survey of the heterosexual idea suggests a new hypothesis. Rather than naming a conjunction old as Eve and Adam, heterosexual designates a word and concept, a norm and role,

* A proposal to investigate and treat our society's "heterosexual conflict" was offered in a 1983 US Justice Department memo by Alfred S. Regnery, then administrator of the Office of Juvenile Justice and Delinquency Prevention. The memo claimed that "heterosexual conflicts . . . are growing and spreading in both virulence and social normalcy," posing a threat to the American family. Quoted by Larry Bush, "Big Brother is Watching You," *Village Voice,* August 7, 1984, p. 23.

an individual and group identity, a behavior and feeling, and a peculiar sexual-political institution particular to the late nineteenth and twentieth centuries.

Because much stress has been placed here on heterosexuality as word and concept, it seems important to affirm that heterosexuality (and homosexuality) came into existence before it was named and thought about. The formulation of the heterosexual idea did not create a heterosexual experience or behavior; to suggest otherwise would be to ascribe determining power to labels and concepts. But the titling and envisioning of heterosexuality did play an important role in consolidating the construction of the heterosexual's social existence. Before the wide use of the word heterosexual, I suggest, women and men did not mutually lust with the same profound, sure sense of normalcy that followed the distribution of "heterosexual" as universal sanctifier.

According to this proposal, women and men make their own sexual histories. But they do not produce their sex lives just as they please. They make their sexualities within a particular mode of organization given by the past and altered by their changing desire, their present power and activity, and their vision of a better world. That hypothesis suggests a number of good reasons for the immediate inauguration of research on a historically specific heterosexuality.[47]

The study of the history of the heterosexual experience will forward a great intellectual struggle still in its early stages. This is the fight to pull heterosexuality, homosexuality, and all the sexualities out of the realm of nature and biology into the realm of the social and historical. Feminists have explained to us that anatomy does not determine our gender destinies (our masculinities and femininities). But we've only recently begun to consider that *biology does not settle our erotic fates.* The common notion that biology determines the object of sexual desire, or that physiology and society together cause sexual orientation, are determinisms that deny the break existing between our bodies and situation and our desiring. Just as the biology of our hearing organs will never tell us why we take pleasure in Bach or delight in Dixieland, our female or male anatomies, hormones, and genes will never tell us why we yearn for women, men, both, other, or none. That is because desiring is a self-generated project of individuals within particular historical cultures. Heterosexual history can help us see the place of values and judgments in the construction of our own and others' pleasures, and to see how our erotic tastes—our aesthetics of the flesh—are socially institutionalized through the struggle of individuals and classes.

The study of heterosexuality in time will also help us to recognize the *vast historical diversity of sexual emotions and behaviors*—a variety that challenges the monolithic heterosexual hypothesis. John D'Emilio and Estelle Freedman's *Intimate Matters: A History of Sexuality in America* refers in passing to numerous substantial changes in sexual activity and feeling: for example, the widespread use of contraceptives in the nineteenth century, the twentieth-century incitement of the female orgasm, and the recent sexual conduct changes by gay men in response to the AIDS epidemic. It's now a commonplace of family history that people in particular classes feel and behave in substantially different ways under different historical conditions.[48] Only when we stop assuming an invariable essence of heterosexuality will we begin the research to reveal the full variety of sexual emotions and behaviors.

The historical study of the heterosexual experience can help us *understand the erotic relationships of women and men in terms of their changing modes of social organization.* Such modal analysis actually characterizes a sex history well underway.[49] This suggests that the eros-gender-procreation system (the social ordering of lust, femininity and masculinity, and baby-making) has been linked closely to a society's particular organization of power and production. To understand the subtle history of heterosexuality we need to look carefully at correlations between (1) society's organization of eros and pleasure; (2) its mode of engendering persons as feminine or masculine (its making of women and men); (3) its ordering of human reproduction; and (4) its dominant political economy. This General Theory of Sexual Relativity proposes that substantial historical changes in the social organization of eros, gender, and procreation have basically altered the activity and experience of human beings within those modes.[50]

A historical view locates heterosexuality and homosexuality in time, helping us distance ourselves from them. This distancing can help us formulate new questions that clarify our long-range sexual-political goals: what has been and is the social function of sexual categorizing? Whose interests have been served by the division of the world into heterosexual and homosexual? Do we dare not draw a line between those two erotic species? Is some sexual naming socially necessary? Would human freedom be enhanced if the sex-biology of our partners in lust was of no particular concern, and had no name? In what kind of society could we all more freely explore our desire and our flesh?

As we move toward 1992 and the one-hundredth birthday of heterosexuality in the United States, a new sense of the historical making of the heterosexual and homosexual suggests that these are ways of feeling, acting, and being with each other that we can together unmake and radically remake according to our present desire, power, and our vision of a future political-economy of pleasure.

Notes

1 This piece follows directly out of my work on "The Invention of the Homosexual, 1880–1950," and "Lesbian and Gay History—Theory and Practice," in *Gay/Lesbian Almanac: A New Documentary* (New York: Harper & Row, 1983), pp. 137–74, 1–19. Since 1982 I have spoken publicly on "The Invention of Heterosexuality." Also see Carole S. Vance, "Social Construction Theory: Problems in the History of Sexuality," in A. van Kooten Niekerk and T. van der Meer, eds., *Homosexuality, Which Homosexuality?* (Holland: An Dekker, 1989).

2 Barbara Welter, "The Cult of True Womanhood: 1820–1860," *American Quarterly*, vol. 18 (Summer 1966); Welter's analysis is extended here to include True Men and True Love.

3 Michael Lynch, "New York Sodomy, 1796–1873," paper presented at the New York Institute for the Humanities, February 1, 1985.

4 George Chauncey, Jr., "From Sexual Inversion to Homosexuality: Medicine and the Changing Conceptualization of Female Deviance," *Salmagundi*, nos. 58–59 (Fall-Winter 1982), 114–46.

5 Walt Whitman, *Leaves of Grass, Facsimile Edition of the 1860 Text* (Ithaca, NY: Cornell University Press, 1961).

6 Michael Lynch, "'Here is Adhesiveness': From Friendship to Homosexuality," *Victorian Studies*, vol. 29, no. 1 (Autumn 1985), 67–96.

7 Hubert Kennedy, *Ulrichs: The Life and Works of Karl Heinrich Ulrichs, Pioneer of the Modern Gay Movement* (Boston: Alvson Publications, 1988).

8 Manfred Herzer to Jonathan Ned Katz, April 16, 1989, and the article by Jean-Claude Féray and Herzer, "(Homo)sexual Studies and Politics in the Nineteenth Century: Karl Maria Kertbeny," *The Journal of Homosexuality*, vol. 19, no. 1 (1990). Also see Herzer, "Kertbeny and the Nameless Love," *Journal of Homosexuality*, vol. 12, no. 1 (Fall 1985), 1–26; and Kennedy, *Ulrichs*, 149–56.

9 Herzer, "Kertbeny and the Nameless Love," pp. 6, 21 n. 6. The term heterosexual appears in the 4th edition of R. Krafft-Ebing, *Psychopathia Sexualis* . . . (Stuttgart: Ferdinand Enke, 1889), 96–97; Herzer to Katz, July 27, 1983.

10 See, for example, Catherine Gallagher and Thomas Laqueur, eds., "The Making of the Modern Body: Sexuality and Society in the Nineteenth Century," *Representations*, no. 14 (Spring 1986), (republished, Berkeley: University of California Press, 1987).

11 Dr. James G. Kiernan, "Responsibility in Sexual Perversion," *Chicago Medical Recorder*, vol. 3 (May 1892), pp. 185–210.

12 R. von Krafft-Ebing, *Psychopathia Sexualis, with Especial Reference to Contrary Sexual Instinct: A Medico-Legal Study*, trans. Charles Gilbert Chaddock (Philadelphia: F.A. Davis, 1892), from the 7th and revised German ed. Preface, November 1892.

13 Dr. Charles H. Hughes, "Erotopathia—Morbid Eroticism," read at the Pan-American Medical Congress, September, 1893; *Alienist and Neurologist,* vol 14, no. 4 (October 1893), pp. 531–78.
14 Mark-André Raffalovich, "Uranism, Congenital Sexual Inversion. Observations and Recommendations," *Journal of Comparative Neurology,* vol. 5 (March 1895), pp. 33–65.
15 W[illiam] A[lexander] Dorland, *The American Illustrated Medical Dictionary,* second ed. (Philadelphia: W.B. Saunders, 1901), p. 300.
16 For the standardization of gender see Lewis Terman and C. C. Miles, *Sex and Personality, Studies in Femininity and Masculinity* (New York: McGraw Hill, 1936). For the standardization of intelligence see Lewis Terman, *Stanford-Binet Intelligence Scale* (Boston: Houghton Mifflin, 1916). For the standardization of work, see "scientific management" and "Taylorism" in Harry Braverman, *Labor and Monopoly Capital: The Degradation of Work in the Twentieth Century* (New York: Monthly Review Press, 1974).
17 See D'Emilio and Freedman, *Intimate Matters,* pp. 194–201, 231, 241, 295–96; Ellen Kay Trimberger, "Feminism, Men, and Modern Love: Greenwich Village, 1900–1925," in *Powers of Desire: The Politics of Sexuality,* eds. Ann Snitow, Christine Stansell, Sharon Thompson (New York: Monthly Review Press, 1983), pp. 131–52; Kathy Peiss, "'Charity Girls' and City Pleasures: Historical Notes on Working Class Sexuality, 1880–1920," in *Powers of Desire,* pp. 74–87; and Mary P. Ryan, "The Sexy Saleslady: Psychology, Heterosexuality, and Consumption in the Twentieth Century," in her *Womanhood in America,* 2nd ed. (New York: Franklin Watts: 1979), pp. 151–82.
18 [Rev. Charles Parkhurst], "Woman. Calls Them Andromaniacs. Dr. Parkhurst So Characterizes Certain Women Who Passionately Ape Everything That Is Mannish. Woman Divinely Preferred. Her Supremacy Lies in Her Womanliness, and She Should Make the Most of It—Her Sphere of Best Usefulness the Home," *The New York Times,* May 23, 1897, p. 16:1.
19 See Lisa Duggan, "The Social Enforcement of Heterosexuality and Lesbian Resistance in the 1920s," in *Class, Race, and Sex: The Dynamics of Control,* ed. Amy Swerdlow and Hanah Lessinger (Boston: G.K. Hall, 1983), pp. 75–92; Rayna Rapp and Ellen Ross, "The Twenties Backlash: Compulsory Heterosexuality, the Consumer Family, and the Waning of Feminism," in Swerdlow and Lessinger; Christina Simmons, "Companionate Marriage and the Lesbian Threat," *Frontiers,* vol. 4, no. 3 (Fall 1979), pp. 54–59; and Lillian Faderman, *Surpassing the Love of Men* (New York: William Morrow, 1981).
20 Havelock Ellis, *Studies in the Psychology of Sex, Volume 1, The Evolution of Sexual Modesty* (Philadelphia: F.A. Davis, 1901). Sigmund Freud, *Three Contributions to the Sexual Theory,* trans. A.A. Brill, intro. James J. Putnam (NY: The Journal of Nervous and Mental Disease Publishing Company, 1910).
21 David Loth, *The Erotic in Literature: A Historical Survey of Pornography as Delightful as it is Indiscreet* (London: Secker & Warburg, 1962), Ch. IX, "The Bars Begin to Drop," pp. 145–70.
22 Mary Ware Dennett, *The Sex Side of Life, An Explanation for Young People* (Astoria, New York: Published by the Author, 1928).
23 Louis Kronenberger, review of André Gide, *The Immoralist, New York Times Book Review,* April 20, 1930, p. 9.
24 Henry James Forman, review of Floyd Dell, *Love in the Machine Age* (New York: Farrar & Rinehart), *New York Times Book Review,* September 14, 1930, p. 9.
25 R.W. Burchfield, ed., *A Supplement to the Oxford English Dictionary* (Oxford, Clarendon Press, 1976), Volume II, H-N, p. 80.
26 Lorenz Hart and Richard Rogers, *Pal Joey* (Columbia Masterworks, ML4364), liner notes by Richard Rogers. I quote (by heart) from the record.
27 Ferdinand Lundberg and Dr. Marnia F. Farnham, *Modern Woman the Lost Sex* (NY: Harper, 1947).
28 Dr. Howard A. Rusk, *New York Times Book Review,* January 4, 1948, p. 3.
29 Alfred Kinsey, Wardell B. Pomeroy, Clyde E. Martin, *Sexual Behavior in the Human Male* (Philadelphia: W.B. Saunders, 1948), pp. 199–200.
30 Kinsey, *Sexual Behavior,* pp. 637, 639.
31 See Steven Epstein, "Gay Politics, Ethnic Identity: The Limits of Social Constructionism," *Socialist Review* 93/93 (1987), pp. 9–54.
32 Gore Vidal, "Someone to Laugh at the Squares With" [Tennessee Williams], *New York Review of Books,* June 13, 1985; reprinted in his *At Home: Essays, 1982–1988* (New York: Random House, 1988), p. 48.
33 Clyde Kluckhohn, "The Complex Kinsey Study and What it Attempts," Section VII, *New York Times Book Review,* September 13, 1953, p. 3.
34 Brooks Atkinson, *The New York Times,* October 1, 1953, p. 35:1.
35 Rosalyn Regelson, "Up the Camp Staircase," *The New York Times,* March 3, 1968, Section II, p. 1:5.

36 Clive Barnes, *The New York Times,* March 22, 1968, p. 52:1. Barnes lavishly praised Zero Mostel's acting of Chayefsky's "fag poet": "It is the humor of the shriekingly heterosexual actor pretending camp, with grotesquely exaggerated mannerisms that are funny simply through their very distance from reality."

37 Judy Klemesrud, "You Don't Have to Be One to Play One," *The New York Times,* September 29, 1968, Section II, p. 1:2.

38 I have not traced when Isherwood first referred to the "heterosexual dictatorship." Isherwood dates to 1929, at age twenty-four, his becoming "suddenly, blindly furious that 'Girls are what the state and the church and the law and the press and the medical profession endorse, and command me to desire.'" *Christopher and His Kind* (New York: Avon Books, 1977), p. 12.

39 Diana Russell and Nicole van de Vens, eds., *Proceedings of the International Tribunal on Crimes Against Women* (Millbrae, California: Les Femmes, 1976), pp. 42–43, 56–57; cited by Adrienne Rich, "Compulsory Heterosexuality and Lesbian Existence," *Signs,* vol. 5, no. 4 (Summer 1980), p. 653.

40 *The Body Politic* (December-January 1977), pp. 19, 21.

41 Lillian Faderman, "Who Hid Lesbian History?," *Frontiers: A Journal of Women Studies,* vol. 4, no. 3 (Fall 1979), p. 74.

42 Rich, "Compulsory Heterosexuality," pp. 631–60.

43 *New York Times Book Review,* August 8, 1982, pp. 10–11.

44 *New York Times Book Review,* October 3, 1982, p. 7.

45 Stephen Farber, "How Conflict Gave Shape to 'Tootsie'," *The New York Times,* p. 1:1, quoting Sydney Pollack. Stanley Keleman, *In Defense of Heterosexuality* (Berkeley, CA: Center Press, 1982), dedicated to "Gail," and to "those who understand that anatomy means the dynamic structure of experience."

46 William H. Masters, Virginia Johnson, Robert Kolodny, *Crisis: Heterosexual Behavior in the Age of* AIDS (New York: Grove Press, 1988).

47 In addition to those already cited in these notes, a few writers have begun the historicizing of heterosexuality. In 1987, GMP in London published *Heterosexuality,* a collection of essays by gay men and lesbians edited by Gillian E. Hanscombe and Martin Humphries; the essay by Jon Ward on "The Nature of Heterosexuality," is the most relevant to historical analysis. In April 1988, at a lesbian and gay studies conference at Brooklyn College, I spoke on that subject, and Henry Abelove and Randolph Trumbach spoke on a separate panel of the same title. In February 1989, Abelove, G.S. Rousseau, and Trumbach participated in a panel of the same title at the University of California, Berkeley. See Marv Shaw, "Inventing Straights: Homosexuality Was a 19th Century Invention; Now Historians Say, So Was Heterosexuality," *Bay Area Reporter,* March 9, 1989. Also see Abelove's "Some Speculations on the History of 'Sexual Intercourse' During the 'Long Eighteenth Century' in England," *Genders,* vol. 6 (November 1989).

48 D'Emilio and Freedman, *Intimate Matters,* pp. 57–63, 268, 356.

49 Ryan, *Womanhood;* John D'Emilio, "Capitalism and Gay Identity" in *Powers of Desire,* pp. 100–13; Jeffrey Weeks, *Coming Out: Homosexual Politics in Britain, from the Nineteenth Century to the Present* (London: Quartet Books, 1977); D'Emilio and Freedman, *Intimate Matters*; Katz, "Early Colonial Exploration, Agriculture, and Commerce: The Age of Sodomitical Sin, 1607–1740," *Gay/Lesbian Almanac,* pp. 23–65.

50 This tripartite system is intended as a revision of Gayle Rubin's pioneering work on the social-historical organization of eros and gender. See "The Traffic in Women: Notes on the Political-Economy of Sex" in *Toward an Anthropology of Women,* ed. Rayna R. Reiter (New York: Monthly Review Press, 1975), pp. 157–210, and "Thinking Sex: Notes for a Radical Theory of the Politics of Sexuality," in *Pleasure and Danger: Exploring Female Sexuality,* ed. Carole S. Vance (Boston: Routledge & Kegan Paul, 1984), pp. 267–329.

4

Critique of compulsory heterosexuality

Steven Seidman

Arguably, the most important concept developed in critical sex studies is the notion of heterosexuality as an institution. This concept allowed an analytical shift from the individual homosexual to a social condition of normative heterosexuality. Politically, the focus changed from an agenda of furthering education and rights to contesting the social inequalities produced by the institutional enforcement of heterosexuality. Conceptualizing heterosexuality as a structural condition made possible a critical social theory of sexuality.

The concept of compulsory heterosexuality was initially formulated by lesbian feminists and gay liberationists in the late 1960s and the early 1970s, chiefly in the United States, the United Kingdom, France, Australia, and the Netherlands. Forged in opposition to the analytical and moral individualism of homophile activists and liberal feminists, the aim was to reveal a socially formed structural order of patterned sexual-gender divisions and hierarchies.

Although their views differ in significant ways, lesbian feminists share with gay liberationists a critique of *sexual voluntarism*. Under conditions of institutionalized normative heterosexuality, individuals no more choose heterosexuality or homosexuality than the laborer chooses wage labor. The critique of compulsory heterosexuality sought to expose the structural constraints obscured by a culture that celebrates sexual freedom.

Even within this critique, lesbian feminists and gay liberationists did not speak entirely with one voice. Lesbian feminists emphasized heterosexuality as an institutionalized part of the social order that fashions a world of gender binarism and hierarchy. Heterosexuality was said to bind women to men, to the roles of wife and mother, and to a private sphere that positioned women as subordinate to men. From this perspective, lesbian feminists argued that the idea of a homosexual identity was a social product of the institution of heterosexuality and thus played a central role in the enforcement of gender binarism and male domination. Gay liberationists resisted a disposition among lesbian feminists to view the heterosexual-homosexual dichotomy exclusively through the lens of gender politics. Liberationists argued that a condition of normative heterosexuality establishes a social order of sexual difference and hierarchy that cannot be collapsed into gender dynamics. Paralleling and intersecting with a hierarchical gender order, normative heterosexuality creates the oppositional figures of the homosexual and the heterosexual alongside the figures of the woman and the man.

Thus, gay liberationists and lesbian feminists argued that normative heterosexuality creates a structural order of gender binarism, heterosexual-homosexual division, male dominance, and heterosexual privilege. This sexual-gender hierarchical order is embedded in Western psyches, classification schemes, social organizations, and public rituals. Under these conditions, heterosexuality becomes compulsory.

By the mid-1970s, lesbian feminism and gay liberationism had faded as political movements. A political culture triumphed in the course of the 1980s and the 1990s that rallied around an agenda of affirming identity and achieving rights and integration. Reformers abandoned the notion of compulsory heterosexuality by appealing to an empirical trend toward the deinstitutionalization of normative heterosexuality. However, lesbian feminism and gay liberationism survived at the edges of a post-Stonewall political culture and experienced a renewal with the advocacy organization ACT UP (AIDS Coalition to Unleash Power). In the course of the 1990s, queer studies reclaimed the notion of the institutionalization of normative heterosexuality, but this appropriation has either edged into a narrow culturalism or has been cast in ahistorical terms. In this essay, I aim to clarify and assess the analytical and sociohistorical status of the concept of institutionalized heterosexuality (cf. Ingraham, 1996, 1999; Jackson, 2006; Renold, 2006; Richardson, 1996; Roseneil, 2002; Wiegman, 2006).

First, I will sketch the concept of compulsory heterosexuality as it initially was developed by lesbian feminists and gay liberationists. In the subsequent three sections, I will outline a queer-inspired critique of the critique of compulsory heterosexuality and then critically engage the effort by some queer theorists to rearticulate compulsory heterosexuality as heteronormativity. In the last section, I will advance a historical rationale for narrowing the application of this concept, at least with respect to the contemporary United States. I also will propose substituting a more sociologically nuanced notion of institutionalized normative heterosexuality for the idea of compulsory heterosexuality.

Compulsory heterosexuality: lesbian feminism and gay liberation

I begin with a somewhat paradoxical historical observation. At the very time when, at least in the United States, the state and institutions such as the criminal justice system, the mass media, and a medical-psychiatric apparatus mobilized a national antigay campaign, the key national homophile organizations of the 1950s and 1960s, the Mattachine Society and the Daughters of Bilitis, rejected the claim advanced by radical theorist Harry Hay that the United States was an antihomosexual society. Instead, homophile activists argued that individuals suspected of homosexuality face prejudice and specific acts of discrimination rooted in ignorance, misinformation, and fear. These activists defended the political goal of assimilation that relied on a strategy of public enlightenment through education and displays of model citizenship. Homophiles anticipated the end of a culture of sexual identity, as well as the end of the very idea of the homosexual (Seidman, 2008).

The cautious politics of these homophile organizations are surely understandable. Given a war-weary United States and the anti-communism sentiment during the Red Scare after World War II, homosexuals were suspect as agents of national subversion. In this context, an agenda of broad institutional and cultural change was almost unthinkable (Johnson, 2004).

The late 1960s and the early 1970s witnessed a sea change in the politics of social movements. Civil rights movements and the antiwar movement were radicalized. Liberation movements shifted criticism from individual prejudice and behavior toward institutions and public culture.

A radical language of social oppression crowded out a reform rhetoric of discrimination. Lesbian and gay politics underwent a dramatic change. Challenging the liberal individualism of homophile politics and liberal feminism, as well as a United States in which women and homosexuals occupied subordinate and outsider roles, two new movements took shape: lesbian feminism and gay liberationism. These movements proposed what was a new idea: that heterosexuality was a social institution and was at the root of the oppression of women and homosexuals.

Lesbian feminists criticized the homosexual politics of the 1950s and 1960s for abandoning gender dynamics and challenged liberal feminism for neglecting heterosexuality. Against liberal feminists, they argued that gender inequality was rooted less in men's attitudes or law than in a sex role system that systematically privileges men (Radicalesbians, 1972/1992). Equal gender rights and respect would not bring about women's empowerment, they believed, because a binary sex-gender order would continue to perpetuate inequality. Lesbian feminists raised the question, Why do women accommodate to a gender order that disempowers them? Although gender-role socialization and male coercion play a role, lesbian feminists argued that heterosexuality is central to understanding the reproduction of a male-dominated binary sex-gender order. Heterosexuality binds women to men and defines women as incomplete without men, prescribing their desires, wants, and roles in a way that make women's self-fulfillment dependent on their relationship with men (Brown, 1975; Bunch, 1975; Rich, 1978/1993; Small, 1975; Solomon, 1975).

But what did lesbian feminists mean by heterosexuality? Departing from sexological and folk discourses, lesbian feminists argued that heterosexuality is neither natural nor only about individual desire, behavior, or identity: Heterosexuality, they insisted, is a socially created institution (Rich, 1978/1993). Specifically, heterosexuality enforces a social order based on sex or gender difference and male dominance (Purple September Staff, 1975; Rich). In the words of the Furies Collective (1975), "Lesbian feminist politics is a political critique of the institution and ideology of heterosexuality as a primary cornerstone of male supremacy" (p. 10). From a lesbian feminist perspective, heterosexuality is not freely chosen:

> True, there are feminists who claim . . . that . . . to be straight is . . . a matter of personal preference. The trouble with this is that we live in a culture which sanctions only heterosexuality. As a result, you cannot convince anyone that you are straight by choice.
>
> *(Purple September Staff, 1975, p. 81)*

Or, as Adrienne Rich (1978/1993) succinctly put it: "Heterosexuality . . . has had to be imposed, managed, organized, propagandized, and maintained by force" (pp. 238–239).

Social institutions, laws, policies, and cultural representations, as well as daily practices of harassment, intimidation, and violence, enforce heterosexuality and gender binarism. Heterosexuality is compulsory in the same sense that wage labor, as Marx argued, is compulsory under capitalism: The legally free laborer has no choice but to exchange his or her labor power for a wage. Similarly, under conditions of compulsory heterosexuality, the social machinery of punishment and regulation is mobilized to enforce a social order based on gender binary, male dominance, and heterosexuality (Bunch, 1975; Rich, 1978/1993; Wittig, 1980/1992).

Lesbian feminists insisted that compulsory heterosexuality and gender binarism have a mutually reinforcing structural relationship. Heterosexuality dictates gender difference but, in addition, a binary gender order normalizes heterosexuality. Thus, heterosexual and homosexual identities are understood as social by-products of a sexist order. Moreover, these sexual identities normalize gender binary—the former by rewards, the latter by sanctions. In their stunning manifesto, "The Woman-Identified-Woman," the Radicalesbians (1972) articulated a social account of sexual identities:

> It should first be understood that lesbianism, like male homosexuality, is a category of behavior possible only in a sexist society—characterized by rigid sex roles and dominated by male supremacy. . . . Homosexuality is a by-product of a particular way of setting up roles . . . on the basis of sex.
>
> *(p. 172)*

Gay liberationism paralleled the rise of lesbian feminism in the late 1960s and the early 1970s. Many liberationists were influenced by the radical currents of the women's movement, including lesbian feminism. However, in opposition to lesbian feminism and to homophile politics, liberationists often defined the aims of a gay movement as sexual freedom (Gay Liberation Front, 1972/1992; Wittman, 1972/1992). Against homophile politics, liberationists sought to shift social analysis and politics away from individual attitudes and behavior to an institutional and cultural level. Heterosexuality was at the center of gay liberationists' sexual theory and politics.

Like lesbian feminists, liberationists also conceptualized heterosexuality as compulsory. Individuals do not choose to organize their lives around heterosexuality, they maintained; instead, heterosexuality is imposed as a condition of social existence. The state, laws, social institutions, culture, and informal social regulations enforce heterosexuality and gender difference as compulsory (Shelley, 1972/1992; Wittman, 1972/1992; Young, 1972/1992). Under social conditions of compulsory heterosexuality, homosexuality becomes a distinct and oppressed social identity. As Byron (1972/1992) put it:

> One is . . . oppressed as a homosexual every minute of every day, inasmuch as one is restrained from acting in ways that would seem normal to a heterosexual. . . . And gay people . . . die a little every day. . . . Everything in society—every movie, every billboard, everything done as second nature in public—reminds the gay person that what he or she is is unnatural, abnormal.
>
> *(p. 59)*

Liberationists agreed with lesbian feminists that compulsory heterosexuality and sexism are mutually reinforcing (Shelley, 1972/1992; Third World Gay Revolution, 1972/1992; Young, 1972/1992). However, they criticized lesbian feminism for marginalizing sexual politics. For lesbian feminists, compulsory heterosexuality is chiefly about enforcing gender difference and male dominance. "The straight norm," claimed the Furies Collective (1975), "is not really a sexual norm at all, but a powerful instrument in the perpetuation of the power relationship between the sexes" (Myron & Bunch, 1975, pp. 10, 83). For gay liberationists, compulsory heterosexuality also underscores a dynamic of sexual difference and hierarchy, not just of power.

Although gender is implicated in the politics of sexuality, liberationists held that the dynamics of homosexual oppression and resistance are not reducible to those of gender politics. In this regard, two Chicago organizations, Third World Gay Revolution and the Gay Liberation Front (1972/1992), stipulated the following:

> The oppression of women and that of gay people are interdependent and spring from the same roots [sexism], but take different forms. Women . . . are oppressed by how they fit into the sex-class structure. Gay people are *persecuted* because we don't fit into that structure at all. . . . Every effort has been made to exterminate us.
>
> *(p. 255)*

Whereas women are denied certain rights and opportunities because of their femininity, lesbians and gay men are denied the right of social existence (Gay Liberation Front, 1972/1992). Responding to the marginalization of sexual politics by lesbian feminism, some women created their own sexual liberationist organizations. For example,

> GLF [Gay Liberation Front] Women . . . are lesbian activists fighting oppression on two fronts: As homosexuals, we work with our gay brothers to fight oppression based on society's exclusion of individuals who love members of the same sex. As women, we work with women's liberation to fight the oppression of all women.
>
> *(Gay Liberation Front Women, 1972/1992, p. 201)*

For members of this organization, homosexual oppression and women's oppression were understood as interrelated but analytically distinct:

> We are discriminated against as women, but lesbians who live openly are fired from jobs, expelled from schools, banished from their homes, and even beaten. . . . Lesbians who hide and escape open hostility suffer equal oppression through psychic damage caused by their fear and guilt. . . . We cannot allow the lesbian issue to be an afterthought.
>
> *(Gay Liberation Front Women, 1972/1992, p. 202).*

Liberationists argued, then, that compulsory heterosexuality creates unique patterns of homosexual subjection, which require a distinctive critical language and politics—for example, notions of the closet, the double life, the gay ghetto, camp, and coming out (Gay Liberation Front, 1972/1992; Shelley, 1972/1992; Wittman, 1972/1992).

To summarize, lesbian feminists and gay liberationists argued that heterosexuality is an institution that creates a structural order of gender binarism, heterosexual-homosexual division, male dominance, and heterosexual privilege. Furthermore, this sexual-gender hierarchical order is said to be embedded in Western psyches, classification schemes, social organizations, and public rituals—from dating and weddings to immigration laws and medical-scientific knowledge. Accordingly, heterosexuality can be said to be institutionalized and compulsory. Under conditions of compulsory heterosexuality, moreover, there is a sense in which homosexuality and gender are also compulsory. Can same-sex desire be anything other than a deviant or polluted homosexual desire under conditions of compulsory heterosexuality? Moreover, can individuals be anything other than men or women under the same conditions?

Compulsory heterosexuality and gender binarism, revisited

The claim that a structural relationship exists between compulsory heterosexuality and a binary gender order is not in doubt. Compulsory heterosexuality is unthinkable without also assuming a dichotomous gender order, and gender binarism would seemingly collapse without compulsory heterosexuality. At issue are a series of assumptions—about the way compulsory heterosexuality produces gender, about the concept of gender, and about the respective power of social structure and individual agency.

According to lesbian feminists and gay liberationists, a social order based on compulsory heterosexuality produces two genders—distinct, oppositional, and hierarchical. I take this claim to be noncontroversial. However, these critics of compulsory heterosexuality also assume a robust notion of gender structuralism that is controversial. Under conditions of compulsory heterosexuality, gender regulation is said to extend across social roles and social spheres, producing a dichotomous gender social order. Gender structuring is also said to extend deeply into individuals' inner life—their psyches, desires, and fantasies—becoming a primary driving force of human action. Self-formation is understood as a process of gendered self-formation. Accordingly, gender can be said to travel with the individual, everywhere and at all times. Under conditions of compulsory heterosexuality, the individual never eludes gender. Men are men whether at home, during sex, in therapy, at work, or in politics.

In short, critics of compulsory heterosexuality theorize a gender order reproduced by psychic and social structures that act with the force of the unconscious—that is, beyond deliberation and intention. This condition of gender structuralism is intended to expose the power of compulsory heterosexuality, thus revealing the agentic-like power of social structure against a culture legitimated by the celebration of individual agency.

As sociologically and politically compelling as this perspective is, it suffers from what I call a normative translation problem. Lesbian feminists and gay liberationists mistakenly assumed that a condition of compulsory heterosexuality successfully translates a normative gender code into a behavioral social reality. To clarify what I mean, consider the workplace. From the standpoint of the critique of compulsory heterosexuality, the workplace would be structured by gender norms that distribute tasks and roles in a patterned way. Women would be assigned feminine-typed tasks and concentrated in feminine-typed occupational sectors, whereas men would monopolize work roles and sectors that possess higher status, salary, and power. This gender pattern would be understood by workers as spontaneously formed to the extent that it was assumed to reflect the essentially different capacities of men and women. A credible argument can be made that a process of normative gender translation was more or less effective in the case of White, middle-class women between roughly the mid-nineteenth and the mid-twentieth centuries in the United States. But this claim loses credibility when we turn to women who were non-White, immigrants, or blue collar, or who pursued careers in politics or the arts.

In the 1960s and 1970s, the era that launched second-wave feminism, problems of normative translation approached a crisis point. As more women pursued paid labor and careers, they challenged the cultural foundation of workplace gender patterns—namely, an ontology of gender difference or the notion of fixed psychosocial differences between men and women. Women, or some women at least, contested the association of high status, power, and salary roles with masculine capacities possessed exclusively or chiefly by men. In their struggle for workplace equality, they claimed either that the capacities requisite for these tasks and roles are not gendered and therefore can be acquired by women who are given the opportunity or, that if such capacities are indeed masculine, then they are not exclusively or chiefly possessed by men. With this strategic move, the normative basis of gender inequality was challenged. Stated differently, workplace gender patterns were then interpreted as being political rather than gender based, as patterns of social inequality.

If, in the 1960s and 1970s in the United States and elsewhere, slippage occurred between normative gender codes and social practices in the workplace, it is likely that such slippage also manifested in many social spheres. Furthermore, if interruptions of normative translation became routine, as the rise of second-wave feminism suggests, it cannot be assumed, as critics have done, that compulsory heterosexuality was empirically concretized as a heterogender structural order. Whether gender binary patterns empirically obtain under conditions of compulsory heterosexuality would depend on the social sphere, its culture, the gender composition of the sector, the broader political context, and so on. A condition of compulsory heterosexuality may indeed have exerted and may still exert normative pressure toward gender binarism. However, to the extent that disruptions of normative gender are frequent enough to unsettle the taken-for-granted status of the ontology of gender difference, gender will be experienced, at least by some women and men, less as a fixed structural order than as a social construct or a site of negotiation and deliberation.

It is not surprising, then, that the gender structuralism of lesbian feminists was challenged by more processual and performative views of gender initially advanced in the 1960s and 1970s by ethnomethodologists and symbolic interactionists and, subsequently, by poststructural feminists. At the center of this challenge was the claim that, despite structural constraints, gender practices have an irreducibly negotiated and agentic aspect. For example, poststructural feminists (Butler, 1989; Fuss, 1995) have argued that people's interior lives are gendered in multiple and contradictory ways. Individuals' psychological identifications move fluidly between and often mix idealizations of men and women. If gender coherence is not internally fixed, then it is established by social actions. To the extent that binary gender norms have regulatory force in social life, individual practices will exhibit dichotomous gender patterns. At the same time, because gender coherence depends on social behavior, there is a presumption of agency that allows individuals to negotiate their gender practices. It follows that, notwithstanding the structural constraints of compulsory heterosexuality, individuals may act in ways that challenge gender norms. In other words, if gender identity is in part a performative accomplishment, then gender must assume a more agentic, fluid, and uneven pattern than is possible in the binary model.

A growing literature on female masculinities offers an instructive illustration of a performative view of gender and suggests more fluid, uneven gender patterns than allowed for by critics of compulsory heterosexuality. C. Jacob Hale (2003; also see Halberstam, 1998; Stryker & White, 2006) has explored some of the ways females express masculinity in the *leatherdyke* culture. Leatherdykes are divided into *boys* and their *daddies,* who are usually butch leatherdykes but can be gay leathermen. Hale counseled against asking whether a leatherdyke daddy is a woman or a man because "such questions . . . presuppose overly simplistic [binary] understandings of how gender categories work and in so doing they reinscribe the hegemonic stranglehold of the dominant sex/gender/sexuality system" (p. 66). Instead, Hale approached the leatherdyke culture from a view of gender "as multiple, context-specific, and purpose-specific" (p. 68). From this perspective, leatherdykes appropriate masculinity not to pass as men, but to explore modes of individuation, eroticism, and power unavailable to conventional femininity. Thus, the leatherdaddy may be a woman at her workplace, but when she steps into the leather world as a daddy, it is as a masculine self. Hale concluded that "gender multiplicity abounds, and we have some, though not unconstrained, agency" (p. 68).

As a theoretical account of gender, the critique of compulsory heterosexuality borders on incoherence. Its political-moral critique drives a gender structuralism that provides consistency, but at considerable cost. If one defends this structuralism in a consistent manner, either agency and transformative change are impossible or else agency becomes an extension of the structural order itself. In this case, the critique of compulsory heterosexuality contributes to suppressing or obscuring everyday acts of gender variance and transgression. Furthermore, a robust notion of agency and a recognition of gender variance significantly weaken the analytical and political force of the notion of compulsory heterosexuality.

Compulsory heterosexuality and sexual politics, revisited

Lesbian feminist and gay liberationist critics of compulsory heterosexuality have also stipulated a sexual order organized around a heterosexual-homosexual hierarchy. The effort, especially by gay liberationists, to analytically differentiate sexual and gender politics has proven to be important in critical sex studies (e.g., Rubin, 1984; Sedgwick, 1990). But what do liberationists assume about the relationship between compulsory heterosexuality and sexuality and about sexual politics?

Liberationists forcefully argued that the compulsory status of heterosexuality is maintained in part by representations of the homosexual as the polluted other compared with the pure heterosexual. However, liberationists often treat the figure of the homosexual in homophobic practices as an abstract other when in fact the polluted homosexual is a concrete other who is always associated with specific psychological dispositions, personality traits, and social behaviors—for example, the salience of lustful or carnal motivations, a narcissistic personality, or manipulative and seductive behavior. At times, in postwar Anglo-European discourses, the homosexual has been presented as a reviled social type, such as a predator, molester, seducer, libertine, or hedonist.

However, liberationists neglected the ways that homophobic representations and practices condition or structure the formation of homosexual identity. Homosexuals may identify with homophobic representations and either revise or reverse the moral meaning of these representations by identifying respectively as normal or queer. Each identity position also suggests a distinct politic: Homophobic identification suggests the closet as resistance; disavowing homophobic identification by linking homosexuality to dispositional and behavioral markers of normal heterosexuality implies a politic of assimilation. Reversing the moral status of the dispositions and behaviors linked to homosexuality suggests a politic of transgression—for example, erotic experimentation or gender fluidity might be championed as liberating. The point I wish to underscore is the following: Compulsory heterosexuality produces not the homosexual but differences, conflicts, and hierarchies among homosexualities at the level of identity, culture, and politics. However, these multiple homosexualities and their stratification were largely ignored by liberationist critics who enforced a sexual politics centered on the homosexual challenge to compulsory heterosexuality.

Liberationists were, for good reasons, preoccupied with how compulsory heterosexuality shaped the personal and social worlds of homosexually oriented individuals. Accordingly, the analysis of the conditions of the closet, coming out, and the formation of individual and collective identity were central in their discourses (Seidman, 2008). However, the concept of compulsory heterosexuality also stipulates differences and hierarchies among *heterosexualites* (those who are behaviorally heterosexual). Specifically, compulsory heterosexuality not only enforces the normative status of heterosexuality but also enforces a normative order within heterosexuality or establishes a standard of so-called normal heterosexuality. Of course, norms of heterosexuality vary across populations and change over time. Still, to the extent that heterosexuality is normative, model heterosexuality will be defined in opposition to the cluster of dispositions, personality traits, and behaviors associated with homosexuality.

If homosexuals are imagined as body- and pleasure-centered, nonmonogamous, and predatory, so-called normal heterosexuality will be associated with person-centeredness, monogamy, and the binding of sex to intimacy and love. Or if, as is increasingly the case in the United States and across Europe, homosexuals are understood as having intimate relationships, these will be represented as unstable and transitory in contrast to heterosexual love, whose normal condition will be described as stable and solid because it is assumed to be founded on deep affectional and social commitments.

Thus, it is not just homosexuality that is disrespected under conditions of compulsory heterosexuality; so, too, are heterosexual practices that deviate from models of what is considered normal heterosexuality. The logic of compulsory heterosexuality suggests that some heterosexuals (e.g., the sex worker, the libertine, or the pornographer) will occupy an outsider social status comparable with that of the homosexual. These figures will experience something of the scandalous and menacing status of the homosexual or the nonnormalized homosexual in the United States or the United Kingdom today.

The notion of compulsory heterosexuality, then, implies differences and hierarchies among homosexualities and heterosexualities. Given these hierarchies, sexual politics exceed the politics of gender preference, sparking, for example, conflicts over the purpose of sexuality (procreation, love, pleasure, expressive values), over norms of intimate behavior and arrangements (marriage, cohabitation, monogamy), over gender norms of sexuality, over norms regulating sex and the private-public sphere, and so on. These conflicts have their own distinct patterns of division and hierarchy, as well as their own strategies of regulation and resistance. Moreover, it is not obvious that the politics of gender preference should be a privileged site of sexual politics (Rubin, 1984; Sedgwick, 1990). By framing sexual politics as a critique of compulsory heterosexuality, as well as by assuming that the heterosexual-homosexual division is the chief axis of sexual injustice, these critics marginalize and suppress sexual conflicts that are not centrally about gender preference.

Queer theory: from compulsory heterosexuality to heteronormativity

The critique of compulsory heterosexuality, developed by lesbian feminists and gay liberationists in the 1960s and 1970s, was supplanted in the 1990s when queer theory appeared as a reconstructed critical sex theory. Queer theorists have not abandoned the idea of compulsory heterosexuality as a structural order, but at least some have restated it in cultural terms, as a critique of the heteronormative structure of representations. Here is how Butler (1989) framed the critique of compulsory heterosexuality:

> I use the term heterosexual matrix . . . to designate . . . a hegemonic *discursive/epistemic model* [italics added] of gender intelligibility that assumes that for bodies to cohere and make sense there must be a stable sex expressed through a stable gender that is oppositionally and hierarchically defined through the compulsory status of heterosexuality.
>
> *(p. 151)*

Some queer theorists have sought to identify the discursive strategies that sustain and resist heteronormativity without reducing such strategies to dichotomies of either repression versus expression or invisibility versus visibility. Instead, they speak of signifying and resignifying or normalizing and reversing, and they underscore the instability of oppositions and hierarchies. Against their lesbian feminist predecessors, queer critics reclaim an emphatic idea of agency by highlighting the role of a signifying subject. However, queer perspectives rarely link the signifying agent to his or her social status or connect text to institution; in the main, they have abandoned the central role that gender played in the critique of compulsory heterosexuality.

Consider (briefly) David Halperin's (1995) "The Queer Politics of Michel Foucault." Heterosexist authority in the contemporary United States, Halperin wrote, is enforced less

> by specific agents of oppression, such as gay-bashers or the police . . . [or] formal, explicit interdictions, such as sodomy laws, [or by] . . . particular, hostile institutions, such as the Supreme Court, but [by] pervasive and multiform strategies of homophobia that shape public and private discourses [and] saturate the entire field of cultural representations.
>
> *(p. 32)*

Having claimed an empirical shift in the social basis of heterosexist authority from social structure to discourse, Halperin (1995) framed a queer critique and politics as a cultural practice of resignification and demystification. He neither addressed nor cited the social structural conditions that make representational resistance possible—such as, for example, the institutional spaces of universities or queer subcultures. The social structural conditions of lesbian and gay subjugation and resistance, as well as the gendered aspects of the politics of heterosexist authority, do little or no analytical work in this queer perspective.

Another key text of queer studies is Diana Fuss's (1991) introduction in *Inside/Out: Lesbian Theories, Gay Theories.* Fuss maintained an exclusive focus on the discursive operation of normative heterosexuality, which is understood in relation to the general trope of inside-out: Heterosexuality and homosexuality gain their meaning and coherence in their relationship of contrast and opposition. In this view, heterosexuality establishes its identity and definitional boundaries not by repressing a preexisting homosexuality but by producing the idea of homosexuality. To secure its normative status, heterosexuality must evoke the homosexual as a threatening other. Paradoxically, homosexuality may actually threaten heterosexuality insofar as the representation engenders desiring subjects who claim to speak on their own behalf or demand to declare and affirm their homosexuality.

Accordingly, heterosexuality must simultaneously produce and exile homosexuality to the space of the invisible and the voiceless—to the closet. Homosexuality then occupies a status as a way of being that is exterior and inferior to heterosexuality. In this stunning example of queer discourse analysis, the heteronormative text is never connected to social structure, institutions, or social dynamics of gendering or racialization. The only constraint in Fuss's (1991) account of the heterosexual-homosexual figure is representational. Fuss has effectively abandoned a notion of compulsory heterosexuality but without providing an epistemological or sociological rationale.

The queer critique of compulsory heterosexuality surrenders too much of the lesbian feminist and gay liberationist institutional and gender-based understanding of power (cf. Butler, 1994). Moreover, in the absence of a social structural perspective, queer critique cannot explain the formation of resisting selves. In fact, queer perspectives have not examined the sociohistorical conditions that make the signifying agent of queer theory and politics possible. In other words, what blinded earlier critics of compulsory heterosexuality to agentic considerations was not only their political investment but also their sociohistorical context—namely, that they were politically engaged at the very time that the conditions of compulsory heterosexuality were being aggressively enforced by a state-driven nationwide antigay politic. It seems reasonable to conjecture that the prominence of a signifying agent in queer perspectives is related to changing social conditions that have made possible new opportunities for individual and collective action. I will briefly explore this conjecture as I consider the sociohistorical scope of the critique of compulsory heterosexuality.

Normative heterosexuality without compulsory heterosexuality

Is the concept of compulsory heterosexuality credible in the contemporary United States? Furthermore, if this notion is abandoned, does that mean surrendering the core of critical sex studies?

For the major U.S. national political organizations, from Lambda Legal Defense to the Human Rights Campaign, their politics seem to rest on the claim that the dominant trend in the United States is the deinstitutionalization of normative heterosexuality. From this perspective, sexual inequality persists but is maintained less by the state and social institutions than by the power of specific individuals, organizations, groups, and political administrations. For reformers such as Bruce Bawer (1993) and Andrew Sullivan (1996), gay and lesbian visibility, tolerance, and integration signal the end of compulsory heterosexuality.

In one respect, I think Bawer and Sullivan are right—there has been a retreat from systemic discriminatory and homophobic practices in many U.S. institutions. Although social incorporation is considerably more mixed at the state level in the United States than in the United Kingdom or western Europe, the integration of gay men and lesbians into bureaucratic and cosmopolitan-type organizations such as civil service agencies or the professions, normalization in key sectors of public and popular culture, and the retreat of the state from a politics of the closet underscore empirical trends supporting the claim of the decline of compulsory heterosexuality (cf. Eskridge, 1999; Gamson, 2002; Raeburn, 2004; Seidman, 2003; Walters, 2002).

Reformers are mistaken, however, in assuming that expanded personal freedom and social integration also indicate the decline of institutionalized normative heterosexuality. I intend this concept to grasp the institutional embeddedness of normative heterosexuality but not necessarily its compulsory status. The latter indicates a regulatory order that reproduces institutionalized normative heterosexuality by means of disenfranchisement, criminalization, and homophobic harassment, as well as violence, sequestration, and cultural pollution. Whether normative heterosexuality is institutionally compulsory is an empirical question.

As I read the empirical record, normative heterosexuality is still institutionalized across all U.S. social sectors, which are, accordingly, organized by patterns of sex-gender division and hierarchy. However, with the exception perhaps of public schools, churches, and the military, normative heterosexuality is probably no longer compulsory in the sense of being a condition of institutional belonging. The conditions of normative heterosexuality across many social sectors in the United States allow for the institutional recognition and integration of lesbians and gay men. In other words, in many social sectors, normative heterosexuality is reproduced in ways that institutionally incorporate gay men and lesbians but continue to position them in a subordinate social status.

For example, gay men and lesbians' enfranchisement has arguably proceeded furthest in the corporate and professional social sectors, which typically have antidiscriminatory policies, gay and lesbian employee associations, domestic partnership coverage, and an official culture of respecting diversity that includes gay and lesbian employees (Raeburn, 2004). In such institutional settings, heterosexuality is not compulsory. However, to the extent that the public face of these institutions, their marketing and public image, their executive hierarchies, and their informal and gendered culture continue to privilege heterosexuality in patterned ways, it is appropriate to speak of the institutionalization of normative heterosexuality.

To take another example, consider patterns of lesbian and gay normalization in U.S. culture. In one sense, normalization indicates the public recognition of lesbians and gays as belonging to a human and national community. Where this symbolic integration obtains, one would expect the weakening of the compulsory status of heterosexuality. At the same time, considerable evidence shows that only lesbians and gay men who exhibit the dispositions and self-presentational traits of an idealized U.S. citizen are recognized as normal and deserving respect. In fact, the legitimation of the normal, respectable gay or lesbian both allows for their integration and stabilizes a moral boundary that separates the normal American—straight or gay—from citizens who fall outside the circle of normality (e.g., trans or libertines, bisexuals or serial monogamists). In other words, in social sectors in which lesbian and gay individuals are integrated and normalized, the dominant axis of sexual hierarchy may no longer be the heterosexual-homosexual division but rather the good versus the bad sexual citizen (Seidman, 2003; Smith, 1997). In such a context, a standard of sexual normality would stipulate moral boundaries that do not privilege gender preference but may privilege (say) a norm of a long-term monogamous relationship or a spiritualized notion of love.

From the vantage point of an American in the 1st decade of the twenty-first century, one sees both a clear trend toward cultural normalization and social integration—and, therefore, the end of the compulsory status of heterosexuality in many social spheres—and the stabilization of institutionalized normative heterosexuality. Why stabilization? Because both defenders of the status quo and reformers can claim—with considerable public credibility, given a U.S. culture of voluntarism—that normalization and integration signal the beginning of the end of sexual inequality and therefore the end of a politics of institutional transformation. Indeed, the frustration of many critics and activists speaks in part to the challenge of persuading a populace of the need for such a politics in a political culture that understands change as achieving first-class citizenship status and assumes that the burden of change rests ultimately on the individual. Unfortunately, many queer critics and activists further undermine the credibility of a transformative political agenda by defending an increasingly irrelevant politic of compulsory heterosexuality. Instead of trying to understand the nuanced patterns of institutionalized sexual-gender social hierarchy, many activists often invoke the specter of a Christian Right threatening a return to the era of the closet.

Conclusion

By way of a conclusion, I want to make explicit some implications of my remarks. Gay liberationists and lesbian feminists invented the idea of compulsory heterosexuality, a concept intended to reveal institutionalized patterns of sexual and gender difference and hierarchy. From this perspective, the identities of man, woman, heterosexual, and homosexual are neither natural nor self-made, but take shape as part of a structural order of compulsory heterosexuality.

The critique of compulsory heterosexuality was a major conceptual breakthrough in the sociology of sexuality. It went beyond labeling theory and script theory that undertheorized social structure, and it also went beyond Marxism and radical feminism that undertheorized sexuality. This new critical sociology of sexuality made possible a politics that challenged liberal strategies of public education and legal reform and radical strategies that continued to look to class movements as the agent of social change. Yet the very structuralism that gives this perspective its analytical and political force also deprives it of a notion of agency that can account for the possibilities of institutional critique and change. Critics of compulsory heterosexuality are unable to explain the possibilities of change from within their own theoretical perspective.

Furthermore, their political and analytical investment in the claim that compulsory heterosexuality produces a binary gender and sexual order does not allow these critics to address either existing forms of gender variation and resistance or sexual political conflicts apart from the politics of gender preference. Ironically, the critique of compulsory heterosexuality has contributed to the marginalization of gender and sexual dissidents and rebels.

I am not suggesting the abandonment of the notion of compulsory heterosexuality, which remains indispensable for understanding the structural sources of sex and gender difference and hierarchy. However, this concept should be used in a more reflexive way that is attentive not only to what it makes possible but also to what it obscures. Additionally, this notion should be approached as having historical preconditions and parameters. I have suggested that this concept is less credible as the end of the 1st decade of the twenty-first century approaches, at least in the United States and likely in the United Kingdom and northern Europe (e.g., Bech, 2007). This decrease in credibility does not mean that a structural sociology should be abandoned in favor of the voluntarism of reformers. Instead, I believe that the concept of compulsory heterosexuality must be distinguished from that of institutionalized normative heterosexuality while recognizing that the former is not always present in the latter case.

Considerable evidence suggests that the conditions of compulsory heterosexuality may describe a unique period in U.S. history, roughly from the 1950s through the 1980s—an era characterized by a state-driven nationwide politic aggressively enforcing institutionalized normative heterosexuality. I also have argued that the notion of institutionalized normative heterosexuality is perhaps preferable to the concept of heteronormativity which, at least in the United States, is often wedded to an exclusively cultural critique. The former concept compels the linking of representations to social structure, once again bringing gender back into the center of the critique and politics of sexuality.

References

Bawer, B. (1993). *A place at the table*. New York: Simon & Schuster.

Bech, H. (2007). The disappearance of the homosexual. In S. Seidman, C. Meeks, & N. Fischer (Eds.), *Introducing the new sexuality studies* (pp. 151–157). New York: Routledge.

Brown, R. M. (1975). The shape of things to come. In N. Myron & C. Bunch (Eds.), *Lesbianism and the women's movement* (pp. 69–78). Baltimore: Diana Press.

Bunch, C. (1975). Lesbians in revolt. In N. Myron & C. Bunch (Eds.), *Lesbianism and the women's movement* (pp. 29–38). Baltimore: Diana Press.

Butler, J. (1989). *Gender trouble: Feminism and the subversion of identity*. New York: Routledge.

Butler, J. (1994). Against improper objects. *Differences: A Journal of Feminist Cultural Studies, 6*(2/3), 1–26.

Byron, S. (1992). The closet syndrome. In K. Jay & A. Young (Eds.), *Out of the closets: Voices of gay liberation* (pp. 58–65). New York: New York University Press. (Original work published 1972)

Eskridge, W., Jr. (1999). *Gaylaw*. Cambridge, MA: Harvard University Press.

Furies Collective. (1975). Introduction. In N. Myron & C. Bunch (Eds.), *Lesbianism and the women's movement* (pp. 9–13). Baltimore: Diana Press.

Fuss, D. (1991). Introduction. In D. Fuss (Ed.), *Inside/out: Lesbian theories, gay theories* (pp. 1–10). New York: Routledge.

Fuss, D. (1995). *Identification papers*. New York: Routledge.

Gamson, J. (2002). Sweating in the spotlight: Lesbian, gay, and queer encounters with media and popular culture. In D. Richardson & S. Seidman (Eds.), *Handbook of lesbian and gay studies* (pp. 339–354). London: Sage.

Gay Liberation Front [Chicago]. (1992). Gay revolution and sex roles. In K. Jay & A. Young (Eds.), *Out of the closets: Voices of gay liberation* (pp. 252–258). New York: New York University Press. (Original work published 1972)

Gay Liberation Front Women [New York City]. (1992). Lesbians and the ultimate liberation of women. In K. Jay & A. Young (Eds.), *Out of the closets: Voices of gay liberation* (pp. 201–205). New York: New York University Press. (Original work published 1972)

Halberstam, J. (1998). *Female masculinity*. Durham, NC: Duke University Press.

Hale, C. J. (2003). Leatherdyke boys and their daddies: How to have sex without women or men. In R. Corber & S. Valocchi (Eds.), *Queer studies* (pp. 61–72). Malden, MA: Blackwell.

Halperin, D. (1995). The queer politics of Michel Foucault. In D. Halperin, *Saint Foucault: Towards a gay hagiography* (pp. 15–124). New York: Oxford University Press.

Ingraham, C. (1996). The heterosexual imaginary. In S. Seidman (Ed.), *Queer theory/sociology* (pp. 168–193). Oxford, England: Blackwell.

Ingraham, C. (1999). *White weddings*. New York: Routledge.

Jackson, S. (2006). Gender, sexuality and heterosexuality. *Feminist Theory, 7*, 105–121.

Johnson, D. (2004). *The lavender scare*. Chicago: University of Chicago Press.

Purple September Staff. (1975). The normative status of heterosexuality. In N. Myron & C. Bunch (Eds.), *Lesbianism and the women's movement* (pp. 79–84). Baltimore: Diana Press.

Radicalesbians. (1992). The woman-identified-woman. In K. Jay & A. Young (Eds.), *Out of the closets: Voices of gay liberation* (pp. 172–176). New York: New York University Press. (Original work published 1972)

Raeburn, N. (2004). *Changing corporate America from inside out*. Minneapolis: University of Minnesota Press.

Renold, E. (2006). "They won't let us play . . . unless you're going out with one of them": Girls, boys and Butler's "heterosexual matrix" in the primary years. *British Journal of Sociology of Education, 27*, 489–509.

Rich, A. (1993). Compulsory heterosexuality and lesbian existence. In H. Abelove, M. Barala, & D. Halperin (Eds.), *The lesbian and gay studies reader* (pp. 227–254). New York: Routledge. (Original work published 1978)

Richardson, D. (1996). Heterosexuality and social theory. In D. Richardson (Ed.), *Theorizing heterosexuality* (pp. 1–21). Buckingham, England: Open University Press.

Roseneil, S. (2002). The heterosexual/homosexual binary: Past, present and future. In D. Richardson & S. Seidman (Eds.), *Handbook of lesbian and gay studies* (pp. 27–44). London: Sage.

Rubin, G. (1984). Thinking sex: Notes for a radical critique of sexuality. In C. Vance (Ed.), *Pleasure and danger* (pp. 267–319). New York: Routledge.

Sedgwick, E. K. (1990). *Epistemology of the closet*. Berkeley: University of California Press.

Seidman, S. (2003). *Beyond the closet*. New York: Routledge.

Seidman, S., & Meeks, C. (2008). Politik der Befreiung, Kulturen der Anpassung: Die Suche nach Authentizität in der amerikanischen Homosexuallenbewegung [Politics of emancipation, cultures of conformity: The search for authenticity in the American homosexual movement]. In N. Pethes & S. Schicktanz (Eds.), *Sexualität als Experiment: Identität, Lust und Reproduktion zwischen science und fiction* (pp. 78–97). Frankfurt, Germany: Verlag.

Shelley, M. (1992). Gay is good. In K. Jay & A. Young (Eds.), *Out of the closets: Voices of gay liberation* (pp. 31–33). New York: New York University Press. (Original work published 1972)

Small, M. (1975). Lesbians and the class position of women. In N. Myron & C. Bunch (Eds.), *Lesbianism and the women's movement* (pp. 49–62). Baltimore: Diana Press.

Smith, A. M. (1997). The good homosexual and the dangerous queer: Resisting the "new homophobia." In L. Segal (Ed.), *New sexual agendas* (pp. 214–231). London: Macmillan.

Solomon, B. (1975). Taking the bullshit by the horns. In N. Myron & C. Bunch (Eds.), *Lesbianism and the women's movement* (pp. 39–48). Baltimore: Diana Press.

Stryker, S., & White, S. (2006). *The transgender studies reader*. New York: Routledge.

Sullivan, A. (1996). *Virtually normal*. New York: Vintage.

Third World Gay Revolution [Chicago] & Gay Liberation Front [Chicago]. (1992). Gay revolution and sex roles. In K. Jay & A. Young (Eds.), *Out of the closets: Voices of gay liberation* (pp. 252–258). New York: New York University Press. (Original work published 1972)

Third World Gay Revolution [New York City]. (1992). What we want, what we believe. In K. Jay & A. Young (Eds.), *Out of the closets: Voices of gay liberation* (pp. 363–367). New York: New York University Press. (Original work published 1972)

Walters, S. (2001). *All the rage*. Chicago: University of Chicago Press.

Wiegman, R. (2006). Heteronormativity and the desire for gender. *Feminist Theory, 7*, 89–103.

Wittig, M. (1992). *The straight mind and other essays*. Boston: Beacon Press. (Original work published 1980)

Wittman, C. (1992). A gay manifesto. In K. Jay & A. Young (Eds.), *Out of the closets: Voices of gay liberation* (pp. 330–341). New York: New York University Press. (Original work published 1972)

Young, A. (1992). Out of the closets, into the streets. In K. Jay & A. Young (Eds.), *Out of the closets: Voices of gay liberation* (pp. 6–30). New York: New York University Press. (Original work published 1972)

Part II
Heterosexualities across the life course

5

Normalizing heterosexuality

Mothers' assumptions, talk, and strategies with young children

Karin A. Martin

> I said, "Someday you will meet a boy that becomes your friend and then makes you feel warm and happy inside. That feeling is called falling in love. When you meet that boy you may decide together to get married like mommy and daddy."
>
> —Mother of a 3-year-old girl

Social scientists have identified not just heterosexism and homophobia as social problems, but also heteronormativity—the mundane, everyday ways that heterosexuality is privileged and taken for granted as normal and natural. Heteronormativity includes the institutions, practices, and norms that support heterosexuality (especially a particular form of heterosexuality—monogamous and reproductive) and subjugate other forms of sexuality, especially homosexuality. While a few researchers have begun to examine the production of heteronormativity in everyday life (e.g., Kitzinger 2005), there is little research on how heterosexuality is normalized for individuals and how people come to understand heterosexuality as natural. Through examining heterosexual mothers' sexual socialization of young children, this article analyzes one way that heterosexuality becomes normalized in individuals' understandings of the social world. I demonstrate that mothers' heteronormativity is manifested in how they think about and parent their children with regard to sexuality. Mothers, themselves enmeshed in a heteronormative social context, monitor, manage, and imagine heterosexuality in their children. Such parenting practices (re)produce heteronormativity as children are taught to understand themselves and the world through a heteronormative lens.

Heterosexuality and heteronormativity

For decades, scholarship in the social sciences has understood that heterosexuality is both socially constructed and hegemonic. Historians have documented the invention of the category of heterosexual persons and demonstrated how macro-socioeconomic structures have both supported and undermined its construction (D'Emilio 1983; Katz 1995). Feminist theorists have examined the compulsory nature of heterosexuality, explicating how it is managed, required, and institutionalized (Ingraham 1994; Rich 1980), and queer theorists have analyzed the abject position of homosexuality (Butler 1990; Sedgwick 1990, 1993). This scholarship demonstrates the social construction of heterosexuality, its normativity, and its privileges, albeit largely at the macro-level. How is heterosexuality or its hegemony constructed within individuals? That is, how do individuals come to understand heterosexuality as normative in the first place? As with some social constructionist accounts of gender (e.g., Martin 1998; Miller 2006), there is no developmental account of heteronormativity. Correspondingly, and as Miller (2006: 446) suggests, any theory "with a 'view from nowhere' in development is somewhat limited."

We do, however, have multiple developmental accounts of sexual identity from which to draw and build. Psychologists have researched sexual identity at the level of the individual, producing multiple theories of how sexual identity is arrived at and transformed across the life course (Bem 1996; Diamond 1998, 2003; Savin-Williams 2005; Troiden 1993). This literature typically focuses on the development of sexual identity among non-heterosexuals, with a few exceptions (e.g., Chodorow 1992; Kitzinger 2005). In trying to explain gay, lesbian, and bisexual identity, much of this scholarship begins from differences in early temperament or innate desires (e.g., Bem 1996; Savin-Williams 2005). While there are many accounts of generic sexual development (most of which are implicitly heterosexual), development of heterosexual *identity* is, comparatively, undertheorized and underresearched. Vague notions of "naturalness" are usually assumed in describing heterosexual identity (Chodorow 1992).

The focus on how individual identities unfold, and how sexual identity labels are taken up by non-heterosexuals, does not tell us much about how heteronormativity is learned and constructed in everyday life at the level of individuals (regardless of whether those individuals become heterosexual or take up another sexual identity). We know little about how, living in a social context thick with heteronormativity, individuals come to accept and privilege what is culturally prescribed as natural and normal.

Heteronormativity (Jackson 2006; Kitzinger 2005), of course, encompasses the many mundane, everyday ways in which heterosexuality is privileged over homosexuality, taken for granted, and seen as natural, ordinary, persistent, and without need of explanation. Jackson (2006) argues that heteronormativity "governs" both gender and sexuality and operates through multiple dimensions of social life (e.g., structure, meaning, everyday practice, and individual subjectivity). Heteronormativity is also normative in a moral sense, defining what is within the bounds of "normal." While some research has begun to examine how these dynamics are reproduced in everyday social life by those "not motivated by heterosexist prejudice or discriminatory intent" (Kitzinger 2005: 478), there is no sociodevelopmental account of how we come to understand which kinds of sexual and romantic relationships are normal. Developmental accounts must also address how heteronormativity is established in childhood. Indeed, there is evidence—discussed next—that such understandings are present in young children and that interaction with parents, most notably mothers, may be especially pivotal.

Sexuality and childhood

Social scientists have long been interested in how children come to understand and employ patterns of social dominance such as race (Lewis 2003; Moore 2001; Van Ausdale and Feagin 1996), gender (Maccoby 1988; Martin 1998; Thorne 1993), and class (Connell 1970; Lareau 2002; Weinger 2000). This research has found that children are cognitively sophisticated and not too "egocentric," as some psychologists have described them, and can make use of "adult," abstract, and complex categories of meaning such as race, class, and gender. Some find that even preschool-aged children are astute learners and users of such categories (Maccoby 1988; Van Ausdale and Feagin 1996).

With respect to sexuality, a substantial body of ethnographic research demonstrates that children understand, enact, and participate in heterosexuality by early elementary school. For example, in her research at two elementary schools, Thorne (1993: 71) finds that "sexual meanings, highlighted by names like 'chase-and-kiss' and 'kissers-and-chasers,' infuse cross-gender [heterosexual] chasing at every age." Furthermore, Best (1983: 116–17) finds that children as young as 2nd grade are engaged with the heterosexual discourses and practices of "boyfriend and girlfriend":

> Boys/men were expected to be attractive, even irresistible, to girls/women, and second grade boys adopted this aspect of the male role with considerable zest. . . . Third grade girls spent endless amounts of time fantasizing about "boyfriends" and marriage. Any gesture of appreciation shown them by boys—the lending of a pencil or an eraser—was viewed as a display of personal interest and would be eagerly discussed with other girls.

These early elementary school practices become more astute and entrenched over time. By the end of primary school, children make sophisticated use of interactive heterosexual performance, as well as heterosexist and homophobic harassment (Renold 2002, 2005). Similarly, in a study of summer camp, McGuffey and Rich (1999) find that boys in middle childhood use homophobia (especially name calling) to police masculinity. This literature shows the ever developing sophistication of children's understandings of the normativity and hegemony of heterosexuality. It also demonstrates that children are well aware of these practices by at least early elementary school.

But what happens before children are ensconced in the practices of elementary school and peer groups? Children learn a lot about gender (and sometimes a bit about sexuality) from preschool teachers and daycare workers (Blaise 2005; Danby 1998; Martin 1998; Skelton 2001; Wallis and VanEvery 2000). Preschool children also learn about gender and sexuality through the media. Children's media, especially films aimed at girls, are filled with hetero-romantic story lines (Do Rozario 2004; Martin, Luke, and Verduzco-Baker 2007; Tobin 2000; Witt 2000).

Research also consistently finds that parents construct gender for their children, and key to this construction is a child's sexuality. This is especially true for boys, because their behaviors and dress are particularly limited in early childhood and often implicate their sexuality (Martin 1998; Thorne 1993). Parenting advice about gender both raises and appeases parents' fears that non-normative gender behavior is a sign of homosexuality (Martin 2005). Parents', especially heterosexual fathers', fears about gender non-normativity are intimately tied to concerns about children's, especially sons', heterosexuality (Kane 2006). Similarly, among parents whose children were sexually abused, McGuffey (2005) finds that fathers use homophobia to reassert and "fix" a son's masculinity after the abuse. These studies suggest the importance of heterosexuality to normative gender identity for parents of young children.

What can we learn about heteronormativity by directly examining parents' sexual socialization practices with their young children? Early childhood is usually seen as a natural precursor to later development and often overlooked. How might parents convey the normativity of heterosexuality to children in early childhood? I examine what mothers—admittedly only one source of sexual socialization, but an important one—convey to children. I am not suggesting that parents' actions will shape or predict (or not) a child's sexual identity. Rather, this article examines how heterosexuality may come to be understood as normative in early childhood, regardless of a child's ultimate sexual identity.

Mothers, children, and heteronormativity

I argue that mothers reproduce heteronormativity in and for their children. It is important to note, however, that mothers are constituted by the very heteronormative context that they then reconstruct for their children. As transmitters of the cultural norms about heterosexuality, mothers are simultaneously constrained by what it means to be a good mother and the many dimensions on which mothers are judged for their mothering (Blum 2007; Hays 1996; Singh 2004). Mothers are particularly under scrutiny concerning their children's sexuality, given the long (and not entirely gone) history of blaming mothers for children's, especially boys', homosexuality (du Plessis 1993). This context shapes mothers' practices and strategies as they parent.

Finally, children are not blank slates merely in the process of becoming adult social actors (Martin et al. 2007; Thorne 1993). Rather, socialization can be understood as a process through which children make meaning from the many pieces of culture they absorb. They simultaneously alter, resist, and manage the conflicting meanings of various pieces of culture, discourse, interactions, and social structures. Children do not necessarily absorb what their mothers tell them without alteration, resistance, and integration with other cultural ideas and knowledge. Socialization is, in these regards, a two way process; children's questions, actions, and reactions all shape what parents say and do with children. This is likely particularly true for issues surrounding sexuality. Experts tell parents to talk to their children about sexuality only when a child asks a question, and parents seem to follow this advice (Frankham 2006). Much sexuality education by parents is thus dependent on a child's inquisitiveness and the available sources of information that might prompt a child to ask a question (Martin et al. 2007). Mothers do not construct heteronormativity on a blank slate, but in interactions with variously knowledgeable and inquisitive children living in varied social contexts.

Research design

The data for this study come from a larger project I conducted on mothers' sexual socialization of young children. Most research on this topic uses small and unsystematic samples (Geasler, Dannison, and Edlund 1995; Moore 2003) and retrospective data (Ward and Wyatt 1994) (likely due to human subjects review boards' requirements and other difficulties in getting access to broader populations of parents and children when researching sexuality). In an attempt to overcome these limitations, I conducted a Web-based survey of U.S. mothers with children ages 3 to 6 years old. The Web survey allowed me to reach a wider range of mothers than could be gathered in interviews or focus groups (Geasler et al. 1995). The survey also allowed me to collect comparable closed- and open-ended answers to a wide range of questions.

Sample

The mothers for the study come from a panel of respondents provided by Survey Sampling International (SSI). SSI is a well-respected provider of Web panels, maintaining a panel of 2.6 million individuals in the United States. From this group, I drew 12,500 e-mail addresses of mothers, with the intent of collecting 500 surveys. I launched the survey in February 2006 with an e-mail invitation to participate. Those who replied to the e-mail answered screening questions to confirm that they fit the sample criteria. The survey was open for eight days, during which I collected 641 responses. I could have collected more responses with follow-up reminders and a longer survey period, but cost prohibited this. Using a Web sample and survey was significantly more cost-effective, and provided a larger sample and more information, than other surveying means (Couper, Traugott, and Lamias 2001). Willingness to participate in Web surveys, and access to the technology to do so, likely shaped the profile of the respondents.

The mothers in the sample were 33.8 years old, on average (see Table 5.1). Most were married (77 percent) and White (88 percent), while about 5 percent were Black, 3 percent Hispanic, 2 percent Asian, and 1 percent American Indian. About 35 percent of mothers had a college degree or more, and approximately half the sample had a household income below $50,000. The other half fell between $50,000 and $150,000, with most at the lower end of this range. Half the mothers worked outside the home, with a mean of 33 hours worked per week. Geographically, the mothers were distributed proportionately across all 50 states. Two mothers described themselves as bisexual.

Respondents were asked to choose their religion from Catholic, Jewish, Muslim, Protestant, no religion, and other. Those who chose Protestant also selected a denomination, and those who chose "other" were asked to explain. I recoded the answers to the religion questions into the variables Catholic (22 percent), Jewish (2 percent), Muslim (.5 percent), Protestant I (15 percent), Protestant II (35 percent), no religion (22 percent), and other (4 percent). This recoding moved many who first reported "other" into one of the Protestant categories, as they also wrote "Baptist," "Christian," or "Methodist." The few remaining in the "other" category are not classifiable in any of the above categories (e.g., Wiccan or Buddhist). I recoded the Protestant denominations into Protestant I and II based on the distinctions made by Laumann and colleagues (1994: 146–47). Protestant I comprises liberal or moderate denominations such as Methodist, Lutheran, Presbyterian, and Episcopalian. Type II Protestants are conservative denominations with evangelical or fundamentalist world views, such as Baptist, Church of Christ, Assembly of God, and those who answered "Christian" or "Born Again."

The Web survey did not produce a random representative sample, but it came closer to representing U.S. mothers of young children on some dimensions than on others. According to an analysis of national data from the Current Population Survey, mothers of 3- to 5-year-olds are slightly younger (about 32.3 years versus 33.8) and slightly less likely to be married (69 percent versus 77 percent) than the mothers in my sample; a similar 36 percent have a college degree or more. The median income of households with children under age 18 according to the 2006 Census is $58,865. Half the mothers in my sample reported a household income below $50,000. Stay-at-home mothers are overrepresented in my sample (50 versus 40 percent). My sample also differs from the general population on race. Whites are overrepresented and other racial/ethnic groups are underrepresented, particularly Blacks (who make up 12.7 percent of the population but only 5 percent of the sample).[1]

Table 5.1 Sample Descriptive Statistics

	Mean	*SD*
Age (N = 640)	33.82	7.12
Number of Children (3 to 6 years) (N = 640)	1.25	.52
Age of Child Considered in Survey (N = 631)	4.60	1.07
Proportion Responding about Girls (N = 632)	.50	.50

(Continued)

Table 5.1 (Continued)

	Mean	*SD*
Proportion Responding about Boys (N = 632)	.50	.50
Annual Household Income, $ (N = 637)		
Less than 30,000	.19	.40
30,000 to 49,999	.30	.46
50,000 to 69,999	.24	.43
70,000 to 89,999	.14	.35
90,000 to 109,999	.06	.25
110,000 to 150,000	.05	.21
More than 150,000	.01	.10
Not Employed (N = 631)	.51	.50
Hours Worked in Paid Employment (N = 314)	.33	.12
Marital Status (N = 638)		
Single	.06	.24
Married	.77	.42
Divorced	.10	.30
Widowed	.00	.04
Domestic partner	.07	.25
Ethnicity (N = 640)		
White/Caucasian	.88	.33
Black/African American	.05	.21
American Indian/Alaskan Native	.01	.12
Hispanic/Latino	.03	.18
Asian	.02	.14
Other	.01	.11
Highest Level of Education (N = 639)		
Less than high school	.02	.12
High school diploma	.20	.40
Some college	.44	.50
Bachelors degree	.25	.43
Some graduate school	.04	.19
Graduate degree	.06	.24
Religion (N = 641)		
Catholic	.22	.41
Protestant I[a]	.15	.36
Protestant II[a]	.35	.48
Muslim	.00	.07
Jewish	.02	.13
No religion	.22	.41
Other	.04	.20

Note: Valid responses N's in parentheses for each variable.

[a] I recoded Protestant denominations into Protestant type I and type II based on the distinctions made by Laumann and colleagues (1994:146–47). Protestant I's comprise liberal or moderate denominations such as Methodists, Lutherans, Presbyterians, and Episcopalians. Type II Protestants include conservative denominations that have evangelical or fundamentalist world views, such as Baptists, Church of Christ, Assembly of God, and those who described themselves as "Christian" or "Born Again."

Method

The survey consisted of open- and closed-ended questions asking mothers what they say (and do not say) to their children about sexuality and reproduction. Some questions asked about the content of what the children were taught, drawing on the Sexuality Information and Education Council of the United States'(SIECUS) guidelines for comprehensive sexuality education for kindergartners (SIECUS 2004). Some questions asked the context (e.g., timing, prompts) for mothers' discussions with children about sexuality and reproduction. Other questions addressed mothers' feelings about these conversations with their children, barriers to educating their children on these topics, other sources of their children's sexual and reproductive knowledge, and demographic information. The questions were not directly framed around heterosexuality but were about sexuality education in general. Most of the questions required simple yes or no answers and some were followed by open-ended questions. For example, the survey began with a broad question: "Have you talked with your child about sex and reproduction or issues surrounding these topics?" For those who said yes, an open-ended question followed, asking the respondent to describe the conversation. The survey used this form of question to ask if and how mothers described "what a wedding is," "falling in love," "divorce," "your own wedding," and "the day your child was born."[2]

I draw at length from two particular questions: "Have you ever wondered if your child might grow up to be gay or lesbian?" and its open-ended follow-up question, "Why or why not?"[3] I also use the answers from the yes-or-no questions: "Have you made a statement to your child that is similar to:" "Some people are homosexual, which means they can be attracted to and fall in love with someone of the same gender," "Two people of the same gender can live in loving, lifetime committed relationships," "Homosexual men and women are also known as gay men and lesbians," "Homosexuality is wrong," and "Making fun of people by calling them gay (e.g., homo, fag, queer) is disrespectful and hurtful."

Results and discussion

While heteronormativity develops from many sources (e.g., media, peers, and other adults), I use evidence from the data to show how mothers' own heteronormative assumptions, talk, and strategies may constitute heteronormativity in their children. Again, mothers are not (solely) "responsible" for children's heteronormativity. Mothers live in a context in which mothering is continuously judged; teaching children about sexuality at all (let alone teaching *young* children anything other than the norm, that is, monogamous, reproductive heterosexuality) is highly suspect if not dangerous. Understanding mothers' practices, however, can illuminate how heteronormativity is reproduced through a mundane, persistent, everyday process that is often without oppressive intention (Kitzinger 2005).

Below, I describe two sets of practices in which mothers engage. The first set of practices assumes one's child is heterosexual and projects that identity onto the child's behavior. These practices are widely shared among mothers in this sample and are used to construct heterosexuality and make it normative. This assumption of a child's heterosexuality colors mothers' sexual socialization of children more generally and may lead to the erasure of gays and lesbians from children's social maps. The second set of practices concerns the strategies mothers use when considering the possibility that their children could one day be gay or lesbian. Mothers are not nearly as uniform in this regard. A few prepare for the future, many passively hope for "the best" (i.e., that their children are heterosexual), and others parent for the prevention of homosexuality.

Notably, mothers' own social contexts (e.g., whether they have close friends or family who are gay or whether they belong to a conservative religion) influence which strategy they pursue.

Assuming heterosexuality and constructing heteronormativity

Most parents presume that their children are heterosexual. This unarticulated, usually unthought, assumption steers much of the heterosexualization of young children. The presumption of heterosexuality at birth is the first step on the way to heteronormativity.

The survey asked mothers if they ever wondered if their 3- to 6-year-olds might grow up to be gay or lesbian; a majority of mothers (74 percent) reported that they had not. Mothers were significantly more likely to wonder about boys than girls (about 8 percent more likely, $p < .05$).[4] Many said they wondered because of a son's non-normative gender behavior (e.g., "he likes dolls" or "he likes his sister's dresses"). This is the only finding illustrating such gender differences. Given the relatively narrow set of behavioral and appearance choices for young boys (Kane 2006; Martin 1998, 2005), this finding is not surprising. However, when no "signs" were present, most mothers claimed they did not wonder. The phrase "ever wondered" does not imply one thinks there is a good chance or even some chance, but asks simply whether the parent had considered the possibility. Heterosexuality's normativity means that most parents understand their children as heterosexual. This attribution of heterosexuality (much like gender attribution) means that mothers then interpret their children's behavior as heterosexual (Kessler and McKenna 1978).

The assumption of heterosexuality frames mothers' understandings of their children's cross-gender play, leading them to prescribe heterosexual romantic interest and desire to many cross-gender interactions. For example, in Table 5.2, Panel A, we see that 25 percent of all mothers (column 1, row A-1) and 36 percent of mothers with 6-year-olds (column 5, row A-1) describe their children as having had a crush on someone of the other gender. Heteronormativity leads mothers to read their children's behavior against the dominant discourse of children as asexual while, at the same time, using adult meanings to understand children's behavior.

For example, one mother of a 3-year-old girl wrote that she did not worry about her child growing up to be lesbian: "She already has boyfriends and has always been interested in having a husband. When her brother was born she asked if he was going to be her husband." Instead of interpreting male peers as "friends," the mother describes them as "boyfriends." Rather than understanding interest in "having a husband" at age 3 as similar to an interest in being a ballerina or a superhero—that is, as a game of pretend not realistically related to one's actual adulthood—the mother believes her child's interest is predictive. Finally, this mother constructs her daughter's confusion about her relationship to a new baby as evidence of proto-heterosexuality, rather than (a perhaps common) childhood misunderstanding of family relationships. Some mothers presented the romantic attractions, flirtatious desires, and love interests of their (elsewhere described as asexual) 3- to 6-year-olds as evidence of the children's heterosexuality and as an explanation for why they did not wonder if their children might grow up to be gay:

> He is already attracted to girls and just does not show any signs that I can see.
>
> My son loves girls—women any age.
>
> She already has crushes on boys.
>
> She seems normal and well adjusted, and she is boy crazy, she falls in love with half of the guys she sees on TV and she is only 5. She is trying to marry Orlando Bloom. She doesn't say anything like that about girls.

> Because he thinks he is already married to a 13-year-old girl who is my daughter's best friend.
>
> At this point she seems to be straight because she has showed interest in little boys her age and she says that they are her boyfriends.
>
> [I don't wonder] because right now all he talks about is his little girlfriends!

In describing their children's heterosexual crushes, none of the mothers described any sexualized behaviors, not even kissing or hand-holding. Rather, mothers imputed romantic interest to their children's playing with, befriending, or talking about peers of the opposite sex.

Mothers, it appears from the data, use different behaviors to discern heterosexuality and homosexuality in children. Mothers used terms like "crushes" and "little girlfriends" to imply a romantic attraction and establish their children's heterosexuality. Mothers who wondered if their children might someday be gay, however, did so not because their sons had crushes on boys (or their girls on girls), but because of a child's non-normative gender behavior. The mothers used imputed desire and attraction to read heterosexuality, but they used gender behavior to read homosexuality.

Furthermore, these data suggest that most mothers do not wonder if their children might someday be gay partly because they find "evidence" of heterosexuality in children's cross-gender behavior and expect that behavior to produce a stable lifetime identity. They operate with a model of sexual identity in which adult sexuality develops linearly from the "signs" in early childhood (Aveline 2006). This is a model of sexuality that gay people themselves often put forward in coming-out stories (Plummer 1995): one is born with a sexual orientation that develops linearly from childhood; gender conformity and cross-gender romantic interests are dismissed as required detours on the way to the "real" gay self. Social scientists have demonstrated that sexual desire, behavior, and identity are frequently inconsistent elements in peoples' lived experiences (Golden 1987; Laumann et al. 1994). Indeed, sexual development is on-going (Diamond 2003, 2006) and social-historical contexts create the possibility of identities and their fluidity (Stein 1997). Mothers do not see such variability in the sexualities they imagine and construct for their children. They envision normative heterosexuality linearly developing from early childhood.

Teaching heterosexuality through love and marriage

Assumptions of heterosexuality likely influence parenting practices by permeating and shaping what mothers teach their children. It is important to note that mothers of 3- to 6-year-olds say little to their children about sexuality itself. Only 3 percent of mothers had said anything about intercourse, and about 50 percent said they had discussed that a baby grows inside the uterus.

Nonetheless, mothers do instruct their children in heterosexuality, and a version that is ultimately normative: it is love-filled, monogamous, married, and reproductive. Mothers discuss romantic love and marriage with young children, and these topics are important and substantive vehicles for heterosexual socialization in early childhood. Although there are more cultural spaces available for homosexuality today, the social constitution of normative heterosexuality has not changed (Johnson 2005: 15): "In its cultural representations, love is hegemonically expressed heterosexuality, and still draws on the 'traditional' scripts of marriage and heterosexual domesticity." Love is culturally understood as natural and good, something acceptable for children to learn about. In learning about romantic love, children learn about heterosexuality. Romantic love is the conduit of that learning, and it is available for children to discover from parents' accounts of love, weddings, and marriage.

Table 5.2 Percentage (N) of Mothers by Age of Children who Reported a Crush, Discussed Falling in Love, and Discussed Marriage and Weddings

		(1) All		*(2) Age 3*		*(3) Age 4*		*(4) Age 5*		*(5) Age 6*		
		%	*(N)*	*%*	*(N)*	*%*	*(N)*	*%*	*(N)*	*%*	*(N)*	*(6) Total N*
Panel A: Crush												
(A-1)	Reports child had a crush on someone (of the other gender)	25	(104)	9	(9)	27	(28)	29	(30)	36	(37)	421
Panel B: Falling in Love												
(B-1)	Discussed falling in love	33	(203)	15	(18)	29	(50)	39	(65)	45	(70)	614
	Of those: [a]											
(B-2)	Heterosexualized falling in love	33	(66)	22	(4)	46	(23)	31	(20)	27	(19)	203
(B-3)	Told child "falling in love will happen to you"	19	(38)	33	(6)	26	(13)	12	(8)	16	(11)	203
(B-4)	Described falling in love as leading to marriage	29	(59)	28	(5)	42	(21)	25	(16)	24	(17)	203
Panel C: Weddings and Marriage												
(C-1)	Described what a wedding is	69	(419)	43	(50)	67	(114)	79	(131)	80	(124)	610
	Of those: [b]											
(C-2)	Described weddings as heterosexual	42	(174)	42	(21)	47	(54)	39	(51)	39	(48)	419
(C-3)	Said same-sex wedding possible	1	(6)	2	(1)	.8	(1)	2	(3)	.8	(1)	419
(C-4)	Described their own wedding	51	(251)	38	(31)	50	(67)	57	(85)	55	(68)	495
(C-5)	Stated: "When you grow up you will get married."	52	(325)	36	(43)	55	(97)	59	(100)	52	(85)	631

[a] 203 mothers reported having a discussion about falling in love with their children. These responses were then coded for heterosexualized falling in love, described love as leading to marriage, and told the children it would happen to them. These are the subsequent three categories. Categories are not mutually exclusive.

[b] 419 mothers talked with their children about weddings. These responses were then coded for those that highlighted the heterosexuality of weddings (e.g., "a man and a woman"). These are reported on the subsequent line.

The data show that mothers teach their children that they will fall in love and marry someone of the opposite gender. First, in Panel B of Table 5.2, we see that 33 percent of mothers reported having discussed "falling in love" with their young children (column 1, row B-1). Of the mothers who described their falling-in-love talk with their children, 33 percent discussed it in heterosexual terms (column 1, row B-2). For example, they explicitly said that love happens between a man and a woman, linking it to their own heterosexual relationships or heterosexual marriage:[5]

> Falling in love is when a man and a woman who are grown ups have deep feelings for one another and want to spend all their time together.
>
> It is something that happens when a lady and a man really like each other, they like each other so much that they start falling in love with each other.
>
> I describe falling in love as a very special friendship between a man and a woman. I describe BEING (not just falling) in love as the way my husband and I feel about each other, wanting to spend time together for the rest of our lives, placing someone else's needs equal to your own, making a life together, working together, compromising, raising a family, etc.

Second, of the mothers who purposefully talked to their children about what it means to fall in love, 19 percent told their children that falling in love is something that will happen to them (column 1, row B-3):

> He asked about my ring. I told him that someday he will meet a nice girl and fall in love, just like mommy and daddy. And then he will get married and give her a ring that says I love you forever. Daddy gave me my ring to tell me he loves me forever and ever.
>
> God has chosen a special person for you to fall in love with. You will know who this person is because God will show you the love.

Through these conversations, children may come to understand that hetero-romantic love is something that will happen to them, not an abstract event that happens to others. Such conversations may play a role in constructing children's understandings of themselves as "supposed to be" heterosexual.

Third, mothers also linked falling in love to getting (heterosexually) married. Of those who reported discussing falling in love with their young children, 29 percent said that love results in marriage (column 1, row B-4). They reported saying things like "falling in love happens when a man and woman marries [sic]" and "[my] child asked why his father and I got married, I told him because we loved each other. And that it takes time to find the right person and when you do you get married. He knows about love. I am not so sure he understands falling in love the way I do at this time."

Apart from the falling-in-love talk, mothers also discussed marriage and weddings quite a bit. In Panel C of Table 5.2, we see that by the time children are 6 years old, 80 percent of mothers have talked to them about weddings (column 5, row C-1). Also, 55 percent of married mothers had described their own weddings to their 6-year-olds (column 5, row C-4). Married and college-educated mothers talked more about weddings than did other mothers, while Black mothers talked about weddings less frequently.[6] Many married mothers reported that their children had seen their wedding pictures or wedding video or were at the mother's wedding. These occasions prompted discussions of weddings, marriages, and their meanings.

Furthermore, 52 percent of children heard from their mothers in some context, "when you grow up you will get married" (column 1, row C-5). For the vast majority, despite there being more talk than ever before of gay marriage, this meant heterosexually married. Indeed, parents often explicitly described marriage as heterosexual. In their descriptors of marriage, more than any other phrases, mothers used "love" and "between a man and a woman." More than the promise, the vow, or even god's role, mothers emphasized love and heterosexuality. One fourth of mothers described both simultaneously, explicitly depicting weddings as being about love and heterosexuality. Like the prescription for falling in love, these comments tell children that the rituals and institutions are about the children themselves and what they will become. When asked what they told their children about weddings, they reported the following:

> When two people, a man and a woman, get together they fall in love and want to spend the rest of their lives together they decide to get married.
>
> My children have both been in weddings as part of the wedding party (flower girls). My youngest isn't curious but my oldest knows that when a man and woman get married it's because they love each other and want to be together forever and maybe have children. She does think you have to marry the first boy you kiss, which, at 5 she's already done. I did tell her that wasn't necessarily true.
>
> When a man and a woman love each other very much, like your mommy and daddy and decided they want to start a family of their own. Mommy dresses in a pretty gown and lots of family and friends come to watch you as you marry your prince.
>
> That two people who love each other have a wedding and get married. The bride gets to wear a white dress and be a princess for a day and the groom is her prince and afterwards they have a party called a reception to celebrate with their family and friends and they get to eat cake. She really liked the eat cake part.
>
> Girls and boys are boyfriend/girlfriend and most of all friends. They decide they want to spend their time and life together so they might get married. Some people live together without being married. Ideally, marriage comes before sex and babies.

Notably, only six mothers described some discussion of same-sex marriage in their talks about weddings and marriage (column 1, row C-3). A few mothers even made it clear that their children understand that same-gender people cannot marry: "She knows that boys marry girls (no same sex relationships). You get married because you are in love." Discussion of marriage with young children may thus also inscribe heteronormativity.

Children's media also echo the connections between love, marriage, and heterosexuality. Although not asked about it specifically, mothers discussed their children's (especially girls') knowledge about love and marriage from the media, particularly movies. In young children's movies, romantic love is constructed as a special and incredibly powerful domain of life that is separate from same-gender friendship and other relationships (Martin and Kazyak 2008). While same-gender friendships are fun or funny, heterosexual love is portrayed as powerful. For example, falling in love can break a spell (*Beauty and the Beast*), cause one to give up her identity (*The Little Mermaid*), be so special that it is off limits even to a powerful genie (*Aladdin*'s genie cannot make people fall in love), or lead children to disobey a parent (all of these and *Pocahontas*). Mothers' comments made the importance of such media clear:

> I often tell my children that someday they will meet a very special person that will make them feel beautiful inside and out. My daughter is a true fan of all that is Disney princess, so she already has her own views on falling in love.
>
> We explained that falling in love is when you want to spend all your time with someone for a very long time. She also watches and reads a lot of Disney stories so she believes that

every girl will meet a prince just like in the stories and they will find each other and fall in love, get married and have babies.

Several mothers also said that their daughters link weddings to the princesses in movies and stories:

[I told her that] a wedding is when two people fall in love and want to stay together forever. They then become husband and wife. It is easy for my daughter to understand because her father and I are married. She has been to weddings and says that brides look like princesses.

[I told her that a wedding is] when a boyfriend and girlfriend decide to try to live together forever (she knows married from prince/princess stories).

The data suggest that children learn that romantic heterosexual love is important from this media, and they then link romantic love to marriage in discussions with their mothers. Media socialization likely builds heteronormativity in conjunction with parents' heterosexual socialization (Martin et al. 2007).

The invisibility of gays and lesbians

Through mothers' assumptions that their children will become heterosexual, most teach their young children that romance, love, weddings, and marriage are heterosexual. By implication, the children should grow up, fall in love, and get married heterosexually. The assumption of a child's heterosexuality also reinforces heteronormativity in another way: gays and lesbians are erased from children's social worlds. Most mothers do not discuss gays and lesbians with their children, nor do children see gays and lesbians depicted in the media (Martin et al. 2007).

In Table 5.3, we see that 62 percent of mothers said nothing to their children about gays and lesbians, not even something negative or disparaging (column 1, first row). Given that 8 percent of mothers told their children that homosexuality is wrong (column 1, last row), that leaves less than one third of mothers who acknowledged gay and lesbian lives, in a way that was at least informational, in discussions with their children. Among this group, 11 percent told their children that "some people are homosexual which means they can be attracted to and fall in love with someone of the same gender" (column 1, second row). Also, 9 percent told their children that homosexuals are also called gays and lesbians (column 1, third row). These mothers reported naming and acknowledging the existence of gays and lesbians for their children. Such processes likely help their children construct more complex understandings of their social world. Such information may also, depending on the context in which it is delivered, disrupt the heteronormativity in children's worlds.

The possibility of homosexuality: parenting strategies

The focus thus far has been on the role of parents' assumptions that their children are heterosexual. There are, nevertheless, important ruptures in heteronormativity. In this section, I examine three strategies mothers use when considering the idea that their children could grow up to be gay or lesbian. This typology emerged from the inductive coding of the open-ended question: "Have you ever wondered if your child might grow up to be gay or lesbian? Why or why not?"[7]

First, as seen in Table 5.4, a few mothers (about 6 percent) described themselves as purposefully parenting to be sure that their children know that gays and lesbians exist (column 5, first row). These mothers want their children to learn that if they are gay or lesbian, their identity will

Table 5.3 Percentage (N) of Mothers by Age of Children and What They Said about Homosexuality to Their Children

	(1) All		*(2) Age 3*		*(3) Age 4*		*(4) Age 5*		*(5) Age 6*		
	%	*(N)*	%	*(N)*	%	*(N)*	%	*(N)*	%	*(N)*	*(6) Total N*
Made no statements about homosexuality or gays and lesbians	62	(394)	76	(91)	70	(123)	56	(95)	51	(85)	631
Stated: Some people are homosexual, which means they can be attracted to and fall in love with someone of the same gender	11	(72)	9	(11)	7	(12)	12	(21)	17	(28)	631
Stated: Homosexual men and women are also known as gay men and lesbians	9	(57)	4	(5)	5	(8)	8	(14)	18	(30)	631
Stated: Making fun of people by calling them gay is disrespectful and hurtful	26	(165)	17	(120)	20	(35)	32	(54)	34	(56)	631
Stated: Two people of the same gender can live in loving, lifetime committed relationships	16	(103)	13	(16)	14	(24)	17	(28)	21	(35)	631
Stated: Homosexuality is wrong	8	(52)	3	(4)	5	(9)	11	(19)	12	(20)	631

be accepted. I call this strategy *preparing for the possibility of homosexuality.* These mothers often describe having out gay family members or close friends. They are more likely to wonder about the possibility of their children being gay and to express acceptance of this wondering:

> Because I know that many kids do [end up gay], and I've known too many GLBT people who have felt very unhappy at their own response to being GLBT. I want to make certain my kids don't add to this in others (because I am certain that they know some kids who are GLBT, even if the kid doesn't know it yet), and because I want them to be happy about finding love, regardless of the gender of the person.
>
> [I] have gay family members, gay and lesbian friends. I want her to know that it would be OK whatever she grew up to be, I don't want her to feel she needs to be heterosexual because it is expected of her.
>
> My sister is a lesbian and I was pretty sure of it before she came out. I even asked her while we were teenagers. She became very angry with me. She did not come out 'til she was 24 years old. We were very close growing up and I think I've been the most accepting of her. It wasn't an issue. I would be accepting of my children because I don't see anything wrong with it. I think the hardest thing is talking to them and making them more open-minded about my sister.
>
> I want to make sure that if he is gay, that he's comfortable with it. I believe that most gay people are born that way. I never tell him he has to be one way or the other, just stuff like: If you want to have kids, you can, but don't have to. You don't have to ever get married if you don't want to.

These mothers not only think it is okay if their children turn out to be gay, but they actively prepare for the possibility. They try to teach their children to be "open-minded," and they try to convey that they do not expect heterosexuality from their children. These parents leave open the possibility for a wide variety of paths.

Much more common than the sentiments of these few mothers, however, are the mothers who employed the strategy I call *hoping for the best*. Of the mothers who imagined the possibility of their children being gay, 62 percent said they would love and support their children if this did turn out to be the case (Table 5.4, column 5, second row). Nonetheless, their comments underscore that they hope their children will not be gay or lesbian (although these mothers expressed a wide range of views on homosexuality). Sometimes their comments include the caveat that although they would not wish this for their children, they would love their children in spite of a gay or lesbian identity, if necessary:

> At this point, I don't see any difference if they are interested in [a] specific gender. And even if they gonna be gay or lesbian, I will support them. Even [if] I don't approve of gay and lesbian.
>
> I have no reason to believe my daughters will grow up and become lesbians but if that is the way it is, I would not love them any less. I would be supportive of them and the way they have chosen to live their lives. My role as a parent is to guide them, mold them into productive human beings and then let them go to live their life and make their own decisions. I think society overall is becoming more receptive to the gay and lesbian community. However, I am not naive enough to believe that they wouldn't encounter some difficulties as many people do not believe in homosexuality but my children will ALWAYS have parents to love and support them no matter what.

> The thoughts are always given to us in everyday life: TV shows, people we meet, etc. However, I know it will not matter to me or my husband if my son ends up to be homosexual over heterosexual. As long as he is a good person and he is happy, it's all we can ask for. We will not promote for him to do this, but we also realize it is a chance we all, as human beings, take.
>
> It could happen to any parent. My husband and I have discussed it and I guess we would be open to the idea although it's not something we exactly want to happen.
>
> I have no reason to wonder if he is going to be gay. If he is I will not love him less. It isn't worth thinking about.
>
> You never know, I'm just keeping an open mind in case it's the case, not that I want it to be. But if I keep an open mind about it I'll be okay.
>
> I am not worried about it as I cannot change what my child's sexual preference is. My child will choose what her sexual preference is when she gets to that stage in her life.

What differentiates these mothers from both those who parent for the possibility of homosexuality and those who parent to prevent homosexuality (as I discuss below), is their passivity with regard to parenting and homosexuality. Regardless of their own views about homosexuality, these mothers seem to share the belief that there is nothing parents can do to shape their children's sexuality. Although they do not say so specifically, they seem to lean toward a biological, immutable understanding of sexuality. These mothers are resigned to the idea that parents cannot change a child's sexuality. Furthermore, although many mothers who "hope for the best" say they will still love a child who turns out to be gay, none suggest that they would like this to be an easy process for their children, nor do they parent in ways that might make it easier for a child who does become gay.

The third group of mothers employ a strategy I call *parenting for prevention*. Table 5.4 shows that 33 percent of mothers actively pursue parenting strategies that attempt to produce or ensure their children's heterosexuality (column 5, row 3). Mothers who belong to conservative religions (Protestant II) (Laumann et al. 1994) are far more likely than others to adopt this strategy

Table 5.4 Parenting Strategies Regarding Homosexuality by Religious Group

	(1)	*(2)*	*(3)*	*(4)*	*(5)*	*(6)*
Parenting Strategies	*No Religion*	*Catholic*	*Protestant I*[a]	*Protestant II*[a]	*Overall*	*Total N*
Preparing for the Possibility (%)	7	8	10	2	6	13
Hoping for the Best (%)	88	79	74	30	62	142
Parenting for Prevention (%)	5	13	16	68	33	75
Total Percent	100	100	100	100	100	
Total N	58	53	31	88	230	230

Note: Jewish (3) and Muslim (1) not included because of small N. Chi square significant, $p < .001$.

[a] I recoded Protestant denominations into Protestant type I and type II based on the distinctions made by Laumann and colleagues (1994:146–47). Protestant I's comprise liberal or moderate denominations such as Methodists, Lutherans, Presbyterians, and Episcopalians. Type II Protestants include conservative denominations that have evangelical or fundamentalist world views, such as Baptists, Church of Christ, Assembly of God, and those who described themselves as "Christian" or "Born Again."

(column 4, row 3). When asked why they did not wonder if their children might one day be gay or lesbian, these mothers said they were parenting in a way that would prevent it, and therefore they did not have to "worry" about it:

> We model a heterosexual healthy marriage life in our family so I believe our daughter sees a correct woman's modeling as do our boys with their dad.
>
> Because I believe that it is a sin. But, there are many, many sins in the Bible. I know that I sin, everyday, even though I try my hardest not to. Still, I pray that my child will also strive not to sin. One way not to sin (or to sin less) is to recognize what you believe is wrong (or sinful). That way you can make an effort not to. I believe that I can teach my children that this is a sin and model a good relationship for them, and this will never be an issue.
>
> Because I think if you raise them with good stability and the right surroundings, things like that do not appear to be normal to him so he would realize in his mind that a same-sex marriage just isn't normal nor is it a part of his lifestyle.
>
> Because he will learn that the Bible does not allow that. We will not allow it. And if he is, he will be committed to a psyc. hospital to find out what is wrong with his mind and brain function!
>
> Because it is biblically wrong and my child will NOT be subjected to any kind of tolerance for that behavior. He is taught to love the person, but hate the sin. We have taught him about Sodom and Gomorrah in the Bible and he knows they were wrong and that is why those cities were destroyed.
>
> It is wrong to be homosexual and I will teach my child the same thing.
>
> I don't believe that children are born gay [but] that it is brought on by environmental influences, or how a child is treated. I don't treat my children like fragile pieces of glass I treat him like he's a boy and expect him to act like a boy.

As is clear from the voices above, one way mothers attempt to prevent homosexuality is to teach their children that it is wrong, often by relying on religious understandings. While mothers told children very little about homosexuality or gay people, 22 percent of those who discussed it explicitly said "homosexuality is wrong." Some mothers think teaching these "values" to children will prevent them from becoming gay. From the data, it is not clear how much children understand and retain these teachings. The data suggest, though, that some children do recall these lessons. For example, a mother of a 5-year-old daughter wrote that she does not worry about her child being gay as her daughter "has said that boys marry girls. It's silly for boys to marry boys and girls to marry girls."

This prevention strategy is significantly associated with conservative religion ($p < .001$). Much has been written about religious conservatives' beliefs that they can turn gays into exgays (Ezren 2006; Moon 2005). My data suggest that this idea has permeated parenting practices such that some parents explicitly think they can prevent gay identities from emerging in their children in the first place. Conservative religious organizations, such as Focus on the Family, publish childcare books that extol this view. They emphasize the importance of a two-parent home, children's affirmation of their identity as male or female, children's identification with the same-sex parent, and the prevention of sexual abuse (see, e.g., Reisser 1997). The "parenting for prevention" mothers echoed all of these practices. While the idea that parenting practices can prevent homosexuality is most explicit and detailed in parenting advice from the far right, this view is prevalent in popular parenting advice from a wide range of perspectives (Martin 2005). In some ways, it is surprising that more mothers did not report engaging in such practices.

Perhaps the strength of the assumption of heterosexuality, especially when children are young, keeps those who are not heavily invested in conservative religious views from actively pursuing such strategies.

In sum, other than a few mothers who consciously parent for the possibility that their children might one day be gay or lesbian, most mothers who consider the possibility do so in ways that solidify the normativity of heterosexuality. Those who employ the "cross your fingers and hope for the best" strategy remain silent about homosexuality, making it invisible to their children. Those who employ the "prevention" strategy give children information suggesting that homosexuality is not normative, not an option for them, and not a positive option for anyone. What is striking is that these strategies are used by parents whose children are under age 6.

Conclusions

The research presented in this article suggests that mothers begin to construct heteronormative understandings for their children in early childhood. This likely contributes to older children's and adults' sense that heterosexuality is natural. Mothers' ascription of heterosexuality to very young children, their discussions of love and marriage that assume heterosexuality, and their prescriptions to their children that they will heterosexually marry when they grow up all contribute to early constructions of heteronormativity. Furthermore, mothers' heteronormative presentation of the world may erase gays and lesbians from children's social worlds. For many young children, gays and lesbians do not exist—the words, symbols, people, and relationships are not part of a child's lexicon. Finally, very few mothers actively parent for the possibility that their children could grow up to be gay. While a few do try to ensure that their children know a gay identity is acceptable, many more mothers actively parent to prevent homosexuality, and, by far, these mothers belong to and are influenced by conservative religions. These mothers think that by teaching that homosexuality is wrong, modeling a good marital relationship, and requiring proper gender roles, they can prevent their children from being gay. The largest group of mothers in this sample said they would still love their children if they grow up to adopt a gay or lesbian identity. Among these mothers, however, none describe actively parenting to give their children knowledge about gay identities or to ensure that their children know such an identity is acceptable.

These findings raise many new questions about how mothers normalize heterosexuality in early childhood. Mothers clearly play an important role in the ways demonstrated here, but they also produce heteronormativity through the books, movies, and other culture to which they expose their children and through the many mundane conversations they have with others that children overhear. Future work should explore how different social contexts of mothering, produced by race, class, religion, and sexual identities, shape mothers' production of normalized heterosexuality. Mothers' identities, social locations, and communities surely differentially shape not only the extent but also how they normalize heterosexuality.

My data focus on mothers and exclude the role of fathers and other caretakers in the construction of heteronormativity. Because mothers are generally more responsible than fathers for children's day-to-day sexual education (Nolin and Petersen 1992), concentrating on their role makes sense. We also know that fathers tend to be more traditional in their gender socialization of children (Kane 2006; Maccoby 1998). Mothers and fathers may therefore differ in the sexual socialization of their children, perhaps especially concerning gender identity. Men also report more homophobic attitudes than do women (Loftus 2001), so there may be other differences as well. Consequently, the results presented here may underestimate the construction of heteronormativity in young children by their parents. Finally, interactions with older siblings may also influence the construction of children's heteronormativity. This study does not address these sources of familial learning.

Children, even very young ones, do not get their information about the social world solely from parents, nor do children always absorb the information and meanings their parents convey in the way parents intend. The version of heteronormativity that mothers offer children is likely disrupted in numerous ways throughout childhood. Future research should examine young children's meaning making directly. What do children hear and retain when parents talk (or are silent) about homosexuality? How do young children interpret such information or combine it with other sources of information? How do they make sense of information from daily life that does not fit their developing notions of heteronormativity (e.g., a peer with two dads, a comment about gay marriage, or the word "gay" itself)? Doing such research with young children will likely be difficult given the sensitivities of parents and human subjects boards. As researchers, we need to find ways to address this gap in our understanding.

In the meantime, this study suggests that mothers convey heteronormativity to children from the time children are very young. These early, mundane, everyday conversations likely lay the foundation for understanding and abiding the larger heteronormative context in which children will develop. In their earliness, their banality, and their embeddedness in routine child care, these conversations demonstrate both how engrained heteronormativity is in the fabric of daily life and how efforts to change this will need to reach the very threads of society.

Notes

1 Using a Web survey likely produced these differences and the biases resulting from them. First, stay-at-home mothers may be more likely to respond to SSI's calls for participants to earn cash and other items while "working" from home. If the choice to stay home reflects their views on gender roles, then these mothers may be more conservative in their sexual values. If so, the analyses may overestimate the extent to which mothers uphold heteronormativity (although there are no differences by employment status). Second, non-Whites are underrepresented, and this too may be due to using a Web survey, given that the digital divide in the United States is partly based on race (DiMaggio et al. 2001).

2 Between 86 and 94 percent of the mothers answered the open-ended questions. Their answers vary in length from a short sentence to a paragraph; the examples here represent the range of lengths. I examined the variation in who answered these questions and found no statistically significant variation by race, household income, or education.

3 Two research assistants first coded the open-ended answers. They read all the answers and generated a set of categories for each question. We then consolidated overlapping categories and produced a set of codes for each open-ended question. Next, they coded all questions independently. We discussed and recoded the few answers (less than 5 percent) that they each coded differently. I used some of these codes to construct the categories and strategies described throughout this article.

4 Details of the logistic regression analyses that include marital status, race, household income, education, and religion as controls are available from the author.

5 The two thirds who did not heterosexualize falling in love this way did not offer same-sex love as a possibility. Rather, their answers consisted of vague or gender neutral descriptions of falling in love, such as "when two people love being with each other—love spending time together, have things in common, and have the same beliefs and love each other unconditionally."

6 Both differences are statistically significant ($p < .05$) based on logistic regression analyses with household income, education, race, marital status, and religion. Details are available from the author.

7 I used half of the answers to this open-ended question to develop this analysis. Among the answers that I did not code into one of the strategies presented here are primarily the brief answers from mothers who said that they just do not think about it, that their children show no sign of being gay, or that their children are too young. A few are answers from mothers who worry that their children might be gay because of gender deviance or because they have a gay or lesbian relative. These non-coded open-ends are evenly distributed across religion (46 percent of those with no religion; 53 percent of Catholics; 54 percent of Protestant I's; and 49 percent of Protestant II's).

References

Aveline, David. 2006. "'Did I Have Blinders on Or What?': Retrospective Sense Making by Parents of Gay Sons Recalling Their Sons' Earlier Years." *Journal of Family Issues* 27:777–802.

Bem, Daryl J. 1996. "Exotic Becomes Erotic: A Developmental Theory of Sexual Orientation." *Psychological Review* 103:320–35.

Best, Raphaela. 1983. *We've All Got Scars: What Boys and Girls Learn in Elementary School.* Bloomington, IN: Indiana University Press.

Blaise, Mindy. 2005. "A Feminist Poststructuralist Study of Children 'Doing' Gender in an Urban Kindergarten Classroom." *Childhood Research Quarterly* 20:85–108.

Blum, Linda M. 2007. "Mother-Blame in the Prozac Nation: Raising Kids with Invisible Disabilities." *Gender & Society* 21:202–26.

Butler, Judith P. 1990. *Gender Trouble: Feminism and the Subversion of Identity.* New York: Routledge.

Chodorow, Nancy J. 1992. "Heterosexuality as a Compromise Formation: Reflections on the Psychoanalytic Theory of Sexual Development." *Psychoanalysis and Contemporary Thought* 15:267–304.

Connell, R. W. 1970. "Class Consciousness in Childhood." *The Australian and New Zealand Journal of Sociology* 6:87–99.

Couper, Mick P., Michael W. Traugott, and Mark J. Lamias. 2001. "Web Survey Design and Administration." *The Public Opinion Quarterly* 65:230–53.

Danby, Susan. 1998. "The Serious and Playful Work of Gender: Talk and Social Order in a Preschool Classroom." Pp. 175–205 in *Gender in Early Childhood,* edited by N. Yelland. New York and London: Routledge.

D'Emilio, John. 1983. "Capitalism and Gay Identity." Pp. 100–113 in *Powers of Desire: The Politics of Sexuality,* edited by A. Snitow, C. Stansell, and S. Thompson. New York: Monthly Review Press.

Diamond, Lisa M. 1998. "The Development of Sexual Orientation among Adolescent and Young Adult Women." *Developmental Psychology* 34:1085–95.

———. 2003. "Was it a Phase? Young Women's Relinquishment of Lesbian/Bisexual Identities Over a Five Year Period." *Journal of Personality and Social Psychology* 84:352–64.

———. 2006. "Careful What You Ask For: Reconsidering Feminist Epistemology and Autobiographical Narrative in Research on Sexual Identity Development." *Signs* 31:471–91.

DiMaggio, Paul, Eszter Hargittai, W. R. Neuman, and John P. Robinson. 2001. "Social Implications of the Internet." *Annual Review of Sociology* 27:307–36.

Do Rozario, Rebecca-Anne C. 2004. "The Princess and the Magic Kingdom: Beyond Nostalgia, the Function of the Disney Princess." *Women's Studies in Communication* 27:34–59.

du Plessis, Michael. 1993. "Mother's Boys: Maternity, Male 'Homosexuality,' and Melancholia." *Discourse* 16:145–73.

Ezren, Tanya. 2006. *Straight to Jesus.* Berkeley, CA: University of California Press.

Frankham, Jo. 2006. "Sexual Antimonies and Parent/Child Sex Education: Learning from Foreclosure." *Sexualities* 9:236–54.

Geasler, Margie J., Linda L. Dannison, and Connie J. Edlund. 1995. "Sexuality Education of Young Children: Parental Concerns." *Family Relations* 44:184–88.

Golden, Carla. 1987. "Diversity and Variability in Women's Sexual Identities." Pp. 18–34 in *Lesbian Psychologies: Explorations and Challenges,* edited by Boston Lesbian Psychologies Collective. Urbana, IL: University of Illinois Press.

Hays, Sharon. 1996. *The Cultural Contradictions of Motherhood.* New Haven, CT: Yale University Press.

Ingraham, Chrys. 1994. "The Heterosexual Imaginary: Feminist Sociology and Theories of Gender." *Sociological Theory* 12(2):203–19.

Jackson, Stevi. 2006. "Gender, Sexuality and Heterosexuality: The Complexity (and Limits) of Heteronormativity." *Feminist Theory* 7:105–21.

Johnson, Paul. 2005. *Love, Heterosexuality, and Society.* New York: Routledge.

Kane, Emily W. 2006. "'No Way My Boys are Going to be Like That!': Parents' Responses to Children's Gender Nonconformity." *Gender & Society* 20:149–76.

Katz, Jonathan. 1995. *The Invention of Heterosexuality.* New York: Dutton.

Kessler, Suzanne and Wendy McKenna. 1978. *Gender: An Ethnomethodological Approach.* Chicago, IL: University of Chicago Press.

Kitzinger, Celia. 2005. "Heteronormativity in Action: Reproducing the Heterosexual Nuclear Family in After-Hours Medical Calls." *Social Problems* 52:477–98.

Lareau, Annette. 2002. "Invisible Inequality: Social Class and Childbearing in Black Families and White Families." *American Sociological Review* 67:747–76.

Laumann, Edward O., John H. Gagnon, Robert T. Michael, and Stuart Michaels. 1994. *The Social Organization of Sexuality: Sexual Practices in the United States.* Chicago, IL: University of Chicago Press.

Lewis, Amanda. 2003. *Race in the Schoolyard: Negotiating the Color Line in Classrooms and Communities.* New Brunswick, NJ: Rutgers University Press.

Loftus, Jeni. 2001. "America's Liberalization in Attitudes toward Homosexuality, 1973 to 1998." *American Sociological Review* 66(5):762–82.

Maccoby, Eleanor E. 1988. "Gender as a Social Category." *Developmental Psychology* 24:755–65.

Martin, Karin A. 1998. "Becoming a Gendered Body: Practices of Preschools." *American Sociological Review* 25:123–222.

———. 2005. "William Wants a Doll. Can He Have One?: Feminists, Child Care Advisors, and Gender-Neutral Child Rearing." *Gender & Society* 19:456–79.

Martin, Karin and Emily Kazyak. 2008. "Romance, Heterosexuality, and Potty-Humor: G-Rated Movies and the Sexual Socialization of Young Children." Unpublished manuscript, Department of Sociology, University of Michigan.

Martin, Karin A., Katherine Luke, and Lynn Verduzco-Baker. 2007. "The Sexual Socialization of Young Children: Setting the Research Agenda." Pp. 231–60 in *Advances in Group Processes: Social Psychology of Gender,* edited by S. Correll. Oxford, UK: Elsevier Press.

McGuffey, C. Shawn. 2005. "Engendering Trauma: Race, Class, and Gender Reaffirmation after Child Sexual Abuse." *Gender & Society* 19:621–43.

McGuffey, C. Shawn and B. Lindsay Rich. 1999. "Playing in the Gender Transgression Zone: Race, Class, and Hegemonic Masculinity in Middle Childhood." *Gender & Society* 13:608–27.

Miller, Patricia H. 2006. "Contemporary Perspectives from Human Development: Implications for Feminist Scholarship." *Signs* 31:445–69.

Moon, Dawne. 2005. "Discourse, Interaction, and Testimony: The Making of Selves in the U.S. Protestant Dispute over Homosexuality." *Theory and Society* 34:551–77.

Moore, Lisa J. 2003. "'Billy, the Sad Sperm with No Tail': Representations of Sperm in Children's Books." *Sexualities* 6:277–300.

Moore, Valerie A. 2001. "'Doing' Racialized and Gendered Age to Organize Peer Relations: Observing Kids in Summer Camp." *Gender & Society* 15:835–58.

Nolin, Mary J. and Karen K. Petersen. 1992. "Gender Differences in Parent-Child Communication about Sexuality: An Exploratory Study." *Journal of Adolescent Research* 7:59–79.

Plummer, Kenneth. 1995. *Telling Sexual Stories: Power, Change, and Social Worlds.* New York: Routledge.

Reisser, Paul. 1997. *Focus on the Family: Complete Book of Baby and Child Care.* Wheaton, IL: Tyndale House Publishers.

Renold, Emma. 2002. "Presumed Innocence: (Hetero)Sexual, Heterosexist and Homophobic Harassment among Primary School Girls and Boys." *Childhood* 9:415–34.

———. 2005. *Girls, Boys and Junior Sexualities: Exploring Children's Gender and Sexual Relations in the Primary School.* New York: RoutledgeFalmer.

Rich, Adrienne. 1980. "Compulsory Heterosexuality and Lesbian Existence." *Signs* 5:631–60.

Savin-Williams, Ritch C. 2005. *The New Gay Teenager.* Cambridge, MA: Harvard University Press.

Sedgwick, Eve K. 1990. *Epistemology of the Closet.* Berkeley, CA: University of California Press.

———. 1993. *Tendencies.* Durham, NC: Duke University Press.

Sexuality Information and Education Council of the United States (SIECUS). 2004. "Guidelines for Comprehensive Sexuality Education: Kindergarten–12th Grade, Third Edition" (http://www.siecus.org/_data/global/images/guidelines.pdf).

Singh, Ilina. 2004. "Doing their Jobs: Mothering with Ritalin in a Culture of Mother-Blame." *Social Science & Medicine* 59:1193–1205.

Skelton, Christine. 2001. *Schooling the Boys: Masculinities and Primary Education.* Philadelphia, PA: Open University Press.

Stein, Arlene. 1997. *Sex and Sensibility: Stories of a Lesbian Generation.* Berkeley, CA: University of California Press.

Thorne, Barrie. 1993. *Gender Play: Girls and Boys in School.* New Brunswick, NJ: Rutgers University Press.

Tobin, Joseph J. 2000. *"Good Guys Don't Wear Hats": Children's Talk about the Media.* New York: Teachers College Press.

Troiden, Richard R. 1993. "The Formation of Homosexual Identities." Pp. 191–217 in *Psychological Perspectives on Lesbian and Gay Male Experiences,* edited by L. D. Garnets and D. C. Kimmel. New York: Columbia University Press.

Van Ausdale, Debra and Joe R. Feagin. 1996. "Using Racial and Ethnic Concepts: The Critical Case of Very Young Children." *American Sociological Review* 61:779–93.

Wallis, Amy and Jo VanEvery. 2000. "Sexuality in the Primary School." *Sexualities* 3:409–23.

Ward, L. M. and Gayle Wyatt. 1994. "The Effects of Childhood Sexual Messages on African American and White Women's Adolescent Sexual Behavior." *Psychology of Women Quarterly* 18:183–201.

Weinger, Susan. 2000. "Economic Status: Middle Class and Poor Children's Views." *Children & Society* 14:135–46.

Witt, Susan D. 2000. "The Influence of Television on Children's Gender Role Socialization." *Childhood Education* 76:322–25.

6

"Your father wouldn't like it"

The social construction of heterosexuality in early childhood

Emily W. Kane

From their earliest years, children are surrounded by a variety of heteronormative influences, drawing them into a social world in which heterosexuality is valorized as a presumed personal identity and a privileged social category. While those influences begin outside children's peer worlds, they are reproduced and refined within peer worlds as well. In this chapter, I draw from my previous work and the work of other scholars to analyze some of the social forces that construct heterosexuality in early childhood, including schools, media, and peer cultures, before moving on to a particular focus on the role of parents.

The social construction of heterosexuality simultaneously involves sexuality and gender. Heteronormativity defines heterosexuality as the normative sexual orientation, and reinforces the foundation on which that socially constructed orientation is built: binary gender categories that are fashioned as fixed, mutually exclusive, opposite, biologically determined, and hierarchically ordered. Scholars and activists concerned with heteronormativity as a social structure recognize that an intersectional analysis is critical, taking into account how gender and sexuality based inequalities are inseparable from other dimensions of inequality such as race, class, nation, and ability. In early childhood, the arenas in which heteronormativity has been explored most frequently include education, media, and the family. For example, Martin et al. (2007) summarize extensive fieldwork in preschool settings, noting that they observed schools "that have as part of their curricular materials for children a 'wedding prop box'" or at which "holiday celebrations, like Valentine's Day, make use of heterosexual imagery in describing love to preschoolers, and that very young children pick up the vocabulary of 'boyfriend-girlfriend'" (p. 251). Gansen (2017) demonstrates the social construction of heteronormativity through observation in preschool classrooms as well, concluding that "before children have salient sexual identities of their own, children are beginning to make sense of heteronormativity and rules associated with sexuality through interactions with their teachers and peers in preschool" (p. 255). Myers and Raymond (2010) focus on schools in which children are just a few years older. They document "concerted heteronormative pressures" in educational institutions, "through curricula, teacher-student interaction, and the formal structuring of activities" (p. 169), but focus their investigation on the active agency of children in co-constructing heterosexuality. Through focus groups with girls in the early elementary grades, they conclude that white girls played a particularly influential role in group interactions through which girls learned that to be an "appropriate girl, they should perform heteronormativity for other girls" and thereby they "reinforced the gender binary in which girls are measured—and measure themselves—by their relationship to boys" (p. 185). Others have highlighted bullying as a peer process through which heteronormative pressures are constructed, with much work focused on older children but some addressing the primary/ elementary school years as well (e.g., Thornberg 2018, whose analysis explicitly recognizes intersecting inequalities of gender, sexuality, and race).

Along with schools and peers, media of various types have been studied in relation to heteronormativity in early childhood. Martin and Kazyak (2009) conduct a content analysis of G-rated children's films in which they persuasively reveal that within these texts, "heterosexuality is constructed through hetero-romantic love relationships as exceptional, powerful, magical, and transformative" (p. 315). Though heterosexuality is constructed as inevitable and ubiquitous, what is particularly striking is the way it is also constructed as exceptional and magical; it is both routine in its frequency, and extraordinary in its magical power to bring joy and fulfillment. Martin and Kazyak (2009) also document a less frequent but still highly consequential pattern: the way female bodies are the subject of the male gaze outside of hetero-romantic relationships in these films, through the exoticization of female characters of color by white male characters.

Wooden and Gillam (2014) interrogate representations of masculinity in Pixar movies, marketed to similarly young children and their families, and also find strong reinforcement of the gender binary and heterosexuality. Another relevant form of media analyzed by scholars is parenting advice books. For example, in one such analysis, Riggs (2008) argues that advice books for fathers are "informed by a range of heteronormative and homophobic assumptions about boys and masculinity" (p. 186). Like others who have studied gendered and sexualized discourse in parenting advice, Riggs (2008) is emphasizing not only the role played by media in distributing that advice, but also the pivotal role parents play in constructing children's gender and sexuality.

Parents and the social construction of heterosexuality

Parents are, of course, especially influential in children's early years, and their part in constructing heterosexuality throughout childhood has been documented in the literature. Martin's (2009) analysis of how mothers normalize heterosexuality with three- to six-year-old children appears in Chapter 5 of this volume. Focused on somewhat older children, McGuffey (2008) offers a nuanced account of how race and gender shape reinforcement of heterosexuality by parents of color whose sons have been sexually abused by men other than a parent. He argues that these parents tend to fear same-sex attraction as a potential outcome of the abuse, and thus "push and encourage their sons' participation into hegemonic forms of masculinity out of their desire for heterosexual boys" (p. 235), also noting that "anxiety over racial subordination . . . increases their investment in traditional gender reaffirmation" (p. 217). Further along the childhood life course, Solebello and Elliott (2011) document active encouragement of children's heterosexual orientation by heterosexual fathers of teenagers, especially for sons. Studies of gay parents find less emphasis on heteronormativity for children, though variations in surveillance based on race and class sometimes limit the openness LGBTQ parents feel in relation to childhood gender expectations (Averett 2016; Berkowitz and Ryan 2011). A new direction in the most recent literature on parental construction of childhood gender and sexuality addresses parents of transgender children, a topic that offers clear potential for exploring the disruption of heteronormativity, but that tends to focus on children beyond early childhood. I return to that recent literature and its implications at the end of this chapter.

My own previous work on parents and the social construction of gender offers a chance to focus in particular on early childhood, and on the way heterosexual fathers shape heteronormativity even for very young children. The remainder of this chapter draws on that previous work, based on qualitative interviews that I conducted with forty-two parents, each of whom had at least one three- to five-year-old child. I focused on that age range as one in which children develop their own sense of gender identity, and thus an age during which their actively expressed wishes and agency are a part of the context in which parents negotiate social expectations of gender. The parents in my study were all from the Northeastern United States, and varied in terms of race, class, gender, sexual orientation, and family structure. For recruitment, I posted announcements in local child care centers, parents' resource organizations, community colleges, local businesses, public housing projects, and I reached out through my own networks (though none of the participants were people I knew prior to the interviews). The process of participation included a brief written questionnaire, followed by a semi-structured interview. The interview began with questions asking interviewees to think back to a time before they had any plans to have children, and recall whether they had a preference for sons or daughters. Moving chronologically, interviewees were then guided through an exploration focused on one child in the three-to-five age range, though briefer questions were also asked about any other children they were parenting. For the focal child, questions started with any gender preferences during pregnancy or adoption/foster care waiting periods, moving into a discussion of the extent to which the child's gender shaped their efforts in decorating, buying clothing, and selecting toys during infancy. The bulk of the interview questions addressed current activities, toys, clothes, behaviors, and gender awareness of the focal child, and the parents' perceptions of the origins of these outcomes, as well as their feelings about their children's behaviors and characteristics in relation to gendered expectations. Interviews ended with some general questions regarding the desirability and feasibility of gender neutrality in childhood. Interviews were taped and transcribed verbatim, and took between one and two hours. Participants were paid a modest honorarium for their time and participation, and were assured of complete confidentiality.

The forty-two interviews include twenty-four mothers and eighteen fathers, from a range of family types (single-parent and two-parent families), class locations (from self-identification as poor/low income to upper-middle class), racial/ethnic groups (including white, Asian-American, and African-American interviewees), and sexual orientations (heterosexual parents, as well as both lesbian mothers and gay fathers). These parents' children include biological children, adopted children, step-children, and foster children. Interviewees' educational backgrounds ranged from less than high school to advanced graduate degrees, with the average years of formal schooling falling between high school graduate and college graduate. Ages ranged from twenty-three to forty-nine years, with the average age at thirty-five years. All of the men interviewed worked outside the home for pay. Among those in heterosexual partnerships, about one-third had a female partner in each of the following categories: full-time homemaker, employed outside the home part-time, and employed outside the home full-time. Among the mothers interviewed, about one-third were full-time homemakers, about one-fifth were employed part-time, and the remainder were employed full-time outside the home. Parents working outside the home employed a range of child care types, including day care centers, home day care, and in-home sitters. Interviewees averaged 2.5 children (with the mode being two), and were roughly evenly split among those having only daughters (26 percent), only sons (29 percent), or at least one of each (45 percent). The children on whom interviews focused included twenty-two sons and twenty daughters. More details of the data collection process and interviewee characteristics are available in a methodological appendix to Kane (2012).

Though I did not ask any questions explicitly about sexuality or sexual orientation, many of the questions focused on ways in which interviewees considered their children typical and atypical of their gender, framed around each interviewee's own definition of typicality. As a result, the kind of gender conformity associated with heteronormativity came up often, and spontaneous mentions of heterosexuality in particular came up sometimes as well.

Heteronormativity across configurations of parenting practice

The primary concepts that frame my analysis in *The Gender Trap* (Kane 2012) are beliefs about the origins of gendered childhoods (how parents balance biological and social explanations) and actions in relation to children's gender (how parents balance actions that reproduce and resist traditionally gendered outcomes). I also focus extensively on accountability, or the ways in which parents feel accountable to judgments by others regarding whether their children perform gender in normative ways.

On the basis of these distinctions, I identify five configurations of parenting practice. I use the term *naturalizers* to refer to parents who view gendered childhoods as rooted in nature and most of whose reported actions reproduce traditionally gendered patterns for their children. These parents sometimes report a sense of accountability to the social judgments of others, whether friends and family or more distant others, but the extent to which they report feeling judged tends to depend on whether their children veer away from traditional gender expectations or not.

Cultivators also report actions that reproduced gendered childhoods, but they view the origins of gendered outcomes as primarily social and tend to see reproducing those outcomes as an everyday part of their work as parents. They express little concern about the judgment of others, engaging in those reproductive actions not out of fear but out of a more routine sense of personal preference for a gender-divided world.

The middle configuration among the five I identify is the *refiners*, parents who hold a balance of biologically and socially deterministic beliefs about the origins of gendered childhoods and engage in a mix of reproductive and resistant actions in relation to childhood gendering. This group tends to feel accountable to potential and actual judgments from others, and that accountability shapes the way they strike the balance between reproductive and resistant actions.

Innovators lean toward seeing gender as socially constructed and engaging in resistant actions, with little concern for social judgments, while *resisters* adopt even more socially determinist beliefs and even more pointedly resistant actions, but with significant concern about accountability to others due to that greater resistance. In terms of heterosexuality and heteronormativity as specific topics within the much wider analysis I offer, I found that the

> majority of parents of both sons and daughters not only assumed that their children would grow up to identify as heterosexual, but they steered them in that direction through routine invocations of heterosexuality. *Resisters* were the only exception, with both gay and straight parents in that group diverging from the general tendency to assume and reinforce children's heterosexuality.
>
> *(Kane 2012, p. 208)*

Apart from *resisters*, the other four parenting types I identify, people who varied by race, class, sexuality, family structure, and political ideology, shared a common tendency to casually assume and interactionally construct heterosexuality as the inevitable orientation for their children. For example, Jerome (a pseudonym), a white, upper-middle-class, heterosexually partnered father classified as a *naturalizer*, repeatedly referred to one of his five-year-old son's friends from preschool as "his girlfriend, his little girlfriend" and spoke proudly of the way his son stands up to other boys if they are "bothering" his "girlfriend."

Gwen, a white, upper-middle-class, heterosexually partnered mother in the *cultivator* category, reported how "cute" she thinks it is that boys in her five-year-old daughter's preschool class have begun to discuss which girl they want to marry. Bob, another *cultivator* who is white, middle-class, and heterosexually partnered, noted how important it was to him that his five-year-old daughter can grow up to "be the executive in the board room and at the same time to be a very feminine woman in her personal life with her husband." This casually taken-for-granted assumption of heterosexual partnership being their children's future destiny (or in Jerome's case the framing of a small child's friendship as a heterosexual romance in the making) was evident among *refiners* and *innovators* as well. *Resisters* were, as noted, the exception, but in the other four groups, one-half to three-quarters of parents made these kinds of comments that assumed their sons and daughters identified or would identify as heterosexual (Kane 2012, p. 181). Such comments, of course, are part of the everyday lives of those children, helping to construct the assumed inevitability of heterosexual orientation.

Another specific finding relevant to the social construction of heterosexuality was the way in which sexuality was spontaneously mentioned by parents "in connection with implied or expressed links between gender nonconformity and non-heterosexual orientation" (Kane 2012, p. 208). At least a few parents from most of the types I identify made this kind of connection, again without any explicit questions focused on sexuality or sexual orientation. But it was absent among the *resisters*, and most common among parents categorized as *cultivators*. *Cultivators* are a logical group among whom to hear about heterosexuality as something they work to produce by encouraging normative gender performance since they are parents who viewed gender as rooted in nature, but also reported a variety of actions they take to craft gendered outcomes, and who had a strong preference for traditional gender divisions. For example, Cameron is a white, middle-class, heterosexually partnered father classified as a *cultivator*. His four-year-old son Ethan expressed some interest in activities and items that Cameron considered more typical for a girl, which bothered him. He reports that Ethan constantly asked for a Barbie doll, so finally Cameron and his wife "got him one, but even then it's got a sport theme, it's a basketball player theme . . . that makes me feel better, it's a more masculine type of Barbie." Especially relevant is Cameron's explanation for why he prefers his son not to want or have what Cameron calls "things that are meant for girls": "maybe I have some deep, deep, deep buried fear that he would turn out . . . well, that his sexual orientation would get screwed up." It is important to note the framing here, that having feminine "things" could possibly lead to a "screwed up" sexual orientation, a potential causal link that led Cameron to "steer (his son) away" from things he considers "meant for girls." Another *cultivator*, Derek, an Asian-American, middle-class, and heterosexually partnered father, also used the word "steer" to describe his response to some concern he feels about his three- and five-year-old sons' interest in more typically feminine items and activities. He noted that he would "like (his) sons to be more masculine," and expanded by talking about his five-year-old son's tendency to cry and withdraw from conflict rather than standing up for himself. Later in the interview, unprompted, he told me that "I guess you wonder if your kid's going to be gay" and "in the back of my mind, and I'm sure a lot of other guys' minds, that's why they'd push their children to the blue shirt over the pink shirt and things like that."

Some *naturalizers* also offered similar comments. Jerome, noted previously, explained that he was raising his son Jack "to be a boy, a man," and therefore would be disappointed if Jack grew up to identify as gay, linking sexual orientation and gender conformity directly. Jamie, another *naturalizer* and a white, low-income single parent, noted a similar concern about her three-year-old son: "if (my son) was acting feminine, I would ask and get concerned on whether or not . . . I would try to get involved and make sure he's not gay."

These examples of linking gender conformity and sexual orientation, and reporting parental action to manage nonconformity and thereby construct heterosexuality, also demonstrate another pattern in my analysis: when such links were made, it was almost always in reference to boys. Even some parents who reported no homophobia or heteronormativity, like white upper-middle-class lesbian mother Brianna, classified as a *refiner*, recognized this tendency in other parents:

> I think it's much more uncomfortable for parents of boys to tolerate their sort of sissy behavior than it is to tolerate tomboy behavior for girls." When I asked her why she thought that was so, she replied, "Homosexuality, the homosexuality issue. There's real fear there. You can be a tomboy, but there's not the fear you are going to be a lesbian, but if you're a boy and you tend to be a sissy, there's the fear that he's going to be a homosexual.

Brianna's analysis matches up well with claims advanced by researchers studying hegemonic masculinity. The fear she identifies is also mentioned in Martin's (2005) article analyzing expert advice on gender conformity in childhood. She contends that the presumption of heterosexuality, and implied links between gender nonconformity and sexual orientation, lead to a stalled revolution in terms of the extent to which many experts and parents are willing to encourage even minor crossing of typical gendered boundaries. Based on a content analysis of best-selling parental advice books, she concludes that heteronormativity limits the degree to which those experts support what she calls "gender neutral child rearing." Therefore, the opening up of gendered constraints requires a revolution in sexuality constraints too: "the success of a gender revolution may require a sexual revolution, which is still missing" (Martin 2005, p. 475).

An additional pattern evident in these examples is that heterosexual fathers are especially likely to report active efforts to craft their young sons' masculinity based on a personal concern about their eventual sexual orientation. Cameron, Derek, and Jerome all express a personal preference for their sons to be heterosexual, while Jamie, the one mother among the examples noted above, focuses more on the potential reactions of others and the societal discrimination her son might face were he to grow up to identify as gay. The quote I used in the title of this chapter, "your father wouldn't like it," was a comment offered by Karen, a white, working-class, heterosexually partnered mother of a five-year-old son. It was part of an explanation she gave her son when she declined to buy a toy he asked for, one she considered more typical for a girl. While she did not explicitly mention sexual orientation, her comment was typical of the concerns raised by quite a few other heterosexually partnered women as they policed their sons' gender conformity in response to anticipated negative responses from their male partners. There were several ways in which heterosexual fathers were implicated in reproducing hegemonic conceptions of masculinity.

> This is evident in the direct endorsement of this type of masculinity that many heterosexual fathers expressed, in the accountability to their male partners that many heterosexual mothers expressed, and in the accountability to the heterosexual world that all the gay and lesbian parents expressed.
>
> *(Kane 2012, p. 207)*

Beyond the gender trap

Though constrained by a deep sense of accountability to the everyday judgments of others, the group I classified as *resisters* did not report routine heteronormativity. Only five parents fell into this classification, but their responses were so notably different that they merited a separate category. Most of those differences related to specifics outside the focus of this chapter and this handbook, but the absence of any assumption that children would grow up to identify as heterosexual and routine actions steering children toward gender conformity as a path toward heterosexuality was one of the differentiating features of this group of parents. Two of these five parents were lesbians and one was a gay man, all white and middle- or upper-middle-class; the other two were heterosexually partnered mothers, one Asian American and middle class, the other white and lower-income. The only interview excerpt that I coded as even possibly heteronormative among these parents was a comment by Tanya, one of the lesbian mothers. Commenting on her hopes and fears for her two sons, ages one and four, she told me: "I want them to grow up to be kind to their girlfriends. I mean that in a lot of different ways, but including in regard to sex." This assumption of heterosexual orientation, though, was followed by another possibility: "And even if they end up having sex with men, whatever, I don't want them to be that sort of stereotypical rogue male." I argue that one might expect gay and lesbian parents to less routinely reinforce heteronormativity, but "neither of the two heterosexual parents in this category made that assumption, and Tanya, the only parent who nearly did so, is one of the gay parents" (Kane 2012, p. 182). Therefore, the way the *resisters* stand out for avoiding routine invocations of heteronormativity is not simply a matter of their sexual orientation, but connected instead to a broader approach to gender structures.

In the conclusion of *The Gender Trap*, I go on to summarize what I consider the implications of heteronormativity among the parents who did invoke it. The routine normalization of heterosexuality as inevitable, as well as fear of non-heterosexual orientation and the linking of gender conformity and sexual orientation especially for boys, all have implications for the way childhoods, and society more broadly, end up constrained by gender. These practices exact a price from boys who do not stick close to traditional expectation regardless of their eventual sexual orientation, and from boys who do stick close but based on fear of social judgments, whether that is their own fear or their parents' fear. "These fears and perceived links between gender and sexuality support dichotomous conceptions of gender and heteronormativity, marginalizing and silencing those who do not identify as heterosexual and exclusively one gender or the other" (Kane 2012, pp. 209–210). Homophobia is also reinforced by those fears and perceived links, along with discrimination, violence, and social exclusion. All of this adds up to "powerful synergies among dichotomous conceptions of gender, heteronormativity, and homophobia" (Kane 2012, p. 210), synergies that make it extremely difficult to loosen gendered restrictions and live outside a strictly binary approach to gender.

Such restrictions are loosened by the parents in my study who resist heteronormativity. And in the several years since my work on this topic was published, an emerging line of scholarship is shedding light on an even more dramatic loosening, among some parents of transgender children. Rahilly (2015) conducted qualitative interviews with twenty-four parents who considered their school-age children significantly gender variant and were not trying to steer those children back toward gender conformity. She argues that "until recently, raising a young child as transgender was culturally unintelligible" but this emerging group of parents represents "new modes of resistance to the normative transmission and regulation of gender practices" (Rahilly 2015, p. 338). Barron and Capous-Desyllas (2017) offer in-depth case studies of four transgender children, ages five to eight, whose parents are also supporting their transition. Though they identify significant obstacles and social judgment faced by these families, they also outline policy approaches that can broaden inclusion and equity for the increasing number of children identifying as transgender, and contribute to raising awareness of parents who allow and affirm their children's gender exploration and transition. Two recent books also explore transgender childhoods. Meadow (2018) and Travers (2018) both offer ground-breaking studies of transgender and gender variant children and their parents, offering even more in-depth consideration of this emerging social phenomenon in which some parents provide resources and encouragement of their children's agency as they seek gender transition or non-binary gender identity. This new and growing body of scholarship reveals the possibility for parents to play a transformative role in breaking down binary conceptions of sex and gender as natural and inevitably unfolding, and crafting new spaces for their children to live outside heteronormative constraints. Such progressive change clearly requires significant support and policy change from medical professionals, schools, social services, and the general public. But these works shed light on the way some parents are advocating for that support and change, working with their children to forge a path into new territory that could transform the constraints of gendered and heteronormative childhoods for transgender children and for all children as well.

Though this literature on transgender children and their families focuses on children from age five onward, some of the children began to identify as gender variant around age three. Taken together with the findings of my own research on parents of preschool children summarized in this chapter, this is a powerful reminder that early childhood is an important period for gendered constraints to be deepened or loosened. Parents alone cannot transform the social construction of gender in early childhood.

> Influenced by a diverse array of religions and cultures, as well as by expert advice, public policy and everyday accountability to others in interaction, parental approaches may be situated in the family, but they are part of a much broader process.
>
> *(Kane 2013, p. 56)*

But alongside, and in concert with or opposition to, those other social forces, parents have a critical role in broadening their children's gendered options and, along the way, reducing heteronormative constraints in society more broadly. And everyone can participate in that effort. From the increasing visibility of parents supportive of transgender childhoods to the way the #MeToo movement has prompted renewed media interest in raising feminist sons (see, for example, McGlynn 2018; Miller 2017; Rich 2018), we may be at a moment of real possibility. But realizing that potential requires broad action. One of the *resisters* noted above, Tanya, told me that she believes most parents "want a better world" for the children, and I argue that this better world includes the hope for a less narrow gendered path. Given the links between gender and sexuality noted earlier in this chapter and throughout this handbook, that less narrow path also opens up spaces relevant to the social construction of sexual orientation. Parents can open up those spaces, but so can all of us.

> Resistant analysis and acts, both large and small, can make a real difference, redefining gendered identities, shifting frameworks of accountability, and pressuring institutions from inside and out. Embracing those resistant analyses and acts, in ourselves and in our responses to those around us, offers a critical opportunity.
>
> *(Kane 2012, p. 218)*

References

Averett, K.H. (2016). The Gender Buffet. *Gender & Society*, 30(2), pp. 189–212.

Barron, C. and Capous-Desyllas, M. (2017). Transgressing the Gendered Norms in Childhood: Understanding Transgender Children and their Families. *Journal of GLBT Family Studies*, 13(5), pp. 407–438.

Berkowitz, D. and Ryan, M. (2011). Bathrooms, Baseball, and Bra Shopping: Lesbian Parents Talk about Engendering their Children. *Sociological Perspectives*, 54(3), pp. 329–350.

Gansen, H.M. (2017). Reproducing (and Disrupting) Heteronormativity: Gendered Sexual Socialization in Preschool Classrooms. *Sociology of Education*, 90(3), pp. 255–272.

Kane, E.W. (2012). *The Gender Trap: Parents and the Pitfalls of Raising Boys and Girls.* New York: New York University Press.

Kane, E.W. (2013). *Rethinking Gender and Sexuality in Childhood.* London: Bloomsbury.

McGlynn, D. (2018). In the #MeToo Era, Raising Boys to Be Good Guys. *New York Times.* Available at www.nytimes.com/(2018)/06/01/well/family/metoo-sons-sexual-harassment-parenting-boys.html [Accessed August 21, 2018].

McGuffey, C.S. (2008). Saving Masculinity: Gender Reaffirmation, Sexuality, Race, and Parental Responses to Male Child Sexual Abuse. *Social Problems*, 55(2), pp. 216–237.

Martin, K.A. (2005). William Wants a Doll, Can He Have One? Feminists, Child Care Advisors, and Gender-Neutral Child Rearing. *Gender & Society*, 19(4), pp. 456–479.

Martin, K.A. (2009). Normalizing Heterosexuality: Mothers' Assumptions, Talk, and Strategies with Young Children. *American Sociological Review*, 74(2), pp. 190–207.

Martin, K.A. and Kazyak, E. (2009). Hetero-Romantic Love and Heterosexiness in Children's G-Rated Films. *Gender & Society*, 23(3), pp. 315–336.

Martin, K.A., Luke, K.P., and Verduzco-Baker, L. (2007). The Sexual Socialization of Young Children: Setting the Agenda for Research. *Advances in Group Processes*, 24, pp. 231–259.

Meadow, T. (2018). *Trans Kids: Being Gendered in the Twenty-First Century.* Berkeley: University of California Press.

Miller, C.C. (2017). How to Raise a Feminist Son. *New York Times.* Available at www.nytimes.com/(2017)/06/02/upshot/how-to-raise-a-feminist-son.html [Accessed August 21, 2018].

Myers, K. and Raymond, L. (2010). Elementary School Girls and Heteronormativity: The Girl Project. *Gender & Society*, 24(2), pp. 167–188.

Rahilly, E.P. (2015). The Gender Binary Meets the Gender-Variant Child. *Gender & Society*, 29(3), pp. 338–361.

Rich, S. (2018). Today's Masculinity is Stifling. *The Atlantic.* Available at www.theatlantic.com/family/archive/(2018)/06/imagining-a-better-boyhood/562232/ [Accessed August 21, 2018].

Riggs, D.W. (2008). All the Boys Are Straight: Heteronormativity in Contemporary Books on Fathering and Raising Sons. *Thymos: Journal of Boyhood Studies*, 2(2), pp. 186–202.

Solebello, N. and Elliott, S. (2011). "We Want Them to Be as Heterosexual as Possible": Fathers Talk about Their Teen Children's Sexuality. *Gender & Society*, 25(3), pp. 293–315.

Thornberg, R. (2018). School Bullying and Fitting into the Peer Landscape. *British Journal of Sociology of Education*, 39(1), pp. 144–158.

Travers, A. (2018). *The Trans Generation: How Trans Kids (and Their Parents) are Creating a Gender Revolution.* New York: New York University Press.

Wooden, S. and Gillam, K. (2014). *Pixar's Boy Stories: Masculinity in a Postmodern Age.* Lanham: Rowman & Littlefield.

7

"Coming out"

Gender, (hetero)sexuality and the primary school

Emma Renold

Introduction: (hetero)sexualising the primary school

Since researchers have explored the school as a specific social and cultural arena for the production and reproduction of sexual and gendered identities, a number of ethnographic studies have begun to problematise and deconstruct dominant school-based sexual and gender identities (Epstein & Johnson, 1994, 1998; Haywood, 1996; Haywood & Mac an Ghaill, 1996; Redman, 1996; Hey, 1997). These studies, however, have predominantly focused on secondary schools, and, to date, there are very few ethnographic studies that locate the primary school as a key site in the production of sexual identities. Primary school studies have instead focused primarily on gender relations (Best, 1983; Clarricoates, 1987; Thorne, 1993; Jordan, 1995; Skelton, 1996, 1997; Francis, 1997) and rarely comment in detail on the dominance of sexuality in the construction of boys' and girls' gendered identities. Nor do they examine sexual relations with the same complexity that they use to explore gender relations. Only very recently has there been a focus on the primary school specifically in terms of its heterosexualising social processes (Epstein, 1997). This article goes some way to redressing this imbalance by illustrating how sexuality, and specifically heterosexuality, is part of the everyday experience in the worlds of primary school children and, furthermore, how heterosexuality underpins most interaction and identity work as they live out the gendered categories 'boy' and 'girl'.

Coming out: researching gender *and* sexuality

The data and analyses presented in this article derive from recently completed doctoral research exploring the salience of gender and sexuality through the accounts by, and observations of, boys and girls in their last year of primary school (see Renold, 1999). The fieldwork took place over a period of a year in two primary schools located in a small, semi-rural town in the east of England.[1] With little existing UK research into how children perceive and construct their gendered identities, I initially (summer, 1994) conducted a 6-week pilot study in two Year 6 [5th grade in the US] classrooms, with a view to identifying, using ethnographic methods, including participant observation, in-depth unstructured exploratory group interviews and focus groups,[2] what it means to occupy and live out the categories 'girl' and 'boy' at school. As in many ethnographic studies, the flexibility and reflexivity of the ethnographic process led to a shift in focus and the inevitable 'Pandora's box' indicative of qualitative research. From examining gender relations, I found myself increasingly exploring sexuality and, in particular, children's interpellation and induction into the processes of 'compulsory heterosexuality' (Rich, 1980) and the intersection and embeddedness of gender and sexuality.

'Coming out', the title for this section, was the phrase scribbled in my field notes as I witnessed the complex daily interactive network of heterosexual performances by both girls and boys as they negotiated their gendered selves. Moreover, by adopting methods that harnessed the 'children's standpoint' (Alanen, 1994), in which children could exercise some control over the focus of the research, previously unreported and private accounts of children's sexual cultures, described by Best (1983) as the 'third hidden curriculum', began to surface. What I offer in this article is an overview of the complex gender/sexual identity formations produced within and between boys' and girls' peer groups. More specifically, I examine the 'acting out' and experiencing of Judith Butler's (1990) 'heterosexual matrix' in which the real expression of masculinity and femininity is embedded within a presupposed heterosexuality. Thus, what follow are accounts by primary school children of how the compulsory nature of heterosexuality is experienced, negotiated and maintained.

Girls and heterosexuality

Embodying fashion: somatic and sartorial ideals

From my first days in the field, I became increasingly aware of the ways in which girls were investing in the production of their bodies as heterosexually desirable commodities. This involved embodying heterosexual somatic (bodily) ideals. Typical daily rituals included checking and regulating arms, legs, hips and thighs, positioning their bodies and others' as 'too fat' or 'too thin' and advocating the need to diet (see Bordo, 1990). Moreover, girls' bodies, as cultural texts, were read by their peers (male and female) almost wholly within a heterosexual framework of desirability:

ER:	Do any of you diet or watch what you eat?
Mandy and Kirsty:	Yeah yeah/
Harriet:	You don't need to Mand.
Mandy:	I do (*quietly spoken*).
ER:	Are you very worried about how thin or fat you are?
Sophie:	Errr no, not really (*sounds unsure*).
Mandy:	Yes yes yes yes yes/
ER:	But it does worry you though?
Mandy and Kirsty:	Yeah, very much.
ER:	Why you two?
Kirsty:	Dunno.
Mandy:	We're just worried about our legs particularly.
Kirsty:	Yeah.
ER:	Because of fashion or
Mandy:	Boys.
Kirsty and Mandy:	Boys.

[. . .]
ER: Does Todd (*Sophie's ex-boyfriend*) ever say anything about the way you look?
Harriet: Yeah he does he calls her/
Sophie: Yeah he says that I'm ugly when I'm not going out with him.
ER: Does he?
Harriet: Yeah but he says that she's really/
Sophie: He thought I had nice legs when I was going out with him.

What I want to emphasise here is not only how girls construct their femininity, or what might be better described as 'hyper-femininity' (McRobbie, 1978), through a specific, culturally coded somatic ideal, but how bodies are only desirable when, through the validation of others, they are heterosexualised. As Sophie recalls, "he thought I had nice legs when I was going out with him". In fact, the ideals that the girls worked with often bore no relation to actual/'real' body size. Sophie for example, was positioned as 'fat', 'ugly', 'thin' and 'pretty' within one school term. 'Attractiveness', it seemed, was contingent on being heterosexually desirable or involved in a heterosexual relationship.

Girls' body projects also involved sartorial expressions through what I have termed the 'flirty fashion' discourse.[3] This incorporated the wearing of mini-skirts, high heels or 'platforms' and a cosmetic culture in which the ultimate goal is being 'attractive' to the opposite sex. The following extracts illustrate the specialised knowledge required to access the 'flirty fashion' discourse and how girls perform their bodies as objects and subjects of heterosexual desire:

Tina: And you know I only wear a lipstick coz I think that eye shadow is a bit too over the top. Sometimes/I put really light colours just a little bit and you can't hardly see it but you feel good.
Danni: I know/
Sally: I put that peach and that white together, Tina I put that peach and that white together.
Tina: Mmm (*nodding approvingly*).
ER: So why do you like wearing it then?
Tina: Coz you like feel fashionable and/
Sally: You just sort of look prettier.
[. . .]
ER: But you're still conscious about how you look/like you still want to be fashionable?
Tina: Yeah yeah/
Sally: Well it depends really, because it depends where there are most boys then er
Danni: If Mosely (*a boy that Sally 'fancies'*) was walking down the street/and she looked really horrible she'd probably hide.
Sally: I'd get mega dressed up.
ER: You'd get mega dressed up?
Sally: Yeah.
ER: What would you wear then?
Sally: Don't know/
Danni: She'd probably wear her 'Love' top.

The girls in this extract took delight and pleasure in the projection of their desirability. Discussions about length of skirt, styles of shoes, combinations of make-up and glittery nail varnish and which lip balms would stain their lips pink very clearly marked these girls as highly visible within the school arena. By drawing ideas and influences from popular magazines such as *Shout, Sugar* and *Just 17*, which seemed to act as 'barometers of girlhood' (McRobbie, 1997), the official school uniform could be transformed to reflect dominant high street fashion, producing a range of unofficial school uniforms. Some of the aforementioned examples could be interpreted as girls internalising the 'male gaze' (see Holland *et al.*, 1998) in so far as they are regulating and producing femininities within normative heterosexual standards of desirability. Many, however, achieved a real sense of agency and power in their new-found 'sexy' bodies, particularly, it could be argued, when being 'sexy' contradicted official (childhood) 'innocent schoolgirl' discourses (Walkerdine, 1996).

A major contradiction in official and unofficial discourses surrounding the production of 'girls' in the primary school is the ambivalent attitude towards sexual knowledge and practice, and notions of an 'innocent' and 'protected childhood'. For example, heterosexuality and heterosexual practices could be actively promoted at the school disco (Rossiter, 1994), yet similar displays of sexual awareness during the school day would, and did, cause concern and were deemed inappropriate. Furthermore, girls with rounded hips, almost fully developed breasts and who were aware of and used their sexuality (often to attract boys) within the school were sometimes treated as sexually deviant. One girl, for example, was referred to me (privately) by her class teacher as a 'tart' because she was openly displaying and enjoying her sexuality with other boys and girls. Thorne (1993), using Douglas's (1966) concept of pollution, also discovered this in her study:

> In our culture we draw sharp divisions between 'child' and 'adult', defining child as relatively asexual . . . and the adult as sexual . . . charged with sexual meaning, fully developed breasts seem uncomfortably out of place on the body of individuals who are still defined as children . . . a sense of pollution derives . . . from the violation of basic lines of social structure.
>
> *(Thorne, 1993, p. 143)*

I would also add, however, that the majority of girls who 'violated' the adult/child binary were not those who possessed pubescent/'adult' bodies, but those who enjoyed using their bodies in a sexual way, 'developed' or not. However, such erotic sexual images and signs present in the 'flirty fashion' and cosmetic cultures are often unspoken and under-researched in primary school studies, although the notion of children possessing sexual knowledge or engaging in sexual activity has provoked wider media debates in the form of moral panics. The next section further explores how some girls within the school are inscribed by discourses more indicative of research on adolescent girls and women.

'Tarty but not too tarty': contradictions in the production of a heterosexual girl

Rossiter (1994, p. 6) argues that the male gaze is an unchangeable ideal and states that 'the girls must obey the rules of discourse that are themselves contradictory'. As the next few extracts illustrate, one of the difficulties the girls faced was being 'tarty, but not too tarty':

(discussing fashionable clothing)

Claire:	I don't like being left out.
Trudy:	You don't want to like, erm, go too far looking like out of the/
Anabel:	*I don't want to look too/tarty*

Trudy: *But/you want to look a bit tarty*
ER: So you want to look attractive but not too tarty?
Al: Yeah yeah/
Anabel: Yeah that's it.
[. . .]
Carrie: I'm not being horrible, but have you seen Trudy's skirt, it's her five-year-old sister's . . . it's like up here (*draws an invisible line well above her knee*).
ER: And you think that's too short?
Carrie: Yeah.
ER: Why have girls started wearing short skirts?
Hannah: Because one person does/then everybody else does.
Carrie: They like to show off their legs.
ER: Why?
Carrie: Coz they want to impress the boys I suppose, like Trudy when she bends down you can see her bum.
Hannah: People really dress up.
Carrie: Yeah Trudy does, she puts blusher and make-up and eye shadow and lipstick.
Janine: She gets carried away with make-up.
ER: Do people think she goes over the top, does everyone?
Carrie: Some people say she's a tart.
ER: Is she?
Carrie: No.
Hannah: Like it happened to Debbie but it blew over.
ER: What happened to Debbie?
Hannah: People calling her a tart/because she wore her skirt up there.
Carrie: Did they? Did they?
ER: So who would? Other girls/or boys as well?
Carrie and Hannah: Girls.
Janine: Girls are bitchy.
ER: How do you know which length skirt to wear/without being called a tart?
Carrie: I think it's just above your knee.
Janine: Or just below.
Carrie: Just above, coz if it's like that it's too
Hannah: Yeah—not like that (*hitches her skirt up well above the knee*).

These extracts echo the sexual double standard that Cowie & Lees (1981), Lees (1987, 1993) and Hey (1997) discovered when teenage girls discussed their sexual reputations. However, comments surrounding 'tarty' and 'tart' refer not to sexual activity but to sexual identities and performances (Lees, 1993). The girls in the extracts stress the difficulty and constant negotiation involved in positioning themselves as fashionable and desiring a fashion that at one moment rendered them attractive and at another labelled them a 'tart' in the regulation of their bodies and their bodily expression. I was particularly struck with the finding that it was the girls themselves doing most of the positioning. However, Rossiter (1994, p. 11) also notes how 'girlfriends were the harshest critics and potential sources of abandonment'. Both through self-surveillance and surveillance of others, the girls seemed to be regulating what Hey (1997, p. 128) describes as the 'socially coercive presence of the male gaze', where discourses of hyper-femininity are bound by the ambivalent notion of 'tart/y'. Ambiguities and inconsistencies surrounding the production of girls as sexual beings is discussed further in the following section as some girls invest in one of the most prestigious legitimators of femininity and heterosexuality; the subject position of 'girlfriend'.

Girlfriends and going out: love letters, messengers and mediators

The study on which this article is based contributes to a growing number of studies which highlight the salience of the heterosexual positions of girlfriend and boyfriend, particularly towards the later years of primary schooling (Thorne & Luria, 1986; Thorne, 1993; Redman, 1996; Adler & Adler, 1998). Breaking the myth that heterosexual relations symbolise entry into 'adolescence', Epstein and others note how 6-year-olds date, dump and two-time and how 4- and 5-year-olds practise heterosexuality (Walkerdine, 1990; Epstein, 1997; Connolly, 1998). This study is no exception.

Heterosexual activity involved a complex daily interactive network, from kissing in the playground or cloakroom, computerised matchmaking diaries, secret love letters, and various tokens of affection (such as teddy bears branded with red hearts on their chests to chocolate love hearts), to blind date competitions, an 'agony aunt' problem-solving magazine and even a telephone 'love line'. Within and outside the school, the heterosexualisation and sexual regulation of girls (and boys) bodies was also constructed through discursive practices such as 'going out', 'dumping' and 'fancying'. Despite the active connotation of the phrase 'going out', couples rarely went anywhere. 'Going out' was a particular discourse which signified and made available the subject positions, 'boyfriend' and 'girlfriend'. For most girls and boys, it also signified monogamy and for a few, legitimate sexual activity, often no more than kissing and holding hands. Some examples follow:

ER:	So what about you Kirsty?
Mandy:	She's going out with Robby, big time, they can't keep their hands off each other (*they laugh*).
Kirsty:	Shut up/
ER:	And before you were going out with/
Kirsty:	James.
ER:	And is it quite serious? (*with new boyfriend*)
Kirsty:	Mmm.
Mandy:	Yeah, you should see them at the park.
ER:	More physical than with James is it?
Kirsty:	Yeah James is immature, well Robby can be/
Mandy:	You should see them at the park.
ER:	(*I laugh*) Is this out of school?
Kirsty:	Yeah, over there (*points behind the school*).
ER:	I don't suppose you can get up to much in school/
All:	(*They laugh*)
Mandy:	Yes . . . mmmmmm.
[. . .]	
Harriet:	Robby's a show-off.
Mandy:	Kirsty don't care, she just wants his body (*Sophie laughs out loud*).
ER:	So do you fancy him physically quite a lot?
Kirsty:	(*Nods vigorously*)
Mandy:	She does.
ER:	What about Pete?

Mandy: (*Laughs and nods*)
ER: OK, what about you two?
Mandy: They're single.
[. . .]
Looking towards the end of the field I see Kirsty, Neil, Mandy and Pete. They are both lying down next to each other, coupled up, facing each other. Neil has now moved on top of Kirsty, straddling her. He then lies on top of her and they start kissing. The two ladies on dinner duty are chatting together approximately 100 metres away. They do not notice Kirsty and Neil. Kirsty then pushes Neil off and trips up Mandy. They trip each other up and then settle back down in their pairs. Neil gets up and does a cartwheel and then swings his hips in a thrusting movement towards Kirsty, they all start laughing.

Surprisingly few girls (seven) were actively going out with boys on a regular basis. Much of the heterosexual activity involved heterosexual gossip networks (who fancied who) and messengers who mediated and relayed love letters, dumping letters and proposals such as 'will you kiss . . .' or 'will you go out with . . .'. Interviews rarely concluded without some discussion of current or past heterosexual relationships. Strikingly, every girl in the study, at some time, positioned herself firmly as heterosexual. Some girls delved back to their infant days. Some constructed fantasy boyfriends. The pressure to story oneself as heterosexually desirable was overwhelming and even involved girls 'going out' with boys who were verbally abusive to them. One girl, Erica, had a boyfriend who routinely called her a 'slag' and a 'slut'. Another girl, Tina, admitted that she would go out with boys she did not 'fancy'. For many, the pressure to perform as heterosexually desirable and to access the position of girlfriend was too overwhelming to resist, so fundamental, it seemed, were heterosexual performances in the construction of and investment in a 'proper' femininity.

The power (?) of love: dumping, being dumped and heterosexual harassment

There were some girls in the study who found their positions as 'girlfriends' and their hetero/sexual knowledge as particularly powerful. Two girls took great delight in challenging the male gaze with a sexual female gaze, with offers of future sexual encounters or relationships to often less desirable, 'effeminate' boys. Other girls, as the following extract reveals, experienced a great deal of power from being able to terminate or 'dump' relationships:

ER: Do the boys get really upset if you dump them?
Tina: No, they just act all tough but I think they're really hurting deep down inside.
ER: What do you mean by acting tough?
Carrie: They say, 'Oh who cares I was going to dump her anyway'.
Sally: Yeah, that's what, that's exactly what Philip said.
ER: Do you have more power if you dump them?
Sally: Yeah you feel like ha-ha-ha.

Dumping (common to both schools) was a time when partners asserted their dominance. There was always a struggle/race to be the first to deliver the 'you're dumped' message. Many girls viewed relationships as 'not serious' and changed their boyfriends quite frequently, much to many boys' dismay. For some, heterosexual relationships often seemed the only domain in the school where they felt they had power over the boys. It was one area where they could assert their dominance. Thus, using boys was not just a way of exploring their sexuality but an area where they could assert their dominance in an unequal field of gender relations, and possibly undermine 'traditional' heterosexual masculinities.

For others, however, being 'dumped' was a hurtful and emotional experience. Skeggs (1997, p. 115) similarly explains that although heterosexual encounters 'offered a space for hedonism, autonomy, camaraderie, pleasure and fun', they were 'simultaneously regulating and generating insecurities' and unhappiness. These unhappy experiences filtered into classroom/working contexts and consolement parties, where friends rallied round. Although some break-ups could be amicable, others could be verbally abusive, as with Sophie's break-up with Todd and his derogatory comments about her body. Other common painful cases included boyfriends choosing other girls over them.

Moreover, while learning how their bodies and new-found sexual knowledge can be exciting, pleasurable and a source of power in particular contexts, girls were also learning how their bodies could also be both threatening and a site of potential and actual danger. During a final interview, three girls disclosed their experiences of sexual harassment, both within and beyond the school gates. However, due to fear of conflict, ridicule and embarrassment, their disclosure not only remained untold, but unchallenged, thus reproducing the boys' behaviours as 'normal' and 'natural'. Such experiences resonate with the well-documented pervasiveness of heterosexual harassment within secondary schools (Jones, 1985; Wolpe, 1988; Halson, 1989; Jones & Mahony, 1989; Kenway & Fitzclarence, 1997) but are underresearched within primary schools (although see Clark, 1990 and Renold, 1999).

Top-girls[4] and tomboys: alternative femininities and heterosexuality

Not all girls invested in the hyper-femininity and heterosexuality discussed so far. Some girls constructed their gender identities by differentiating from 'girlie' femininities and challenged the 'male gaze' through embodiments of alternative dress and fashion. The following accounts explore how some girls' views destabilised the gendered status quo:

Hayley: I wouldn't do that, I wouldn't want to look like that coz they're so skinny and I wouldn't want to be anorexic or anything/
Jo: No coz a lot of people go anorexic just to look like the models.
ER: So you're quite wary of that are you?
All: Yeah.
Harriet: I don't care what they/look like, I look like I wanna look like.
Jo: I don't care what they look like/

The challenge of dominant bodily ideals led some girls to a kind of somatic flexibility that challenged dominant body discourses and provided a discursive space within which they could transform dominant notions of (bodily) femininity. It can be suggested that their critique of somatic idealism led to moments of freedom, choice and agency to 'be' and to 'look' exactly how they liked. However difficult it was to achieve, it was not impossible, and became a source of strength and independence (from dominant 'body' discourses) for some girls. Such transformations and alternative feminine performances were particularly marked in their style of dress:

Harriet: I just wear jeans and stuff/
Amanda: Some people like something that's comfy and then some people think 'oh I've got to look like tarty'/

Harriet: Yeah going around and getting all the boys around you.
ER: So you don't feel like that at all?
Harriet: No, if boys like you then they like you for the way you are not coz of how you look or how fashionable you are.
ER: What about you Amanda, do you feel the same or not?
Amanda: Yeah the same because you can't, I mean the boys can't fancy you like just coz you've got good clothes on/
Harriet: Yeah, they fancy you just . . . they should go out with the clothes not you (*laughs*).
[. . .]
Amanda: . . . we don't really care/
Harriet: We don't care very much about what we look like/
Amanda: I don't care whether I look fashionable or not and she does/she like puts make-up on just to go to like Tesco's (*talking about sister*).

The girls (Harriet and Amanda) in these extracts have rejected the 'flirty-fashion' of the majority of girls, favouring instead 'comfy' over 'tarty'. Their style could be described as 'sporty', swapping high heels for trainers and cycling shorts (under their skirts) for mini-skirts. Disliking and rejecting the notion that bodies are only heterosexual objects of desire for (predominantly male) others, when Harriet says "they should fancy you, not your clothes", their sporting fashion does not overtly signify their sexuality, but fitness, comfort, practicality and perhaps, most of all, their flight from 'girlie' femininities. Thus, it could be suggested that their choice of clothes symbolised rejection of dominant heterosexual discourses as much as it rejected dominant fashion and body discourses.

Resisting and/or rejecting hyper-feminine discourses and practices, however, only seemed possible through active heterosexual performances and competencies (see also Hey, 1997). Although they did not 'throw themselves into romance' (Davies, 1982), there were moments when they were subject to the patriarchal surveillance of the male gaze (almost literally) when all four of them waited for 3 days for one boy, Pete, to pick one of them for his girlfriend. Girls who resisted hyper-feminine discourses but who did not engage in heterosexual practices or who were not positioned as heterosexually desirable were denigrated and rendered 'non-girls', signified by insults such as 'weirdos' and even 'boys' (Renold, 1999). Thus, it seemed that alternative femininities could only be constructed if girls projected and secured their heterosexuality.

A significant departure from the hyper-feminine heterosexuality of the 'girlie-girls' was that boys were not solely pursued or perceived as potential boyfriends. Harriet neatly summed this up when she declared that "boys aren't just for boyfriends and girls aren't just for girlfriends". However, many of the girls reported the difficulty of mixed-sex platonic relationships (see also Clarke, 1990; Thorne, 1993; Rossiter, 1994):

Harriet: The other people on the table, all I do is talk to them, I don't want to be boyfriends or girlfriends or anything.
Mandy: Yeah.
Harriet: Like Pete, her boyfriend (Mandy), I just to talk to him, it's not . . . he's just like a friend, not boyfriend or girlfriend . . . coz you need some boys to talk to sometimes, not just all girls all the time but you don't want to get in a . . . like a relationship with them . . . but you still do.

Thus, even at this age and even before sexual activity is involved, the pressure to heterosexualise mixed-sex interactions is very strong, thus preventing the development of boys' and girls' friendships. The only girl in the study who successfully managed to interact with boys (through football and friendships) was Erica, a self-defined tomboy. However, towards the end of Year 6, even she began to feel the pressures of compulsory heterosexuality, with her public disclosures of elaborate romantic dreams about older boys. The demise of the 'tomboy' subject position and the experiences of Harriet and her friends' mixed-sex friendships signals all too clearly how the heterosexual matrix underscores most boys' and girls' gender identities and interactions with an increasing pressure as girls reach the end of their primary school years. As other studies are beginning to illustrate, however, boys and men are also subject to the heterosexual matrix and the 'male gaze', which similarly regulates and constitutes their sexual and gender identities (Mac an Ghaill, 1994; Connolly, 1998; Holland *et al.,* 1998).

Boys and heterosexuality

There has been a growing volume of educational research into the production of male heterosexualities within the secondary and post-16 sectors (Mac an Ghaill, 1994, 1996; Kehily & Nayak, 1996, 1997; Haywood, 1996). However, with a few exceptions (Redman, 1996; Epstein, 1997), there is a lack of critical and detailed exploration of the diversity and ambiguities surrounding boys' heterosexual cultures within primary school research. This section, following Mac an Ghaill (1994) and Connell (1995), explores how hegemonic masculine performances are inextricably tied to dominant notions of heterosexuality. Yet, where a legitimate femininity involved successful heterosexual performances, hegemonic masculinity could be secured through the subject position of 'boyfriend' *and* through the discourses and practices of fighting and football (Renold, 1997). Nevertheless, with the pressure for girls to secure boyfriends and the status of 'boyfriend' as a key signifier of hegemonic masculinity, the majority of boys invested, albeit tenuously, in the production and projection of their heterosexuality. The following accounts reveal the complex ways in which boys construct, define and maintain their heterosexual identities through compulsory heterosexuality, misogyny and homophobia (Mac an Ghaill, 1994) and how integral heterosexual performances are to the production of proper 'boys'.

Girls and girlfriends: fears, frustrations and shattered fantasies

Over the year, nine out of a total of 21 boys publicly engaged in 'fancying', 'asking girls out' and being 'boyfriends'. Although its acceptable and assumptive status created pressures to conform for boys and girls, 'coming out' as heterosexual was, for boys, often a complex and contradictory process fraught with fears and frustrations:

Liam: Aaron hangs around with Kirsty.
Aaron: I don't.
Liam: Yeah, Aaron hangs around with Kirsty.
Aaron: I don't, I play footy.
Liam and Martin: Aaron fancies Kirsty.
Liam and Martin: Aaron fancies Kirsty, Aaron fancies Kirsty, Aaron fancies Kirsty, Aaron fancies Kirsty/
ER: OK OK (*they quieten down*) . . . (*Aaron picks up the tape recorder*)
Aaron: I hate Kirsty's guts.

Liam: All right, Aaron doesn't really fancy her but he does, he did a few years, a few weeks ago.
Aaron: I, I've been out with her three times but er, but/
Liam: He likes her but/
Aaron: But she's a fat cow.

Competing discourses surrounding the sexually innocent child and the sexual adolescent created contradictions and conflicts for many girls. Boys' contradictions, however, lay in their ambivalent attitude towards proximity to girls, which could, at any given time, give rise to teasing behaviours associated with fear of the 'feminine' and/or an expression and confirmation of boys' heterosexual masculinity. Teasing and ridicule often led to misogynistic discourses and the objectification of girls ("fat cow"). In an attempt to resecure 'masculinity', boys would draw on alternative hegemonic discourses and generate examples like Aaron's comment (in response to being teased about fancying Kirsty): "no I don't, I play footy". The following extract further illustrates the confusions and anxieties when heterosexual relationships were secured:

ER: What do you think has been the hardest thing to cope with being a Year Six?
Colin: Girls.
ER: Martin?
Martin: SATS.
Colin: Girlfriends.
Martin: Yeah, coz if you have a girlfriend you have everyone saying 'oh can you come and kiss me/, can you come and kiss meee' (*singsong*).
ER: And you don't want to?
Colin: NO.
[. . .]
Colin: On the practice walk, Samantha asked him out.
ER: Did she?
Darren: Yeah but now she wants to go out with Adrian.
ER: So what happened to the other girls, did they dump you/or did you?
Darren: They dumped me, they always dump me, it's not fair.
Colin: They always dump me.
[. . .]
ER: What about you Aaron?
Aaron: I did have Claire but she's a cow.
ER: Why is she a cow?
Aaron: Because she always uses me, the last time she used me/
Liam: Go on, and let's get the popcorn.
ER: What happened last time?
Aaron: Well when I was going out with her, I, I, she dumped me right, and I go, 'why did you dump me?' and she didn't say anything and about an hour later she goes, 'I was using you anyway'.

Some boys were teased for not having a girlfriend. However, for the majority of boys, who sporadically engaged in heterosexual practices of 'fancying' and 'going out', these relationships were riddled with a combination of unease and tension. When asked what were the most difficult times during their final year at primary school, Martin, Colin and Darren said "girlfriends". Martin, for example, expressed his anxiety of heterosexual behaviour, not wanting to 'kiss' his girlfriend. Alternatively, Darren's frustration at "always being dumped" positioned him as powerless and he viewed girls as merciless manipulators ("they just use you"). Neither one of these boys experienced the dominant and powerful subject position associated within the wider heterosexual discourses of patriarchy. They, and others, were confronted with girls who would dump them if they so desired.

"I play football instead": compulsory heterosexuality?

ER: So what about you three, any girlfriends David? (*shakes his head*) Ryan? (*shakes his head*) Jake? (*shakes his head*) So no girlfriends/
Ryan: I got up to novice two in carting.
[. . .]
Darren: I still like a girl I used to go out in the comp with called Amanda.
ER: I remember . . . what about you Timothy?
Timothy: I haven't got a girlfriend.
ER: Would you like one?
Timothy: No, not really/
Pete: No he's more into football.
ER: You're more into football are you?
Timothy: (*Nods*)

Not all boys engaged in heterosexual boyfriend/girlfriend relationships. Some expressed a desire for a 'proper' relationship proceeding primary school, which involved intimate sexual activities. A couple of boys stressed that they were "too young" or "not ready" to have a girlfriend. Their position as (non-sexual) 'children' within primary school discourses seemed to make acceptable the absence of heterosexual performances. However, unless they successfully performed as 'tough-guys', 'footballers' or were 'sporting competent', their 'heterosexuality' would be called into question and they would often be 'homosexualised' and denigrated as 'gay' (explored further in the following section). In fact, the foregoing extracts emphasise the two routes through which boys defined their hegemonic masculinity; girlfriends and sport (Connolly, 1994). Pete, for example, offers the latter ("he's more into football") as if the two subject positions of boyfriend and footballer are interchangeable. In a similar way, Ryan's positioning, as successful 'sportsman', immediately follows his negative response to having a girlfriend. Being competent at sport was not always a sufficient signifier for heterosexual masculinity.

Misogyny, homophobia and heterosexual assertions

In the pursuit of hegemonic masculinity, undermined by the refusal of girls to occupy passive and sexual subject positions, heterosexual identifications were defined through misogynistic and homophobic discourses, and heterosexual fantasies. The following four extracts illustrate the overt ways in which boys formed their heterosexual identities. These included the following:

(1) Symbolic sexual performances
Juliet starts singing a song when pupils have been told to be quiet. Darren spins round on his chair and leans forward in front of Juliet. He then mouths the word 'fuck' at her, I am not sure why. He looks annoyed at something.

(2) Public sexual innuendoes

Mrs Fryer tries to quieten the class down. She asks them to put their lips together. Adrian shouts out 'oo err, I'm not kissing everyone in this class'. Many of the boys and girls start laughing. Mrs Fryer looks at me, smiles, rolls her eyes and gives Adrian a long look (of disapproval?).

(3) Sexual storytelling

Jake is telling Ryan a story concerning Nick Park's characters, 'Wallace and Grommit'. I overhear the sentence, 'yeah, and Wallace is fucking a sheep covered in Mustard and he's going "uh uh uh uh" ' (Jake mimes fucking a sheep). They both burst into laughter.

. . .

Jake is laughing and joking with his friends. He tells them with a serious, but cocky face, 'I had Pamela Anderson in my bedroom last night'. He then explains how he has a picture of Pamela Anderson directly above his bed. They all fall about laughing again.

(4) Sexual objectification of girls (and women—see earlier)

ER: So what about you Darren?

Pete: Well, he's been out with Mandy, I mean, not Mandy, I mean, er er Victoria about three times in the past three months init? Or something like that and once he went out with her for about a month didn't ya?

Darren: Mmm.

ER: What happened, why aren't you seeing her any more?

Pete: Because she, because he called her a fucking bitch and/

Darren: I . . . I just always get in a stress over some things, like I was in a stress that time/ and I don't know why.

These extracts parallel Mac an Ghaill's findings in so far as the boys' 'sex talk' and sexual performances seemed 'publicly to validate their masculinity to their friends' (and, as extracts 1 and 2 illustrate, to other girls in their class) and went some way to reinforcing dominant heterosexual masculinities, while subordinating femininities. Such performances, particularly their misogyny and sexual objectification of women, also went some way to reinstating boys' heterosexual dominance, often undermined and denied through conventional and 'real' boyfriend/girlfriend relationships. Further heterosexual assertions included overt homophobia and essentialist naturalised discourses surrounding homosexual practices:

As Colin walks into the classroom, he clips Aaron around the head. Aaron responds with 'get off ba-by' to which Colin, horrified, shouts, 'urgh, you gay'. Aaron laughs this off and tells me about the latest fight between two girls in the playground.

. . .

ER: When you say gay Jake, what do you mean by that?

Jake: You know, like/really sad.

Sean: A bender (*Sean, Ryan and Jake laugh*)/

Ryan: And you can sound gay can't you/

David: Simon (*peer*)/he sounds gay.

Ryan: Our next door neighbour/

[. . .]

Jake: You know that 'supermarket sweep' (*game show*)?

ER: Yeah.

Jake: Well, there was this man on there/

David: And he (*host of show*) goes, 'you're really pretty aren't you'.
Jake: Yeah, and he won it right, about £2000 and he goes up to him and he can't stop kissing him (*laughing*), he kisses him about 2000 times/
Ryan: Yeah that's like Michael Barrymore/
Jake: Yeah and/he smacked Michael Barrymore in the other day/
Sean and Ryan: Yeah (*they all cheer and clap*)/
David: Who did?
ER: Why is that good?
Sean: Coz he's gay.

Discourses of homophobia were expressed vehemently by boys who did not engage in overt heterosexual boyfriend/girlfriend relationships and more frequently than by boys who *did* 'have girlfriends' and who *were* 'going out'. At times, these discourses were particularly disturbing, such as the explanation, "coz he's gay", offered to my questioning of their delight at Michael Barrymore being "smacked in". This appeared as little less than an advocacy of 'queer bashing'. Aside from homophobic narratives communicated in the group interviews, homophobic performances infiltrated classroom and playground interactions. These were directed at boys who got too close to other boys and those boys who failed or chose not to access hegemonic masculine discourses/practices. Differentiating oneself, and subordinating homosexualities, by shouting out or positioning other boys as 'gay' were all ways in which these boys asserted and attempted to make coherent their heterosexual identities. The extracts also reveal how homophobic performances are more about gender than sexual practices and are a means of regulating and policing the boundaries of hegemonic heterosexual masculinities, as Kehily & Nayak, quoting Butler, explain:

> We see homophobic performance as a style which gives masculinity the appearance of substance, produced through the 'regulatory fiction of heterosexual coherence'.
>
> *(Butler, 1990, p. 137, cited in Kehily & Nayak, 1996, p. 225)*

The pressure and struggle that some boys experienced in forming heterosexual relationships and their perceived powerlessness (being dumped, being used) produced contradictory heterosexual identities (Holland *et al.*, 1998). Thus, homophobic performances and misogyny seemed to offer a way of producing 'heterosexual coherence', which in turn signified a coherent 'masculine' identity.

Conclusions

While by no means exhausting the complex ways in which children forge their sexual identities, I have shown throughout how girls and boys are subject to the pressures of a compulsory heterosexuality and in different ways and to different ends struggle in the constitution and conflation of their gendered and sexual identities. The majority of girls in the study produced their femininity through dominant notions of heterosexuality, policed through the surveillance and regulation of their own and others' bodies and behaviours. Those who challenged 'girlie' hyper-femininities, by rejecting the notion that girls exist solely for the objectification and pleasure of boys, seemed only to be successful, however, when they were accompanied by competent heterosexual performances and relationships. Interestingly, there was no simple powerful/powerless binary divide in the boyfriend/girlfriend positions, but the sexual double standard, however, remained in the contradictory and arbitrary discourses of 'tarty' and 'tart'.

Moreover, the disclosures of sexual harassment and feelings of anxiety and despair for those girls whose femininity pivoted on heterosexual desirability and the securing of boyfriends illustrate the persistence of age-old sexual inequalities.

For the majority of boys in the study, overt heterosexual practices, such as being a boyfriend, were not the only routes to the formation of their masculine identities. Fighting and football were alternative signifiers, thus challenging the notion of compulsory heterosexuality for boys. However, not to participate in sporting or fighting practices involved being subject to ridicule and ostracism in the form of heterosexist and homophobic jibes and insults (Renold, 1997). Furthermore, the conflation of femininity and homosexuality rendered proximity to girls (even within the discourse of heterosexuality) a fragile and ambiguous experience. Many boys resorted to defining and asserting their heterosexuality through discourses, gestures and practices of misogyny and homophobia.

In light of these findings, however, raising awareness of children's sexuality free from sensationalism and scandal will be no easy task given the current and past surge of restrictive, prohibitive and oppressive sound-bites and clauses (Epstein & Johnson, 1994, 1998). This article, for example, was written against a backdrop of governmental moralising rhetoric surrounding sexual scandals of pregnant 12-year-old schoolgirls and a call for the values of marriage (and thus, by default, the institution of heterosexuality) to be part of the primary school curriculum (Dennis, 1999). On a more positive note, however, recent debates, such as the National Union of Teachers' response to government curriculum proposals for the year 2000, offer encouragement. Commenting on the new personal, social and health education framework for 5–16-year-olds, general secretary Doug McAvoy tells of the bullying that children experience through homophobic insults and jokes and requests that children in primary schools should learn about lesbian and gay sexuality beyond the knowledge they pick up on the playground (Cassidy, 1999).

Although underdeveloped in this article, my findings support these proposals in so far as the pressures of compulsory heterosexuality to conform have particularly damaging consequences for those boys and girls who are positioned as Other to the normalising and regulatory (heterosexual) gendered scripts. I would also add that sexuality needs to be included as an equal opportunities issue that can deal with the *everyday* realities of boys' and girls' early sexual experiences. As Epstein (1999) concludes, 'we need to grasp the nettle of sex education and develop a broader sexuality education, in schools, where sexuality in its broadest sense is recognised, and where difference is valued and respected'. In this way, not only can the more damaging practices of misogyny, heterosexism and homophobia be legislated against, but 'hidden injuries', 'paradoxical pleasures' and the more 'fluid forms of dominance and subordination' (Kenway *et al.*, 1997, p. 22) can also be recognised. However, only a curriculum and policy framework that is sensitive to and reflects pupils' *own* sexual cultures can support children's experience of their developing sexual and gendered identities.

Key to transcripts

( ) Background information (includes body movement, emotion, name of speaker, interruptions, tone of voice)

. . . Pause

/ Moment when interruption begins

" "Direct quotation

??? Inaudible responses

[. . .] Different extract from same interview or extract from a different interview to follow

Notes

1 Pupils attending both schools were predominantly white English and from a range of socio-economic backgrounds.
2 The main study involved visiting one Year 6 classroom in each site, for 2/3 days (each), every fortnight, for a period of a year (1994/95).
3 I am using the Foucauldian understanding of discourse as socially organised frameworks of meaning which are shaped by and shape/regulate our behaviour, and which can delimit what can be said and done at particular moments in time (Foucault, 1978).
4 'Top-girls' was initially a term used by a group of boys to describe a dominant group of girls. I maintained the term, drawing further on the feminist evocations surrounding Carol Churchill's (1990) play, *Top Girls,* which resonated with the feminist discourses engaged with by the girls who accessed what I have termed the 'top-girl' subject position (see Renold, 1999).

References

Adler, P.A. & Adler, P. (1998) *Peer Power: pre-adolescent peer culture and identity* (New Brunswick, NJ, Rutgers University Press).

Alanen, L. (1994) Gender and generation: feminism and the child question, in J. Qvortrup, M. Brady, G. Sgritto & H. Winterberger (Eds) *Childhood Matters: social theory, practice and politics* (Aldershot, Avebury).

Best, R. (1983) *We've All Got Scars: what girls and boys learn in elementary school* (Bloomington, IN, Indiana University Press).

Bordo, S. (1990) Reading the slender body, in: M. Jacobus, E. V. Keller & S. Shuttleworth (Eds) *Body/Politics: women and the discourses of science* (London, Routledge).

Butler, J. (1990) *Gender Trouble: feminism and the subversion of identity* (London, Routledge).

Cassidy, S. (1999) Teach primary pupils about gays, says NUT, *Times Educational Supplement,* 9 July.

Churchill, C. (1990) *Top Girls* (London, Methuen).

Clark, M. (1990) *The Great Divide: gender in the primary school* (Melbourne, Curriculum Development Centre).

Clarricoates, K. (1987) Child culture at school: a clash between gendered worlds, in: A. Pollard (Ed.) *Children and their Primary Schools: a new perspective* (London, Falmer Press).

Connell, R.W. (1995) *Masculinities: knowledge, power and social change* (Cambridge, Polity Press).

Connolly, P. (1995) Boys will be boys? Racism, sexuality and the construction of masculine identities amongst infant boys, in J. Holland & M. Blair (Eds) (1995) *Debates and Issues in Feminist Research and Pedagogy* (Clevedon, Multilingual Matters).

Connolly, P. (1998) *Racisms, Gendered Identities and Young Children: social relations in a multi-ethnic, inner-city primary school* (London, Routledge).

Cowie, C. & Lees, S. (1981) Slags or drags, *Feminist Review,* 9, pp. 17–31.

Davies, B. (1982) *Life in the Classroom and Playground: the accounts of primary school children* (London, Routledge).

Davies, B. (1993) *Shards of Glass: children reading and writing beyond gendered identities* (Cresskill, NJ, Hampton Press Inc.).

Douglas, M. (1966) *Purity and Danger: an analysis of concepts of pollution and taboo* (London, Routledge).

Epstein, D. (1997) Cultures of schooling/cultures of sexuality, *International Journal of Inclusive Education,* 1, pp. 37–53.

Epstein, D. (1999) Sex and sensibilities, *Times Educational Supplement,* 2 July.

Epstein, D. & Johnson, R. (1994) On the straight and narrow: the heterosexual presumption, homophobias and schools, in: D. Epstein (Ed.) *Challenging lesbian and Gay Inequalities in Education* (Buckingham, Open University Press).

Epstein, D. & Johnson, R. (1998) *Schooling Sexualities* (Buckingham, Open University Press).

Foucault, M. (1978) *The Will to Knowledge: the history of sexuality,* Vol. I (trans. R. Hurley) (Harmondsworth, Penguin).

Francis, B. (1997) Power plays: children's constructions of gender and power in role plays, *Gender and Education,* 9, pp. 179–191.

Halson, J. (1989) The sexual harassment of young women, in L. Holly (Ed.) *Girls and Sexuality: teaching and learning* (Milton Keynes, Open University Press).

Haywood, C. (1996) Out of the curriculum: sex talking, talking sex, *Curriculum Studies,* 4, pp. 229–251.

Haywood, C. & Mac an Ghaill, M. (1996) Schooling masculinities, in: M. Mac an Ghaill (Ed.) *Understanding Masculinities: social relations and cultural arenas* (Buckingham, Open University Press).

Hey, V. (1997) *The Company She Keeps: an ethnography of girls' friendships* (Buckingham, Open University Press).

Holland, J., Ramazanoglu, C., Sharpe, S. & Thomson, R. (1998) *The Male in the Head: young people, heterosexuality and power* (London, Tufnell Press).

Jones, C. (1985) Sexual tyranny: male violence in a mixed secondary school, in: G. Weiner (Ed.) *Just a Bunch of Girls* (Milton Keynes, Open University Press).

Jones, C. & Mahony, P. (Eds) (1988) *Learning Our Lines: sexuality and social control in education* (London, Women's Press).

Jordan, E. (1995) Fighting boys and fantasy play: the construction of masculinity in the early years of school, *Gender and Education,* 5, pp. 157–167.

Kehily, M.J. & Nayak, A. (1996) Playing it straight: masculinities, homophobias and schooling, *Journal of Gender Studies,* 5, pp. 211–229.

Kehily, MJ. & Nayak, A. (1997) Lads and laughter: humour and the production of heterosexual hierarchies, *Gender and Education*, 9, pp. 69–87.

Kenway, J. & Fitzclarence, L. (1997) Masculinity, violence and schooling: challenging poisonous pedagogics, *Gender and Education,* 9, pp. 117–133.

Kenway, J. & Willis, S. with Blackmore, J. & Rennie, L. (1997) Are boys victims of feminism in schools? Some answers from Australia, *International Journal of Inclusive Education,* 1, pp. 19–35.

Lees, S. (1987) The structure of sexual relations in school, in M. Arnot & G. Weiner (Eds) *Gender and the Politics of Schooling* (London: Hutchinson).

Lees, S. (1993) *Sugar and Spice: sexuality and adolescent girls* (London, Penguin).

Mac an Ghaill, M. (1994) *The Making of Men: masculinities, sexualities and schooling* (Buckingham, Open University Press).

Mac an Ghaill, M. (1996) Deconstructing heterosexualities within school arenas, *Curriculum Studies*, 4, pp. 191–207.

McRobbie, A. (1978) Working class girls and the culture of femininity, in: Women's Study Group (Eds) *Women Take Issue* (London, Hutchinson).

McRobbie, A. (1997) More! New sexualities in girls and women's magazines, in: A. McRobbie (Ed.) *Back to Reality? Social Experiences and Cultural Studies* (Manchester, Manchester University Press).

Redman, P. (1996) Curtis loves Ranjit: heterosexual masculinities, schooling, and pupils' sexual cultures, *Educational Review*, 48, pp. 175–182.

Renold, E. (1997) 'All they've got on their brains is football': sport, masculinity and the gendered practices of playground relations, *Sport, Education and Society,* 2, pp. 5–23.

Renold, E. (1999) Presumed innocence: an ethnographic exploration into the construction of sexual and gender identities in the primary school, unpublished dissertation, University of Wales, Cardiff.

Rich, A. (1980) Compulsory heterosexuality and lesbian existence, *Signs,* 5, pp. 631–660.

Rossiter, A.B. (1994) Chips, Coke and rock 'n' roll: children's mediation of an invitation to a first dance party, *Feminist Review*, 46, pp. 1–19.

Skeggs, B. (1997) *Formations of Class and Gender* (London, Sage).

Skelton, C. (1996) Learning to be tough: the fostering of maleness in one primary school, *Gender and Education*, 8, pp. 185–197.

Skelton, C. (1997) Primary boys and hegemonic masculinities, *British Journal of Sociology of Education*, 18, pp. 349–369.

Thorne, B. (1993) *Gender Play: boys and girls in school* (Buckingham, Open University Press).

Thorne, B. & Luria, Z. (1986) Sexuality and gender in children's daily worlds, *Social Problems*, 33, pp. 176–190.

Walkerdine, V. (1990) *Schoolgirl Fictions* (London, Verso).

Walkerdine, V. (1996) Popular culture and the eroticization of little girls, in: J. Curran, D. Morely & V. Walkerdine (Eds) *Cultural Studies and Communications* (London, St Martin's Press).

Wolpe, A.M. (1988) *Within School Walls: the role of discipline: sexuality and the curriculum* (London, Routledge).

8

The ambiguity of "having sex"

The subjective experience of virginity loss in the United States

*Laura M. Carpenter**

What do we mean when we talk about sex? At the turn of the twenty-first century in the United States, there exists no single answer to this question. Different individuals and social groups attach diverse meanings to sexual activity, variously understanding sex as an expression of intimacy, a route to physical pleasure, or a sacred part of marriage. People even disagree about which sexual acts constitute "real" sex, as became apparent during the 1998 independent council investigation of President Clinton, in which classifying certain sexual activities as sex or as foreplay was a major point of contention. In short, the meaning of the term *sex* is ambiguous in the contemporary U.S. Because sexuality comprises a central part of personal identity, what sex means matters profoundly to the women and men who must negotiate their sexual lives in an atmosphere of diverse beliefs. It is also consequential for researchers who study sexual attitudes and conduct, and for policy makers who seek to address sexuality-related issues.

The experience of virginity loss offers one vantage point from which to explore the ambiguity surrounding sex and the consequences of that ambiguity for personal identity. Societal concerns about sexuality often crystallize around virginity loss, both because it is widely perceived as one of the most significant turning points in sexual life and because of the emphasis public health and policy professionals place on first coitus and sexual initiation. In this paper, I concentrate on two subjective aspects of virginity loss. First, to what sexual experiences do women and men refer when they talk about virginity loss or the first time they had sex? Which events do they posit as producing the transition from virgin to nonvirgin identity and who do they see as eligible to make that transition? Second, how do people interpret virginity loss? How do the meanings that individuals attach to virgin and nonvirgin identity shape their expectations and choices about the transition between those identities?

In answering these questions, I address several short-comings of the literature on early sexual experiences. First, relatively little research has explored the subjective meanings of virginity loss (di Mauro, 1995). Although first experiences with vaginal intercourse—which researchers often

* The author would like to thank Robin L. Leidner, Constance A. Nathanson, Frank F. Furstenberg, Jr., Demie Kurz, Harold J. Bershady, Sangeetha Madhavan, Gloria Y. Gadsden, Sara Kinsman, Eileen Lake, Shara Neidell, and Eva Skuratowicz for their assistance at various stages of this project.

identify as "virginity loss"—have been staples of research on sexual behavior since the 1960s, the preponderance of literature on early sexuality has focused on its public health dimensions (Ericksen, 1999; Sprecher, Barbee, & Schwartz, 1995). Second, most studies of virginity loss have focused primarily or exclusively on the experiences of young women and on people who identify themselves as heterosexual, despite a growing body of empirical and anecdotal evidence that beliefs and behavior vary meaningfully across and within gender and sexual orientation (this evidence includes Elder, 1996; Hart, 1995; Holland, Ramazanoglu, & Thomson, 1996; Rubin, 1990; Thompson, 1995; Tolman, 1994). Third, many of the studies that are sensitive to meaning rely on data gathered more than a decade ago, before the advent of HIV/AIDS as a public problem and the full impact of the New Right backlash against liberal sexual ideology (e.g., Brumberg, 1997; Rubin, 1990; Thompson, 1995).

Theoretical background

My analysis relies on an understanding of sexuality as profoundly shaped by social factors or *socially constructed* (Gagnon & Simon, 1973; Laws & Schwartz, 1977; Stein, 1989; Vance, 1991). Different cultural groups, both within and across societies, interpret different activities as sexual and imbue different sexual practices with specific meanings. At the same time, individuals actively interpret and reinterpret their sexual experiences over their lifetimes, thereby creating their identities as sexual beings. The patterned ways in which cultures and individuals approach sexuality can be understood as *interpretive frames,* schemas that enable people to "locate, perceive, identify, and label" occurrences within their life and the social world at large (Goffman, 1974, p. 21).

Diverse ways of framing specific aspects of sexuality, such as virginity loss, may be available in a given society at a single time. The frames that are available serve as part of the cultural "toolkit" with which individuals construct their sexual identities (Swidler, 1986). In the contemporary West, sexuality constitutes a central feature of identity; individuals are to a great degree defined by themselves and others, both socially and morally, in terms of their sexuality (Foucault, 1978; Giddens, 1992; Plummer, 1995; Weeks, 1985). Early sexual experiences, perhaps especially virginity loss, appear to be crucial steps through which individuals develop a sense of their identities as sexual beings (Gagnon & Simon, 1973; Holland et al., 1996).

In modern social life, identity (or self) comprises an ongoing project on which people expend considerable creative effort (Giddens, 1992). Sociologists typically theorize identity as a bridge linking the individual and society. One can usefully distinguish between *social identity*, the identities people attribute or impute to others, and *personal identity,* the meanings people attribute to their own selves (Snow & Anderson, 1987).[1] Social and personal identity are not necessarily congruent. For instance, a young woman may be perceived by her friends as a virgin (social identity) while knowing herself to be a nonvirgin (personal identity). Identity comprises multiple dimensions, of which sexual identity (incorporating virginity status) is only one. Various dimensions of identity are intertwined in ways that depend in part on individuals' interpretations of those dimensions. For example, people who interpret virginity as a stigma might associate virgin identity with "loser" or "geek" identity, whereas people who frame virginity as a valuable gift might link virgin identity with traditional feminine identity.

Different interpretive frames imply different evaluations of virgin and nonvirgin identity. A person may embrace or distance himself from a particular social or personal identity, depending on his and others' interpretations of it. Should he desire a different identity than the one he has, he may work to obtain a new one, either in fact (as when a virgin seeks to lose his virginity) or in appearance (as when a virgin portrays himself as a nonvirgin). Not static, identity changes over the life course, as when people adopt new social roles or statuses. Transitions from one identity to another comprise rites of passage or status passages; virginity loss, entailing the transition from virgin to nonvirgin identity, constitutes just such a passage (Glaser & Strauss, 1971; Turner, 1969; van Gennep, 1908). (Although the literature on status passages typically assumes congruence between social and personal identity, transitions can presumably occur independently at either level.) Undergoing a rite of passage involves relinquishing one identity in order to replace it with another. Therefore, how people approach a status passage and how they conduct themselves afterwards depend in part on their beliefs about both the initial and new identities (as well as on the beliefs of those around them).

Definitions and interpretations of virginity loss serve as tools for constructing sexual identity at both the social and personal levels. The ways people define virginity loss determine the point at which they see themselves—and others—as moving from virgin to nonvirgin identity as well as whom they deem eligible to make that transition. Not least because they imply evaluations of the desirability of virgin and nonvirgin identity, interpretations of virginity loss influence individuals' conduct, including their decisions about when to lose virginity (i.e., when to adopt a new personal and/or social identity) and how to present themselves to others (i.e., what social identity to claim, possibly distinct from personal identity). As we will see, the ambiguity of virginity loss affords people some, if limited, discretion in constructing their sexual identities.

Changing meanings and definitions of virginity loss

Although the loss of virginity has been almost universally recognized as an important rite of passage, comprising part of the transition from childhood to adulthood, beliefs about the meaning of and criteria for making the transition from virginity to nonvirginity have varied considerably (Muuss, 1970; Schlegel, 1995). Within the U.S., notions about the meaning of virginity loss—rooted in a Christian tradition venerating virginity (Aries, 1985)—have changed significantly over time. In the mid- to late-nineteenth century U.S., virginity implied purity and innocence from sexual experience and desire, and was seen as a natural and necessary state for unmarried women (Nathanson, 1991; Welter, 1983). Virginity loss was framed as an irrevocable loss of innocence and, if it took place outside of marriage, as the onset of moral corruption, madness, and even death. After about 1900, new ways of framing virginity loss became ascendant, accompanied by changes in sexual conduct. At the beginning of the century, young men typically saw their own virginity as a neutral or negative attribute, whereas young women perceived theirs as a thing of value. Yet, in contrast with previous eras, the belief that virginity was valuable for women did not preclude a growing proportion of young women and men from framing virginity loss as appropriate within the context of serious premarital relationships. From about 1920 on, young people increasingly opted to lose their virginity before marriage, typically with the person they planned to marry (Brumberg, 1997; D'Emilio & Freedman, 1988; Modell, 1983; Rubin, 1990).

This pattern prevailed until the mid 1960s, when young people, especially young women, more and more came to approve of and engage in premarital sexual intercourse with partners whom they did not expect to marry (Hofferth, Kahn, & Baldwin, 1987; Jessor & Jessor, 1975; Reiss, 1960; Zelnik & Shah, 1983). Although men's virginity continued to be framed as neutral or stigmatizing, for women a new frame emerged in which virginity was neither desirable nor undesirable (Rubin, 1990). By the 1980s, some young women even adopted frames more typical of men, perceiving virginity as an embarrassment or unwanted constraint (Brumberg, 1997; Rubin, 1990; Thompson, 1995), a stance which may have grown more prevalent during the 1990s (Sprecher & Regan, 1996). Over this period, gender differences in the prevalence and timing of first coitus narrowed considerably, largely due to changes in women's conduct (King, Balswick, & Robinson, 1977; Sherwin & Corbett, 1985; though see Ehrenreich, Hess, & Jacobs, 1986).

These broad changes did not, however, entirely displace traditional notions positing virginity as a virtue in women but as a negative trait in men (Ferrell, Tolone, & Walsh, 1977; Moffatt, 1987; Sprecher & Regan, 1996; Thompson, 1990). Beginning in the mid 1980s, frames casting virginity as valuable gained renewed popularity in certain segments of society. For instance, members of the New Right promoted a new frame advocating premarital virginity for both men and women; some proponents even claimed that virginity could be regained, provided sufficient repentance and commitment to future chastity (Dobie, 1995; Ingrassia, 1994). Indeed, one study found that, between 1990 and 1995, an increasing proportion of young men expressed pride and happiness about remaining virgins (Sprecher & Regan, 1996). As a consequence of these many changes, diverse ways of framing virginity loss—and sex in general—coexist in the present-day U.S. (D'Emilio & Freedman, 1988; Seidman, 1991).

Concern with specifying exactly which sexual acts could result in virginity loss appears to be a recent phenomenon, part of a general tendency, beginning in the late nineteenth century and accelerating over the course of the twentieth, to approach human sexuality as a medical, rather than a moral, matter. Public health experts' focus on "risk behaviors" is one prominent recent expression of the medicalization of sexuality (Nathanson, 1991; Tiefer, 1995; Weeks, 1985). Before the twentieth century, virginity loss was probably understood as resulting from vaginal intercourse, but not from partnered sexual activities such as manual stimulation (van de Walle & Muhsam, 1995). Yet, the primary conceptualization of virginity loss was in moral terms—as an irreversible transition from innocence (and virtue) to experience (and corruption)—rather than in terms of the performance of specific physical acts (Nathanson, 1991). Popular literature in the highly sexually-restrictive late nineteenth century included more than one cautionary tale in which young women lost their virtue without engaging in a genital sexual act (Welter, 1983). Attempts to establish physical criteria for virginity loss could be seen as early as the 1830s, with the "invention" of petting—noncoital sexual contact intended not to compromise premarital virginity (Rothman, 1983). But it was not until the 1920s that popular understandings of virginity loss came to center on delineating the sexual activities in which virgins could engage without losing virginity. From then on, the practice of engaging in noncoital genital sexual activity with the express intent of retaining virginity became increasingly widespread. Scholars have referred to this phenomenon as *technical virginity* (Newcomer & Udry, 1985). Technical virgins almost invariably equate virginity loss with first coitus, although, as Rubin (1990) notes, the content of "everything but" coitus has changed over time, most notably to include oral sex. In every era, virginity loss appears to have been understood as possible only between a woman and a man.

In contemporary popular and academic literature, the term *virginity loss* denotes first coitus. As one advice manual for teen women explains, "Unless his penis penetrates your vagina, you're a virgin" (Solin, 1996, p. 85). Similarly, social scientists often use the terms *nonvirgin* and *virgin* as shorthand to describe people who have and have not experienced vaginal intercourse (e.g., Jessor & Jessor, 1975; Schuster, Bell, & Kanouse, 1996). Few modern scholars appear to have consciously considered the possibility that virginity loss could refer to an experience other than first coitus. Yet, despite this apparent consensus, the definition of virginity remains somewhat ambiguous. In the one study (to my knowledge) to investigate explicitly how young people define virginity loss, only four fifths of respondents agreed that a woman would lose her virginity "if her vagina [was] fully penetrated by a penis" (Berger & Wenger, 1973, p. 669). Furthermore, anecdotal evidence suggests that young lesbians and gay men have recently begun to reframe virginity loss as including sex between same-sex partners (Elder, 1996; Hart, 1995), rather than deeming virginity loss as irrelevant to their own experiences as was common in the past (Raymond, 1994).

Definitions of sex are similarly ambiguous. On the one hand, when (heterosexual) women and men in the U.S. and Britain use the term sex, they almost always refer to vaginal-penile intercourse (Holland et al., 1996; Wight, 1994). However, Sanders and Reinisch (1999) found that many (41%) college students thought of oral-genital contact as sex and even more (81%) considered anal-genital contact sex. In light of the definitional ambiguity surrounding both sex and virginity loss, the common formula defining virginity loss as occurring the first time a person has sex appears deceptively straightforward.

Data and research methods

This study relies on data from in-depth case studies of 61 women and men, the majority of whom lived in the greater Philadelphia metropolitan region. Of the 33 women, 22 (67%) self-identified as heterosexual, 7 (21%) as lesbians, and 4 (12%) as bisexual. Of the 28 men, 17 (61%) described themselves as heterosexual, 9 (32%) as gay, and 2 (7%) as bisexual. Respondents came from diverse backgrounds. Almost 80% were White, 10% were African-American, 7% were Latino, and 5% were Asian-American. Two thirds were from middle-class backgrounds, as measured by parental education and occupation, and the remaining one third were from working-class backgrounds. Fifty-five percent of respondents were both White and from middle-class backgrounds. One third (21) were raised main-line Protestant, one fourth (16) Roman Catholic, one sixth (10) evangelical Protestant, one eighth (8) Jewish, and one tenth (6) nonreligious. Fifty-six of the 61 described themselves as nonvirgins at the time of the interview. Of these 56, 88% reported losing their virginity during adolescence (at age 16.4 on average).

Respondents ranged in age from 18 to 35, with an average age of about 25. Age distributions differed little by gender or by sexual orientation. My goal of situating virginity loss in the broader context of earlier and later sexual experiences prompted my decision to interview young adults (over age 17) rather than adolescents. Although I did not limit the sample to nonvirgins, in selecting respondents 18 or older, I could be assured that the vast majority would have become sexually active prior to the interview (Laumann et al., 1994). Interviewing young adults also facilitated comparison across sexual orientation. Because people who identify themselves as lesbian, gay, or bisexual seldom do so, especially publicly, before their late teens (Raymond, 1994), locating nonheterosexual adolescents to interview would have proved difficult. The upper limit of the age range, 35, was set to include people who became sexually active before as well as after HIV/AIDS became a prominent public health issue, but to exclude those who became teenagers before the so-called Sexual Revolution was well established (in the early 1970s).

To locate study participants, I used the purposive snowball sampling method. Initial respondents were recommended by professional contacts and special-interest organizations; I then asked every person I interviewed to introduce me to others who might agree to take part in the study. Snowball sampling offered several advantages crucial to achieving my research aims. Recruiting study participants through their own social networks may have helped overcome reluctance to participate in research on a topic typically perceived as very private (Sterk-Elifson, 1994; Thompson, 1995). (Although large-scale sexuality surveys have successfully employed random samples—e.g., Laumann, Gagnon, Michael & Michaels, 1994—such methods may not be appropriate for gathering in-depth subjective accounts of sexual experiences.) Snowball sampling moreover enabled me to identify gay and bisexual women and men, who are not numerically common, readily "visible," or evenly distributed throughout the U.S. population (Biernacki & Waldorf, 1981).

Drawbacks of snowball samples include their nonrandom, nonrepresentative nature, which prevents the researcher from directly generalizing findings to a broader population. Additionally, because social networks tend to be relatively homogeneous, the members of each snowball are likely to hold similar beliefs.[2] To counter this potential source of bias and to increase sample diversity, I started several snowballs in each of the four main gender-sexual orientation categories and limited each snowball to five members.[3] The typically small size of snowball samples also hinders the ability to generalize. Yet, a small, nonrandom sample may be sufficient for researchers who are concerned primarily with discovering the range of ideas or behaviors available in a given culture, rather than their prevalence in a population. Indeed, one of the most striking aspects of the 61 interviews I conducted is the frequency with which different respondents raised the same general themes. Glaser and Strauss (1967) refer to this phenomenon as saturation. Given the focus of my research, then, the advantages of the snowball sampling method outweighed the drawbacks.

Interview methods

To gather data for this project, I relied on in-depth, semi-structured interviews. Most questions were open ended so that participants could speak freely and at length about what they perceived as the salient aspects of virginity loss, thereby enabling me to collect a wealth of detailed data on subjective interpretations and experiences. Yet every interview asked about the same categories of information—the definition and meaning of virginity loss, learning about virginity loss, personal sexual history, and virginity-related social interactions—facilitating comparisons among respondents. In-depth interviews provide respondents with the opportunity, often lacking in traditional social science surveys, to explain experiences that defy simple categorization. They also enhance participants' ability to ascertain the trustworthiness of the interviewer, and thus may promote more extensive, detailed, or truthful accounts. Conversely, closed-ended questions presume a priori knowledge of the possible range of understandings that people bring to phenomena like virginity loss. Exploratory studies such as mine provide a necessary foundation for surveys seeking to illuminate the subjective aspects of virginity loss.

Interviews lasted from 1 to 3 hours and took place at a location chosen by the respondent (typically the respondent's home or office, or my office). Participants were informed that their identities would remain confidential and anonymous and that they could stop the interview at any time; they were not compensated for taking part in the study. The Human Subjects Committee of the Institutional Review Board of the University of Pennsylvania approved the study design, interview protocol, and consent form.

I conducted every interview in person between April 1997 and October 1998. This period overlapped with the independent council investigation of the relationship between President Bill Clinton and Monica Lewinsky, which arguably prompted a national consciousness raising about the definitional ambiguity of sex. Twenty-five interviews took place in or after late January 1998, when allegations that Lewinsky had performed fellatio on Clinton were first widely publicized. Five of these 25 respondents mentioned the Clinton-Lewinsky controversy during our interviews; 6 of the 25 self-identified as heterosexual. People seldom question the commonsense equation of sex with vaginal-penile intercourse, unless they have personally experienced (and recognized) desire for same-sex partners. (The seeming "naturalness" of heterosexuality is a key component of the phenomenon Rich, 1980, named *compulsory heterosexuality*.) Therefore, although I expected that gay and bisexual respondents would have interrogated the sex-coitus equation during the process of coming out (and thus well before the interviews), I was concerned that the extraordinary circumstances of the Clinton-Lewinsky investigation might have prompted heterosexual respondents to revise their definitions of virginity loss, thus biasing later interviews. Fortunately, the timing of the interviews appeared not to affect their content. Regardless of when I spoke with them, most heterosexual respondents initially defined virginity loss with a simple statement such as "[Virginity loss is] the first time having sex" (Lavinia, 30, heterosexual), by which they meant vaginal intercourse.[4] In contrast, virtually every lesbian, gay, or bisexual participant responded by raising the issue of sex between same-sex partners, often referring more generally to the existence of different ways of defining sex.

Methods of analysis

To code and analyze interview data, I relied primarily on the systematic procedures referred to as *grounded theory* (Glaser & Strauss, 1967). Developed to optimize analysis of qualitative data, the grounded theory approach stresses the inductive development of the analytic categories guiding the researcher's inquiries. This strategy helps the researcher focus on the meaning of experiences to study participants. My analysis thus seeks to represent faithfully the means through which real people make sense of their social world. To uncover patterns in respondents' talk about virginity loss, I read transcripts of each interview several times, allowing salient themes to emerge from them. For example, I did not ask study participants whether they saw virginity as a gift or as a stigma; that respondents thought about virginity in these metaphorical terms emerged during the course of the interviews and analysis. Using these emergent themes, along with key topics as cited in the relevant literature, I developed a guide for coding the interviews, which I then reread, identifying these themes and topics as they appeared.

Findings

Defining virginity loss

Participants in my study were in complete agreement about a few aspects of the definition of virginity loss. In particular, every respondent believed that vaginal-penile intercourse would constitute virginity loss, if it were the first partnered sexual activity in which a woman or man had engaged. Furthermore, every respondent stipulated that a person could not lose her or his virginity without the involvement of a human partner and the stimulation—by more than manual means alone—of at least one partner's genitalia. Less agreement existed regarding other sexual acts that could take place between a woman and a man.[5] About one fourth (17) of respondents believed that a woman or a man who engaged in oral sex with an opposite-sex partner would lose her or his virginity. For example, Marty (26, heterosexual) said of oral sex, "That's fooling around, in my terminology." More respondents—56%—thought that anal intercourse between a man and a woman could constitute virginity loss.[6]

The prevalence of anti-gay sentiment in the U.S. notwithstanding, a majority of study participants claimed that it was possible to lose one's virginity with a same-sex partner. Four fifths of respondents (49) believed that both men and women could lose their virginity with a same-sex partner. Another 10% believed that men could lose their virginity with same-sex partners, but that women could not. Only 4 respondents argued that virginity loss could take place only through coitus. Respondents who saw same-sex virginity loss as possible took two different perspectives regarding the sex, or sexual orientation, of the virgin and her/his partner. About half of participants (29) posited different standards of virginity loss for sex between same- and opposite-sex partners. For example, Meghan (22, heterosexual) said: "I guess virginity has to be defined within each type of relationship, like woman-woman, man-man, heterosexual . . . If that is their way of making love . . . I think probably no, they wouldn't be a virgin." Another one third (20) believed that anal sex, oral sex, and coitus were equally capable of resulting in virginity loss, regardless of the sex of the partners involved. For example, Seth (19, gay) explained: "I think of oral sex as sex, and I think of anal sex as sex, and I think of vaginal sex as sex. Those are kind of like the three things that I think of as sex." (On the tendency to create hierarchies among sexual acts, see Rubin, 1984.)

Definitions of virginity loss varied by sexual orientation, in ways that correspond to the particular concerns of people who are heterosexual and people who are not. For example, all but one of the nonheterosexual respondents contended that both women and men could lose their virginity with partners of either sex, compared with just under three fourths of heterosexual participants. Lesbians, gay men, and bisexuals were also considerably more likely than heterosexual women and men to say that vaginal, oral, and anal sex would all result in virginity loss, regardless of the sex of the actors (59% and 18%, respectively). Several respondents suggested that people who support such a single-standard definition of virginity may do so out of a desire to establish equal status or acceptance for gay sex, an issue arguably of greater concern to gay and bisexual women and men than to their heterosexual counterparts.

There was little agreement about nonconsensual sex experiences. Just under half of the respondents (26) believed that rape would constitute virginity loss. For example, Karen (21, heterosexual) said: "[Rape] would definitely be intercourse, so I wouldn't consider them a virgin. Unfortunately." About one third (22) felt that a person absolutely could not lose their virginity as a result of rape. According to Matt (24, heterosexual):

> I guess losing your virginity is at least partially defined by the experience you gained about sex and relationships. And I think that there's so much that's strange about [rape and molestation] that they may not really fall into that category.

The remaining 13 participants fell somewhere in between these two extremes, arguing that although a person who was raped was technically (i.e., physiologically) no longer a virgin, in many ways they still were. For instance, Carrie (20, heterosexual) said:

> I see virginity as definitely something that you can choose into, and people . . . don't get to choose into rape . . . If their only sexual experience has been something like a rape, I would call them a virgin even though technically, um, something did happen.

In short, respondents disagreed as to whether nonconsensual sex should be categorized as a form of sex, albeit an undesirable one, or whether it was, in some sense, not really sex at all. They also disagreed as to whether virginity loss could or should occur only on a voluntary basis.

Beliefs about virginity loss and nonconsensual sex were patterned by gender, consistent with the distinctive concerns women and men have regarding sexuality. Nearly two thirds of women in the study said that rape could never or could only technically constitute virginity loss, compared with only half of men. This gender difference appears to stem from a variety of social factors, especially women's greater susceptibility to rape and the greater likelihood that women respondents had themselves experienced a nonconsensual sexual encounter. (For national data, see Laumann et al., 1994.) One fourth (8) of the women in the study had been victims of forced sex, compared with only one man. None of these nine respondents believed that virginity could be lost through coerced sex.

Another dimension of social identity along which definitions of virginity loss were patterned was age. Younger respondents (25 and under) were more likely than their older counterparts to view same-sex virginity loss as possible (91% and 67% of younger and older respondents, respectively) and to believe that nonconsensual sex could not or could only technically result in virginity loss (55% and 15% of younger and older respondents, respectively). The extent to which younger participants thought it possible to lose virginity with a same-sex partner suggests a growing legitimization of gay and lesbian sexuality in the U.S. over time. Similarly, the greater tendency of younger respondents to exclude rape from their definitions of virginity loss may indicate partial incorporation of feminist ideas about rape into mainstream understandings of sexuality. It is noteworthy that younger respondents appear to be redefining virginity loss rather than choosing to abandon the concept of virginity altogether. Their decisions stand as testimony to the continuing social significance of the categories of virgin and nonvirgin in the face of a changing sexual landscape.

Identifying personal virginity-loss experiences

Another way to evaluate what people mean when they talk about virginity loss is to look at which experiences they identify as the point at which they lost their own virginity. Of the 56 respondents who were not virgins at the time of the interview, four fifths said that they had lost their virginity the first time they engaged in coitus. Eight participants reported losing their virginity the first time they gave or received oral sex and 2 identified the first time they had anal sex as the point at which they lost their virginity. (Five of the respondents who identified a first same-sex encounter as the point at which they lost their virginity did so only in retrospect; at the time of the encounter, they had not yet questioned the common definition of virginity loss as a person's first experience with coitus.)

Which experiences respondents identified as resulting in their own loss of virginity varied by sexual orientation. All 37 nonvirgin heterosexual respondents and 4 of 5 nonvirgin bisexual respondents reported losing their virginity the first time they engaged in coitus. In contrast, only one third of gay and lesbian respondents said that they lost their virginity via coitus. Lesbians were quite a bit more likely than gay men to have lost their virginity through coitus: 4 of 6 nonvirgin lesbian respondents had done so, compared with only 1 of 8 nonvirgin gay men. Only one respondent, a gay man named Seth, reported losing his virginity with an opposite-sex partner by engaging in some act other than coitus (reciprocal oral sex). Of the 48 respondents who had ever engaged in coitus, 2 did not currently identify their first experience of coitus as the point at which they lost their virginity. Sarah (33, lesbian) said she lost her virginity the first time she performed oral sex on another woman; she engaged in one act of coitus 2 years later. As an adult, Geoff (30, gay) pinpointed his loss of virginity as the first time he exchanged oral sex with another boy (at age 5); but as a teen, he had thought of himself as losing his virginity the first time he engaged in coitus (at age 12).

Interpreting virginity loss

Over the course of their lives, the women and men who participated in my study drew primarily on three distinctive metaphors to make sense of virginity and the experience of virginity loss. About half (30) of them at some point likened virginity to a gift and virginity loss to gift-giving. For instance, Kelly (24, heterosexual) said that virginity is:

> . . . supposed to be something special and cherished and wonderful and something to keep and you give to someone who is. . . . I don't know if lose is the right word. . . . I'll say you give to someone, whenever you find the right person.

Just over half (34) of respondents compared virginity and virginity loss to stages in a broader process or rite of passage. According to Emma (24, heterosexual):

> I see everything in life as kind of a process and, losing your virginity is kind of the start of a process. . . . In general . . . the first time with anything tends to be a little awkward at best, you know. And so . . . it's just kind of the start of something that progresses.

Finally, just over one third (23) of participants at some point turned to the metaphor of virginity as a stigma to understand their experiences. As Kendall (28, gay) recalled:

> I think almost every teen-like movie . . . was about getting laid or not getting laid, and what an idiot you were for not getting laid. And then girls, you know, hemming and hawing, "Should I put out? Should I not put out?" Growing up it's always been a stigma, it's always been a bad thing . . . to be a virgin. I'm sure I knew a lot more virgins than let on. But, couldn't be a virgin in public.

As described here, the three primary interpretive frames are best understood as ideal types (see Weber, 1946). In practice, the boundaries between the frames, and the experiences of those who employed them, were somewhat indistinct. Moreover, about one third of respondents reported that their perspectives on virginity had changed over time, often in response to new experiences.

These metaphorical interpretive frames profoundly shaped respondents' expectations, experiences, and retrospective evaluations of virginity loss. When people think metaphorically, they compare two phenomena and expect those phenomena to resemble one another (Lakoff & Johnson, 1980). Thus, respondents who spoke of virginity as a gift anticipated the experience of "giving" their virginity to resemble giving a gift more generically. Perceiving virginity as a very valuable gift, not least because of its nonrenewable nature, these women and men were concerned primarily with finding partners who would appreciate the worth of their gift and, more important, reciprocate it with a gift of similar value (typically the recipient's own virginity or increased commitment to the relationship). The norm of reciprocity stipulates that every gift must be returned; therefore, a single gift can set in motion an endless series of exchanges, each of which strengthens the bond between the givers. Yet, while a giver can increase the odds of reciprocity by selecting a recipient who seems likely to return her gift, she cannot compel reciprocation. Givers are, therefore, always somewhat subject to the whims of recipients (at least in societies like the contemporary U.S., where social controls are relatively weak). (For more details, see Mauss, 1925; Schwartz, 1967.)

In a similar manner, participants who interpreted virginity as part of a process expected the experience of virginity loss to resemble other familiar processes, such as education or marriage, which entail a transition from one social status to another. These men and women believed that virginity loss, like social transitions in general, would increase their knowledge (about sexuality or themselves) and leave them feeling transformed. Adherents to the process frame saw virginity loss as both an inevitable and a desirable transition, but disagreed as to whether it was rapid and dramatic or gradual and incremental. (On the sociological aspects of status passages, see Glaser & Strauss, 1971; Turner, 1969; van Gennep, 1908.)

Finally, respondents who viewed virginity as a stigma were eager to discard that stigma as soon as practically possible. They typically emphasized the importance of not incurring additional stigmas, such as a reputation for sexual ineptitude, during the campaign to lose virginity. Cognizant of the ever-present possibility that their stigma could be discovered, exposed, and derided by others, many in this group sought to conceal their virginity so long as it existed. These concerns are characteristic of people who bear a temporary stigma. (For a classic statement on stigma, see Goffman, 1963.)

Patterns by gender and sexual orientation

Study participants drew on different interpretive frames to understand virginity depending in part on their gender. Women and men were equally likely to have ever seen virginity loss as part of a larger process, as we see in Table 8.1. However, almost twice as many women as men had thought about virginity as a gift (61% of women, compared with 36% of men). Conversely, men were nearly three times more likely than women to have ever viewed virginity as a stigma (57% of men and 21% of women). This pattern is consistent with the resilient, if evolving, sexual double standard (Ferrell, et al., 1977; Moffatt, 1987; Rubin, 1990). Notably, gender differences were more pronounced among older respondents (26 and over), suggesting a possible weakening of the double standard over time.

Interpretations of virginity were also patterned by sexual orientation. As shown in Table 8.1, the propensity ever to interpret virginity as a stigma varied little by sexual orientation. However, many more lesbians and gay men adhered to the process frame than did their heterosexual counterparts (73% and 46%, respectively). Conversely, heterosexual respondents were more likely to have ever thought of virginity as a gift than were their gay and lesbian counterparts (54% compared with 31%). Bisexual respondents fell somewhere in between, with two thirds interpreting virginity as a gift and two thirds viewing it as a stage in a process. Gay and bisexual respondents were especially likely to have seen virginity loss as part of a process, in part because, for them, virginity loss was closely intertwined with the process of coming out.

Interpretations, expectations, and conduct

These interpretive frames are of particular interest because each was associated with a fairly distinctive constellation of sexual beliefs and conduct, including sexual behavior and presentation of self before and after virginity loss, relationships with virginity-loss partners, contraceptive use during virginity loss, and satisfaction with the experience of virginity loss overall. Here, I briefly discuss the ways that interpretive approaches to virginity loss shaped respondents' decisions about how to present themselves to others, especially their virginity-loss partners. In presenting

Table 8.1 Interpretation of Virginity Ever by Gender and Sexual Orientation

	Gift	*Stigma*	*Process*	*Other*[a]	*Total*[b]
Women	61% (20)	21% (7)	52% (17)	9% (3)	54% (33)
Men	36% (10)	57% (16)	61% (17)	11% (3)	46% (28)
Heterosexual	54% (21)	38% (15)	46% (18)	5% (2)	143% (39)
Lesbian/gay	31% (5)	38% (6)	73% (12)	25% (4)	167% (16)
Bisexual	67% (4)	33% (2)	67% (4)	0% (0)	167% (6)
Total	49% (30)	38% (23)	56% (34)	10% (6)	153% (61)

[a] Four respondents (three gay men and one lesbian) at some point interpreted virginity as irrelevant to their own experience; two respondents (both heterosexual women from evangelical Protestant backgrounds) described maintaining virginity as a way to honor one's commitment to God.

[b] Percentages total more than 100 because some respondents reinterpreted virginity over time.

themselves as virgins or nonvirgins, participants claimed particular social identities, sometimes based on and sometimes despite their personal identities (see Table 8.2).

Before losing their virginity, respondents who viewed virginity as a gift typically spoke openly about their virginity status with people they knew. In fact, they were often quite proud of being virgins. These men and women invariably discussed their virginity with their sexual partners, in part to ensure that their partners realized what a special gift they were about to receive. Such self-disclosure also served as a way to encourage reciprocity. Bryan (18, heterosexual), who had made a point of discussing his virginity with his girlfriend before they had sex, explained, "If you feel as though you're not loved as much as . . . you love this other person, and you actually decide to have sex with this person, I think you kind of feel slighted." Communication about virginity status may have been facilitated by the nature of the relationship adherents to the gift frame had with their virginity-loss partners: They were the group most likely to lose their virginity in serious dating relationships and to be in love with their partners or to describe them as "soulmates." Respondents who interpreted virginity as a gift were the most likely to use contraceptives when they lost their virginity (79% did), a tendency apparently

Table 8.2 Selected Aspects of Virginity-loss (VL) Experiences by Interpretation of Virginity Loss

	Interpretation of virginity loss		
Aspect of experience	*Gift*	*Stigma*	*Process*
Presentation of self before/after VL.	Most likely to be proud of virginity; most likely to be ashamed of virginity loss.	Most likely to conceal virginity; most likely to brag about virginity loss (when possible).	Typically open about virginity status before and after VL, but neither proud nor ashamed.
Communication with VL partner.	Invariably admitted own virginity to VL partner. Failure to discuss reciprocity concerns could lead to dissatisfaction.	Least likely to admit virginity to VL partner. Concealed virginity often undetected (esp. among younger virgins), but discovery could be devastating.	Typically told partners about own virginity. Able to overcome physically or emotionally unpleasant experiences by talking with partner.
Relationship to VL partner.	Most likely to lose virginity in a serious dating relationship, when in love, or with a "soulmate."	Most likely to lose virginity with a stranger or "temporary" partner (e.g., a friend).	If hetero- or bisexual, typically dating VL partner. If lesbian or gay, VL often with friend (VL part of coming out process).
Contraceptive use at VL (for those whose VL was coitus).	Most likely to use contraceptives (79%); most likely to use the Pill (36% of users), often in combination with condoms.	Least likely to use contraceptives (59%); often unwilling to discuss contraception with VL partner, for fear of appearing inexperienced.	Second-most likely to use contraceptives (67%); non-users often planned to use, but didn't because VL encounter unplanned.
Overall satisfaction with VL experience.	Most dependent for satisfaction on the conduct of VL partners (due to emphasis on reciprocation).	Typically satisfied merely by losing virginity, but devastated if ridiculed by VL partner.	Pleasurable experiences common. Where VL not pleasurable, generally satisfied with VL as a "learning experience."

related to both willingness to communicate and the relationship between partners. (Data are for respondents who lost their virginity by engaging in coitus.) On the downside, however, the five respondents (all women) whose partners failed to reciprocate described their virginity-loss experiences as emotionally devastating and as diminishing their value as persons. The norm of reciprocity effectively empowers recipients at the expense of givers; therefore, participants who saw virginity as a gift were particularly vulnerable to distressing virginity-loss experiences precisely because they framed virginity as a gift.

From a policy perspective, encouraging young people to interpret virginity as a gift—a stance consistent with many abstinence-only sex education programs—is a double-edged sword, protecting against one negative potential consequence of sexual activity (pregnancy and/or STD transmission) but increasing the likelihood of another deleterious consequence (emotional distress due to partner's nonreciprocation). In contrast, even adherents to the stigma frame whose partners ridiculed them experienced virginity loss as positive on balance, inasmuch as they lost their stigma. Participants who saw virginity loss as a process achieved the goal of gaining knowledge merely through losing their virginity, thus their partners could in practice wield little power over them. I discuss the relationship among interpretive frames, gender, and sexual agency in more detail elsewhere (Carpenter, 2000).

In contrast, participants who saw virginity as a stigma were extremely reluctant to admit their virginity to anyone they knew. Many worked to disguise their virginity, either actively—by falsifying their sexual histories—or passively—by allowing or encouraging others to assume that they were no longer virgins. Not surprisingly, people who interpreted virginity as a stigma were the most likely to conceal their virginity from their virginity-loss partners. For instance, Bill (31, heterosexual) decided not to tell his partner that he was a virgin because "It was so obvious to me that she wasn't [a virgin], that I felt demeaned by, if I had [told her]." Indeed, many respondents in this group lost their virginity with relative strangers, from whom they might more easily conceal their sexual status. Most clandestine virgins avoided detection by their partners; however, the three respondents whose partners either ridiculed them as virgins or as sexually incompetent were profoundly dissatisfied with the manner in which they lost their virginity (albeit relieved to have expunged their stigma). Men were far less successful than women at concealing their virginity and sexual inexperience, perhaps due to popular stereotypes of men as sexually active and women as sexually passive. Respondents who lost their virginity at relatively advanced ages were also less successful at concealment, apparently because their similarly-aged partners were already sexually experienced. The desire of adherents to the stigma frame to avoid being stigmatized as virgins also affected their use of contraceptives. The group least likely to employ a form of contraception (59% did), a number of these respondents declined to discuss contraception—or to insist on practicing safer sex—precisely in order to avoid appearing inexperienced or foolish to their partners. Bill recalled:

> I was so nervous, it was my first time and . . . I didn't want to look foolish, so I ended up having sex with her without any protection. And she said that she was okay, she had that taken care of. And I didn't go into any great details, I was just so nervous.

Finally, women and men who thought of virginity loss as a step in a process were typically frank about their virginity status, seeing it as cause for neither pride nor shame. Almost all of these respondents told their virginity-loss partners that they were virgins, which may have facilitated later discussions of awkward or unpleasant aspects of virginity loss. In fact, people who interpreted virginity as part of a process proved to be the best-equipped to work through physically or emotionally negative experiences by talking with their partners, generally in ways that helped ensure more positive sexual experiences later on. For example, Jennifer (25, heterosexual) expected virginity loss with her boyfriend of three months to be physically and emotionally enjoyable. Instead, she found sexual intercourse to be so unpleasant and tedious that she had no desire to have sex again. She had, however, enjoyed losing her virginity on an emotional level; this, plus her boyfriend's support and encouragement were crucial in convincing her that the physical aspects of sex would improve over time. She said:

> I didn't even enjoy it. . . . It just made me think it was a waste of my time [laughs]. . . . I told him, "That's it?" He's like, "Isn't that enough?" [laughs]. And I said, "No" [laughs]. He had lost his virginity with a girl he had been with before. And so I think going through it with her . . . he kind of knew that it wasn't that pretty the first time.

Respondents who saw virginity as a stage in a process were almost as likely as adherents to the gift frame to use contraceptives when they lost their virginity (67% did), probably for much the same reasons: open communication and close relationships with partners. Interestingly, of the four adherents to the process frame who lost their virginity without using contraceptives, three had at some point discussed contraception with their partners and had planned to use condoms. However, consistent with their understanding of virginity loss as stemming naturally out of a series of experiences, these young people lost their virginity when "one thing led to another" in circumstances where contraceptives were unavailable.

Discussion

These findings demonstrate that considerable ambiguity surrounds the definition and interpretation of virginity loss. This ambiguity provides young women and men with a degree of flexibility: Within constraints, they may choose which specific definitions and interpretations of virginity and nonvirginity they will use in constructing their sexual identities. In recent decades at least, virginity loss has by and large been defined with reference to physiological rather than to moral criteria, and has been specifically equated with first coitus. Indeed, participants in my study defined virginity loss almost exclusively in physiological terms, with scarcely any mention of virtue or sin. Not one respondent disputed the common belief that otherwise sexually inexperienced individuals would lose their virginity the first time they engaged in coitus. However, a majority contended that, with same-sex partners, people could also lose their virginity without engaging in vaginal intercourse. Moreover, about half believed that nonconsensual coitus could not truly result in virginity loss. Given the popular equation of virginity loss with "first sex," new definitions of virginity loss suggest new understandings of sex in general. Defining virginity loss to include same-sex encounters implies an understanding of "real" sex that challenges heterosexist norms. Likewise, defining virginity loss to exclude rape implies that coercive sexual acts are not "really" sex. My study thus corroborates previous findings of disagreement over the definition of virginity loss (Berger & Wenger, 1973) and sex (Sanders & Reinisch, 1999). It also advances the literature by revealing definitional ambiguities related to sex with same-sex partners and to coercive sex (both previously unexamined).

Definitions of virginity loss constitute claims about identity, for how people define virginity loss determines how and when they believe the transition between virgin and nonvirgin identity occurs. To the extent that virginity loss forms an important part of the passage from childhood to adulthood, different definitions of virginity loss render people differentially eligible for achieving status as sexual adults. For example, the traditional equation of virginity loss with first coitus effectively denies nonvirgin identity and sexual adulthood to people who do not wish to engage in vaginal intercourse. Conversely, defining virginity loss as possible through oral or anal sex with same-sex partners extends the status passage of virginity loss to gay, bisexual, and heterosexual people alike. By a similar token, to exclude coercive sex from the definition of virginity loss is to claim that the transition from virgin to nonvirgin identity cannot be imposed by another but rather must be chosen by the person making the transition.

Given their implications for identity, it is not surprising that definitions of virginity loss were patterned by group membership, reflecting group concerns. Lesbian, gay, and bisexual respondents, whose sexual repertoires depended less on coitus than did those of their heterosexual counterparts, were considerably more likely to argue that oral and anal sex could result in virginity loss, especially between same-sex partners. These men and women thereby proposed assigning virgin and nonvirgin social identity in ways consistent with their understanding of themselves as sexual adults for whom coitus is not the central sexual act. These criteria moreover correspond with many of these respondents' own experiences of adopting nonvirgin personal identity without engaging in vaginal intercourse. Likewise, women respondents, far more likely than men to experience coercive sex, were disproportionately likely to argue that virginity loss could not occur without the virgin's consent. They therefore asserted that virgin and nonvirgin identity are to some extent voluntary.

By challenging traditional definitions of virginity loss, individuals and social groups can help alter prevailing criteria for assigning social identity and possibly also promote greater social equity. The definitional ambiguity of virginity loss allows people some discretion in choosing the point at which they adopt personal identity as nonvirgins, as when a self-identified lesbian rejects heteronormative definitions to locate her own loss of virginity at her first sexual encounter with another woman. A person whose own definition of virginity loss diverges considerably from prevailing understandings may find that others assign her a social identity that differs from her personal identity. Yet, as more individuals adopt nontraditional definitions of virginity loss, new criteria for assigning social identity may emerge and supplant older approaches. Younger respondents were more likely than their older counterparts to offer nontraditional definitions, suggesting that such changes may be underway.

Previously, scholars have established that diverse interpretations of virginity loss and sex are available in the contemporary U.S. (D'Emilio & Freedman, 1988; Seidman, 1991; Thompson, 1995). Participants in my study framed virginity loss in ways corresponding roughly to previously described understandings of virginity as valuable, stigmatized, and relatively neutral. However, my research presents a more subtle and useful picture of diverse perspectives on virginity loss. Because metaphorical ways of thinking posit similarities between two phenomena—in this case, between virginity loss and gift-giving, stigma, and learning processes—it is possible to illuminate virginity loss by drawing on sociological knowledge about the phenomena with which people compare it. The metaphorical frames for virginity loss that emerged as respondents recalled their experiences may therefore offer a particularly promising framework for future research on early sexual experiences.

My findings further extend previous studies by demonstrating the continuing evolution of interpretations of virginity loss. Like researchers before me, I found that women and men tended to interpret virginity loss differently, with women more apt to view virginity as a valuable gift and men more likely to see virginity as a stigma. Also as in earlier studies, a handful of women and men in my project embraced gender atypical views of virginity; younger participants were considerably more likely to cross this gender boundary. Yet, my interviews revealed a third way of interpreting virginity loss—as a step in a longer process—which largely transcended gender; such an interpretation has seldom been mentioned in previous research (Rubin, 1990, notes a value-neutral stance toward virginity among women but not among men). These findings suggest an ongoing trend whereby the meanings attributed to virginity loss are increasingly dissociated from gender.

Like definitions, interpretations of virginity loss serve as tools for the construction of sexual identity. When a person decides to lose her virginity, she is effectively electing to adopt a new personal identity and potentially a new social identity, should she (or another) choose to disclose her new status. Respondents based their choices about virginity loss (and related phenomena like self-presentation and contraception) on their interpretations of virginity and on what those interpretations imply about virginity and nonvirginity as identities. Adherents to the gift frame viewed virginity as a worthy personal and social identity which they were proud to claim. They strove to maintain their identity as virgins (at both levels) until they were able to make the transition to an equally respectable nonvirgin identity—one which signaled the deepening of a committed relationship with a loving, reciprocating partner. In contrast, respondents who saw virginity as a stigma endeavored to conceal their personal identity when they were virgins, to project a nonvirgin social identity (even when discrepant with personal identity), and to achieve the nonvirgin personal identity they desired under almost any circumstance. People who drew on the process frame perceived both virginity and nonvirginity as acceptable social and personal identities, depending on individual circumstances, and typically adopted a social identity congruent with their personal identity both before and after virginity loss. They spoke of deciding to undergo the transition to nonvirgin personal identity when the time felt "right." The interpretive ambiguity of virginity loss allowed respondents to select from among different approaches to virginity loss, each associated with different stances toward virgin and nonvirgin identity. These diverse interpretations guided people's choices about virginity loss—the adoption of nonvirgin identity—along different paths with distinctive consequences.

Conclusion

In this paper, I have explored ambiguities in the definition and interpretation of virginity loss as a specific case of the ambiguities of "sex." I have also shown how individuals use definitions and interpretations of virginity loss as tools for constructing sexual identity at both the social and personal levels. Definitions of virginity loss and sex are ambiguous; with the exception of coitus, people disagree about which sexual activities can result in virginity loss and thus, by extension, about which activities are "really" sex. A similar ambiguity pertains to interpretations of virginity loss and sex, for different people ascribe diverse meanings to all manner of sexual experiences. Different definitions of virginity loss enable people to construct personal identity in different ways, by allowing them to choose, within constraints, the point at which they move from virgin to nonvirgin identity. Diverse interpretations of virginity loss likewise guide people's choices about losing virginity—and adopting a new identity—along different paths, based in part on what specific interpretive frames imply about virgin and nonvirgin identity. Having changed dramatically in the past, definitions and interpretations of virginity loss and sex continue to evolve, often apparently in response to social movements like feminism and gay rights.

Taken together, my findings challenge researchers to broaden their understandings of virginity loss and sex. Scholars need to realize that women and men in the contemporary U.S. do not simply equate virginity loss and sex with coitus. Although a few studies have adopted relatively inclusive definitions of sex (e.g., Laumann et al., 1994), more need to follow suit. In addition, researchers must bear in mind the coexistence of diverse approaches to virginity loss and sex, which may not directly correspond with gender or other aspects of social identity. Recognizing that definitions and interpretations of virginity loss vary is an important step toward developing a thorough understanding of adolescent sexuality. Such knowledge is important for its own sake as well as for the success of future research, sex education curricula, and public policy initiatives. For example, given diverse perspectives on virginity loss, survey participants may approach the same questions from different interpretive standpoints. Likewise, sex education programs that assume homogeneity in beliefs may fail to affect their audiences as intended.

The research reported here can be usefully extended in several ways. In light of previous studies suggesting distinctive patterns by racial-ethnic background (Aneshensel, Fielder, & Becerra, 1989; Horowitz, 1983; Schuster et al., 1996; Smith & Udry, 1985), and given the relative racial and ethnic homogeneity of my sample, future research should evaluate the ambiguities of virginity loss and sex among a more diverse group. Especially crucial from a public policy perspective, future investigations should also seek to establish the prevalence of these patterns in a large probability sample. Finally, research on the depiction of virginity loss in mass media would expand scholars' knowledge about the cultural resources young people possess when they approach early sexual experiences. Young people construct their identity as sexual beings in part through virginity loss, but in the contemporary U.S. the meaning of virginity loss is ambiguous, as is the meaning of sex. Better understanding of the many potential meanings of virginity loss thus constitutes a crucial step in developing the comprehensive picture of adolescent sexuality on which sex education, research, and adolescents themselves depend.

Notes

1 Snow and Anderson (1987) identify a third dimension of identity, *self-concept,* which refers to a person's overarching view of herself or himself as a social, moral, and physical being and serves as a "working compromise" between social and personal identity (p. 1348).
2 Focusing on an event that typically preceded the interview by several years may help mitigate this type of selection bias. While adult friends probably hold similar views on sexuality, shared beliefs about virginity per se may be less salient in adult than teen friendships (on teen peers, see Billy & Udry, 1985; Kinsman, Romer, Furstenberg, & Schwartz, 1998; Thompson, 1990). None of the clusters of friends I interviewed included people who had known one another at the time of their own virginity loss.
3 People who are willing to participate in sexuality research may be unusually comfortable talking about sexuality or may perceive their own conduct and attitudes as consonant with social norms. Nonetheless, my sample included several very conservative and several radical respondents. Regrettably, I have no way to ascertain how many people were not included among potential participants because acquaintances declined to recommend them.
4 To preserve confidentiality, all respondents are identified by pseudonyms.
5 I did not ask separate questions about fellatio and cunnilingus, nor did I inquire specifically about perceptions of giving versus receiving oral sex. Respondents' remarks at various junctures indicated disagreement as to whether performing oral sex would be sufficient to cause virginity loss.
6 Qualitative researchers typically favor terms such as *many, seldom,* and *often* over percentage statistics for fear that readers will misinterpret the latter as representing the distribution of beliefs and behaviors among a broader population. Yet, words like "many" can be vague and imprecise. For the sake of precision in meaning, I use both percentage statistics and qualitative expressions. In no case should the reader assume that these percentages can be directly generalized to young adults in the U.S. overall.

References

Aneshensel, C. S., Fielder, E. P., & Becerra, R. M. (1989). Fertility and fertility-related behavior among Mexican-American and non-Hispanic white female adolescents. *Journal of Health and Social Behavior, 30,* 56–76.

Aries, P. (1985). St. Paul and the flesh. In P. Aries & A. Bejin (Eds.), *Western sexuality: Practice and precept in past and present times* (pp. 36–39). Oxford, England: Blackwell.

Berger, D. G., & Wenger, M. G. (1973). The ideology of virginity. *Journal of Marriage and the Family, 35,* 666–676.

Biernacki, P., & Waldorf, D. (1981). Snowball sampling: Problems and techniques of chain referral sampling. *Sociological Methods and Research, 10,* 141–163.

Billy, J. O. G., & Udry, J. R. (1985). Influence of male and female best friends on adolescent sexual behavior. *Adolescence, 20,* 21–32.

Brumberg, J. J. (1997). *The body project.* New York: Random House.

Carpenter, L. M. (2000, August). Gender and the meaning and experience of virginity loss in the contemporary United States. Paper presented at the Annual Meeting of the American Sociological Association, Washington, DC.

D'Emilio, J., & Freedman, E. B. (1988). *Intimate matters: A history of sexuality in America.* New York: Harper & Row.

di Mauro, D. (1995). *Sexuality research in the United States: An assessment of the social and behavioral sciences.* New York: The Social Science Research Council.

Dobie, K. (1995, January/February). Hellbent on redemption. *Mother Jones, 20,* 50–54.

Ehrenreich, B., Hess, E., & Jacobs, G. (1986). *Re-making love: The feminization of sex.* New York: Doubleday.

Elder, L. (1996). *Early embraces.* Los Angeles: Alyson Publications.

Ericksen, J. A. (1999). *Kiss and tell: Surveying sex in the twentieth century.* Cambridge: Harvard University Press.

Ferrell, M. Z., Tolone, W. L., & Walsh, R. H. (1977). Maturational and societal changes in the sexual double-standard: A panel analysis (1967–1971; 1970–1974). *Journal of Marriage and the Family, 39,* 255–271.

Foucault, M. (1978). *The history of sexuality.* New York: Vintage.

Gagnon, J. H., & Simon, W. (1973). *Sexual conduct: The social sources of human sexuality.* Chicago: Aldine.

Giddens, A. (1992). *The transformation of intimacy.* Stanford, CA: Stanford University Press.

Glaser, B. G., & Strauss, A. L. (1967). *The discovery of grounded theory: Strategies for qualitative research.* Chicago: Aldine.

Glaser, B. G., & Strauss, A. L. (1971). *Status passage.* Chicago: Aldine-Atherton.

Goffman, E. (1963). *Stigma: Notes on the management of spoiled identity.* New York: Simon and Schuster.

Goffman, E. (1974). *Frame analysis: An essay on the organization of experience.* Cambridge, MA: Harvard University Press.

Hart, J. (1995). *My first time.* Los Angeles: Alyson Publications.

Hofferth, S. L., Kahn, J. R., & Baldwin, W. (1987). Premarital sexual activity among U.S. teenage women over the past three decades. *Family Planning Perspectives, 19,* 49.

Holland, J., Ramazanoglu, C., & Thomson, R. (1996). In the same boat? The gendered (in)experience of first heterosex. In D. Richardson (Ed.), *Theorising heterosexuality* (pp. 143–160). Bristol, PA: Open University Press.

Horowitz, R. (1983). *Honor and the American dream: Culture and identity in a Chicano community.* New Brunswick, NJ: Rutgers University Press.

Ingrassia, M. (1994, October 17). Virgin cool. *Newsweek, 124,* 58–69.

Jessor, S. L., & Jessor, R. (1975). Transition from virginity to nonvirginity among youth: A social-psychological study over time. *Developmental Psychology, 11,* 473–484.

King, K., Balswick, J. O., & Robinson, I. E. (1977). The continuing premarital sexual revolution among college females. *Journal of Marriage and the Family, 39,* 455–459.

Kinsman, S. B., Romer, D., Furstenberg, F. F., Jr., & Schwartz, D. F. (1998). Early sexual initiation: The role of peer norms. *Pediatrics, 102,* 1185–1193.

Lakoff, G., & Johnson, M. (1980). *Metaphors we live by.* Chicago: University of Chicago Press.

Laumann, E. O., Gagnon, J. H., Michael, R. T., & Michaels, S. (1994). *The social organization of sexuality: Sexual practices in the United States.* Chicago: University of Chicago Press.

Laws, J. L., & Schwartz, P. (1977). *Sexual scripts: The social construction of female sexuality.* Hinsdale, IL: Dryden Press.

Mauss, M. (1925). *The gift.* New York: Norton.

Modell, J. (1983). Dating becomes the way of American youth. In L. P. Moch & G. D. Stark (Eds.), *Essays on the family and historical change* (pp. 91–126). College Station, TX: Texas A & M University Press.

Moffatt, M. (1987). *Coming of age in New Jersey.* New Brunswick, NJ: Rutgers University Press.

Muuss, R.E. (1970). Puberty rites in primitive and modern societies. *Adolescence, 1970,* 109–128.
Nathanson, C. A. (1991). *Dangerous passage: The social control of sexuality in women's adolescence.* Philadelphia: Temple University Press.
Newcomer, S. F., & Udry, J. R. (1985). Oral sex in an adolescent population. *Archives of Sexual Behavior, 14,* 41–46.
Plummer, K. (1995). *Telling sexual stories.* London: Routledge.
Raymond, D. (1994). Homophobia, identity, and the meanings of desire: Reflections on the cultural construction of gay and lesbian adolescent sexuality. In J. M. Irvine (Ed.), *Sexual cultures and the construction of adolescent identities* (pp. 115–150). Philadelphia: Temple University Press.
Reiss, I. L. (1960). *Premarital sexual standards in America.* Glencoe, IL: Free Press.
Rich, A. (1980). Compulsory heterosexuality and lesbian existence. In A. Snitow, C. Stansell, & S. Thompson (Eds.), *Powers of desire: The politics of sexuality* (pp. 177–205). New York: Monthly Review Press.
Rothman, E. K. (1983). Sex and self-control: Middle-class courtship in America, 1770–1870. In M. Gordon (Ed.), *The American family in socio-historical perspective* (pp. 393–10). New York: St. Martin's Press.
Rubin, G. (1984). Thinking sex: Notes for a radical theory of the politics of sexuality. In C. S. Vance (Ed.), *Pleasure and danger: Exploring female sexuality* (pp. 267–319). Boston: Routledge.
Rubin, L. (1990). *Erotic wars: What happened to the sexual revolution?* New York: Farrar, Strauss & Giroux.
Sanders, S., & Reinisch, J. M. (1999). Would you say you "had sex" if . . . ? *Journal of the American Medical Association, 281,* 275–277.
Schlegel, A. (1995). The cultural management of adolescent sexuality. In P. R. Abramson & S. D. Pinkerton (Eds.), *Sexual nature, sexual culture* (pp. 177–194). Chicago: University of Chicago Press.
Schuster, M. A., Bell, R. M., & Kanouse, D. E. (1996). The sexual practices of adolescent virgins: Genital sexual activities of high school students who have never had vaginal intercourse. *American Journal of Public Health, 86,* 1570–1576.
Schwartz, B. (1967). The social psychology of the gift. *American Journal of Sociology, 73,* 1–11.
Seidman, S. (1991). *Romantic longings: Love in America, 1830–1980.* New York: Routledge.
Sherwin, R., & Corbett, S. (1985). Campus sexual norms and dating relationships: A trend analysis. *The Journal of Sex Research, 21,* 258–274.
Smith, E. A., & Udry, J. R. (1985). Coital and non-coital sexual behaviors of white and black adolescents. *American Journal of Public Health, 75,* 1200–1203.
Snow, D. A., & Anderson, L. (1987). Identity work among the homeless: The verbal construction and avowal of personal identities. *American Journal of Sociology, 92,* 1336–1371.
Solin, S. (1996). *The* Seventeen *guide to sex and your body.* New York: Simon and Schuster.
Sprecher, S., Barbee, A., & Schwartz, P. (1995). "Was it good for you, too?": Gender differences in first sexual intercourse experiences. *The Journal of Sex Research, 32,* 3–15.
Sprecher, S., & Regan, P. C. (1996). College virgins: How men and women perceive their sexual status. *The Journal of Sex Research, 33,* 3–15.
Stein, A. (1989). Three models of sexuality. *Sociological Theory, 7,* 1–13.
Sterk-Elifson, C. (1994). Sexuality among African-American women. In A. S. Rossi (Ed.), *Sexuality across the life course* (pp. 99–126). Chicago: University of Chicago Press.
Swidler, A. (1986). Culture in action: Symbols and strategies. *American Sociological Review, 51,* 273–286.
Thompson, S. (1990). Putting a big thing into a little hole: Teenage girls' accounts of sexual initiation. *The Journal of Sex Research, 27,* 341–361.
Thompson, S. (1995). *Going all the way: Teenage girls' tales of sex, romance, and pregnancy.* New York: Hill and Wang.
Tiefer, L. (1995). *Sex is not a natural act and other essays.* Boulder, CO: Westview.
Tolman, D. L. (1994). Doing desire: Adolescent girls' struggles for/with sexuality. *Gender and Society, 8,* 324–342.
Turner, V. (1969). *The ritual process.* Ithaca, NY: Cornell University Press.
van de Walle, E., & Muhsam, H. V. (1995). Fatal secrets and the French fertility transition. *Population and Development Review, 21,* 261–279.
van Gennep, A. (1908). *The rites of passage.* Chicago: University of Chicago Press.
Vance, C. S. (1991). Anthropology rediscovers sexuality: A theoretical comment. *Social Science and Medicine, 33,* 875–884.
Weber, M. (1946). The social psychology of world religions. In H. H. Gerth & C. W. Mills (Eds.), *From Max Weber: Essays in sociology* (pp. 267–301). Oxford, England: Oxford University Press.

Weeks, J. (1985). *Sexuality and its discontents.* London: Routledge.

Welter, B. (1983). The cult of true womanhood: 1820–1860. In M. Gordon (Ed.), *The American family in socio-historical perspective* (pp. 372–392). New York: St. Martin's Press.

Wight, D. (1994). Boys' thoughts and talk about sex in a working class locality of Glasgow. *The Sociological Review, 42,* 703–738.

Zelnik, M., & Shah, F. K. (1983). First intercourse among young Americans. *Family Planning Perspectives, 15,* 64–70.

9

Hooking up

Hot hetero sex or the new numb normative?

Rachel Kalish and Michael Kimmel

'Here at Cornell, nobody dates', says Troy, age 21, a junior. 'We go out in groups to local bars. We go to parties. And then after we're good and drunk, we hook-up. Everyone just hooks up.' When asked whether this involves sex, he half-smiles: 'Hmm . . . maybe, maybe not. That's sort of the beauty of it, you know? Nobody can really be sure.'

This conversation echoes the majority of conversations we have had with young people all across America. Among US college students, 'hooking up' defines the current form of social and sexual relationships. Dating in college, at least the traditional dinner-and-a-movie iteration, seems to be obsolete (England and Thomas 2007). Instead, groups of same-sex friends go out together to meet sexual partners in a casual setting like a bar or a party (Paik 2010; Ronen 2010). Two people run into each other and, after a few drinks they decide to go back to one or the other's residence, where some sexual interaction occurs. There is no expectation of a further relationship. Hook-ups can morph into something else: friends with benefits or a dating relationship (Paik 2010; England, Shafer, and Fogarty 2008), but that requires some additional, and complex, negotiation.

Many adults find this behaviour promiscuous and irresponsible (Stepp 2007). What is this hooking-up culture all about? What does it mean exactly? What's the *point* of all that sex? The *Online College Social Life Survey* was developed in an effort to find out. It has now been administered to about 14,600 students at 19 campuses—large and small, public and private—in the United States.[1] We asked participants about their experiences of various sexual behaviours, orgasm, drinking behaviour, and romantic relationships. We asked both women and men, gay and straight (but mostly straight). Most were between 18 and 24. Many of the findings are unsurprising; after all, young adulthood since the 1960s has been a time of relative sexual freedom and well-documented experimentation (Becker 1972). What may be surprising, though, is how many young people accept that hooking up—recreational sex with no strings attached—is the *best* arrangement available to them (Paul 2006; Bogle 2008; England and Thomas 2007). Once, sexual promiscuity co-existed with traditional forms of dating, and young people could manoeuvre between the two on their way towards serious romantic relationships (Paik 2010). Now, hooking up is all there is; relationships begin and end with sex. Hooking up has become the alpha and omega of young adult romance (Paik 2010; England, Shafer, and Fogarty 2008).

Although hooking up might seem utterly mutual—after all, women and men both participate—what appears on the surface turns out to be a bit more complex. Despite enormous changes in the sexual attitudes of young people in America, the gender politics of campus sex do not seem to have changed very much at all. Sex on campus remains 'guys' sex'. Women are welcome to act upon their sexual desires, but guys run the scene. Women who decide not to join the party can look forward to going to sleep early and alone. Women who do join the party run the risk of encountering the same old double standard that no amount of feminist progress seems able to eradicate fully (Schalet 2010; Ronen 2010; Paul 2006; Allen 2003; Crawford and Popp 2003). Though women may accommodate themselves to men's desires—indeed, some feel they have to accommodate themselves to them—the men's rules rule. Yet many pro-active young women embrace their sexuality and enter into what may not be an even playing field, negotiating their own levelling mechanisms (Allen 2003). They are free to want sex, and free to have it. While the hook-up culture on many US campuses facilitates the separation of sex from emotion, allowing young women to adopt a traditionally 'male' model of sexual behaviour, campus politics sometimes requires some nuanced identity work on the part of young women to escape social scorn or stigma for their sexual behaviour, and the ambiguity of the term 'hooking up' allows them that (Epstein et al. 2009).

Hooking up at American colleges is not only about sex, it is also a form of communication (Epstein et al. 2009). It can be about conquest, but the hook-up culture can also be used to stratify students. As often as we heard young women telling us that they discuss who has hooked up with whom, we also heard young women describing their concerns about their hook-up partners telling friends, or worrying about getting a reputation based on their hook-ups.

Is there a relationship between hooking up and pleasure? After nearly half a century of feminist campaigns enlarging the erotic possibilities for women, encouraging sexual agency and autonomy, is hooking up a bold step forward for women, enabling them to pursue pleasure for its own sake, or a gigantic step backwards, a coercive strategy to force women to play by 'men's rules' in the sexual marketplace, delimiting the possibilities for autonomous erotic pleasure?

We argue that this either/or framing is problematic. Hooking up is both a step forward for women who seek to expand their erotic repertoire and explore various facets of heterosexual desire. At the same time, as the new normative sexual experience among American university students, it structures that very erotic exploration into definable and normative constructs, constraining the very impulses it enables. In gendered terms, we argue that it represents a moment in what might be called 'the masculinisation of sex', the employment of gendered meanings to understand heterosexual desire. Women's sexual experience comes increasingly to resemble men's; indeed, the criteria by which heterosexual pleasure is measured are gendered criteria (Crawford and Popp 2003; D'Emilio and Freedman 1997). Just as friendship and love have been increasingly 'feminised'—criteria of female friendships have come to define what friendship and love actually mean (see Cancian 1987)—so, too, have we witnessed a parallel masculinisation of sex. Indeed, this is the flip-side of the feminisation of love; masculine notions that sex and love are separate, and that the non-relational pursuit of sex is an end in itself, are expressions of that gradual separation. Women are increasingly taking on these behaviours, at times to the chagrin of some traditional critics.

While hooking up may be seen as a gender-neutral terrain on which heterosexual desire is played out, we argue that many of its features can reproduce gender inequality (Bogle 2008). Hooking up most closely resembles the socio-sexual patterns of mainstream gay male subculture of the pre-HIV era, in which groups of friends would go to a bar, find a potential sex partner, and engage in some sexual activity with no expectation of a future romantic or emotional relationship (Levine 1998). While same-sex sexuality could be constructed relatively independently of gender relations, empirically, it seems that the gender of the actor is more critical than the gender of the person's partner; that is, the sexualities of lesbians were organised around different gendered normative structures than the sexualities of gay men (see Michael et al. 1995). Even when lesbians constructed a gender-non-normative sexuality, it was organised through a repudiation of traditional notions of femininity; that is, constructed through gender (see Califia 1988).

We argue that hooking up enables the expansion of the heterosexual erotic repertoire while at the same time constraining some of the very expressions it is supposed to be liberating. It does both because it is a deeply gendered sexual project that takes place on a gender-unequal terrain, and therefore reproduces the masculinisation of sex, with varying consequences for women. While others are quick to point out the negative consequences for women (Stepp 2007; Glenn and Marquardt 2001), we aim to highlight the positive aspects of hooking up for agentic and sex-positive young American women.

Historical American campus sexual patterns

In the 1930s, sociologist Willard Waller (1937) described American campus romance as a complex dance that he called 'rating-dating-mating': a competitive romantic marketplace in which students rated themselves in reference to both the other sex and the evaluations of their peers. They then sought to date appropriately. In order to have a 'Class A' rating, men 'must belong to one of the better fraternities, be prominent in activities, have a copious supply of spending money, be well-dressed, be "smooth" in manners and appearance, have a "good line", dance well and have access to an automobile'. Women, by contrast, may need 'good clothes, a smooth line, ability to dance well', but paramount, was her already-determined 'popularity as a date', since her 'prestige depends on dating more than anything else' (Waller 1937, 730). What is immediately striking about Waller's comment, written nearly three-quarters of a century ago, is how accurate it continues to be.

In Waller's time, all this rating and dating was ultimately in the service of mating: relationships between committed intimate partners that would lead, eventually, to marriage. Today, this sequence has been all but abandoned among young Americans. They still rate themselves and each other. Men have to be cool, women effortlessly perfect. But the idea of dating seems obsolete. Today, American campus culture is not about dating to find an appropriate mate; it's more about mating to find an appropriate date!

'A date for me is like when a guy calls you up and says, "would you like to go someplace," you know, like to dinner, or to a movie', says Debbie, a 21-year-old senior at the University of Virginia. 'That never happens here!', she laughs. 'Now it's like you see a guy at a party and he says, "What are you doing now? Can I walk you home?" It's like, you know, the beginning of the date is like the end of the date. He walks you home, and then you hook-up.'

In some ways this is not news. College campuses have always been places of sexual experimentation, freedom, and predation (Becker 1972). Many of the reasons are obvious: young people are out from under direct parental control and feel freer to experiment with different activities. Being away from home means they are also freed from the critical scrutiny of their high school and neighbourhood friends, free to try on new identities with different cliques (Becker 1972). Living in close proximity to many age-mates fosters close friendships. In college, the shift from family to peers as a regulator of mate selection is cemented. This emphasis on friendships lessens the primacy of romantic relationships (Roseneil 2005) and also allows mate selection to serve as a form of communication among peers.

Stated simply, *a college student today will never again be in a place where there are so many sexually active unmarried people.* Nor will college students ever again be around so many sexually active people *like themselves,* with roughly similar class and race characteristics (since homogamy is often present in college sexual activity). Prior to college, not as many people are sexually active (Michael et al. 1995). After college, not as many people are sexually available, either in terms of their physical proximity or in terms of their relationship status. College is the quintessential gathering place for middle-class Americans aged 18–22 (Bogle 2008). Before and after college, such casual couplings need to be a bit better planned—before because they live with their parents, and after, because they have to leave their home or apartment.

Hooking up

In recent years, scholarly researchers and intrepid journalists have bravely waded in to demarcate the term 'hooking up', to map its boundaries and explain its strange terrain. Yet these definitions are vague and contradictory. One research group refers to it as 'a sexual encounter which may or may not include sexual intercourse, usually occurring on only one occasion between two people who are strangers or brief acquaintances' (Paul and Hayes 2002, 642–43). Another study maintains that hooking up 'occurs when two people who are casual acquaintances or who have just met that evening at a bar or party agree to engage in some forms of sexual behavior for which there will likely be no future commitment' (Lambert, Kahn, and Apple 2003, 129).

Our collaborative research project, the *Online College Social Life Survey,* found that hooking up covers a multitude of behaviours, including kissing (61 per cent) and nongenital touching (51 per cent), oral sex but not intercourse (24 per cent), manual stimulation of the genitals (38 per cent), and intercourse (23 per cent). It can mean 'going all the way'. Or it can mean 'everything but'. By their senior year, we found that students had averaged nearly seven hook-ups during their collegiate careers. A little less than half (42 per cent) say they have never hooked up, while slightly less than a third (28 per cent) have hooked up 10 times or more.[2] So some American undergraduates avoid the hook-up culture, while others dive in. Regression analyses show that the students who hook up more are those who are younger, white, and less religious (Kalish 2007).

As a verb, 'to hook up' means to engage in any type of sexual activity with someone without a relationship. Hooking up is used to describe casual sexual encounters on a continuum from 'one-and-done' (a hook up that takes place only once with someone who may or may not be a stranger) to 'sex buddies' (acquaintances who meet regularly for sex but rarely if ever associate otherwise), to 'friends with benefits' (friends who do not care to become romantic partners, but may include sex among the activities they enjoy together) (Paul 2006; Paik 2010).

Part of what makes the hook-up culture so difficult to define and describe is the simple fact that young men and women experience it in very different ways. They may be playing the same game, but they are playing by a different set of rules, and they define 'winning' and even 'scoring' in totally different ways. Gender is the key to understanding these campus sexual patterns or, rather, the different ways in which these behaviours are interpreted by American men and women. Yet we must also recognise another institution that inherently shapes hook-up culture and those who participate: heterosexuality.

The institution of heterosexuality is still pervasive in shaping young people and especially impacts their enactment of gender (Allen 2003; Tolman, Striepe, and Harmon 2003). The institution of heterosexuality inundates society with the notions that heterosexual behaviours are optimal, denigrating any other behaviours (Rich 1983). Tolman, Striepe, and Harmon assert that:

> Ideologies of masculinity and femininity, which infuse constructions of adolescent male and female sexuality, fit together to reproduce particular and limited forms of sexuality . . . the notion that adolescent boys are sexual predators fits together with the notion that

> adolescent girls are supposed to be sexually passive. Both notions represent and reproduce compulsory heterosexuality.
>
> *(2003, 10)*

In the context of American hook-up culture, this operates in differentiating perceptions and behaviours by gender. For males, hooking up becomes a form of homosocial communication, by which they communicate and earn status with peers. For females, compulsory heterosexuality, in tandem with gendered notions of femininity, prioritises romance, which 'disable[s] them from being agentic and authentic about their bodies and sexual relationships' (Tolman, Striepe, and Harmon 2003, 9) which we will discuss below.

Deliberate vagueness

The phrase 'hooking up' itself is deliberately vague, which is why any attempt to define it concretely will inevitably fall short. In fact, it is that very vagueness and ambiguity that characterises it; according to Alice, a sophomore at the University of Maine:

> But see, hooking up and having sex can be two different things. It's really hard. When people say, 'We hooked up' you don't really know what they mean by that. They could be having sex every night and you're assuming that they probably just made out or something like that.

(Note that names and colleges have been changed to protect the anonymity of the respondents.)

That vagueness serves men and women in different ways. When a young male says he 'hooked up' with someone, he may or may not have had sex with her, but he is certainly hoping that his friends think he has. A woman, on the other hand, is more likely to hope they think she has not (Schalet 2010).

In a sense, hooking up retains certain features of older dating patterns: male domination, female compliance, and double standards. Although hooking up may seem to be mutually desired by both males and females, our research indicates that males initiate sexual behaviour most of the time (less than a third of respondents said this was mutual). Hook-ups are twice as likely to take place in his room as in hers. Hooking up enhances his reputation whereas it can damage hers. Men who hook up a lot are seen by their peers as studs; women who hook up a lot are seen as sluts who 'give it up' (Allen 2003; Crawford and Popp 2003; Paul 2006). This may be why many young women prefer to hook up in the guy's room; enduring a 'walk of shame' home early in the morning may be less damaging to her reputation than having a steady stream of guys entering and exiting her dorm room.

The vagueness of the term itself—hooking up—turns out to be a way to protect the reputation of the woman while enhancing that of the man (Epstein et al. 2009). In addition to that conceptual vagueness after the fact, hook-ups are also characterised by vagueness before and even during the fact. Most hook-ups share three elements: spontaneity; the nearly inevitable use of alcohol; and the absence of any expectation of a relationship.

Planned spontaneity

This spontaneity is nonetheless carefully planned. American males have elaborate rituals for what has become known as 'the girl hunt' (Grazian 2007). There are 'pre-game' rituals such as drinking before you go out to bars, since consuming alcohol, a requirement, is expensive and it is more cost effective to begin the buzz before you set out (Kimmel 2008).

When men claim that the hook-up is spontaneous, they are referring not to whether or not the hook-up will take place, but with whom. Women have a different view of spontaneity. Since they know that hooking up is what the guys want, the girls cannot be 'spontaneous' about it. They have to think—whether or not, with whom, under what conditions—and plan accordingly. They have to decide how much they can drink, how much they can flirt, and how to avoid any potentially embarrassing or even threatening situations. The males lounge in comfort of the illusion of alcohol-induced spontaneity; the women are several steps ahead of them.

Yet the illusion of spontaneity remains important for both males and females. It is a way of distancing yourself from your own sexual agency, a way of pretending that sex just happens (Tolman 2002). It helps young people to maintain invulnerability around the whole thing. It is better to appear less interested, that way no one will know the extent of your disappointment if your plans do not come to fruition. Such a posture complicates the pursuit of pleasure, especially for women.

This distance from sexual agency is interesting for women since, in many cases, it can be their earliest attempts at embodying their sexual agency, and then they feel disentangled from their own agentic sexuality. The double standard that exists makes this an attractive alternative for women who are coming into their sexuality but are doing so in an environment where women who seek out sex are stigmatised (Ronen 2010; Allen 2003). So, rather than risking the potentially devastating label of 'slut' by going out deliberately to seek sex, sex-positive young women can wade into the hook-up scene and enact their sexuality as they choose while being able to fall back on the idea that the sex 'just happened' (Tolman 2002). The ambiguity of the term as well as the presence of alcohol also offer potential ways for sexually agentic women to evade stigma.

The inevitability of alcohol

Virtually all hooking up is lubricated with copious amounts of alcohol, likely more alcohol than sex: 'A notable feature of hook-ups is that they almost always occur when both participants are drinking or drunk' (Glenn and Marquardt 2001, 15). In our study, men averaged nearly five drinks on their most recent hook-up, women nearly three. Alcohol is seen as germane to the US college environment (Bogle 2008). In qualitative interviews, more students discussed feeling pressure to drink than they did to hook up. Hooking up, it appears, may be optional, but on the American college social scene, intoxication is not.

To say that alcohol clouds one's judgment would be an understatement. Drinking is *supposed* to cloud judgment. Drinking gives the drinker 'beer goggles', which typically expand one's notion of other people's sexual attractiveness (Paul 2006).

Yet that is only part of the story. The other part is to cloud *other people's* judgment. If you were drunk, you do not have to take responsibility for what happens. For males, this means that if they get rejected they can attribute it to drunkenness. The same holds true for their sexual performance if they do find a willing partner. In fact, drunkenness provides a convenient excuse for all sorts of potential sexual disasters, from rejection to premature ejaculation to general ineptitude born of inexperience. For a lot of guys, the liquid courage provided by alcohol is the only thing that makes them able to withstand the potential for rejection that any sexual advance entails in the first place (Epstein et al. 2009).

For women, alcohol may allow for a wider range of behaviours to be expressed, and it may also encourage young women to be more agentic in their sexuality, perhaps by talking to a potential partner rather than waiting for him to approach her. As mentioned above, women who are more forthright about their sexual desires can fall back on intoxication as an excuse should their behaviour be scrutinised by peers. At modern US colleges, it is still easier for young women to say 'Oh, I was drunk' rather than say 'well, I just wanted to get laid'. Intoxication is normative for young women, but actually wanting sex is more problematic, and problematised.

The absence of expectations

One of the key features of hooking up is that it is strictly a 'no-strings-attached' event. Young Americans in college—and this applies to both women and men—seem generally wary of relationships. The focus is always on what it costs, rather than what it might provide. And if you consider the prevalence of divorce (D'Emilio and Freedman 1997), their cynicism is neither surprising nor unfounded. Hooking up is seen as being a lot easier than having a relationship. Students constantly say that having a relationship, actually dating, takes a lot of time, and 'like, who has time to date?' asks Greg, a junior at the College of Wooster in Ohio. 'I mean, we're all really busy, and we have school, and classes, and jobs, and friends, and all.' Students want relationships someday, but they do not want to waste precious party time in college to put in the effort that a relationship requires.

Young women today are more comfortable with their sexuality than any generation in history (Siegel 2007). There are certainly women who prefer hooking up to relationships. Women also hook up to avoid emotional entanglements that would distract them from their studies, professional ambitions, friendship networks and other commitments. Or they hook up because they do not think they are ready for a commitment and they just want to hang out and have fun (Stepp 2007). Yet many also do it because it is the only game in town. If they want to have sexual relationships with men—and by all appearances they certainly do—then this is the field on which they must play. Some women may want more, some may not, but since more is not available either way, they take what they can get, but they try to do so in a manner that works best for them.

Hooking up and relationships: 'the talk'

In general, women tend to be more ambivalent about hook-up culture; some report feeling sexy and desirable, others feel it is cheap and rarely leads anywhere (Stepp 2007). When it comes to forming an actual relationship, the women are the ones who attempt to negotiate whether the hooking up will proceed to a deeper level of intimacy. 'Are we a couple or not?' she asks, and the decision is up to her male partner.

Most American students indicate that they want to get married someday, just not now and probably not until their early 30s (D'Emilio and Freedman 1997). Their relationship phobias are less related to fears of commitment, and more to do with the time commitment involved. US students do not see the need to expend time working at a relationship, especially if they can have the sexual aspect without the effort. Hooking up, for guys, is less a relationship path than it is for some women. In fact, it serves an entirely different purpose.

Male hook-ups: homosocial interaction

In some ways hooking up represents the sexual component of young men's more general aversion to adulthood. They do not want girlfriends or serious relationships in part because they do not feel themselves ready and also in part because they see relationships as 'too much work'. Instead, they want the benefits of adult relationships, which for them seem to be exclusively sexual, with none of the responsibility that goes along with adult sexuality: the emotional connection, caring, mutuality, and sometimes even the common human decency that mature sexual relationships demand. Put simply, hooking up *is* the form of relationship guys want with girls (Kimmel 2008).

Yet it is more complicated than simple pleasure seeking on the part of men, because as it turns out pleasure is not the first item on the hook-up agenda. In fact, pleasure barely appears on the list at all (Paul 2006). If sex were the goal, a man would have a much better chance of having more (and better) sex if he had a steady girlfriend. The actual experience of sex pales in comparison to the experience of talking about sex (Epstein et al. 2009; Kimmel 2008):

> When I've just got laid, the first thing I think about—really, I shouldn't be telling you this, but really it's the very first thing, before I've even like 'finished'—is that I can't wait to tell my crew who I just did. Like, I say to myself, 'Omigod, they're not going to believe that I just did Kristy!'

So says Ted, a 21-year-old junior at Wisconsin:

> Like I just know what will happen. They'll all be high fiving me and shit. And Kristy? Uh, well, she'll probably ask me not to tell anyone, you know, to protect her reputation and all. But, like, yeah, right. I'm still gonna tell my boys.

Hooking up has less to do with guys' relationships with women and a lot more to do with guys' relationships with other guys. 'It's like the girls you hook-up with, they're like a way of showing off to other guys', says Jeff, a fraternity member at the University of Northern Iowa:

> I mean, you tell your friends you hooked up with Melissa, and they're like, 'whoa, dude, you are one stud.' So, I'm into Melissa because my guy friends think she is so hot, and now they think more of me because of it. It's totally a guy thing.

He looks a bit sheepish. 'Don't get me wrong', he adds, with little affect. 'I mean, yeah, Melissa is very nice and blah blah blah. I like her, yeah. But', he lights up again, 'the guys think I totally rule'.

Ted's and Jeff's comments echo those heard from young men all across America. Hooking up is a way that men communicate with other men; it is about homosociality. It is a way that males compete with each other, assert their masculinity, establish a pecking order, and attempt to move up in their rankings (Epstein et al. 2009). Seen in this light, the hook-up culture, at least for men, is more than a desperate bid simply to keep up. It is a way to keep up, and keep quiet about it, while being rather noisy at the same time.

Young women are far more concerned with how much information is out there about their hook-up behaviours. Yet young women will also rate each other not as much by with whom they hook up, as males do, but by how often they hook up. There is a fine line demarcating the 'correct' number of hook-up partners, so many young women worry about protecting their privacy, and their reputations (Paul 2006).

Female hook-ups: balancing agency and expectations

Increasing numbers of women are diving into the hook-up culture, yet their experiences are internalised differently from their male peers. While hook-up culture may be an example of previously marginalised behaviours moving back into the centre, the double standard does still exist, and the ramifications of it are acutely felt by young women, who manoeuvre between expressing their sexual desires, and restricting those desires to enact stereotypical gender role expectations (Tolman, Striepe, and Harmon 2003; Allen 2003; Paul 2006).

While males see hooking up as a form of communication, women's experiences with hooking up can be grouped into different categories, related to her expectations of the hook up. Some American women hook up to achieve a relationship or to express their feelings towards a male partner, in line with traditional notions of femininity; some do it to have fun or to enjoy their own sexuality, which would be seen as more transgressive. In qualitative interviews, when asked why they hook up, the most common response was 'for fun', followed by 'because I like him'. It is a small proportion of women who hook up for the sole purpose of finding a relationship, possibly because their male counterparts do not cooperate, or because experience leads them to alter their expectations (Paul 2006).

Women, however, repeatedly stressed the need to 'be smart' to avoid getting hurt. Emily, a junior at Stony Brook University in New York, tells us: 'If you go into it with Disneyish expectations and equate hook-ups with a relationship, you'll get hurt.' Emily, and others like her, are able to enjoy hooking up, and feel empowered doing so. Such sex-positive young women provide proof that women can engage in casual sexual behaviours without negative consequence (Eisenberg et al. 2009), which directly counters the more pervasive narrative that hooking up is inherently damaging for young women (Stepp 2007; Glenn and Marquardt 2001).

We go one step further and see potential benefits of hook-up behaviours for young heterosexual women. Through hooking up, emergent adults learn what to expect in heterosexual interactions (Paul 2006), yet they can also learn about their own sexuality. While faking orgasm (discussed below) is not instructive in teaching males how to provide female pleasure, young women have the opportunity to learn how to be agentic sexually through the hook-up culture (Allen 2003).

Hooking up vs good sex

Mature sexual relationships are complex; fulfilling sex often occurs in the context of committed relationships (Gottman 1995). Hooking up may provide quantitative evidence of sexual prowess, but it cannot answer the qualitative insecurities that invariably attend sexual relationships. Hooking up may make one feel more like a man when talking with other guys, but it does not help—indeed, it may actually hinder—healthy and mutually satisfying sexual relationships with women. Hooking up offers sex without entanglements, but it is attended by so many possibilities for crises and misunderstanding that it can still become quite entangled. Since there is so much surface interaction in hook-up culture, but so little actual connection, most of this stays buried.

With all this hooking up, friends with benefits, and booty calls, guys should feel they have it made. Yet there is a creeping anxiety that continually haunts men's sexual activities. They worry that perhaps they are not doing it enough, or well enough, or they are not big enough or hard enough. Though the *evidence* suggests that men are in the driver's seat when it comes to sex, they *feel* that women have all the power, especially the power to say no.

And these days, those women have a new 'power': the power to compare. Many men become suddenly uneasy when the topic of women's sexual expectations came up in conversation. Jeff, a sophomore at UC San Diego, said:

> Uh, this is the tough part, you know. I mean, well, like, *we're* supposed to have hooked up a lot, but now so are they, and they, like, talk about it in ways that we guys never would. So, like, you feel like you have to be this fabulous lover and they have to come at least three times,

> and like, your, you know, your, uh, dick isn't the biggest she's ever seen, and like you always feel like you're being measured and coming up a bit . . . [he laughs uncomfortably], short.

Men often feel a lot of pressure to hook up and to let their friends know about it. They feel a lot of pressure to be great in bed. In Bogle's (2008) study, some students estimated that some of their friends were hooking up 25 times every semester. While the individual men in Bogle's survey believed that, in terms of their own experiences, hooking up meant kissing and other sexual play, they willingly believed that their *friends* were actually having full intercourse. 'It's always the *other* student who, they believed, actually had intercourse every time they hooked up', Bogle writes (2008, 90).

When we asked men to estimate the percentage of other males on their campus who had sex on any given weekend, the average answer given was about 80 per cent. That is, it was commonly believed that four out of every five men on campus had had sex. In actually, the figure of 80 per cent is the percentage of senior men who have *ever* had vaginal intercourse in our college survey. The actual percentage of college males having sex on any given weekend is between 5 per cent and 10 per cent of men surveyed. This gives one an idea of how pervasive the hook-up culture is, how it distorts perceptions, and the sorts of pressures one might feel. How can he feel like a man if he is the only one not getting laid? If so many women are available, sexually promiscuous, and hooking up as randomly as the men are, what is wrong with him if he is the only one who is unsuccessful?

As it turns out, men's insecurity is not altogether unfounded. In our survey, in their most recent hook-ups, regardless of what actually took place, only 19 per cent of the women reported having an orgasm, as compared to 43 per cent of the men. When women received cunnilingus, only about a quarter experienced an orgasm, though the men who reported they had performed cunnilingus on their partner reported that she had an orgasm almost 60 per cent of the time. This orgasm gap extends to intercourse as well. Women report an orgasm 19 per cent of the time; the men report that the women had an orgasm 39 per cent of the time. (The women, unsurprisingly, are far better able to tell if the men had orgasms, and reporting rates are virtually identical.)

Many women fake orgasm, and most do so 'to make that person feel good, to make them feel like they've done their job', as one woman put it in an interview. Some women said that they faked it 'just really to end it,' because 'they're like bored with it' (England, Shafer, and Fogarty 2008, 538). 'He was, like, trying so hard to make me come', says Trish, a senior. 'And there was like no way it was going to happen. I felt so bad for him. I mean, I had gone down on him and he came already, and he was, like, trying to be a good sport about it, but really . . . So I just faked it and he felt good and I felt relieved.'

The hook-up culture is also a source of pressure for women, but perhaps not the pressure one would expect. Women feel pressured to enjoy sex, or to let their partner think they enjoyed the sex. Given that many young women are still socialised to be nurturing, it is not surprising that young women may put their partner's needs ahead of theirs (Tolman, Striepe, and Harmon 2003) by faking orgasm to validate their partner's sexual skills (England, Shafer, and Fogarty 2008). Additionally, non-academic discourse on hooking up tells the story of young women desperate for relationships so they hook up with strangers in a quest for attention (Stepp 2007). Yet, in interviews with young women, not a single one said they hook up because they felt pressure. Instead, they indicated that they hook up because they are bored, attracted to someone, or, dare we say it, horny. The pressure young women face is pressure to be 'on the scene', to have the 'right' look to attract the 'right' guys. Once those guys are attracted, women are not as much concerned with the pressure to hook up as they are with the worry that their hook-up partner will not demand too much of their time, or tell their guy friends about the hook up.

Hooking up and gender politics

Anti-feminist jeremiads fret constantly about women's lost modesty, chastity, or even their capitulation to male standards of sexual conduct. Conservative columnists complain about ever-loosening sexual mores, and use the gender inequality of hook-up culture to advise women to keep their legs crossed (Stepp 2007). Women, they counsel, must remember the message that their grandmothers might once have told them: 'Men want only one thing.' So women, if they yearn for commitment and marriage, have to re-learn how to just say no.

Such advice ignores the pleasure-seeking behaviours and intentions of both women *and* men, and assumes that women are naturally chaste and virginal, were it not for those rapaciously predatory men. Such an image is outdated to women who have shown themselves fully capable of seeking and enjoying sex in ways that their mothers—and certainly those grandmothers!—could never have imagined.[3] Both women and men are pleasure-seeking creatures (Allen 2003), especially on campus, and it allows young American men to continue to avoid being accountable if the focus of all the advice is only on women.

The truth is, hooking up is not the end of the world. It is a time out, like college. More importantly, it is a political time out; that is, it is experienced differently, and unequally, by women and men. Focusing all one's moralising attention on young women only perpetuates that inequality, rather than challenges it.

Hooking up: the new normative?

What these earnest warnings miss, of course, is that not the opposition between hooking up and courtship, but that hooking up *is* today's culture of courtship. It is certainly not true that all the women are hooking up in order to develop relationships, nor are all guys hooking up in the hopes of avoiding precisely the relationships that the women are seeking (Allen 2003). Most actually want relationships. But, most say, not quite yet.

American college students today will get married—eventually. It will be about eight years later than their mothers and fathers did. They will do that by choice, because they want to establish careers, enjoy relationships, and develop autonomy before marriage (D'Emilio and Freedman 1997). The contemporary culture of courtship is not their parents' culture of courtship, but it is no less a 'culture' and no less legitimate.

The students interviewed in depth following our quantitative survey were convincing on this score. Hooking up, in their minds, is not an alternative to relationships. It is the new pathway to forming relationships. Even if only a small percentage of hook-ups result in relationships, most relationships do begin with a hook up. For some, hooking up is most definitely in the service of some future relationship—just not this particular one. Sociologist Kathleen Bogle argues that hooking up has become the normative path to relationships on campus. 'There's something about the way people define college life as a time to party and a time to kick back', she told a journalist. 'They're postponing marriage, so they have time to play the field' (Jayson 2007).

Hooking up can be a nice distraction from school work that does not require a great input of time; time which many students need to devote to classes, work, internships, and other things that make them attractive candidates to graduate schools or on the job market. For American college women today, it is *that* market that takes precedence over the marriage market. Just as they will 'play the field' by applying to a variety of graduate programs or internships, so do they enjoy the sexual sampling and exploration that the hook-up culture enables.

Notes

1 A list of participating schools is available on request.
2 Our numbers seem to square with other surveys or, perhaps, run a bit to the conservative side, since we have a large sample of colleges in our pool and virtually all other surveys were done only at the researcher's own university.
3 For examples of this, see Stepp (2007) and Glenn and Marquardt (2001).

References

Allen, Louisa. 2003. Girls want sex, boys want love: Resisting dominant discourses of (hetero)sexuality. *Sexualities* 6 (2): 215–36.

Becker, Howard S. 1972. 'What do they really learn at college?'. In *College and student: Selected readings in the social psychology of higher education,* edited by K.A. Feldman. New York: Pergamon.

Bogle, Kathleen A. 2008. *Hooking up: Sex, dating and relationships on campus.* New York: New York University Press.

Califia, Pat. 1988. *Sapphistry: The book of lesbian sexuality.* Tallahassee, FL: Naiad Press.

Cancian, Francesca. 1987. *The feminization of love.* New York: Cambridge University Press.

Crawford, Mary, and Danielle Popp. 2003. Sexual double standards: A review and methodological critique of two decades of research. *Journal of Sex Research* 40 (1): 13–27.

D'Emilio, John, and Estelle B. Freedman. 1997. *Intimate matters: A history of sexuality in America.* 2nd ed. Chicago: University of Chicago Press.

Eisenberg, Marla E., Diann M. Ackard, Michael D. Resnick, and Diane Neumark-Sztainer. 2009. Casual sex and psychological health among young adults: Is having 'friends with benefits' emotionally damaging? *Perspectives on Sexual and Reproductive Health* 41 (4): 231–7.

England, Paula, Emily Fitzgibbons Shafer, and Alison C.K. Fogarty. 2008. Hooking up and forming romantic relationships on today's college campuses. In *The gendered society reader,* edited by M.S. Kimmel and A. Aronson. New York: Oxford University Press.

England, Paula, and Ruben J. Thomas. 2007. The decline of the date and the rise of the college hook up. In *Family in transition,* edited by A.S. Skolnik and J.H. Skolnik. 14th ed. Boston: Allyn & Bacon.

Epstein, Marina, Jerel P. Calzo, Andrew P. Smiler, and L. Monique Ward. 2009. 'Anything from making out to having sex': Men's negotiations of hooking up and friends with benefits scripts. *Journal of Sex Research* 46: 414–24.

Glenn, Norval, and Elizabeth Marquardt. 2001. *Hooking up, hanging out, and hoping for Mr. Right: College women on dating and mating today.* Institute for American Values report to the Independent Women's Forum New York: Institute for American Values.

Gottman, John. 1995. *Why marriages succeed or fail.* New York: Simon & Schuster.

Grazian, David. 2007. The girl hunt: Urban nightlife and the performance of masculinity as a collective activity. *Symbolic Interaction* 30 (2): 221–43.

Jayson, Sharon. 2005. Teens define sex in new ways. *USA Today,* 18 October: 1.

Kalish, Rachel. 2007. Perceived norms and hook ups among college students: Evidence from the College Social Life Survey. Unpublished manuscript, Department of Sociology, Stony Brook University, New York.

Kimmel, Michael S. 2008. *Guyland: The perilous world where boys become men.* New York: Harper.

Lambert, Tracey A., Arnold S. Kahn, and Kevin J. Apple. 2003. Pluralistic ignorance and hooking up. *Journal of Sex Research* 40: 129–33.

Levine, Martin. 1998. *Gay macho: The life and death of the homosexual clone.* New York: New York University Press.

Michael, R.T., J.S. Gagnon, E.O. Laumann, and G. Kolata. 1995. *Sex in America: A definitive survey.* New York: Warner Books.

Paik, Anthony. 2010. The contexts of sexual involvement and concurrent sexual partnerships. *Perspectives on Sexual and Reproductive Health* 42 (1): 33–42.

Paul, Elizabeth L. 2006. Beer goggles, catching feelings, and the walk of shame: The myths and realities of the hookup experience. In *Relating difficulty: The processes of constructing and managing difficult interaction,* edited by D.C. Kirkpatrick, S. Duck, and M.K. Foley. Mahwah, NJ: Lawrence Erlbaum.

Paul, Elizabeth L., and Allison Hayes. 2002. The casualties of 'casual' sex: A qualitative exploration of the phenomenology of college students' hookups. *Journal of Social and Personal Relationships* 19 (5): 639–63.

Rich, Adrienne. 1983. Compulsory heterosexuality and lesbian existence. In *Powers of desire: The politics of sexuality*, edited by A. Snitow, C. Stansell, and S. Thompson. New York: Monthly Review Press.
Ronen, Shelly. 2010. Grinding on the dance floor: Gendered scripts and sexualized dancing at college parties. *Gender and Society* 24 (3): 355–77.
Roseneil, Sasha. 2005. Living and loving beyond the boundaries of heteronorm: Personal relationships in the 21st century. In *Families in society: Boundaries and relationships*, edited by Linda McKie and Sarah Cunningham-Burley. Bristol: Policy Press.
Schalet, Amy. 2010. Sexual subjectivity revisited: The significance of relationships in Dutch and American girls' experiences of sexuality. *Gender and Society* 24 (3): 304–29.
Siegel, Deborah. 2007. *Sisterhood interrupted: From radical women to grrrls gone wild*. New York: Palgrave.
Stepp, Laura Sessions. 2007. *Unhooked: How young women pursue sex, delay love, and lose at both*. New York: Riverhead Books.
Tolman, Deborah L. 2002. *Dilemmas of desire: Teenage girls talk about sexuality*. Cambridge, MA: Harvard University Press.
Tolman, Deborah L., Meg Striepe, and Tricia Harmon. 2003. Constructing a model of adolescent sexual health. *Journal of Sex Research* 40 (1): 4–13.
Waller, Willard. 1937. The rating and dating complex. *American Sociological Review* 2: 727–34.

10

"Speaking as a heterosexual"

(How) does sexuality matter for talk-in-interaction?

*Celia Kitzinger**

Compared with the accumulation of research on the speech and language of lesbian, gay, bisexual, and transgender (LGBT) people (e.g., Chesbro, 1981; Jacobs, 1996; Kulick, 1998, 2000; Leap, 1996; Livia & Hall, 1997), the talk of heterosexuals *qua* heterosexuals has been much less studied. As Cameron and Kulick (2003) pointed out, "One of the privileges enjoyed by dominant groups in general is that their identities and modes of behaviour are rarely scrutinized in the same way as the identities and behaviours of subordinated groups" (p. 153). Animated in part by the analytic interest in how dominant groups construct the social world (see also Wilkinson & Kitzinger, 1993, 1996), this article draws on a series of conversations accumulated by conversation analysts over the course of a couple of decades of data collection and inspects them for the varying ways in which the co-conversationalists display their heterosexuality to one another and, thereby, to us as analysts.

As I show, virtually all the talk on which the classic findings of conversation analysis (CA) are based is produced by heterosexuals, who reproduce in their talk a normative taken-for-granted heterosexual world. Whatever their *internal* sexual desires and fantasies, and however they might *privately* describe their own sexual orientations, the *public* identities they display in interaction are insistently heterosexual—and over the course of the interactions in which they are engaged, these co-conversationalists reflect and reproduce a profoundly heteronormative social order. Nowhere in the data sets on which CA is founded does anyone announce that they (or anyone else they know) are heterosexual or preface a turn with, "Speaking as a heterosexual . . .," yet the heterosexuality of the interactants is continually made apparent.

In drawing attention to the displayed heterosexuality of the speakers in the classic CA data sets, it is not my intention either to advance the claim that nonheterosexuals speak differently from heterosexuals, or to mount a challenge to the general applicability of classic CA findings.[1] Rather, by analyzing these data sets for what they reveal about how heterosexuality is produced in talk, my intention is to further open up the analytic opportunities within CA for studying

* Thanks to Sue Wilkinson, Deborah Cameron, Don Zimmerman, and Geoff Raymond for helpful comments on an earlier draft of this article.

the taken for granted. These classic data sets may well reflect the social worlds of many ordinary heterosexual British and American people in the 1960s to 1980s at the times these data were collected. It was—and maybe still is—possible to treat heterosexuality as universal, to display one's own and other people's heterosexuality without being heard thereby as doing anything special, and to display an assumption of living in a world apparently almost entirely devoid of LGBT people. These data sets offer, then, an intriguing anthropological insight into the ordinary lives of heterosexual people and the local moment-by-moment social construction of their heterosexual worlds.

In researching the production of normative heterosexuality in the quotidian interaction of heterosexual speakers, this article makes an important contribution to LGBT studies. As research on race and gender has targeted the dominant identities of Whiteness and maleness, so LGBT studies has increasingly targeted the dominant identity of heterosexuality for deconstruction. "Like whiteness in a white supremist society, heterosexuality is not only socially produced as dominant but is also taken-for-granted and universalizing" (Ingraham, 2001, p. 73). Writing from the perspective of "queer sociology," Seidman (1996) argued that, given the history of sociology as a "de-naturalizing force," heterosexuality should be inspected for the ways in which it is produced as a *natural* or *normal* way to be; and from the (contested) field of "queer linguistics," Cameron and Kulick (2003) insisted that "more attention should be given to the language in which heterosexual identities and desires are made manifest" (p. 153). As I show, a distinctive feature of these "displays" of heterosexuality is that they are not usually oriented to as such by either speaker or recipient. Rather, heterosexuality is taken for granted as an unquestioned and unnoticed part of their life worlds. Unlike those performances of gendered or racialized identities that are actively "worked up"—such as Agnes's self-presentation as female (Garfinkel, 1967) or telephone sex workers' constructions of varying racial identities in conformity with the sexual preferences of their clients (Hall, 1995)—these cointeractants are generally "giving off" rather than actively displaying their heterosexual identities. They are simply allowing their heterosexuality to be inferred in the course of some activity in which they are otherwise engaged. I suggest that this very inattentiveness to heterosexuality as a possible identity category, and the ease with which interactants make heterosexuality apparent without being heard as "talking about" heterosexuality, both reflects and constructs heteronormativity.

In analyzing the construction of normative heterosexuality in ordinary talk, I am also contributing to CA in two ways. First, a recurrent concern of CA is with the deployment of "membership categories" (e.g., Sacks, 1995a, Lecture 6) and "person reference forms" (e.g., Schegloff, 1996) in ordinary conversation. Family and kinship terms are among the categories whose use Sacks began to explore—most famously in "the baby cried, the mommy picked it up" discussion (Sacks, 1972b) but also at various locations scattered throughout his work, including an interrogation of the use of inferences attached to *wife*, *sister*, and *child* in a counselling call (Sacks, 1995a, p. 116) and the (hypothetical) deployment of (heterosexual) "couple" inferences to disguise otherwise stigmatized identities (Sacks, 1995a, p. 593). The analysis presented here builds on that work and adds to it an exploration of the way in which person reference forms (such as "my husband/wife" or "her mother-in-law") also make available—at least to a recipient for whom such things matter—the inference of that person's heterosexuality; an inference not usually overtly oriented to as such by speakers or recipients in the data set under consideration, but that nonetheless shows us, as analysts, the production of normative heterosexuality as an ongoing, situated, practical accomplishment.

Second, in focusing on an interactional feature not oriented to as such by the participants themselves, I adopt an unusual analytic strategy (however, see Sacks, 1995b, pp. 175–187)—and one I would advocate for those interested in uncovering the kinds of social worlds on which (as I show) the practices and actions of speakers depend, and that they reproduce in their talk. As I have suggested elsewhere (Kitzinger, 2000, in press-a, in press-b; Land & Kitzinger, 2005), it is precisely the fact that sexist, heterosexist, and racist assumptions are routinely incorporated into everyday conversations without anyone noticing or responding to them as such that constitutes a culture. How is it, for example, that an unquestioned set of mundane heterosexual assumptions regularly surface in talk in which participants do not notice (or orient to) their own heterosexual privilege; and precisely, how does this failure to orient constitute and reconstitute a heterosexist culture? These questions "uncover the practical reasoning through which the taken-for-granted world is accomplished (and resisted)—the resources members have for sustaining a social world in which there are 'women' and 'men,' 'heterosexuals' and 'homosexuals,' 'normal people' and the rest of us" (Kitzinger, 2000, p. 173). As conversation analysts, we can avoid "going native"—that is, rather than taking for granted the heterosexual kinship system displayed and deployed by social members, we can treat the language through which heterosexuality is displayed with the same "outsiders'" curiosity that has animated the analysis of the subcultural argot of pickpockets (Maurer, 1964), drug addicts (Agar, 1973), or dance musicians (Becker, 1963). We can interrogate it for what it shows us about the local production of a culture.

Finally, the normative heterosexuality analyzed in this article constitutes a backdrop against which to analyze the strategies of LGBT people both in concealing their identities and in making them—or allowing them to become—apparent (see Kitzinger, 2000; Land & Kitzinger, in press; Wilkinson & Kitzinger, 2003). More generally, the approach adopted here advances a method for researching the production and reproduction of culture through mundane interaction. As such, it is a contribution to the long tradition of sociological research that aims to explicate the "seen-but-unnoticed" or tacit presuppositions of everyday life.

The data

In this article, I draw on data sets collected and analyzed by the founders of CA (Sacks, Schegloff, and Jefferson) and by other leading conversation analysts (notably Drew, Goodwin, Heritage, Lerner, Maynard, Pomerantz, and Zimmerman) to show how co-conversationalists routinely produce themselves (and each other) as heterosexual. Data sets widely used in CA publications include conversations between friends and colleagues (e.g., HGII, TG, SN-4, Upholstery Shop); telephone calls to and from private homes (e.g., the Rahman, Heritage, Holt, SBL, and NB corpora); dinnertime conversations (Virginia, Automobile Discussion, Chicken Dinner); and institutional data such as the group therapy session (Sacks, 1995a, 1995b), suicide prevention center calls (Sacks, 1972a, 1995a, 1995b), and 911 emergency calls (Zimmerman, 1992). In researching this article, I have drawn on the original recordings and existing transcripts of these data when I have had access, and on the published versions of the data when I did not. Most of these data sets are in the form of audio rather than video recordings, and most are telephone conversations: Hence, my analysis focuses on audible rather than visually accessible heterosexual displays—on how people talk heterosexuality into being rather than on how heterosexuality is displayed through visual or body deployment. In most of these data, the members of heterosexual couples are neither jointly present nor in interaction with each other. This means that individuals are presenting themselves as heterosexual without the assistance of a co-present heterosexual partner—and I have limited my analysis in this article to such displays.[2]

In presenting this analysis, I also speculate as to how interactions do—or might—run off differently when speakers display not *hetero-* but *homosexuality*, and what this tells us about the social world. In so doing, I draw on published self-report data from LGBT people, from the rare instances in which an LGBT identity is made available or discussed in the classic CA corpora, and on a limited amount of my own data featuring lesbians in interaction with heterosexuals (see also Land & Kitzinger, in press).

Heterosexual and other identity categories

As Schegloff (1997a)—and others—argued, the fact that someone can be categorized with reference to a particular identity category does not make that identity automatically relevant in any particular interaction. The interactants in these data sets are not, of course, describable *only* as members of the heterosexual category: They could also be labelled using other conventional sociological categories such as those indexing their gender, class, ethnicity, age, nationality, and so on; and such categories are sometimes more clearly relevant, even for those people who are, at other times, hearably heterosexual. In Fragment 1, for example, Emma (whose talk I later analyze as displaying her heterosexuality) is not talking "as a heterosexual" but "as a White person." She has called her sister with some "hot-off-the-press" news about the marines who have just arrived in her street—one of her neighbors (Larry) having charitably collected them from the local navy base to join his family for Thanksgiving dinner. The importance Emma attaches to telling her news is displayed through her production of it as the reason for the call—and because Lottie has company (her "no" at 07 is designed as a "go ahead" despite this and not as a denial of it), the telling and receipt of this news turns out to be the *only* business of this call:

Fragment 1
[NB:IV:12:R]
((Earl answered the call and has passed the phone to his wife, Lottie))

01	Lot:	Ye:ah.
02	Emm:	Lottie?y[ih
03	Lot:	[Yeh
04		(.)
05	Emm:	Yihknow Larry went down'n got those guys f'm
06		Pen'lt'n I didn'know yih had ↓comp'ny..hh [h h]
07	Lot:	[No:.]
08		(.)
09	Emm:	An:d uh (.) th- ↑two of'm'r goin acro:ss sstreet
10		th'tooiss (.) kyoo and ↑one of'm (.) u-dow:n
12		the street goin with Larry is £da::rk.h£
13		(.)
14	Emm:	.hh.hh There's uhv u-there's four of'm 'n £↓one
15		of'm's colored,£

These co-interactants of course already know each other to be White: Their shared ethnicity is here made relevant by Emma's invocation of an alternative ethnicity, labelled "dark" (Line 12) and "colored" (Line 15)—and later in this call, "Black." Although, on evidence I show from her conversations elsewhere, Emma *is* heterosexual, it is her ethnicity and not her heterosexuality that is relevant in this fragment (see also Sacks, 1995b, pp. 175–187, on the construction of ethnicity in a call in the SBL corpus).

It is not just that these speakers are sometimes speaking in terms that produce them as being of particular ethnicities and at other times in terms that produce them as heterosexuals: The two can be done at one and at the same time. Toward the beginning of the conversation in Fragment 2, Hyla and Nancy have been talking about the plot of the play they are to attend that evening, which revolves around the conflict between a young woman with a Jewish boyfriend and her aunt who is a "real bigot" and "hates anyone who isn't a Catholic." The subsequent conversation ranges over a variety of topics, including Hyla's thwarted desires for a "nice Jewish boy" called Richard, who promised, but has so far failed, to contact her: The two young women have collaborated in enacting a fantasy phone call in which Richard asks Hyla to marry him. Now, in response to Nancy's question about clothing for that evening, Hyla says she is "not gonna get dressed up":

Fragment 2
[HGII]

01	Hyl:	Yihknow who do I aftih look nice for.
02		(.)
03	Hyl:	hh [h-h h- h h h]
03	Nan:	[Well you nev]er know who's g'nna be
04		in the pla:y I mean we are
05		si[tting close t'the(steh-]heh)]
06	Hyl:	[k h h-.h h-h h-hhh-hh-hh(eh heh)] eh eh e-=
07	Nan:	=·hhe:hh=
08	Hyl:	=·hhh[Maybe the Jewish [gu:]y, hunh=
09	Nan:	[He'll look out en [go,]
10	Nan:	=He'll go, Jhuliet Juliet- Nancy. Hy[la.]
11	Hyl:	[uhh]=
12		uh.uh[.uh
13	Nan:	[.hhe:hhh hhhh
14		(.)
15	Hyl:	.hhhhh er maybe the Jewish guy thet's:
16		[hh[henh [henh [hnh [heh
17	Nan:	[A: [right [Maybe [he's [really Jewi(h)sh
18		[.hhhhh [w'l go back stage en gitiz autograph

Here, in response to Hyla's renewed complaint about her lack of a boyfriend who it is worth "looking nice for" (her girlfriend to whom she is speaking is clearly *not* worth looking nice for), Nancy invokes the romantic possibilities of the leading actor: He might look out of the play and call their names as Romeo did to Juliet—and he might be *really* Jewish, and thereby, a suitable romantic partner for her friend. In this conversation, Hyla's Jewishness and her heterosexuality are co-produced through the fantasy of romance with the "really Jewish" guy—although only the Jewish category is named, whereas her (and his) heterosexuality are simply assumed.[3]

In brief, other categorical identities (not just ethnicity but also class, age, sex, nationality, etc.) may be invoked such that a single speaker may be heard to be speaking as a member of one of these other categories in addition to, and even at the same time as, producing himself or herself as heterosexual.

Speaking as heterosexuals: co-constituting a heteronormative world

The question I am using the data sets to address, then, is how people produce themselves and others as heterosexual and—in so doing—co-constitute a normative heterosexual world. I begin by considering those occasions on which heterosexuality is displayed through talk that is explicitly oriented to (hetero)sex or to (hetero)relationships (as in Fragment 2, shown earlier).

The most explicit (hetero)sexual references in these conversations are in the form of sexual joking, banter, reports of (hetero)sexual activity, and innuendo. Paul Drew's (1987) classic analysis of "po-faced receipts of teases" includes data in which a sister teases her brother by alleging (in the presence of their parents) that he spent the night with his girlfriend (p. 228); a young woman being teased about her supposed sexual interest in a (male) member of a rock band (p. 228); and a newly married heterosexual couple whose complaint about the apparent structural deterioration of their new home is met with a teasing suggestion that this is attributable to their "bumping around" ("that is, in bed"; p. 229). The "dirty joke" that forms the centrepiece of one of Sacks's (1995b, Lecture 9) most celebrated lectures begins, "there was these three girls and they just got married?" (p. 470), and employs the taken-for-granted cultural commonplace of a honeymoon—with all its sexual implications—in developing a joke about fellatio between the bride and her new husband (also see Sacks, 1974). Overall, the data support the (previously undocumented) claim that "talk about sexuality is often about heterosexual desires and activities, again reinforcing the presumption of universal heterosexuality" (Eckert & McConnell-Ginet, 2003, p. 207).

A second fairly explicit way in which heterosexuality is displayed in these conversations is through topic talk about heterosexual relationships—typically marriage or marriage-related topics such as engagements, weddings, marital troubles, and so forth. The civil institution of marriage is available in England and the United States to two persons over the age of consent irrespective of their race or ethnicity, religion, nationality, or class—subject only to the constraint that they must be of different sexes. In both countries there was—and in some social contexts still is—social disapproval of interracial marriages or of marriages between couples of (say) different religious backgrounds or social classes (Romano, 2003), but in neither country—during the years in which these data were collected—was that social opprobrium formally encoded in laws banning such marriages as was then (and still is) the case for same-sex couples.[4] No country in the modern history of the world permitted same-sex marriage until 2001; hence, all references in the data sets to marriage (and to associated institutions such as engagements, weddings, honeymoons, divorces, etc.) index different-sex couples and, thereby, heterosexuality. In indexing heterosexuality in this way, speakers treat it as the taken-for-granted normative default way to be—and do so independently of whether they approve of the particular heterosexual relationship they are talking about.

Therefore, in the course of the activities in which they are otherwise engaged, Shelley displays her own heterosexuality with talk about plans for her forthcoming wedding (SN-4; Schegloff, 1995, pp. 225–227), and Kevin displays his own heterosexuality in telling a friend about plans for his wedding anniversary (Holt: U.88-2-2). Speakers display the heterosexuality of other (nonpresent) parties when, for example, a family friend attempts to diffuse a mother–daughter argument by launching a funny story about a wedding ("Well why don't I change the subject an' tell ya about thuh wedding," Virginia 17:25), thereby displaying the heterosexuality of the bride and groom; and when, in updating Mom on recent events, Lesley reports the news of Janet's engagement (Holt 1.8); and when two friends, Ava and Bee, discuss whether a mutual acquaintance is married yet (TG); and when Ann tells her friend Jenny about the manager of a department store who "married this mother who already had a little boy" (Rahman B.1.13). In Fragment 3 (which follows), Ron tells family news, displaying the heterosexuality of his two sons, each of whom is located with reference to his place of residence; his marriage; and (at least by implication in Shawn's case) his job. The news about Shawn is his geographical relocation, to which mention of his wife is subordinated; the news about Michael is his 1-year-old marriage:

Fragment 3
[Holt SO88(II)-2-2]

Ron:	.hhh Just to bring you up to date with our
	family uh:m: .t.hh our eldest son u: Shawn
	u-who lives with iz wife in Taunton, ih he
	now practices in Bridgewa↑ter?
	(.)
Les:	eeYe:s,?
Ron:	.t He transferred from Newt'n Abbott to r-.hhh=
Les:	=[Oh lovely.]
Ron:	=[(Tauntonn)]so th[(at he c'n be)]=
Les:	[Nice an' handy for you.]=
Les:	=[↑ Y e : s ?]
Ron:	=[So that's very]u-That's very[good,?
Les:	[.hhhheeyah
Ron:	Uh:m: Michael is still: soldiering on very
	happily as uh::um (.) policeman (.) in:
	ee[Yeovil.]
Les:	[Yeo↑vil?]
	(0.2)
Les:	Good,?
	(.)
Ron:	And has: uhm: uh seems to be quite happy
	[an-n(.)d he'n Ginny've just been married=
Les:	[.p.t.khhhhh
Ron:	twelve ↑months =
	(.)
Les:	eeYes,
	(0.2)

Across the data sets, there is a fair amount of talk that takes a negative or critical stance toward particular (past, current, or possible future) marriages: Nancy berates her estranged husband (NB.II calls; see Drew, 1987, pp. 238–239; Jefferson, 1984, p. 195); Emma—whose husband has just left her—confides her marital problems to her daughter and sister (NB.IV.4; see Drew & Holt, 1988, pp. 408–410); Billy and his girlfriend Gail are "definitely not married" ("They have a prob'm [. . .] Definite pro:b'm," TG); the early warning signs that might have led to the separation of Jean Claude's parents are reported ("you know the mum did an awful lot independently," Holt: J86:1:4); and a complaint about a mother-in-law criticizes her as a wife (she "nagged- (1.0) uhr 'er own husband'," Holt: 2.9). In Fragment 4, Nancy is reporting her aunt's account of the marriage of a (now divorced) man:

Fragment 4
[NB.II.4]

Nan: =She knew im w'n'e ↑wz ↓merr↑ied?h
(0.2)
Emm: [M m :]hm?
Nan: [A::n'] to iz first wi:fe:? who she said
was en ⋆absolute bitch how a ni:ce guy ⋆ever
merried a woman like that she'd never know.
They never had inny children?
Emm: °M[m :] hm:,°]
Nan: [.hh] .hhh] A:n' she said she wz so:
re↓lie:ved en so was: her friend Helen (0.2)
Rob's a:nt .hhhhh wen::: Ro:b js decided duh
call a halt tih the whole thi:ng?

Clearly, it is not the case that all heterosexual relationships are treated as acceptable, good, or desirable ones: Negative representations derive from considerations of recipient design and local interactional concerns, such as building a complaint about a mother-in-law (Holt 2.9) or explaining the failed first marriage of a man in whom the speaker herself has a romantic interest (Fragment 4). However, nowhere in the data is heterosexuality itself treated as problematic: Instead, even in the course of complaining about it, the different-sex definition of marriage is underwritten and reinscribed simply through being treated as taken-for-granted.

Although sexually explicit jokes and topic talk about heterosexual relationships and rituals constitute the most overt ways in which these people reveal their own (and others') heterosexuality, these are perhaps the least analytically interesting, precisely because of their explicitness. As Schegloff (2000) said, the relevances that shape the formulated experience exhibited in talk-in-interaction are made apparent "not only in what persons choose overtly to talk about; perhaps there least of all" (p. 718). In the remainder of this article, I move from talk about heterosexual sex and heterosexual relationships to show the extent to which heterosexuality forms a taken-for-granted backdrop that shapes talk in which people are explicitly oriented to other topics and actions entirely. I consider ways in which speakers make apparent their own or others' heterosexuality (or, more precisely, their own or others' location within heterosexual relationships) in contexts in which neither the (hetero)sex nor the (hetero)relationship constitute the topic of the talk. In the examples that follow, heterosexuality is deployed, indexed, alluded to, or relied on as a taken-for-granted common place in the course of some action other than topic talk in which the speakers are engaged. I suggest that it is in and through this talk, far more than in talk about (hetero)sex and (hetero)relations, that we can gain an analytic purchase on the mundane ways through which heteronormativity is produced and reproduced in ordinary talk-in-interaction.

It is common for speakers to mention their heterosexual involvements (dates, engagements, weddings, marriages) without being thereby engaged in topic talk about them. In Fragment 5, the caller is clearly making available a hearing of herself as heterosexual: She has a date with a man and is concerned about whether he really wants her. She is not, however, announcing her heterosexuality, nor is the information about her date tonight conveyed as simply news or topic talk. Rather, she makes available the information that she is heterosexual as part of the main action she is engaged in—describing her feelings of being "nothing" and (despite her date tonight) like someone "no man" would want. Her heterosexuality is a taken-for-granted background resource she draws on in displaying the suicidal feelings that have led her to make this call:

Fragment 5
[From Sacks, 1995a, p. 66]

01	Cal:	I'm a grown woman an attractive woman I have a
02	Clt:	[Do you have any]
03	Cal:	[real nice date] good looking guy for a date
04		tonight and and I somehow I'm feeling that
05		I'm nothing ((smiling sigh))
06	Cal:	And I know nobody's a nothing But I am. It's
07		like everybody else is somebody and somewhere
08		along the line I muffed up.
//		((possible break))
09	Cal:	And I do think what man wants a neurotic
10		childless forty year old woman. No man.

In Fragment 6, Robbie refers to her marriage in the course of a conversation about Kent—an area of England where her co-conversationalist Lesley grew up, and coincidently, which it turns out, was also where Robbie herself was "born and bred." She invokes her marriage by way of giving an account for having left Kent. (The towns of Sevenoaks and Chipstead are both in Kent.) Just as the previous fragment was not talk about a date but a display of the speaker's suicidal feelings, so this fragment is not talk about a marriage, but a display of Kentish credentials:

Fragment 6
[Holt: 5.88.1.5]

01	Rob:	An' then um .p.hhh (0.3) u-u- We moved to
02		Sevenoaks: t'be nearer an' ↑al:ways round Seven-
03		well no Sevenoaks 'n then we went t'Chipstead f'r
04		awhi: [le ( )=
05	Les:	[hYe:s:.
06	Rob:	=outsi:de Sevenoaks (ever hea[rd'v it)
07	Les:	[Ye:s.
08	Les:	Yes ye:s.
09	Rob:	But um ↑Oh no: born 'n br- twenty one yea:rs.
10		(0.2)
11	Les:	Ah:.
12		(0.2)
13	Rob:	Yes 'n then: well I- I moved w'n I married
14		(0.3)
15	Les:	Ah:.
16		(.)
17	Rob:	Lovely place
18		(.)
19	Les:	Ye:s::. Y[e:s.

20 Rob: [( ) I suffer from (.) severe
21 Kentitis when we come ↓back. he[re,

In these instances, the display of heterosexuality (of the suicide caller, of Robbie) is done in the service of some other action (presenting oneself as a potential suicide or as Kentish) to which it is merely incidental.

One interactional problem for LGBT people in heteronormative contexts may be a difficulty in making apparent their homosexuality in the service of some action in which they are engaged without having the revelation of their sexual identity treated by the recipient as the main action. It may well be harder for someone with a same-sex date to deploy it, as the speaker does in Fragment 5, as evidence for the depth of her depression without having the thereby-revealed fact of her homosexuality topicalized as possibly related to her suicidal feelings. It may harder for someone with a same-sex partner to refer to events (such as a geographical relocation) with reference to her relationship with that partner, not just because she lacks a straightforward term (*married*) to describe the role of that relationship in her life, but also because she runs the risk of being heard to have made a gratuitous reference to her counternormative sexuality. Fragment 7 comes not from the main data corpus but from a field observation of my own: It is a conversation (as it turns out, the *entire* conversation) between two women encountering each other for the first time during lunch at an academic conference:

Fragment 7
[Author: FN: 2003]

01 Ali: How long have you been vegetarian?
02 May: Since I met my partner. She's vegetarian.
03 Ali: Oh. ((turns to person seated other side of her and does not address May again over the course of nearly 1 hr))

Ali's question to May was prompted by Ali's request to the serving person for the vegetarian option and is hearable as a topic proffer. May's response answers the question first with a formulation of duration that makes her couple relationship available, and then with an account for the relevance of that formulation that (via the proterm) makes her lesbianism available. Ali receives the answer as news—but that is *all* she does: Having initiated the interaction and launched vegetarianism as a topic for discussion with May, she now abandons it, and the conversation with May, altogether without providing any account for her withdrawal from the conversation (compare the account analyzed in Goodwin, 1987). The absence of any rationale from Ali for failing to follow up on her question (e.g., "let me just say hi to X . . .") leaves May to surmise the likely reason for the shift in attention—and that may be sufficient to convey to May that the reason lies in her having incidentally made available her lesbian identity.[5]

The single most common way in which speakers display both their own and others' heterosexuality is (as May displays her lesbianism in Fragment 7) via person reference forms—especially nonrecognitional ones. How to refer to a person unknown to another (i.e., the deployment of nonrecognitional person reference forms) has been described as "a central problem of sociology" (Sacks, 1995a, p. 41). According to Schegloff (1996) it is

> . . . an immense territory, and one of deep importance for sociology [. . .] Most significant in this regard is its inclusion of all the category terms for types of persons in a culture's inventory, by reference to which are composed a society's understanding(s) of "the sorts

> of people" there are, what they are like, how the society and the world works—in short, its culture.
>
> *(p. 465)*

In the rest of this section I show how nonrecognitional person reference often deploys terms from the heterosexual kinship system (e.g., husband, mother-in-law), thereby locating the speaker, or those about whom she or he is speaking, as heterosexual (also see Kitzinger, in press-a). Widespread use of heterosexual kinship terminology displays the extent to which "how the society and the world works" is organized with reference to heterosexual marriage.

Husband and wife

By referring to their husbands, female callers position themselves as wives; by referring to their wives, male callers position themselves as husbands,[6] thereby displaying, incidentally, in the course of the action in which they are otherwise engaged, their location within heterosexual marital units. Whether these people are really heterosexual (whatever that means exactly), the speakers' selection of person reference terms like husband or wife makes that inference available to their recipient—and people who identify themselves as lesbian or gay (or who have same-sex sexual partners) are commonly described as "passing for straight" if they remain within heterosexual marriages.

The data set includes many instances of people referring to their husband or wife without being oriented thereby to "speaking as a heterosexual"—especially (but far from exclusively) in interactions with strangers. In data from suicide counselling calls reported by Sacks (1972a, 1995a), the terms husband and wife are frequently used, as in Fragment 8 (which follows), in which the loss of a wife is provided as an instance of a "personal problem" that has caused the caller to feel suicidal. The reference term here (wife) evokes the culturally understood inferences of an intimate and caring relationship, such that the loss of such a category member renders understandable the caller's depression:

Fragment 8
[From Sacks, 1972a, p. 50]

01 A: Has there been some personal problem or difficulty
02 that you're experiencing?
03 B: Yes. I just lost my wife and I feel awfully
04 depressed.

In Fragments 9 (also from the suicide prevention calls) and 10 (to emergency police), the callers refer to their husband—thereby rendering *ordinary* and *natural* the action they are performing, as callers, in contacting the call takers for help on behalf of this other person. (See the parallel analysis on the use of wife and husband terms in out-of-hours doctor's calls; Kitzinger, in press-a):

Fragment 9
[From Sacks, 1995a, p. 73]

01 A: Hello this is Mr Smith
02 B: Say, my husband is suicidal and, I mean,
03 he's attempted it about half a dozen times.

Fragment 10
[IND PD 59, in Schegloff, 1997a, p. 525)

01	Pol:	What's the trouble lady,
02	Cal:	I don't know my husband's sitting in his chair
03		I don't know what's wrong with him he can't talk
04		or move or anything.

The use of the kinship categories *husband* and *wife* mobilizes the inferences that attach to such relationships, obviating the need for the caller to account for the other's depression, or her concern on behalf of the other. Whatever other interactional hurdles these speakers encounter, their invocation of a different-sex spouse is not problematic. Rather, the sheer ordinariness of one spouse calling on behalf of another makes the use of these kinship terms a powerful resource for "doing being ordinary" (Sacks, 1984) with all the interactional benefits (of not having to provide accounts, explanations, justifications, etc.) that attach to being an ordinary person doing a natural activity. By contrast, in Fragment 11, someone calling for help on behalf of a friend presents an epistemically downgraded version of the history of the person she calls about ("I believe . . .," Line 02) and finds herself giving an account as to why it is she, rather than a family member, who is calling:

Fragment 11
[From Sacks, 1972a, p. 69]

01	Cal:	. . . I'm calling for a friend who's had a history of
02		mental disturbance; I believe attempted suicides
03		were involved at that time . . .
04	Clt:	. . . What is your relationship to her?
05	Cal:	Just a friend.
06	Clt:	Just a friend. I see.
07	Cal:	Her family moved out about a year ago.
08	Clt:	No family. I see.
09	Cal:	Not in this part of the country.

Relational categories (e.g., husband–wife, neighbor–neighbor, friend–friend) "constitute loci for rights and obligations" (Sacks, 1972a, p. 40), with spouses (and parents–children) treated as preeminent among these (also see Kitzinger, in press-a). For lesbians and gay men calling about a suicidal partner or depressed by a partner's death, there is no readily available and taken-for-granted term comparable to *my husband* or *my wife* on which to draw. Lesbians and gay men do not have easy access to a person reference term like husband or wife, which no longer renders appropriate the need for an account (Sacks, 1995a, pp. 23–24) as to why they are the person calling or why that, in itself, constitutes an unremarkable account as to why they might be depressed.

Spousal references are deployed as offering nonaccountable reasons for a range of emotions (e.g., depression, Fragment 8) and decisions (e.g., geographical relocation, Fragment 6). In Fragment 12, the patient deploys the person reference term *husband* as a resource in managing the issue of "doctorability" (Heritage & Robinson, 2005):

Fragment 12

01	Pat:	(I'm here on fal[se pre- pretenses.)<I think
02	Doc:	[.hh

03 Doc: [<Yes.
04 Pat: [ehh! hih heh heh heh!
// ((five lines omitted))
05 Pat: I asked my husband yesterday 'cause I could feel:
06 (0.8) (cause) I: could feel this li'l mo:le coming.
07 An:d: uh (0.5) (he) (.) I: hh thought I better
08 letchya know-<uh well I asked my husband 'f it was
09 in the same place you took off thuh (0.5) thee (mm)
10 thee: °([ )
11 Doc: [That's why you've come in be[cause of the
12 mo:le

In Fragment 13, Mrs. Mears has telephoned the owner of a house she would like to rent: The house has been advertised in the newspaper and the owner is unknown to her. When the owner asks for her name (Line 03), she gives both her own name—using the title "Mrs.," which identifies her as a married woman—and the name of her husband, whose title implies his membership in the medical profession. In this instance, her heterosexual marital status provides her with a resource to lay claim to "a possible extra qualifier for renting a house" (Sacks, 1995a, p. 758):

Fragment 13
[SBL 1.3; see Sacks, 1995a, p. 757[7]]

01 Own: I'll continue to try to get the: tenant: and see:
02 'n let her know that someone wants to see it.
03 .hhh Do you mind giving me you:r na:me.
04 Mea: mm We:ll my na:me is Missus Mears. My husband
05 is Doctor Mears
06 Own: Uh tha- How do you spell that.

References to husbands and wives have the effect (neither intended nor oriented to in any of these calls) of displaying the caller's heterosexuality and their location within the legitimate and socially sanctioned legal status of marriage. These invocations of spouses are designed to achieve interactional goals related to the immediate sequential contexts in which they occur. There is no sense that these are contrived self-presentations of heterosexuality: What the speakers are working up is an account for depression, a reason for relocation, the doctorability of their complaint, or their eligibility as tenants; their production of themselves as heterosexual is guileless. Their conformity with heteronormative expectations makes available to them resources for engaging in these other activities—resources not available to LGBT interactants.[8] Any attempt to deploy parallel terms invoking a same-sex partner is (even in the 21st century) likely to derail the interaction by displaying the speaker's counternormative lesbian or gay identity (see Land & Kitzinger, in press).

Finally, it is worth noticing that there are very few instances in these data corpora in which one spouse refers to the other using a person reference form other than one of the following four: my husband/wife; the person's name; "Mum," "Dad," or variants thereof when talking to their children (e.g., Schegloff, 1992, p. 1323, Excerpt 22); or the relevant proterm (he or she). The massive numerical predominance of these four reference forms reflects a socially normative practice, such that when reference forms other than these are deployed, something special is being done interactionally—as, for example, when the nonnormative formulation is employed in the service of a request to the co-interactant. Therefore, a truck driver produces a locally initial reference to his wife as "the lady that answers the door"—a formulation that is recipient designed for the police dispatcher in the service of the request he is making for a message to be delivered (IPD ND 1); and a caller to an out-of-hours doctor's office produces a locally initial formulation of her husband as "a patient of Doctor [name]'s," thereby recipient designing her talk to display her husband's entitlement to medical care from this doctor's practice in the service of her request for a home visit (DEC 2-1-15 FOOD POISONING; Kitzinger, in press-a). However, the "unmarked," nonrecognitional reference form for married different-sex partners is wife or husband—meaning that the (legally imposed) absence of these terms for same-sex partners often presents a significant interactional hurdle in terms of forwarding the actions in which they are engaged.

In-law terminology

American and European kinship terminology includes the concept of *in-law* in consideration of family composition, and its use constitutes either the speaker, or one of the speaker's relatives, as located within a marital heterosexual relationship. In Fragment 14, Lesley has called a plumber and, having made contact with someone she takes to be his wife, she formulates her request so as to display both her recipient's presumed heterosexual marital status and her own via her selection of *mother-in-law* as a person reference form for the person subsequently referred to as "Mrs. Nan Field" (a husband is a prerequisite for a mother-in-law). The person reference form is not, of course, selected to display Lesley's marital status, but to render unnecessary an account as to why it is she who is calling on behalf of this person:

Fragment 14
[Holt:l:6]

Les: Could you:r husband call on my mother in law please
(0.4)
Les: a:nd uh have a look at he:r um: (1.0) .h uh her
bathroo:m,

In Fragment 15, Emma is offering an account as to why her daughter may not be able to visit her for Thanksgiving:

Fragment 15
[NB.4.9]

Emm: .hh Her hu- u-her father in la:w's in the ho:spit'l

Emma launches her turn with what sounds as though it is probably headed for "her husband's father" and repairs it to "her father in law"—thereby perhaps rendering the relationship between the sick man and her daughter more personal and immediate (and hence, more compelling a reason for her daughter not to visit her). In any event, either version refers to the same role-occupant in a kinship system that is organized around marriage. Without having designed her turn to achieve this, Emma is displaying that she has a married heterosexual daughter.

Likewise, in the course of a reporting designed as a prelude to inviting the recipient to co-participate in the event (see Drew, 1984, pp. 139–140), Guy displays that he has a heterosexual daughter (married to his son-in-law):

Fragment 16
[NB:1:1:2]

G: .hhhhhh Hey uh, hh My son'n law's down,
'nd uh thought w'might play a little golf
either this afternoon er tomorrow. Wouldju
like tuh (0.9) hh get out? hh

In designing a turn as a challenge (Schegloff, 1997a, p. 523) to Curt's claim that one particular racer (the "he" in Curt's first turn) is "the only good regular out there" (in the races), Gary incidentally displays that he has a heterosexual sister (married to his brother-in-law):

Fragment 17
[AutoDiscussion (transcript simplified), from Schegloff, 1997a, p. 523]

Cur: He- he's about the only regular <he's about the only
good regular out there'z, Keegan still go out?
Mik: Keegan's out there, he's he run,
(0.5)
Gar: [Whaddayah mean my brother in law's out there]

People in same-sex couples (and unmarried different-sex partners) do not have unproblematic access to terminology that would locate their partner's parents and siblings in relationship to them (as mother- or father-in-law and brother- or sister-in-law do for married heterosexuals). Nor, of course, do the parents and siblings of people in same-sex couples have access to the terminology of son- or daughter-in-law or brother- or sister-in-law to refer to their relative's same-sex partner. Creative solutions may include using these terms anyway despite their factual inaccuracy; deploying various circumlocutions (e.g., "my daughter's friend/partner/girlfriend" for the person who might otherwise be a daughter-in-law) and inventing variants that signal same-sex couples' exclusion from equal marriage rights (e.g., my own parents used *daughter-out-of-law* as a nonrecognitional referent for my partner; a lesbian author refers to her lover's brother as "my brother-if-there-were-a-law"; MacLean 1995).

Identification of other with reference to their spouse

In Fragments 18 and 19, speakers use a person reference form that identifies the person they are speaking about as some other person's spouse: "Mr. Quinn's wife" and "Mittie's husband." The speakers are recipient designing the turns with reference to how they figure their interactant knows this person, and they display an analysis that Mr. Quinn and Mittie are people clearly known to recipient, such that the talked-about people can be located with reference to them:

Fragment 18
[H:088:1:8:5]

Leslie: Well a'course um:: Mister Quinn's wife has had lumps
removed fr'm 'er neck hasn't she

Fragment 19
[Schenkein, in Schegloff, 1997a, p. 519)

Joe: Oh you know, Mittie- Gordon, eh- Gordon,
Mittie's husban' died.

In Fragment 20 the speaker is engaged in a search for the name of "that guy" and is producing "clues" for his recipients: He first attempts an identification of him with reference to his workplace and then with reference to his wife:

Fragment 20
[AutoDiscussion (transcription simplified)]

Cur: Didju know that guy up there et-oh. What the'hell
is's name usetuh work up't (Steeldinner) garage did
their body work. for 'em.
(2.0)
Cur: Oh:: he meh- uh,
(0.5)
Cur: His wife ra[n off] with Bill McCa:nn.

Schegloff (1996) pointed out that person reference provides "the terms through which people are observed, noticed and experienced" (p. 438)—and what we see in each of Fragments 18 through 20 is that those terms are formulated with reference to the heterosexual marital relationship and, hence, reproduce heteronormativity. There is no reason, in principle, why people in same-sex (or unmarried) couples should not also be located with reference to whichever member of the couple is presumed best known to the recipient of the talk (e.g., "Jenny's girlfriend" or "Bob's partner"), and data from LGBT speakers would presumably reveal this to be the case. When such formulations run off smoothly and without interactional trouble, they reflect and reproduce a world in which same-sex and unmarried coupledom is accepted and taken for granted. The absence of such same-sex formulations in the data set on which CA has relied reflects the insistently conventional (married) heterosexuality of the speakers from whom the data are collected.

The production of (heterosexual) couples

When speakers refer to two persons in a couple relationship, such references are generally done so as to display the couple relationship. This is most explicit when terms like *boyfriend* or *husband* are used, as in Fragments 21 and 22:

Fragment 21
[Terasaki, 1976, p. 53, as cited in Levinson, 1983, p. 351]

D: Y'wanna know who I got stoned with a
few w(hh)eeks ago? hh!
R: Who.
D: Mary Carter'n her boy(hh)frie(hhh)nd.hh

Fragment 22
[Rahman.B.2.14]

Ver: .h ’R yih[go]in yih won’t be goin t’th’town
tomorrow will you.
Jen: .h Well ah hahftih go ah:’m ah’v got s’m::
eh:: Liz en uhr husb’n coming foh:: (0.7)
e s- uh s- |supper

The use of two first names conjoined by an “and” may convey heterosexual coupledom when one name is male and the other female, and when the activities in which these two people are engaged (e.g., visiting or eating out with friends) is culturally understood to be a coupled activity:

Fragment 23
[NB.II.5]

Emm: .t.hh Uh Kay en Errol w’r s’pozetuh come ↓DO:WN
uh: la:s’ ni:ght,

Fragment 24
[NB.IV.4]

Emm: .hhh ↑We were spoze tih gone ou’tuh dinner with
Bill’n Gladys

List formulations typically use prosody and tempo to produce people in pairs of (heterosexual) couples as in Fragment 25:

Fragment 25
[Holt X(C)-2-1-4]

Kat: I [thought maybe we c’d g- have a get together of,=
Les: [.hh
Kat: =Melissa ’n Brian: ’n (0.5) Sarah ’n that bloke,
(.) oh: uh Cli[ve?

By pairing together the (identifiably different sex) names of the four people (with a pause between the two pairings), Katherine’s talk produces them as two heterosexual couples. (An LGBT version might have been, “Melissa ’n Sarah ’n (0.5) Brian ’n that bloke, (.) oh: uh Clive”.)

Heterosexual couples are also produced by referring to them by a shared surname:

Fragment 26
[SBL.3.2]

Cla: So anywa:y she: cancelled’er cla:ss out but (.)
a:n:’ (.) the Gra:hams c’dn come on Tue:sdee
[so:]it’s] [too ba::d,

Fragment 27
[NB.II.3]

01 Emm: .t.hh (.) So we jis: (.) le:ft 'n .hh .hh .hh
02 Cliff Brow:n wz there remember he usetih be ar
03 nei:ghbor?
04 Lot: ↑Ye::[a h :.]
05 Emm: [The Br]o::wns 'n[:
06 Lot: [Ye:ah,

As with pairs of male–female first names, pluralized shared surnames are used to produce lists of people as couples—as in "the Havershams and the Coles" in Fragment 28:

Fragment 28
[Holt X(C)-1-1-1]

01 Les: .tk.hhhh –Anyway we had a very good evening o:n
02 Saturda:y
03 (.)
04 Mum: ↑Ye:s?
05 Les: We went to North Cadbury: an' Gordon came too an:d
06 Kenneth Haversham and the Havershams 'n the Coles were
07 there

Although the children of heterosexual married couples often have the same surname as their parents (and in the worlds in which these co-interactants live, married couples and their children *always,* it seems, have the same surname), these children are not apparently necessarily or automatically understood as included in a reference to the Grahams; the Browns; or, as in the earlier instance, the Havershams. Kenneth (whom, as is evident from conversation elsewhere in this corpus, is their son) is named separately from the Havershams, his parents.

Many of these methods of producing the heterosexual couple are surely also available to and about same-sex couples (and, as Fragment 21 illustrates, to unmarried couples): References to "Jenny and her girlfriend," to visiting "Maria and Alice," or to a guest list including "Margaret and Sophie, and Bill and Mark" must be commonplace in the nonheteronormative contexts they reflect and constitute. Thus far, at least, I am not suggesting that the practices available to do person reference are distinctively different for same-sex and different-sex couples—only that they may be deployed differently in the heterosexist contexts they thereby reveal themselves to be oriented to.

Pronominal heterosexuality: the use of locally initial proterms

Another method through which (heterosexual) couples are produced in the classic CA data sets is through speakers' use of pronouns—in particular, first-person plural proterms (we, us, our). Across the (noninstitutional) data sets, use of a locally initial and unspecified *we* is normatively treated by co-interactants as meaning the speaker and his or her spouse. The *we* (Line 01) in Fragment 28 (shown earlier) is one such instance. Lesley's "Anyway" (Line 01) marks a disjuncture from the previous talk (about the death of a mutual acquaintance) to a new topic. Therefore, her *we* is a locally initial person reference invoking an unspecified collectivity. The fact that she is using it to mean "my husband and I" is apparent from her subsequent addition of Gordon (the couple's son)—thereby displaying that he was not initially understood as one of the *we* (a move that is paralleled—in Line 06—by the separate naming of Kenneth Haversham, their son, from the Havershams).

In Fragment 29, Lesley moves from the first-person singular ("I'm teaching tomorrow," Line 01) to the first-person plural ("we'll be up . . ." and "we'll be able to lie in . . .") without specifically naming who else is included in her *we*—although this person (Mark, who is, of course, known by Mum to be Lesley's husband) is finally named at Line 19:

Fragment 29
[Holt X(C)1-1-1]

01	Les:	Well I'm teaching tomorrow so:,
02	Mum:	Oh: goody:. [hee!
03	Les:	[we:'ll be up[e- aa-
04	Mum:	[heh heh eh-eh h=
05	Les:	We'll be able to LIE: I:N:. Becuz U:SUALLY WE'RE UP
06		at SIX 'n toMORROW is eh we'll be able t' l get up at
07		six thirty.
08		(0.6)
09	Mum:	Oh. u-Why::,
10		(.)
11	Mum:	he he hn- [Why are]you why: six thirty.
12	Les:	[Becuz]
13	Les:	Becuz I always ↑do when I'm teaching.
14		(0.3)
15	Mum:	Oh I see:,
16		(0.4)
17	Mum:	An' you usually get up at si:x.
18		(0.7)
19	Les:	Well ye:s, cz Mark has: (.) does 'n (.) hour's overtime
20		befo:re sk- work starts.
21		(1.0)
22		Mum: Oh:-:.

In Fragments 30 and 31, a locally initial *we* is used by Emma (Fragment 30, Line 08) and Jo (Fragment 31, Lines 04, 14, 17), respectively. In both of these instances, however, the other person who constitutes the speaker's *we* is never named. This causes no apparent difficulty for the co-interactants who seem to be assuming that *we* invokes the husbands with whom—it is evident from other calls in the corpora—Emma and Jo are co-constituted as couples:

Fragment 30
[NB.II.3]

01	Lot:	...lo:,
02	Emm:	£G'morning Letitia£=
03	Lot:	=u.-hHow'r YOU:.=
04	Emm:	=FI:NE HOW'R [YOU:.

05	Lot:	[eh he:h heh WUDIYIH kno:w.=
06	Emm:	=.hhh Jis got down last -ni:ght.eh
07	Lot:	OH YOU DI[:D?
08	Emm:	['hhh We BEEN tuh PA:LM SPRI:NGS.
09		(0.2)
10	Lot:	Oh: God ah be't it's [ho:[:t.

Fragment 31
[SBL:2:1:3:R]

01	Cla:	...Clai:re Moh::r.
02	Jo:	Well how are yuh.hh
03	Cla:	Fi:ne how'r you:.
04	Jo:	We're jis fi:ne.
05	Cla:	Were you eading?
06	Jo:	t hhhh
07		(0.5)
08	Jo:	S'm gra:pes, uhh huhhh=
09	Cla:	=heh hheh Ah-ah wz dus lookin et mi: [ne
10	Jo:	[ehh hehh he[h h e h]=
11	Cla:	[eghh heh]=
12	Jo:	=[heh]
13	Cla:	=[hhh]hh It's so ˆho::t.ˆOh[: ['hhh [hhhhhh] [hhhhh]
14	Jo:	[Oh it ['s [We jis]got [i::n,]
15		(.)
16	Cla:	Oh[d i d] yuh?]
17	Jo:	[We've b]een a]way f'almiss two weeks you kno:w,

As elsewhere in the analyses advanced in this article, I am pointing to the *absence* of trouble in the co-conversationalists' talk: The ease with which an unspecified locally initial *we* is managed and deployed reflects "how the society and the world work" (Schegloff, 1996, p. 465) in relation to heterosexual married couples. The locally initial use of *we* in these instances seems to rely, in part, on (and to reproduce) the overarching primacy of the couple as a collectivity in relation to which Anglo Americans locate themselves; and, in part, on the kinds of activities in which the collectivity indexed as *we* is reportedly engaged: a shared evening event (Fragment 28), sleeping and rising together (Fragment 29), and vacations (Fragments 30 and 31). These are culturally understood to be the kinds of activities in which couples engage (although, of course, others may also do so); the combination of an unspecified *we* engaged in activities culturally understood as "the sorts of things couples do together" makes available—indeed, may in some circumstances mandate—the hearing of *we* as "the couple of which I am a part." For the members of different-sex married couples whose talk is displayed earlier, this *we* reproduces them as the married couples they already know themselves to be. The same sort of *we* is presumably routinely used by heterosexual unmarried couples and same-sex couples who are open about their status as couples and is treated with caution by closeted same-sex couples or different-sex couples *not* wanting to reveal their relationships. This analysis of *we* in normative situations offers analytic purchase on the deployment (or avoidance) of it in relation to nonnormative arrangements.

It is also common practice for speakers to use the pronouns *he* or *she* as a method for referring to just one member of a couple and for distinguishing the one from the other—a practice that is, of course, possible only when the members of the couple can be differentiated by sex. In deploying a proterm as an unproblematic person reference for one member of a couple unknown to the cointeractant, a speaker also thereby conveys that the couple is composed of people of different sexes. In Fragment 32, Lesley is offering some assistance to someone whose husband—encountered recently at a party political meeting—has apparently lost his job, and whom she knows vaguely but has not seen (as transpires later in the call) for many months. She gives as the reason for the call—the offer of possible help from "friends in Bristol" (clearly treated as unknown to her recipient—both through her use of a nonrecognitional reference and, of course, because the purpose of her call is to put the recipient and her husband in touch with them). It is worth looking in some detail at how these friends in Bristol are produced as a couple, and as a heterosexual couple:

Fragment 32: Three heterosexual couples
[Holt:2:3]

```
Mar:   One three five?
       (.)
Les:   Oh hello, it's um: Leslie Field he:re,
Mar:   Oh ↑hello:,
Les:   Hello, .tch.h I ↑hope you don't mind me getting
       in touch but uh- we metchor husband little while
       ago at a Liberal meeting.
       (0.3)
Mar:   Ye:[s?
Les:      [.hh And he wz: (0.3) i-he told us something of
       what'd happen:ed,
       (0.5)
Les:   to him .hh An:' I wondered haa- (0.2) i-he said he
       m::ight have another position in vie:[w,
Mar:                                        [Mmhm,
Les:   .hh (.) Uhm (0.3) .tch Well I don't know how that
       went, .h uh (.) It's just thet I wondered if he
       hasn:'t (0.3) uh we have friends in: Bristol
Mar:   Ye:s?
Les:   who:-(.) uh: thet u-had the same experience.
Mar:   Oh↑::.
Les:   And they uhm: .t (0.2) .hh He worked f'r a printing
       an:' paper (0.9) uh firm [u-
Mar:                            [Ye:s,
Les:   uh[:- which ih puh- uh: part'v the Paige Group.
Mar:     [Yeh,
       (.)
Les:   .hh And he now has: u-a:: um (1.1) I don't think you'd
       call it a consultancy (0.2) They find positions for
       people: in the printing'n paper (0.4) indus[try:,
Mar:                                              [Oh I see: [:.
Les:                                                         [ hh
       An:d if: i-your husband would li:ke their addre [ss.
Mar:                                                   [Y e :[: s,
```

Les: [<As
they're specialists,
Mar: Ye::s?
(.)
Les: Uhm: my husband w'd gladly give it [t o h i m .]

First, the relevance of hearing the friends in Bristol as a couple is supplied by a local context in which couples (specifically, married heterosexual couples) are indexed in the preceding talk. At Line 06, Lesley's *we* (rather than, say, *I*) produces her as a member of some unspecified collectivity on whose behalf she is "getting in touch" (likewise, see her *us,* Line 10; and *we,* Line 18)—and hence, as proposed in my analysis of *we* mentioned earlier, is likely to be heard as invoking her marital unit. Lesley also references the marital relationship of her co-interactant ("your husband," Line 06)—such that the relevant interactional units are constituted as two married couples. The friends in Bristol are first hearable as a married couple, then, in the context of the two other married couple relationships already indexed in this talk. The subsequent pronoun repair from *they* to *he* (at Line 22) extracts one member of the couple from the collectivity and is performed because, although the "experience" (Line 20) of unemployment and its consequences on their lives was presumably a shared event for both members of the couple already indexed in the plural (with "friends," Line 18), it was only one member of the couple who lost a job—the one who "worked for a printing and paper firm" (Lines 22–23), and for whom the proterm *he* is appropriate. Notice that *he* is treated as serving to differentiate the member of the couple who was employed (and subsequently lost employment) from the other, and hence produces the other as female. If both members had been male, *he* would not have been usable in differentiating the two members of the couple from one another, and a different formulation—for example, "one of them," "the employed one," and so forth—would have been necessary to do so.

In Fragment 33, Ros and Bea are two nurses talking about a case that Bea is working on and about which it turns out Ros has independent information. In Line 01, she is checking this information with Bea:

Fragment 33
[SBL 1.1.10]

Ros: =Isn't she the one: who- hh I ↑think
ah hheahrd about ?it.? Th'daughter in law
told me wasn't she playing
go:[lf out et th]e V a l l e]y Clu:b?=
Bea: [Y e : s]thet's ↑i t]
Bea: =Thet's ↑the -o:ne.
Ros: En had'n aneurism.
Bea: Yhe:s:,
Ros: Suddenl*y.
Bea: Mm hm,
Ros: nThey thought et first she wz hit witha
golf: (0.5) ball uhr bat er something but
it wasn't that i[t w'ss:]uh-
Bea: [Uh-hah.]
Ros: a ruptured aneurism hhh And i-*u-*u-th*i-
(0.3) they didn'wan'Doctor Reeves'n Saint

17		Joh:n they took'er dow:n tih U.C.L.A★:.
18	Bea:	Yhe:s:.
19		(0.3)
20	Bea:	Ah-hah.
21	Ros:	An'it (0.3) Ah'it left'er (0.4) quite
22		permanently damaged ?I s[uppose?
23	Bea:	[tk
24	Bea:	Uh:pparently,
25		(.)
26	Bea:	Uh ↑he is still hopef★ul.
27		(.)
28	Ros:	The husb★'n.
29	Bea:	Ah hah end yih never jus' (.) eh yih js'
30		never saw such devotion in yer l★i:fe.

At Line 26, Bea treats a locally initial *he* as adequate reference for a husband who has so far not been introduced into the conversation. And indeed, Ros correctly identifies this proterm as referring to the husband (Line 28)—of whose existence she presumably has prior knowledge (via the daughter-in-law, Line 02), but who is indexed here only by a proterm with no clear prior referent. Like the locally initial use of *we* to mean the (heterosexual, married) couple as a collectivity, the locally initial use of *he* in Fragment 33, combined with a range of contextual knowledge, relies on (and reproduces) a category-bound activity (here hopefulness for a spouse's recovery) to index a spouse and (thereby) the centrality of the husband-wife relationship.

Fragment 34 is quoted by Sacks (1995a, pp. 762–763) and (with reference to Sacks's, 1995a, earlier argument) by Schegloff (1996, p. 475, Footnote 19)—both of whom point to the use of a locally initial *he* at Line 06, which "it appears clear" (Schegloff), is "obviously" (Sacks) a reference to Mr. Hooper:

Fragment 34
[From Sacks, 1995a, pp. 762–763]

01	A:	How is Missuz Hooper.
02	B:	Uh oh, about the same.
03	A:	mm, mm mm mm. Have they uh th-uh
04		Then she's still continuing in the same way.
05	B:	Yes, mm hm.
06	A:	Well I hope uh he can con- uh can, carry on
07		that way, be [cause-
08	B:	[Well he wants to make a chay- a change,

Sacks (1995a) said,

> Focussing on "I hope he can carry on," there's no "he" being talked about; no person that could be referred to via "he" has been introduced. Who's "he"? Obviously in this case "he" is Mr Hooper. The topic is Mrs Hooper's illness. The introduction of him in such a way as requires the use of Mrs Hooper to find who "he" is, may be one way that, that Mr Hooper is being talked of subtopically is done.
>
> *(p. 763)*

As in Fragments 32 and 33, a locally initial *he* (Line 06; i.e., a locally subsequent reference form in a locally initial position) is understood and treated by the co-interactants as referring to a husband. What makes it "obviously" (Sacks, 1995a, p. 763) the case that *he* indexes the husband? First, the use of the title Mrs. (Line 01) indexes the existence of a husband (at least at some point), whereas the use of a first and last name would not, and Miss would be counterindicative—but in any event, the interactants seem to share some information about Mrs. Hooper and presumably both know of the husband's existence (part of what Schegloff, 1996, p. 457, perhaps meant when he said that the *he* reference "invoke[es] recipient's (B's) knowledge of the matters being talked about to solve what—that is relevant to this topic—this person reference could be referring to"). The plural proterm *they* at Line 03 (also used in Fragment 32, Line 22) is hearable as possibly inviting the recipient to understand Mrs. Hooper as part of an (unspecified) collectivity. The invocation of another as part of a collective *they* may, like the invocation of oneself as part of a collective *we,* produce the heterosexual (married) unit as the collectivity generally understood as thereby referenced.[9] The subsequent production of a locally initial *he* (Line 06) (possibly hearable as extracting a male from the *they* at Line 03) produces a male person as needing to carry on in the context of Mrs. Hooper's illness. The apparent ease with which the speakers produce and understand this locally initial *he* as Mrs. Hooper's husband displays (for us as analysts) the extent to which coping with a wife's illness is an activity category bound to husband, and that this category boundedness is a *resource* that is relied on by the speaker who deploys—and the recipient who makes sense of—the locally initial proterm. The "knowledge of the matters being talked about" (Schegloff, 1996, p. 457) is not merely knowledge specific to the individual circumstances of Mrs. Hooper (in Fragment 34) or the friends in Bristol (in Fragment 32, about whom the recipient in fact has no prior knowledge): It rests also on cultural knowledge about what categories of people care about and for each other, and possibly share a single family income—categories produced here in terms of the heterosexual married couple. Through the invocation of husbands and wives with locally initial proterms (we, he, she), speakers treat the existence of such persons as a taken-for-granted feature of their social worlds.

Across these conversations, then, a couple is understood as composed not just of two people, but specifically of two people of different sexes. This assumption is most flagrantly apparent in Fragment 35, in which Lesley tells her friend, Joyce, that she has ordered roses as a present for her ruby wedding anniversary—and that, in recognition of that specific occasion, she has ordered "a couple, a male and a female." (Line 02 is the final assessment of someone they have been discussing in the sequence that Lesley treats as finished when she launches Line 01.):

Fragment 35
[Holt 10_88–1-08]

Les: The other thing [i s I]
Joy: [°She's dr]ead,fu[1.°
Les: [I wz g'nna mention
to you, .hhhh is I've ordered th- (.) the roses, I've
ordered as it wz your- (0.2) k- your ruby wedding I (.)
ordered a cou:ple. a ma:le 'nd a £ fema:le hhuh heh
he [h hn
Joy: [Oh: he-how l:o:[v e]ly. oh-:-:-:
Les: [.hh]E:dward Mo::rse an' Eena
Harkn[ess.
Joy: [Oh::: Edward Morse is one I l::o:::ve.=

Through her selection of different-sex roses, Lesley displays the extent to which heterosexuality is displayed as integral to her understanding of a marriage.[10] The couple whose anniversary is being celebrated are specifically produced, through the gift she has selected for them, as a male and a female. Of course, they happen to be categorizable as male and female—but that is not the only way of categorizing them, and it is the selection of this particular (sex-based) category system that constitutes Lesley's report of her gift as specifically heterosexual. Alternative categories she might have used—that sound implausible only because of the primacy of the male–female distinction in our taken-for-granted understanding of married coupledom—might have been a climbing rose and a bush rose (producing the couple as composed of a tall and a short member); or a red rose and a white rose (producing them as originating respectively from the English counties of Lancashire and Yorkshire, of which these flowers are emblems). Any actual marriage is (almost) as likely to be between two people of different heights and geographical regions as between two people of different sexes: However, the former two category systems are treated as incidental to the Euro-American definition of marriage, whereas the latter category system is central to it. The dominant cultural understanding of marriage—reflected and reconstituted in Lesley's formulation of her gift—is (as the marriage amendments in 17 U.S. states now instantiate[11]) the union of one man and one woman. It is not likely that Lesley, living in rural England in the mid-1980s, was defending marriage against the incursions of equal marriage activists; her selection of different-sex roses simply reflects and reconstitutes the taken-for-granted heteronormativity of her culture.

Speaking as a homosexual

There is only one identifiably homosexual speaker in the data sets reviewed here: a caller to the suicide prevention center in the data collected by Sacks (1972a, 1995a, 1995b). Although many of the suicide calls involve problems in heterosexual relationships (spousal deaths, divorces or abandonments; see Sacks, 1972a, pp. 52, 56), and although many callers make apparent that they *are* heterosexual (e.g., calls 9, 14, 16, 17, 19, 23, and 24 in Sacks, 1972a), nobody calls the suicide line *because* they are heterosexual. Rather, heterosexuality in these calls, as elsewhere in the data corpora collectively, is a taken-for-granted backdrop. By contrast with these suicidal heterosexuals, the one suicidal homosexual caller presents his sexual orientation as the reason for the call (Sacks, 1972a, pp. 65–66; 1995a, pp. 46–47). This speaker is alone in these data corpora in orienting to his talk as conveying information about his sexual orientation (i.e., he is speaking as a homosexual in a way that no heterosexual in these data is ever speaking as a heterosexual):[12]

Fragment 36
[From Sacks, 1995a, p. 46]

01	Clt:	Is there anything you can stay interested in?
02	Cal:	No, not really.
03	Clt:	What interests did you have before?
04	Cal:	I was a hair stylist at one time, I did some
05		fashions now and then, things like that.
//		((lines omitted))
70	Clt:	Have you been having some sexual problems?
71	Cal:	All my life.
72	Clt:	Uh huh. Yeah.

73	Cal:	Naturally. You probably suspect, as far as the
74		hair stylist and, uh, either one way or the
75		other, they're straight or homosexual, something
76		like that.

Sacks (1995a) commented,

> In this case, although it might not be proper for this man to say about himself that he's troubled by possible homosexual tendencies, he finds a way to invoke a subset of occupational categories, "hair stylist . . . fashions . . . and things like that," which constitutes an adequate basis for inferring homosexuality. And in his subsequent talk he proposes that such an inference has "probably" been made by the other.
>
> *(p. 47)*

By contrast, the inference of heterosexuality (made on the basis of different-sex partners and spouses) is never oriented to as such by interactants. These casual and unoriented to displays of heterosexuality in the service of local interactional goals constitute a mundane instance of heterosexual privilege by those who take for granted, as others cannot, their access to the culture's kinship terminology and their own conformity with a heteronormative social order.

Conclusion

The field sometimes known as "queer linguistics" (Kulick, 2002) has overwhelmingly focused on deviant groups: for example, gay men (Chesbro, 1981; Leap, 1996), lesbians (Moonwomon-Baird, 1997), *travesti* (Kulick, 1998), *hijras* (Hall & O'Donovan, 1996), and sex workers (Hall, 1995). As Cameron and Kulick (2003) pointed out, "understanding the processes that maintain the hegemony of heterosexuality requires attention to be given not only to the cases in which bodies/relations/desires 'deviate' from the norm, but also to those cases in which they do not" (p. 149). In this article, I have focused on instances in which apparently nondeviant heterosexuals produce themselves as such, and I have drawn attention to the utterly banal and commonplace nature of these heterosexual performances. I have shown various ways in which, without any orientation to so doing, speakers "give off" their heterosexuality, and I have argued that the cointeractants in these data sets are not actively "doing being heterosexual" or flaunting their heterosexuality—but are simply getting on with the business of their lives, treating their own and others' heterosexuality as entirely unremarkable, ordinary, taken-for-granted and displaying it incidentally in the course of some other action in which they are engaged. For the "normal" heterosexual participant, nothing special is happening. For any deviant LGBT participant in (or eavesdropping on) the conversations in the data corpora from which these fragments have been extracted, a clamorous heterosexuality is everywhere apparent.

In pointing to the pervasive heterosexuality of the speakers on whose talk the foundational findings of CA are based, I am drawing attention to a feature of these data corpora not previously noted in the literature. The fragments I have cited have been used by other conversation analysts as instances of a reporting as a prelude to an invitation (Fragment 16, Drew, 1984); an insertion repair (Fragment 17, Schegloff, 1997a); a pre-announcement (Fragment 21, Levinson, 1983), among other technical features. Look, for example, at Fragments 37 through 39 (which follow), which exemplify (as argued in this article) instances of heteronormativity—but each of which is used elsewhere in the CA literature to illustrate some technical feature of talk-in-interaction:

an upgraded second assessment (Fragment 37, Pomerantz, 1984, p. 60), a try-marked sequence (Fragment 38, Sacks & Schegloff, 1979, p. 19), and the use of "oh" as a successful outcome of a search (Fragment 39, Heritage, 1984, pp. 299–300), respectively:

Fragment 37
[NB:VII.13] (From Pomerantz, 1984, p. 60)

01 E: ... yihknow he's a goodlooking fel'n
02 eez got a beautiful wi:fe.=
03 M: =Ye:s::. Go:rgeous girl-

Fragment 38
(From Sacks & Schegloff, 1979, p. 19)

01 A: ... well I was the only one other than
02 than the uhm tch Fords? Uh Mrs. Holmes Ford?
03 You know [the the cellist?
04 B: [Oh yes. She's she's the cellist.
05 A: Yes.
06 B: Ye[s
07 A: [Well she and her husband were there...

Fragment 39
[Goodwin: G91:250] (From Heritage, 1984, pp. 299–300)

01 A: ... This girlfr- er Jeff's gi:rlfriend,
02 the one he's gettin' married to, (0.9) s
03 brother.=he use'to uh,
// ((13 lines of data omitted. During this
// period the setting is disrupted by the
// leaving of some of the participants))
17 A: What was I gonna say.= Oh:: anyway.=
18 She use'ta, (0.4) come over....

The observation that these data instances display the heterosexuality of the "good looking fella" and his wife (Fragment 37), the Fords (Fragment 38), and Jeff and his girlfriend (Fragment 39) is entirely irrelevant to and inconsequential for the technical findings of upgraded second assessment, try-marked sequences, and the deployment of *oh*. I am emphatically *not* suggesting that other analysts' failure to comment on the heterosexuality of the talk compromises their technical analyses in any way. This point is worth emphasizing in the light of previous criticisms of CA for having allegedly made invalid generalizations about interactional practices on the basis of the restricted categories of speakers whose talk constitutes its data (e.g., Coates, 2002; Eckert & McConnell-Ginet, 2003, p. 111). The displayed heterosexuality of the speakers in CA's classic data corpora is utterly irrelevant to the overwhelming majority of the analyses on which the foundational discoveries of conversational practices (such as turn taking, sequence organization, preference, repair, etc.) are based.

In conclusion, I consider further the implications of my findings for LGBT studies, CA, and future work connecting the two. First, for LGBT studies, this analysis offers evidence to counter a common criticism of LGBT activists: The charge that we flaunt our sexuality (e.g., ". . . do you have to let everyone know? Why flaunt it?"; Manahan, 1982, p. 68). One response is to draw attention to the many ways in which heterosexuals display their heterosexuality in ordinary everyday interaction. This study documents some of those displays and shows how, in the everyday talk analyzed here, heterosexuality is "naturalized"—constructed as an invisible (unoriented to) category. Parallel claims have been made about Whiteness: "In daily interaction white people view and experience whiteness as a 'neutral,' that is, a 'normal' state of being, an empty racial category" (Moore, 2002, p. 63); and the method employed here could also be used to study this—and, indeed any other—hegemonic identity. This study, then, contributes to LGBT research on "coming out" and "passing" by revealing the pervasive backdrop of taken-for-granted heterosexuality against which such activities are conducted. As Goffman (1963) said, those who must strategize whether and how to disclose potentially discrediting information in mixed contexts "will have to be alive to aspects of the social situation that others treat as uncalculated and unattended. What are unthinking routines for normals can become management problems for the discreditable" (p. 88).

As the analysis presented in this article shows, the range of interactional activities from which closeted same-sex couples are excluded, or that they must actively monitor and manage if they are not to reveal their homosexuality, is vast—ranging from the appropriate receipt of explicit talk about heterosexual sex and relationships (while not being able to reciprocate without fabrication), through to the management of pronouns. Given the pervasiveness of heterosexual self-display as revealed in these data, the *failure* to display oneself as heterosexual must also be an indicator of possible homosexuality—and presumably constitutes one element of the so-called "gaydar" (the ability of lesbians and gays to spot each other as such from clues missed by most heterosexuals). Given the frequency with which heterosexual speakers reveal other people's heterosexuality through mundane references to their partners, this analysis also indicates the kinds of problems faced by parents of lesbians and gays when (like Ron in Fragment 3) conveying family news: "families of lesbians and gays must also decide whether or not to come out about their own queer family members" (Bernstein & Reimann, 2001, p. 7). This research, then, lays some empirical groundwork for using CA to explore the relation between the casual disclosure of sexual identity by heterosexual people who are doing "nothing special" and the management issues attendant on disclosing a lesbian or gay identity—"the love that is famous for not daring to speak its name" (Sedgwick, 1993, p. 45). We can use the foundational discoveries of CA (turn taking, sequence organization, repair, etc.) to explore how sexual identities are interactionally managed, displayed, negotiated, and concealed (see Kitzinger, 2000; Land & Kitzinger, in press). Most fundamentally, this analysis has begun to explore the ways in which a mundane taken-for-granted world is produced through everyday talk in interaction.

The implications of this analysis for CA are also far reaching. Conversation analysts (e.g., Schegloff, 1996) have noted the importance of person reference terms as a central component of our understanding of culture. The analyses presented here have contributed to CA a closer examination of practices of person reference in relation to the production of the (heterosexual) marital relationship. I have shown how categorical references to husband and wife are deployed with reference to culturally understood inferences (which they thereby reproduce) of the intimacy, care, co-residence, and single economic unit constituted by the married couple; and the activities in which they are understood to be jointly engaged (co-visiting, co-vacationing, co-hosting, sleeping in the same bed). I have shown how heterosexual couples are produced as such through practices of naming and how nonrecognitional person references reflect and reproduce a kinship system that positions individuals in terms of heterosexual relationships either through their own marriages or those of others and how these reference forms are deployed in the interests of local interactional goals. My analysis also displays what may turn out to be a routine (rather than exceptional) use of locally subsequent reference forms in locally initial positions (Schegloff, 1996) as a device for displaying (at least heterosexual) coupledom.

Inspection of the data based on which the field of CA has relied does seem to show that heterosexual displays are a commonplace and taken-for-granted feature of social interaction. As analysts, we might want not to take a member's perspective on this but rather to treat the interactant's everyday world as problematic and to explore how, and in the service of what other actions, their heterosexuality is assumed and deployed. We might notice that heterosexuality is available to them as a resource; we might consider what kind of world they are reflecting and reproducing in their talk. More broadly, we might ask what is happening when nothing special is happening: when the second is in a preferred relation to the first; when the yes–no question is followed by a yes–no answer; when the recognitional referent is recognized or the nonrecognitional referent is treated as adequate; when the punchline of the story is promptly and properly received and the second story is treated as fitted to the first; when presumed ordinary experiences are treated as ordinary—what is happening *then,* how is *that* done, and what kind of world must we be living in that these things run off smoothly? This kind of analysis may enable us better to understand (as activists and as conversation analysts) the routine achievement of a taken-for-granted world (Schegloff, 1986).

Notes

1 Other researchers have pointed to the allegedly male (e.g., Coates, 2002) or "white, middle-class Anglo-American" (Eckert & McConnell-Ginet, 2003, p. 111) nature of the data sets on which conversation analysis (CA) is based and have suggested that key findings of CA (e.g., turn taking) may be limited to those categories of speakers whose talk constituted the data. It should be noted, in considering these critiques, that some of the most frequently cited and painstakingly analyzed data in early CA come from talk involving people who are African American (e.g., the Upholstery Shop data) and identifiably working class (e.g., the Automobile Discussion data), and that the classic data sets overwhelmingly involve talk between women (e.g., the SBL, Trio, NB, Rahman, and Holt corpora).

2 There is some foundational conversation analyis data involving both members of heterosexual couples in interaction, generally over meals or drinks in one couple's home (e.g., Automobile Discussion, Chicken Dinner). Lerner (1992) specifically analyzed such data with reference to how collectivities (such as the couple) become consequential social units in ordinary conversation.

3 Also see also the following:

[MC:I:15] (From Jefferson, 1978, p. 233)

```
01 Har:  I said "And-and-and-" "What ih-" "Is her
02       boyfriend a nice ma:n Joey?" He sz "Oh
03       he's very nice, he's a colored man." hhhhhhh
04       [HAH hah!
```

This produces the woman under discussion, Joey, and the interactants, Harmony and Lil, as White in the course of topic talk. It also treats women having boyfriends *per se* as unremarkable—what is remarked on is the ethnicity of this particular boyfriend and not the fact of his existence (although, in fact, it turns out that the point of the telling is Joey's misunderstanding in that the colored man is some sort of paid employee and not a boyfriend at all).

4 The right to marry and found a family is a fundamental human right (Article 16 of the Universal Declaration of Human Rights, http://www.un.org/Overview/rights.html), advanced in the face of Nazi bans on marriage between Jews and Aryans, the U.S. antimiscegenation laws, and the South African apartheid regime's prohibition of mixed marriages between races. Campaigns for equal marriage rights today include the following: in the United Arab Emirates, the right to marry for different-sex Muslims and Christians (banned by *Shari'a* law; http://web.amnesty.org/library); in Israel, equal marriage rights for different-sex Palestinians and Israelis (subject to apartheid marriage laws by Israel's new law on marriage and citizenship; Mariner, 2003); and, across most of the world, the right to marry a same-sex

partner. There are currently only two national governments in the world that permit same-sex marriage: the Netherlands (since 2001) and Belgium (since 2003). Since 2003, most of the Canadian provinces and territories have enacted equal marriage legislation, and this is likely to be reflected at the federal level in 2005. In the United States, only the state of Massachusetts has equal marriage legislation, and this is very unlikely to become federal policy. (For more information on the equal marriage debates, see Kitzinger & Wilkinson, 2004a, 2004b).

5 I am grateful to Geoff Raymond for drawing my attention to the relevance of Goodwin's (1987) analysis to this data fragment.

6 In telephone conversations, the maleness or femaleness of the caller is attributed on the basis of voice quality (only two gender misidentifications are apparent in the hundreds of calls in these data sets) and in co-present interactions, on the basis of the appearance of the speaker. Recipients' confidence in their ability to make correct gender attributions on the basis of voice quality is such that, in the small amount of telephone data we have so far collected in which lesbians refer to their partners in ways that identify them as female (e.g., as girlfriend, partner, wife, or using a female proterm or identifiably female name), there is no instance in which they are subsequently treated as male (see Land & Kitzinger, in press). Clearly, this confidence may be misplaced (and exploited; see Hall, 1995).

7 I have access to the original audiodata and have retranscribed this fragment, which is why it departs somewhat (especially Line 03) from the version given by Sacks (1995a, p. 757).

8 In a survey of language use among gay men, Harvey (1997) found that 4 of the 53 respondents reported referring to their same-sex partner as their wife or husband—a usage he described as "parodic appropriation" (p. 68). I have no recorded naturalistic data in which someone in a same-sex couple can be heard as referring to a same-sex partner using the terminology appropriate to a different-sex spouse (i.e., wife from a gay man or husband from a lesbian). Those instances in which a woman refers to her same-sex partner as her wife (see Land & Kitzinger, in press) result in major interactional difficulties.

9 Of course *we* and *they* are also used as locally initial proterms by speakers who thereby index that they are speaking in some institutional capacity, or about persons acting in an institutional capacity (Schegloff, 1996, p. 477, Footnote 25)—and the speaker at Line 03 is also hearable as possibly launching a question about the medical professionals involved in Mrs. Hooper's treatment.

10 And to sexual relationships in general—elsewhere, in discussing her teenage son's plans to attend an all night party, she relies on the notion that sex segregation means no possibility of sexual activity:

[Holt X(C) 2-1-2]

Les: [Well ↑I don't mind i- I mean (.) I don't mind 'im
taking the sleep ing bag. an' staying the night.
providing they're a::ll (.) u-bo[y:s.

11 As of November 2004.

12 The only talk *about* non-heterosexual people I have found in the data corpora are the following: talk about actors who play "fags" in the movies, including what is apparently a quote from some such movie ("Tell them I'm not a fag"; Chicken Dinner); a news report about "fags" in Detroit ("Isn't that the place they say where if two fags split up one's got to pay the other one alimony?"; "Too way ahead out there"; Chicken Dinner); and what Drew (1987) described as "three teasing attributions to Vic of homosexuality" (p. 224; Upholstery Shop)—to which Vic's retort is that he would rather be a "faggot" than marry the female prostitute with whom he reports having been sexually involved.

References

Agar, M. (1973). *Ripping and running: A formal ethnography of urban heroin addicts.* New York: Seminar Press.

Becker, H. S. (1963). *Outsiders.* New York: Free Press.

Bernstein, M., & Reimann, R. (2001). Queer families and the politics of visibility. In M. Bernstein & R. Reimann (Eds.), *Queer families, queer politics: Challenging culture and the state* (pp. 1–24). New York: Columbia University Press.

Cameron, D., & Kulick, D. (2003). *Language and sexuality.* Cambridge, England: Cambridge University Press.

Chesbro, J. W. (Ed.). (1981). *Gayspeak: Gay male and lesbian communication.* New York: Pilgrim Press.

Coates, J. (2002). *Men talk: Stories in the making of masculinities.* Oxford, England: Blackwell.

Drew, P. (1984). Speakers' reportings in invitation sequences. In J. M. Atkinson & J. Heritage (Eds.), *Structures of social action: Studies in conversation analysis* (pp. 129–151). Cambridge, England: Cambridge University Press.

Drew, P. (1987). Po-faced receipts of teases. *Linguistics, 25,* 219–253.

Drew, P., & Holt, E. (1988). Complainable matters: The use of idiomatic expressions in making complaints. *Social Problems, 35,* 398–417.

Eckert, P., & McConnell-Ginet, S. (2003). *Language and gender.* Cambridge, England: Cambridge University Press.

Garfinkel, H. (1967). *Studies in ethnomethodology.* Englewood Cliffs, NJ: Prentice Hall.

Goffman, E. (1963). *Stigma.* London: Penguin.

Goodwin, C. (1987). Unilateral departure. In G. Button & J. R. Lee (Eds.), *Talk and social organization* (pp. 206–216). Clevedon, England: Multilingual Matters.

Hall, K. (1995). Lip service on the fantasy lines. In K. Hall & M. Bucholtz (Eds.), *Gender articulated: Language and the socially constructed self* (pp. 183–216). New York: Routledge.

Hall, K., & O'Donovan, V. (1996). Shifting gender positions among Hindi-speaking hijras. In V. L. Bergvall, J. M. Bing, & A. F. Freed (Eds.), *Rethinking language and gender research: Theory and practice* (pp. 228–266). London: Longman.

Harvey, K. (1997). Gay men, straight men and a problem of lexical choice. In K. Harvey & C. Shalom (Eds.), *Language and desire: Encoding sex, romance and intimacy* (pp. 60–82). London: Routledge.

Heritage, J. (1984). A change-of-state token and aspects of its sequential placement. In J. M. Atkinson & J. Heritage (Eds.), *Structures of social action: Studies in conversation analysis* (pp. 299–345). Cambridge, England: Cambridge University Press.

Heritage, J., & Robinson, J. (2005). Accounting for the visit: Giving reasons for seeking medical care. In J. Heritage & D. W. Maynard (Eds.), *Communication in medical care: Interaction between physicians and patients.* Cambridge, England: Cambridge University Press.

Ingraham, C. (2001). Heterosexuality: It's just not natural. In D. Richardson & S. Seidman (Eds.), *Handbook of lesbian and gay studies* (pp. 73–82). London: Sage.

Jacobs, G. (1996). Lesbian and gay male language use: A critical review of the literature. *American Speech, 71,* 49–71.

Jefferson, G. (1978). Sequential aspects of storytelling in conversation. In J. N. Schenkein (Ed.), *Studies in the organization of conversational interaction* (pp. 219–248). New York: Academic.

Jefferson, G. (1984). On stepwise transition from talk about a trouble to inappropriately next-positioned matters. In J. M. Atkinson & J. Heritage (Eds.), *Structures of social action: Studies in conversation analysis* (pp. 191–222). Cambridge, England: Cambridge University Press.

Kitzinger, C. (2000). Doing feminist conversation analysis. *Feminism & Psychology, 10,* 163–193.

Kitzinger, C. (in press-a). Heteronormativity in action: Reproducing the heterosexual nuclear family in "after hours" medical calls. *Social Problems.* Special Section: Language, interaction, and social problems.

Kitzinger, C. (in press-b). How talk-in-interaction reproduces normative social worlds without "intention," "belief" or "prejudice." *Discourse Studies: Discourse, Interaction and Cognition.*

Kitzinger, C., & Wilkinson, S. (2004a). The re-branding of marriage. *Feminism & Psychology, 14,* 127–150.

Kitzinger, C., & Wilkinson, S. (2004b). Social advocacy for equal marriage: The politics of "rights" and the psychology of "mental health." *Analyses of Social Issues and Public Policy, 4,* 173–194.

Kulick, D. (1998). *Travesti: Sex, gender and culture among Brazilian transgendered prostitutes.* Chicago: University of Chicago Press.

Kulick, D. (2000). Gay and lesbian language. *Annual Review of Anthropology, 29,* 243–285.

Kulick, D. (2002). Queer linguistics? In K. Campbell-Kibler, R. J. Podesva, S. J. Roberts, & A. Wong (Eds.), *Language and sexuality: Contesting meaning in theory and practice* (pp. 65–68). Stanford, CA: CSLI Publications.

Land, V., & Kitzinger, C. (in press). Speaking as a lesbian: Correcting the heterosexist presumption. *Research on Language and Social Interaction.*

Leap, W. L. (1996). *Word's out: Gay men's English.* Minneapolis: University of Minnesota Press.

Lerner, G. H. (1992). Collectivities in action: Establishing the relevance of conjoined participation in conversation. *Text, 13,* 213–245.

Levinson, S. C. (1983). *Pragmatics.* Cambridge, England: Cambridge University Press.

Livia, A., & Hall, K. (Eds.). (1997). *Queerly phrased: Language, gender and sexuality.* Oxford, England: Oxford University Press.

MacLean, J. (1995). An afternoon with my if-there-were-a-laws. In K. Jay (Ed.), *Dyke life: A celebration of the lesbian experience* (pp. 23–26). New York: HarperCollins.

Manahan, N. (1982). Homophobia in the classroom. In M. Cruikshank (Ed.), *Lesbian studies: Present and future* (pp. 66–69). New York: The Feminist Press.

Mariner, J. (2003, August 13). Israel's apartheid marriage laws: A wall of separation through the heart. *Counterpunchorg.* Retrieved September 13, 2003, from www. ccmep.org/2003.articles/Palestine/081303_israels_apartheid_marriage_law.htm

Maurer, D. W. (1964). *Whiz mob: A correlation of the technical argot of pickpockets with their behavior pattern.* New Haven, CT: College and University Press.

Moonwomon-Baird, B. (1997). Toward a study of lesbian speech. In A. Livia & K. Hall (Eds.), *Queerly phrased: Language, gender and sexuality* (pp. 202–203). New York: Oxford University Press.

Moore, V. A. (2002). The collaborative emergence of race in children's play: A case study of two summer camps. *Social Problems, 49,* 58–78.

Pomerantz, A. (1984). Agreeing and disagreeing with assessments: Some features of preferred/dispreferred turn shapes. In J. M. Atkinson & J. Heritage (Eds.), *Structures of social action: Studies in conversation analysis* (pp. 57–101). Cambridge, England: Cambridge University Press.

Romano, R. (2003). *Race mixing: Black–White marriage in post-war America.* Cambridge, MA: Harvard University Press.

Sacks, H. (1972a). An initial investigation of the usability of conversational data for doing sociology. In D. Sudnow (Ed.), *Studies in social interaction* (pp. 31–74). New York: Free Press.

Sacks, H. (1972b). On the analysability of stories by children. In J. J. Gumperz & D. Hymes (Eds.), *Directions in sociolinguistics: The ethnography of communication* (pp. 329–345). New York: Holt, Rinehart & Winston.

Sacks, H. (1974). An analysis in the course of a joke's telling in conversation. In R. Bauman & J. Sherzer (Eds.), *Explorations in the ethnography of speaking* (pp. 337–354). Cambridge, England: Cambridge University Press.

Sacks, H. (1984). On doing "being ordinary." In J. M. Atkinson & J. Heritage (Eds.), *Structures of social action: Studies in conversation analysis* (pp. 413–429). Cambridge, England: Cambridge University Press.

Sacks, H. (1995a). *Lectures on conversation: Volume I.* Oxford, England: Blackwell.

Sacks, H. (1995b). *Lectures on conversation: Volume II.* Oxford, England: Blackwell.

Sacks, H., & Schegloff, E. A. (1979). Two preferences in the organization of reference to persons in conversation and their interaction. In G. Psathas (Ed.), *Everyday language: Studies in ethnomethodology* (pp. 15–21). New York: Irvington.

Schegloff, E. A. (1986). The routine as achievement. *Human Studies, 9,* 111–151.

Schegloff, E. A. (1992). Repair after next turn: The last structurally provided defense of intersubjectivity in conversation. *American Journal of Sociology, 97,* 1295–1345.

Schegloff, E. A. (1995). *Sequence organization.* Unpublished manuscript.

Schegloff, E. A. (1996). Some practices for referring to persons in talk-in-interaction. In B. A. Fox (Ed.), *Studies in anaphora* (pp. 437–485). Amsterdam: Benjamins.

Schegloff, E. A. (1997a). Practices and actions: Boundary cases of other-initiated repair. *Discourse Processes, 23,* 499–545.

Schegloff, E. A. (1997b). Whose text? Whose context? *Discourse & Society, 8,* 165–187.

Schegloff, E. A. (2000). On granularity. *Annual Review of Sociology, 26,* 715–720.

Sedgwick, E. K. (1993). Epistemology of the closet. In H. Abelove, M. A. Barale, & D. M. Halperin (Eds.), *The lesbian and gay studies reader* (pp. 45–61). London: Routledge.

Seidman, S. (1996). *Queer theory/sociology.* Cambridge, MA: Blackwell.

Wilkinson, S., & Kitzinger, C. (Eds.). (1993). *Heterosexuality: A "Feminism & Psychology" reader.* London: Sage.

Wilkinson, S., & Kitzinger, C. (Eds.). (1996). *Representing the other: A "Feminism & Psychology" reader.* London: Sage.

Wilkinson, S., & Kitzinger, C. (2003). Constructing identities: A feminist conversation analytic approach to positioning in action. In R. Harre & F. Moghaddam (Eds.), *The self and others: Positioning individuals and groups in personal, political and cultural contexts* (pp. 157–180). Westport, CT: Praeger.

Zimmerman, D. H. (1992). The interactional organization of calls for emergency assistance. In P. Drew & J. Heritage (Eds.), *Talk at work: Interaction in institutional settings* (pp. 418–469). Cambridge, England: Cambridge University Press.

11

A heterosexual life

Older women and agency within marriage and the family

Jenny Hockey, Angela Meah and Victoria Robinson

Jean Brown[1] was born in 1928 in Lancashire and grew up during the Second World War. She offered her life history as a contribution to a study of the making of heterosexual relationships in East Yorkshire.[2] Now widowed, Jean married Harry in 1949 and her children and grandchildren currently live in East Yorkshire, though Jean herself has remained in Lancashire. The aim of this study was to identify cross-generational continuities and differences in the way in which heterosexual relationships were conceptualised and made within extended families. Qualitative interviews, conducted with representatives of three generations in twenty-two families in East Yorkshire, included discussion about how individuals acquired sexual knowledge, began making heterosexual relationships, set up families and dealt with divorce and death. A life history approach gave information about events which both contextualised and were contained within individuals' lives; in addition it yielded accounts of how people made sense of their experience and the emotions it had engendered (Alasuutari, 1995, p. 50).

If we see Jean's life history as an example of how heterosexuality was understood and experienced between two world wars, as well as an older widow's reflections on her earlier, married life, then we also need to recognise it as the product of an engagement with Angela Meah, the study's research associate. In other words, we need to ask how their commonalities and differences may have enabled certain dimensions of heterosexuality to be highlighted while others were downplayed. For example, Jean and Angela share the same social class and regional identity, being born within fifteen miles of each other. Yet they differ markedly in age and educational background. While Jean is seventy-five, has always lived and worked in the same area, Angela is thirty and has three higher degrees, her PhD involving fieldwork alone in difficult conditions in South Africa. Both women have experienced heterosexual relationships but how they engage with the conditions of heterosexuality is profoundly influenced by both the commonalities and the differences between them.

The question we raise is how, as twenty-first century feminist academics, we might interpret the gendered life histories of women born between two world wars. What light might their narratives shed on the question of women's agency within the context of 'institutionalised heterosexuality' (VanEvery, 1996)? In asking this question, we draw on Jackson's view of heterosexuality. She argues that 'as institution, practice, experience and identity heterosexuality is not merely sexual' (1996, p. 30). It is this broader notion of the interconnectedness of many domains of life – paid employment, family life, domestic and emotional labour, sexual practice – at the site of heterosexuality, which underpins this paper. We are therefore contemplating lives which took shape around seventy years ago, but do so using political and intellectual resources developed and refined only during the last thirty. As authors, our own ages range between thirty and late fifties. To some extent, therefore, we must acknowledge a *generational* distance which might parallel a *political* distance from the gendered values which informed older women's upbringing. Yet with one author nearing sixty, this paper is not simply a young woman's investigation of chronological and generational distance, of the older woman as 'other'. Nonetheless, the interview data to be discussed here were produced via an interaction between women of *different* ages, one being seventy-five, the other thirty. As noted, many factors divide them, yet they share important commonalities. The data themselves, however, were produced at a particular moment within the history of heterosexuality and this, too, informs the process of their production. The life story of Jean, the older woman, conforms to the profile of traditional or hegemonic heterosexuality, containing few surprises for the reader with a similar background, or with female relatives and friends from Jean's generation. Though she shares a working class background with Angela, Jean never accessed the educational opportunities which made Angela economically independent, and empowered her to engage critically with the conditions of her own heterosexuality. Should Jean's 'traditional' heterosexual history therefore be viewed as the outcome of a set of patriarchal relationships and practices oriented towards her family's well-being, rather than her own? Engaging critically with feminist and social gerontology debates around the notion of agency, we address the question of whether she nonetheless demonstrates 'a creative capacity that is irreducible to structural conditions' (Wray, 2003, p. 514).

In an account of (hetero) sex, Smart argues that 'heterosexuality may be many things', even though 'at times we need to collectivise this diversity (for example when recognizing heterosexual privilege and its naturalization)' (1996, p. 170). With respect to sexual knowledge, Jean grew up within institutionalised silences and omissions – indeed the implicit injunctions to passivity, characteristic of women's lives before World War Two. Yet she spoke directly about her sexual history and the pleasure she found and took within it. Arguing that 'there can be multiple meanings (although not any old random meanings) attached to different sexualities at the same time' (1996, p. 167), Smart enjoins that we 'retain a politics and pleasure in more fragmented heterosexualities' (1996, p. 174). She refers to the heterosexual women who 'wrote of "being" heterosexual in *Heterosexuality: a Feminism and Psychology Reader*' (Wilkinson & Kitzinger, 1993): 'We can certainly see radically different heterosexual identities emerging in which these women are far from being the dupes of patriarchy, are far from homophobic, are far from accepting male sexual dominance, and are far from seeking their own missing penises as Freud would have us do. Some of them also seem to be having a good time even if they feel they should do so quietly' (1996, p. 177).

Jean evaded this pressure to 'do so quietly'. Not only did she describe her sexual experience openly when interviewed, introducing the topic herself by saying, *We weren't all virgins that walked down the aisle*; but she also answered her children's questions about sex *honestly and straightforwardly*. She said *there was no, not sort of forbidden territory, no barriers, really; I'd walk about with underwear on, you know, and things like that* . . . . Engaging with feminist debates around the concept of agency, we ask about Jean's 'creative capacity' (Wray, 2003, p. 514) within the conditions of possibility afforded by the institution of heterosexuality. For a woman of her generation, did she demonstrate resistance to the heterosexual imperative that women should remain silent or euphemistic about sexual knowledge and experience? In addressing this question, it is important to recognise that our evidence is data generated within an interview between two women who may have spoken with particular ease, given that they shared a specific working class, regional accent. Though situated within the potentially more dominant role of 'educated interviewer', as a younger woman capable of speaking frankly about sexual matters, Angela's age-based distance from Jean may also have influenced what was said. Bearing this contextual information in mind, what we undertake here is an exploration of apparent contradictions visible within Jean's account of a 'traditional' heterosexual life history.

Structure, agency and feminist theory

Davis takes issue with 'feminist common sense' which, in her view, 'both traditionally and in the present, tends to treat power within gender relations as basically top-down and repressive. Women are regarded as the inevitable victims of male supremacy, helpless and hapless at the hands of the evil-intentioned, omnipotent male' (1991, p. 79). Interrogating (hetero)sex, Smart also argues that feminists have inadvertently augmented male power by overinflating the penis. She asks, 'must we simply reassert that all heterosexual sex is oppression?' (1996, pp. 161–162). Such critiques of monolithic, top-down repressive gender power remind us of the diversity of heterosexualities which women and men inhabit; *and* the agency of women (and men) within institutionalised heterosexuality. Failure to acknowledge this reduces all women to a single position; that of 'cultural dupe' (Jackson, 1999), or 'dope' (Davis, 1991, p. 80). Davis calls for a theory of gendered power which allows us 'to reinstate women to the position of agency without falling into the concomitant stance of blaming them for social inequalities' (1991, p. 82). To provide a nuanced interpretation of the way Jean fulfilled a traditional role within a male breadwinner family and undertook extended emotional labour on behalf of her mother, her husband, her daughter and grand-daughter, we require a theoretical framework which allows us to understand her life as something more complex than just 'collusion'.

Similar debates within the sociology of ageing are relevant here. Bury (1995) points out dangers in 'structured dependency' theory, a political economy of the life course which privileges exclusion from paid work as the basis for older adults' relatively low social status. Introduced as a corrective to biologically based views of ageing which privileged individual adjustment to 'inevitable' decline, structured dependency theory, like early second wave feminism, highlighted structural features of older adults' oppressive conditions. In both cases, however, the relationship between structure and agency needs to be addressed, for as Bury says, it is 'important in developing a perspective on ageing, since it challenges the portrayal of older people (especially women) as passive victims of circumstance' (1995, p. 16). Wray also argues that within the gerontological literature 'there has been a tendency to overemphasise the effects of structural disadvantages and overlook the power of women to resist and transform social structures' (2003, p. 512). The more micro-level life course approach which Bury advocates also has problems, however – ranging from proselytising injunctions to age 'positively', to the postmodern critique of life course stages which privileges consumerism and 'choice'. Nonetheless a life course perspective does consider how macro-level factors such as income and health mesh with individual biographies, though *differences* between older adults remain neglected, and here gender is crucial.

Ingrisch's use of a life history approach *does* attend to gender and is relevant for micro-level data such as Jean's. Highlighting the way Women's Studies has largely confined itself to 'the contradictions between women's socially prescribed roles and the reality of their daily lives' among women *under sixty,* she brings older women out of the margins, giving them a voice 'through their life histories' (1995, p. 42). Using a grounded theory approach, she attempts to 'reconstruct the informal logic of life' (1995, p. 43). Her work can be compared with a 'positive ageing' approach to women's later lives which suggests they might challenge and resist gender roles which were 'barely questioned in young adulthood' (Ginn & Arber, 1995, p. 8). While certain categories of older women access the education, independence and good health which encourage the reinvention of gendered identities in later life, the wider scope of a life history approach provides a more subtle way of interpreting an entire heterosexual life course such as Jean's. Rather than approaching her apparently 'empowered' testimony as an eventual reinvention of her gendered identity *in the present,* we focus on that more extended trajectory of her life course and consider the nature of her agency across the whole series of discursive practices which have constituted her heterosexual history. Thus, for example, although Jean adhered to a traditional gendered division of labour until her fifties, she retained her office job, becoming sole breadwinner when Harry was made redundant at fifty-eight. While she insisted on a corresponding reversal of domestic labour, she took responsibility for his contribution, orchestrating his involvement to help him overcome the depression of job loss: *And so, I went and did this job, so I used to leave him a list every day, things to shop, and I never let him do a big shop. I made him go out every day and buy a bit of something, so that got him out of the house, you know.* Jean's heterosexual life history, therefore, reveals considerable subtlety in the overlap between conformity and reinvention, the relationship between the two shifting across the time of Jean's life with Harry. Indeed her account of and reflections on a lifetime's heterosexual experience provide data which resonate with Brah's perspective on the relationship between experience, subjectivity and agency. In Brah's view 'to think of experience and subject formation as processes is to reformulate the question of agency' (1996, p. 117). Rather than conceiving of the 'I' which takes action as a 'unified, fixed, already existing entit(y)' (1996, p. 117), Brah draws attention to contradictory, inevitably incomplete processes of identity formation within which agency manifests itself. The data we discuss here indeed reflect this way of understanding the relationship between experience, subjectivity and agency.

Conceptualising agency

Whilst advocating a life course approach to ageing and gender, Bury (1995, p. 28) sees no real attempt to theorise the relationship between agency and structure across time. Instead this method has been used to chart the horizontal unfolding of lives at the micro level, then noting the impact of historical and structural factors upon them. This will not help a feminist interpretation of the contradictions within Jean's narrative. Let us consider the example of 'falling in love': when Jean met Harry at the age of fifteen she knew he was *the one* because she *couldn't stop thinking about him. Sort of tingles up your spine, just sort of knew, this is something special.* When Angela asked her how she knew he was *the right person* for her, Jean said, *just a, a feeling, really . . . couldn't get him out of my head.* And she went on: . . . *dancing with him, never being bored with him, never being bored, and he was a good hard-working man.* Meyer points out that when early second wave feminists 'launched their attacks on the male–female love relationship stating that this relationship was corrupted by power inequalities' (1991, p. 24), they were using a structural argument. Individual choice and agency were absent from their explanations. Jackson too is sceptical of this reductionist approach, arguing that 'romanticism and realism can coexist at different levels of our subjectivities. It is perfectly possible to be critical of heterosexual monogamy, dismissive of romantic fantasy and still fall passionately in love' (1999, p. 118). Rather than seeing women 'in love' as inevitably disillusioned cultural dupes, Jackson argues that young women can privilege romantic love with a considerable realism: 'It may be the case that women are expecting more out of heterosexual relationships and are less likely to remain in them if these expectations are not realised' (1999, p. 121). The example of romantic love, therefore, need not exclude the exercise of agency by heterosexual women.

With different data, Davis, too, takes up this question. Having taped consultations between male GPs and female patients, she anticipated a relatively naked exercise of male power. Yet, as she says, 'it was abundantly clear that, just as male doctors could be nice and friendly while exercising control, patients were often surprisingly recalcitrant and rebellious. In fact, the patients routinely exercised power in all sorts of subtle, sneaky and even somewhat unorthodox ways' (1991, p. 76). While post functionalist sociology has indeed tried to recover the social actor as 'competent and knowledgeable', Davis argues that 'this stance . . . seems to disappear as soon as the participants turn out to have a gender' (1991, p. 79). She argues for attention to the microscopic or trivial ways in which gender power is actually enacted, including an acknowledgment of the resources available to both women as well as men. Without this, the possibility of change is denied, both theoretically and practically. 'Political nihilism', Davis says, is all that remains to us (1991, p. 82). Wray adds that older women's agency cannot be extrapolated from their structural position: 'access to resources alone does not translate into empowerment, but is also related to perceptions of their value' (2003, p. 514). Thus, although Jean had always committed herself to the needs of her immediate and her extended family, her previous paid employment and involvement in community activities constituted bases for her self-perception as *independent* in widowhood: *I mean, some people can't live alone. I can, because I'm independent, you know, doesn't bother me, living alone.* Both Davis and Wray adhere to a version of Giddens' structuration theory, yet Davis criticises its lack of 'empirical and theoretical grounding' (1991, p. 83). In what follows, we respond to calls for a more nuanced and empirically grounded account of women's agency through a detailed exploration of Jean's life history.

Growing up heterosexual

As we begin to read the interview, generational difference is evident: Angela is wary of assuming that someone of Jean's age will articulate details of more private or emotional aspects of her experience. Jean's age is something Angela explores tentatively: *Can I ask first, if it's not too personal a question, what year were you born?* When it comes to sexual and reproductive knowledge, Jean highlights the generational distance between them – and their possible lack of a common language: . . . *they didn't call it periods in my day, you were "unwell".* She goes on: *We didn't have "sex", we "made love", you know, these days it's all sex, sex, sex, in't it?* How Jean's age and sexual experience might intersect remains uneasy territory for Angela who says: *Now you might tell me to mind my own business here, what was the sex like as you got older?* What is evident, however, is that despite *differences* in the ways in which sexual and reproductive knowledge might be articulated, the two women speak about it with similar directness. Through the following account we seek to disentangle the continuities and the changes which both unite and separate them.

We begin by noting how Jean's subjectivity develops within a culture implicitly organised according to heterosexual principles. However, we then identify aspects of her life history which suggest a position of sustained resistance to such frameworks. Finally we turn to data which attest to Jean's capacity to direct the course of events within her own life, yet with the apparent outcome of reproducing institutionalised heterosexuality. It is particularly via these final data that we attend to the complexities of agency as a life long process through which Jean inhabits the categories of heterosexuality.

For Jean, little explicit sexual and reproductive knowledge was made available within the family as she grew up, an experience shared by many of the younger, middle-aged women interviewed. As Jean said, . . . *there wasn't an awful lot of discussion. You were expected to know really.* This 'omission' can be construed as an aspect of Jean's socialisation into heterosexuality: of her mother she says *all I can remember her saying is that, [SIGH] you had to keep yourself, that was my mother's thing, "Keep yourself clean". You had to keep yourself clean.* Along with this possibility of female 'dirtiness' came the danger of washing your hair whilst menstruating – a contradiction in terms, yet one which signalled unspecified threats associated with growing up female. Among her peers, however, this process was marked by pairing off with boys, a necessary pre-requisite for social status. When she went behind the bike sheds with Arthur Bradshaw at the age of twelve, the exchange involved simply a kiss on the lips and an invitation to the cinema which her parents would forbid. Yet Jean felt like *Cock of the North* because *he was a real bonny lad, he was, and all the girls liked him, everybody talked to him, he was absolutely gorgeous.* Already, therefore, she experienced heterosexuality as contradictory, 'unspeakable', but a marker of social status. That it might frame her developing subjectivity was something she experienced not just within the family and peer group, but also at an institutional level: for example, in the double seats for 'courting couples' at the cinema. This more macro-level example of everyday life being organised according to heterosexual principles had a temporal as well as spatial dimension. Double seats were given up on marriage, the intimacies of a darkened cinema giving way to those of the bedroom. Indeed the 'fixed abode' of the marital home was pre-figured in the way these seats were allocated: as Jean said, *ours were 17 and 19 and if ever we went, you know, these were our seats.* Heterosexuality's spatially marked trajectory was thus segmented into temporally bounded stages: 'courting', led on to 'marriage', 'the hegemonic form of heterosexuality' (VanEvery, 1996, p. 40). Women's agency, however, was expressed in their recollections of this highly 'structured' marker of heterosexual status. Like women from all three generations, Jean's memory of her wedding in 1949, over fifty years earlier, is richly textured: the toastmaster's red jacket; her white chiffon velvet dress; the twenty-five carnations which made up her bouquet; the potato pies her mother made for the reception. History and biography intersect as Jean acknowledges the constraints of that post-war era and how they were nonetheless partially overcome at her wedding: *we had some belting wedding presents and that kind of thing, and went to Fleetwood* [LAUGHS], *fabulous Fleetwood.* She goes on: *we didn't have a fabulous spread, it was ham and something, but in those days it was very good.* Heterosexuality also provided the organising principle for the gifts given to guests: quarter pound boxes of Black Magic and Cadbury's Milk Tray for every *lady* and *each man got a cigar.* Moreover, the public nature of this transition to heterosexual coupledom is evident in its 'performative' aspects: Jean recalls the vicar's wife, a former student at RADA, telling her *I shall be sat at the back and I hope to hear every word.*

Growing up heterosexual led to a traditional domestic division of labour on marriage: Jean would ensure that tea was on the table for Harry, particularly when he felt left out after their daughter arrived. They passed on a model of family life which restricted sexual expression to within its confines, warning their daughter not to *let them down* by becoming pregnant and exposing them to gossip. As Harry's parents aged, Jean cared for them, organising her paid employment around her domestic role, Harry taking on the male breadwinner role. When Harry died at sixty-three, Jean spent months in a daze, struggling to believe what had happened. She said she still thought of herself as Harry's wife, and couldn't imagine being with anybody else. For the rest of her life, we can speculate, Jean will continue to identify as the heterosexual partner of the young man she met when she was fifteen.

Threaded through Jean's account, however, is evidence of her reflexivity, of an alternative perspective which allowed her to view these conditions critically. For example, she flouted the unexplained injunction against washing her hair whilst menstruating; she suspected the playground stories of how babies *popped out* of the *brown line down your stomach* and *then it sort of sealed up.* Of this she says, *I used to think, it's a funny how-do-you-do this,* then asking a friend's mother, since her own mother *hadn't got the words.*

Having countered the 'ignorance' engendered among young women by actively seeking out this knowledge, she was better placed to make sense of sounds coming from her parents' bedroom. Indeed, her resistance to the implicit injunction to navigate a route into heterosexuality without any explicit knowledge of its bodily implications did not stop here. In her parents' bedroom she discovered their copy of Marie Stopes' *Married Love,* helped herself to its contents and, indeed, read it with Harry, her boyfriend. Of this episode, she said, *and I think that was an absolute marvellous help, you know.* When they put theory into practice, she was sixteen and a half. Their sexual relationship developed in both their homes, whilst their parents were out, a decision Jean made on the basis of her own experience: *I enjoyed it too much to feel guilty,* she said.

Jean's most valued memories were of her wedding and the birth of her children, yet despite her lack of higher education, when she and her peers were all having babies she *got to the stage when I wanted conversation that didn't dwell on babies.* Although her married life with Harry seemed to mesh seamlessly with the requirements of hegemonic heterosexuality, Jean deliberately ensured that she always had '*a life apart from him'*: flower arranging for the local church; pottery classes; girl guide leadership; Sunday School teaching; committee work. Harry's redundancy at fifty-eight *shattered* him. He coped *very badly, very badly,* Jean said, *he was ill with that, he'd always been the breadwinner.* When she was offered full-time work, Jean went to Harry and said *from now on, I'm the breadwinner, so you can take over all my jobs [. . .] including the cooking . . . and it's not demeaning.*

On the basis of this account, can we conceptualise Jean as an agent of change, working across the currents of hegemonic heterosexuality? What is the status of her refusal of its limitations? Jean is also profoundly committed to a traditional form of heterosexuality, reproducing rather than just resisting its patterning of everyday life. In these final extracts from Jean's narrative we critically consider the assumption that as a patriarchal institution, heterosexuality denies women agency, rendering them passive within a particular set of ideological and material conditions. These are data which cannot easily be interpreted as 'resistance', yet which reveal a woman for whom heterosexuality is a self-directed system of thought and practice.

As already noted, Jean readily recalls the materialities of her wedding. As a key heterosexual 'moment', it figures alongside descriptions of her first kiss with Arthur Bradshaw; first sex, lying in the grass on a summer Sunday teatime; her first home in *a little two-up and two-down cottage*; and years later, discovering her husband *stone cold* in their bed after his brain haemorrhage. These transitional moments in Jean's heterosexual life reflect the traditional structures which inform the lives of many women and men, both then and now. First sex, for example, she describes almost as an inevitability: *we'd gone down to the common and that, I mean, loads of other people went as well, and we were down there, and, you know, afterwards, lying down in the grass, and got kissing, and went a little bit further, and a bit further and, then it happened* [SIGH]. When Angela puts to Jean the late twentieth century perception of a sexually innocent older generation for whom pre-marital sex was *not the done thing,* Jean's response is, *it was actually, but people didn't talk about it, I mean, it happened, with most of my friends, but you didn't talk about it, you didn't brag about it, like they do now.* Yet Jean's account suggests that she was empowered with the resources to direct her sexual practice according to her own wishes. Thus, for example, although her immediate response to this *spontaneous* first sex was *oh God, what if I have a baby,* she dealt with her anxiety promptly: *after that he, we never did without, um, Durex.*

Indeed, when Jean met Harry she was only fifteen. He was nineteen, which did not go down *terribly well* with her mother. Jean, however, reminded her parents that whilst there was an age difference, at least his family was local and known to her own – which would not have been the case if, like all her friends, she had gone off to Bolton Palais and found boyfriends among the solders, sailors and airmen who frequented it. Having secured parental consent through this rhetorical strategy, Jean and Harry began courting, yet, as Jean said, over time *he started . . . taking me for granted, and I had no intention of being taken for granted.* Taking control of the situation, she told him: *I wanted a break, and, I made an excuse of another lad, but he were nothing.* She maintained her position of strength for three months until Harry's mother asked her to take him back because he was *crying and upset and not eating, and his life were at an end and all this, that and the other.* Jean took him back and *he never ever took me for granted afterwards.* Their long marriage was, therefore, on the terms chosen by Jean. Not only did Jean find a house for them, but she talked her father into agreeing a wedding date prior to the official age of consent. Before the birth of their daughter, Jean and Harry shared the housework, though Jean took responsibility for its organisation, preparing the tea which he would cook on his return home. Indeed when Angela asked Jean whether she felt their relationship changed after marriage, she said *Yeah, I think, I felt a bit more responsibility, yeah, I felt a bit more responsible for one another, really.* This taking of responsibility is evident in much of Jean's narrative. For example, after difficulties with breast-feeding her first child, she resisted hospital birth for her second, taking note of the doctor's criticism of its quality of care. Finding a midwife from among her local contacts, she managed to secure a home birth for her second child.

As Jean and Harry's parental roles developed, this challenged their status as a heterosexual couple. Jean was quick to modify her possessive attitude to their daughter and actively ensure the involvement of both Harry and the extended family. After she caught herself just about to tell her mother-in-law not to pick up their daughter, she describes reflecting: *She just doesn't belong to you, you know, and from then on, I was sort of very, very careful, and as Harry walked through the door, you know, I'd pick her up and give him, where before, I'd sort of, I'd held onto her.* When the stitching she received after the birth compromised their sexual relationship, she again actively sought out medical advice and with Harry's patience, determined to gradually retrieve the pleasure she valued so much.

Harry's support at this time was something she not only appreciated but also committed herself to reciprocating when he lost confidence in himself after redundancy. Thus she deliberately chose not to take the initiative sexually: *particularly during that period when he, things were a bit rough for him, I never, ever made any overtures, because I didn't want him to feel, if he couldn't, he was a failure.* Clearly there are complex processes at work here as Jean actively adopts a 'passive' role, one aimed at helping rescue Harry's masculine identity.

As noted above, Jean also organised the breadwinner role reversal in such a way as to provide Harry with support during his depression. Indeed, emotional labour characterises much of Jean's account. She reflects actively on the nature of relationships between different family members, on her family members' motivations and agendas, always with the aim of overcoming differences and making up for inadequacies. In addition she provides emotional support for a grandchild with serious mental health problems. At various points she provides evidence that her family see her as someone with strength and a capacity for independence. Her daughter rarely *puts her foot down* on Jean's behalf, conscious that Jean is more than able to defend herself when necessary; and Harry, she says, hoped not to survive her since he felt he would not cope alone as well as she would. She recalls his words after the sudden death of a work colleague: *"I don't want be left on my own, Jean will cope a lot better than I will", he said, "but not yet". But you see, six months later, you know, he'd gone.*

When Angela asked Jean what advice she would pass on to her grandchildren about the ingredients of a successful relationship, Jean identified *hard work* and *tolerance,* as well as *love.* In the data with which we completed this paper, there is considerable evidence of Jean's 'hard work', particularly in orchestrating the emotional lives of her family's members. While this 'labour' is one characteristically undertaken by women, when viewed within this body of empirical data, it becomes evident that, like the women Jackson (1999) identifies as pursuing 'love' with realistic ambitions, Jean too feels empowered to realise her vision of heterosexual family life. Rather than entering into relations of dependency which would locate a male partner as the source of its fulfilment, Jean herself is the agent through which that life is brought into being.

Conclusion

While Rich (1980) has characterised heterosexuality as intrinsically about the absence of choice for women, VanEvery's account (1996) of the lives of women who challenge hegemonic constructions of heterosexuality and gender whilst still identifying as heterosexual and/or engaging in heterosexual sex raises the question of women's *choice*. In the data presented here we have used a life course approach both to gather and to interpret what was said. This means that the context within which we consider our material extends not only temporally, but also at a theoretical level in that it has both macro as well as micro level resonances. Thus if we place Jean's busy engagement with the conditions of her own heterosexual life in the broader context of data pertaining to a spread of topics, stretching across a seventy-year period, we can see that her 'engagement' stands alongside positions of resistance. As described, she refused to remain ignorant of sexual knowledge, engineered her parents' approval of an older boyfriend and her early marriage to him, purposefully took on the breadwinner role in later life, maintained separate leisure interests and actively managed her husband's depression. Yet in doing heterosexuality 'her way', Jean also tailored her paid employment to the demands of her family and undertook extensive emotional labour on their behalf.

Jackson (1996) describes heterosexuality as institution, practice, experience and identity. As our data indicate, the institution of heterosexuality profoundly shaped Jean's earlier life; and in terms of her future identity, she cannot envisage herself as anything other than Harry's wife. Yet when we consider heterosexuality as practice and as experience, Jean's life history indicates that within these two areas, she not only exercised considerable agency, but also reflected extensively upon how her practice might shape her experience of heterosexuality. These are the data which our life history approach allowed us to access (Alasuutari, 1995, p. 50). While we may separate out heterosexuality into its constituent elements, as Jackson (1996) does, it remains important to recognise the interrelationship between these different aspects and acknowledge the way practice and experience themselves produce an institution and an identity we recognise as 'heterosexual'. In that Jean chose what she would *not* accept, we need to recognise, as contemporary feminists, that there are important forms of agency at work in her choices of what she desired and *would* work hard for.

Notes

1 The names used for informants and individuals referred to in the data are pseudonyms.
2 We are grateful to the Economic and Social Research Council for funding this project.

References

Alasuutari, P. (1995) *Researching Culture. Qualitative Method and Cultural Studies,* Sage, London.

Brah, A. (1996) *Cartographies of Diaspora*, Routledge, London.

Bury, M. (1995) 'Ageing, gender and sociological theory', in *Connecting Gender and Ageing,* eds S. Arber & J. Ginn, Open University Press, Buckingham.

Davis, K. (1991) 'Critical sociology and gender relations', in *The Gender of Power,* eds K. Davis, M. Leijenaar & J. Oldersma, Sage, London.

Ginn, J. & Arber, S. (1995) '"Only connect": gender relations and ageing', in *Connecting Gender and Ageing,* eds S. Arber & J. Ginn, Open University Press, Buckingham.

Ingrisch, D. (1995) 'Conformity and resistance as women age', in *Connecting Gender and Ageing,* eds S. Arber & J. Ginn, Open University Press, Buckingham.

Jackson, S. (1996) 'Heterosexuality and feminist theory', in *Theorising Sexuality,* ed. D. Richardson, Open University Press, Buckingham.

Jackson, S. (1999) *Heterosexuality in Question,* Sage, London.

Meyer, J. (1991) 'Power and love: conflicting conceptual schemata', in *The Gender of Power,* eds K. Davis, M. Leijenaar & J. Oldersma, Sage, London.

Rich, A. (1980) 'Compulsory heterosexuality and lesbian existence', *Signs,* Vol. 5, no. 4, pp. 631–660.

Smart, C. (1996) 'Collusion, collaboration and confession: on moving beyond the heterosexuality debate', in *Theorising Sexuality,* ed. D. Richardson, Open University Press, Buckingham.

VanEvery, J. (1996) 'Heterosexuality and everyday life', in *Theorising Sexuality,* ed. D. Richardson, Open University Press, Buckingham.

Wilkinson, S. & Kitzinger, C. (1993) *Heterosexuality: a Feminism and Psychology Reader,* Sage, London.

Wray, S. (2003) 'Women growing older: agency, ethnicity and culture', *Sociology,* Vol. 37, no. 3, pp. 511–528.

Part III

Straight identities and intersections of race, class, and gender

12

Prisons for our bodies, closets for our minds

Racism, heterosexism, and Black sexuality

Patricia Hill Collins

White fear of black sexuality is a basic ingredient of white racism.

—Cornel West

For African Americans, exploring how sexuality has been manipulated in defense of racism is not new. Scholars have long examined the ways in which "white fear of black sexuality" has been a basic ingredient of racism. For example, colonial regimes routinely manipulated ideas about sexuality in order to maintain unjust power relations.[1] Tracing the history of contact between English explorers and colonists and West African societies, historian Winthrop Jordan contends that English perceptions of sexual practices among African people reflected preexisting English beliefs about Blackness, religion, and animals.[2] American historians point to the significance of sexuality to chattel slavery. In the United States, for example, slaveowners relied upon an ideology of Black sexual deviance to regulate and exploit enslaved Africans.[3] Because Black feminist analyses pay more attention to women's sexuality, they too identify how the sexual exploitation of women has been a basic ingredient of racism. For example, studies of African American slave women routinely point to sexual victimization as a defining feature of American slavery.[4] Despite the important contributions of this extensive literature on race and sexuality, because much of the literature assumes that sexuality means *hetero*sexuality, it ignores how racism and heterosexism influence one another.

In the United States, the assumption that racism and heterosexism constitute two separate systems of oppression masks how each relies upon the other for meaning. Because neither system of oppression makes sense without the other, racism and heterosexism might be better viewed as sharing one history with similar yet disparate effects on all Americans differentiated by race, gender, sexuality, class, and nationality. People who are positioned at the margins of both systems and who are harmed by both typically raise questions about the intersections of racism and heterosexism much earlier and/or more forcefully than those people who are in positions of privilege. In the case of intersections of racism and heterosexism, Black lesbian, gay, bisexual, and transgendered (LGBT) people were among the first to question how racism and heterosexism are interconnected. As African American LGBT people point out, assuming that all Black people are heterosexual and that all LGBT people are White distorts the experiences of LGBT

Black people. Moreover, such comparisons misread the significance of ideas about sexuality to racism and race to heterosexism.[5]

Until recently, questions of sexuality in general, and homosexuality in particular, have been treated as crosscutting, divisive issues within antiracist African American politics. The consensus issue of ensuring racial unity subordinated the allegedly crosscutting issue of analyzing sexuality, both straight and gay alike. This suppression has been challenged from two directions. Black women, both heterosexual and lesbian, have criticized the sexual politics of African American communities that leave women vulnerable to single motherhood and sexual assault. Black feminist and womanist projects have challenged Black community norms of a sexual double standard that punishes women for behaviors in which men are equally culpable. Black gays and lesbians have also criticized these same sexual politics that deny their right to be fully accepted within churches, families, and other Black community organizations. Both groups of critics argue that ignoring the heterosexism that underpins Black patriarchy hinders the development of a progressive Black sexual politics. As Cathy Cohen and Tamara Jones contend, "Black people need a liberatory politics that includes a deep understanding of how heterosexism operates as a system of oppression, both independently and in conjunction with other such systems. We need a black liberatory politics that affirms black lesbian, gay, bisexual, and transgender sexualities. We need a black liberatory politics that understands the roles sexuality and gender play in reinforcing the oppression rooted in many black communities."[6] Developing a progressive Black sexual politics requires examining how racism and heterosexism mutually construct one another.

Mapping racism and heterosexism: the prison and the closet

> We regarded the struggle in prison as a microcosm of the struggle as a whole. We would fight inside as we had fought outside. The racism and repression were the same; I would simply have to fight on different terms.
>
> —Nelson Mandela

Like Nelson Mandela's view, when it comes to racism in the United States, life for African American women and men can be compared to being in prison.[7] Certainly the metaphor of the prison encapsulates the historical placement of African Americans in the U.S. political economy. The absence of political rights under chattel slavery and Jim Crow segregation and the use of police state powers against African Americans in urban ghettos have meant that Black people could be subjugated, often with little recourse. Moreover, prisons are rarely run solely by force. Routine practices such as strip searches, verbal abuse, restricting basic privileges, and ignoring physical and sexual assault among inmates aim to control prisoners by dehumanizing them. Visiting his brother Robbie, who was incarcerated on a life sentence in a Pennsylvania prison, author John Wideman describes this disciplinary process:

> The visitor is forced to become an inmate. Subjected to the same sorts of humiliation and depersonalization. Made to feel powerless, intimidated by the might of the state. Visitors are treated like both children and ancient, incorrigible sinners. We experience a crash course that teaches us in a dramatic, unforgettable fashion just how low a prisoner is in the institution's estimation. We also learn how rapidly we can descend to the same depth. . . . We suffer the keepers' prying eyes, prying machines, prying hands. We let them lock us in without any guarantee the doors will open when we wish to leave. We are in fact their prisoners until they release us. That was the idea. To transform the visitor into something he despised and feared. A prisoner.[8]

As direct recipients of the anti–civil rights agenda advanced under conservative Republican administrations, contemporary African Americans living in inner cities experienced the brunt of punitive governmental policies that had a similar intent.[9] Dealing with impersonal bureaucracies often subjected them to the same sorts of "humiliation and depersonalization" that Wideman felt while visiting his brother. Just as he was "made to feel powerless, intimidated by the might of the state," residents of African American inner-city neighborhoods who deal with insensitive police officers, unresponsive social workers, and disinterested teachers report similar feelings.

African American reactions to racial resegregation in the post–civil rights era, especially those living in hyper-segregated, poor, inner-city neighborhoods, resemble those of people who are in prison. Prisoners that turn on one another are much easier to manage than ones whose hostility is aimed at their jailers. Far too often, African Americans coping with racial segregation and ghettoization simply turn on one another, reflecting heightened levels of alienation and nihilism.[10] Faced with no jobs, crumbling public school systems, the influx of drugs into their neighborhoods, and the easy availability of guns, many blame one another. Black youth are especially vulnerable.[11] As urban prisoners, the predilection for some Black men to kill others over seemingly unimportant items such as gym shoes, jewelry, and sunglasses often seems incomprehensible to White Americans and to many middle-class Black Americans. Privileged groups routinely assume that all deserving Americans live in decent housing, attend safe schools with caring teachers, and will be rewarded for their hard work with college opportunities and good jobs. They believe that undeserving Blacks and Latinos who remain locked up in deteriorating inner cities get what they deserve and do not merit social programs that will show them a future. This closing door of opportunity associated with hyper-segregation creates a situation of shrinking opportunities and neglect. This is the exact climate that breeds a culture of violence that is a growing component of "street culture" in working-class and poor Black neighborhoods.[12]

Given this context, why should anyone be surprised that rap lyrics often tell the stories of young Black men who feel that they have nothing to lose, save their respect under a "code of the street."[13] Ice Cube's 1993 rap "It Was a Good Day," describes a "good" day for a young Black man living in Los Angeles. On a "good" day, he didn't fire his gun, he got food that he wanted to eat, the cops ignored him and didn't pull him over for an imaginary infraction, and he didn't have to kill anyone. Is this art imitating life, or vice versa? Sociologist Elijah Anderson's ethnographic studies of working-class and poor Black youth living in Philadelphia suggests that, for far too many young African American males, Ice Cube's bad days are only too real.[14] Just as male prisoners who are perceived as being weak encounter relentless physical and sexual violence, weaker members of African American communities are preyed upon by the strong. Rap artist Ice T explains how masculinity and perceived weakness operate:

> You don't understand anyone who is weak. You look at gay people as prey. There isn't anybody in the ghetto teaching that some people's sexual preferences are predisposed. You're just ignorant. You got to get educated, you got to get out of that jail cell called the ghetto to really begin to understand. All you see is a sissy. A soft dude. A punk.[15]

Women, lesbian, gay, bisexual, and transgendered people, children, people living with HIV, drug addicts, prostitutes, and others deemed to be an embarrassment to the broader African American community or a drain upon its progress or simply in the wrong place at the wrong time become targets of silencing, persecution, and/or abuse. This is what prisons do—they breed intolerance.

The experiences of people in prison also shed light on the myriad forms of African American resistance to the strictures of racial oppression. No matter how restrictive the prison, some prisoners find ways to resist. Often within plain sight of their guards, people who are imprisoned devise ingenious ways to reject prison policies. Nelson Mandela recounts the numerous ways that he and his fellow prisoners outwitted, undermined, tricked, and, upon occasion, confronted their captors during the twenty-seven years that he spent as a political prisoner in South African prisons. Craving news of the political struggle outside, prisoners communicated by writing in milk on blank paper, letting it dry to invisibility and, once the note was passed on, making the words reappear with the disinfectant used to clean their cells. They smuggled messages to one another in plastic wrapped packages hidden in food drums.[16] In the case of solitary confinement where an inmate could be locked up for twenty-three hours a day in a dark cell, just surviving constituted an act of resistance. As Mandela observes, "Prison is designed to break one's spirit and destroy one's resolve. To do this, the authorities attempt to exploit every weakness, demolish every initiative, negate all signs of individuality—all with the idea of stamping out that spark that makes each of us human and each of us who we are."[17] Mandela and his fellow prisoners recognized the function of actual prisons under racial apartheid and of apartheid policies as an extension of prison.

Recognizing that their everyday lives resemble those of prison inmates often politicizes individuals. Autobiographies by African Americans who were imprisoned because of their political beliefs, for example, Angela Davis and Assata Shakur, or who became politicized during their imprisonment, for example, Malcolm X or George Jackson, point to the significance of actual incarceration as a catalyst for resistance. In the 1980s, many poor and working-class African American youth who were locked up in urban ghettos and facing the closing door of opportunity refused to turn their rage upon one another. Instead, many chose to rap about the violence and intolerance around them and, in the process, created an influential hip-hop culture that reached youth all over the world. Crafted in the South Bronx, an urban landscape that had been abandoned by virtually everyone, African American, Latino, and Afro-Caribbean youth created rap, break dancing, tagging (graffiti), fashions and other cultural creations.[18] Ice Cube's rap about his good day represents the tip of an immense hip-hop iceberg. With few other public forums to share their outrage at a society that had so thoroughly written them off, Black youth used rap and hip-hop to protest the closing door of opportunity in their lives and to claim their humanity in the face of the dehumanization of racial segregation and ghettoization. Without strategies of noncooperation such as those exhibited by Mandela and his colleagues and without developing new forms of resistance such as hip-hop, Black people simply would not have survived.

What is freedom in the context of prison? Typically, incarcerated people cannot voluntarily "come out" of prison but must find a way to "break out." Under chattel slavery, the history of the Underground Railroad certainly reflected the aspirations of enslaved Africans to break out of the prison of slavery and to flee to the quasi freedom offered by Northern states. But just as gender, age, skin color, and class affect the contours of oppression itself, these very same categories shape strategies of resistance. As African American women's slave narratives point out, men and young people could more easily break out by running away than women, mothers, and older people. Then as now, African American women are often reluctant to leave their families, and many sacrifice their own personal freedom in order to stay behind and care for children and for others who depend on them. Under Jim Crow segregation, very light-skinned African Americans faced the difficult choice of "passing" and leaving their loved ones behind. More recently, as prime beneficiaries of the antidiscrimination and affirmative action policies of the civil rights movement, many middle-class and affluent African Americans have moved to distant White suburbs. Such actions certainly reflect a desire to escape the problems associated with poor and working-class Black neighborhoods. If one can "buy" one's freedom, as Nike ads proclaim, why not exercise personal choice and "just do it"?

In other situations, African Americans have recognized the confines of the prison and, through unruly, spontaneous uprisings or through organized political protests, have turned upon their jailers. A series of urban uprisings in cities such as New York, Detroit, Miami (1980), Los Angeles (1992), and Cincinnati (2001) typify the explosive reactions of many poor and working-class African Americans to bad schools, terrible housing, no jobs, little money, and dwindling prospects. The catalyst is usually the same—police brutality against unlucky African American citizens. More organized Black protests also reflect this process of turning upon the jailers of racism and refusing to cooperate with unjust laws and customs. Historically, social formations that kept African Americans impoverished and virtually powerless—chattel slavery, labor exploitation of the Jim Crow Southern agriculture, and the continuing growth of urban ghettos—all sparked organized African American political protest. The abolitionist movement, the formation of the NAACP (1909) and the Urban League (1910), the size of Marcus Garvey's Black Nationalist United Negro Improvement Association (1920s), the many organizations that participated in the civil rights and Black Power movements, and the increased visibility of Black youth through hip-hop culture reflect resistance to racism.

Racism may be likened to a prison, yet sexual oppression has more often been portrayed using the metaphor of the "closet."[19] This metaphor is routinely invoked to describe the oppression of lesbian, gay, bisexual, and transgendered people. Historically, because religion and science alike defined homosexuality as deviant, LGBT people were forced to conceal their sexuality.[20] For homosexuals, the closet provided some protection from homophobia that stigmatized LGBT sexual expression as deviant. Being in the closet meant that most hid their sexual orientation in the most important areas of their lives. With family, friends, or at work, many LGBT people passed as "straight" in order to avoid suspicion and exposure. Passing as straight fostered the perception that few gays and lesbians existed. The invisibility of gays and lesbians helped normalize heterosexuality, fueled homophobia, and supported heterosexism as a system of power.[21]

Because closets are highly individualized, situated within families, and distributed across the segregated spaces of racial, ethnic, and class neighborhoods, and because sexual identity is typically negotiated later than social identities of gender, race, and class, LGBT people often believe that they are alone. Being in the private, hidden, and domestic space of the closet leaves many LGBT adolescents to suffer in silence. During the era of racial segregation, heterosexism operated as smoothly as it did because hidden or closeted sexualities remained relegated to the margins of society *within* racial/ethnic groups. Staying in the closet stripped LBGT people of rights. The absence of political rights has meant that sexual minorities could be fired from their jobs, moved from their housing, have their children taken away in custody battles, dismissed from the military, and be targets of random street violence, often with little recourse. Rendering LGBT sexualities virtually invisible enabled the system of heterosexism to draw strength from the seeming naturalness of heterosexuality.[22]

Since the 1980s, gay, lesbian, bisexual, and transgendered people have challenged heterosexism by coming out of the closet. If the invisibility of sexual oppression enabled it to operate unopposed, then making heterosexism visible by being "out" attacked heterosexism at its core. Transgressing sexual borders became the hallmark of LGBT politics. The individual decision to come out to one's family or friends enabled formerly closeted LGBT people to live openly and to unsettle the normalization of heterosexuality. Transgression also came to characterize one strand of gay group politics, moving from the gay and lesbian identity politics of the first phase of "gay liberation" to more recent queer politics.[23] Gay pride marches that embrace drag queens, cross-dressers, gay men who are flamboyantly dressed, individuals with indeterminate gender identities, and mannish lesbians push the envelope beyond accepting the LGBT people who are indistinguishable from everyone else, save for this one area of sexual orientation. Through public, visible, and often outrageous acts, "queering" normal sexuality became another hallmark of LGBT politics. The phrase, "we're queer, we're here, get used to it" embraces a clear stance of defiance. At the same time, another strand of gay politics strives to be seen as "good gay citizens" who should be entitled to the same rights as everyone else. Practices such as legitimating gay marriages and supporting adoptions by gay and lesbian couples constitute another expression of transgression. By aiming for the legitimacy granted heterosexual couples and families, gay and lesbian couples simultaneously uphold family yet profoundly challenge its meaning.[24]

Racism and heterosexism, the prison and the closet, appear to be separate systems, but LGBT African Americans point out that *both* systems affect their everyday lives. If racism and heterosexism affect Black LGBT people, then these systems affect *all* people, including heterosexual African Americans. Racism and heterosexism certainly converge on certain key points. For one, both use similar state-sanctioned institutional mechanisms to maintain racial and sexual hierarchies. For example, in the United States, racism and heterosexism both rely on segregating people as a mechanism of social control. For racism, segregation operates by using race as a visible marker of group membership that enables the state to relegate Black people to inferior schools, housing, and jobs. Racial segregation relies on enforced membership in a visible community in which racial discrimination is tolerated. For heterosexism, segregation is enforced by pressuring LGBT individuals to remain closeted and thus segregated from one another. Before social movements for gay and lesbian liberation, sexual segregation meant that refusing to claim homosexual identities virtually eliminated any group-based political action to resist heterosexism. For another, the state has played a very important role in sanctioning both forms of oppression. In support of racism, the state sanctioned laws that regulated where Black people could live, work, and attend school. In support of heterosexism, the state maintained laws that refused to punish hate crimes against LGBT people, that failed to offer protection when LGBT people were stripped of jobs and children, and that generally sent a message that LGBT people who came out of the closet did so at their own risk.[25]

Racism and heterosexism also share a common set of practices that are designed to discipline the population into accepting the status quo. These disciplinary practices can best be seen in the enormous amount of attention paid both by the state and organized religion to the institution of marriage. If marriage were in fact a natural and normal occurrence between heterosexual couples and if it occurred naturally within racial categories, there would be no need to regulate it. People would naturally choose partners of the opposite sex and the same race. Instead, a series of laws have been passed, all designed to regulate marriage. For example, for many years, the tax system has rewarded married couples with tax breaks that have been denied to single taxpayers or unmarried couples. The message is clear—it makes good financial sense to get married. Similarly, to encourage people to marry within their assigned race, numerous states passed laws banning interracial marriage. These restrictions lasted until the landmark Supreme Court decision in 1967 that overturned state laws. The state has also passed laws designed to keep LGBT people from marrying. In 1996, the U.S. Congress passed the Federal Defense of Marriage Act that defined marriage as a "legal union between one man and one woman." In all of these cases, the state perceives that it has a compelling interest in disciplining the population to marry and to marry the correct partners.[26]

Racism and heterosexism also manufacture ideologies that defend the status quo. When ideologies that defend racism and heterosexism become taken-for-granted and appear to be natural and inevitable, they become hegemonic. Few question them and the social hierarchies they defend. Racism and heterosexism both share a common cognitive framework that uses binary thinking to produce hegemonic ideologies. Such thinking relies on oppositional categories. It views race through two oppositional categories of Whites and Blacks, gender through two categories of men and women, and sexuality through two oppositional categories of heterosexuals and homosexuals. A master binary of normal and deviant overlays and bundles together these and other lesser binaries. In this context, ideas about "normal" race (whiteness, which ironically, masquerades as racelessness), "normal" gender (using male experiences as the norm), and "normal" sexuality (heterosexuality, which operates in a similar hegemonic fashion) are tightly bundled together. In essence, to be completely "normal," one must be White, masculine, and heterosexual, the core hegemonic White masculinity. This mythical norm is hard to see because it is so taken-for-granted. Its antithesis, its Other, would be Black, female, and lesbian, a fact that Black lesbian feminist Audre Lorde pointed out some time ago.[27]

Within this oppositional logic, the core binary of normal/deviant becomes ground zero for justifying racism and heterosexism. The deviancy assigned to race and that assigned to sexuality becomes an important point of contact between the two systems. Racism and heterosexism both require a concept of sexual deviancy for meaning, yet the form that deviance takes within each system differs. For racism, the point of deviance is created by a *normalized White heterosexuality* that depends on a *deviant Black heterosexuality* to give it meaning. For heterosexism, the point of deviance is created by this very same *normalized White heterosexuality* that now depends on a *deviant White homosexuality*. Just as racial normality requires the stigmatization of the sexual practices of Black people, heterosexual normality relies upon the stigmatization of the sexual practices of homosexuals. In both cases, installing White heterosexuality as normal, natural, and ideal requires stigmatizing alternate sexualities as abnormal, unnatural, and sinful.

The purpose of stigmatizing the sexual practices of Black people and those of LGBT people may be similar, but the content of the sexual deviance assigned to each differs. Black people carry the stigma of *promiscuity* or excessive or unrestrained heterosexual desire. This is the sexual deviancy that has both been assigned to Black people and been used to construct racism. In contrast, LGBT people carry the stigma of *rejecting* heterosexuality by engaging in unrestrained homosexual desire. Whereas the deviancy associated with promiscuity (and, by implication, with Black people as a race) is thought to lie in an *excess* of heterosexual desire, the pathology of homosexuality (the invisible, closeted sexuality that becomes impossible within heterosexual space) seemingly resides in the *absence* of it.

While analytically distinct, in practice, these two sites of constructed deviancy work together and both help create the "sexually repressive culture" in America described by Cheryl Clarke.[28] Despite their significance for American society overall, here I confine my argument to the challenges that confront Black people.[29] Both sets of ideas frame a hegemonic discourse of *Black sexuality* that has at its core ideas about an assumed promiscuity among heterosexual African American men and women and the impossibility of homosexuality among Black gays and lesbians. How have African Americans been affected by and reacted to this racialized system of heterosexism (or this sexualized system of racism)?

African Americans and the racialization of promiscuity

Ideas about Black promiscuity that produce contemporary sexualized spectacles such as Jennifer Lopez, Destiny's Child, Ja Rule, and the many young Black men on the U.S. talk show circuit have a long history. Historically, Western science, medicine, law, and popular culture reduced an African-derived aesthetic concerning the use of the body, sensuality, expressiveness, and spirituality to an ideology about *Black sexuality*. The distinguishing feature of this ideology was its reliance on the idea of Black promiscuity. The possibility of distinctive and worthwhile African-influenced worldviews on anything, including sexuality, as well as the heterogeneity of African societies expressing such views, was collapsed into an imagined, pathologized Western discourse of what was thought to be essentially African.[30] To varying degrees, observers from England, France, Germany, Belgium, and other colonial powers perceived African sensuality, eroticism, spirituality, and/or sexuality as deviant, out of control, sinful, and as an essential feature of racial difference.[31]

Western religion, science, and media took over 350 years to manufacture an ideology of Black sexuality that assigned (heterosexual) promiscuity to Black people and then used it to justify racial discrimination. The racism of slavery and colonialism needed ideological justification. Toward this end, preexisting British perceptions of Blackness became reworked to frame notions of racial difference that, over time, became folded into a broader primitivist discourse on race. Long before the English explored Africa, the terms "black" and "white" had emotional meaning within England. Before colonization, white and black connoted opposites of purity and filthiness, virginity and sin, virtue and baseness, beauty and ugliness, and God and the devil.[32] Bringing this preexisting framework with them, English explorers were especially taken by Africans' color. Despite actual variations of skin color among African people, the English described them as being *black*, "an exaggerated term which in itself suggests that the Negro's complexion had powerful impact upon their perceptions."[33] From first contact, biology mattered—racial difference was embodied. European explorers and the traders, colonists, and settlers who followed were also struck by the differences between their own cultures and those of continental Africans. Erroneously interpreting African cultures as being inferior to their own, European colonial powers redefined Africa as a "primitive" space, filled with Black people and devoid of the accoutrements of more civilized cultures. In this way, the broad ethnic diversity among the people of continental Africa became reduced to more generic terms such as "primitive," "savage," and "native." Within these categories, one could be an Ashanti or a Yoruba, but each was a savage, primitive native all the same. The resulting primitivist discourse redefined African societies as inferior.[34]

Western natural and social sciences were deeply involved in constructing this primitivist discourse that reached full fruition in the nineteenth and early twentieth centuries.[35] Through laboratory experiments and field research, Western science attempted to understand these perceived racial differences while creating, through its own practices, those very same differences. For example, Sarah Bartmann's dissection illustrates this fascination with biological difference as the site of racial difference, with sexual difference of women further identified as an important topic of study.[36] Moreover, this perception of Africa worked with an important idea within nineteenth-century science, namely, the need to classify and rank objects, places, living things, and people. Everything had its place and all places were ranked.[37] With its primitiveness and alleged jungles, Africa and its peoples marked the bottom, the worst place to be, and a place ripe for colonial conquest. Yet at the same time, Africa was dangerous, different, and alluring. This new category of primitive situated Africans just below Whites and right above apes and monkeys, who marked this boundary distinguishing human from animals. Thus, within Western science, African people and apes occupied a fluid border zone between humans and animals.

With all living creatures classified in this way, Western scientists perceived African people as being more natural and less civilized, primarily because African people were deemed to be closer to animals and nature, especially the apes and monkeys whose appearance most closely resembled humans. Like African people, animals also served as objects of study for Western science because understanding the animal kingdom might reveal important insights about civilization, culture, and what distinguished the human "race" from its animal counterparts as well as the human "races" from one another. Donna Haraway's study of primatology illustrates Western scientists' fascination with identifying how apes differed from humans: "the study of apes was more about humans. Moreover, the close proximity to apes and monkeys that Africans occupied within European derived taxonomies of life such as the Great Chain of Being worked to link Africans and animals through a series of overlapping constructs. Apes and Africans both lived in Africa, a place of wild animals and wild people. In both cases, their source of wildness emerged from their lack of culture and their acting out of instinct or bodily impulses."[38] This family resemblance between African people and animals was not benign—viewing Africans and animals alike as embodied creatures ruled by "instinct or bodily impulses" worked to humanize apes and dehumanize Black people.

In this context, studying the sexual practices of African people and animals took on special meaning. Linking African people and animals was crucial to Western views of Black promiscuity. Genital sexual intercourse or, more colloquially, the act of "fucking," characterized animal sexuality. Animals are promiscuous because they lack intellect, culture, and civilization. Animals do not have erotic lives; they merely "fuck" and reproduce. Certainly animals could be slaughtered, sold, and domesticated as pets because within capitalist political economies, animals were commodities that were owned as private property. As the history of animal breeding suggests, the sexual promiscuity of horses, cattle, chickens, pigs, dogs, and other domesticated animals could be profitable for their owners. By being classified as proximate to wild animals and, by analogy, eventually being conceptualized as being animals (chattel), the alleged deviancy of people of African descent lay in their sexual promiscuity, a "wildness" that also was believed to characterize animal sexuality. Those most proximate to animals, those most lacking civilization, also were those humans who came closest to having the sexual lives of animals. Lacking the benefits of Western civilization, people of African descent were perceived as having a biological nature that was inherently more sexual than that of Europeans. The primitivist discourse thus created the category of "beast" and the sexuality of such beasts as "wild." The legal classification of enslaved African people as chattel (animal-like) under American slavery that produced controlling images of bucks, jezebels, and breeder women drew meaning from this broader interpretive framework.[39]

Historically, this ideology of Black sexuality that pivoted on a Black heterosexual promiscuity not only upheld racism but it did so in gender-specific ways. In the context of U.S. society, beliefs in Black male promiscuity took diverse forms during distinctive historical periods. For example, defenders of chattel slavery believed that slavery safely domesticated allegedly dangerous Black men because it regulated their promiscuity by placing it in the service of slave owners. Strategies of control were harsh and enslaved African men who were born in Africa or who had access to their African past were deemed to be the most dangerous. In contrast, the controlling image of the rapist appeared after emancipation because Southern Whites feared that the unfettered promiscuity of Black freedmen constituted a threat to the Southern way of life. In this situation, beliefs about White womanhood helped shape the mythology of the Black rapist. Making White women responsible for keeping the purity of the White race, White men "cast themselves as protectors of civilization, reaffirming not only their role as social and familial 'heads,' but their paternal property rights as well."[40]

African American women encountered a parallel set of beliefs concerning Black female promiscuity. White Americans may have been repulsed by a Black sexuality that they redefined as uncivilized "fucking," but the actions of White men demonstrated that they simultaneously were fascinated with the Black women who they thought engaged in it. Under American slavery, all White men within a slave-owning family could treat enslaved African women within their own families as sexual property. The myth that it was impossible to rape Black women because they were already promiscuous helped mask the sexual exploitation of enslaved Black women by their owners. Using enslaved Black women for medical experimentation constituted another form of control. As individuals who are trained to watch, dissect, and cast a critical eye on biological and social phenomena, scientists became voyeurs *extraordinaire* of Black women's bodies. For example, between 1845 and 1849, Marion Sims, now remembered variously as the Father of American Gynecology, the Father of Modern Gynecology, and the Architect of the Vagina, conducted surgical experiments on slave women in his backyard hospital in Montgomery, Alabama. Aiming to cure vaginal fistulas resulting from hard or extended childbirth, Sims discovered a way to peer into Black women's vaginas. Placing Lucy, a slave woman, into knee-chest position for examination, Sims inserted a pewter spoon into her vagina and recounts, "introducing the bent handle of the spoon I saw everything, as no man had ever seen before. The fistula was as plain as the nose on a man's face."[41]

The events themselves may be over, but their effects persist under the new racism. This belief in an inherent Black promiscuity reappears today. For example, depicting poor and working-class African American inner-city neighborhoods as dangerous urban jungles where SUV-driving White suburbanites come to score drugs or locate prostitutes also invokes a history of racial and sexual conquest. Here sexuality is linked with danger, and understandings of both draw upon historical imagery of Africa as a continent replete with danger and peril to the White explorers and hunters who penetrated it. Just as contemporary safari tours in Africa create an imagined Africa as the "White man's playground" and mask its economic exploitation, jungle language masks social relations of hyper-segregation that leave working-class Black communities isolated, impoverished, and dependent on a punitive welfare state and an illegal international drug trade. Under this logic, just as wild animals (and the proximate African natives) belong in nature preserves (for their own protection), unassimilated, undomesticated poor and working-class African Americans belong in racially segregated neighborhoods.

This belief in Black promiscuity also continues to take gender-specific forms. African American men live with the ideological legacy that constructs Black male heterosexuality through images of wild beasts, criminals, and rapists. A chilling case was provided in 1989 by the media coverage of an especially brutal crime that came to be known as the "Central Park Jogger" panic. In this case, a White woman investment banker jogging in Central Park was raped, severely beaten, and left for dead. At the time, the police believed that she had been gang-raped by as many as twelve Black and Latino adolescents. The horror of the crime itself is not in question, for this attack was truly appalling. But as African American cultural critic Houston A. Baker points out, what was also noteworthy about the case was the way in which it crystallized issues of race, gender, class, and sexuality in the mass media. The assault occurred during a time when young Black men and hip-hop culture were becoming increasingly visible in urban public space. Lacking spacious basement recreation rooms and well-tended soccer fields, African American and Latino youth set up their equipment on streets and in public parks, creating public hip-hop theaters. Graffiti, breakdancing, and enormous boom boxes blasting the angry lyrics of gangsta rap effectively "blackened" urban spaces. Baker describes how public space became a site of controversy: "Urban public space of the late twentieth-century [became] . . . spaces of audiovisual contest. It's something like this: 'My billboards and neon and handbills and high-decibel-level television advertising are purely for the public good. Your boom boxes and graffiti are evil pollutants. Erase them, shut them down!'"[42]

The attack in Central Park occurred in this political, social, and cultural context. The "park panic" that followed the incident drew upon this fear of young Black men in public space, as evidenced by their loudness, their rap music, and their disrespect for order (graffiti). In doing so, it referenced the primitivist ideology of Blacks as animalistic. Media phrases such as "roving bands" and "wolf pack" that were used to describe young urban Black and Latino males during this period were only comprehensible *because* of long-standing assumptions of Black promiscuity. Drawing upon the historical discourse on Black promiscuity, the phrase "to go buck wild" morphed into the new verb of "wilding" that appeared virtually overnight. Baker is especially insightful in his analysis of how the term "wilding" sounded very much like rapper Tone-Loc's hit song "Wild Thing," a song whose content described sexual intercourse. "Wilding" and "Wild Thing" belong to the same nexus of meaning, one that quickly circulated through mass media and became a plausible (at least as far as the media was concerned) explanation for the brutality of the crime.[43] Resurrecting images of Black men as predatory and wild, rape and "wilding" became inextricably linked with Black masculinity.

The outcome of this case shows how deeply entrenched ideologies can produce scenarios that obscure the facts. Ironically, twelve years after five young Black males were convicted of the crime, doubts arose concerning their guilt. A convicted murderer and serial rapist came forward, confessed to the rape, and claimed he had acted alone. After his story was corroborated by DNA testing, the evidence against the original "wolf pack" seemed far less convincing than in the climate created by "wilding" as the natural state of young Black men. In 2003, all of the teenagers originally convicted of the crime were exonerated, unfortunately after some had served lengthy jail terms.[44]

African American women also live with ideas about Black women's promiscuity and lack of sexual restraint. Reminiscent of concerns with Black women's fertility under slavery and in the rural South, contemporary social welfare policies also remain preoccupied with Black women's fertility. In prior eras, Black women were encouraged to have many children. Under slavery, having many children enhanced slave owners' wealth and a good "breeder woman" was less likely to be sold.[45] In rural agriculture after emancipation, having many children ensured a sufficient supply of workers. But in the global economy of today, large families are expensive because children must be educated. Now Black women are seen as producing too many children who contribute less to society than they take. Because Black women on welfare have long been seen as undeserving, long-standing ideas about Black women's promiscuity become recycled and redefined as a problem for the state.[46]

In her important book *Killing the Black Body: Race, Reproduction, and the Meaning of Liberty*, legal scholar Dorothy Roberts claims that the "systematic, denial of reproductive freedom has uniquely marked Black women's history in America."[47] Believing the unquestioned assumption of Black female promiscuity influences how poor and working-class Black women are treated. The inordinate attention paid to the sexual lives of adolescent Black women reflects this ongoing concern with an assumed Black female promiscuity.[48] Rather than looking at lack of sex education, poverty, sexual assault, and other factors that catalyze high rates of pregnancy among young Black women, researchers and policy makers often blame the women themselves and assume that the women are incapable of making their own decisions. Pregnancy, especially among poor and working-class young Black women, has been seen as evidence that Black women lack the capacity to control their sexual lives. As a visible sign of a lack of discipline and/or immorality, becoming pregnant and needing help exposes poor and working-class women to punitive state policies.[49] Arguing that Black women have been repeatedly denied reproductive autonomy and control over their own bodies, Roberts surveys a long list of current violations against African American women. Black women are denied reproductive choice and offered Norplant, Depo-Provera, and similar forms of birth control that encourage them to choose sterilization. Pregnant Black women with drug addictions receive criminal sentences instead of drug treatment and prenatal care. Criticizing two controversial ways in which the criminal justice system penalizes pregnancy, Roberts identifies the impossible choice that faces women in these situations. When a pregnant woman is prosecuted for exposing her baby to drugs in the womb, her crime hinges on her decision to have a baby. If she has an abortion she can avoid prosecution, but if she chooses to give birth, she risks going to prison. Similarly, when a judge imposes birth control as a condition of probation, for example, by giving a defendant the choice between Norplant or jail, incarceration becomes the penalty for her choice to remain fertile. These practices theoretically affect all women, but, in actuality, they apply primarily to poor and working-class Black women. As Roberts points out, "prosecutors and judges see poor Black women as suitable subjects for these reproductive penalties because society does not view these women as suitable mothers in the first place."[50]

African Americans and the whitening of homosexuality

Depicting people of African descent as symbols of embodied, natural sexuality that "fucked" like animals and produced babies installed Black people as the essence of nature. Moreover, the concern with Black fertility linked perceptions of promiscuity to assumptions of heterosexuality. Within this logic, homosexuality was assumed to be impossible among Black people because same-sex sexual practices did not result in reproduction:

> Among the myths Europeans have created about Africa, the myth that homosexuality is absent or incidental is the oldest and most enduring. For Europeans, black Africans—of all the native peoples of the world—most epitomized "primitive man." Since primitive man is supposed to be close to nature, ruled by instinct, and culturally unsophisticated, he had to be heterosexual, his sexual energies and outlets demoted exclusively to their "natural" purpose: biological reproduction. If black Africans were the most primitive people in all humanity—if they were, indeed, human, which some debated—then they had to be the most heterosexual.[51]

If racism relied on assumptions of Black promiscuity that in turn enabled Black people to "breed like animals," then Black sexual practices that did not adhere to these assumptions challenged racism at its very core. Either Black people could not be homosexual or those Blacks who were homosexual were not "authentically" Black.[52] Black people were allegedly not threatened by homosexuality because they were protected by their "natural" heterosexuality. In contrast, Whites had no such "natural" protection and thus had to work harder at proving their heterosexuality. By a curious twist of logic, these racist assumptions about an authentic Blackness grounded in a promiscuous heterosexuality helped define Whiteness as well. In this context, homosexuality could be defined as an internal threat to the integrity of the (White) nuclear family. Beliefs in a naturalized, normal hyper-heterosexuality among Black people effectively "whitened" homosexuality. Within a logic that constructed race itself from racially pure families, homosexuality constituted a major threat to the White race.[53]

Contemporary African American politics confront some real contradictions here. A discourse that constructs Black people as the natural essence of hyper-heterosexuality and White people as the source of homosexuality hinders developing a comprehensive analysis of Black sexuality that speaks to the needs of straight and gay Black people alike. Those African Americans who internalize racist ideologies that link Black hyper-heterosexuality with racial authenticity can propose problematic solutions to adolescent pregnancy, rape, sexual violence, and the troubling growth of HIV/AIDS among African Americans. Such beliefs generate strategies designed to regulate tightly the sexual practices of Black people as the fundamental task of Black sexual politics. This position inadvertently accepts racist views of Blackness and advocates an antiracist politics that advocates copying the heterosexist norms associated with White normality. Such beliefs also foster perceptions of LGBT Black people as being less authentically Black. If authentic Black people (according to the legacy of scientific racism) are heterosexual, then LGBT Black people are less authentically Black because they engage in allegedly "White" sexual practices. This entire system of sexual regulation is turned on its head when heterosexual African Americans reject promiscuity yet advocate for a Black eroticism.

In a similar fashion, visible, vocal LGBT Black people who come out and claim an erotocism that is not predicated upon heterosexuality also profoundly challenge the same system. The historical invisibility of LGBT African Americans reflects this double containment, both within the prison of racism that segregates Black people in part due to their alleged sexual deviancy of promiscuity and within the closet of heterosexism due to the alleged sexual deviancy of homosexuality. The closets created by heterosexism were just as prominent within Black communities as outside them. For example, the Black Church, one of the mainstays of African American resistance to racial oppression, fostered a deeply religious ethos within African American life and culture.[54] The Black Church remains the linchpin of African American communal life, and its effects can be seen in Black music, fraternal organizations, neighborhood associations, and politics.[55] As religious scholar C. Eric Lincoln points out, "for African Americans, a people whose total experience has been a sustained condition of multiform stress, religion is never far from the threshold of consciousness, for whether it is embraced with fervor or rejected with disdain, it is the focal element of the black experience."[56]

At the same time, the Black Church has also failed to challenge arguments about sexual deviancy. Instead, the Black Church has incorporated dominant ideas about the dangers of promiscuity and homosexuality within its beliefs and practices.[57] Some accuse the Black Church of relying on a double standard according to which teenaged girls are condemned for out-of-wedlock pregnancies but in which the men who fathered the children escape censure. The girls are often required to confess their sins and ask for forgiveness in front of the entire congregation whereas the usually older men who impregnate them are excused.[58] Others argue that the Black Church advances a hypocritical posture about homosexuality that undercuts its antiracist posture: "Just as white people have misused biblical texts to argue that God supported slavery, and that being Black was a curse, the Bible has been misused by African Americans to justify the oppression of homosexuals. It is ironic that while they easily dismiss the Bible's problematic references to Black people, they accept without question what they perceive to be its condemnation of homosexuals."[59]

One reason that the Black Church has seemed so resistant to change is that it has long worried about protecting the community's image within the broader society and has resisted *any* hints of Black sexual deviance, straight and gay alike. Recognizing the toll that the many historical assaults against African American families have taken, many churches argue for traditional, patriarchal households, and they censure women who seemingly reject marriage and the male authority that creates them. For women, the babies who are born out of wedlock are irrefutable evidence for women's sexual transgression. Because women carry the visible stigma of sexual transgression—unlike men, they become pregnant and cannot hide their sexual histories—churches more often have chastised women for promiscuity. In a sense, Black churches historically preached a politics of respectability, especially regarding marriage and sexuality, because they recognized how claims of Black promiscuity and immorality fueled racism. In a similar fashion, the Black Church's resistance to societal stigmatization of all African Americans as being sexually deviant limits its ability to take effective leadership within African American communities concerning all matters of sexuality, especially homosexuality. Black Churches were noticeably silent about the spread of HIV/AIDS among African Americans largely because they wished to avoid addressing the sexual mechanisms of HIV transmission (prostitution and gay sex).[60]

Within Black churches and Black politics, the main arguments given by African American intellectuals and community leaders that explain homosexuality's presence within African American communities show how closely Black political thought is tethered to an unexamined gender ideology. Backed up by interpretations of biblical teachings, many churchgoing African Americans believe that homosexuality reflects varying combinations of: (1) the loss of male role models as a consequence of the breakdown of the Black family structure, trends that in turn foster weak men, some of whom turn to homosexuality; (2) a loss of traditional religious values that encourage homosexuality among those who have turned away from the church; (3) the emasculation of Black men by White oppression; and (4) a sinister plot by White racists as a form of population genocide (neither gay Black men nor Black lesbians have children under this scenario).[61] Because these assumptions validate only one family form, this point of view works against both Black straights and gays alike. Despite testimony from children raised by Black single mothers, families headed by women alone routinely are seen as "broken homes" that somehow need fixing. This seemingly pro-family stance also works against LGBT African Americans. Gay men and lesbians have been depicted as threats to Black families, primarily due to the erroneous belief that gay, lesbian, and bisexual African Americans neither want nor have children or that they are not already part of family networks.[62] Holding fast to dominant ideology, many African American ministers believe that homosexuality is unnatural for Blacks and is actually a "white disease." As a result, out LGBT African Americans are seen as being disloyal to the race.

Historically, this combination of racial segregation and intolerance within African American communities that influenced Black Church activities explains the deeply closeted nature of LBGT Black experiences. The racial segregation of Jim Crow in the rural South and social institutions such as the Black Church that were created in this context made living as openly gay virtually impossible for LGBT African Americans. In small town and rural settings of the South, it made sense for the majority of LBGT Black people to remain deeply closeted. Where was the space for out Black lesbians in Anita Hill's close-knit segregated community of Lone Tree in which generations of women routinely gave birth to thirteen children? Would coming out as gay or bisexual Black men make any difference in resisting the threat of lynching in the late nineteenth century? In these contexts, Black homosexuality might have further derogated an already sexually stigmatized population. Faced with this situation, many African American gays, lesbians, and bisexuals saw heterosexual passing as the only logical choice.

Prior to early-twentieth-century migration to Northern cities, Black gays, lesbians, and bisexuals found it very difficult to reject heterosexuality outright. Cities provided more options, but for African Americans residential housing segregation further limited the options that did exist. Despite these limitations, gay and lesbian Black urban dwellers did manage to carve out new lives that differed from those they left behind. For example, the 1920s was a critical period for African American gays, lesbians, and bisexuals who were able to migrate to large cities like New York. Typically, the art and literary traditions of the Harlem Renaissance have been analyzed through a race-only Black cultural nationalist framework. But LGBT sexualities may have been far more important within Black urbanization than formerly believed. Because the majority of Harlem Renaissance writers were middle-class, a common assumption has been that their response to claims of Black promiscuity was to advance a politics of respectability.[63] The artists of the Harlem Renaissance appeared to be criticizing American racism, but they also challenged norms of gender and sexuality that were upheld by the politics of respectability.

Contemporary rereadings of key texts of the Harlem Renaissance suggest that many had a homoerotic or "queer" content. For example, new analyses locate a lesbian subtext within Pauline Hopkins's novel *Contending Forces*, a homoerotic tone within the short stories of Black life detailed in *Cane*, and an alternative sexuality expressed in the corpus of Langston Hughes's work.[64] British filmmaker Isaac Julien's 1989 prizewinning short film *Looking for Langston* created controversy via its association of Hughes with homoeroticism. Julien's intent was not to criticize Hughes, but rather, to "de-essentialize black identities" in ways that create space for more progressive sexual politics. At a conference on Black popular culture, Julien explains this process of recognizing different kinds of Black identities: "I think blackness is a term used—in the way that terms like 'the black community' or 'black folk' are usually bandied about—to exclude others who are part of that community . . . to create a more pluralistic interreaction [*sic*] in terms of difference, both sexual and racial, one has to start with de-essentializing the notion of the black subject."[65] Basically, rejecting the erasure of gay Black male identities, Julien's project creates a space in which Hughes can be both Black and queer.

Middle-class African Americans may have used literary devices to confront gendered and sexual norms, but working-class and poor African Americans in cities also challenged these sexual politics, albeit via different mechanisms. During this same decade, working-class Black women blues singers also expressed gendered and sexual sensibilities that deviated from the politics of respectability.[66] One finds in the lyrics of the blues singers explicit references to gay, lesbian, and bisexual sexual expression as a natural part of lived Black experience. By proclaiming that "wild women don't get no blues," the new blues singers took on and reworked longstanding ideas about Black women's sexuality. Like most forms of popular music, Black blues lyrics talk about love. But, when compared to other American popular music of the 1920s and 1930s, Black women's blues were distinctive. One significant difference concerned the blues' "provocative and pervasive sexual—including homosexual—imagery."[67] The blues took on themes that were banished from popular music—extramarital affairs, domestic violence, and the short-lived nature of love relationships all appeared in Black women's blues. The theme of women loving women also appeared in Black women's blues, giving voice to Black lesbianism and bisexuality.

When it came to their acceptance of Black gays, lesbians, and bisexuals, urban African American neighborhoods exhibited contradictory tendencies. On the one hand, Black neighborhoods within large cities became areas of racial and sexual boundary-crossing that supported more visible lesbian and gay activities. For example, one community study of the lesbian community in Buffalo, New York, found racial and social class differences among lesbians. Because Black lesbians were confined to racially segregated neighborhoods, lesbians had more house parties and social gatherings within their neighborhoods. In contrast, White working-class lesbians were more likely to frequent bars that, ironically, were typically located near or in Black neighborhoods.[68] In her autobiography *Zami*, Audre Lorde describes the racial differences framing lesbian activities in New York City in the 1950s where interracial boundaries were crossed, often for the first time.[69] These works suggest that African American lesbians constructed sexual identities within African American communities in urban spaces. The strictures placed on all African American women who moved into White-controlled space (the threat of sexual harassment and rape) affected straight and lesbian women alike. Moreover, differences in male and female socialization may have made it easier for African American women to remain closeted within African American communities. Heterosexual and lesbian women alike value intimacy and friendship with their female relatives, their friends, and their children. In contrast, dominant views of masculinity condition men to compete with one another. Prevailing ideas about masculinity encourage Black men to reject close male friendships that come too close to homoerotic bonding.

On the other hand, the presence of Black gay, lesbian, and bisexual activities and enclaves within racially segregated neighborhoods did not mean that LGBT people experienced acceptance. Greatly influenced by Black Church teachings, African Americans may have accepted homosexual individuals, but they disapproved of homosexuality itself. Relations in the Black Church illustrate this stance of grudging acceptance. While censuring homosexuality, Black churches have also not banished LGBT people from their congregations. Within the tradition of some Church leaders, homosexuality falls under the rubric of pastoral care and is not considered a social justice issue. Ministers often preach, "love the sinner but hate the sin."[70] This posture of "don't be too out and we will accept you" has had a curious effect on churches themselves as well as on African American antiracist politics. For example, the Reverend Edwin C. Sanders, a founding pastor of the Metropolitan Interdenominational Church in Nashville, describes this contradiction of accepting LGBT Black people, just as long as they are not too visible. As Reverend Sanders points out: "the unspoken message . . . says it's all right for you to be here, just don't say anything, just play your little role. You can be in the choir, you can sit on the piano bench, but don't say you're gay."[71] Reverend Sanders describes how this policy limited the ability of Black churches to deal with the spreading HIV/AIDS epidemic. He notes how six Black musicians within Black churches died of AIDS, yet churches hushed up the cause of the deaths.

As Reverend Sanders observes, "Nobody wanted to deal with the fact that all of these men were gay black men, and yet they'd been leading the music for them."[72]

The dual challenges to racism and heterosexism in the post–civil rights era have provided LGBT Black people with both more legal rights within American society (that hopefully will translate into improved levels of security) and the potential for greater acceptance within African American communities. As a result, a visible and vocal Black LGBT presence emerged in the 1980s and 1990s that challenged the seeming separateness of racism and heterosexism in ways that unsettled heterosexual Black people and gay White people alike. Rejecting the argument that racism and heterosexism come together solely or even more intensively for LGBT African Americans, LGBT African American people highlighted the connections and contradictions that characterize racism and heterosexism as mutually constructing systems of oppression. Working in this intersection between these two systems, LGBT African Americans raised important issues about the workings of racism and heterosexism.

One issue concerns how race complicates the closeting process and resistance to it. Just as Black people's ability to break out of prison differed based on gender, class, age, and sexuality, LGBT people's ability to come out of the closet displays similar heterogeneity. As LGBT African Americans point out, the contours of the closet and the costs attached to leaving it vary according to race, class, and gender. For many LGBT Whites, sexual orientation is all that distinguishes them from the dominant White population. Affluent gay White men, for example, may find it easier to come out of the closet because they still maintain many of the benefits of White masculinity. In contrast, in part because of a multiplicity of identities, African American gay, lesbian, bisexual, and transgendered individuals seem less likely than their White counterparts to be openly gay or to consider themselves completely out of the closet.[73] Race complicates the coming-out process. As Kevin Boykin recalls, "coming out to my family members, I found, was much more difficult than coming out to my friends. Because my family had known me longer than my friends had, I thought they at least deserved to hear the words 'I'm gay' from my own lips. . . . On the other hand, precisely because my family had known and loved me as one person, I worried that they might not accept me as another. Would they think I had deceived them for years?"[74] Gender and age add further layers of complexity to the coming-out process, as the difficulties faced by African American lesbians and gay African American high school youth suggest.[75]

Another related issue concerns the endorsement of "passing" and/or assimilation as possible solutions to racial and sexual discrimination. Black LGBT people point to the contradictions of passing in which, among African Americans, racial passing is routinely castigated as denying one's true self, yet sexual passing as heterosexual is encouraged. Barbara Smith, a lesbian activist who refused to remain in the closet, expresses little tolerance for lesbians who are willing to reap the benefits of others' struggles, but who take few risks themselves:

> A handful of out lesbians of color have gone into the wilderness and hacked through the seemingly impenetrable jungle of homophobia. Our closeted sisters come upon the wilderness, which is now not nearly as frightening, and walk the path we have cleared, even pausing at times to comment upon the beautiful view. In the meantime, we are on the other side of the continent, hacking through another jungle. At the very least, people who choose to be closeted can speak out against homophobia. . . . [Those] who protect their closets never think about . . . how their silences contribute to the silencing of others.[76]

Even if the "wilderness" is not nearly as frightening as it once was, the seeming benefits of remaining closeted and passing as straight may be more illusory than real. Because of the ability of many LGBT individuals to pass as straight, they encounter distinctive forms of prejudice and discrimination. Here racism and heterosexism differ. Blackness is clearly identifiable, and in keeping with assumptions of color blindness of the new racism, many Whites no longer express derogatory racial beliefs in public, especially while in the company of Blacks. They may, however, express such beliefs in private or behind their backs. In contrast, U.S. society's assumption of heterosexuality along with its tolerance of homophobia imposes no such public censure on straight men and women to refrain from homophobic comments in public. As a result, closeted and openly LGBT people may be exposed to a much higher degree of interpersonal insensitivity and overt prejudice in public than the racial prejudice experienced by Blacks and other racial/ethnic groups.[77]

Black churches and African American leaders and organizations that held fast in the past to the view of "don't be too out and we will accept you" faced hostile external racial climates that led them to suppress differences among African Americans, ostensibly in the name of racial solidarity. This version of racial solidarity also drew upon sexist and heterosexist beliefs to shape political agendas for all Black people. For example, by organizing the historic 1963 March on Washington where Martin Luther King, Jr. gave his legendary "I Have a Dream Speech," African American civil rights leader Bayard Rustin played a major role in the civil rights movement. Yet because Rustin was an out gay man, he was seen as a potential threat to the movement itself. Any hint of sexual impropriety was feared. So Rustin stayed in the background, while Martin Luther King, Jr. maintained his position as spokesperson and figurehead for the march and the movement. But the question for today is whether holding these views on race, gender, and sexuality makes political sense in the greatly changed context of the post–civil rights era. In a context where out-of-wedlock births, poverty, and the spread of STDs threatens Black survival, preaching abstinence to teens who define sexuality only in terms of genital sexual intercourse or encouraging LGBT people to renounce the sin of homosexuality and "just be straight" simply miss the mark. Too much is at stake for Black antiracist projects to ignore sexuality and its connections to oppressions of race, class, gender, and age any longer.

Racism and heterosexism revisited

On May 11, 2003, a stranger killed fifteen-year-old Sakia Gunn who, with four friends, was on her way home from New York's Greenwich Village. Sakia and her friends were waiting for the bus in Newark, New Jersey, when two men got out of a car, made sexual advances, and physically attacked them. The women fought back, and when Gunn told the men that she was a lesbian, one of them stabbed her in the chest.

Sakia Gunn's murder illustrates the connections among class, race, gender, sexuality, and age. Sakia lacked the protection of social class privilege. She and her friends were waiting for the bus in the first place because none had access to private automobiles that offer protection for those who are more affluent. In Gunn's case, because her family initially did not have the money for her funeral, she was scheduled to be buried in a potter's grave. Community activists took up a collection to pay for her funeral. She lacked the gendered protection provided by masculinity. Women who are perceived to be in the wrong place at the wrong time are routinely approached by men who feel entitled to harass and proposition them. Thus, Sakia and her friends share with all women the vulnerabilities that accrue to women who negotiate public space. She lacked the protection of age—had Sakia and her friends been middle-aged, they may not have been seen as sexually available. Like African American girls and women, regardless of sexual orientation, they were seen as approachable. Race was a factor, but not in a framework of interracial race relations. Sakia and her friends were African American, as were their attackers. In a context where Black men are encouraged to express a hyper-heterosexuality as the badge of Black masculinity, women like Sakia and her friends can become important players in supporting patriarchy. They challenged Black male authority, and they paid for the transgression of refusing to participate in scripts of Black promiscuity. But the immediate precipitating catalyst for the violence that took Sakia's life was her openness about her lesbianism. Here, homophobic violence was the prime factor. Her death illustrates how deeply entrenched homophobia can be among many African American men and women, in this case, beliefs that resulted in an attack on a teenaged girl.

How do we separate out and weigh the various influences of class, gender, age, race, and sexuality in this particular incident? Sadly, violence against Black girls is an everyday event. What made this one so special? Which, if any, of the dimensions of her identity got Sakia Gunn killed? There is no easy answer to this question, because *all* of them did. More important, how can any Black political agenda that does not take *all* of these systems into account, including sexuality, ever hope adequately to address the needs of Black people as a collectivity? One expects racism in the press to shape the reports of this incident. In contrast to the 1998 murder of Matthew Shepard, a young, White, gay man in Wyoming, no massive protests, nationwide vigils, and renewed calls for federal hate crimes legislation followed Sakia's death. But what about the response of elected and appointed officials? The African American mayor of Newark decried the crime, but he could not find the time to meet with community activists who wanted programmatic changes to retard crimes like Sakia's murder. The principal of her high school became part of the problem. As one activist described it, "students at Sakia's high school weren't allowed to hold a vigil. And the kids wearing the rainbow flag were being punished like they had on gang colors."[78]

Other Black leaders and national organizations spoke volumes through their silence. The same leaders and organizations that spoke out against the police beating of Rodney King by Los Angeles area police, the rape of immigrant Abner Louima by New York City police, and the murder of Timothy Thomas by Cincinnati police said nothing about Sakia Gunn's death. Apparently, she was just another unimportant little Black girl to them. But to others, her death revealed the need for a new politics that takes the intersections of racism and heterosexism as well as class exploitation, age discrimination, and sexism into account. Sakia was buried on May 16 and a crowd of approximately 2,500 people attended her funeral. The turnout was unprecedented: predominantly Black, largely high school students, and mostly lesbians. Their presence says that as long as African American lesbians like high school student Sakia Gunn are vulnerable, then every African American woman is in danger; and if all Black women are at risk, then there is no way that any Black person will ever be truly safe or free.

Notes

1 The field of postcolonial studies contains many works that examine how ideas generally, and sexual discourse in particular, was essential to colonialism and to nationalism. In this field, the works of French philosopher Michel Foucault have been pivotal in challenging prior frameworks heavily grounded in Marxism and in Freudian psychoanalysis. Here I rely on two main ideas from the corpus of Foucault's work. The first, expressed in his classic work *Discipline and Punish*, concerns the strategies that institutions use to discipline populations and get them to submit under conditions of oppression (Foucault, Michel. 1979. *Discipline and Punish: The Birth of the Prison*. New York: Schocken). The second idea concerns the normalization of such power through the use of hegemonic ideologies. Volume I of Foucault's *The History of Sexuality* uses sexuality to illustrate this normalization of power (Foucault, Michel. 1980. *The History of Sexuality Vol. I: An Introduction*. New York: Vintage Books). Despite the enormous impact that Foucault has had on studies of power, few works analyze his treatment of race. Ann Stoler's *Race and the Education of Desire* is exemplary in this regard (Stoler, Ann Laura. 1995. *Race and the Education of Desire: Foucault's History of Sexuality and the Colonial Order of Things*. Durham, N.C.: Duke University Press). Stoler examines how Foucault's analyses of sexuality in European societies can be read also as an analysis of race. In this chapter, I rely on many of Stoler's insights. For a comprehensive overview of works on Foucault and sexuality that do not deal with race, see Stoler 1995, 19, n. 1. For a description of the specific manipulation of sexual discourse within colonialism, see McClintock, Anne. 1995. *Imperial Leather: Race, Gender, and Sexuality in the Colonial Contest*. New York: Routledge; Gilman, Sander L. 1985. *Difference and Pathology: Stereotypes of Sexuality, Race, and Madness*. Ithaca, N.Y.: Cornell University Press; and Young, Robert J. C. 1995. *Colonial Desire: Hybridity in Theory, Culture and Race*. New York: Routledge, 90–117.

2 Jordan, Winthrop D. 1968. *White Over Black: American Attitudes toward the Negro*, 1550–1812. New York: W. W. Norton, 3–43.

3 Jordan 1968, 136–178.

4 See, for example, White, Deborah Gray. 1985. *Ar'n't I a Woman? Female Slaves in the Plantation South*. New York: W.W. Norton.

5 Despite the marginality of all LGBT Black people, subpopulations did not place issues of sexuality on the public agenda at the same time or in the same way. Black lesbians raised issues of heterosexism and homophobia in the 1980s, fairly early in modern Black feminism. For classic work in this tradition, see Combahee River Collective. 1982. "A Black Feminist Statement." *But Some of Us Are Brave*. Ed. Gloria T. Hull, Patricia Bell Scott, and Barbara Smith, 13–22. Old Westbury, N.Y.: Feminist Press; Lorde, Audre. 1982. *Zami, A New Spelling of My Name*. Freedom, Calif.: Crossing Press; Smith, Barbara, ed. 1983. *Home Girls: A Black Feminist Anthology*. New York: Kitchen Table Press; and Clarke, Cheryl. 1983. "The Failure to Transform: Homophobia in the Black Community." *Home Girls: A Black Feminist Anthology*. Ed. Barbara Smith, 197–208. New York: Kitchen Table Press. For a representative sample of more recent works, see Clarke, Cheryl. 1995. "Lesbianism: An Act of Resistance." *Words of Fire: An Anthology of African-American Feminist Thought*. Ed. Beverly Guy-Sheftall, 241–251. New York: The New Press; Gomez, Jewell, and Barbara Smith. 1994. "Taking the Home Out of Homophobia: Black Lesbian Health." *The Black Women's Health Book: Speaking for Ourselves*. Ed. Evelyn C. White, 198–213. Seattle: Seal Press; Moore, Lisa C., ed. 1997. *Does Your Mama Know? An Anthology of Black Lesbian Coming Out Stories*. Austin, Texas: Redbone Press; Gomez, Jewelle. 1999. "Black Lesbians: Passing, Stereotypes and Transformation." *Dangerous Liaisons: Blacks, Gays, and the Struggle for Equality*. Ed. Eric Brandt, 161–177. New York: The New Press; Greene, Beverly. 2000. "African American Lesbian and Bisexual Women." *Journal of Social Issues* 56, no. 2: 239–249; Smith, Barbara. 1998. *The Truth That Never Hurts: Writings on Race, Gender, and Freedom*. New Brunswick, N.J.: Rutgers University Press. In contrast, works by gay Black men achieved greater prominence later. See, for example, Hemphill, Essex, ed. 1991. *Brother to Brother: New Writings by Black Gay Men*. Boston: Alyson Publications; Riggs, Marlon T. 1992. "Unleash the Queen." *Black Popular Culture*. Ed. Gina Dent, 99–105. Seattle: Bay Press. *Tongues Untied*, the documentary by the late Marlon Riggs, represents an important path breaking work in Black gay men's studies in the United States (*Tongues Untied*. 1989. Marlon T. Riggs. 1 videocassette (55 min.): San Francisco, CA: Frameline). More recently, work on Black masculinity that analyzes homosexuality has gained greater visibility. See Hutchinson, Darren Lenard. 1999. "'Claiming' and 'Speaking' Who We Are: Black Gays and Lesbians, Racial Politics, and the Million Man March." *Black Men on Race, Gender, and Sexuality*. Ed. Devon W. Carbado, 28–45. New York: New York University Press; Riggs, Marlon T. 1999. "Black Macho Revisited: Reflections of a SNAP! Queen." *Black Men on Race, Gender, and Sexuality*. Ed. Devon W. Carbado, 306–311. New York: New York University Press; Thomas Kendall. 1996. "'Ain't Nothin' Like the Real Thing': Black Masculinity, Gay Sexuality, and the Jargon of Authenticity." *Representing Black Men*. Ed. Marcellus Blount and George P. Cunningham, 55–69. New York: Routledge; Carbado, Devon W. 1999. "Introduction: Where and When Black Men Enter." *Black Men on Race, Gender, and Sexuality*. Ed Devon W. Carbado, 1–17. New York: New York University Press; Hawkeswood, William G. 1996. *One of the Children: Gay Black Men in Harlem*. Berkeley: University of California Press; Simmons, Ron. 1991. "Some Thoughts on the Challenge Facing Gay Intellectuals." *Brother to Brother: New Writings by Black Gay Men*. Ed. Essex Hemphill, 211–228. Boston: Alyson Publications.

6 Cohen, Cathy J., and Tamara Jones. 1999. "Fighting Homophobia versus Challenging Heterosexism: 'The Failure to Transform' Revisited." *Dangerous Liaisons: Blacks, Gays, and the Struggle for Equality*. Ed. Eric Brandt. New York: The New Press, 88.

7 Mandela, Nelson. 1994. *Long Walk to Freedom: The Autobiography of Nelson Mandela*. Boston: Little, Brown, 341. Foucault suggests that the prison serves as an exemplar of modern Western society (Foucault 1979). The techniques used to discipline and punish deviant populations constitute a punishment industry. Prisons operate by controlling populations via disciplining the body. Foucault's work on sexuality also emphasizes regularization and discipline, only this time via creating discourses of sexuality that also aim to control the body (Foucault 1980). For an analysis of Foucault's treatment of race, sexuality, and gender, see Stoler 1995.

8 Wideman, John Edgar. 1984. *Brothers and Keepers*. New York: Penguin, 52.

9 For works that detail the effects of welfare state policies on African Americans, see Quadagno, Jill. 1994. *The Color of Welfare: How Racism Undermined the War on Poverty*. New York: Oxford University Press; Brewer, Rose. 1994. "Race, Class, Gender and U.S. State Welfare Policy: The Nexus of Inequality for African American Families." *Color, Class and Country: Experiences of Gender*. Ed. Gay Young and Bette J. Dickerson, 115–127. London: Zed; Neubeck, Kenneth J., and Noel A. Cazenave. 2001. *Welfare Racism: Playing the Race Card against America's Poor*. New York: Routledge. For general works on state policy and African American economic well-being, see Squires, Gregory D. 1994. *Capital and Communities in Black and White: The Intersections of Race, Class, and Uneven Development*. Albany: State University of New York Press; Massey, Douglas S., and Nancy A. Denton. 1993. *American Apartheid: Segregation and the Making of the Underclass*. Cambridge, Mass.: Harvard University Press; Oliver, Melvin L., and Thomas M. Shapiro. 1995. *Black Wealth/White Wealth: A New Perspective on Racial Inequality*. New York: Routledge. For analyses of jobs and urban economies, see Wilson, William Julius. 1996. *When Work Disappears: The World of the New Urban Poor*. New York: Knopf; Wilson, William Julius. 1987. *The Truly Disadvantaged: The Inner City, the Underclass, and Public Policy*. Chicago: University of Chicago Press.

10 West, Cornel. 1993. *Race Matters*. Boston: Beacon Press.

11 In the 1980s, homicide became one of the leading causes of death of young Black men (Oliver, William. 1994. *The Violent Social World of Black Men*. New York: Lexington Books). For work on the vulnerability of Black youth in

inner cities, see Anderson, Elijah. 1978. *A Place on the Corner.* Chicago: University of Chicago Press; Anderson, Elijah. 1990. *Streetwise: Race, Class, and Change in an Urban Community.* Chicago: University of Chicago Press; Anderson, Elijah. 1999. *Code of the Street: Decency, Violence and the Moral Life of the Inner City.* New York: W. W. Norton; Canada, Geoffrey. 1995. *Fist, Stick, Knife, Gun: A Personal History of Violence in America.* Boston: Beacon Press; Kaplan, Elaine Bell. 1997. *Not Our Kind of Girl: Unraveling the Myths of Black Teenage Motherhood.* Berkeley: University of California Press; Kitwana, Bakari. 2002. *The Hip Hop Generation: Young Blacks and the Crisis in African-American Culture.* New York: Basic Books.

12 Anderson 1999.

13 Anderson 1999.

14 Anderson 1978; 1990; 1999

15 As quoted in Cole, Johnnetta Betsch, and Beverly Guy-Sheftall. 2003. *Gender Talk: The Struggle for Women's Equality in African American Communities.* New York: Ballantine, 139.

16 Mandela 1994, 367–368.

17 Mandela 1994, 341.

18 Rose, Tricia. 1994. *Black Noise: Rap Music and Black Culture in Contemporary America.* Hanover, N.H.: Wesleyan University Press, 21–61; George, Nelson. 1998. *Hip Hop America.* New York: Penguin, 1–21.

19 Sociologist Steve Seidman traces the emergence and decline of the closet as a metaphor describing contemporary LGBT politics (Seidman, Steven. 2002. *Beyond the Closet: The Transformation of Gay and Lesbian Life.* New York: Routledge). Seidman dates the closet as reaching its heyday in the 1950s and early 1960s during the early years of the cold war. In his research, he was surprised to find that many contemporary gay Americans live outside the social framework of the closet. Seidman suggests that the two main ways that gay life has been understood since 1969, namely, the coming-out narrative or the migration to gay ghettoes, may no longer be accurate: "as the lives of at least some gays look more like those of straights, as gays no longer feel compelled to migrate to urban enclaves to feel secure and respected, gay identity is often approached in ways similar to heterosexual identity—as a thread" (Seidman 2002, 11). Unfortunately, Seidman's methodology did not allow him to explore the ways in which Black LGBT people have similar and different experiences.

20 Both science and religion advanced different justifications for stigmatizing homosexuals. Until recently, Western medicine and science viewed sexuality as being biologically hardwired into the human species and obeying natural laws. Heterosexual sexual practices and reproduction were perceived as the "natural" state of sexuality, and all other forms of sexual expression were classified as deviant. Religion offered similar justifications. Promiscuity and homosexuality emerged as important categories of "unnatural" sexual activity that normalized monogamous heterosexuality within the context of marriage and for purposes of reproduction.

21 This is Foucault's argument about biopower, the normalization of practices that enable society to discipline individual bodies, in this case, sexual bodies, and groups, in this case, straights and gays, as population groups that become comprehensible only in the context of discourses of sexuality. This view prevailed until shifts within the study of sexuality in the 1980s and 1990s.

22 Seidman, Steven. 1996. "Introduction." *Queer Theory/Sociology.* Ed. Steven Seidman. Malden, Mass.: Blackwell, 6.

23 The term *queer* often serves as an umbrella term for lesbian, gay, bisexual, transgendered, and anyone else whose sexuality transgresses the status quo. Not everyone claims the term as an identity or statement of social location. Some argue that the term erases social and economic differences among lesbians and gay men, and others consider it to be derogatory. Still others use the term to acknowledge the limitless possibilities of an individual's sexuality. They see terms such as *gay*, *lesbian*, and *bisexual* as misleading in that they suggest stable sexual identities. Beyond these ideological differences, I do not use the term *queer* here because LGBT African American people do not prefer this term. When participants in the *National Black Pride Survey 2000* were asked which label from a very extensive list came closest to describing their sexual orientation, 42 percent self-identified as gay, 24 percent chose lesbian, 11 percent chose bisexual, and 1 percent marked transgendered. In contrast to high levels of agreement on gay and lesbian, "queer" was one of the least popular options (1 percent). As the survey reports, "Black GLBT people do not readily, or even remotely, identity as 'queer'" (Battle, Juan, Cathy J. Cohen, Dorian Warren, Gerard Fergerson, and Suzette Audam. 2002. *Say It Loud, I'm Black and I'm Proud: Black Pride Survey 2000.* New York: The Policy Institute of the National Gay and Lesbian Task Force, 19).

24 LGBT politics and the "queering" of sexuality has been one important dimension of the post–civil rights era and Seidman contends that the postcloseted world of the post–civil rights era has shown greater acceptance of LGBT people. Yet, suggests Seidman, acceptance may come with a price. Today, LGBT people are under intense pressure to fit the mold of the "good gay citizen," to be monogamous and to look and act normal. This image may be safe, but it continues to justify discrimination against those who do not achieve this ideal (Seidman 2002).

25 Here I use the framework of "domains of power" to examine the convergence of racism and heterosexism. Briefly, race, sexuality, gender, class, and other systems of oppression are all organized through four main domains of power. The structural domain of power (institutional policies), the disciplinary of power (the rules and regulations that regulate social interaction), the hegemonic domain of power (the belief systems that defend existing power arrangements), and the interpersonal domain of power (patterns of everyday social interaction) are organized differently for different systems of oppression. Here I use this model as a heuristic device to build an argument about the interconnections of racism and heterosexism. For a discussion of the framework and its applicability in Black feminist politics, see chapter 12 of *Black Feminist Thought* (Collins, Patricia Hill. 2000. *Black Feminist Thought: Knowledge, Consciousness, and the Politics of Empowerment.* New York: Routledge, 273–290).

26 For a discussion of the *Loving* decision and its effects on interracial marriage, see Root, Maria P. P. 2001. *Love's Revolution: Interracial Marriage.* Philadelphia: Temple University Press. For the full definition of the Defense of Marriage Act, see U.S. Census Bureau. 2000. "Technical Note on Same-Sex Unmarried Partner Data from the 1990 and 2000 Censuses." Web page [accessed March 16, 2003]. Available at http://www.census.gov/population/www/cen2000/samesex.html.

27 Racism and heterosexism share this basic cognitive frame, and it is one shared by other systems of power.

28 Clarke 1983.

29 Both sets of ideas also serve as markers for constructing both heterosexuality and homosexuality within the wider society. Prior to the social movements of the civil rights era that called increased attention to both racism and heterosexism, racial protest was contained within the prisons of racially segregated neighborhoods and LGBT protest within the invisibility of individual closets.

30 Mudimbe, V. Y. 1988. *The Invention of Africa: Gnosis, Philosophy, and the Order of Knowledge.* Bloomington: Indiana University Press; Appiah, Kwame Anthony. 1992. *In My Father's House: Africa in the Philosophy of Culture.* New York: Oxford University Press.

31 Young 1995, 90–117; McClintock 1995.

32 Jordan 1968, 7.

33 Jordan 1968, 5. Jordan suggests that the reactions of the English differed from those of the Spanish and the Portuguese who for centuries had been in close contact with North Africa and who had been invaded by peoples both darker and more civilized than themselves. The impact of color on the English may have been more powerful because England's principal contact with Africans came in West Africa and the Congo, areas with very dark-skinned Africans. Thus, "one of the fairest-skinned nations suddenly came face to face with one of the darkest peoples on earth" (Jordan 1968, 6).

34 Torgovnick, Marianna. 1990. *Gone Primitive: Savage Intellects, Modern Lives.* Chicago: University of Chicago Press, 18–20.

35 Historically, scientific racism has made important contributions to creating and sustaining myths of Black promiscuity as well as constructing a normalized heterosexuality juxtaposed to the alleged deviancy of White homosexuality. The scientific racism of medicine, biology, psychology, anthropology, and other social sciences constructed both Black promiscuity as well as homosexuality and then spent inordinate time assisting state and religious institutions that aimed to regulate these practices. For general discussions of race and science, see Gould, Stephen Jay. 1981. *The Mismeasure of Man.* New York: Norton; Harding, Sandra, ed. 1993. *The "Racial" Economy of Science: Toward a Democratic Future.* Bloomington: Indiana University Press; Zuberi, Tukufu. 2001. *Thicker than Blood: How Racial Statistics Lie.* Minneapolis: University of Minnesota Press.

36 Fausto-Sterling. 1995. "Gender, Race, and Nation: The Comparative Anatomy of 'Hottentot' Women in Europe, 1815–1817." *Deviant Bodies: Critical Perspectives on Difference in Science and Popular Culture.* Ed. Jennifer Terry and Jacqueline Urla, 19–48. Bloomington: Indiana University Press.

37 Foucault 1979.

38 Haraway, Donna. 1989. *Primate Visions: Gender, Race, and Nature in the World of Modern Science.* New York: Routledge, Chapman & Hall, 262. In this context, studying animals that were clearly not human but close to it might reveal what granted Europeans their humanity and Africans their putative bestiality. Here the interest in animal behavior as a form of human behavior uninterrupted by culture appears. Within primatology, monkeys and apes have a privileged relation to nature and culture, in that "simians occupy the border zones" (Haraway 1989, 1). "In Africa, the primate literature was produced by white colonists and western foreign scientists under no pressure until well after independence to develop scientific, collegial relations with black Africans. African primates, including the people imagined as wildlife, modeled the 'origin of man' for European-derived culture. . . . Africa became a place of darkness, one lacking the enlightenment of the West. India has been used to model not the 'origin of man,' but the 'origin of civilization.' Both are forms of 'othering' for western symbolic operations, but their differences matter" (Haraway 1989, 262).

39 Collins 2000, 69–96.

40 Wiegman, Robyn. 1993. "The Anatomy of Lynching." *American Sexual Politics.* Ed. John C. Fout, and Maura Tantillo, 239.

41 Quoted in Kapsalis, Terri. 1997. *Public Privates: Performing Gynecology from Both Ends of the Speculum.* Durham, N.C.: Duke University Press, 37. Understandings of Black women's promiscuity also build upon a deep historical theme within Western societies that links deviant sexuality with disease. The hypervisible, pathologized portion of Black women's sexuality centered on the icon of the whore, the woman who demands money for sexual favors. This image is pathologized in that prostitutes were associated with ideas about disease and pollution that bore stark resemblance to ideas about the threat of racial pollution so central to conceptions of whiteness grounded in purity (Giddings, Paula. 1992. "The Last Taboo." *Race-ing Justice, En-Gendering Power.* Ed. Toni Morrison. New York: Pantheon, 419).

42 Baker, Houston A. 1993. *Black Studies, Rap, and the Academy.* Chicago: University of Chicago Press, 43.

43 Baker 1993, 33–60.

44 Dwyer, Jim. 2002. "Reinvestigation of Park Jogger Case Leaves Some Officials with Doubts" *New York Times*, A15. September 28. This case also resembles the well-known case of the Scottsboro boys in which a group of Black men were convicted of allegedly raping White women. They too were eventually exonerated.

45 White 1985.

46 Gould 1981; Zucchino, David. 1997. *The Myth of the Welfare Queen.* New York: Scribner; Amott 1990; Brewer 1994; Neubeck and Cazenave 2001.

47 Roberts, Dorothy E. 1997. *Killing the Black Body: Race, Reproduction, and the Meaning of Liberty.* New York: Pantheon Books, 4.

48 In a context in which the United States has the highest teen pregnancy rate in the Western world, the even higher rates of teen pregnancy among African American adolescents is a cause for alarm. Many factors influence high rates of pregnancy among young Black women. For example, adult men, some of whom may have coerced girls to have sex with them, father most of the babies born to teen mothers. Studies show that as many as one in four girls are victims of sexual abuse (Roberts 1997, 117).
49 See Gould 1981; Lubiano, Wahneema. 1992. "Black Ladies, Welfare Queens, and State Minstrels: Ideological War by Narrative Means." *Race-ing Justice, En-Gendering Power.* Ed. Toni Morrison, 323–63. New York: Pantheon Books; Zucchino 1997; Neubeck and Cazenave 2001.
50 Roberts 1997, 152.
51 As quoted in Cole and Guy-Sheftall 2003, 165.
52 For a discussion of the type of racial reasoning that generates ideas of racial authenticity, see Cornel West's "The Pitfalls of Racial Reasoning" (West 1993, 21–32).
53 These same pressures fostered views of homosexuals as invisible, closeted, and assumed to be White. Normalized White heterosexuality became possible and hegemonic only within the logic of both racism and heterosexism.
54 The general use of the term "the Black Church" refers to Black Christian churches in the United States. This includes any Black Christian who worships and is a member of a Black congregation. The formal use of the term refers to independent, historic, and Black-controlled denominations that were founded after the Free African Society in 1787. For a listing, see Monroe, Irene. 1998. "Louis Farrakhan's Ministry of Misogyny and Homophobia." *The Farrakhan Factor: African-American Writers on Leadership, Nationhood, and the Minister Louis Farrakhan.* Ed Amy Alexander. New York: Grove Press, 297, n. 1. For a general history of the Black Church, see Lincoln, C. Eric. 1999. *Race, Religion, and the Continuing American Dilemma.* New York: Hill & Wang. For analyses of Black women's participation in the Black Church, see Douglas, Kelly Brown. 1999. *Sexuality and the Black Church: A Womanist Perspective.* Maryknoll, N.Y.: Orbis; Gilkes, Cheryl Townsend. 2001. *If It Wasn't for the Women: Black Women's Experience and Womanist Culture in Church and Community.* Maryknoll, N.Y.: Orbis; Higginbotham, Evelyn Brooks. 1993. *Righteous Discontent: The Women's Movement in the Black Baptist Church 1880–1920.* Cambridge, Mass.: Harvard University Press.
55 See, Patillo-McCoy, Mary. 1999. *Black Picket Fences: Privilege and Peril among the Black Middle Class.* Chicago: University of Chicago Press, especially Patillo-McCoy, Mary. 1998. "Church Culture as a Strategy of Action in the Black Community." *American Sociological Review* 63 (December): 767–784.
56 Lincoln 1999, xxiv.
57 Douglas 1999.
58 Cole and Guy-Sheftall 2003, 116.
59 Cole and Guy-Sheftall 2003, 120.
60 Cohen, Cathy J. 1999. *The Boundaries of Blackness: AIDS and the Breakdown of Black Politics.* Chicago: University of Chicago Press, 276–288.
61 Simmons 1991.
62 For a discussion of the family networks of Black gay men in Harlem, see Hawkeswood 1996. Also, see Battle et al. 2002, 13–17.
63 Higginbotham 1993, 185–229.
64 Somerville, Siobhan B. 2000. *Queering the Color Line: Race and the Invention of Homosexuality in American Culture.* Durham, N.C.: Duke University Press.
65 Julien, Isaac. 1992. "Black Is, Black Ain't: Notes on De-essentializing Black Identities." *Black Popular Culture.* Ed. Gina Dent. Seattle: Bay Press, 274.
66 Davis, Angela Y. 1998. *Blues Legacies and Black Feminism: Gertrude "Ma" Rainey, Bessie Smith and Billie Holiday.* New York: Vintage.
67 Davis 1998, 3.
68 Kennedy, Elizabeth Lapovsky, and Madeline D. Davis. 1994. *Boots of Leather, Slippers of Gold: The History of a Lesbian Community.* New York: Penguin Books.
69 Lorde 1982.
70 Monroe 1998, 281.
71 Comstock, Gary David. 1999. "'Whosoever' Is Welcome Here: An Interview with Reverend Edwin C. Sanders II." *Dangerous Liaisons: Blacks, Gays, and the Struggle for Equality.* Ed. Eric Brandt. New York: The New Press, 156.
72 Comstock 1999, 156.
73 Boykin, Keith. 1996. *One More River to Cross: Black and Gay in America.* New York: Anchor Books, 90.
74 Boykin 1996, 19.
75 Moore 1997; McCready, Lance. 2001. "When Fitting In Isn't an Option, or, Why Black Queer Males at a California High School Stay Away from Project 10." *Troubling Intersections of Race and Sexuality: Queer Students of Color and Anti-oppressive Education.* Ed. Kevin K. Kumashiro, 37–54. New York: Rowman & Littlefield.
76 Smith, Barbara. 1990. "The NEA Is the Least of It." 66.
77 Boykin 1996, 81.
78 "Skeleton in Newark's Closet: Laquetta Nelson Is Forcing Homophobia Out into the Open" 2003.

13

Displaying heterosexuality in an inner city

Carissa M. Froyum

Economic restructuring during the 1960s and 1970s resulted in concentrated poverty and social isolation in formerly thriving, class-integrated black neighborhoods (Wilson 1996; Massey and Denton 1988; Rankin and Quane 2000). For teens growing up now, inner cities are places of vulnerability and potential victimization. The threat of violence, especially gang (or "crew") and drug-related violence, is nearly omnipresent for boys in the most disadvantaged neighborhoods (Anderson 1999; Lauritsen and White 2001; Lauritsen 2003), while girls routinely face sexual violence at the hands of male peers and older men (Benson et al. 2003; Lauritsen 2003; Miller 2008). Moreover, few conventional, institutional routes to status and power are available due to widespread racism and poverty (Pyke 1996). As a result, inner-city teens often espouse fear, despair, hopelessness, and fatalism (Anderson 1999; Bolland 2003; Edin and Kefalas 2005; Kaplan 1997).

While inner-city life has garnered much research attention, we still know too little about how youths protect themselves and combat their vulnerability. We do know that boys display a compensatory form of masculinity through the "cool pose" and instigating fights (Anderson 1999; Miller 2008). Boys seem to use their bodies to intimidate others as a way to establish respect and garner safe passage in neighborhoods. We know much less about how girls combat vulnerability; the literature tends to frame them as passive victims rather than active social subjects who create meaningful strategies for resisting victimization and despair (see Cobbina et al. 2008; Edin and Kefalas 2005; Jones 2004, 2008; Kaplan 1997; Miller 2008; Stack 1974 for excellent exceptions). This study, however, treats inner-city teens as active subjects who respond to and adapt to their environment, making use of the social tools at their disposal. I do so by examining how teens use heterosexuality and heteronormativity to ideologically and interactionally bolster status, meaning, and identity in an environment that deflates them.

Inner-city vulnerability

Inner cities are plagued by violence targeted at young men of color (Anderson 1999; Lauritsen and White 2001; Lauritsen 2003; Miller 2008). Anderson's (1999) ethnography illustrates that a violence-ridden "code of the street" results. Threats and stickups become a form of social control as young men fight over turf and respect. Boys learn that "might makes right," and losing fights or walking away makes them susceptible to future attacks. Disadvantaged neighborhoods struggle to protect boys against the ensuing violence (Lauritsen 2003), and incarceration is so common it constitutes a life stage for black men with little education (Pettit and Western 2004).

Although the literature often overlooks it, danger in the inner city leads to fear, a sense of vulnerability, alienation, and sadness among boys. Boys often feel abandoned by police and politicians and develop resentment toward them (Anderson 1999; Cobbina et al. 2008; Miller 2008). They also develop a fatalism about their own futures, believing they will die young (Anderson 1999).

Sexual and intimate violence are common experiences among girls (Benson et al. 2003; Cobbina et al. 2008; Edin and Kefalas 2005; Miller 2008). Miller (2008) found that sexual harassment and victimization were commonplace. Studies show that boys gang rape girls (Bourgois 1996), "run trains" (Miller 2008, pp. 134–243), and "hit and run" (Anderson 1999). Domestic violence is similarly problematic in disadvantaged neighborhoods and households with more employment instability and financial strain (Benson et al. 2003). In Edin and Kefalas (2005, pp. 94–98), women reported that domestic violence was the "chief culprit" in their destroyed relationships.

In response, girls justifiably fear for their safety and often see boys as sexual predators (Tolman et al. 2003). Girls also report feeling pressured to engage in sexual acts. In Miller (2008), girls felt especially vulnerable in neighborhoods that sat outside the protective reach of male family members and friends. Gendered narratives, furthermore, lead youth to interpret girls' victimization as their own fault: girls dressed too provocatively, were too "fast," or failed to protect themselves properly.

Combating vulnerability

When inner-city life threatens their physical, social, and psychological wellbeing, teens use the available social resources to establish respect and status, often in gendered ways. The most prominent finding is that while low status boys have few institutional resources for establishing themselves as real men, they strive to garner other boys' respect and a sense of control through their physical capital in the neighborhood (Anderson 1999; Connell 1995; Messerschmidt 2004; Pyke 1996). Their ability to dominate others in order to establish themselves as men does not lie in their position as professionals or high-powered bosses. Rather, their bodies become the primary resource for identity making. Anderson explains: "Manhood and respect are two sides of the same coin; physical and psychological well-being are inseparable, and both requires a sense of control, of being in charge" (1999, p. 91). They often achieve this sense of control, dominance, and importance by presenting intimidating and threatening fronts.

Research is much less likely to frame girls as actively combating their vulnerability, but the studies that do also illustrate a gendered process. Girls seem to use motherhood, in particular, to construct themselves as mature, worthy, and competent (Edin and Kefalas 2005). Kaplan's (1997) study showed that girls became mothers to create love, meaning, and control in their lives. Fewer studies still address girls' sexual strategies outside of motherhood. Some girls adopt the strategies of boys: living by the "code of the street," fighting, or joining gangs as coping strategies, although not as ways to enact femininity (Jones 2008; Miller 2001). Miller and colleagues (Cobbina et al. 2008; Miller 2008) found that girls avoided going outside, avoided particular boys, sought intervention from others, established networks of men to protect themselves, ignored harassing behavior, or stood up for themselves directly to persons harassing them.

This chapter argues that heterosexuality is a primary instrument of resistance for both boys and girls, and their sexual strategies draw on gendered ideologies and practices. Heterosexuality allows boys and girls to establish their importance with each other and demonstrate their domination over others (or, at least, their ability to resist being dominated) within a dangerous and degrading social context.

Methods and data

Urban Youth Network (UYN) is an urban youth service organization for mostly black inner-city teenagers and their families. The data come from fieldwork and interviews that I conducted at UYN's summer day camp over seven weeks. The kids, aged between twelve and seventeen, who attended the camp were all African American, except for one white girl. Almost all of them were from low-income, working poor families. The vast majority of them were heterosexual. I also conducted in-depth interviews with twenty teens and informal interviews with staff. Eleven of the teen interviewees were girls, and nine were boys. Interviews covered their family background, gender ideologies, ideas about manhood and womanhood, friendships, dating experiences, and plans for the future.

My methods followed the grounded theory approach in which data collection and analysis are simultaneous (Charmaz 2001). The study was designed to theorize social processes by generalizing across social situations or specifying the influence of context on particular processes. Each day, I recorded "notes on notes" as a way to organize patterns and to conduct early analysis. I then wrote detailed extended field notes and self-reflection. More thorough analysis came in the form of analytic memos.

The life of UYN teens

The lives of UYN youths were full of instability and transitions. Drug addiction was prevalent in the city, along with the crime and violence that accompany it. Several boys had already been arrested, and many felt discriminated against by the police. A few shared stories of abuse. Most twelve- or thirteen-year-old boys and girls at UYN had not started to date seriously, and their heterosexual interactions seemed playful. By age fourteen, though, teens had started talking with romantic interests on the phone or had developed short-lived boyfriend–girlfriend relationships. Out of the twenty teenagers interviewed, only one-quarter reported having experienced sexual intercourse. Women remained a fairly stable but taken-for-granted presence for many teens. Twelve of those interviewed lived with their mothers (three with their fathers), and others lived with an aunt or grandmother. The teens struggled to make sense of the chaotic environment that surrounded them. Neighborhood and family instability fostered a lack of control and efficacy (Anderson 1999; Kaplan 1997). Creating a sense of control, status among peers, and a positive sense of self, in turn, were of the utmost importance.

Heterosexual ideologies

Even though inner cities are places of physical and psychological vulnerability for both boys and girls (Cobbina et al. 2008; Miller 2008), heterosexual boys in this study rarely considered themselves to be *sexually* vulnerable. Rather, heterosexuality was a primary medium for them to feel in control and establish themselves as important and dominant. Nearly every teen in this study viewed sexuality through an essentialist framework that played off of and reinforced heteronormative stereotypes that positioned boys as sexual subjects. They believed that the laws of nature determined that boys and girls had opposite, if not complementary, sexual natures, because boys had penises and girls had vaginas. Boys' sexuality was seen not only as pleasurable but as something boys were *entitled* to enjoy and seek (Allen 2003; Tolman et al. 2003). These sexual natures, which they often tied to religious beliefs or endowment by God, contrasted to supposedly unnatural same-sex sexuality. As Keisha put it: "You can't stick a vagina in a vagina."

Male heterosexual entitlement became a dominant ideological framework for establishing a boy's status among other boys. They labeled sexually dominant boys—and themselves—"pimp," "player," and "baller." Boys also bragged publicly about their heterosexual experiences, the girls with whom they had sex, or their physical endowment. During one group discussion about manhood, for example, two boys sat whispering together. When a staff person called them out for not paying attention, Shawn matter-of-factly explained: "He's talking about a girl he's busted." Asia reported that boys in her school bragged: "I got the biggest . . . [penis]." Even boys who struggled to garner girls' sexual attention bragged about their sexual adeptness. Tad nicknamed himself "Sexual Vanilla" as a way to highlight his sex appeal and light complexion. Even Ethan, who reported being sexually coerced by a girl at age eleven, framed himself as sexually appealing and entitled rather than as a victim.

By propping themselves up through heterosexual nicknames and boasting, boys reinforced that they were entitled to sexual self-interest and control by drawing on essentialist heteronormative ideologies: they were male and had a penis, which meant their (strong) sex drive was natural. Within this framework, all the youth expected boys to be heterosexual beings who pursued sexual gratification through girls, even at the expense of others. This sense of heteromale sexual entitlement justified playing "the game" of getting pleasure through heterosexuality or control through manipulation (Staiger 2005). Teens emphasized the uncontrollability of male sexuality. Girls' understanding of male sexuality often made them uncomfortable, and they played up stereotypical beliefs as a way to ease the tension. Keisha, for instance, bantered about boys who would not wait two months to have sex: "Some boys can't hold it that long!" Tamika labeled boys who thought about "getting laid" as the "typical guy."

Boys who were sexually active directly described male heterosexual impulses as uncontrollable. An unrelenting sex drive became justification for cheating on a girlfriend, for example. They dismissed cheating, particularly when the cheating boy had not declared his commitment to a girlfriend or was still adjusting to hormonal changes. Even though they recognized cheating as hurtful to girls and perhaps guilt inducing, boys were *supposed* to test the waters. Ethan, for example, described the experience of puberty as: "When you get a certain age, your hormones start jumping and some dudes just can't control it." For Michael cheating became a natural response to "temptations."

Thus, the heteronormative notion of male sexual entitlement gave boys situational control in which their sexual desires and actions could serve as sources of domination in their relationships, self-importance, and identity formation.

The dominant ideology for girls, on the other hand, was one of female heterosexual vulnerability. When a girl has sex for the first time, the teens described her virginity as "taken," "lost," or given away (see Carpenter 2002). Keisha explained sex as: "Boys can go with you and want to *do it to you* [emphasis added]." Other times teens said boys tried to "hit it," "bust" a girl, or "get it." The commonality of harassing experiences along with the perception that boys were sex-crazed and girls were sexually vulnerable fueled girls' perceptions that heterosexuality was bad, disgusting, and painful. To some, sexual intercourse was not only undesirable but gross or "nasty"; and girls who engaged in it were themselves nasty and bad.

Despite the skepticism and fear, heterosexual relationships remained an important source of affirmation and status for girls. Most UYN girls retained romanticized images of intimacy with boys. Alayna was attracted to the emotional connection she felt with Vernon: "We talk about everything . . . When I would say something to him, he would say something back to me that

I would say to someone. It's like there's another me but a boy really." "I could tell him anything," Asia said of her former boyfriend. "He could tell me everything. Everything we did, we did it together." Most girls thought that serious relationships would bring stability, commitment, and security. Alayna believed that marriage was the ultimate relationship for this reason. "I would like that to be the feeling that I have throughout the whole marriage, through thick and thin, through God do us part." Grace agreed: "I would know how a person would feel about me no matter what."

Heterosexuality affirmed the girls' importance as people: they are worthy of being invested *in*. They could see themselves as special and as deserving of hours of conversation, being treated to a meal, or declarations of love.

Ideologically, then, heterosexuality provided teens status, meaning, and feelings of importance, which were otherwise frequently lacking in their lives.

Bolstering heterosexuality

Teens demonstrated their heterosexuality publicly in several ways that bolstered their status among their peers. Below, I show that boys sexually objectified girls and whipped girls, while girls touted their virginity. Both groups dissociated themselves from homosexuality.

Sexually objectifying girls

Boys routinely demonstrated their heterosexuality through the public objectification of girls. Throughout camp, they sexually harassed girls or degraded them as sex objects. During one fifty-minute group, Shawn, for example, repeatedly propositioned a girl to sit on his lap, for his sexual pleasure. When pressed by an adult to stop, he brushed off his comments as "just kidding" (see also Hill 2007). He continued, nonetheless, to make sexual gestures at the girl from across the room: gazing at her, licking his lips, sticking out his tongue at her, and then licking at her. Later during the same group, he tried to peek at girls' underwear.

Some boys tried to overpower girls' commitment to their own virginity by sexually objectifying it. A few boys articulated a preference for "virgin girlfriends" because they viewed girls' virginity as assets. "I'd rather have a virgin girlfriend," Ethan explained. "Shows respect for themselves. They love their property. Nobody trespassing or interfering with them. Not being a virgin is like somebody getting in their space and they're not saving themselves." In commodifying girls' bodies as "property," Ethan reframed girls' intentional virginity as attractive and inviting for the right boy rather than as a rejection of boys' manipulation and control. Ethan assumed that *he* was the right boy. In this way, girls' bodies were not vehicles of sexual pleasure for themselves but for boys. A virginal status also supposedly alleviated concern over sexually transmitted diseases because the girls were categorized as "clean."

At other times, sexual objectification was not targeted at a specific girl by an individual boy, but a group of boys exerted toward girls in general. When preparing to go swimming, a group of boys "joked" that girls should leave their swimming suits at home, insisting that girls wear bikinis, thongs, or bras instead. In doing so, boys symbolically undressed girls from a one-piece suit to a bikini to undergarments. The staff's inaction to their comments, as in most cases at UYN, reinforced the naturalness of the boys' right to exert power through heterosexual means.

"Get you whipped"

Boys in romantic relationships with girls demonstrated their heterosexual prowess by trying to control girlfriends to gain status. Some UYN boys intentionally and publicly manipulated girls' emotions so that they could boss them around. Once girls had fallen in love, they were more willing to do what they were told and to be subordinate to their male partners. UYN young people referred to these dominated people as "whipped." An exchange between Donte and Shirlisa illustrates the power within whipping. Donte was seeing Shantell when he began a flirtation with Shirlisa. When Shirlisa found out, Donte denied it. But Shirlisa did not believe him and demanded that he decide between the girls. He chose her. Their relationship quickly evolved into an ongoing power struggle. It came to a head when Donte degraded her in front of his male friends, declaring to her, "I can get you whipped." This declaration was a direct challenge to her. Being or getting whipped meant that Donte had successfully controlled her—she was in love with him and therefore would follow his orders. He had essentially trained her to be his servant. That day when she came to check up on Donte who was sitting with a group of friends, he tested his control over her. Shirlisa described the situation, which I walked in on during the camp:

> I wanted to come in and sit down for a little while, you know, just to see what he was talking about. And then he said, "Go get me a drink" or "Get out of the room" or something. That's when he's got control. But I don't do that. Ain't nobody going to control me.

Donte made these demands in front of a group of boys and me. In her interview, as shown above, Shirlisa claimed to refuse to be controlled by Donte. During the real exchange, however, Shirlisa never protested Donte's requests, and she laughed uneasily in submission. Donte repeatedly bragged to his friends how he had never been whipped, and the boys around them laughed with Donte about whipping girls.

Shevron took a similar approach to Donte by blending heterosexual courtship, public challenges, and domination. Shevron, a popular boy among girls, routinely degraded Natasha in public by sexually teasing her in front of others. Shevron, for instance, bragged in front of a crowd that Natasha wanted to have sex with him. At first she vehemently denied his claim—equally loudly so that everyone could hear. In the next round of exchanges, though, Shevron upped the ante by grinning and blurting that *she* propositioned *him* to have sex over the weekend. Rather than expressing genuine annoyance, however, Natasha responded with increasingly flirtatious obstinacy. She yelled back exaggerated retorts that indicated her supposed nonchalance about the relationship: "Don't nobody want you, boy!" Other times she yelled in his face and threatened to steal him (hit him) while pumping her fist into her palm—all the while smiling broadly.

Both of these examples illustrate the public declarations of whipping someone, in order to impress male peers. Doing so allowed boys to increase their status through public displays of heterosexuality and domination.

Touting virginity

Girls touted their virginity and used their virgin status to proclaim their moral worth rooted in heterosexuality (Bettie 2000; Schalet et al. 2003). They considered a girl who successfully guarded her heterosexuality to be worthwhile, admirable, and strong, particularly if she struggled to do so. That made virgins' own heterosexual struggle a sign of character rather than, say, a rejection. This strategy of moralizing virginity was particularly salient for girls who were active in churches or had a group of friends who supported each other's virginity. A virgin symbolized not only strength and self-control but also goodness. In turn, sexual intercourse and sexual feelings became things to avoid and deflect out of moral honor and prudence. Shirlisa, Shantell, Alayna, and Keisha all declared themselves to be virgins during interviews, even though sexual status was a point of contention in public. Shirlisa, for example, embraced her virginal status as something to "save" as a gift to her future husband.

While most of the girls explained their decision to not have sex in terms of "saving" themselves for marriage, Alayna's understanding of adultery connected sexual inhibition with immorality. She recently learned that her sexual thoughts and feelings themselves were sinful:

> I'm still a virgin. I'm pretty well rounded and I carry myself with a certain respect. It's a good thing to be because it also says in the bible that thou shall not commit adultery. And this weekend I learned that you commit adultery if you look at someone and you know that you want them, you know that they look good. That's committing adultery because that's not your husband. That's like having a boyfriend, walking away from you, looking at somebody else saying she looks good. That would be wrong.

In Alayna's mind just being attracted to a boy—let alone engaging in any sexual activity—was a sin and would make her a bad person. Her embrace of abstinence not only motivated her to keep her sexual feelings for a boy in check but it provided emotional rewards: she was a strong, moral, and godly person for doing so.

A virgin status, then, was symbolic of girl strength, especially to conservative elders or within circles of friends like Keisha's. Virginity also served as a protective barrier to deflect unwanted sexual advances while projecting heteronormativity. Girls did this through claiming to figure out what boys "really want" and then asserting their commitment to remaining a virgin. Keisha employed her friends, all of whom she described as virgins, to protect against boys' manipulation:

> We don't fall into them because we know they're lying. Say we had a boyfriend. We talk to each other about it. My friends are like, "You know he's lying. You know he's lying."
>
> [My friends] be like, "Yeah, we know. I know." And so they are like, "You better not be yeah [having sex]." "You know I'm not."

These assertions allowed girls to reject boys in socially legitimated ways that raised their status.

Dissociating from homosexuality

Finally, heterosexual teens distanced themselves from their gay or lesbian peers/family members whom they believed might be a contagion on them. While teens viewed heterosexuality as natural, they also recognized flexibility in sexual behavior; and they all had contact with people who were lesbian, gay, or bisexual, and feared that people "turned gay" through exposures. To minimize what they experienced as social risk, teens distanced themselves from gay/lesbian individuals or publicly teased, harassed, or threatened them. Trenton's mom advised him, and he took to heart, to "never talk to a gay person . . . Gay people aren't the kind of people you want to be around." Boys, especially, legitimated violence as an appropriate response to sexual innuendo. Darius, for example, said he would hit any boy who touched him.

Teens also dissociated from behavior that their peers would perceive as "gay." Teens frequently changed their appearance or behavior in order to be seen as straight (Froyum 2007). Shantell dressed more feminine to avoid being teased. Boys avoided bending over while dancing because "I'm not gay." Justin refused to bowl so he wouldn't "look like a fag."

Conclusions

This study examined how teens do heterosexuality as a way to combat their vulnerability within an inner city. Instability and violence threaten the physical and psychological wellbeing of teens, producing a vulnerability too often ignored in the literature. While the threats themselves are gendered—boys risk being attacked when they fail to establish themselves as dominant and girls face physical and sexual violence because they are girls—both boys and girls combat them by drawing on the social resources available to them to create a sense of control and meaningful identities. This study shows that heterosexuality is a primary medium for doing so and that both boys and girls mediate their vulnerabilities through heterosexuality, albeit in gendered ways that have gendered consequences.

Boys drew on gender ideologies that both informed and justified their sexual strategies. Because their ideologies characterized males as naturally sexually compelled and entitled, boys were able to establish themselves as high status, important, and in control by enacting sexual domination over girls. Boasting of sexual conquests, cheating, sexual objectification of girls, and getting girls whipped were all public declarations to status done by boys. In this way, doing sexuality was a direct attempt to establish themselves as important in the eyes of their male peers at the direct expense of girls' value and sense of trust and safety in hetero-relationships. Furthermore, boys justified—and some girls became resigned to—these manipulative behaviors through gendered narratives of boys' sexual temptations and natural doggedness.

Girls often came to resent and even fear boys as sexual predators, and they dreaded the loss of control that seemed inevitable in many romantic relationships. Yet it was through their relationships with boys that girls were able to gain status and culturally legitimated identities as girlfriend (and later as wife and mother). These statuses provided girls the semblance of stability, admiration from other girls, and a worthwhile sense of self, as well as potential access to material resources. The resulting social context was the ultimate paradox for girls: they remained dependent upon the very people who hurt them in order to bolster status in opposition to them.

Both boys and girls bolstered their heterosexuality by distancing themselves from gay individuals or gay-typed behavior. These heteronormative ideologies and interactions allowed otherwise marginalized individuals to establish meaning and status among their peers.

References

Allen, L., 2003. Girls want sex, boys want love: Resisting dominant discourses of (hetero)sexuality. *Sexualities*, 6(2), 215–236.

Anderson, E., 1999. *Code of the street: Decency, violence, and the moral life of the inner city*. New York: W.W. Norton & Company.

Benson, M.L., Fox, G.L., DeMaris, A., and Van Wyk, J., 2003. Neighborhood disadvantage, individual economic distress and violence against women in intimate relationships. *Journal of Quantitative Criminology*, 19(3), 207–235.

Bettie, J., 2000. Women without class: Chicas, cholas, trash, and the presence/absence of class identity. *Signs: Journal of Women in Culture & Society*, 26(1), 1–35.

Bolland, J.M., 2003. Hopelessness and risk behaviour among adolescents living in high-poverty inner-city neighbourhoods. *Journal of Adolescence*, 26, 145–158.

Bourgois, P., 1996. In search of masculinity. *British Journal of Criminology*, 36(3), 412–427.

Carpenter, L.M., 2002. Gender and the meaning and experience of virginity loss in the contemporary United States. *Gender & Society*, 16(3), 345–365.

Charmaz, K., 2001. Grounded theory. In: Emerson, R.M. ed. *Contemporary field research: Perspectives and formulations*. Second edn. Prospect Heights: Waveland Press, 335–352.

Cobbina, J.E., Miller, J., and Brunson, R.K., 2008. Gender, neighborhood danger, and risk-avoidance strategies among urban African-American youths. *Criminology*, 46(3), 673–709.

Connell, R.W., 1995. *Masculinities*. Berkeley: University of California Press.

Edin, K. and Kefalas, M., 2005. *Promises I can keep: Why poor women put motherhood before marriage*. Berkeley: University of California Press.

Froyum, C.M., 2007. "At least I'm not gay": Heterosexual identity making among poor black teens. *Sexualities*, 10(5), 603–622.

Hill, H.D., 2007. Steppin' out: Infidelity and sexual jealousy among unmarried parents. In: England, P. and Edin, K. eds. *Unmarried couples with children*. New York: Russell Sage Foundation, 104–132.

Jones, N., 2004. "It's not where you live, it's how you live": How young women negotiate conflict and violence in the inner city. *The ANNALS of the American Academy of Political and Social Science*, 595, 49–62.

Jones, N., 2008. Working "the code": On girls, gender, and inner-city violence. *Australian and New Zealand Journal of Criminology*, 41(1), 63–83.

Kaplan, E.B., 1997. *Not our kind of girl: Unraveling the myths of black teenage motherhood*. Berkeley: University of California Press.

Lauritsen, J.L., 2003. *How families and communities influence youth victimization*. Washington, DC: US Department of Justice.

Lauritsen, J.L. and White, N.A., 2001. Putting violence in its place: The influence of race, ethnicity, gender, and place on the risk for violence. *Criminology & Public Policy*, 1(1), 37–60.

Massey, D.S. and Denton, N.A., 1988. Suburbanization and segregation in U.S. metropolitan areas. *American Journal of Sociology*, 94(3), 592–626.

Messerschmidt, J.W., 2004. *Flesh and blood: Adolescent gender diversity and violence*. Lanham: Rowman & Littlefield.

Miller, J., 2001. *One of the guys: Girls, gangs, and gender*. New York: Oxford University Press.

Miller, J., 2008. *Getting played: African American girls, urban inequality, and gendered violence*. New York: New York University Press.

Pettit, B. and Western, B., 2004. Mass imprisonment and the life course: Race and class inequality in U.S. incarceration. *American Sociological Review*, 69, 151–169.

Pyke, K.D., 1996. Class-based masculinities: The interdependence of gender, class, and interpersonal power. *Gender & Society*, 19(5), 527–549.

Rankin, B. and Quane, J., 2000. Neighborhood poverty and the social isolation of inner-city African American families. *Social Forces*, 79(1), 139–164.

Schalet, A., Hunt, G., and Joe-Laidler, K., 2003. Respectability and autonomy: The articulation and meaning of sexuality among the girls in the gang. *Journal of Contemporary Ethnography*, 32(1), 108–143.

Stack, C., 1974. *All our kin: Strategies for survival in a black community*. New York: Harper & Row.

Staiger, A., 2005. "Hoes can be hoed out, players can be played out, but pimp is for life": The pimp phenomenon as strategy of identity formation. *Symbolic Interactionism*, 28(3), 407–428.

Tolman, D.L., Spencer, R., Rosen-Reynoso, M., and Porche, M.V., 2003. Sowing the seeds of violence in heterosexual relationships: Early adolescents narrate compulsory heterosexuality. *Journal of Social Issues*, 59(1), 159–178.

Wilson, W.J., 1996. *When work disappears: The world of the new urban poor*. New York: Vintage Books.

14

Straight women

Doing and undoing compulsory heterosexuality in post-closeted American culture

James Joseph Dean

How does heterosexuality shape women's femininities? This question is often implicitly addressed, or altogether absent, in scholarship on women's formations of gendered selves (for exceptions see Budnick 2016; Hamilton 2007; Jackson 1999, 2006; Richardson 1996). Through the frame of a post-closeted cultural dynamic, this chapter's analysis intervenes in the systems of compulsory heterosexuality and male domination. On the one hand, I provide an account of the homophobic practices and claims to privilege of some straight women. On the other, I explore how other straight women enact antihomophobic practices but maintain straight privilege, while others reject straight privilege at times and develop what I call a *queered straight identification*.

In this chapter, I draw on the concept of compulsory heterosexuality to theorize and understand straight women's identity enactments, detail the background of this study, and provide an overview of the continuum I developed to sketch the range of homophobic to antihomophobic practices that straight women discussed with me during the in-depth interviews I conducted.

I employ the late Adrienne Rich's ([1980] 1993) concept of compulsory heterosexuality in order to theorize how heterosexuality organizes normative femininity. Focusing on how heterosexuality shapes women's femininities, I show that the continuing analytical purchase of the concept of compulsory heterosexuality is that it points our attention to the differential structural enforcement of heterosexuality on women. It shows the ways in which bisexual, lesbian, and queer women's sexualities in today's context are often variably caught and resituated in processes of commodification and heterosexist dynamics. Often these heterosexist dynamics are situated from the standpoint of straight men, as seen in mass media representations such as straight male pornography or in public displays of same-sex kissing by ostensibly straight women who use these acts to titillate straight men, explore non-straight behaviors in straight spaces, or identify as bisexual or "heteroflexible" (Clark 1993; Hamilton 2007; Rupp and Taylor 2010).

Rich's conception of compulsory heterosexuality as a political institution highlights how heterosexuality is a structural norm and system of power that creates hierarchies that differentially value, reward, and enfranchise heterosexuals over non-heterosexuals. More than this, her concept captures how male domination works to make heterosexuality compulsory for women in different ways than for men, due to women's different structural positions in social institutions, particularly in normative roles as wives in marriages and mothers in families. Rich ties her concept to social institutions as well as representations in culture, thus providing a rigorous sociological account of how gender and sexual orders work together in support of compulsory heterosexuality.

In sum, Rich's theory argues for a tight connection between male domination and the enforcement of heterosexuality on women, and the concept of compulsory heterosexuality embeds two claims. First, the theory claims that women's desires, roles, and identities are defined as dependent on relations with men; thus, heterosexuality enforces gender differences and binary conceptions of sex and gender. Second, it claims that a binary gender order makes heterosexuality seem as if men and women are "natural," necessary, and compulsory complements to one another as a result of the reduction of species survival, reproduction, and romantic relationships to heterosexual relations (Butler 1990, 1992; Rich [1980] 1993; Seidman 2009).

However, over the last third of the twentieth century, lesbians and gay men have become integrated into a variety of social institutions; thus, while normative heterosexuality's dynamics still subordinate gay men and lesbians, American society is witnessing the weakening of compulsory heterosexuality in social institutions, such as corporate workplaces, multiple mass media outlets, and in county, state, and federal courtrooms where legal changes now support and condition the inclusion of out lesbians and gays as well as their representations within these spheres (Eskridge 1999; Gamson 2002; Ghaziani 2011; Raeburn 2004; Seidman 2002; Stein 2010; Walters 2001; Weeks 2007).

Moreover, compulsory heterosexuality not only subordinates lesbians and gay men but also normalizes and circumscribes the recognition of the multiple forms of heterosexualities that exist. Taking a Foucauldian (1978) approach, we may see compulsory heterosexuality as producing differences, conflicts, and hierarchies among heterosexualities at the level of identity, culture, and politics. For instance, a heterosexual normative model of identity, which links itself to monogamy and procreation within marital relations and views sexuality as a private matter, claims a hierarchical position over non-monogamous, nonmarried, nonprocreative, and nonprivate sexual practices in the lives of these *other* straight men and women as well as non-heterosexuals, as the rest fail to meet the normative standard of this specific formulation of heterosexuality (Richardson 1996; Rubin 1984; Seidman 2002, 2009). In this sense, scholars should think of "normative heterosexualities" in the plural, recognizing the multiplicity of hierarchies among heterosexualities in its normative construction.

For example, the sociologist Laura Hamilton (2007), in her study of Greek fraternity parties at a Midwestern university, finds that heterosexual women will kiss other women to garner heterosexual male attention. She quotes one college woman as saying, "Guys said, 'Do it, do it!' just screwing around . . . [They] were like, 'These girls are going to kiss!' So you think you're cooler and guys think you're cooler" (p. 164). Here, same-sex intimacy between women with straight men watching confirms the women's heterosexual statuses, as opposed to creating doubt or suspicion of them as lesbian or bisexual (Rupp and Taylor 2010). To underscore the point, it almost goes without saying that the converse situation of two straight men kissing with women watching at, say, a college sorority party would not generally confirm the straight status of these individual men.

Whereas research shows that straight men tend to be more verbally and physically demonstrative in their homophobic displays than heterosexual women (Gallup 1995; Herek 1988), Hamilton's study calls our attention to the homophobic practices that straight women use to avoid, marginalize, and exclude lesbians in order to remain un-stigmatized by their presence in college. Hamilton and other sociologists demonstrate that straight femininities draw on specifically gendered practices, such as bodily capital (the value of one's body's shape), beauty, and charm in garnering straight men's recognition and bolstering the value of their straight femininity in erotic markets (Bernstein 2007; Bettie 2004; McCall 1992).

The study

Data for this research are based on twenty-nine in-depth interviews with fourteen self-identified black straight women and fifteen self-identified white straight women. The interviews lasted from 1.5 to 2.5 hours on average. I conducted the interviews from 2004 to 2005 in "Orangetown," a city in the northeastern United States. As is standard practice to protect the real identities of one's respondents and their exact geographical location, all respondents' names, along with the city and names of the places mentioned in this book, have been changed in order to maintain confidentiality.

The research design purposefully sampled for race and gender to analytically compare them along the axis of heterosexuality. The black female respondents' ages range from twenty to eighty, while the white female respondents' ages range from twenty to sixty-one. Among the black women, ten are single; three are married; two are divorced and single. Five of the white women are single; four are married; four are divorced and currently single; two are currently married but divorced from a previous marriage. (For a more detailed description of the study and its participants, see Dean's 2014 book.)

This case study is based on a nonrandom snowball sample and is limited by its lack of generalizability beyond the reported interviews (Burawoy et al. 1991). I used social distance theory in order to capture a diverse range of straight women's accounts and the range of their homophobic and antihomophobic stances. The subjects in this study ranged from those who have daily interaction with Orangetown's active and "out" lesbian, gay, and queer community to those who had little daily interaction with this neighborhood and community.

The interview guide used open-ended questions that inquired about the following: how respondents let others know they were heterosexual and what social cues they used to decide if someone was gay or straight; their experiences with LGBTQ persons coming out to them; their comfort in socializing in gay/queer spaces; and their definition of homophobia. I used the terms straight and heterosexual interchangeably during the interviews.

Analysis involved transcribing and coding the interview data into over thirty-five thematic memos (Charmaz 2007). I present an analytical continuum of straight femininities. This continuum emerged from the memo analyses, and I present the range of the sample, from homophobic expressions of straight femininities to antihomophobic ones.

The straight identity practices continuum

This chapter uses a continuum that I call *the straight identity practices continuum* to map homophobic stances of straight femininities, on one end, moving to antihomophobic ones, on the other end. I use this analytical continuum to empirically explore a range of homophobic and antihomophobic practices by straight women, moving from those who establish strongly aversive boundaries to those with weak boundaries, and, finally, to those who blur boundaries between straightness and queerness. My discussion of these practices derives from interview data, and I take the practices the women report to me as conventional ways of speaking and acting that they treat as matters of commonsense knowledge and everyday competence. By social distance, I mean the practices these women use to negotiate boundaries in associating themselves with or disassociating themselves from gay, lesbian, and queer individuals, symbols, and social spaces.

I present case studies of black and white straight femininities and show how race shapes and frames straight women's homophobic and antihomophobic stances. Aspects of the lives of straight women are sketched with the purpose of illustrating a series of positions on the continuum.

The following analysis divides straight femininities into three sections. The first section explores the homophobic end of the continuum and how straight women in this category enact homophobic stances (generally based on their Christian religious beliefs) that condemn homosexuality. The second section analyzes those straight women who fall into the *weak boundaries* category; it illustrates a series of antihomophobic stances by straight women who contest homophobic prejudice and discrimination yet are not willing to blur normative boundaries of heterosexuality. The *blurred boundaries* category is discussed in the last section. Here, I focus on a more "activist" set of straight women whose identity practices blur identity boundaries between heterosexuality and homosexuality.

In the second and third sections, I suggest that we approach understanding *antihomophobic* practices as plural and constitutive in the establishment of straight femininities. By antihomophobia, I mean practices that aim to counter prejudice and discrimination against lesbians, gays, bisexuals, and queers as well as practices that may expose, and sometimes renounce, straight status and privilege. However, I note that not all practices are reducible to homophobia or antihomophobia; some identity practices are non-homophobic and thus neither enact homophobic nor antihomophobic practices. Nonetheless, in these sections, I highlight straight women's antihomophobic practices that help to give rise to a post-closeted culture of openly lesbian, gay, bisexual, transgender, and queer (LGBTQ) individuals and representations of them.

Compulsory heterosexuality and strongly aversive boundaries

Here I use the continuum of straight identity practices to map a range of interactional practices through which straights enact boundaries of social distance. In this section I analyze the identity practices of the eight out of the twenty-nine straight women who fall into the strongly aversive category. Five of these women are black and the other three are white. My conceptualization of identity practices draws on the in-depth interviews I conducted with fourteen black and fifteen white straight women.

Straight women in the *strongly aversive* category use identity practices that are more understated, subtle, and nuanced in establishing their straight identities in interactions with lesbians and gay men. For instance, all of the eight women who fell into this grouping stated that they have lesbian or gay acquaintances, friends, coworkers, or even family members who are part of their circle of friends or extended familial relations. Many of them also reported having gone to gay bars on occasion, stating that they did not feel particularly anxious about being viewed as possibly lesbian or bisexual while there. Nonetheless, all of these eight straight women express homophobic views that define homosexuality as socially and morally inferior to heterosexuality, and it is this key characteristic that establishes their coding into the strongly aversive grouping on the continuum.

Although I use the same analytical frame of homophobic to antihomophobic practices in categorizing where each woman lies on the continuum, straight women's practices of homophobia have less to do with constructing strongly aversive boundaries of social distance; instead, the issue of same-sex marriage and its condemnation due to religious worldviews proved salient in their homophobic practices. In part, the social capital women gain through marriage, the establishment of families, and statuses such as wife and mother are informing these straight women's homophobic prejudices, as the desire to maintain these privileges emerges in their homophobic responses to this issue (Bourdieu 2001; Chodorow 1978; Hays 1996; Moore 2011).

At their most extreme, these straight women's homophobic practices reproduce the norm of compulsory heterosexuality that would turn homosexuality back into a closeted identity that does not merit respect, recognition, or rights. Generally, these respondents invoked Christian religious beliefs to justify their homophobic practices. Religious views act as a clear moral compass, dividing the world into sacred and profane divisions (Alexander 1988; Durkheim [1912] 1995), and for these straight women religious beliefs have an aura of being beyond reproach. However, as sociologists we must view religious practices as choices; thus, individuals and their faiths must be held accountable for the positions they hold on social issues.

For four of the five black women and one of the three white women in this group, Christian religious judgments, compulsory heterosexuality, and homophobia intersect in prejudices that construct only heterosexual identities and relationships as morally right, good, and blessed, while homosexual ones are constructed as morally wrong, bad, and damned. The issue that most clearly brought this to the fore was same-sex marriage. At the time of my interviews in 2004 and 2005, the Massachusetts State Supreme Court had just rendered its decision legally sanctioning same-sex marriages on November 18, 2003 and started issuing licenses on May 17, 2004, making it the first state to legalize same-sex marriage.

In post-closeted culture, straights face competing cultural logics: on one hand, they negotiate a logic of the cultural normalization of homosexuality, which promotes tolerance, acceptance, and a liberalization of attitudes toward gays. On the other hand, straight individuals may draw on homophobic cultural logics, which are often based in social-psychological schemas of abnormality and unhealthiness or religious ones of Christian immorality and sinfulness. Homophobic and antihomophobic practices and discourses exist side by side in the complex contexts of today's post-closeted culture; they are competing logics and discourses that configure and reconfigure the changing environment of contemporary sexual identity politics in American society. In my interviews, this complex context is illustrated by the way practices of cultural normalization or antihomophobia and homophobia are combined in the same heterosexual person.

Consider Martha Lewis, a fifty-four-year-old black woman who wears her hair in small dreadlocks to her shoulders. She recently went back to college and finished a BA and a master's degree in Christian counseling in 2000. Martha has been married and divorced twice and has a thirty-seven-year-old son from her first marriage and a twenty-five-year-old daughter from her second. She is conventionally feminine in appearance and wore professional dress attire when I interviewed her at work.

At the beginning of the interview, Martha tells me that she has enjoyed socializing in gay bars with straight women friends in the past. She relates this story:

> The women I went out with, we were all heterosexual . . . We were just out and a friend of mine who, this particular friend has a lot of friends who are homosexual and knows where they go hang out to party. So she said it was a really neat place and I said, "Well, come on. Let's go." So we did. A couple of ladies asked us to dance and we would do that. But, my one friend she got hit on. Well, she is the one friend who has the homosexual friends, so maybe they had seen her out and maybe assumed. That could be it, but my other friend and myself were never hit on. We were asked to dance and we had a great time, like girlfriends dancing.

Her ease in socializing in gay establishments led me to initially think she would be supportive of gay and lesbian people. Similarly, when she tells me about a gay male friend whom she met in her social work program, saying, "A classmate of mine . . . who is homosexual, we still stay in touch.

I love him very much and we really got to talk a lot," I am led to believe that she is strong in her support and acceptance of lesbian and gay individuals and their relationships.

However, toward the end of the interview, when I inquire further about other lesbian or gay individuals who have come out to her and her thoughts on their identity, relationships, and the issue of same-sex marriage, she explains that she views homosexuality as a choice that is wrong in the eyes of God and her Christian faith. Given Martha's age, fifty-four, and the fact that she grew up before Stonewall, her tolerance has clear limits.

For Martha, being lesbian or being a woman in a relationship with another woman is to enter a non-Christian existence defined by sin. Furthermore, she views civil rights as a term reserved for racial minorities like blacks, as these minorities in her mind did not "choose" to be born with darker skin. The logic of choice and free will, though, is not an acceptable legitimating strategy for Martha's strong Christian religious beliefs that condemn homosexuality. As the interview progressed, I pushed Martha to defend her notion that sexuality was a choice by asking her whether she viewed her own heterosexuality as a choice or was it just homosexuality she thought of as a choice. As a result of my questions, she became defensive but also perhaps more candid in her responses. Here is our exchange:

> James: Okay, so in your mind then the problem with homosexuality is that it is against Christianity?
>
> Martha: I didn't say it is a problem. Why did you say that, "the problem with homosexuality?"
>
> James: Well, if you see it as a choice that is wrong, then . . .
>
> Martha: Who am I to say if it is right or wrong? It is just my choice. I think we all have choices. Then we have to suffer the consequences of those choices or reap the benefits of those choices. I am not God so I am not going to say anything. It's just that I choose to be heterosexual. Your choice is your choice and that is something that you have to work out with God. Because when you are before God, the playing ground is all level so [*clears throat*] excuse me, it is not a problem. Right or wrong, it is just what the Bible says. I didn't see him say he made Jack and Jack or whatever. He even says it was an abomination, so we will just go from his word, and his word is kind of specific there, but again it is a person's choice.

Religious teachings are a core principle of her belief system, and many devoutly religious Americans like her base their judgments on a polarizing logic according to which behaviors, identities, and relations are either morally pure or impure. So, whether or not Martha actually views her own heterosexuality or others' homosexuality as choices, as she says, remains dubious for me. Nonetheless, under the pressure of my questioning and with a growing sense of defensiveness, her quote demonstrates that she views homosexuality as "an abomination" because it goes against Christian scripture. Her religiosity, in short, is the fulcrum on which her homophobia turns.

Like Martha, Beth Moore, a twenty-six-year-old white woman who describes herself as a strongly religious Christian woman, also takes issue with gays and lesbians being able to get married. Similarly, Beth defines a marriage as a relationship that is religiously sanctioned. And since Christian scripture condemns homosexuality, Beth does not support gay marriages, although she would support civil unions for gay men and lesbians:

> I don't agree with gay marriage. I think that marriage is a religious thing. I think that civil unions are different than marriage, but I also think that marriage is something that is consecrated by a priest in a church. To me, it seems like more or less a religious thing, whereas a

> civil union, like being married by a judge or something like that; it's not the religious aspect of being, I mean you're still in a union; it's still a union. I just think marriage has religious connotations to it.

While religious beliefs and attitudes toward same-sex marriage capture an important aspect of homophobic practices, the interactions between straights and lesbians and gays provide another significant indicator as well. For example, Beth described being friends with her lesbian teammates with whom she played hockey in college. However, when her lesbian teammates started dating, she was the last to know. She says,

> I was kind of the last to know of our group of friends. So I had kind of figured [it out]. [Due to] the time that they were spending together and just talking to our other friends, I kind of figured it out before they told us what was going on.

Although it is hard to be sure of why Beth's lesbian teammates told her last, it seems plausible to assume that they might have avoided telling Beth if they thought she would be disapproving of their relationship. Lesbians and gay men may use boundaries of social distance between themselves and homophobic straights as well, trying to avoid potential acts of disrespect and misrecognition of their relationships and lives.

Although most of the black, along with one of the white, straight women I interviewed justified the norm of heterosexuality in relationships and marriages through a Christian morality, there was one exception to this among the five. This exception is Nia Gray, a twenty-one-year-old black woman who is a graduate student in Orangetown, a small city in the northeastern United States. Raised by a working-class Jamaican mother, along with her twin sister and nine other siblings in Brooklyn, New York, Nia views heterosexuality as a central aspect of her self-identity. When I ask why heterosexuality is "very" important to her, Nia says:

> Because considering the fact that I want to have children. I want to have the whole ideal family life. I want to get married. I want to have a husband there who will rub my back, my feet, and all of that stuff. I think that it will create more of a balance in my life. I think being with a female would create an imbalance.

Nia defines straight identity as including marriage, children, and an "ideal family life" while viewing homosexual identities and relations as excluding those possibilities.

Although she has gay and lesbian acquaintances, Nia feels that homosexuality is socially and morally inferior to heterosexuality. For example, one of the first individuals to come out to her was a close childhood friend, Lori Keith, whom Nia considered to be like family since they had grown up together. Nia told me that when Lori came out to her, she let Lori know that she would still be her friend. I asked Nia whether she had become more supportive of lesbian and gay people because of that experience. This is our exchange:

> Nia: I think it just made me question where I stood as far as that issue was concerned, considering that, OK, this is somebody who's like my sister. Am I so close-minded that I'm just gonna say forget her? Forget all that we've been through? I was like nah, nah, I'm not going to do that. And I just decided that I don't exactly support it, but I tolerate it. I tolerate it.
>
> James: What's the difference for you between support and tolerate?

Nia: Support, meaning I endorse it. Tolerate is like, OK, I don't like it, but I'm willing to put up with you because you're family or because we've been through so much. I wouldn't cut you out of my life just for that. So like I said, I wouldn't endorse it. I wouldn't be a supporter, like, yay, gay and lesbian rights, they should get married and all that stuff. I wouldn't do that. No.

For some straight women like Nia, having contact with close friends who are lesbian does not translate into stronger forms of support, such as supporting their right to marry.

However, the issue of how Nia "successfully" performs a straight identity in everyday life is an anxious topic for her. Nia is a petite young black woman, who by her own admission prefers to dress casually in jeans and sneakers and to forgo wearing skirts, high heels, or cosmetics. Since she says that she cannot tell if a woman is a lesbian unless the woman is extremely stereotypical, Nia says that the only way another individual would know that she is straight would be by her telling them directly or talking about men. With the increasing visibility of LGBTQ individuals and the withering of the closet, post-closeted contexts create situations where anyone is viewed as possibly being lesbian or gay. Therefore, Nia fears that this pattern of LGBTQ visibility means that the traditional presumption of a straight sexuality will be further undermined and will put more pressure on her to more conventionally perform her straight femininity.

Several women have flirted with Nia and tried to seduce her, by asking her whether she was interested in them sexually, as in the case of her childhood friend Lori, or by inviting her to have a bottle of wine and talking about having had sex with another woman and enjoying it, as in the case of her summer roommate Yolanda Jones. And while Nia has turned down each woman's sexual proposition, she still fears being tempted to have sex with a woman and worries about becoming bisexual, although she says she has never had sex with a woman. She tells me,

> I just hope that me personally I don't get turned out. That's my fear. I don't want to get turned out. But I know it can happen . . . I don't think that all people who turn gay choose it; I think that full-blown lesbians, yeah. But then there's bisexuals [*sic*] who based on experience gives me a doubt and just think, "I want to be pleased, whether it's by a man or a woman. I don't care." And I think that's based on experience. And like I said, I've even thought it and that's only because it's so prevalent now. I feel like even my own sexuality is being attacked because I'm getting women who are coming at me this way.

Because Nia does not enact a clear straight feminine identity performance, her main way of projecting her heterosexuality is to draw boundaries between straights and openly lesbian and gay people in her social circles. Consequently, she has a mostly straight group of other black friends. By condoning her friends' homophobic jokes, she reinforces her status as heterosexual. That is, since her identity practices do not clearly perform a clear straight femininity, Nia relies on social distance and homophobic displays to do this work for her.

And yet Nia's straight femininity is a source of tension for her on a number of levels. For her, normative straight femininity is too confining, limiting, and even oppressive. From her strong personality to her appearance with her hair in dreadlocks, Nia feels in conflict with the normative boundaries of black straight femininity. For example, when I ask her how she thinks of her own self-identity in general, Nia says, "Different from other females. I consider myself more masculine in my mind and certain things that I chose to do, sports, just my aggressive tendencies. I consider myself a masculine female."

In understanding her homophobic attitudes, though, Nia primarily associates her negative views toward homosexuality with her Caribbean cultural background and says that her mother and family would not accept her if she was lesbian.

> Because you know in our community they, we, they don't stand for that [homosexuality]. I'm from a Caribbean background and all the sounds that they make concerning homosexuality, all gay people are supposed to die. And kill them, shoot them, all that stuff. Yeah, that definitely makes it hard for people to come out because it's like a death sentence almost to come out with it. Like they'll [my mother and family would] tell me I need spiritual guidance; I'm lacking in some area. I'm unbalanced, that I'm an unbalanced person. Yeah, it'd be hard. It would be very hard.

Nia is clear that a homosexual identity would bring shame, rejection, and a kind of social death to any individual who would be openly gay or lesbian in her Caribbean culture and black community in Brooklyn, as she knows that her childhood friend Lori was disowned and shunned by her family and friends, including Nia's mother. Nia's story illustrates an individual who tolerates but does not support her lesbian friends or their struggle for legal rights. Her homophobic practices are based on views that grew out of her Caribbean family's values and the larger black community she grew up in.

Shifts in compulsory heterosexuality: weak boundaries, antihomophobic practices, and "fag hags"

The identity practices of straight women who integrate lesbian and gay friends, fellow church members, coworkers, and kin into their social circles are an important social force in promoting antihomophobic practices and supporting a post-closeted cultural dynamic that offers new relational arrangements from friendship to religious alliance to workplace collegiality in straights' and lesbian and gay individuals' lives. Unlike the previous respondents, these straight women engage in antihomophobic practices that position gays and lesbians as equals deserving of respect, recognition, and rights. The fourteen out of twenty-nine respondents who fall into this category describe weaker levels of religiosity overall, and generally strong religious beliefs were a barrier to tolerance and support of gay men and lesbians. Eight white and six black women compose the weak boundaries position on the continuum. However, six out of the fourteen straight women in this group did express moderate or high levels of religiosity, and so I describe these women as a counterpoint to those from the previous section, showing that Christian religious beliefs are compatible with supporting and accepting lesbian and gay individuals and their relationships. Three black and three white women make up the six strongly religious straight women.

The key characteristic that defined one as belonging to this category, and not the next, is that these women did flag their straight status and maintain straight privilege to various extents. These women used a gender strategy of embodying conventional femininity in performing a straight status in everyday life as a way of maintaining straight privilege. Unlike the next group of straight women, these straight women do not blur normative heterosexual boundaries by letting themselves be viewed as lesbian or bisexual, nor do the majority (eleven out of the fourteen) report experiencing same-sex fantasies or engaging in same-sex acts. The next group, in contrast, blurs normative hetero/homo boundaries and reports various kinds of experiences of sexual fluidity.

Although straight women in this "middle" group are less concerned with lesbians and gay men embodying gender-conventional practices, these straight women do take for granted and therefore naturalize the homo/heterosexual binary division that views sexual identities as static, uniform, and fixed. This sense of the homo/heterosexual binary is evidenced in their descriptions of gay identities as uniform or fixed and, again, their retention of straight privilege while generally being egalitarian in their views of lesbian and gay people, their relationships, and legal rights.

Furthermore, in this group, straight women who defined their Christian beliefs as important to their self-identities stated that they had joined reconciling Methodist churches that accepted lesbian and gay members or that they simply did not accept their faith's stance on gay identities and relationships. For example, Stephanie Phillips, a black woman who grew up as a teenager in the 1960s in Pittsburgh, and belonged to a traditional black Baptist church back then, explains, "They [her black community in Pittsburgh] were very repressed. They were all religious and everything. There wasn't any shacking up when I was [growing up], then in the '60s, people got married—old and young."

In contrast, Stephanie now attends a liberal Methodist church that she helped to become a reconciling congregation that actively accepts gays and lesbians as members. Within the United Methodist Church, churches that belong to the Reconciling Congregations Program embrace gay members and the adoption of liberal attitudes toward homosexuality (Moon 2004). She tells me:

> At my church, the Methodist as a denomination is split between being reconciling and non-reconciling . . . and so this church is basically white with a smattering of black, but there were myself and maybe ten other people who wanted that church to recognize gays and lesbians straight up by naming them in the mission statement and in doing that, we educate [others about these issues].

Reconciling Methodist congregations signal the growing institutional support for including gays and lesbians within mainstream Protestant denominations (Moon 2004), and straight women like Stephanie are active participants in creating an inclusive religious congregation and a post-closeted dynamic in their religious communities.

Other straight women with religious backgrounds like Margaret O'Riordan maintained their memberships in the Catholic Church but disavowed the Church's stance on homosexuality. Margaret, born in 1970, is married with four kids, attends mass weekly, and belongs to a women's Bible study group, and even studied to be a nun in her early twenties. Not surprisingly, she defines herself as a "hardworking Catholic woman," and her faith remains an integral part of her life. However, on the issue of same-sex marriage and the Catholic Church's stance against it, Margaret and the Church part ways:

> I know the Catholics don't want it. I know that I'm supposed to believe that it's just a man and a woman, but you know God created everybody. So that's the way that it is in my book . . . I think that everybody should be allowed to do what they want to do and be with whom they want to be with.

Margaret maintains a strong identity as a Catholic, but she deviates from the Church's stance on some issues.

In contrast to the religiosity of Stephanie and Margaret, Vanessa is a twenty-seven-year-old light-skinned black woman who was raised in the Methodist faith, but does not ascribe much importance to religion. Vanessa moved to Orangetown after finishing her bachelor's degree in merchandising in New York City and now works as a manager at a retail store in the mall. Her close friendships with gay men have had a kind of domino effect, leading her to become friends with their gay friends and so on. This is how Vanessa explains her friendships with gay men:

> Gay guys can have a closer relationship with females, I think [than straight men]. We perceive gay guys like your girlfriends. You tell them things that you wouldn't tell your [straight] guy friends. A lot of straight guys I don't think know how to be friends with a female. They just don't know how to have that relationship. It's either you're sleeping with them or not. You just can't have that relationship. They just can't hang out and watch a movie. For a lot of them [straight men]. I'm not saying every single straight guy. I do have straight guy friends, but I think a lot of straight guys can't. And you can have that relationship with a gay guy. You like the same things. You like the same corny movies.

Here Vanessa tells me that her friendships with gay men can often be closer and more intimate than her friendships with straight men, who she thinks more readily want a sexual, not a platonic, relationship.

Vanessa is conventionally feminine, and although she says it is unusual that she does not date at her age, twenty-seven, she says that moving back to New York City and saving money to do that are her goals right now. Since she does not date, as she plans to move soon, Vanessa says that the only way people know that she is straight is through comments she makes about men whom she finds attractive and through her conventional feminine appearance. Further, while she does not avoid or consciously wear anything in particular to indicate her heterosexuality, she assumes that most people think she is straight. Even though she is friends with many gay men and goes on occasion to gay bars with her friend Leonard Bray, she still does not worry about being taken as a lesbian while there. "A lot of people already knew me [at the bar]," she explains, "and they knew that I was just hanging out with Leonard. And nobody tried to hit on me while I was there."

Because of her close friendships with gay men, Vanessa has become well aware of gay men's identity practices, some of their different sexual preferences (e.g., being a top, a bottom, or versatile when it comes to anal sex), and now routinely notes when she interacts with or thinks she sees gay men and lesbians in public places like the retail store where she works.

> Sometimes I can tell. I'm not saying I can always tell. I'm not 100 percent, but I can mostly tell when someone is homosexual . . . I can tell by the way they talk, the way they act. I'm not being judgmental and putting a label on anyone, but I'm a pretty good judge. My closest friend is gay. I know that there are different types. My friend Leonard does act more feminine and he does wear, not like girls' clothes, but he wears tight T-shirts and you can tell. Whereas lesbians, especially when they do dress more mannish and depending on the way they're acting, you can tell that they're lesbians.

Furthermore, she even somewhat seriously questions the heterosexuality of coworkers whose interests make her suspect they might be gay, although one is married and the other is engaged. Her "insider" knowledge of gay life means that she no longer assumes that an outer heterosexual identity indicates an inner heterosexual desire. This is how she explains it to me:

> There are two guys who probably don't know that they're gay. They probably aren't gay, but just their actions. They do act a little bit more feminine. I've worked with them closely. The one guy is always talking about Madonna and just stuff that straight men don't usually talk about or [are] into. It's not necessarily because they're in fashion, but God knows. Just like the stuff, Madonna, different TV shows that they talk about [make them seem possibly gay].

Vanessa's friendships with gay men, then, have made her part of a rich symbolic world of gay and straight identity codes, where gender practices, taste preferences, and social interests indicate a gay or possibly gay identity (Muraco 2012; Nardi 1999). Moreover, within gay subculture, straight women like Vanessa are labeled and readily given roles as "fag hags"—straight women who are open to and supportive of gay men, readily befriending them (Moon 1995; Muraco 2012). While the term "fag hag" is arguably degrading, there exists no popular cultural equivalent label for gay men's friendships with straight men, nor lesbians' friendships with straight women or men. Straight women and gay men, then, have an established social relationship indicated by slang terms like "fag hag," portrayed on TV shows like *Will & Grace*, and increasingly prominent in post-closeted cultural contexts, as indicated by Vanessa's friendships with gay men that situate her *within* and a part of gay male subculture.

This notwithstanding, Vanessa and the other straight women in this group, it is important to note, aimed to maintain a clear straight identity status and its accompanying privilege by embodying conventional femininity, by expressing sexual interest in men, and by not blurring heterosexual/homosexual identity practices, which might possibly mark them as lesbian or bisexual. I acknowledge, of course, that their straight identity status is also simply descriptive of their felt experiences, but these straight women did not want to be viewed as lesbian or bisexual, nor did the majority of them include conscious experiences of same-sex desires, fantasies, or sexual encounters as part of their self-practices. The limit of these straight women's antihomophobic stances is, then, shown by their performances of a clear straight femininity and the socially vested privileges it grants.

The declining significance of compulsory heterosexuality: blurring boundaries, antihomophobias, and sexual fluidity

The distinction between the previous straight feminine practices and the ones in this section is that these heterosexual women consciously permit themselves to be viewed as lesbian or bisexual in some situations. They purposefully blur boundaries between homosexuality and heterosexuality, and it is this key point that constitutes their antihomophobic practices that challenge compulsory heterosexuality. By letting themselves be viewed as homosexual, these women surrender straight privilege and contest the norm of heterosexuality. It is also important to note that women in this group defined religion as of minimal importance to their self-identities; they described themselves as having low levels of religiosity or as nonreligious altogether.

A total of seven out of the twenty-nine women fell into this last group, both claiming experiences of same-sex intimacy and blurring normative heterosexual boundaries in a variety of public contexts in daily life. Four are white and the other three are black. Sexual fluidity among these women seems to be conditioned by their antihomophobic practices. In contrast, the heterosexual women in the previous section did not blur boundaries, nor did they generally report experiences of sexual fluidity or make sexual fluidity part of a queered identification. For example, when I asked Vanessa, "Do you think you ever might have a sexual experience with someone of the same sex?" she said, "I can't say never. At this point in time, no. I'm not attracted to women like that. I want a man." This was the typical kind of response to this question among women in the previous group.

For the following women, in contrast, sexual fluidity practices ranged from fantasies and thoughts about being involved with a woman to having had sexual encounters with women at different times over the course of their lives. The question, then, is how do these women project a straight identity? Importantly, each one of them does come out as straight at different times to express interest in someone or to decline someone's interest in them. Moreover, they identify as heterosexual, not bisexual, which maintains a heterosexual subjectivity for themselves and the significant others in their lives. Further, if they feel uncomfortable, anxious, or fearful when blurring boundaries, then employing conscious gender-conventional practices is a readily available strategy for reemphasizing their straight status and recuperating its privilege, as is disclosing an interest in men by discussing a boyfriend, husband, or male partner.

At this end of the continuum, the sexual identity practices of these heterosexual women blur boundaries of homo/heterosexuality and enact sexually fluid behaviors that both challenge the homo/heterosexual binary division and draw attention to the socially constructed character of the sexual and gender institutional orders, which their micro identity practices aim to render fluid, contested, and in flux.

Driving to a neighboring city from Orangetown to interview Jennifer Dowd, I met a single straight woman who thinks of herself as a liberal and politically minded Irish American. Jennifer enjoys her work but also has her own local radio show, where she brings attention to issues ranging from the environment and immigration to the poor and economically disadvantaged. Previously married, she's now single and in her forties. Raised Catholic, she no longer keeps faith with the Church.

Explaining to me how her interactions with lesbian coworkers have indicated to her that she does not clearly perform a straight femininity, Jennifer tells me that she isn't concerned about being recognized as heterosexual in any number of public contexts. For example, Jennifer's last job was at a chemical company, and as she started to get to know her colleagues, she was approached by two lesbian coworkers, who she intuited might have a romantic, as well as collegial, interest in getting to know her. One of the women, Susan Davis, who was out at work, flirted with Jennifer, inviting her out on a lunch date. Jennifer chose not to "come out" as straight at work to Susan, stating that she did not feel it was appropriate to discuss personal relationships in that context. However, on their lunch date, Jennifer did let Susan know that she wasn't interested in women. Commenting on why she thinks her lesbian coworkers perceived her as lesbian, Jennifer says,

> I don't scream as some straight woman; that's for sure. I always thought just having short hair was perceived as being somewhat gay. The other thing is I think sometimes just being single people think, "Oh, well, maybe," if the person's not married that they're gay. I don't think it's all that clear-cut whether somebody's gay or straight looking. I think some people are more to the type, like a woman who's got very long hair, wears frilly skirts and has long polished fingernails is seen as definitely heterosexual, whereas I have short little stubby fingernails. I'm more of a hippie and I'm not into makeup, which I think is read as gay a lot.

Although Jennifer says that she has not changed her appearance to avoid being viewed as lesbian, her statement illustrates that she recognizes a certain set of gendered practices as codes for lesbianism (i.e., short hair, nonpolished nails, an absence of makeup), and she codes being married, having long hair, wearing makeup, and conventionally feminine clothes as gender identity practices that project a normative straight femininity.

Further, if being perceived as a lesbian meant she had a strong personality as a woman, then Jennifer was fine with that stereotypical association.

> If people thought I was gay in part because I was single or in part because I was sort of a strong personality and because I was fighting a kind of very male structure, [then] that didn't seem like such a bad thing.

Age enters here into Jennifer's performance and self-image, though, as being in her forties makes salient her single status as possibly indicating a lesbian identity; whereas when she was in her twenties, her age might not have been relevant to the question of whether she projected a clear heterosexual status.

If Jennifer sometimes blurs boundaries by associating with lesbian coworkers, Erica Harris goes even further in her everyday life. Erica routinely breaks down boundaries of normative heterosexuality, blurs identity practices of straight femininity, and enacts an active antihomophobic practice in her everyday life.

Erica is a twenty-two-year-old black woman who manages a local restaurant on Main Street in Orangetown. In everyday life, Erica challenges boundaries between gays and straights in two main ways. First, her straight, lesbian, and gay friends and coworkers are integrated into her personal and professional lives. She lives and works in an area called Center City in downtown Orangetown where, like her friends and coworkers, gays and straights interact regularly. Second, in public Erica regularly holds her straight, lesbian, and bisexual female friends' hands and often greets them with a kiss on the lips. She says that she hugs, kisses, and holds the hands of both her male and female friends in public, and she makes no distinction between whether the women are straight, lesbian, or bi.

It is, perhaps, not surprising that Erica openly discusses her own same-sex encounter without a sense of shame. Growing up post-Stonewall and in contexts of LGBTQ cultural visibility seems to have laid the groundwork for her to feel comfortable talking about the encounter without much anxiety.

> I'm the kind of person who's willing to try anything and again try to not box everything into this is the way it is. This is the way it should be. This is the way it's gonna be. I'm able to be malleable, and I'm also somebody who does not view same-sex relationships as wrong. What I did was fine. It's a piece of my life story now.

As well, she says that this experience caused her to rethink her own straight identity and how an identity category reduces the complicated and messy nature of one's experiences. Erica describes sexual identities as fluid, contextual, and dependent on the circumstances one finds oneself in:

> I consider myself heterosexual. Just the same way, like I said before, politically, I consider myself black. But I'm more than that in terms of my ethnic makeup. Just as in sexuality, I'm more than just a straight female. I'm attracted to different things. I don't make myself any promises that I'll never change. I believe that a lot of things are based on the individual person. Give me a woman who does everything right for me and we'll see. This particular woman did not.

Erica's antihomophobia extends beyond blurring sexual identity practices and giving up her heterosexual privilege: her identity practices demonstrate a queering of straight femininity. A queered heterosexual identification contests essentialist and unified conceptions of heterosexuality and replaces them with a fluid, contextual, and dynamic conception of sexualities. Erica's antihomophobic practices are also aimed at changing the worldview of her unenlightened acquaintances and friends. For example, she takes some of her homophobic straight male friends to gay bars to show them that gays are just as diverse, "normal," and often unremarkably ordinary as heterosexuals:

> For example, going to a place like The Pub [a gay bar on Main Street], some friends, if I even bring that up, they're like, "What am I? Fresh meat?" I'm like, "Honey, you're not that cute."

> And I think it's that they are not able to understand that there's not one kind of gay person. Not everybody is going to be threatening to you. That threatening persona, that threatening gay man [who's effeminate and aggressively flirtatious] . . . That's what my friends think they are going to encounter anytime they go into a place that is not completely heterosexual, which is unbelievable to me. So, what do I do? I drag them in there anyway.

In short, Erica attempts to replace her homophobic friends' stereotypical perceptions of gay individuals and spaces with lived interactional experiences, hoping that experiential reality corrects homophobic prejudice.

Sociologists distinguish between the terms "identity" and "identification." Identification is defined as an attachment to a group of people, while identity indicates a central aspect of one's self-definition. This is a useful distinction for understanding individuals like Jennifer and Erica who self-identify as heterosexual but have strong identifications with gay and lesbian friends and the larger gay community they belong to as allies and friends.

Furthermore, each of these straight women not only blurs boundaries of normative heterosexuality but also recognizes straight privilege as part of a culture that aims to value heterosexuality over homosexuality. While each woman will disclose her straight status at various times to signal her interest in men or to decline someone's interest in her, they each practice an antihomophobia that challenges binary sexual identity categories, and in doing so they carve out space for lesbian, gay, bisexual, and queer people and subcultures through their own identity practices.

The continuum and the limits of compulsory heterosexuality

Compulsory heterosexuality remains central to the contemporary social organization of straight women's identity practices, particularly straight women who use homophobic practices based in religious views of homosexuality as a sin, but even pro-gay straight women who subtly maintain straight privilege and naturalize the homo/heterosexual binary enact it as well. The continuum provides insight into how straight women and their recurrent identity practices resist, incorporate, and reconfigure the homophobic and antihomophobic dynamics present in the complicated contexts of post-closeted culture.

On one end, even the most homophobic straight women illustrate a degree of tolerance toward lesbian and gay individuals, and some were even comfortable socializing in lesbian and gay spaces. However, this tolerance belies their homophobic prejudices, which were often based in religious worldviews, but also social ones, that judge homosexual identities as abnormal, gay relationships as inferior, and marriage as the exclusive privilege and legal right of straight women and men. Although their Christian moral beliefs appear genuine, they also seem to feel compelled to offer a legitimizing rationale for their homophobic prejudices, one that would be seen as beyond criticism, and even beyond their own personal choice. Religious beliefs often invoke the discourses of piety and tradition to that effect, aiming to seem as if they are unchangeable and thus beyond criticism. Consequently, these straight women's choices to invoke religious rationales to validate their opinions of homosexual identities and relations as inferior make sense given that religious discourses provide cover and lend authority to one's beliefs.

With the exception of Martha, the other four black straight women did not want to be viewed as entirely unsupportive or intolerant of lesbian and gay identities, relations, and same-sex marriage. Still, four out of five black women cited their Christian faith as their justification for opposing gay identities and rights. Only one of the white women, Beth, invoked her Christian faith in disapproving of gay marriage, while the other two white women and Nia, the remaining black woman, adopted social views of homosexuality as deviant and abnormal to substantiate their homophobic attitudes.

Overall, the eight straight women in this category displayed weaker homophobic practices than the straight males I interviewed (see Dean 2013, 2014). For instance, looking at the cases of the most homophobic straight women respondents, I noted that several of them have socialized in gay bars and dance clubs without a sense of anxiety. This was not the case for the homophobic straight men, who generally would not enter a gay bar, for instance. Unlike the men in my larger study, the straight women respondents did not express a preoccupation with or anxiousness about being potentially perceived as lesbian or bisexual in gay spaces in particular, or more generally in their everyday lives. Generally, even the homophobic straight women exhibited a sense of self that was less defensive about their own styles of dress, bodily comportment, and general appearance being perceived as possibly homosexual in everyday interactions, although there were exceptions to this, as we saw in the case of Nia.

The issue of same-sex relationships and marriages provoked prejudicial responses from all eight straight women in this category. All of these women viewed the idea of same-sex marriage as either violating Christian scripture (Brumbaugh et al. 2008; Finlay and Walther 2003; Fisher et al. 1994; Olson, Cadge, and Harrison 2006) or as socially deviant and thus culturally illegitimate. Their disapprobation of lesbian and gay relationships and same-sex marriages evidences their wish to maintain the exclusivity of these roles, statuses, and institutions as strictly heterosexual privileges. In effect, they do this by imposing a second-class status on lesbian and gay relations and by denying them the civil right to marry. These straight women, then, illustrate their possessive investment in straight identity as the superior sexuality by marking homosexual relations and same-sex marriages as inferior.

Further, I suggest that these women's investment in heterosexual marriage preservation makes sociological sense, due to the social capital straight women accrue by entering into matrimony and motherhood (Bourdieu 2001; Di Leonardo 1987). The social statuses of wife and mother are traditional routes to prestige and power in society, and they remain culturally normative roles and ideals, even when contemporary American society is experiencing marriage deinstitutionalization, with increasing rates of cohabitation and with over a third of all births to unmarried women today (Cherlin 2004).

The middle spectrum of the continuum includes straight women, some strongly religious and others less so, who embrace lesbians and gay men as trusted friends, fellow church members, and valued coworkers. These fourteen straight women's pro-gay practices embrace both the conventional and the unconventional gender expressions of their lesbian and gay friends, workmates, and kin. However, by retaining their straight status and privilege through the avoidance of practices that would make indistinct their straight sexuality, as well as their view of gay and lesbian sexualities as the identity of a fixed minority, these straight women promote lesbian and gay equality while simultaneously naturalizing the homo/heterosexual division.

In the weak boundaries category of the continuum, three of the six black women reported strong Christian faiths, but they did not use their religious beliefs to condemn homosexuality; rather, they sought to embrace lesbian and gay individuals as members of their religious communities and as intimate friends, as did the three white women who defined their religious beliefs and church membership as key parts of their self-identities. In addition, the black straight women on this side of the continuum, regardless of whether they were religious or not, generally drew on their experiences with racism in understanding the homophobic prejudice lesbian women and gay men negotiate in American society.

The seven straight women in the third category, who blur identity practices of homo/heterosexuality and enact sexuality as fluid, challenge gender and sexual institutional orders through their micro-practices, and demonstrate the socially constructed character of the institutional orders as well. Significantly, these straight women document the ability of individuals to variably reconfigure institutional orders through micro-identity practices of sexuality and gender. At various times and places these women's identity performances and antihomophobic stances reject straight privilege, making sexually fluid experiences part of their straight femininities and illustrating the development of queered identifications among some straight women today. They are in part the creators of a post-closeted culture where the discourse and regulatory norm of compulsory heterosexuality is withering in the lives of straight women who consider themselves allies, activists, and members of lesbian, gay, and queer communities today.

References

Alexander, J., 1988. *Durkheimian sociology: cultural studies.* Cambridge: Cambridge University Press.

Bernstein, E., 2007. *Temporarily yours: intimacy, authenticity, and the commerce of sex.* Chicago: University of Chicago Press.

Bettie, J., 2004. *Women without class: girls, race, and identity.* Berkeley: University of California Press.

Bourdieu, P., 2001. *Masculine domination.* Cambridge: Polity.

Brumbaugh, S.M., Sanchez, L.A., Nock, S.L., and Wright, J.D., 2008. Attitudes toward gay marriage in states undergoing marriage law transformation. *Journal of Marriage and Family*, 70(2), 345–359.

Budnick, J., 2016. Straight girls kissing? *Gender & Society*, 30(5), 745–768.

Burawoy, M., et al., 1991. *Ethnography unbound: power and resistance in the modern metropolis.* Berkeley: University of California Press.

Butler, J., 1990. *Gender trouble.* New York: Routledge.

Butler, J., 1992. *Bodies that matter: on the discursive limits of "sex".* London: Routledge.

Charmaz, K., 2007. *Constructing grounded theory.* Los Angeles: Sage.

Cherlin, A.J., 2004. The deinstitutionalization of American marriage. *Journal of Marriage and Family*, 66(4), 848–861.

Chodorow, N., 1978. *The reproduction of mothering: psychoanalysis and the sociology of gender.* Berkeley: University of California Press.

Clark, D., 1993. Commodity lesbianism. In *The lesbian and gay studies reader*, ed. Henry Abelove, Michèle Aina Barale, and David Halperin, pp. 186–201. New York: Routledge.

Dean, J.J., 2013. Heterosexual masculinities, anti-homophobias, and shifts in hegemonic masculinity: the identity practices of black and white heterosexual men. *The Sociological Quarterly*, 54(4), 534–560.

Dean, J.J., 2014. *Straights: heterosexuality in post-closeted culture.* New York: New York University Press.

Di Leonardo, M., 1987. The female world of cards and holidays: women, families, and the work of kinship. *Signs: Journal of Women in Culture and Society*, 12(3), 440–453.

Durkheim, É., (1912) 1995. *The elementary forms of religious life.* New York: Free Press.

Eskridge, W.N., 1999. *Gaylaw: challenging the apartheid of the closet.* London: Harvard University Press.

Finlay, B. and Walther, C.S., 2003. The relation of religious affiliation, service attendance, and other factors to homophobic attitudes among university students. *Review of Religious Research*, 44(4), 370–393.

Fisher, R.D., Derison, D., Polley, C.F., Cadman, J., and Johnston, D., 1994. Religiousness, religious orientation, and attitudes towards gays and lesbians. *Journal of Applied Social Psychology*, 24(7), 614–630.

Foucault, M., 1978. *The history of sexuality.* Vol. 1, *An introduction.* New York: Vintage.

Gallup, G.G., 1995. Have attitudes toward homosexuals been shaped by natural selection? *Ethology and Sociobiology*, 16(1), 53–70.

Gamson, J., 2002. Sweating in the spotlight: lesbian, gay and queer encounters with media and popular culture. In *Handbook of lesbian and gay studies*, ed. Diane Richardson and Steven Seidman, pp. 339–354. Thousand Oaks: Sage.

Ghaziani, A., 2011. Post-gay collective identity construction. *Social Problems*, 58(1), 99–125.

Hamilton, L., 2007. Trading on heterosexuality. *Gender & Society*, 21(2), 145–172.

Hays, S., 1996. *The cultural contradictions of motherhood.* New Haven: Yale University Press.

Herek, G.M., 1988. Heterosexuals' attitudes toward lesbians and gay men: correlates and gender differences. *Journal of Sex Research*, 25(4), 451–477.

Jackson, S., 1999. *Heterosexuality in question.* London: Sage.

Jackson, S., 2006. Interchanges: gender, sexuality and heterosexuality: the complexity (and limits) of heteronormativity. *Feminist Theory*, 7(1), 105–121.

McCall, L., 1992. Does gender fit? Bourdieu, feminism, and conceptions of social order. *Theory and Society*, 21(6), 837–867.

Moon, D., 1995. Insult and inclusion: the term fag hag and gay male community. *Social Forces*, 74(2), 487–510.

Moon, D., 2004. *God, sex, and politics: homosexuality and everyday theologies*. Chicago: University of Chicago Press.

Moore, M.R., 2011. *Invisible families: gay identities, relationships, and motherhood among Black women*. Berkeley: University of California Press.

Muraco, A., 2012. *Odd couples: friendships at the intersection of gender and sexual orientation*. Durham, NC: Duke University Press.

Nardi, P.M., 1999. *Gay men's friendships: invincible communities*. Chicago: University of Chicago Press.

Olson, L.R., Cadge, W., and Harrison, J.T., 2006. Religion and public opinion about same-sex marriage. *Social Science Quarterly*, 87(2), 340–360.

Raeburn, N.C., 2004. *Changing corporate America from inside out: lesbian and gay workplace rights*. Minneapolis: University of Minnesota Press.

Rich, A., (1980) 1993. Compulsory heterosexuality and lesbian existence. In *The lesbian and gay studies reader*, ed. Henry Abelove, Michèle Aina Barale, and David Halperin, pp. 227–254. New York: Routledge.

Richardson, D., 1996. *Theorising heterosexuality: telling it straight*. Buckingham: Open University Press.

Rubin, G., 1984. Thinking sex. In *Pleasure and danger: exploring female sexuality*, ed. Carole Vance, pp. 267–319. Boston: Routledge and Kegan Paul.

Rupp, L.J. and Taylor, V., 2010. Straight girls kissing. *Contexts*, 9(3), 28–32.

Seidman, S., 2002. *Beyond the closet: the transformation of gay and lesbian life*. Florence: Taylor & Francis.

Seidman, S., 2009. Critique of compulsory heterosexuality. *Sexuality Research and Social Policy*, 6(1), 18–28.

Stein, A., 2010. The incredible shrinking lesbian world and other queer conundra. *Sexualities*, 13(1), 21–32.

Walters, S.D., 2001. *All the rage: the story of gay visibility in America*. Chicago: University of Chicago Press.

Weeks, J., 2007. *The world we have won: the remaking of erotic and intimate life*. London: Routledge.

15

"Guys are just homophobic"

Rethinking adolescent homophobia and heterosexuality

C.J. Pascoe

Teenage masculinity

Kevin, a high school student in suburban San Francisco, sits at an IHOP, short of money for dinner. His friend, Craig, agrees to lend him money, but only on the following condition – that Kevin repeat a series of confessional phrases which Craig can videotape and place on YouTube. Kevin buries his head in his hands asking, "You're going to take a video of this and post it on YouTube aren't you?!" Craig ignores Kevin's plea saying, "Anyway, repeat after me. I Kevin James Wong."

Kevin: I, Kevin James Wong.
Craig: 17 years old.
Kevin: (WHO AT THIS POINT STARTS TO GIGGLE EMBARRASSEDLY): 17 years old.
Craig: Senior at Valley High School.
Kevin: Senior at Valley High School.
Craig: In Santa Clarita.
Kevin: In Santa Clarita.
Craig: Am now confessing.
Kevin: Am now confessing.
Craig: That I, Kevin Wong.
Kevin: That I, Kevin Wong.
Craig: Am a homosexual male.
Kevin: Am a homosexual male.

They dissolve into laughter as their friend Jesse jumps into the frame behind Kevin. Craig posted the video on YouTube and eagerly showed it to me as I interviewed him in a local Starbucks. He and his friends giggled as they continued to show me other YouTube videos, one of which featured them imitating men engaging in anal intercourse and then bursting into fits of laughter.

About two years before I watched Craig's video in that Santa Clarita coffee shop I found myself two hours away, at a high school in Riverton, California, where a group of fifth graders had been bussed in for the day to participate in the local high school's performing arts day. As I looked around the outdoor quads decorated with student artwork and filled with choirs singing and bands playing, a student from River High, Brian, ran past me to the rear quad yelling to a group of the elementary school boys. He hollered at them, pointing frantically, "There's a faggot over there! There's a faggot over there! Come look!" The group of boys dashed after Brian as he ran down the hallway, towards the presumed "faggot." Peering down the hallway I saw Brian's friend, Dan, waiting for the boys. As the boys came into his view, Dan pursed his lips and began sashaying towards them. He swung his hips exaggeratedly and wildly waved his arms on the end of which his hands hung from limp wrists. To the boys Brian yelled, referring to Dan, "Look at the faggot! Watch out! He'll get you!" In response, the 10-year-olds screamed in terror and raced back down the hallway. I watched Brian and Dan repeat this drama about the predatory faggot, each time with a new group of young boys.

Kevin, Craig, Brian and Dan enacted similar scenes containing similar messages: men or boys who do not conform to normative understandings of masculinity and sexuality should be mocked, humiliated and possibly feared. I have spent the better part of the last decade interviewing teens about and observing their behavior around definitions of masculinity and sexuality. Across a variety of geographic settings, boys from a range of class and racial/ethnic groups report sentiments much like those expressed by Kevin, Craig, Brian and Dan. Conversations with and observations of these boys indicate that homophobic taunts, jokes, teasing and harassment are central to the ways in which contemporary American boys come to think of themselves as men.

The homophobia articulated by Kevin, Craig, Brian and Dan seems representative of many American youth. Nationally, 93 percent of youth hear homophobic comments at least occasionally and 51 percent on a daily basis (National Mental Health Association 2002). Interestingly, in one state, 80 percent of youth who have been targeted with anti-gay harassment identify as heterosexual (Youth Risk Behavior Survey – Washington 1995). While this harassment is primarily directed at boys, girls suffer from sexualized harassment as well. The American Association of University Women (2001) documents that 83 percent of girls have been sexually harassed at school. These cursory statistics point to an educational experience in adolescence characterized in part by sexualized and gendered aggression directed from boys at other boys *and* at girls.

This type of joking and teasing can have dire consequences. Ninety percent of random school shootings have involved straight-identified boys who have been relentlessly humiliated with homophobic remarks (Kimmel 2003). For instance, Michael Carneal and Andy Williams, both involved in rampage school shootings, had been harassed for being gay (Kimmel 2003; Newman et al. 2004). Michael Carneal's school newspaper actually published a report outing him as gay (though he did not self-identify as such) (Newman et al. 2004). Eric Mohat, a 17-year-old high school student in Ohio who enjoyed theater and playing music, shot himself in 2007 after hearing homophobic taunts. Similarly, Carl Joseph Walker Hoover, an 11-year-old middle school student in Massachusetts, suffered homophobic harassment from his classmates for performing well academically. He hung himself as a desperate response to the teasing. Lawrence King, having been bullied relentlessly since third grade for his non-traditional gender presentation, was shot and killed by a fellow student in 2008 whom he had asked to be his Valentine.

While certainly the sort of joking and minor humiliation exhibited in the two opening stories does not match the level of violence in these examples, a problematic intersection of gender and sexuality undergirds all of them. Practices that seem to reflect basic homophobia – imitating same-sex eroticism, calling someone queer or mincing about with limp wrists – are also about policing gendered identities and practices. Through making homophobic jokes, calling other boys gay and imitating effeminate men, boys attempt to assure themselves and others of their masculinity. For contemporary American boys, the definition of masculinity entails displaying power, competence, a lack of emotions, heterosexuality and dominance. Says Kevin, for instance, to be masculine is to be "tough." The ideal man is "strong" and he "can't be too emotional" adds Erik. Maleness does not confer masculinity upon a given boy. Rather masculinity is the repeated signaling to self and others that one is powerful, competent, unemotional, heterosexual and dominant.

This signaling appears in two ways, through practices of repudiation and confirmation. Repudiatory practices take the form of a "fag discourse," consisting of homophobic jokes, taunts, and imitations through which boys publicly signal their rejection of that which is considered unmasculine. Boys confirm masculine selves through public enactments of compulsive heterosexuality which include practices of "getting girls," physically confining girls under the guise of flirtation and sex talk. For many contemporary American boys masculinity must be repeatedly proven, as one's identity as masculine is never fully secured. This essay unpacks adolescent boys' public enactments of homophobia and heterosexuality, examining them as sexualized as well as gendered processes which have ramifications for all teenagers – male, female, straight and gay.

The fag discourse

Boys repeatedly tell me that "fag" was the ultimate insult for a boy. Darnell stated, "Since you were little boys you've been told, 'hey, don't be a little faggot.'" Jeremy emphasized that this insult literally reduced a boy to nothing, "To call someone gay or fag is like the lowest thing you can call someone. Because that's like saying that you're nothing." Indeed, much like the boys terrorized by Brian and Craig, boys often learn long before adolescence that a "fag" is the worst thing a guy could be. Thus boys' daily lives often consist of interactions in which they frantically lob these epithets at one another and try to deflect them from themselves.

Many boys explained their frequent use of insults like queer, gay and fag by asserting that, as Keith put it, "guys are just homophobic." However, analyzing boys' homophobic practices as a "fag discourse" shows that their behavior reflects not just a fear of same-sex desire, but a specific fear of *men's* same-sex desire. Many told me that homophobic insults applied primarily to boys, not to girls. While Jake told me that he didn't like gay people, he quickly added, "Lesbians, okay, that's good!" Now lesbians are not "good" because of some enlightened approach to sexuality, but because, as Ray said, "To see two hot chicks banging bodies in a bed, that's like every guy's fantasy right there. It's the truth. I've heard it so many times." So their support of lesbians is more about heterosexual fantasy than about a progressive attitude (Jenefsky and Miller 1998).

Furthermore, several boys argued that fag, queer and gay had little to do with actual sexual practices or desires. Darnell told me, "It doesn't have anything to do with being gay." Adding to this sentiment, J. L. said, "Fag, seriously, it has nothing to do with sexual preference at all. You could just be calling somebody an idiot, you know?" As David explained, "Being gay is just a lifestyle. It's someone you choose to sleep with. You can still throw a football around and be gay." David's final statement clarifies the distinction between popular understandings of these insults and teens' actual use of them. That is, that they have to do with men's same-sex eroticism, but at their core discipline gendered practices and identities (such as the ability, or lack thereof, to throw a football). In asserting the primacy of gender to the definition of these seemingly homophobic insults, boys reflect what Riki Wilchins (2003) calls the Eminem Exception, in which Eminem explains that he doesn't call people "faggot" because of their sexual orientation, but because they are weak and unmanly. While it is not necessarily acceptable to be gay, if a man were gay *and* masculine, as in David's portrait of the football-throwing gay man, he does not deserve the insult.

What renders a boy vulnerable to homophobic epithets often depends on local definitions of masculinity. Boys frequently cited exhibiting stupidity, femininity, incompetence, emotionality or same-sex physicality as notoriously non-masculine practices. Chad, for instance, said that boys might be called a fag if they seemed "too happy or something" while another boy expounded on the dangers of being "too smiley." Ironically, these insults are pitched at boys who engage in seemingly heterosexual activities. Kevin, when describing his ideal girlfriend said, "I have to imagine myself singing, like serenading her. Okay, say we got in a fight and we broke up. I have to imagine myself as a make-up gift to her singing to her out of her window." Kevin laughed as he said that when he shares this scenario with his friends "the guys are like, 'dude you're gay!'"

Because so many activities could render a boy vulnerable to these insults, perhaps it is little surprise that Ben asserted that one could be labeled for "anything, literally anything. Like you were trying to turn a wrench the wrong way, 'dude you're a fag.' Even if a piece of meat drops out of your sandwich, 'you fag'" While my research shows that there are particular set of behaviors that could get a boy called the slur, it is no wonder that Ben felt a boy could be called it for "anything." In that statement he reveals the intensity and extent of the policing boys must do of their behaviors in order to avoid the epithet.

The sort of homophobic harassment detailed above has as much to do with definitions of masculinity as it does with actual fear of other gay men (Corbett 2001; Kimmel 2001). Being subject to homophobic harassment has as much to do with failing at masculine tasks of competence, heterosexual prowess or in any way revealing weakness as it does with a sexual identity. Homophobic epithets such as fag have gender meanings *and* sexual meanings. The insult is levied against boys who are not masculine, even momentarily, and boys who identify (or are identified by others) as gay. This sets up a very complicated daily ordeal in which boys continually strive to avoid being subject to the epithet, but are simultaneously constantly vulnerable to it.

This sort of homophobia appears frequently in boys' joking relationships. Sociologists have pointed out that joking is central to men's relationships in general (Kehily and Nayak 1997; Lyman 1998). Through aggressive joking boys cement friendship bonds with one another. Boys often draw laughs through imitating effeminate men or men's same-sex desire. Emir frequently imitated effeminate men who presumably sexually desired other men to draw laughs from students in his introductory drama class. One day his teacher, disturbed by noise outside the classroom, turned to close the door saying, "We'll shut this unless anyone really wants to watch sweaty boys playing basketball." Emir lisped, "I wanna watch the boys play!" The rest of the class cracked up at his imitation. No one in the class actually thought Emir was gay, as he purposefully mocked both same-sex sexual desire and an effeminate gender identity. This sort of ritual reminded other youth that masculine men didn't desire other men, nor did they lisp or behave in other feminine manners. It also reminded them that men who behaved in these ways were worthy of laughter and derision.

These everyday joking interchanges, however, were more than "just jokes." For some boys, such as Lawrence King, the intolerance for gender differences espoused by these joking rituals has serious, if not deadly, consequences. Ray and Peter underscore this in their conversation. Ray asserted "I can't stand fags. Like I've met a couple. I don't know. The way they rub you. Gay people I don't care. They do their thing in their bedroom and that's fine. Feminine guys bother me." Peter, his friend, continued "If they try to get up on you. I'll kill you." Ray and Peter illuminated the teenage boys' different responses to gay and effeminate men as Ray espouses tolerance for the presumably gender normative former and Peter threatens violence against the latter. In this sense the discourse runs a continuum from joking to quite violent harassment. While boys said that the "fag" insult was more about failing at masculinity, than about actually being gay, it seemed that a gay and unmasculine boy suffered the most under this "gender regime" (Connell 1987).

As a talented dancer who frequently sported multicolored hair extensions, mascara and wore baggy pants, fitted tank tops and sometimes a skirt, Ricky violated norms of gender *and* sexuality. He told me that harassment started early, in elementary school. "I'm talking like sixth grade,

I started being called a fag. Fifth grade I was called a fag. Third grade I was called a fag." Though he moved schools every two years or so, this sort of harassment continued and intensified as he moved into high school. At his school's homecoming game (for which Ricky had choreographed the half time show) he was harassed until he left after hearing things like "there's that fucking fag" and "What the fuck is that fag doing here? That fag has no right to be here." When watching him dance with the school's all female dance team other boys reacted in revulsion. Nils said, "It's like a car wreck, you just can't look away." J. R., the captain of the football team, shook his head and muttered under his breath, "That guy dancing, it's just disgusting. Disgusting!" shaking his head and stomping off. Even though dancing is the most important thing in his life, Ricky didn't attend school dances because he didn't like to "watch my back" the whole time. He had good reason for this fear. Brad said of the prom, "I heard Ricky is going in a skirt, it's a hella short one." Sean responded with "I wouldn't even go if he's there." Topping Sean's response Brad claimed, "I'd probably beat him up outside."

The harassment suffered by Ricky featured none of the joking or laughter exhibited in other interchanges. Very real threats of violence undergirded boys' comments about him. Ricky told me that he walked with his eyes downcast in order to avoid guys' eye contact, fearing that they'd see such eye contact as a challenge. Similarly he varied his route home from school each day and carried a rock in his hand to protect himself. For many boys, in order to maintain a sense of themselves as masculine, they felt they had to directly attack Ricky, a symbol of what they feared most, of unmasculine nothingness.

Compulsive heterosexuality

If daily life for many boys entails running a gauntlet of homophobic insults, how do they avoid being permanently labeled as Ricky was? Boys defend against homophobic teasing and harassment by assuring others of their heterosexuality. By engaging in a number of cross-gender rituals, a boy can relatively successfully defend himself against ending up in Ricky's position, the object of harassment, derision and violence. In the same way that boys' homophobia is not specifically about a sexual identity, compulsive heterosexuality[1] is not only about expressing love, desire and intimacy, but about showing a sexualized dominance over girls' bodies. The sort of gendered teasing in which boys engage takes a toll on girls as well as other boys. In my research I found three components of compulsive heterosexuality: rituals of getting girls, rituals of touch, and sex talk.

Perhaps the most obvious example of "getting girls" is having a girlfriend. Having a girlfriend seems a normal teen behavior. For boys who are identified as feminine and teased for unmasculine practices, having a girlfriend functions as some sort of protection against homophobic harassment. Justin told me that some boys have girlfriends "so they look like they're not losers or they're not gay." David told me that a lot of the kids at his high school think that he is gay because of his preppy clothing choices and his lisp such that for him "it's better to have a girlfriend . . . because people think I'm gay. I get that all the time." In order to defend against teasing and harassment boys like David need to establish a sort of baseline heterosexuality by proving they can "get a girl." Because of the difficulty in avoiding all of the behaviors that might render one vulnerable to teasing, having a girlfriend helps to inure one to accusations of the "fag discourse."

Similarly, cross-gender touching rituals establish a given boy's heterosexuality. These physical interchanges may first appear as harmless flirtation, but upon closer inspection actually reinforce boys' dominance over girls' bodies. The use of touch maintains a social hierarchy (Henley 1977). Superiors touch subordinates, invade their space and interrupt them in a way subordinates do not do to superiors and these superior–inferior relationships are often gendered ones. Boys and girls often touch each other as part of daily interaction, communication and flirtation. In many instances cross-sex touching was lightly flirtatious and reciprocal. But these touching rituals ranged from playful flirtations to assault-like interactions. Boys might physically constrain girls under the guise of flirtation. One time in a school hallway a boy wrapped his arms around a girl and started to "freak" her, or grind his pelvis into hers as she struggled to get away. This sort of behavior happened more often in primarily male spaces. One day for instance, in a school weight room, Monte wrapped his arms around a girl's neck as if to put her in a headlock and held her there while Reggie punched her in the stomach, albeit lightly, and she squealed. A more dramatic example of this was during a passing period in which Keith rhythmically jabbed a girl in the crotch with his drumstick, while he yelled "Get raped!" These examples show how the constraint and touching of female bodies gets translated as masculinity, embedding sexualized meanings in which heterosexual flirting is coded as female helplessness and male bodily dominance.

While people jokingly refer to boys' sex talk as "boys will be boys" or "locker room" talk, this sex talk plays a serious role in defending against acquiring an identity like Ricky's. Boys enact and naturalize their heterosexuality by asserting "guys are horndogs" or by claiming that it is "kind of impossible for a guy" to not "think of sex every two minutes" as Chad does. Thinking about boys' sexual performance in terms of compulsive heterosexuality shows that asserting that one is a horndog and cannot help but think about sex is actually a gendered performance. Boys' sex talk often takes the form of "mythic story telling" in which they tell larger than life tales about their sexual adventures, their bodies and girls' bodies that do not reflect love, desire or sensuality, but rather dominance over girls' bodies. Pedro, for instance, laughed and acted out having sex with his girlfriend by leaning back up against the wall, legs and arms spread and head turning back and forth as he continued to say proudly "I did her so hard when I was done she was bleeding. I tore her walls!" The boys surrounding him cheered and oohed and aahed in amazement. Violence frequently frames these stories. Much like the touching rituals in which boys establish dominance over girls' bodies, these stories show what boys can make girls bodies do. Rich, after finishing lifting weights in his school's weight room, sat on a weight bench and five boys gathered around him as he told a story, after much urging, about sex with his now ex-girlfriend. He explained that they were having sex and "she said it started to hurt. I said we can stop and she said no. Then she said it again and she started crying. I told her to get off! Told her to get off! Finally I took her off," making a motion like he was lifting her off of him. He continued, "There was blood all over me! Blood all over her! Popped her wall! She had to have stitches." Boys start cracking up and moaning. Not to be outdone, other boys in the circle begin to chime in about their sexual exploits. Even those who don't have stories about themselves, asserted their knowledge of sex through vicarious experiences. Troy joined the discussion with a story about his brother, a professional basketball player for a nearby city. He "brought home a 24 year old drunk chick! She *farted* the whole time they were doing it in the other room! It was *hella* gross!" All the boys crack up again. Adam, not to be outdone, claimed "My friend had sex with a drunk chick. He did her in the butt! She s*** all over the place!" The boys all crack up again and yell out things like "Hella gross!" or "That's disgusting!" These graphic, quite violent stories detail what boys can make girls bodies do – rip, bleed, fart and poop.

To understand the role of sexuality in maintaining gender inequality it is important to look at sexuality, and specifically heterosexuality, not as a set of desires, identities or dispositions, but as an institution. Adrienne Rich (1986) does this when she argues that heterosexuality is an institution that systematically disempowers women. Similarly, compulsive heterosexuality is a set of practices through which boys reinforce linkages between sexuality, dominance and violence. This heterosexuality is a defensive heterosexuality, not necessarily a reflection of an internal set of emotions.

Conclusion

Many boys' school-based lives involve running a daily gauntlet of sexualized insults, as they simultaneously try to lob homophobic epithets at others and defend themselves from said epithets. In this sense masculinity becomes the daily interactional work of repudiating the labels of fag, queer or gay. Unpacking the definition of what appears to be homophobia clarifies the gender policing at the heart of boys' harassment of one another and of girls. Homophobic epithets may or may not have explicitly sexual meanings, but they always have gendered meanings. Many boys are clearly terrified of being permanently labeled as gay, fag or queer, since to them such a label effectively negates their humanness. As a part of boys' defensive strategy, girls' bodies become masculinity resources deployed in order to stave off these labels.

The practices of compulsive heterosexuality indicate that control over girls' bodies and their sexuality is central to definitions of adolescent masculinity. If masculinity is, as boys told me, about competence, heterosexuality, being unemotional, and dominance, then girls' bodies provide boys the opportunity to ward off the fag discourse by demonstrating mastery and control over them. Engaging in compulsive heterosexuality also allows boys to display a lack of emotions by refusing to engage the empathy that might mitigate against such a use of girls and their bodies. It is important to note that many of these boys are not unrepentant sexists or homophobes. In private and in one-on-one conversations, many spoke of sexual equality and of tender feelings for girls. For the most part these were social behaviors that boys engaged in when around other boys, precisely because they are less reflections of internal homophobic and sexist dispositions and more about constituting a masculine identity, something that is accomplished interactionally.

This gendered homophobia, as well as sexualized and gendered defenses against it, comprises contemporary adolescent masculinity. Fear of any sort of same-sex intimacy (platonic or not) polices boys' friendships with one another. The need to repudiate that which is not considered masculine leads to a very public renunciation of same-sex desire. Heterosexual flirtation becomes entwined with gendered dominance. What this means is that the public face of adolescent sexuality is rife with reproduction of gender inequality, through processes of the fag discourse and compulsive heterosexuality.

Note

1 This concept draws upon Adrienne Rich's (1986) influential concept of "compulsory heterosexuality" as well as Michael Kimmel's (1987) notion of "compulsive masculinity."

References

A.A.U.W. 2001. *Hostile Hallways*. Washington, DC: American Association of University Women.

Connell, R. W. 1987. *Gender and Power*. Stanford, CA: Stanford University Press.

Corbett, Ken. 2001. "Faggot = Loser." *Studies in Gender and Sexuality* 2(1): 3–28.

Henley, Nancy. 1977. *Body Politics: Power, Sex, and Nonverbal Communication*. Englewood Cliffs, NJ: Prentice-Hall.

Jenefsky, Cindy and Diane H. Miller. 1998. "Phallic Intrusion: Girl-Girl Sex in Penthouse." *Women's Studies International Forum* 21(4): 375–85.

Kehily, Mary J. and Anoop Nayak. 1997. "'Lads and Laughter': Humour and the Production of Heterosexual Masculinities." *Gender and Education* 9(1): 69–87.

Kimmel, Michael. 2001. "Masculinity as Homophobia: Fear, Shame, and Silence in the Construction of Gender Identity." Pp. 266–87 in *The Masculinities Reader*, ed. S. Whitehead and F. Barrett. Cambridge: Polity Press.

——. 1987. "The Cult of Masculinity: American Social Character and the Legacy of the Cowboy." Pp. 235–49 in *Beyond Patriarchy: Essays by Men on Pleasure, Power and Change*, ed. M. Kaufman. New York: Oxford University Press.

Kimmel, Michael S. 2003. "Adolescent Masculinity, Homophobia, and Violence: Random School Shootings, 1982–2001." *American Behavioral Scientist* 46(10): 1439–58.

Lyman, Peter. 1998. "The Fraternal Bond as a Joking Relationship: A Case Study of the Role of Sexist Jokes in Male Group Bonding." Pp. 171–93 in *Men's Lives*, Fourth ed., ed. M. Kimmel and M. Messner. Boston, MA: Allyn and Bacon.

National Mental Health Association. 2002. *What Does Gay Mean? Teen Survey Executive Summary.*

Newman, Katherine, Cybelle Fox, David J. L. Harding, Jal Mehta and Wendy Roth. 2004. *Rampage: The Social Roots of School Shootings.* New York: Basic Books.

Rich, Adrienne. 1986. "Compulsory Heterosexuality and Lesbian Existence." Pp. 23–74 in *Blood, Bread and Poetry.* New York: W.W. Norton.

Wilchins, Riki. 2003. "Do You Believe in Fairies?" *The Advocate*, February 4, p. 72.

Youth Risk Behavior Survey – Washington. 1995. Washington, DC: NYRBS.

16

"Sprinkle some gay on my straight"

Hybrid hegemonic masculinities in a post-gay era

Tristan Bridges and Kendall Ota

> People always think I'm gay . . . always! . . . They see what I wear and . . . and they see how I talk . . . I always tell people that I . . . come out as straight every time I meet someone . . . I mean, I was in the closet and I didn't even know it . . . [Pursing his lips] I like to sprinkle some gay on my straight.
>
> *(Peter, 22, Guys for Gender Justice)*

Peter is a young, straight, white man still living at home. He is a "part-time environmentalist and feminist," but his father is quick to respond, "It's not a job if you don't get paid, Pete." Peter is a member of a pro-feminist group of men Tristan studied and, like those in two other groups of straight men in this study, Peter talked about some aspects of his gender performance as "gay," though he identifies as straight.

When pressed about his sexuality in front of friends, Peter will say things like, "I'm straight. Like I'm only sexually attracted to women. And I'm *really* sexually attracted to women. But I'm like a gay straight . . . like a straight-lite." And Peter is not alone. Tristan met straight, white men with very different gender and sexual politics who liked to describe aspects of themselves as "gay." This paradoxical practice produced a consequence we describe in detail in this chapter: it shores up their masculine identities as *hetero*sexual. This is surprising, in part, because a great deal of theory and scholarship has discussed homophobia and sexual prejudice as integral components of masculine identity. While this practice appears to challenge this relationship, we argue that this relationship is better understood here as reconfigured.

Little scholarship examines queer practices and performances among heterosexuals (e.g., Schippers 2000). We examine what motivates such practices, what they mean, how they are intended, and what kinds of consequences they have. Here, we explore the ways straight men make use of gay culture and "gay aesthetics" (Bridges 2014) to authenticate and accessorize their heteromasculine identities and obscure their relationship with power and inequality. To do this, we need to understand sexuality as both a *sexual* and *cultural* category (e.g., Halperin 2012; Ward 2008, 2015), building on "hybrid masculinity" to make sense of these practices and their meanings (e.g., Bridges 2014; Bridges and Pascoe 2014, 2018; Pascoe and Bridges 2017).

Gendered homophobia and the challenge of measuring change

Raewyn Connell first defined hegemonic masculinity as a cultural ideal that sustains or legitimizes men's dominance over women and *some* men (Connell 1987, 1995; Connell and Messerschmidt 2005). Hegemonic masculinity achieves this position by being situated against other configurations of gender practice. Connell (1987, 1992, 1995) argues that gay men have long occupied a foil against which "masculine" identity is constructed. Indeed, masculinity has a long-standing relationship with homophobia. Since "gay" emerged as a sexual identity, masculinity has been linked to establishing distance from it (Connell 1992; Mosse 1996; Chauncey 1994; Ibson 2002, 2018). Yet, Peter and other men in this study appear to call this relationship into question.

Indeed, men's sexual prejudice has shifted a great deal in very recent history. While high levels of anti-gay prejudice among men were among the early empirical examples (e.g., Kite 1984; Herek 1986) that gave rise to the modern theories of homophobia as connected with masculinity (e.g., Lehne 1976; Connell 1987, 1992, 1995; Kimmel 1994; Corbett 2001; Pascoe 2007), more recent surveys indicate radically lower levels of sexual prejudice among men.

Some scholars suggest that homophobia has become much less attached to masculinity. Anderson (2009) argues, for instance, that the masculinities practiced by young men today are more "inclusive"—less hierarchical and homophobic (see also McCormack 2012). The behavior and comments from Peter shared at the beginning of this chapter could support this conclusion. Yet, scholarship examining the meanings, extent, and consequences of what appears to be a transformation in the relationship between masculinity and homophobia has also come to different conclusions.[1] To make sense of this apparent paradox, we summarize theory and scholarship on "hybrid masculinity" (Bridges 2014; Bridges and Pascoe 2014, 2018) and introduce the concept hybrid *hegemonic* masculinity.

Hybrid hegemonic masculinities

Hybrid masculinities broadly refer to those gender projects that selectively incorporate elements of gender culturally associated with various "Others" (Demetriou 2001; Bridges and Pascoe 2014). Men occupying identities with concentrated collections of privilege (young, straight, educated, white, cisgender) are not the *only* people mobilizing "hybrid" configurations of masculinity, but the hybrid masculine practices associated with *this* group are distinct. As such, we refer to those hybrid masculine practices as configurations of *hybrid hegemonic masculinity.*

Since the article upon which this chapter is based was first published (Bridges 2014), the theorization of hybrid masculinity has further developed (e.g., Bridges and Pascoe 2014, 2018; Pascoe and Bridges 2017). Collectively, this work examines gender practices that blur various forms of social difference yet leave social dominance unquestioned. Scholarship on hybrid hegemonic masculinities supports the notion that they work to legitimate patriarchy and other forms of power and inequality while obscuring this process as it takes place (Bridges and Pascoe 2014, 2018; Connell and Messerschmidt 2005).

The adoption of identity practices deemed "soft," "feminine," "gay," and more appears to be widespread or recognized among men in socially dominant groups (e.g., Messerschmidt and Messner 2018). Messner (1993) first analyzed this dynamic in the 1990s, arguing that the shifts were "more style than substance." And, following Bridges (2014) and Bridges and Pascoe (2014, 2018; see also Pascoe and Bridges 2017), scholars have built on this framework to examine the motivations, meanings, and consequences associated with identity projects that work to recuperate power and privilege whilst appearing to challenge them.

For instance, Aboim (2010) found that Portuguese heterosexual men were more involved in domestic labor than previous generations, but that they also adopted discourses framing men as "better" than women at "feminine" tasks around the house. Rather than challenging inequality, Aboim (2010) argues they are "reinventing" gender hegemony. Groes-Green (2012) comes to a similar conclusion among heterosexual men in Mozambique. Similarly, Jóhannsdóttir and Gíslason (2018) examine how broad cultural orientations toward gender and sexual equality in Iceland exist comfortably alongside "lingering" forms of gender and sexual prejudice. And Young's (2017) ethnographic study of men participating in Hawaiian cock-fighting communities shows these men who practice femininities in ways that work to reproduce gender inequality.

Pfaffendorf (2017) uncovered the construction of a hybrid hegemonic masculinity within a therapeutic boarding school for elite boys. McDowell (2017) discovered that Christian hardcore punk music fans cultivate "softer" forms of masculinity that shore up gender hegemony—something scholars examining evangelical Christians in the United States have found in other arenas of social life (e.g., Donovan 1998; Heath 2015; Gerber 2014; Diefendorf 2015). In another arena, scholars have addressed straight men's adoption of gender egalitarian discourse in ways that promote less change than their discourses suggest (e.g., Lamont 2015; Elliot 2019).

Scholarship examining hybrid hegemonic masculinities has uncovered significant transformations in the *expression* of structures and systems of power and inequality (e.g., Messner 1993, 2007; Demetriou 2001; Arxer 2011; Bridges 2014; Messerschmidt 2010, 2018; Barry 2018). This work supports an emergent body of scholarship on what is sometimes referred to as "modern" prejudice—those new forms of inequality that are less easily captured by traditional measures. For instance, Doan, Loehr, and Miller (2014) discovered that while attitudes toward gay rights have liberalized in the "post-gay" era, heterosexual privilege and sexual inequality are also maintained in more subtle forms. Similarly, Brodyn and Ghaziani (2018) identify practices they call "performative progressiveness" to describe the "misalignment" between progressive *attitudes* and *actions*. And Sumerau and Grollman (2018) describe similar discursive tactics as "obscuring oppression" (see also Pascoe and Hollander 2015).

We now turn to examining how the shifting practices associated with homophobia among men and emergent practices that seem to challenge the relationship between homophobia and masculinity can be understood as *hybrid* configurations of hegemonic masculinity that simultaneously *obscure* and *secure* power and inequality.

Data/methods

Three separate groups of men were studied ethnographically over the course of two years. Each was selected for variation in gender-political affiliation (anti- to pro-feminist) and level of reflexivity surrounding gender/sexual inequality. The groups vary along both axes: fathers' rights activists, pro-feminist activists, and a group without gender-political affiliation—bar regulars. Most of the men in this study are white (56 of 63) and 61 of 63 identify as heterosexual.

Men Can Parent Too[2] is a fathers' rights activist organization helping fathers navigate divorce and custody proceedings and organizing to actively protest what they see as gender inequality in those proceedings. Talking to these men about gender inequality is easy. If you ask about what it looks like, they offer answers similar to Chris, a 38-year-old journalist who has limited access to seeing his children from a previous marriage: "Gender inequality is such a load of shit. Women complain more and we live in a goddamned society that rewards complainers."

Guys for Gender Justice is a pro-feminist group who meet to discuss gender and sexual inequality, raise money and volunteer for non-profit feminist organizations, and engage in various gender and sexual violence prevention work with boys and young men. These men are passionate about gender and sexual inequality. As one member, Seth, said, "It's a privilege to not have to think about gender inequality because you're basically on the quote-unquote *right* side in that you benefit from it."

The Border Boys are a group of bar regulars. Their "meetings" are less structured and organized than the other groups, but they meet at least as frequently. As a group, they think far less about gender and inequality, though gender, sexuality, and inequality are regular topics of conversation when they get together. When asked about gender inequality, men in this group were likely to say things like Travis, a 31-year-old manager at a gas station, did: "It's like . . . I'm not saying gender inequality is not *an* issue. I'm just sort of saying it's not *my* issue."

The pattern of identification we address in this chapter (straight men's reliance upon and use of gay aesthetics) was not observed among every member of each group. Rather, this practice was performed by some men in each group. Thus, this chapter is principally concerned with the further grounded theorization of "hybrid hegemonic masculinities" to examine the motivations behind and consequences associated with straight men's use of gay aesthetics to bolster their *heterosexual* masculine identities.

Straight men's use of "gay aesthetics"

The aesthetic elements of sexualities are those performative and symbolic aspects that coalesce around specific sexual collectivities and give rise to distinctive sexual cultures (Ghaziani 2017). Bridges defines "sexual aesthetics" as the "cultural and stylistic distinctions utilized to delineate symbolic boundaries between gay and straight cultures and individuals" (Bridges 2014: 62; see also Halperin 2012). But, sexual aesthetics are best identified by *how they are used* rather than from what they are composed as they do *not* refer to the universal components of gay identity and culture. Rather, gay aesthetics are used in ways that suggest universal elements of gay identity and culture. Thus, when Matt (a Border Boy), told his friends, "I can tell a dude's gay by the way he walks," he implied a set of criteria he uses to assess gay men's sexuality. Analyzing gay aesthetics does not depend on Matt's criteria being accurate; what matters is that he believes they are. This means that we can think of gay culture as something analytically distinct from collections of gay individuals (Halperin 2012).

Men in each of the three groups had different understandings of what comprised gay aesthetics. Indeed, sexual aesthetics differ by groups and individuals and over time. For example, in Pascoe's (2007) study of masculinity and sexuality in high school, she found that specific behaviors were understood as "gay" when enacted by white boys, but not black boys, like dancing and a concern with clothing and appearance. Despite variation in what qualified as gay aesthetics, men in each group relied on them in similar ways—suggesting universal elements of sexual identity and culture.

For instance, at a group meeting of Guys for Gender Justice, conversations about having been "mistaken for gay" were a common topic of conversation. At one meeting, Shane jokingly shared about how he responds to his apparent illegibility as heterosexual:

> People sometimes think I'm gay . . . I take it as an opportunity to help gay people . . . I'll usually say something like, "Because I'm stylish? Or because I'm nice to people? . . . What? Because I'm healthy and care about my clothes and the way I look?" You know? Like, "Oh, because I have good taste in music?"

Shane was joking. He describes resisting heterosexism by strategically reframing the implications of being thought to be gay. Rather than being insulted, Shane claims to perform a "post-gay" discursive maneuver whereby he situates the comment as complimentary. While intending to neutralize difference, Shane is simultaneously reinforcing the boundaries separating "gay" and "straight" by (re)classifying a collection of behaviors and tastes as "gay" in ways that situate him as both *different from* and *better than* "most men." Thus, in addition to resisting heterosexism, Shane's comments also work to distinguish him from other men as politically progressive—authenticating his feminist politics.

Men in each of the three groups engaged in similar uses of gay aesthetics toward different ends. Though their gender politics and levels of reflexivity surrounding gender and sexual inequality differ, each subjectively identified aspects of their performance of masculinity as "gay" in ways that discursively distinguish them from other men. Below, we describe the different evidence men in each group relied upon to frame themselves as "gay." Subsequently, we describe how these findings offer a powerful illustration of hybrid hegemonic masculinity in practice.

What qualifies as "gay"?

One of the Border Boys, Richard, opened up about how emotionally available he is and that this is an important element of his own understanding of masculinity. "I'm emotional, man. I cry at movies. I cry when my friends hurt my feelings . . ." He continued: "I'm not your average man . . . all masculine and all that . . . And if that makes me gay, then fuck it, I'm gay." Then he paused and added, "But, of course, I'm not *gaaaay*." When asked to explain, Richard delineated his understanding of gay aesthetics:

> Well . . . it's gay if you [cocks his wrists] . . . if you're all pansy . . . It's gay to talk like *this* [affects his voice]. But it's also gay if you're, like into how you look too much . . . It's gay if you're all emotional . . . like if you cry . . . or even if you care too much about your friends . . . It's gay to read or . . . like, if you like *novels* [affecting his voice] rather than books . . . It's gay to be into gay rights . . . or even women's rights. That's totally gay!

As Richard explains the types of things that might label men "gay," he unpacks some of the elements that make up sexual aesthetics. He identifies elements associated with specific *tastes* (concern with appearance, interest in specific kinds of literature and culture), *behaviors* (bodily comportment and styles of speech), and *ideologies* (support for specific causes or issues). And while Richard identifies these three elements, he and the other Border Boys only relied on two when they talked about themselves as "gay." In fact, each group relied on a different number of these elements when they invoked gay aesthetics, and tastes were the most common (see Table 16.1). Below, we briefly explore these different aesthetic elements.

Table 16.1 Elements of gay aesthetics used by group

	Tastes	*Behaviors*	*Ideologies*
Men Can Parent Too	✓		
The Border Boys	✓	✓	
Guys for Gender Justice	✓	✓	✓

"Gay" tastes

As with Richard's subjective assessment of his literary tastes as "gay," straight men in each of the groups identified some of their tastes as "gay." Nathan, a paving contractor in Men Can Parent Too, shared:

> I have always been the kinda' guy who is just really into some girly kind of stuff. Having daughters was like . . . I mean, I don't want to call it gay, but doing that kind of girly kind of thing . . . I'm fine with that . . . playing dress-up or playing house or like rocking out to girly music . . . I'm that kind of dad . . . [My ex] used to tease me . . . like, "Honey, are you *gay*?" (laughs).

Another member of Men Can Parent Too, Ralph, expressed a similar sentiment after telling me that the other men he works with as a security guard "are just not the same kinda' guy as me." He shared,

> All of 'em . . . want action . . . I'm just trying to be a dad and make a paycheck . . . I actually am not all into this action . . . I don't drink beer . . . I really don't like it. I mainly drink wine. But, I'm gay like that and it doesn't bug me.

When pressed to explain, Ralph continued: "Oh, no . . . no no no. I'm not a fag or something like that. I just mean I'm into kinda' gay stuff like that, you know?"

Here, Ralph and Nathan's subjective identification of some of their tastes as "gay" also involves a strategic reassertion of their straight identities. These two examples help illustrate how straight men can discursively rely on gay aesthetics in ways that bolster their *heterosexual* identities. These men's reliance upon gay aesthetics enables them to discursively distance themselves from stereotypes of masculinity that have sustained feminist critique. This tactic is not necessarily indicative of a weakening relationship between masculinity and homophobia but, rather, is an illustration of hybrid hegemonic masculinity that shores up and legitimates gender and sexual inequalities in historically new ways (e.g., Demetriou 2001; Bridges and Pascoe 2014, 2018).

This gender maneuver enables each to engage in what Bridges (2015) refers to as "practiced indifference," whereby some groups of men occupying identities with concentrated collections of privilege are able to appear relaxed, content, and at ease with an increasingly varied range of gender performances.

Men in each of the groups did this, relying on specific tastes to subjectively situate themselves as gay(ish), providing some discursive distance between themselves and the systems of power from which they benefit. Travis (a Border Boy) works as a manager at a gas station. Somewhat ironically, Travis identified his interest in women as among his "gay" qualities:

> I'm into hanging out with women . . . I'm not a man's man or whatever . . . I like art, jazz, and . . . I hate to say it this way, but I just actually think I'm a lot better than [the Border Boys] . . . Sure, some of that is gay . . . but I mean . . . sometimes I feel like I really get along with gay men . . . we just have a lot of things in common, with one *really* big difference.

Echoing Ralph's use of gay aesthetics to distinguish himself from other men, Travis accomplishes something similar. While Travis never uses "fag," he did find a way of strategically "outing" himself as straight by highlighting the "*really* big difference" between having "gay" tastes and being gay.

Men from Guys for Gender Justice participated in this practice too. As Peter's comment opening this chapter suggests, that he likes "to sprinkle some gay on [his] straight," he works to discursively "out" himself as straight alongside his identification with gay aesthetics. And while all of the men in this study relied on gay aesthetics to distinguish themselves from "most men," some (notably those in Guys for Gender Justice) also relied on gay aesthetic tastes as symbolic evidence of their gender politics. Men in Guys for Gender Justice relied on gay aesthetics in an effort to authenticate their feminist and progressive credentials (see also Kolb 2014). As one member, Gary, put it, "If people thinking you're gay doesn't bug you, it's a good sign you're on the right side." Or, as another member, Peter, put it more bluntly, "It's basically impossible to be homophobic if people think you're gay." Peter and Gary's "performative progressiveness" (Brodyn and Ghaziani 2018) is different from Ralph and Travis's use of gay aesthetics. But each engaged in a more general process of indirectly identifying as straight through a disavowal of gay identity.

While Connell (1992) identified "straight gay" men as relying on straight aesthetics alongside their gay identities, comparing the motives of her "straight gay" men with the "gay straight" we describe here is useful. Connell (1992) argued that the "straight gay" men in her study relied on straight aesthetics with practical intent: for the purposes of safety and gender identification. The straight men relying on gay aesthetics in this chapter, however, did not discuss sexual aesthetics as a part of systems of power and inequality. And this distinction helps to situate the consequence of these practices as working to simultaneously *secure* and *obscure* relations of power and inequality even if this is not these men's intention.

"Gay" behaviors

A second element of gay aesthetics upon which men in Guys for Gender Justice and the Border Boys both relied were *behavioral*. The notion that there are "tells" of gay identities has a long and troubled history and speaks to the co-constitutive nature of gender and sexuality (e.g., Pascoe 2007; Schippers 2000; Ward 2015). Gender transgressive behavior was described as "gay" by men in all three groups, though only men in Guys for Gender Justice and the Border Boys claimed to participate in such behavior. Among the Border Boys, some regularly engaged in behavior they framed (jokingly) as emasculating because of its association with gay sexual identities. Meanwhile, among Guys for Gender Justice, discussion of engaging in "gay" behavior more often came up during conversations about having been mistaken as gay.

On one night, Eric (the Border Boys) walked into the bar in his typical attire: jeans, a white t-shirt, and a black leather jacket. As soon as he entered, another Border Boy, Matt, commented loudly enough that all the men at the bar could hear: "Eric! Why do you always come here looking like you're trying to hustle burly gay men at some skeezy after-hours place." The bar laughed as Matt mocked Eric. Eric sauntered over in an effete style and facetiously confronted Matt and then sardonically sang the chorus to the Village People's "Macho Man," twirling before sitting down and saying "I'm macho as fuck," to raucous laughter.

Other men among the Border Boys sometimes described their own behavior as gay. Henry plays in a band and is often chided for caring too much about his appearance. After being teased by Travis one night, Henry responded, "That's just me. I'm not gay . . . but I've got flair, dude." Continuing, and affecting his voice with a lisp, "I've got tons of flair and I don't care." Jeffrey joined in, "This is my fucking voice, man. It's the way I talk . . . I can't help that." Jeffrey has a higher-pitched voice and is sometimes mocked as "gay" by others for his careful enunciation. Both Henry and Jeffrey laughed at themselves for fitting what they frame as "gay" behavioral cues. And their "practiced indifference" about this is a masculinizing practice (Bridges 2015).

Behavioral gay aesthetics were more commonly invoked by men in Guys for Gender Justice, particularly when sharing "mistaken for gay" stories. Consider the following exchange after Bradley shared that a coworker mistakenly insinuated that he might be gay.

Bradley: She just walked up . . . called me "girlfriend," but like, "grrrlfreeend." She's new and just like totally was like, "Yep. That guy is gay as a feather boa." [laughs from the group]

Rob: [laughing] No! It's just . . . I get that from women too though. Like other women [nurses] I work with initially assume. And women patients. They'll be like, "Do you have a boyfriend?" or like, older women will say some stuff like, "I support gay marriage" like out of the blue. I'll laugh. I mean . . . fair assumption. Male nurse. Kind. Gets a decent haircut. Women feel comfortable talking to me. These are signs people! [laughing].

This kind of exchange was not uncommon among Guys for Gender Justice. This "practiced indifference" works as a hybrid hegemonic masculine strategy through the strategic assimilation of gender transgressive behavioral practices to distinguish themselves from other men. As Messerschmidt (2010) writes, "In practice, of course, incorporation and oppression can occur together" (2010: 39). This interplay between hegemony and subversion is similar to Schippers's (2000) analysis of gender and sexual performances among straight participants in alternative hard rock subculture. Here, these men appear to be challenging gender hegemony—and many understand their actions this way. And yet, these practices simultaneously *obscure* and *secure* the same systems of inequality they seem designed to challenge.

"Gay" ideologies

The third dimension of gay aesthetics that Richard identified is ideological, suggesting that political and ideological perspectives can be marked with sexual meaning. Feminism was the most frequently cited political commitment imbued with sexual connotations, but environmentalism and pacifism were also discussed this way. Situating masculinity and feminism as contradictory positions men's engagements with feminism as implicitly gender transgressive (e.g., Bridges 2010). Men in Guys for Gender Justice were acutely aware of this. After telling Tristan all of the members of the group identified as heterosexual, Dan joked, "it's funny, 'cause we're all involved in this totally *gay* thing." He explained:

> It's . . . gay to be into gay rights . . . or even women's rights. It's gay to be anti-violence. I once got told I was gay because I was *against* violence against women . . . I got called gay for bringing up Exxon Valdez . . . Being pro-environment is apparently gay . . . Guys invest in types of masculinity that are ruining the world . . . literally ruining the world.

Only men in Guys for Gender Justice subjectively identified their own political commitments as "gay" in this way. And here, similar to the ways men in each group subjectively identified certain elements of their own tastes or behaviors as "gay," this practice was also an act of *distinction*—allowing some men to distinguish themselves from "Other" men (those "ruining the world"). Gay aesthetics are used here to discursively *authenticate* these men's politically progressive identities, consistent with Kolb's (2014) research on men doing victims advocacy work receiving symbolic rewards Kolb calls "progressive merit badges." Here, these pro-feminist men's use of gay aesthetics allows them to symbolically bestow such badges upon themselves.

Another member, Saul, made this clear as well. When Tristan first met Saul as a part of this study, he was sporting a t-shirt proclaiming "Feminist chicks dig me!" on the front and carrying a messenger bag with pins and ribbons denoting political commitments—an AIDS awareness ribbon, anti-war and anti-gun pins, Planned Parenthood paraphernalia, and more. Explaining why he joined Guys for Gender Justice, Saul shared:

> I initially got involved with a sexual violence resource center as a volunteer . . . All the ladies I worked with there . . . they all totally thought I was gay . . . It's funny how people think you're gay if you, like, are for gay marriage . . . Apparently even being against sexual violence is gay . . . It's like clothes . . . I don't wear straight guy clothes and I don't have straight guy politics . . . and to be perfectly honest, that's one of a few reasons I'm different from most guys. I'm better.

Almost every member of this group discussed the ways their involvement with Guys for Gender Justice was related to their gender and sexual identities. And it was a common tactic to subjectively identify their politics as "gay" in ways similar to Dan and Saul, symbolically authenticating their feminist political identities.

Clearly, these straight men's use of gay aesthetics to distinguish themselves from "most men" is meaningfully different from the "fag discourse" that Pascoe (2007) identified and other overt sexual prejudice and discrimination considered fundamental to contemporary masculinity (e.g., Connell 1992, 1995; Herek 1986; Lehne 1976). We argue here, however, that as a hybrid hegemonic masculine practice, this behavior produces similar consequences. Systems of power and inequality are enormously elastic, such that the mechanisms through which durable inequalities like those based on gender and sexuality persist transform and adapt to changing historical circumstances (Bridges and Pascoe 2014, 2018). These straight men's reliance on gay aesthetics works in ways that allow *some* men to obscure gender and sexual power and inequality in ways that have the effect of symbolically securing their status and position in systems of power and inequality despite the appearance of calling that position into question.

Conclusion

Despite trends toward increasing levels of gender and sexual progressivism, gender and sexual inequalities persist in new and transforming ways. A growing collection of work on hybrid hegemonic masculinity highlights the flexibility of existing systems of power to preserve inequalities. In this chapter, we develop a more precise description of these practices as configurations of hybrid hegemonic masculinity to demonstrate the multiplicity of meanings and consequences. In the case of the straight, white men described here, gay aesthetics allow these men to discursively distinguish themselves from and obscure systems of structured advantage from which they benefit. While seemingly rupturing those symbolic boundaries between "gay" and "straight," we show here that they simultaneously maintain gender and sexual inequality. In discursively constructing "gay straight" identities, these men also reconstruct those same systems of power and inequality they appear to challenge.

Gender and sexuality are challenging to study, in part, because they do not stand still. The types of practices, beliefs, and interests labeled "masculine," "feminine," "gay," and "straight" are incredibly complex and subject to more flexibility than many imagine. This makes studying transformations in masculinities and their relationships with gender and sexual inequality challenging. We are here interested in highlighting the very *instability* of masculinity by focusing on the motivations and meanings of some of its component parts when they appear to have transformed in ways that challenge previous work on the relationship between masculinity and homophobia. While research has tended to situate this relationship as either "enduring" or "in decline," the men's gender and sexual practices in this study help to illustrate why neither of these answers are nuanced enough to understand these contemporary transformations.

Notes

1 For critiques of "inclusive masculinity" as a framework, see de Boise (2015) and O'Neill (2015).
2 Groups and participants in this study were assigned pseudonyms for anonymity.

References

Aboim, Sofia. 2010. *Plural Masculinities: The Remaking of the Self in Private Life.* New York and London: Routledge.

Anderson, Eric. 2009. *Inclusive Masculinity: The Changing Nature of Masculinities.* New York: Routledge.

Arxer, Steven L. 2011. "Hybrid Masculine Power: Reconceptualizing the Relationship between Homosociality and Hegemonic Masculinity." *Humanity & Society* 35: 390–422.

Barry, Ben. 2018. "(Re)Fashioning Masculinity: Social Identity and Context in Men's Hybrid Masculinities through Dress." *Gender & Society* 32(5): 638–662.

Bridges, Tristan. 2010. "Men Just Weren't Made to Do This: Performances of Drag at 'Walk a Mile in Her Shoes' Marches." *Gender & Society* 24(1): 5–30.

Bridges, Tristan. 2014. "A Very 'Gay' Straight? Hybrid Masculinities, Sexual Aesthetics, and the Changing Relationship between Masculinity and Homophobia." *Gender & Society* 28(1): 58–82.

Bridges, Tristan. 2015. "Cosmopolitan Masculinities and Gender Omnivorousness: Transformations in Gender and Inequality." *Feminist Reflections* (blog), January 29. Available at: https://thesocietypages.org/feminist/2015/01/29/cosmopolitan-masculinities-and-gender-omnivorousness-transformations-in-gender-and-inequality/.

Bridges, Tristan and C.J. Pascoe. 2014. "Hybrid Masculinities: New Directions in the Sociology of Men and Masculinities." *Sociology Compass* 8(3): 246–258.

Bridges, Tristan and C.J. Pascoe. 2018. "On the Elasticity of Gender Hegemony: Why Hybrid Masculinities Fail to Undermine Gender and Sexual Inequality," pp. 254–274 in *Gender Reckonings*, edited by J.W. Messerschmidt, P.Y. Martin, M.A. Messner, and R. Connell. New York: New York University Press.

Brodyn, Adriana and Amin Ghaziani. 2018. "Performative Progressiveness: Accounting for New Forms of Inequality in the Gayborhood." *City & Community* 17(2): 307–329.

Chauncey, George. 1994. *Gay New York.* New York: Basic Books.

Connell, Raewyn. 1987. *Gender and Power.* Stanford: Stanford University Press.

Connell, Raewyn. 1992. "A Very Straight Gay: Masculinity, Homosexual Experience, and the Dynamics of Gender." *American Sociological Review* 57(6): 735–751.

Connell, Raewyn. 1995. *Masculinities.* Stanford: Stanford University Press.

Connell, Raewyn W. and James Messerschmidt. 2005. "Hegemonic Masculinity: Rethinking the Concept." *Gender & Society* 19(6): 829–859.

Corbett, Ken. 2001. "Faggot = Loser." *Studies in Gender and Sexuality* 2(1): 3–28.

de Boise, Sam. 2015. "I'm Not Homophobic, 'I've Got Gay Friends': Evaluating the Validity of Inclusive Masculinity." *Men and Masculinity* 18(3): 318–339.

Demetriou, Demetrakis. 2001. "Connell's Concept of Hegemonic Masculinity: A Critique." *Theory and Society* 30: 337–361.

Diefendorf, Sarah. 2015. "After the Wedding Night: Sexual Abstinence and Masculinities over the Life Course." *Gender & Society* 29(5): 647–669.

Doan, Long, Annalise Loehr, and Lisa R. Miller. 2014. "Formal Rights and Informal Privileges for Same-Sex Couples: Evidence from a National Survey Experiment." *American Sociological Review* 79(6): 1172–1195.

Donovan, Brian. 1998. "Political Consequences of Private Authority: Promise Keepers and the Transformation of Hegemonic Masculinity." *Theory and Society* 27: 817–843.

Elliot, Karla. 2019. "Negotiations between Progressive and 'Traditional' Expressions of Young Australian Masculinity." *Journal of Sociology* 55(1): 108–123.

Gerber, Lynne. 2014. "Grit, Guts, and Vanilla Beans: Godly Masculinity in the Ex-Gay Movement." *Gender & Society* 29(1): 26–50.

Ghaziani, Amin. 2017. *Sex Cultures.* Malden, MA: Polity Press.

Groes-Green, Christian. 2012. "Philogynous Masculinities: Contextualizing Alternative Manhood in Mozambique." *Men and Masculinities* 15(2): 91–111.

Halperin, David. 2012. *How to Be Gay.* Cambridge, MA: Harvard University Press.

Heath, Melanie. 2015. "Manhood Over Easy: Reflections on Hegemonic, Soft-Boiled, and Multiple Masculinities," pp. 155–164 in *Exploring Masculinities*, edited by C.J. Pascoe and T. Bridges. New York: Oxford University Press.

Herek, Gregory. 1986. "On Heterosexual Masculinity." *American Behavioral Scientist* 29(5): 563–577.

Ibson, John. 2002. *Picturing Men: A Century of Male Relationships in Everyday American Photography.* London: Smithsonian Institution Press.

Ibson, John. 2018. *The Mourning After: Loss and Longing among Midcentury American Men.* Chicago: University of Chicago Press.

Jóhannsdóttir, Ásta and Ingólfur V. Gíslason. 2018. "Young Icelandic Men's Perceptions of Masculinity." *Men and Masculinities* 26(1): 3–19.

Kimmel, Michael S. 1994. "Masculinity as Homophobia," pp. 119–141 in *Theorizing Masculinities*, edited by H. Brod and M. Kaufman. Thousand Oaks: Sage Publications.

Kite, Mary E. 1984. "Sex Differences in Attitudes toward Homosexuals: A Meta-Analytic Review." *Journal of Homosexuality* 10(1–2): 69–81.

Kolb, Kenneth. 2014. *Moral Wages: The Emotional Dilemmas of Victims Advocacy Counseling.* Berkeley: University of California Press.

Lamont, Ellen. 2015. "The Limited Construction of an Egalitarian Masculinity: College-Educated Men's Dating and Relationship Narratives." *Men and Masculinities* 18(3): 271–292.

Lehne, Gregory K. 1976. "Homophobia Among Men," pp. 68–88 in *The Forty-Nine Percent Majority*, edited by D. David and R. Brannon. Reading, MA: Addison-Wesley.

McCormack, Mark. 2012. *The Declining Significance of Homophobia: How Teenage Boys are Redefining Masculinity and Heterosexuality.* New York: Oxford University Press.

McDowell, Amy D. 2017. "Aggressive and Loving Men: Gender Hegemony in Christian Hardcore Punk." *Gender & Society* 31(2): 223–244.

Messerschmidt, James. 2010. *Hegemonic Masculinities and Camouflaged Politics.* Boulder: Paradigm Publishers.

Messerschmidt, James W. 2018. *Hegemonic Masculinity: Formulation, Reformulation, and Amplification.* New York: Rowman & Littlefield.

Messerschmidt, James W. and Michael A. Messner. 2018. "Hegemonic, Nonhegemonic, and 'New' Masculinities," pp. 35–56 in *Gender Reckonings*, edited by J.W. Messerschmidt, P.Y. Martin, M.A. Messner, and R. Connell. New York: New York University Press.

Messner, Michael. 1993. "'Changing Men' and Feminist Politics in the United States." *Theory and Society* 22(5): 723–737.

Messner, Michael. 2007. "The Masculinity of the Governator." *Gender & Society* 21(4): 461–480.

Mosse, George L. 1996. *The Image of Man.* New York: Oxford University Press.

O'Neill, Rachel. 2015. "Whither Critical Masculinity Studies? Notes on Inclusive Masculinity Theory, Postfeminism, and Sexual Politics." *Men and Masculinities* 18(1): 100–120.

Pascoe, C.J. 2007. *Dude, You're a Fag: Masculinity and Sexuality in High School.* Berkeley: University of California Press.

Pascoe, C.J. and Jocelyn Hollander. 2015. "Good Guys Don't Rape: Gender, Domination, and Mobilizing Rape." *Gender & Society* 30(1): 67–79.

Pascoe, C.J. and Tristan Bridges. 2017. "Fag Discourse in a Post-Homophobic Era," pp. 352–358 in *Inequality in the 21st Century*, edited by D.B. Grusky and J. Hill. Boulder: Westview Press.

Pfaffendorf, Jessica. 2017. "Sensitive Cowboys: Privileged Young Men and the Mobilization of Hybrid Masculinities in a Therapeutic Boarding School." *Gender & Society* 31(2): 197–222.

Schippers, Mimi. 2000. "The Social Organization of Sexuality and Gender in Alternative Hard Rock." *Gender & Society* 14(6): 747–764.

Sumerau, J.E. and Eric Anthony Grollman. 2018. "Obscuring Oppression: Racism, Cissexism, and the Persistence of Social Inequality." *Sociology of Race and Ethnicity* 4(3): 322–337.
Ward, Jane. 2008. "Dude-Sex: White Masculinities and 'Authentic' Heterosexuality among Dudes Who Have Sex with Dudes." *Sexualities* 11(4): 414–434.
Ward, Jane. 2015. *Not Gay: Sex Between Straight White Men*. New York: New York University Press.
Young, Kathryne M. 2017. "Masculine Compensation and Masculine Balance: Notes on the Hawaiian Cockfight." *Social Forces* 95(4): 1341–1370.

17

Doing gender, doing heteronormativity*

"Gender normals," transgender people, and the social maintenance of heterosexuality

Kristen Schilt and Laurel Westbrook

In "Feminism, Marxism, Method and the State," Catherine MacKinnon (1982, 533) argued that "sexuality is the linchpin of gender inequality." This argument echoed earlier conceptualizations of heterosexuality as a compulsory, institutionalized system that supports gender inequality (Rich 1980). Despite these important insights, however, theorizing heterosexuality did not become central to feminist sociology (Ingraham 1994). Rather, it was queer theory that picked up the theoretical mantle, turning the gaze onto how the "heterosexual matrix" (Butler 1989) maintains inequality between men and women (see Seidman 1995). Shifting the object of analysis from the margins (women, homosexuals) to the center (men, heterosexuals) allowed for the theorization of heteronormativity—the suite of cultural, legal, and institutional practices that maintain normative assumptions that there are two and only two genders, that gender reflects biological sex, and that only sexual attraction between these "opposite" genders is natural or acceptable (Kitzinger 2005). Heterosexuality plays a central role in "maintaining the gender hierarchy that subordinates women to men" (Cameron and Kulick 2003, 45). Yet the relationship between heterosexuality and gender oppression remains undertheorized in social science research.

In this article, we bring attention to the everyday workings of heteronormativity by examining potential challenges to this "sex/gender/sexuality system" (Seidman 1995): people who live their lives in a social gender that is not the gender they were assigned at birth. People who make these social transitions—often termed "transgender" people—disrupt cultural expectations that gender identity is an immutable derivation of biology (Garfinkel 1967; Kessler and McKenna 1978). In social situations, transgender people—as all people—have "cultural genitalia" that derive from their gender presentation (Kessler and McKenna 1978). Yet in sexual and

* AUTHORS' NOTE: We are extremely grateful to Beth Schneider, Jane Ward, Dana Britton, and the anonymous reviewers at *Gender & Society* for the detailed and thoughtful feedback that they provided on earlier versions of this article. In addition, we wish to thank Wendy Brown, Karl Bryant, Richard Juang, Dawne Moon, Charis Thompson, Barrie Thorne, Aliya Saperstein, and Mel Stanfill for comments on previous versions of this work. Portions of this research have been supported by funding from the Regents of the University of California.

sexualized situations—interactional contexts that allow for the performance of both gender and heterosexuality—male-bodied women and female-bodied men present a challenge to heteronormativity. As we demonstrate, analyzing these situations can illuminate the relationship between the maintenance of gender and the maintenance of (hetero)sexuality.

Taking methodological insights from queer theory, we consider how cisgender men and women[1]–whom Garfinkel (1967) terms "gender normals"—react to transgender people. This focus inverts the typical model of using transgender people (the margins) to illuminate the workings of everybody else (the center) (see Garfinkel 1967; Kessler and McKenna 1978; West and Zimmerman 1987). We draw on two case studies: an ethnographic study of transmen who socially transition from female to male (FtM) in the workplace and a textual analysis of media narratives about the killings predominantly of transwomen who socially transition from male to female (MtF). Attention to how gender normals react to the discovery of what they perceive as a mismatch between gender identity and biological sex in these public and private relationships reveals the interactional precariousness of the seemingly natural heterosexual gender system. We argue that these responses demonstrate that the processes of "doing gender" (West and Zimmerman 1987) are difficult to separate from the maintenance of heteronormativity. Our case studies show that doing gender in a way that does not reflect biological sex can be perceived as a threat to heterosexuality. Cisgender men and women attempt to repair these potential ruptures through the deployment of normatively gendered tactics that reify gender and sexual difference. These tactics simultaneously negate the authenticity of transmen and transwomen's gender and sexual identities and reaffirm the heteronormative assumption that only "opposite sex" attraction between two differently sexed and gendered bodies is normal, natural, and desirable.

Literature review

The persistence of gender inequality is well documented within sociology. Behind this reproduction of inequality are cultural schemas about the naturalness of a binary gender system in which there are two, and only two, genders that derive from biology (chromosomes and genitalia) (West and Zimmerman 1987). These schemas constitute and are constituted by our current gender order—the patterns of power relations between men and women that shape norms for femininity and masculinity by defining what is gender-appropriate in arenas such as romantic partner selection, occupational choice, and parental roles. The gender order is hierarchical, which means there is consistently a higher value on masculinity than on femininity (Connell 1987; Schippers 2007).

Ethnomethodological theories of gender (see Garfinkel 1967; Kessler and McKenna 1978; West and Zimmerman 1987) argue that an empirical focus on social interactions makes the mechanisms that maintain this gender system visible, as "social interactions can reflect and reiterate the gender inequality characteristic of society more generally" (Fenstermaker, West, and Zimmerman 2002, 28). This theoretical body of work examines what has come to be termed "doing gender" (West and Zimmerman 1987)—the interactional process of crafting gender identities that are then presumed to reflect and naturally derive from biology. As masculinity and femininity are not fixed properties of male and female bodies, the meanings and expectations for being men and women differ both historically and across interactional settings. Normative expectations for men and women maintain gender inequality, as strictures of masculinity push men to "do dominance" and strictures of femininity push women to "do submission" (West and Zimmerman 1987). Taken together, these expectations about natural gender differences translate into an unreflexive production of doing inequality that reproduces the hierarchical gender system more broadly (Fenstermaker, West, and Zimmerman 2002).

Fully illuminating the mechanisms that uphold gender inequality, however, requires a more thorough analysis of the interplay between gender and sexuality—what some feminists have termed the connection between patriarchy and compulsory heterosexuality (Rich 1980)—than is offered in these theories. Heterosexuality—like masculinity and femininity—is taken for granted as a natural occurrence derived from biological sex. Heterosexual expectations are embedded in social institutions, "guarantee[ing] that some people will have more class status, power, and privilege than others" (Ingraham 1994, 212). The hierarchical gender system that privileges masculinity also privileges heterosexuality. Its maintenance rests on the cultural devaluation of femininity and homosexuality. Showing the effects of this socialization, violent crimes against gay men—individuals who are culturally stereotyped as feminine (Hennen 2008)—typically are propagated by men (Franklin 2000). The gender system must be conceived of as *heterosexist*, as power is allocated via positioning in gender and sexual hierarchies. As such, understanding the persistence of gender inequality necessitates an understanding of the relationality between heterosexuality and gender.

Heterosexuality requires a binary sex system, as it is predicated on the seemingly natural attraction between two types of bodies defined as opposites. The taken-for-granted expectation that heterosexuality and gender identity follow from genitalia produces heteronormativity—even though in most social interactions genitals are not actually visible. People do not expect a mismatch between "biological" credentials and gender presentations but rather assume that gendered appearances reflect a biologically sexed reality (West and Zimmerman 1987). This assumption is not always warranted. Transgender people—people who live with a social gender identity that differs from the gender they were assigned at birth—can successfully do masculinity or femininity without having the genitalia that are presumed to follow from their outward appearance.

In many social interactions, transgender people's private bodies matter little, as—if they "pass" in their desired social gender—their appearance is taken to be proof of their biological sex. Sexual encounters, however, can disrupt the taken-for-granted assumptions that people who look like women have vaginas and people who look like men have penises. In these situations, gender normals, particularly men, can have strong, even violent reactions. A question arises: Is the reaction related to (trans)gender or (hetero)sexuality? Framed as a (trans)gender issue, this violence operates as a disciplinary force on bodies that transgress the seemingly natural gender binary. Yet (hetero)sexuality is also an important factor as "the heterosexual framework that centers upon the model of penis-vagina penetration undoubtedly informs the genital division of male and female" (Bettcher 2007, 56). Transgender people have their claim to their gender category of choice challenged in these situations on the basis of genitalia, which in turn calls the heterosexuality of cisgender people they have been sexual with into question. How people respond to breaches to naturalized attitudes about gender and sexuality can illuminate the processes and mechanisms behind the everyday unfolding of not just doing gender but also doing heteronormativity.

Methods

The first case study examined reactions to open workplace transitions—situations in which transgender people announce their intention to undergo a gender transition and remain in the same job. Between 2003 and 2007, Schilt conducted in-depth interviews with 54 transmen in Southern California and Central Texas. Generating a random sample of transmen is not possible, as there is not an even dispersal of transmen by state or transgender-specific neighborhoods from which to sample. Respondents were recruited from transgender activist groups, listservs, support groups, and personal contacts. After the interview, each respondent was asked if he felt comfortable recommending any coworkers for an interview about their experience of the workplace transition. Fourteen coworkers (10 women and four men) of eight transmen in professional and blue-collar jobs were interviewed.

There were few demographic differences between transmen from the two regions. Thirty-five of these men had openly transitioned at one point in their lives, 19 in California and 16 in Texas. The majority were white (86 percent), with relatively equal numbers of queer, bisexual, and gay men and heterosexual men. The average age of California respondents was higher than that of the Texas respondents (35 vs. 25). California transmen also had a wider range of years of transition—from the mid-1980s to the mid-2000s—while all of the transmen interviewed in Texas openly transitioned in the early to mid-2000s. In both states, most transmen transitioned in professional occupations or in service industry/retail occupations (72 percent), with a minority transitioning in blue-collar occupations and "women's professions."

In the second case study, Westbrook systematically collected all the available nonfiction texts produced by the mainstream news media in the United States between 1990 and 2005 about the murders of people described as doing gender so as to possibly be seen as a gender other than the one they were assigned at birth. Texts included those identifying a murder victim as wearing clothing, jewelry, and/or makeup associated with a gender other than the one they were labeled at birth; naming a murder victim as *transsexual, transgender*, a *cross-dresser*, or a *transvestite*; and/or describing the victim of fatal violence as *a man in a dress, a man posing as a woman, passed as a man, a woman posing as a man, female impersonator*, or *a woman who is really a man*. For this article, we will refer to this group of people using the term "transgender."

In total, Westbrook collected and analyzed 7,183 individual news stories about 232 homicides. Most texts came from searches of the databases Lexis Nexis and Access World News and included print newspaper articles and news magazine articles produced for a general audience. To gather these texts, Westbrook compiled a list of names of people identified as transgender murder victims by transgender activists and then searched for articles about these victims. She then assembled a list of names and terms used to describe victims in these news stories, such as "posed as a woman," and performed a new search using those terms. This process was repeated a number of times. The extensiveness of the search makes these texts a census of all available stories, not just a sample, and all cases identified by transgender activists were written about at least once in the mainstream press.

Westbrook analyzed texts using the qualitative data analysis software Atlas.ti. Coding focused on how each news story explained the act of violence being reported, with explanations conceptualized as "frames"—ways that people make sense of the world by highlighting certain aspects of an event while ignoring others (Benford and Snow 2000; Goffman 1986). News media framings of this violence were analyzed not in an attempt to access what "really happened" in these interactions but as reflections of dominant explanations of why such violence may occur. The mainstream news media both reflect and shape dominant belief systems (Ferree et al. 2002; Gamson et al. 1992); as such, attention to media framings of violence against transgender people provides useful insight into the sex/gender/sexuality system.

Although journalists framed the violence in many ways, more often than not they described the violence as a response to actual or perceived deception of the perpetrator by the transgender person. Westbrook coded stories as using this deception framing if they explicitly claimed that the perpetrator felt deceived and, as a result, killed the victim. Stories that described the killing as resulting from anger at a "discovery" that the victim was really a man, really a woman, or transgender were also included under the code "deception frame." In examining these stories, Westbrook also attended to the genders of the victim(s) and perpetrator(s) and the context in which the crime occurred, including the relationship between the victim and perpetrator and location of the crime. Other variables of interest, such as race and class of those involved, were rarely mentioned in news stories and so were not part of the analysis.

There are some potential limitations to this comparative model. The first lies in the populations we compare. While transmen and transwomen are lumped together as "transgender" in many situations, their experiences do not mirror one another. Still, we find these comparisons to be fruitful for our analyses for several reasons. First, while the selection of transmen in the first case study was purposive, the focus on transwomen in the second case study was not. The lack of any documented incidents involving heterosexual cisgender women killing transmen suggests that the tactics used to police gender and sexual transgressions are themselves gendered—a point we develop in our analysis. Second, this comparison reveals how responses to transmen and transwomen vary across public and private sexualized/sexual relationships. This comparison illuminates how criteria for membership in gender categories differ in sexual, as compared to nonsexual, situations.

Doing gender and heteronormativity in public relationships

Open workplace transitions—situations in which a transgender employee informs her employers that she intends to begin living and working as a man—present an interesting empirical setting for examining how gender and heteronormativity "work" in public relationships. Reactions to this announcement could play out in multiple ways. Transmen could be fired for making a stigmatized identity public, thus neutralizing this potential challenge to the binary gender order. They could experience no change to their workplace experiences. Or they could be repatriated as men by being expected to follow the men's dress and behavioral codes and being moved into new jobs or positions that employers see as better suited to masculine abilities and interests.

The experiences of transmen in both Texas and California are largely consistent: They are incorporated into men's jobs and men's workplace cultures. These incorporations are not seamless, however. When transmen's (hetero)sexuality is raised at work, heterosexual men often encourage an open display of shared sexual desire for women—emphasizing their new sameness with transmen. Heterosexual women, in contrast, police the boundaries of who can be counted as a man—negating their new "oppositeness" with transmen. In sexualized situations, transmen's masculinity is simultaneously reinforced—as men frame them as heterosexual men—and challenged—as women position them as homosexual women.

Reaffirming "natural" gender difference

Employers and coworkers find new ways to do gender "naturally" by incorporating transmen into the workplace as one of the guys. On an organizational level, some employers rehire transmen as men, institutionally sanctioning their transition into a man's career track. Preston received a directive from his boss that he should adopt the men's dress code at his blue-collar job, which meant the removal of a single earring he had worn unproblematically for years as a woman in the same workplace. John's employer in his service industry job required that he retain the women's uniform until he started testosterone—at which point he could legitimately don a men's uniform. Employers also issue top-down dictates that give transmen access to men's restrooms and lockers and ask coworkers to change names and pronouns with their transgender colleague. These employer responses show how gender boundaries can shift—former women can be accepted as men—without a change in structural gender relations or organizational policies.

When transmen receive top-down support for their workplace transitions, men and women coworkers often show their adherence to these dictates by enlisting transmen into masculine "gender rituals" (Goffman 1977). For the first few weeks of Jake's transition, heterosexual men colleagues began signaling in an obvious way that they were treating him like a guy:

> A lot of my male colleagues started kind of like slapping me on the back [laughs]. But I think it was with more force than they probably slapped each other on the back. . . . And it was not that I had gained access to "male privilege" but they were trying to affirm to me that they saw me as a male. . . . That was the way they were going to be supportive of me as a guy, or something of the sort [laughs].

The awkwardness of these backslaps illustrates his colleagues' own hyperawareness of trying to do gender with someone who is becoming a man. Jake felt normalized by this incorporation and made frequent references to himself as a *trans*man to disrupt his colleagues' attempts to naturalize his transition.

Women also engage transmen in heterosocial gender rituals, such as doing heavy lifting around the office. The change is so rapid that many transmen are, at first, not sure how to make sense of these new expectations. Kelly, who transitioned in a semiprofessional job, notes,

> Before [transition] no one asked me to do anything really and then [after], this one teacher, she's like, "Can you hang this up? Can you move this for me?" . . . Like if anything needed to be done in this room, it was me. Like she was just, "Male? Okay you do it." That took some adjusting. I thought she was picking on me.

Ken describes a similar experience in his semiprofessional workplace. While his coworkers were slow to adopt masculine pronouns with him, his women coworkers did enlist him in carrying heavy items to the basement and unloading boxes. This enlistment into heterosocial gender rituals suggests that while open transitions might make gender trouble for coworkers who struggle with how they should treat their transgender colleague, this disruption does not make them reconsider the naturalness of the gender binary. Treating transmen as men gives them their "rightful" place in the dichotomy—and allows schemas about men and women's natural differences to go unchanged.

Interviews with coworkers illuminate how they grapple with this potential breach to their ideas about gender. Heterosexual men emphasized that if they were not discussing the transition in an interview, it would not cross their minds. They position this transition from female to male as "natural" for a masculine woman. One man in a blue-collar job says,

> I chuckle to myself every now and then, how just natural it seems. [It] took a while for the pronouns to catch on but now it just comes out naturally. It just seems like a natural fit. It just seems like my inclination or my intuition at the beginning was correct; it just seemed, like, natural that she should go through with something like this because she was gonna be more comfortable as a man than as a woman.

Another man says he was unsurprised about the transition because his colleague "was an unattractive woman." As many transmen move from being masculine (e.g., gender-nonconforming) women to gender-conforming men, their decisions to transition can be seen as a natural fit for someone who was viewed as doing femininity unsuccessfully. Many transmen also move from being gender nonconforming women who are assumed to be lesbians to gender-conforming men who are assumed to be heterosexual—a move that coworkers can justify as confirmation of the naturalness and desirability of a heteronormative gender system.

Women coworkers express more hesitation about seeing transmen as men. Several women discuss their concern about what they perceive as mismatch between their colleague's gender presentation—male—and his biological sex—female. One woman who works with a transman in a female-dominated job says,

> It's a hard thing for me [to say I see him as a man]. . . . On some levels yes, but in other ways, no. If I think about it, I start thinking about his body. I feel that his body would be different than any man that I would know. . . . When I think a lot about it, I definitely think about his body and what's happened to it. I wouldn't think of him as I would another male friend.

Another woman in a blue collar job makes a similar comment, saying,

> I can't say yes [I see him as a man] but I can't really say no. The appearance has changed. You know . . . he always looked like a guy . . . dressed like a guy . . . and what's changed is that his hair is cut short. But I can't really say I accept him as a guy.

These comments demonstrate the power of gender attributions as, on one hand, these women see their colleagues as men because they look like men. However, when they think too much about their bodies—what they see as an authentic and unchangeable sexed reality—they are hesitant to include them in the category of man.

Yet, showing the power of institutionally supported public relationships, many coworkers will validate transmen's new social identities as men regardless of their personal acceptance of this identity—in effect "passing" as supportive colleagues. While sociologists have positioned transgender people as gender overachievers who attempt to be 120 percent male or female (see Garfinkel 1967), coworkers' adherence to these gender rituals suggests that in these public interactions, gender normals may have more anxiety about how gender *should* be done than the person who is transitioning. Whether or not this adherence reflects authentic support for transmen *as men*, it maintains the idea of natural gender differences that create "opposite" personality types with different abilities and interests.

Gendered responses to heterosexuality

The incorporation of transmen as one of the guys at work is not seamless. Where this incorporation comes apart highlights the connection between doing gender and maintaining heteronormativity. While the workplace often is framed as nonsexual, interactions can become sexualized, as in sex talk and sexual banter; and/or sexual, in ways both consensual and nonconsensual (Williams, Giuffre, and Dellinger 1999). Heterosexual women's perception of a mismatch between their colleague's biological sex and gender identity comes to the forefront in (hetero)sexualized interactions. Women can accept transmen as men when doing masculine roles at work—heavy lifting, killing spiders—but not in sexualized relationships with female-bodied people. Illustrating this, Preston remembers telling a woman coworker that he had a new girlfriend. He was shocked when she yelled across the room, "How do you have sex if you don't have a dick?" Her comment shows that in his coworker's mind, Preston does not have the essential signifier of manhood and therefore cannot *really* have penis-vagina intercourse—the hallmark of heterosexuality.

In sexualized situations, women frame transmen as deceptive—tricking women into seemingly heterosexual relationships without the necessary biological marker of manhood. At a volunteer organization Peter participated in for many years, before and after his transition, he developed a flirtatious relationship with a woman volunteer. He says, "We were flirting a bit and someone noticed. She pulled me aside and said, 'Does she know about you? I am concerned she doesn't know about you. What is going on between you two? This is totally inappropriate.'" Having known his co-volunteers for several years, he was surprised to realize they saw him as suspicious and threatening. Chris encountered a similar experience in his first job as a man. Hired as a man, he planned not to come out as transgender at work. However, his transition became public knowledge when a high school colleague recognized him. While she originally agreed not to tell anyone, she changed her mind. He says, "So basically for the first time in my life—I was nineteen—I had girls *like* like me, you know. And I think what happened was [this former classmate] was thinking, 'Oh that's sick, I better warn them.'" While his coworkers continued to treat him as a man in nonsexual interactions, a woman he had set up a date with cancelled. He had no further romantic interest shown to him by women at that job. His experience shows how women's acceptance of transmen's gender can be negated in sexualized interactions. In these situations, women regender transmen as biological females passing as men in an attempt to trick women into homosexuality.

Conversely, rather than policing transmen's heterosexuality, heterosexual men encourage it by engaging them in sex talk about women. Kelly notes,

> I definitely notice that the guys . . . they will say stuff to me that I know they wouldn't have said before [when I was working as a female]. . . . One guy, recently we were talking and he was talking about his girlfriend and he's like, "I go home and work it [have sex] for exercise."

He adds that this same coworker went out of his way to avoid him before his transition. The coworker later told Kelly that he was uncomfortable with gays and lesbians. This disclosure reflects heteronormativity, as becoming a presumably heterosexual man can be viewed more positively than being a lesbian. While some transmen personally identify as gay or queer men, heteronormativity ensures that their coworkers imagine they are transitioning to become heterosexual men. These responses show that when an open transition has employer support, heterosexual men are willing in many cases to relate to transmen they see as heterosexual on the basis of shared sexual desire for women. Illustrating this, one coworker describes taking his transman colleague to Hooters because they both enjoy looking at "scantily clad women."

As heteronormativity requires men to ignore other men's bodies, heterosexual men do masculinity, and simultaneously uphold their heterosexuality, by ignoring the bodily details of transmen's transitions. Cisgender men are hesitant to admit any interest in genital surgery. Those who did ask questions about genital surgery in their interview qualified that this interest was purely "scientific," rather than prurient. Ignoring genitalia gives transmen a "sameness" with heterosexual men at work. This sameness allows cisgender men to enlist transmen into discussions of heterosexuality that never go beyond the theoretical. Heterosexual women, in contrast, now have an "oppositeness" with transmen, making them and other women at work part of a potential dating pool. This transition moves transmen's heterosexuality closer to practice than theory—a move that accounts for the reactive, policing steps to thwart transmen's heterosexuality by placing emphasis on genitalia. Perhaps drawing on their own surprise at learning that someone who looks like a man might not have a penis, they want to alert other women who could be "tricked" into homosexuality.

These experiences illustrate that while both cisgender men and women treat transmen as socially male in nonsexualized public interactions, there are gender differences in responses to sexualized public interactions. In these situations, men gender transmen as heterosexually male on the basis of gender presentation, while women gender them as homosexually female on the basis of biological sex. When gender category and heterosexual authenticity are policed through reference to genitalia, the choice of targets is gendered. Further illustrating this, heterosexual cisgender men often engage in policing and harassing behaviors toward transwomen's public workplace transitions (Schilt 2009; Schilt and Connell 2007). This difference suggests that cisgender people react more strongly toward transgender people who become the "opposite gender" but are presumed to still be the "same sex," as they—and their entire gender—now run the risk of unwittingly engaging in homosexuality. Yet the public context of these relationships still mediates the methods used to enforce heteronormativity. As the next section shows, in private, sexual relationships, men show more extreme reactions.

Doing gender and heteronormativity in private relationships

Examining media accounts of killings of transgender people provides important insight into the beliefs that maintain gender inequality and heteronormativity. Journalists frame a minority of the murders of transpeople in the United States between 1990 and 2005 as caused by reasons wholly, or mostly, unrelated to their membership in the group "transgender." These sorts of cases—the result of personal conflict, random violence, or membership in categories such as "woman" or "person of color"—account for about 33 percent of transgender homicides in which reporters provide a cause for the violence. Journalists attribute the other 67 percent to reasons more closely related to being transgender. Articles describe homophobia or transphobia as the primary cause of violence in only 6 percent of the total cases, while in the majority of cases, 56 percent, journalists depict violence as resulting from private, sexual interactions in which the perpetrator feels "tricked" into homosexuality by "gender deceivers." An additional 5 percent depict the murder as resulting from cisgender men defending themselves from unwanted sexual advances.

As with reactions to public, sexualized relationships, the response patterns in these private, sexual interactions are gendered. Almost 95 percent of reported cases involve a cisgender man murdering a transwoman, while no articles describe a cisgender woman killing a transman.[2] The gendered pattern of violence represented in mainstream news stories echoes, although significantly exceeds, that for all reported homicides in the United States, as 65.3 percent involve a male offender and male victim and 2.4 percent of cases are females killing females (Bureau of Justice Statistics 2007). While reports of homicides, whether they be from the Bureau of Justice Statistics or transgender activists and the mainstream news, are unlikely to include every murder in the United States, the extremity of the gender gap in identified fatal violence against transgender people demonstrates that, while doing masculinity and doing violence are socially linked, the combined threat to both gender and sexuality posed by transgender bodies in private, sexual relationships can result in hypergendered responses by cisgender men.

Gender and heterosexuality in private

Most of the transgender homicides covered in the mainstream news media occur in what can be understood as private relationships, such as those between lovers, family members, friends, acquaintances, and strangers met on the street or in bars; or outside the realm of socially authorized public relationships, such as people engaged in illegal activities like prostitution and drug dealing. Of the 136 cases in which journalists identify the relationship between the perpetrator and victim, only one is said to be a relationship between coworkers, and it occurs far outside the realm of legally sanctioned working relationships—an MtF prostitute portrayed as killing her transsexual madam in an argument over money (Grace 2003). Similarly, although many of these murders occurred in public spaces, such as in parks and on the street, they rarely took place within the more regulated spaces of retail stores or other places of business.

Almost two-thirds of the reported fatal violence in these private interactions transpired within sexual relationships of short duration, such as the victim and perpetrator engaging in a physical sexual encounter for the first time, or the perpetrator or victim propositioning the other for a sexual relationship (either with or without the exchange of money). Many articles describe the perpetrators and victims as strangers or very recent acquaintances. In these narratives, cisgender men approach or are approached by a woman for sex and the pair immediately go to a place where they can engage in such an encounter. Upon becoming sexual, the cisgender man discovers the transwoman's penis and reacts with physical violence. Articles explain the resulting violence as caused by the perpetrators feeling deceived by the transwomen about their "true gender" and "tricked" into a homosexual encounter.

News articles described the murder of Chrissey Johnson (nee Marvin Johnson) in such a way:

> *Man charged in death of transvestite*
>
> A Baltimore man has been arrested for killing a 29-year-old man whom he had brought home believing the victim was a woman. The police said that Allen E. Horton, 22, went into a rage Saturday night when he discovered Marvin Johnson, who was dressed as a woman, was really a man, a police spokesman said yesterday.
>
> (Washington Times *1993)*

News coverage frames fatal sexual encounters between cisgender men and transwomen sex workers similarly, as this description of the murder of Jesse Santiago (nee Jesus) shows:

> *Man kills transvestite, then himself, police say*
>
> A bizarre case of mistaken sexual identity ended in the fatal screwdriver stabbing of a transvestite Bronx prostitute and the suicide of his killer early yesterday, police said. It began late Friday night when 47-year-old Augustin Rosado propositioned what he believed was a female prostitute in the University Heights section. The two headed to Rosado's fourth-floor furnished room in a transient hotel on Cresten Avenue, police said. Once inside, Rosado discovered the prostitute was a male transvestite and flew into a rage, stabbing the unidentified 30-year-old man repeatedly with a screwdriver and hitting him with a metal pipe, police said. . . . A detective working on the case said it is nearly impossible to tell on sight which prostitutes plying their trade in the area are men and which are women. "Some of these transvestites look sexier than some women," he said. "I could see how someone could be surprised."
>
> *(Jamieson 1992)*

The "deception" in these frames is a dual one; articles portray victims as lying both about their gender and about their sexual orientation. Showing how the sexual context of the relationship matters, reporters never use the deception frame for cases in which there has been no sexual interaction between the transgender person and a cisgender person. This lack of the deception frame in these nonsexual situations highlights the salience of genitalia as the key determiner of gender and sexual identity in sexual situations.

Gender "deception" and the precariousness of (male) heterosexuality

Accusations of false doings of gender in sexual interactions dominate the news coverage of the murder of transwomen by cisgender men through phrases such as "secret," "lied," "tricked," "misled," "avoid detection," "posed as a woman," "true gender," "really a woman," "true identity," "double life," "fooled," "deceit," "pretended," "masquerade," and "gender secret." One typical news story opened,

> Gregory Johnson's friends and a cousin think they know why someone shot the 17-year-old boy and his 18-year-old friend, and then left their bodies to burn beyond recognition inside a blazing SUV. Rage. Johnson, they say, was a sweet and funny young man who liked to dress as a woman, fooling his dates. They suspect one of them became enraged upon learning the truth and killed Johnson and his female friend.
>
> *(Horne and Spalding 2003)*

Journalists, and the people they quote, say that transwomen victims misportrayed their gender through the clothing they wore, the names they used, and often the timbre of their voices. To utilize gender deception as the explanation for violence requires an underlying conception of a true gender that the victim intentionally did not display to the perpetrator. Indeed, the phrase "true gender" is often used in these articles, and the idea of a truth of gender is constructed using other terms; for example, reporters often say that victims had a "gender secret" and were "actually" or "really" another gender. "True gender" in these stories functions both as a synonym for "sex" as well as a reference to the ways that journalists and perpetrators feel that the victims *should* have been doing gender. Although these victims presented as women socially, in the minds of the journalists and perpetrators, they were *really* men for the purposes of sexual interactions because they had penises. Descriptions of the murder of MtF Gwen Araujo, who had not had genital surgery, illustrate this point, as journalists regularly defined her "true gender" as male.

> *Passion blamed for teen's slaying: client's discovery of victim's true gender led to chaos, attorney for one murder suspect says*
>
> A defense attorney for one of three men charged with killing a transgender teen described his client Thursday as a quiet, even-tempered man caught up by ungovernable passions the night he discovered he had unwittingly had sex with a man. "What followed was absolute pandemonium and chaos," said attorney Michael Thorman, who described the killing as "classic manslaughter," not murder. . . . The four men met Araujo, whom they knew as "Lida," in the summer of 2002. Merel and Magidson, according to Nabors, had sex with Araujo, but became suspicious about the teen's gender after comparing notes. On Oct. 3, 2002, the men confronted Araujo at Merel's house in Newark, a San Francisco suburb, and demanded: "Are you a woman or a man?" Another woman at the house found out the truth by grabbing Araujo's genitals. Uproar ensued. The 17-year-old Araujo was punched, choked, hit with a skillet, kneed in the face, tied up and strangled. Araujo was buried in a remote area near Lake Tahoe; about two weeks later Nabors led police to the victim's body.
>
> *(Associated Press 2004)*

In sexual interactions such as this one, "true gender" is often determined by touching the genitals, showing that truth here is determined by bodily, rather than social, criteria. In sexual relationships, biological sex and social gender are expected to "match." As a result, women with penises are seen as sexual deceivers.

We can see the importance of the shape of genitals, rather than transgender status, in determining "true gender" by comparing journalists' explanations of murders of transwomen who have and have not had genital surgery. Between 1990 and 2005, the mainstream news reported on the murder of six transwomen who had had genital surgery. None of them were said to have been killed because they "deceived" their sexual partner about their "true gender." Journalists do not use the deception frame to explain the murder of postoperative transwomen, as they possess the "correct" biological credentials to do gender as women in sexual interactions. In contrast, journalists portray transwomen who have not had genital surgery as being truly men and, as such, engaging in a double deception—about both their gender and sexual orientation—if they have sex with heterosexual men. Shawn Wilson assumed that Robert Gibson must be a homosexual after discovering Gibson's male genitalia during a sexual encounter:

> *Man to stand trial in stabbing death of female impersonator*
>
> A 21-year-old man was ordered yesterday to stand trial on a murder charge in the stabbing death of an El Cajon hairdresser who moonlighted as a female impersonator. Shawn Keith Wilson told police after his arrest that he allowed 32-year-old Robert Howard Gibson to perform a sex act on him, then "tripped out" when he realized that Gibson was a man. Gibson was stabbed 25 times late on the night of July 30. . . . Shortly after Wilson's arrest, [Wilson's friend, Laree] Stemen told detectives that Wilson had told her that a homosexual "tried to rape him."
>
> *(Wolf 1998)*

Transwomen who desire men are assumed to be gay men because they have penises and want to engage in sex with other people with penises. Without the biological credentials to prove their desire as heterosexual, they are presumed to be homosexual.

In many of these murder cases, journalists and perpetrators portray transwomen as deceptive gay men, seeking to trick innocent heterosexual men into homosexuality. This "trick" carries a heavy social weight through what we term the "one-act rule of homosexuality." Similar to the idea that anyone with one drop of black blood is black (Davis 1991), both straight and gay people often believe that engaging in sexual encounters with people of the same sex demonstrates an innate, previously hidden, homosexuality, no matter what sexual identity one may personally avow (Ward 2006). In interviews and court testimony, the accused killers of Gwen Araujo articulate a belief that for a man to have sex with a person who has male-shaped genitals makes him homosexual, even if he were unaware of those genitals at the time. Mainstream news stories describe one of the convicted killers as starting to cry and repeating "I can't be gay" over and over again when the group of men "discovered" that Gwen Araujo had testicles. The punishment for attempting to "trick" someone into homosexuality is death—the only way to literally destroy the evidence of the violation of the one-act rule. Because the "true gender" for sexual encounters is determined by genital shape, self-identity is not sufficient for deciding either gender or sexuality. Thus, heterosexual men are constantly at risk of losing their claim to heterosexual status—just as transwomen are at risk of losing their claim to their chosen gender identity—because both gender and sexuality are produced in interaction. Individuals alone cannot determine their gender or sexuality and must, instead, prove them through fulfilling the appropriate criteria, including having the "right" genitals and never desiring someone with the "wrong" genitals.

The belief that gender deception in a sexual relationship would result in fatal violence is so culturally resonant that, even in cases where there is evidence that the perpetrator knew the victim was transgender prior to the sexual act, many people involved in the case, including journalists and police officers, still use the deception frame.[3] In one such case, that of the murder of Chanelle Pickett (nee Roman Pickett) by William Palmer in 1995, Palmer claimed that he only discovered that Pickett had male genitals once they were engaged in sex. Countering this, a few news articles include quotes from friends of Pickett's who said that Palmer was a regular at transgender hangouts and intentionally pursued transwomen who had not had genital surgeries. Despite these claims, journalists usually explain the murder as resulting from the discovery of Pickett's gender. During the trial, both framings of the violence were told, and the jury found the deception narrative more convincing, convicting Palmer of only assault and battery and sentencing him to two years in jail. Following the logics of heteronormativity and gender inequality, people often ignore counterevidence in these cases and accept the violence as justified.

In mainstream news media portrayals, when faced with the discovery of the transgender status of a sexual partner, men and women respond differently. We cannot account for this gap by only attending to questions of gender. Instead, we must look to the intersections of gender and sexuality. When heterosexual cisgender men and women discover that their sexual partner is transgender, this new information could challenge their claims to heterosexuality, as well as to their gender category of choice. As we saw with the cases of cisgender men, their masculinity is challenged as they feel "raped" and feminized through their connection to homosexuality. To repair this breach, they respond with violence—a masculine-coded act. Because of the interconnectedness of gender and sexuality, cisgender men reclaim their heterosexuality by emphasizing their masculinity. News articles described how when Jose Merel feared that his sexual contact with Gwen Araujo would mark him as gay, his friend Nicole Brown attempted to sooth him through references to his masculinity, saying, "This is not your fault. You were a football player." By highlighting his participation in a masculine sport, she tries to cleanse him of homosexual stigma.

But while cisgender men can repair the sexuality breach by emphasizing masculinity through violence, cisgender women cannot use the same tactic. To do violence and, thus, do masculinity would further destabilize women's claims to both femininity and heterosexuality. Given that masculine behavior in women is associated with lesbianism, cisgender women who wish to emphasize heterosexuality must respond differently—either ending the relationship or accepting their partner in one way or another. This gender difference can be seen clearly in portrayals of the life of Brandon Teena. Before he was killed by two men enraged by his sexual encounters with the local women, he had several heterosexually identified cisgender women partners "discover" his "true gender," but not one responded with fatal violence. Thus, men, not women, can use violence to repair the breach in gender and the challenge to their sexuality caused by the discovery of transgender status in private, casual sexual relationships. The extremity of men's responses shows the depth of the threat of transgender bodies to heteronormativity within sexual situations and the need to neutralize that threat through hypergendered reactions.

Conclusion

This article examines how responses by gender normals to transmen and transwomen demonstrate the ways gender and (hetero)sexuality are interrelated. The sex/gender/sexuality system rests on the belief that there are two, and only two, opposite sexes, determined by biology and signaled primarily by the shape of genitals. The idea of sexual difference naturalizes sexual interactions between "opposite" bodies; within this logic it seems obvious, to paraphrase a slang phrase, to "insert tab A into slot B." Sex between two tabs or two slots, in contrast, is unnatural. Similarly, this sex/gender/sexuality system rests on the belief that gendered behavior, (hetero) sexual identity, and social roles flow naturally from biological sex, creating attraction between two opposite personalities. This belief maintains gender inequality, as "opposites"—bodies, genders, sexes—cannot be expected to fulfill the same social roles and, so, cannot receive the same resources.

The case studies in this article improve our understandings of the workings of a heteronormative gender system predicated on people being clearly categorized as one of two sexes. Much of the literature on violence against transpeople points to gender norm transgression as the cause of violence and assumes that all transgender people are at risk for the same type of violence across social situations. Our two studies complicate this explanation. In public interactions not coded as sexual, self-identity and gender presentation can be sufficient to place someone in his or her gender category of choice—particularly in situations where this new identity is supported by people in authority positions. This adherence reflects the accountability to situational norms in public interactions (Goffman 1966). Highlighting the importance of these public norms, when open workplace transitions do not receive top-down support, cisgender men and women are more likely to express resistance to their transgender colleague (Schilt 2009)—even when they have worked unproblematically for many years with their transgender colleague prior to his or her transition. This resistance is heightened when public interactions become sexualized. In these situations, responses that police heterosexuality are, in themselves, gendered: cisgender women regulate transmen's sexualized behaviors through talk and gossip, whereas cisgender men police transwomen through aggressive verbal harassment (Schilt 2009; Schilt and Connell 2007).

Examining gender normals' reactions to private, sexual interactions with transmen and transwomen presents something of a paradox, however. The majority of cases in the textual analysis present cisgender men murdering transwomen after learning that their sexual partner is transgender. Yet although surely interactions occur in which cisgender women "discover" that the transmen with whom they have been sexually intimate were assigned female at birth, there were no reported cases of cisgender women reacting violently to such a discovery. The gender gap in use of violence to repair the breach in gender and (hetero)sexuality occurs because violence can be used to claim masculine, but not feminine, heterosexuality. Although the one-act rule of homosexuality may well apply equally to men and women, a woman cannot undo the violation by responding with violence.

The extremity of the violence cisgender men use to punish transwomen in private, sexual situations highlights gender inequality in the forms of the cultural devaluation of femininity, homosexuality, and, particularly, males choosing to take on characteristics coded as feminine. The violent reactions from men illustrate the real-life outcomes of gender socialization that requires men to demonstrate their own masculinity and heterosexuality through the devaluation and ridicule of male homosexuality and any presentations—by men or by women—of femininity (Hennen 2008; Pascoe 2007). Similarly, the intense harassment of transwomen by cisgender men in the workplace derives from the valuation of masculinity over femininity. Whereas transmen may face less censure because they are adopting the socially respected traits of masculinity, transwomen are understood as committing the double sin of both abandoning masculinity and choosing femininity.

These gender differences further suggest the importance of the context of interactions (nonsexual/sexualized/sexual; public/private). Sexual and nonsexual situations require different degrees of "oppositeness." Heterosexual interactions entail both opposite genitals as well as opposite gendered behavior. By contrast, nonsexual heterosocial interactions only require opposite gendered behavior, so self-identity can be accepted without biological credentials. As genitals are not visible in nonsexual situations, and are not needed to engage in any of the expected behaviors of the interaction, they are not required to establish membership in a gender category for nonsexual relationships. By contrast, genitals are a central part of the social interaction of a sexual encounter, and so are used both to determine the genders of the people involved as well as the sexual orientation of the encounter. Thus, the criteria for gender membership are different in social versus (hetero)sexual circumstances; only in sexual situations is there a requirement that gender (self-presentation) equals sex (genitals). Accepting transgender people's self-identity in nonsexual situations does not threaten cisgender people's claims to heterosexual status. Men can be *homosocial* with other men, including those who lack the biological credentials for maleness, without being *homosexual*. In sexualized circumstances, however, heterosexuality is threatened by the one-act rule of homosexuality. Cisgender men stand to lose not just their sexual identity but also their standing as "real" men.

Illustrating the connection between gender and sexuality, gender normals react most strongly to transgender people who become, via gender transitions, part of the "opposite gender." The content of these reactions, however, is mediated by the context of the relationship (public/private) and the degree of sexualization of the interaction. In the public context of the workplace, cisgender men and women can incorporate transmen as men into interactions coded as gendered—lifting boxes, backslapping. When interactions become sexualized, however, men emphasize their sameness with transmen while women reject their new oppositeness. These patterns suggest that when a transgender person is not a potential sexual partner, biological credentials (the "right" genitalia) are not required to claim membership in a gender category. By contrast, when the transgender person is in theory part of a potential pool of sexual partners, the criteria for gender membership becomes much more strict—cultural genitals are no longer enough and biological genitals are a necessity.

Examining the reactions of cisgender people to transgender people helps to illuminate the mechanisms that uphold the heteronormative sex/gender/sexuality system and illustrates the lengths to which gender normals will go to maintain a gender/sexual order that occurs "naturally." However, it would be a mistake to assume cisgender sexual desire for transgender bodies "must be paid for in blood," as Halberstam (2005) has argued. Some cisgender people—men, women, gay, straight, bisexual, pansexual—seek sexual and romantic partnerships with people they know to be transgender. Under a heternormative system, this open desire for transgender bodies typically is framed as pathological or fetishistic (Serano 2009). Future research should examine the purposeful sexual and romantic relationships between cisgender and transgender people outside of this pathological frame, as these relationships have the potential to create (hetero)sexual trouble within a heteronormative gender system.

Notes

1 *Cis* is the Latin prefix for "on the same side." It compliments *trans*, the prefix for "across" or "over." "Cisgender" replaces the terms "nontransgender" or "bio man/bio woman" to refer to individuals who have a match between the gender they were assigned at birth, their bodies, and their personal identity.

2 Of the reported murders in which both the gender of the victim and perpetrator were known, 94.9 percent (149 of 157 cases) were instances of cisgender men killing transwomen. The remaining cases included three in which a cisgender woman killed a transwoman (1.91 percent), two in which a transwoman killed another transwoman (1.27 percent), and three in which one or more cisgender men killed a transman (1.91 percent).

3 Perpetrators may claim deception, even when none occurred, to try to reduce both legal and social castigation. As desire for opposite gender transgender bodies is culturally understood as *homosexual* desire, following the belief that genitalia determine gender in sexual interactions, perpetrators may claim they

were deceived to try to cleanse themselves of the stigma from the one-act rule of homosexuality. They may also make such a claim to attempt to reduce criminal charges from homicide to manslaughter.

References

Associated Press. 2004. Passion blamed for teen's slaying: client's discovery of victim's true gender led to chaos, attorney for one murder suspect says. *Los Angeles Times*, 16 April.

Benford, Robert, and David Snow. 2000. Framing processes and social movements: An overview and assessment. *Annual Review of Sociology* 26:611–39.

Bettcher, Talia. 2007. Evil deceivers and make believers: On transphobic violence and the politics of illusion. *Hypatia* 22:45–62.

Bureau of Justice Statistics. 2007. Homicide trends in the U.S.: Trends by gender. http://www.ojp.usdoj.gov/bjs/homicide/gender.htm (accessed 7 March, 2009).

Butler, Judith. 1989. *Gender trouble: Feminism and the subversion of identity*. New York: Routledge.

Cameron, Deborah, and Don Kulick. 2003. *Language and sexuality*. Cambridge: Cambridge University Press.

Connell, R. W. 1987. *Gender & power*. Berkeley: University of California Press.

Davis, Floyd James. 1991. *Who is Black? One nation's definition*. University Park: Pennsylvania State University Press.

Fenstermaker, Sarah, Candace West, and Don Zimmerman. 2002. Gender inequality: New conceptual terrain. In *Doing gender, doing difference*, edited by Sarah Fenstermaker and Candace West, 25–40. New York: Routledge.

Ferree, Myra Marx, William Anthony Gamson, Jurgen Gerhards, and Dieter Rucht. 2002. *Shaping abortion discourse: Democracy and the public sphere in Germany and the United States*. Cambridge: Cambridge University Press.

Franklin, Karen. 2000. Antigay behaviors among young adults: Prevalence, patterns and motivators in a noncriminal population. *Journal of Interpersonal Violence* 15:339–62.

Gamson, William A., David Croteau, William Hoynes, and Theodore Sasson. 1992. Media images and the social construction of reality. *Annual Review of Sociology* 18:373–93.

Garfinkel, Harold. 1967. *Studies in ethnomethodology*. Englewood Cliffs, NJ: Prentice Hall.

Goffman, Erving. 1966. *Behavior in public places: On the social organization of groups*. New York: Free Press.

———. 1977. The arrangement between the sexes. *Theory & Society* 4 (3): 301–31.

———. 1986. *Frame analysis: An essay on the organization of experience*. Boston: Northeastern University Press.

Grace, Melissa. 2003. Nabbed in tricky transsexual slay. *Daily News* (New York), 21 May.

Halberstam, Judith. 2005. *In a queer time and place: Transgender bodies, subcultural lives*. New York: New York University Press.

Hennen, Peter. 2008. *Faeries, bears, and leathermen: Men in community queering the masculine*. Chicago: University of Chicago Press.

Horne, Terry, and Tom Spalding. 2003. Dating habits may have led to teen's death. *Indianapolis Star*, 26 July.

Ingraham, Chyrs. 1994. The heterosexual imaginary: Feminist sociology and theories of gender. *Sociological Theory* 12:203–19.

Jamieson, Wendell. 1992. Man kills transvestite, then himself, police say. *Newsday* (Melville, NY), 9 February.

Kessler, Suzanne, and Wendy McKenna. 1978. *Gender: An ethnomethodological approach*. Chicago: University of Chicago Press.

Kitzinger, Celia. 2005. Heteronormativity in action: Reproducing the heterosexual nuclear family in after-hours medical calls. *Social Problems* 52 (4): 477–98.

MacKinnon, Catherine. 1982. Feminism, Marxism, method and the state: An agenda for theory. *Signs: Journal of Women in Culture and Society* 7 (13): 515–44.

Pascoe, C. J. 2007. *Dude, you're a fag: Masculinity and sexuality in high school*. Berkeley: University of California Press.

Rich, Adrienne. 1980. Compulsory heterosexuality and lesbian existence. *Signs: Journal of Women in Culture and Society* 5 (4): 631–60.

Schilt, Kristen. 2009. (Trans)gender at work: The persistence of gender inequality. Manuscript.

Schilt, Kristen, and Catherine Connell. 2007. Do workplace gender transitions make gender trouble? *Gender, Work and Organization* 14 (6): 596–618.

Schippers, Mimi. 2007. Recovering the feminine other: Masculinity, femininity, and gender hegemony. *Theory & Society* 36 (1): 85–102.

Seidman, Steven. 1995. Deconstructing queer theory or the under-theorization of the social and the ethical. In *Social postmodernism: Beyond identity politics*, edited by Linda Nicholson and Steven Seidman. Cambridge: Cambridge University Press.

Serano, Julia. 2009. Why feminists should be concerned with the impending revisions of the DSM. http://www.feministing.com/archives/015254.html (accessed 6 May, 2009).

Ward, Jane. 2006. Straight dude seeks same: Mapping the relationship between sexual identities, Practices, and cultures. In *Sex matters: The sexuality and society reader*, 2nd ed., edited by Mindy Stombler. Needham Heights, Massachusetts: Allyn & Bacon.

Washington Times. 1993. Man charged in death of transvestite. 4 January.

West, Candace, and Don Zimmerman. 1987. Doing gender. *Gender & Society* 1 (2): 125–51.

Williams, Christine, Patti Giuffre, and Kirsten Dellinger. 1999. Sexuality in the workplace. *Annual Review of Sociology* 25:73–93.

Wolf, Leslie. 1998. Man to stand trial in stabbing death of female impersonator. *San Diego Union-Tribune*, 21 October.

Part IV
Straight states

18

Introduction to "The Straight State: Sexuality and Citizenship in Twentieth Century America"

Margot Canaday

For all orderly processes, we must in some way classify man.

—Dr. Dahlgren, surgeon, U.S. Public Health Service, testifying in *Rosenberg v. Fleuti*

Measured against other Western democracies at the dawn of the twentieth century, the American state—slow to develop, small in size, and limited in capability—stood out as distinctive.[1] Fifty years later, a period of expansion had produced a state that was finally European in its heft, but still exceptional in another way: in terms of its homophobia. "There appears to be no other major culture in the world," Alfred Kinsey wrote in 1953, in which homosexual relationships were "so severely penalized."[2] Not only was the United States "the only major power in the world" that excluded homosexuals from its armed services and government employment, the sociologist Donald Webster Cory wrote a decade later, "but the homosexual is the only individual who is punished in this manner, not only for any activities that may be indulged in, but for harboring the desire to perform such activities."[3] Those suspected of homosexuality were purged from the civil service and military in astounding numbers at midcentury. They were also barred from certain federal benefits, faced increased FBI and Post Office surveillance and explicit immigration and naturalization exclusions, as well as the stain of alleged political subversion.[4] It seems a paradox. How did a state that was so late in coming construct such a vast apparatus for policing homosexuality, and why?

Unlike comparable European states, which were well established *before* sexologists "discovered" the homosexual in the late nineteenth century, the American bureaucracy matured during the same years that scientific and popular awareness of the pervert exploded on the American continent. This study examines three of the "engines" of the twentieth-century state—the Bureau of Immigration, the military, and the federal agencies that administered welfare benefits—to demonstrate how federal interest in homosexuality developed in tandem with the growth of the bureaucratic state. In emphasizing the relationship between state formation and homosexual identity, I not only seek to put the history of sexuality into closer dialogue with political and legal history, but to complicate what has now become a standard interpretation within the field of gay and lesbian history as well. Namely, that extreme state repression of sex and gender nonconformity in the mid-twentieth century was a result of the sudden visibility of gays and lesbians during and after World War II.

That explanation is not exactly wrong, but it is incomplete. World War II was a watershed moment in the state's relationship to homosexuality, yet homosexuality was not a new phenomenon for state officials during and after the Second World War. Rather, federal bureaucrats had been aware of traits and behaviors that were coming to be associated with homosexuality for at least half a century. The regulatory response to this knowledge before the war, however, was fairly anemic. Viewing this period through the McCarthyist lens of what came after, it is hard to understand how federal officials could be both so aware and yet seemingly so indifferent to perversion during these years.

This sluggish federal response loses some of its mystery if we center the processes of twentieth-century state-building, and the way that states must "puzzle before they power."[5] Federal officials were confronted with evidence of sex and gender nonconformity as they did the things that bureaucrats do—whether keeping undesirables out of the country, peopling an army, or distributing resources among the citizenry. But they initially encountered this evidence without a clear conceptual framework to analyze the problem. Even so, they worried about those whose bodies or behaviors seemed perverse to them. Over time, they worked toward an understanding of what this phenomenon was and why it might be significant, and they made some minimal attempts at regulation. Yet when perversion was policed in this early period, it was often through regulatory devices aimed at broader problems: poverty, disorder, violence, or crime, for example.

As the state expanded, however, it increasingly developed conceptual mastery over what it sought to regulate. This itself was part of the work of state-building, part of a longer process of the state coming to know and care about homosexuality. After the Second World War, an increasingly powerful state wrote this new knowledge into federal policy, helping to produce the category of homosexuality through regulation. From the mid-1940s into the late 1960s, the state crafted tools to overtly target homosexuality. In contrast to the earlier period, policies were enacted that *explicitly* used homosexuality to define who could enter the country and be naturalized, who could serve in the military, and who could collect state benefits. A homosexual-heterosexual binary, in other words, was being inscribed in federal citizenship policy during these years. Indeed, this study's examination of three of the arenas where the meaning of American citizenship was most sharply articulated over the course of the twentieth century—in immigration, the military, and welfare—reveals the emergence of that binary as one of the organizing categories of federal policy in the postwar United States.

Regulation, of course, changed what was regulated. The state did not, I argue, simply encounter homosexual citizens, fully formed and waiting to be counted, classified, administered, or disciplined. This was not, as political theorist Jacqueline Stevens has written in a slightly different context, simply a matter of "pre-constituted groups" either coming into or being blocked from the public sphere.[6] Rather, the state's identification of certain sexual behaviors, gender traits, and emotional ties as grounds for exclusion (from entering the country, serving in the military, or collecting benefits) was a catalyst in the formation of homosexual identity.[7] The state, in other words, did not merely implicate but also *constituted* homosexuality in the construction of a stratified citizenry.

Homosexuality is thus a legal category as much as a medical or psychiatric one. This study not only sets the federal regulation of homosexuality in longer historical view, but also offers an account of the *bureaucratization* of homosexuality—something forged, in short, through legal and administrative processes. To uncover those processes is to challenge the law's own tendency to authorize homosexuality as somehow pregiven or even natural in its constitution. "The power exerted by a legal regime consists less in the force that it can bring to bear against violators of its rules," writes the legal historian Robert Gordon, "than in its capacity to persuade that the world described in its image and categories is the only attainable world."[8]

Before laying out the argument in greater detail, a fuller discussion of three of the main terms that frame this study will be necessary.

The state

The state is notoriously difficult to conceptualize and write about.[9] "The domain we call the state is not a thing, a system, or a subject," political theorist Wendy Brown writes, "but a significantly unbounded terrain of powers and techniques, an ensemble of discourses, rules, and practices, cohabiting in limited, tension-ridden, often contradictory relation with one another."[10] While I appreciate Brown's conception, this is hardly a clear recipe for historical research. Historians, for their part, have responded to the vastness and complexity of the state (until fairly recently) by not writing about the state at all. Indeed, it is remarkable how limited the historiography on the U.S. state still is, given the lengthy period of time for which American history *was* political history and vice versa.[11] Yet ignoring the state is less of an option than it once was, largely because social scientists working outside of history have made the case for its significance so powerfully. The state was a "central actor in its own right," historian Brian Balogh observes in his discussion of the work of Theda Skocpol and Steven Skowronek, "an autonomous force and one that had to be reckoned with in writing the nation's history." While those social scientists who advocate "bringing the state back in" have stirred historians' interest, historians have generally not adopted their approach wholesale.[12] The best work on the state by historians takes state institutions seriously, but incorporates rather than jettisons the "society" or "culture" side of the binary, blending social and cultural with legal and political history.[13]

This study, accordingly, takes a "state-building from the bottom up" or "social history of the state" approach. We can see the state through its practices; the state is "what officials do."[14] And by officials, I mean not only top decision-makers but bureaucrats at all levels. This is, moreover, not only a "people" but a "places" approach to the state. In locating the places of the state, my method similarly hovers close to the ground. I am as likely to find the state at a Veterans Administration (VA) office in Florida or in an immigration inspector's booth on the border, as in the halls of Congress or before the bar of the Supreme Court. Focusing on these kinds of spaces provides an opportunity to think about the state as not only "intervening" in, but as "intervened" by sexuality as well. The state does not just direct policy at its subjects; various state arenas are themselves sites of contest over sex/gender norms, and therefore structured by those norms.[15] This is, in large measure, what it means to say that we have a "straight state."

In contrast to numerous historical studies that examine one modality of state power over time (the growth of the welfare state or the national security state, for example), my study looks at the state's regulation of one issue (homosexuality) across several venues of federal authority. While I undoubtedly sacrifice some depth for breadth, this broad cross-sectional view illuminates the gradual construction of a legal apparatus to deal with same-sex erotic behavior and gender inversion across state institutions. But despite broad convergence over time, the state is not a monolith, and officials created and implemented policies in ways that were generally sensitive to the needs of the agencies they represented. For instance, an alien discovered to have defective genitalia in the early years of the twentieth century most likely would have been excluded at the border as perverse. The same condition, though, might not have prevented a would-be soldier from being inducted into the army. Across the bureaucracy, sex and gender nonconformity figured in different ways.

An alternative approach might look vertically at local-state-federal interaction rather than horizontally, as I do, across several institutions of the federal state. At a historiographical moment when political and legal historians are turning their attention especially to governance at state and local levels, why shouldn't this be my approach?[16] I focus on the federal government for a simple reason. Numerous commentators at midcentury noted that there was "no crime against being homosexual."[17] This is true. There was no crime. But there was a policy against being homosexual, and it was federal in nature. States and localities generally policed homosexual acts; sometimes the feds did as well. Yet in addition, it was the federal government that gradually developed the tools to target homosexual personhood or status, the condition of *being* a homosexual.[18] The federal government, moreover, never defined homosexual status in the abstract, but always as a part of defining citizenship. Indeed, it is most likely that because citizenship is (since Reconstruction) a national category, the federal government played such an important role in shaping homosexual identity. Now, to take each of the two categories that the federal state filled with meaning in turn:

Citizenship

In contrast to American historical writing on the state, there has been an explosion of historical work on citizenship in recent years.[19] That work—which complements a booming industry in citizenship studies throughout the academy—uses citizenship in a myriad of ways. Citizenship has been long understood as a set of rights, a tradition exemplified by the work of British sociologist T. H. Marshall.[20] More recent work emphasizes citizenship as obligation.[21] In addition to liberal and republican paradigms, contemporary scholarship on citizenship also includes communitarian, social democratic, feminist, and multicultural critiques.[22] Sociologists Will Kymlicka and Wayne Norman have usefully pointed out that this vast scholarship can be broken down into two broad categories. Some accounts describe citizenship as practice, with the emphasis on the activity of being a citizen. Other accounts treat citizenship as status, whether defined legally or culturally. Scholarship in this vein concerns citizenship as identity, seeks to identify the attributes of good citizens, and to determine the way in which individuals are incorporated into the status of citizenship.[23] While each of my chapters necessarily touches on the practices of citizenship—soldiering, immigrating, or the act of claiming benefits—this project takes its driving questions from the literature on citizenship as status.

In the American tradition, the legal status of citizenship is simple. According to Linda Kerber, one either is or is not a citizen. In contrast to some European nations, there are no formal categories here of first- and second-class citizenship. But the preoccupation of historians in recent years, including Kerber, has been to examine the "distinctions that were historically experienced"—how, in Nancy Cott's words, citizenship "can be delivered in different degrees of permanence or strength."[24] This study adds sexuality to the ascriptive tradition of American citizenship that Rogers Smith lays out, and makes the case that the trajectory of American citizenship in the twentieth century has not been one of continual expansion, but is defined rather by the persistent "nexus of exclusion and inclusion."[25] As the state moved to enfranchise women and dismantle Jim Crow, it was gradually working to construct a boundary in law and policy that by midcentury explicitly defined the homosexual as the anticitizen.[26] What was an inchoate and vague sort of opposition between citizenship and perversion in the early twentieth century became a hard and clear line by midcentury.

Sometimes, as in the case of aliens who were deported because they engaged in homoerotic behavior, homosexuality was defined as outside of citizenship through formal legal expulsion. More often, those suspected of sexual perversion were not formally excluded from citizenship status. One who was denied the right to serve in the military or access to state benefits, for example, would (if not an alien) retain the right to reside in the country.[27] Citizenship is thus best understood through an approach that considers "threshold questions" regarding access to the nation-state (i.e., immigration) alongside, as legal scholar Linda Bosniak writes, "questions about the nature and quality of citizenship as practiced within the political community" (in this study, access to welfare benefits or military employment). Just as few historical studies of the state treat multiple modalities of state power simultaneously, few studies of citizenship consider immigration and naturalization policy in tandem with other aspects of citizenship. In analyzing them together, I hope to show, in Bosniak's formulation, that "citizenship's threshold and its substantive character are interwoven," and to highlight that "political communities exist in a wider world."[28] Indeed, while certainly not transnational in scope, this study suggests a flow of people, practices, and ideas about sexuality across borders that impacted national belonging for aliens and citizens alike.

Yet whether talking about "threshold" questions of membership or "internal" questions about the way that already-existing citizens actually experienced their citizenship, it is critical to note that many of those who engaged in same-sex erotic practices or expressed gender nonconformity were never vetted by the state at all.[29] Indeed, state policies directed at sex/gender nonconformists have generally not operated by targeting large numbers—and this was especially true for the earlier period. As important as documenting the legal construction of a barrier for sexual minorities in terms of who would be able to immigrate, soldier, and collect benefits, then, is to determine the terms of inclusion within citizenship. The historical evolution of the policies that have over time configured citizenship in relation to homosexuality reveals that, in the words of political theorist Lisa J. Disch, "otherness is immanent to citizenship." Citizenship fosters "internal differentiation and hierarchy," Disch writes, by incorporating some into citizenship in a way that highlights their subordination or "degraded status."[30] And citizenship's mode of incorporation—whether formally inclusionary or exclusionary at any given moment—was not only productive of difference, I argue, but also identity. Over the course of the early to mid-twentieth century, the state crafted citizenship policies that crystallized homosexual identity, fostering a process by which certain individuals began to think of their sexuality in political terms, as mediating and mediated by their relationship to the state.

Homosexuality

Homosexuality is perhaps the most vexing of all, because its meaning changed so much in the years that this study covers, and that change, as I have already suggested, was itself in part a result of the processes of state formation I write about here. Historians of sexuality—critiquing Michel Foucault's assertion that the homosexual had emerged as a "species" by the turn of the century—have argued that the appearance of the homosexual as a personality type in medical literature was, in George Chauncey's words, but "one of several powerful (and competing) sexual ideologies."[31] Alongside the medical ideologies were popular frameworks (which Chauncey writes about), and the ideologies of state officials regarding the sexual cultures and types they encountered as their various bureaucracies expanded. Whatever the extent to which Foucault was correct about the invention of homosexuality during these years, Progressive-era officials used the word homosexuality somewhat interchangeably with "pervert," "degenerate," "pederast," and "sodomite." Moreover, these labels generally did not refer to a kind of person who engaged in sexual activity with a member of the same sex. The homosexual was instead a perverted type whose perversion was defined primarily by gender inversion (mannishness in women and effeminacy in men) rather than by sexual behavior per se.[32] And perversion was a fuzzy category, loosely associated with degeneracy, and sometimes manifested as well through morphology (for example, defective genitalia or "poor physique"). Most state authorities in the early twentieth century shared with the populations they policed a notion that men who had sex with perverts (as long as they were masculine and took the "active" role in sexual relations) engaged in immoral behavior (like stealing or whoring), but were not themselves perverse. There was not yet a clear moral axis that cleaved the population into homosexuals and heterosexuals. Rather, a hazier divide existed—something more akin to perverts and normals.

Although "normal" individuals who engaged in sexual relations with persons of the same sex fell outside the moral economy of perversity in early twentieth-century America, they do not fall outside the purview of this history of homosexuality and federal policy. For this is not, actually, a history of federal interest in what homosexuality is at any given moment, but rather a history of federal interest in *what becomes* homosexuality by midcentury. In short, I am writing about a process more than a thing. My approach is, following David Halperin, genealogical. Halperin writes that homosexuality signifies "the effect of a cumulative process of overlay and accretion," in which a variety of "prehomosexual discourses" are held together in an "unstable convergence."[33] Conceptually, I begin with that convergence—homosexuality at midcentury—and follow it backward in time. I follow the threads as they separate; as long as they remain subject to federal policing, they remain part of the story. Or, to put this in another way that follows the chronological movement of this study, I am tracing the "accretion" that over time results in the modern notion of homosexuality as defined by sexual object choice. This was a broadening of the early twentieth-century paradigm—the "normal" man, for example, who was masculine and had sex with other men became a homosexual by midcentury, but the gender invert didn't stop being one. Government policy played a critical role in widening the definitional parameters of what made one homosexual; policing this broader configuration required, in turn, a greater investment of state resources.

The regulation of homosexuality in women was also affected by the overall broadening of homosexuality that state policies had helped to bring about. In the early years of the twentieth century, the emphasis placed on gender difference in defining sexual normativity meant that same-sex eroticism among men and same-sex eroticism among women were seen as distinct kinds of things. As a result, men and women were subject to different forms of policing. Indeed, the federal regulation of male and female sexual deviance occurred on two separate tracks during the first part of the twentieth century, such that state policing of women was almost entirely focused on deviant *heterosexuality*.[34] The new understanding of homosexuality that began to crystallize as mid-century approached was characterized by a binarism between heterosexuality and homosexuality. Everyone was either one or the other, and the defining feature of homosexuality was same-sex sexual activity (whether the act in question concerned two men or two women). In minimizing the definitional importance of gender, this new framework treated sex between men and sex between women as similar acts, and thus subjected women to regulation as *homosexuals*.

Yet it wasn't only that homosexuality came to be seen as pertaining to women as well as men that led to increased policing among women as midcentury approached. Federal officials also had to decide that homosexuality among women was a problem that deserved federal attention. Their slowness to do so (even as government resources for policing expanded) reflects the way that state policies configured citizenship and homosexuality in relation to one another. Gendered ideologies of citizenship, in other words, shaped the gendered regulation of perversion—male perverts mattered so much to the state because male citizens did.[35] Until almost midcentury, a relatively small regulatory apparatus and genuine state indifference to female perversion meant that women were rarely targeted by legal instruments that were used to vet those who engaged in same-sex sexual behavior or manifested gender inversion. Such tools were deployed against women only as they were more fully incorporated into the arena of first-class citizenship—most visibly, when they were permanently integrated into the military during the early years of the cold war. As women were more completely drawn into citizenship, then, state officials became more focused on lesbianism.

Moving forward

This study is comprised of two chapters on each of three cases: immigration, the military, and welfare. Thematically, the project is layered. The outer layer, chapters 1 and 6, is immigration. Moving inward, the next layer, chapters 2 and 5, is the military. Finally, the nucleus of the study, chapters 3 and 4, focuses on welfare. The organization of part I of the book (immigration-military-welfare) is mirrored in part II (welfare-military-immigration). The three cases, moreover, each serve two functions in the structure of the project: immigration, military service, and welfare represent major components of citizenship; and, the Bureau of Immigration, the military establishment, and the federal agencies that administered welfare programs all played a major role in the rise of the twentieth-century state. Across several state arenas and over time, then, the six chapters reveal a variety of federal institutions all engaged (but at different stages) in the same enterprise: defining homosexuality and citizenship in relation to one another through the construction of policies that established individuals who exhibited gender inversion or engaged in homoerotic behavior as either outside of or degraded within citizenship.

I proceed throughout by keeping my finger on the arenas where the state was experiencing growth more generally, because the process of state-building itself drew the regulatory eye to sexual/gender deviance. So, for example, I begin with immigration, one of the earliest federal bureaucracies, and the first to leave substantial documentation of its response to sexual perversion. The military's adoption of psychiatric and other forms of screening for recruits during World War I led to a growing awareness of sexual "abnormalities" among the troops, so I shift my focus from immigration to the military during this period. (Actual bureaucrats followed this same trajectory, as for example, a Dr. Thomas Salmon, who began his career by inspecting immigrants for the Public Health Service [PHS], and then went on to be the head of psychiatry for the American Expeditionary Forces during the First World War.)[36] The crisis of the Depression inaugurated new experiments with government social provision, and I next examine how New Dealers dealt with rumored and actual homosexuality in work camps for single male transients—the "runaway boys and men." The subsequent chapter focuses on the denial of GI Bill benefits to soldiers discharged for homosexuality during and after World War II. With the dawn of the McCarthy era, I take advantage of the unique opportunity that the 1950s' military provides to examine federal policies on homosexuality that were derived from the regulation of women. My last chapter circles back to immigration policy because it allows me to follow the story from where I began with the Bureau of Immigration to the Immigration and Naturalization Service (INS) and the federal courts. Here especially, I "bring the law back in," as William Novak writes, to political history, considering the courts alongside the administrative agency as just another venue through which the modern state is created.[37]

Readers should be forewarned that in organizing my study by these cases, I do not claim complete coverage of every federal arena where the state acted to define homosexuality. I do not, for example, look at the federal civil service's antihomosexual purge at midcentury because of the comprehensive way this story has been told elsewhere.[38] I also deliberately (if somewhat gingerly) step over World War II.[39] I do not ignore the war but neither do I make it the hub, preferring to engage this story through the World War II–era VA bureaucracy and its implementation of benefits (and hence the welfare-warfare state). I do so because I think welfare has been incredibly understudied in its relationship to sexuality, and because the state was as concerned with using its resources to *settle* men *down* after wartime (think marriage, home, and reproduction) as it was with anything they may have done "over there." Indeed, mobility was a central problematic for the state's regulation of sexuality—the subjects of regulation in this study are all, in one way or another, people on the move. So GI Bill benefits aimed to domesticate men after World War II, but were also a reaction to the memory of so many single men out drifting and "on the bum" during the preceding decade. This inchoate opposition between mobility and settlement evolved into an explicit differentiation between homosexuals and heterosexuals across the temporal span of World War II, and we can see the homosexual-heterosexual binary emerging out of federal welfare policy in this key moment of American state-building. For all these reasons, the state's welfare function makes most sense at the center of this study.

Finally, a note about my semantic choices for the years before homosexuality became a hegemonic term: whenever possible, I try to use the language that federal officials used. Officials not only used a variety of terms, they adopted new terminologies at different rates, depending on the labels they heard used by the sexual cultures with which they came into contact, and on how "up" they were on the current medical literature. State officials also made up terms for bureaucratic usage. So, for instance, immigrants were excluded for a "lack of sexual development," which was closely associated with sexual perversion. "I would first observe that this term in exactly these words will . . . not be found in any of the standard works of medicine," Surgeon General H. S. Cumming wrote to Commissioner-General of Immigration W. W. Husband in 1922. "These words were used by the medical officers [involved] in order to make plain to the non-medical examiners what the condition was which they were certifying."[40] The surgeon general's concern, like that of many of the state officials who will appear in the following chapters, was less technical precision than to find the words and concepts with which to navigate a sex and gender terrain still coming into view.

Notes

1 See, for example, many of the essays in, and especially the introduction to, Margaret Weir, Ann Shola Orloff, and Theda Skocpol, eds., *The Politics of Social Policy in the United States* (Princeton, NJ: Princeton University Press, 1988); Brian Balogh, "The State of the State among Historians," *Social Science History* 27 (Fall 2003): 456; Meg Jacobs and Julian E. Zelizer, "The Democratic Experiment: New Directions in American Political History," in *The Democratic Experiment: New Directions in American Political History*, ed. Meg Jacobs, William J. Novak, and Julian E. Zelizer (Princeton, NJ: Princeton University Press, 2003), 2. My representation of the early twentieth-century state as a fledgling bureaucracy refers to the federal state. William Novak has argued convincingly that state and local governments were quite vigorous in nineteenth-century America. See William J. Novak, *The People's Welfare: Law and Regulation in 19th Century America* (Chapel Hill: University of North Carolina Press, 1996). I do not find Novak's more recent article applying this notion of a vigorous state more broadly (across all levels of government) as persuasive. William J. Novak, "The Myth of the 'Weak' American State," *American Historical Review* 113 (June 2008): 752–72. Several scholars (Richard John, Jerry Mashaw, and Richard White, among others) have identified pockets of federal authority throughout American history. Yet relative to what existed in Europe at that moment, as well as to what came later, the tools and resources available to the federal state in 1900 were limited.

2 Alfred C. Kinsey, *Sexual Behavior in the Human Female* (Philadelphia: Saunders, 1953), 483. Kinsey's observation was not unique: "In contrast to England and the United States, the majority of European states do not proscribe homosexual acts between consenting adults. Austria, Germany, and Norway are the only European countries that do so, but in Norway the law is not enforced. In Belgium, homosexual conduct is punishable only if there is an assault, if the sexual object is a minor, or if there is a violation of public decency. Similar situations obtain in Denmark, Greece, Italy, the Netherlands, Sweden, and Switzerland. In France, homosexuality between consenting adults has not been a crime since the *Code Napoléon* went into force in 1810" (Thomas S. Szasz, "Legal and Moral Aspects of Homosexuality,"

in *Sexual Inversion: The Multiple Roots of Homosexuality,* ed. Judd Marmor [New York: Basic Books, 1965], 127–28). See also Institute for Sex Research, "The Challenges and Progress of Homosexual Law Reform," 10–11, vertical file, "Legal Aspects of Homosexuality," Kinsey Institute, Indiana University, Bloomington.

3 Donald Webster Cory, *The Lesbian in America* (New York: MacFadden-Bartell, 1965), 221.

4 The earliest study of state homophobia at midcentury was John D'Emilio's *Sexual Politics, Sexual Communities: The Making of a Homosexual Minority in the United States, 1940–1970* (Chicago: University of Chicago Press, 1983). For a recent study that looks exclusively at the civil service purge, see David K. Johnson, *The Lavender Scare: The Cold War Persecution of Gays and Lesbians in the Federal Government* (Chicago: University of Chicago Press, 2004).

5 Hugh Heclo, *Modern Social Politics in Britain and Sweden: From Relief to Income Maintenance* (New Haven, CT: Yale University Press, 1974), 305.

6 Jacqueline Stevens, *Reproducing the State* (Princeton, NJ: Princeton University Press, 1999), 56.

7 On the state's role as an agent that identifies (and a related critique of the concept of identity), see Rogers Brubaker and Frederick Cooper, "Beyond 'Identity,'" *Theory and Society* 29 (2000): 1–47.

8 Robert W. Gordon, "Critical Legal Histories," *Stanford Law Review* 36 (January 1984): 109.

9 Stevens, *Reproducing the State*, 57.

10 Wendy Brown, *States of Injury: Power and Freedom in Late Modernity* (Princeton, NJ: Princeton University Press, 1995), 174–75.

11 Despite that long reign, political historian Morton Keller could lament to his colleague William Leuchtenburg in 1986 that there was still "close to *everything* to be learned about the State." William E. Leuchtenburg, "The Pertinence of Political History: Reflections on the Significance of the State in America," *Journal of American History* 73 (December 1986): 594. Of course, it depends who you talk to—where, for example, Brian Balogh saw a paucity of historical scholarship on the U.S. state, William Novak saw an abundance. Both assessments were made in articles written in 2003. In part, these disparate assessments might reflect differences between political (Balogh) and legal (Novak) history. Balogh, "The State of the State among Historians," 455–63; William J. Novak, "The Legal Origins of the Modern American State," in *Looking Back at Law's Century*, ed. Austin Sarat, Bryant Garth, and Robert A. Kagan (Ithaca, NY: Cornell University Press, 2002), 250.

12 Balogh, "The State of the State among Historians," 458–59. The works that Balogh discusses include Theda Skocpol, "Bringing the State Back In," in *Bringing the State Back In*, ed. Peter B. Evans, Dietrich Rueschemeyer, and Theda Skocpol (New York: Cambridge University Press, 1985), 3–37; Stephen Skowronek, *Building a New American State: The Expansion of National Administrative Capacities, 1877–1920* (New York: Cambridge University Press, 1982). See also Julian E. Zelizer, "Stephen Skowronek's *Building a New American State* and the Origins of American Political Development," *Social Science History* 27 (Fall 2003): 425–41.

13 William Novak's *The People's Welfare* is an excellent example of this, as are many of the essays in Jacobs, Novak, and Zelizer, *The Democratic Experiment.* Note, however, that almost no attention is paid in this volume to sexuality, the full significance of which I think political history has yet to appreciate. See also George Steinmetz, ed., *State/Culture: State Formation after the Cultural Turn* (Ithaca, NY: Cornell University Press, 1999).

14 John R. Commons, quoted in Novak, *The People's Welfare*, 8.

15 For a related argument about race, see Michael Omi and Howard Winant, *Racial Formation in the United States: From the 1960s to the 1990s* (New York: Routledge, 1994), 82.

16 Scholarship exemplifying this approach includes Novak, *The People's Welfare*; Thomas J. Sugrue, "All Politics Is Local: The Persistence of Localism in Twentieth-Century America," in *The Democratic Experiment: New Directions in American Political History*, ed. Meg Jacobs, William J. Novak, and Julian E. Zelizer (Princeton, NJ: Princeton University Press, 2003), 301–26; Laura Edwards, "Status without Rights: African Americans and the Tangled History of Law and Governance in the Nineteenth-Century U.S. South," *American Historical Review* 112 (April 2007): 365–93. Localism has long been the dominant paradigm in LGBT history. See Marc Stein, "Theoretical Politics, Local Communities: The Making of U.S. LGBT History," *GLQ* 11 (2005): 605–24.

17 Alfred A. Gross, *Strangers in Our Midst: Problems of the Homosexual in American Society* (Washington, DC: Public Affairs Press, 1962), 93; Edward H. Knight, "Overt Male Homosexuality," in *Sexual Behavior and the Law*, ed. Ralph Slovenko (Springfield, IL: Charles C. Thomas Publishers, 1965), 434.

18 "The Consenting Adult Homosexual and the Law: An Empirical Study of Enforcement and Administration in Los Angeles County," *UCLA Law Review* 13 (1966): 658.

19 A sampling of that work includes Linda Gordon, *Pitied But Not Entitled: Single Mothers and the History of Welfare, 1890–1935* (Cambridge, MA: Harvard University Press, 1994); Rogers M. Smith, *Civic Ideals: Conflicting Visions of Citizenship in U.S. History* (New Haven, CT: Yale University Press, 1997); Candace Lewis Bredbenner, *A Nationality of Her Own: Women, Marriage, and the Law of Citizenship* (Berkeley: University of California Press, 1998); Nancy F. Cott, "Marriage and Women's Citizenship in the United States," *American Historical Review* 103 (December 1998): 1440–74; Katherine Franke, "Becoming a Citizen: Reconstruction Era Regulation of African American Marriages," *Yale Journal of Law and the Humanities* 11 (1999): 251–309; Linda K. Kerber, *No Constitutional Right to Be Ladies: Women and the Obligations of Citizenship* (New York: Hill and Wang, 1999); Mary L. Dudziak, *Cold War Civil Rights: Race and the Image of American Democracy* (Princeton, NJ: Princeton University Press, 2000); Alexander Keyssar, *The Right to Vote: The Contested History of Democracy in the United States* (New York: Basic Books, 2000); Alice Kessler-Harris, *In Pursuit of Equity: Women, Men, and the Quest for Economic Citizenship in 20th Century America* (Oxford: Oxford University Press, 2001); Nancy F. Cott, *Public Vows: A History of Marriage and the Nation* (Cambridge, MA: Harvard University Press, 2002); Evelyn Nakano Glenn, *Unequal Freedom: How Race and Gender Shaped American Citizenship and Labor* (Cambridge, MA: Harvard University Press, 2002); Lizabeth Cohen, *A Consumers' Republic: The Politics of Mass Consumption in Postwar America* (New York: Knopf, 2003); Erika Lee, *At America's Gates: Chinese Immigration during the Exclusion Era, 1882–1943* (Chapel Hill: University of North Carolina Press, 2003); Mae M. Ngai, *Impossible Subjects: Illegal Aliens and the Making of Modern America* (Princeton, NJ: Princeton University Press, 2003); Meg Jacobs, *Pocketbook Politics: Economic Citizenship in Twentieth-Century America* (Princeton, NJ: Princeton University Press, 2004); Nancy MacLean, *Freedom Is Not Enough: The Opening of the American Workplace* (Cambridge, MA: Harvard University Press, 2006).

20 Marshall's classic work is "Citizenship and Social Class," in *The Citizenship Debates: A Reader*, ed. Gershon Shafir (Minneapolis: University of Minnesota Press, 1998), 93–112.

21 Kerber, *No Constitutional Right to Be Ladies*.

22 For examples of these various approaches, see Gershon Shafir, ed., *The Citizenship Debates: A Reader* (Minneapolis: University of Minnesota Press, 1998).

23 Will Kymlicka and Wayne Norman, "Return of the Citizen: A Survey of Recent Work on Citizenship Theory," in *Theorizing Citizenship*, ed. Ronald Beiner (Albany: State University of New York, 1995): 283–322.

24 Linda K. Kerber, "The Meanings of Citizenship," *Journal of American History* 84 (December 1997): 834, 837; Cott, "Marriage and Women's Citizenship," 1441.

25 Ursula Vogel, "Marriage and the Boundaries of Citizenship," in *The Condition of Citizenship*, ed. Bart van Steenbergen (Thousand Oaks, CA: Sage, 1994), 77; Smith, *Civic Ideals*. This is a way of thinking about citizenship historically that has been well articulated by scholars of race and gender.

26 I am not suggesting here that state-sponsored racism and sexism were eliminated in the twentieth century—only that citizenship expanded to formally include certain groups at precisely the same moments that it contracted to formally exclude others. Moreover, I argue that past exclusions continue to shape the way that those who are newly included experience citizenship.

27 The right to serve in the military is more accurately understood as *the right to fulfill the obligation* to serve in the military. But fulfilling that obligation is a way to obtain the entitlements (i.e., rights) of full citizenship. So, for instance, military service is a prerequisite for certain government benefits. On the way that the obligations and rights of citizenship are necessarily linked, see Kerber, *No Constitutional Right to Be Ladies*, xxi–xxiii.

28 Linda Bosniak describes a "division of labor" between immigration scholars who take up the "threshold" issue of access to national citizenship, and political and constitutional theorists who are more interested in the quality and experience of citizenship for those who are already members of the nation-state. "Most political and constitutional theorists presume a bounded citizenry and devote themselves to asking what the nature of relations should be among the already recognized citizens. In contrast, alienage as a category raises questions about the way in which the citizenry's boundaries are constituted in the first instance." See Linda Bosniak, "Universal Citizenship and the Problem of Alienage," *Northwestern University Law Review* 94 (Spring 2000): 964–65, 971. Bosniak's division of labor generally holds true for American historians, although some gender historians have bridged the gap. See, for example, Cott, *Public Vows*.

29 Bosniak, "Universal Citizenship and the Problem of Alienage," 971.

30 Lisa J. Disch, review of *Being Political: Genealogies of Citizenship*, by Engin F. Isin, *Environment and Planning D: Society and Space* 21 (June 2003): 380–82. Disch asks, "How can inclusion emancipate if those

groups who imagine themselves to be outsiders are already necessary to and presupposed by the citizen body—but in a degraded status?"

31 Michel Foucault, *The History of Sexuality: An Introduction, Vol 1* (New York: Vintage Books, 1978), 48; George Chauncey Jr., *Gay New York: Gender, Urban Culture, and the Making of the Gay Male World, 1890–1930* (New York: Basic Books, 1994), 27.

32 It was that perverts wanted to be penetrated *like women*, rather than the fact that they had sex with men, that made them perverse.

33 David Halperin, "How to Do the History of Male Homosexuality," *GLQ* 6 (2000): 90–91.

34 See Estelle Freedman, "The Prison Lesbian: Race, Class, and the Construction of the Aggressive Female Homosexual, 1915–1965," *Feminist Studies* 22 (Summer 1996): 397–415. For a related point about the development of psychiatry, see Elizabeth Lunbeck, *The Psychiatric Persuasion: Knowledge, Gender, and Power in Modern America* (Princeton, NJ: Princeton University Press, 1994).

35 Despite women's suffrage, citizenship policies defined the typical citizen as male. Women were excluded from military service; naturalization cases from the 1870s through the 1920s concerned men; women's citizenship could be gained or lost based on the alienage or native birth of their husbands; single women were effectively excluded from the 1870s on by immigration provisions barring prostitutes and public charges; and welfare state provision channeled resources toward men as breadwinners. See Cott, "Marriage and Women's Citizenship"; Kessler-Harris, *In Pursuit of Equity*.

36 Earl Bond, *Thomas W. Salmon: Psychiatrist* (New York: W. W. Norton, 1950).

37 Novak, "The Legal Origins of the Modern American State," 272. On the relationship between the courts and the administrative state, see also Reuel Schiller, "'Saint George and the Dragon': Courts and the Development of the Administrative State in Twentieth-Century America," *Journal of Policy History* 17 (2005): 110–24. This point is not meant to suggest that *only* my last chapter involving federal court cases falls within the purview of legal history. The emphasis of the preceding chapters is on the realm of administrative law—for example, the Bureau of Immigration's Boards of Special Inquiry, adjudicative boards within the Veterans Administration, or the investigative arm of the cold war military. Law is, as Robert Gordon notes, "the work of anyone . . . whose task is the administration of public policy" ("Critical Legal Histories," 66).

38 See especially Johnson, *The Lavender Scare*.

39 Two extremely skillful accounts that deal with homosexuality and World War II are Allan Bérubé, *Coming Out Under Fire: The History of Gay Men and Women in World War II* (New York: Plume, 1991); Leisa D. Meyer, *Creating G.I. Jane: Sexuality and Power in the Women's Army Corps* (New York: Columbia University Press, 1996).

40 File no. 55255/070, box 1815, Records of the Immigration and Naturalization Service, RG 85, National Archives, Washington, DC.

19

Uganda's anti-homosexuality bill

Reflections from a transnational frame

Marcia Oliver

What does it mean to think about sexuality transnationally, or within a transnational frame? The concept "transnational" refers to the movement of people, ideas, practices, institutions, and capital across national borders. Transnational movement affects sexuality in diverse and often unpredictable ways, like the global circulation of Western (particularly Western European and North American) cultural ideals of normative heterosexuality (e.g., standards of beauty) or lesbian and gay identities via mass media technologies; the movement of people across borders in search of sexual ventures or freedom from persecution; or people who engage in sexual labor as a means to support themselves and their families after migrating to a new country.

The movement of information and people across borders also plays a major role in facilitating transnational activism and solidarities around issues of global justice, such as campaigns to end war and torture, neoliberal development, violence against women, or homophobic policies and regimes. Yet, not all forms of transnational activism set out to challenge global economic and socio-cultural inequalities or support the human rights claims of marginalized or non-normative populations. For instance, transnational activism can also include conservative or right wing movements – many of which are concerned with defending and (re)installing "traditional" institutions and values across the globe, especially concerning gender (e.g., women's roles in society and rights to bodily autonomy) and sexuality (e.g., gay and lesbian sexualities). Take, for example, the growing activism in recent years that supports greater criminalization of homosexual behavior and harsher penalties for gay people. This is perhaps most evident by the horrific acts of violence committed by the Islamic State against gay men or the recent wave of anti-gay legislation that has been passed (or reinstated) in different parts of the world, including Russia, Iran, India, and a number of sub-Saharan African countries (e.g., Uganda, Nigeria, and Gambia).

A transnational frame enriches our analyses of sexuality and sexual politics by focusing on the specific sites where transnational flows of ideas, resources, and people are happening to better understand how global and domestic factors – institutional, cultural, economic, political, religious – intersect to produce, reinforce, reconfigure, and oftentimes challenge sexual injustice and violence in particular contexts.

This chapter focuses on the emergence of recent anti-gay legislation in Uganda, a country in the Great Lakes Region in East Africa. It reflects on some of the assumptions informing global reactions to Uganda's Anti-Homosexuality Bill, which has been widely criticized by scholars and human rights activists for perpetuating ahistorical and deeply problematic accounts of "African" sexuality. What kinds of accounts about "African" sexuality do we hear from both opponents and supporters of the legislation? On the one hand, Western critics of the legislation have often engaged in racist and imperialist campaigns that equate "African" countries with unbridled homophobia and violence, while "Western" countries represent "modern" sexual liberation and freedom. Accompanying this racialized discourse is the paternalistic assumption that "African" sexual minorities are passive "victims" in need of Western protection and liberation. For example, in a recent BBC documentary, *The World's Worst Place to be Gay*?, Scott Mills names Uganda as the world's most dangerous place to be gay, which (like other Western commentaries) tends to reduce homophobia to an ahistorical and monolithic account of "African" morality or culture. The colonial origins of homophobic laws and violence are ignored (more on this point below), as are the more recent interventions of U.S. evangelicals in supporting and promulgating anti-gay sentiments in Africa. These accounts also erase the continued violence and exclusionary practices that lesbian, gay, and transgendered people face in the Western world (see Mogul et al. 2011); the many voices that support LGBTI rights and equality in Africa; and the significant gains that have been made in the struggle to recognize sexual minority rights across the continent (see Ward 2013), such as the legalization of same-sex marriage in South Africa (2007) and the numerous African countries that have signed statements in support of gay and lesbian rights in the UN General Assembly (2008) and Human Rights Council (2011).

On the other hand, there are those who have shown support for the legislation within Uganda and from other African nations by denouncing homosexuality as "unAfrican" and an immoral imposition from the West. In making such claims, religious and political elites employ a fictive and essentialist understanding of "African" culture that erases the colonial roots of Christianity (and the colonial re-making or African sexualities as "naturally" heterosexual and reproductive) and the sexual pluralism and diversity that comprise African cultures (as elsewhere in the world). In other words, it is not homosexuality that was imported to Africa, but rather the institutionalization of legalized homophobia through colonial laws that define homosexuality as a crime "against the order of nature" (Penal Code Act 1950). This chapter aims to provide readers with a more situated and critical reading of Uganda's Anti-Homosexuality Bill that accounts for both the transnational and domestic dynamics that have fueled its emergence, its formulation and key provisions, and support by many of the country's conservative religious and political leaders.

Uganda's Anti-Homosexuality Bill: mapping its emergence, demise, and return

Post-colonial Uganda is part of the Great Lakes Region in East Africa, bordered by Sudan in the North, Kenya in the East, Tanzania and Rwanda in the South and the Democratic Republic of Congo in the West. With a population of roughly 37 million, the vast majority of Ugandans are Christian, identifying primarily with one of the "two traditional pillars of Ugandan Christian life": the Anglican Church of Uganda or the Roman Catholic Church (Ward 2015: 128). These two pillars of Christian life are themselves a product of Uganda's colonial history – marked by the arrival of French (Catholic) and British (Protestant) missionaries in the late nineteenth century. With Britain formally declared the protectorate and authority of Uganda in 1894, the Anglican Church of Uganda became the informal established church of the colonial state, despite Catholicism's greater popularity with the rural masses. By the time Uganda gained independence in 1962, Christianity was deeply embedded within Ugandan society.

Colonial rule was principally concerned with breaking down old forms of life and creating the conditions that would bring new forms of life into being that would ensure civilization, security and trade. Many of Uganda's pre-colonial customs and laws were altered by colonial and missionary interventions, subjecting personal and social relationships to greater restrictions and surveillance. Those aspects of Ugandan culture that were perceived as "immoral" or against the laws of "nature" were targeted by colonial authorities who implemented a range of "civilizing" practices that were often informed by Christian and Victorian sensibilities about gender, sexuality, and morality. For instance, colonial laws based on Judeo-Christian values were enacted to encourage Ugandans to adopt the bourgeois (white) patriarchal family as the site for sexual expression and procreation (such as increasing bridewealth rates to impede customary marriages and encourage Christian ones). Integral to these "civilizing" projects were depictions of "African" bodies and sexualities as distinct from the West as primitive, deviant, excessive and ruled by desire (Tamale 2011). Imagining "African" sexualities as rooted in "nature" led to the absurd conclusion that African sexualities could not be anything but heterosexual and reproductive (Lewis 2011). This narrow representation of African sexualities informs the establishment of colonial sodomy laws that criminalize homosexuality (e.g., Uganda's Penal Code), as well as the recent social and political campaigns to intensify anti-gay legislation in the country (e.g., Anti-Homosexuality Act 2014).

In 2009, ruling-party Member of Parliament (MP) David Bahati introduced Uganda's Anti-Homosexuality Bill "to protect the cherished culture of the people of Uganda" and to "strengthen the nation's capacity to deal with emerging internal and external threats to the traditional heterosexual family," such as "sexual rights activists seeking to impose their values of sexual promiscuity on the people of Uganda" (Bill No. 18. 2009). In February 2014, President Yoweri Museveni signed an amended version of the Bill into law. Although same-sex activity has long been prohibited under colonial law, the Anti-Homosexuality Act (AHA) sought to further criminalize same-sex sexuality to include "attempted" homosexuality, the "promotion" of homosexuality, "conspiracy to commit" homosexuality, and "aiding and abetting" homosexuality. It also imposed mandatory testing for HIV and life imprisonment for certain acts classified as "aggravated homosexuality," such as when the offender is HIV-positive.

International and national responses to the legislation were divided, with support voiced mainly by other African nations considering similar legislation and some of Uganda's (mostly Pentecostal) religious leaders and political elites (many of whom have connections with conservative evangelical actors and organizations in the United States). The Bill initiated extensive criticism both within and outside Uganda, ranging from LGBTI communities to progressive religious leaders (like retired Ugandan Bishop Christopher Ssenyonjo), from human rights activists to public health and HIV/AIDS experts, and from academics to state leaders and Western donors (including the U.S. and Britain). One of the most significant initiatives to emerge in response to the legislation – which led to the Anti-Homosexuality Act's (AHA) annulment in August 2014 – was a petition launched in the Constitutional Court of Uganda by a coalition of gay, lesbian, and transgender activists, academics, members of parliament, journalists and human rights organizations. Just months after the law was passed, the Constitutional Court of Uganda ruled in favor of the petition and struck down the legislation on the grounds that it was passed without parliamentary quorum. Although the court's decision represents a significant win by human rights advocates, it is noteworthy that the judicial reasoning was based on a procedural technicality, not on a normative or moral rejection of the substantive content of the Bill (such as opposing the AHA on the grounds that it violates Ugandans' constitutionally guaranteed rights to privacy, freedom from discrimination and cruel and degrading treatment, to dignity, and freedom of expression, thought, and assembly). At the time of this writing a revised version of the anti-gay legislation has been drafted (though not yet tabled in Parliament), despite President Museveni's recent warnings that the country's economic security and trade relations with key donors would be severely undermined should parliamentary members pursue additional anti-gay legislation (Vision Reporter 2014).

To some critics this revised Bill, entitled "The Prohibition of Promotion of Unnatural Sexual Practices Bill, 2014," is even more repressive and far-reaching than the country's previous Anti-Homosexuality Act. As its title suggests, the revised Bill reveals a much more concerted effort to prohibit the promotion of "unnatural" sexual practices, defined as "a sexual act between persons of the same sex, or with or between transsexual persons, a sexual act with an animal, and anal sex, within the meaning of section 145 of the Penal Code Act" (Draft Legislation 2014: 2). From a social constructionist perspective, the very language of "unnatural" sexual practices reflects a naturalistic view of sexuality, which functions to normalize reproductive heterosexuality as the only socially acceptable form of sexuality. All non-heterosexual forms of sexuality are rendered "unnatural" and, in this instance, criminal. Like the previous Anti-Homosexuality Act, anyone convicted of promoting "unnatural" sexual activities is liable to imprisonment for seven years, where promotion is understood broadly to mean "recruiting, encouraging, soliciting, or inciting a person to engage in unnatural sexual practices by providing premises, distributing textual or visual material or any other means to interest a person in unnatural sexual practices" (Draft Legislation 2014: 2). The revised Bill makes it a criminal offence for any person to lease or sublease premises for the purpose of engaging in "unnatural" sexual activities, raising fears among lesbian, gay, and transgender communities that if the Bill is passed they will face even greater violence and state persecution, including homelessness. Frank Mugisha, a gay-rights activist in Uganda, warns of the far-reaching consequences that the "promotion" aspect of the Bill will have on all Ugandans, including landlords who rent to LGBTI Ugandans, international aid and non-governmental organizations that provide services or advocate for LGBTI people, hotels that provide space for LGBTI meetings, journalists, academics, or LGBTI activists that disseminate information about homosexuality, and personal or organizational Twitter or Facebook accounts that contain LGBTI-related material (Johnston 2014).

Mugisha's concerns have not gone unwarranted. During a recent fieldwork trip in Uganda (August 2014), my colleagues and I witnessed first hand the chilling and harmful effects that the Anti-Homosexuality Act has on democratic governance, freedom of expression, and the lives of marginalized populations. Just weeks after President Museveni signed the Bill into law, the government began restricting the activities of one of the country's largest human rights organizations, the Refugee Law Project (RLP), under allegations that it "promotes" homosexuality under the guise of its human rights work. More specifically, the organization was denied access to refugee settlements throughout the country and was prohibited to work with refugee clients at its Kampala headquarters. Although the RLP has been particularly active in opposing the anti-gay law and organizing a coalition of civil society organizations to contest it (known as the Civil Society Coalition on Human Rights and Constitutional Law), the vast majority of its work focuses on providing legal assistance, mental health and psychosocial support, and conducting research and policy advocacy on issues that affect the more than 380,000 refugees and asylum seekers in the country (such as peace-building and transitional justice initiatives). As of summer 2015, the Refugee Law Project had resumed its work with refugees and asylum seekers after a 10-month suspension.

Homosexuality, Western conservatives, and political power in Uganda

The Anti-Homosexuality Act was not the first time that debates over homosexuality entered public discourse in Uganda; there has been a dramatic increase in public talk about homosexuality since the late 1990s (Hassett 2007; Tamale 2007). Nor was the legislation simply the product of Uganda's conservative political and religious leaders. As I have argued elsewhere (Oliver 2013), the wording and timing of the Anti-Homosexuality legislation were themselves influenced by both transnational and domestic factors. Of particular significance is the influence of the U.S. Christian Right (hereafter CR) in supporting anti-gay sentiments in Africa and, in particular, the crafting of the Anti-Homosexuality Act in Uganda. Although the CR has been tremendously successful in shaping gender and sexuality-related policies and laws in the U.S. for decades, the gay rights movement has made significant headway in shifting public attitudes toward greater tolerance and acceptance of gay and lesbian rights and marriage equality (especially among younger generations), culminating in the recent U.S. Supreme Court ruling (2015) that declared a fundamental right to marriage for same-sex couples. With its influence waning at home, the CR has turned its attention outward to the global realm, and more specifically to Africa, to spread its "pro-family" agenda. In 2005, the BBC's *Focus on Africa* reported: "Africa is being colonized and Christianized all over again. The colonizers this time are American, not Europeans, and the brand of belief they are bringing to Africa is Evangelical Christianity" (cited in Huliaras 2008). Although there is nothing "natural" about the Christian Right's vision of the family, it informs a worldwide alliance of conservative religious faiths committed to defending a particular vision of the family as "inscribed in nature and defined by heterosexual marriage whose primary purpose is procreation" (Buss 2004: 57).

The CR's global influence can be seen in U.S. foreign policies on HIV/AIDS prevention (especially the emphasis on abstinence and fidelity programs) and family planning; the elaborate communications network of CR broadcasting across sub-Saharan Africa (e.g., the Christian Broadcasting Network and the Trinity Broadcasting Network); its increased presence and activism within the United Nations over issues of gender, sexuality, and women's rights; as well as the dramatic increase in the number of Western conservative organizations working (and financing projects) in Africa since the 1990s. An important factor in this development is the recent controversies over homosexuality within the worldwide Anglican Communion, which has provided fertile ground for CR actors to join forces with conservative Episcopalians and allies in the global South to defend biblical orthodoxy on matters of human sexuality.

With global Christianity now concentrated in the global South (with over 30 million of its 80 million worldwide membership residing in Africa, notably in Nigeria, Uganda and Kenya) (Kaoma 2009), African bishops have become a powerful force in Anglican Communion politics. In the lead up to the 1998 Lambeth Conference (a large meeting that takes place every 10 years of bishops of the Anglican Communion to discuss key issues of the day), U.S. conservatives sought alliances with church leaders in the global South to oppose the more tolerant and liberal positions on sexuality supported by some Western Anglican provinces (Hassett 2007). Western efforts to build alliances with Southern Anglicans paid off: at the 1998 Lambeth Conference, African bishops were integral to passing a resolution that declared homosexuality to be "incompatible with Scripture" and recommended against the blessing of same-sex unions and the ordination of homosexuals as bishops. Moreover, following the U.S. Episocopal Church's decision in 2003 to ordain Gene Robinson (an openly gay man) as Bishop of the Diocese of New Hampshire, several Southern provinces severed ties with the Episcopal Church, rejected funding from the more liberal Western churches (Duin 2005), and offered their churches to U.S. conservatives who have broken ties with the Episcopal Church U.S.A. As Daly (2001) notes, the Church of Uganda is a significant player in the U.S. conservative Episcopal movement's growing international network: it is the second largest Anglican Church in the worldwide Communion (with roughly 8 million members or 30% of the country's population) and has become a popular "spiritual home" for many Western conservatives (see also Hassett 2007).

The transnational linkages between U.S. and Ugandan conservative evangelicals have been well documented (Kaoma 2009; Sharlet 2008; Hassett 2007), with some of the most vocal religious and politically engaged anti-gay Ugandan activists having connections with CR actors and organizations (such as the secretive CR group known as the Family, or the Fellowship, California mega-church Pastor Rick Warren, and Lou Engle from The Call). As Reverend Kopya Kaoma's (2009) research reveals, it is many of the same U.S. evangelical organizations supporting anti-gay sentiments in Africa that have long been active in domestic anti-gay politics in the U.S. For him, and other human rights activists, the rise in homophobia throughout Africa is directly linked to the global anti-gay activism and alliance building of U.S. Christian conservatives. Just months before the Anti-Homosexuality Bill was introduced in Parliament, the Family Life Network (a fundamentalist Christian NGO in Uganda) organized a seminar that featured three prominent U.S. conservative Christians who spoke about the "truth" of homosexuality and the "dark and hidden" global agenda of homosexuality. Scott Lively from California's Abiding Truth Ministries was one of the speakers at the Kampala-based seminar. Speaking to religious leaders, parliamentarians, police officers, teachers, and concerned parents, he reiterated a number of claims that are well established in CR anti-gay discourse and literature: homosexuality as an irrefutable sin condemned by God; homosexuality as distinct from race (as a chosen, rather than innate, behavior) and undeserving of human rights; homosexuality as predatory (especially towards children); and the existence of a global gay agenda that promotes homosexuality and aims to destroy the moral foundations of society and human civilization itself (see Oliver 2013).

The direct influence of CR strategies and literature on Uganda's recent anti-gay campaigns is clearly apparent in a follow up meeting that was held just days after the anti-gay seminar, where the organizer (Stephen Langa of Uganda's Family Life Network) described Richard Cohen as one of "the most authoritative writers who has written on the subject [of homosexuality]" (Langa 2009). For those of you who may not be familiar with Richard Cohen, this is particularly alarming not only because in 2002 he was expelled from the American Counseling Association for ethics violations, but also because his text, "Coming Out Straight" (2000), cites the widely discredited research of Dr. Paul Cameron (director of the Family Research Institute, Colorado Springs) that claims homosexuals are more likely to abuse children. This outrageous assertion was a centerpiece of Langa's performance, exemplified by his claim that "what we're dealing with here is not a joke . . . they don't care about you. They want your children!" (Langa 2009), as was a dramatic narration of a passage from Michael Swift's (1987) "Gay Revolutionary," which is a staple in numerous CR publications (Herman 1997). Despite the text's explicit satirical nature, conservative anti-gay campaigns often use it as "evidence" of a powerful global gay movement that promotes homosexuality and aims to recruit the world into its "immoral" ways.

In some sense, there is nothing particularly unique about the anti-gay rhetoric that was affirmed at these meetings in Kampala: Christian Right actors have been formulating their anti-gay positions in the U.S. for decades and, as part of their efforts to build a transnational conservative Christian alliance, have increasingly distributed CR anti-gay literature and built alliances throughout Africa and elsewhere in the world (such as Kenya, Nigeria, Zimbabwe, and Russia) (see Federman 2014; Baptiste 2014). Similar anti-gay sentiments are well established in the Ugandan press and circulated by Ugandan conservative religious and political leaders (see Oliver 2013). For instance, years before Scott Lively told his Kampala audience that gay rights are not human rights because unlike race, "there is no definitive study that has ever proved that homosexuality is innate" (2009), Pastor Martin Ssempa wrote in a letter to Human Rights Watch (a U.S.-based organization):

> I can certainly understand why organizations like yours [Human Rights Watch] want people to think that homosexuality is fixed, like race, and cannot be changed, because you know that would make people more sympathetic to your "sexual rights" agenda which conflicts with the strong family values of Uganda.
>
> *(Ssempa 2007)*

Within this letter, Ssempa not only denies LGBT rights by reiterating the CR positioning of homosexuality and race as distinct and mutually exclusive categories, he also equates Human Rights Watch with the encroaching "global gay agenda" that promotes homosexuality and threatens to destroy Ugandan culture and "traditional" family values. For Ssempa, and other conservative anti-gay activists, heterosexuality is "natural" and exists outside power relations, which (as critical sexuality and gender scholars note) ignores the multiple power relations that produce and regulate sexuality in socially desirable, albeit narrow, ways according to hetero-patriarchal and reproductive norms.

While it is apparent that many Ugandan anti-gay positions – including the wording of the Anti-Homosexuality Act – are profoundly shaped by CR strategies and discourse, these positions are not determined by the CR. Rather, conservative evangelicals in Uganda make claims to "African" culture and national sovereignty to denounce homosexuality as "un-African" and a neo-colonial imposition from the West. For instance, President Museveni has commended the Church for "resisting homosexuality, a decadent culture being passed on by the Western nations"; Archbishop Orombi has publically claimed that "homosexuality is against our culture"; and James Buturo, the former Ethics and Integrity Minster, has asserted that "we shall not allow those people from the West to define our identity and destiny" (see Oliver 2013: 98). Statements such as these rely on a particular conception of "African" culture, as historically fixed, homogenous, and fundamentally different from the West. The claims to African culture made by conservative religious and political leaders are particularly powerful; they speak to and manipulate very real social anxieties that many Ugandans experience every day in relation to family and the nation, especially concerning the power of money to influence "corruptive" and "immoral" behavior (Sadgrove et al. 2012). This is particularly significant in a context of global neoliberalism, which has produced deeper inequalities and greater socio-economic difficulties for the vast majority of Ugandans.

Human rights activists draw on a number of strategies to counter the conservative claim that homosexuality is "un-African" or "against African culture," like pointing to the colonial roots of Christianity and, it follows, the institutionalization of the monogamous heterosexual family itself. Sexual pluralism long comprised African cultures and traditions. As historical and anthropological research shows, there is ample evidence of sexual and familial diversity in pre- and post-colonial Africa (Nyanzi 2013), including the expression of same-sex intimacies, which have acquired many different social meanings over time and in different contexts ranging from sin to special powers to the noblest form of love, as well as a way to establish hierarchy or exercise political resistance through history (Hoad 2007; Tamale 2014).

Other critics have shown how the "resurrection of official gay-bashing" (Olopade 2012) distracts the Ugandan public from the government's neglect of socio-economic issues and official abuses of authority (abuses that, for the most part, have been met with silence by both Western donors and conservative Christians). Sylvia Tamale, for instance, argues that anti-gay rhetoric serves as a "political tool" for conservative leaders to maintain power and divert attention away from more pressing socio-economic and political problems. In her words:

> Instead of blaming political mismanagement and corruption for high unemployment, the high cost of living, and poor health facilities, the population is encouraged to focus, inter alia, on red herrings such as "the vice of homosexuality" and "the evil of prostitution" which are fished out of the sea of morality particularly when electoral accountability is looming.
>
> *(Tamale 2013: 39)*

The Anti-Homosexuality Bill was introduced to Parliament just 16 months before Uganda's presidential elections. With debates over sexual morality taking the center stage in the international and national imagery, other pressing social, economic and political issues were marginalized and displaced from mainstream public discourse, such as the illiberal and authoritarian practices of Museveni's regime. For example, human rights activists in Uganda have widely criticized Museveni's grip on political power (since 1986), his use of violent tactics to crush political dissent (such as the recent Walk-to-Work campaign led by opposition leader Kizza Besigye) and restrictions on civil liberties (including freedom of assembly, media, and association), government corruption and reckless state expenditures on fighter jets and political campaigning and events – while millions of Ugandans face high unemployment, poor wages and working conditions, rising inflation, excessive living costs, and poor social welfare services.

I began this essay with a question: what does it mean to think about sexuality transnationally? In turning our focus to Uganda, we've learned that the rise in anti-gay sentiments and the emergence of the Anti-Homosexuality Act cannot be viewed in a vacuum, but must be seen in relation to a series of transnational and domestic factors. Of particular significance is the colonial re-shaping of African sexualities and the enactment of legal codes that criminalized homosexuality, the power and influence of Western Christian conservatives in supporting (and arguably inciting) the rise in anti-gay sentiments in Africa, and the instrumentalization of sexuality by diverse political and religious actors to support self-serving agendas. For conservative religious leaders both within and outside Uganda, anti-gay campaigns may serve to bolster their public standing and social relevance in global Christian politics; for Uganda's political elite, anti-gay rhetoric may help to sustain one's hold on political power and detract attention away from socio-economic and political misconduct; and for Western donors, anti-gay legislation may provide the necessary justification to impose aid conditionalities on African governments and nongovernmental organizations. One of the most significant (albeit unintended) effects of transnational anti-gay activism in Uganda (and elsewhere in Africa) has been the vibrant activism of LGBTI groups and human rights allies across the continent. Not only have they exposed the repressive and unconstitutional effects of anti-gay legislation on the lives of sexual minorities (and Africans more broadly) but, to close with the words of Sylvia Tamale, have made "the question of sexuality an intrinsic part of the democratic struggle on the continent, and not peripheral to it" (Tamale 2013:42).

Acknowledgements

The author extends her gratitude to the many people in Uganda who gave their time and insights to her research over the years. She acknowledges the Uganda National Council for Science and Technology for granting her permission to conduct this research and the financial support from the Centre for International Governance Innovation, Waterloo, Canada (P.I. Dr. Suzan Ilcan, University of Waterloo). The author also thanks members of the Canadian Network for Critical Sociology (especially Elisabeth Rondinelli) and the editors of this collection for their helpful comments and suggestions.

Bibliography

Baptiste, Nathalie (2014). It's not just Uganda: Behind the Christian Right's onslaught in Africa. *The Nation*, 4 April 2014. URL: www.thenation.com/blog/179191/its-not-just-uganda-behind-christian-rights-onslaught-africa.

Bill No. 18 (2009). The Anti-Homosexuality Bill, Uganda. October.

Buss, D. (2004). The Christian Right, globalization, and the "natural family." In M.A. Tétreault & R. Denemark (Eds.), *Gods, Guns & Globalization: Religious radicalism and international political economy* (pp. 57–78). Boulder: Lynne Rienner Publishers, Inc.

Daly, L. (2001). A church at risk: The Episcopal "Renewal Movement." *IDS Insights*, 2(2), 1–2. URL: www.idsonline.org/publications.html.

Draft Legislation (2014). *The Prohibition of Promotion of Unnatural Sexual Practices, Bill*, 2014. 29 October 2014.

Duin, Julia (2005). African bishops reject aid. *The Washington Times*, 7 June 2005. URL: www.washingtontimes.com/news/2005/jun/07/20050607-115436-7061r/?page=all

Federman, Adam (2014). How U.S. Evangelicals fueled the rise of Russia's "pro-family" Right. *The Nation*, 27 January 2014. URL: www.thenation.com/article/177823/how-us-evangelicals-fueled-rise-russias-pro-family-right.

Hassett, M. (2007). *Anglican Communion in Crisis: How Episcopal dissidents and their African allies are reshaping Anglicanism*. Princeton: Princeton University Press.

Herman, D. (1997). *The Antigay Agenda: Orthodox vision and the Christian Right.* Chicago and London: The University of Chicago Press.

Hoad, N. (2007). *African Intimacies: Race, homosexuality and globalization.* Minneapolis: University of Minnesota Press.

Huliaras, A. (2008). The evangelical roots of U.S. Africa policy. *Survival,* 50(6), 161–182.

Human Rights Watch (2011). *UN Human Rights Council: A stunning development against violence.* URL: www.hrw.org/news/2011/03/22/un-human-rights-council-stunning-development-against-violence.

Johnston, Chris (2014). Uganda drafts new anti-gay laws. *The Guardian*, 8 November 2014. URL: www.theguardian.com/world/2014/nov/08/uganda-drafts-anti-gay-laws-prison-promotion-homosexuality.

Kaoma, K. (2009). *Globalizing the Culture Wars: U.S. conservatives, African churches, and homophobia.* Somerville: Political Research Associates.

Langa, S. (2009). Follow up meeting on the homosexuals' agenda, 15 March 2009. Kampala. URL: www.boxturtlebulletin.com/2009/02/28/10171.

Lewis, Desiree (2011). Representing African sexualities. In S. Tamale (Ed), *African sexualities: A reader.* (p. 45). Cape Town: Pambazuka Press.

Lively, S. (2009). Seminar on exposing the homosexuals' agenda, 5 March 2009. Kampala. URL: http://wn.com/Scott_Lively.

Mogul, Joey, Ritchie, Andrea, & Whitlock, Kay (2011). *Queer (In)Justice: The criminalization of LGBT people in the United States.* Boston: Beacon Press.

NCAVP [National Coalition of Anti-Violence Programs] (2014). 2013 Report on LGBTQ and HIV-Affected Hate Violence. URL: http://avp.org/resources/reports/term/summary.

Nyanzi, Stella. (2013). Dismantling reified African culture through localised homosexualities in Uganda. *Culture, Health & Sexuality: An International Journal of Research, Intervention and Care* 15(8): 952–967.

Oliver, Marcia (2013). Transnational sex politics, Conservative Christianity, and antigay activism in Uganda. *Studies in Social Justice,* 7(1): 83–105.

Olopade, D. (2012). Gay bashing, a government diversion. *International Herald Tribune*, 22 February. URL: http://latitude.blogs.nytimes.com/2012/02/22/gay-bashing-in-uganda-is-a-diversion-from-government-malfeasance/

Sadgrove, J., Vanderbeck, R., Andersson, J., Valentine, G. & Ward, K. (2012). Morality plays and money matters: Towards a situated understanding of the politics of homosexuality in Uganda. *Journal of Modern African Studies,* 50(1): 103–129.

Sharlet, J. (2008). *The Family: The secret fundamentalist at the heart of American power.* New York: Harper Collins.

Ssempa, M. (2007). Homosexuality is against our culture. *New Vision*. URL: http://www.newvision.co.ug/new_vision/news/1219820/homosexuality_culture.

Tamale, Sylvia (2007). *Homosexuality: Perspectives from Uganda.* Kampala, Uganda: Sexual Minorities Uganda (SMUG).

Tamale, S. (2011). Introduction. In S. Tamale (Ed.), *African Sexualities: A reader* (pp. 1–7). Cape Town: Pambazuka Press.

Tamale, Sylvia (2013). Confronting the politics of non-conforming sexualities in Africa. *African Studies Review*, 56(2): 31–45.

Tamale, Sylvia (2014). Exploring the contours of African sexualities: Religion, law and power. *African Human Rights Law Journal,* 14(1): 150–177.

Vision Reporter (2014). Museveni calls for fresh debate on homosexuality. *New Vision*, 3 October 2014. URL: www.newvision.co.ug/news/660387-museveni-calls-for-fresh-debate-on-homosexuality.html.

Ward, Kevin (2013). Religious institutions and actors and religious attitudes to homosexual rights: South Africa and Uganda. In C. Lennox & M. Waites (Eds.), *Human Rights, Sexual Orientation and Gender Identity in The Commonwealth: Struggles for Decriminalization and Change* (pp. 409–427). London, UK: Institute of Commonwealth Studies.

Ward, Kevin (2015). The role of the Anglican and Catholic Churches in Uganda in public discourse on homosexuality and ethics. *Journal of Eastern African Studies*, 9(1): 127–144.

20

One is not born a bride

How weddings regulate heterosexuality

Chrys Ingraham

All aspects of our social world – natural or otherwise – are given meaning. Culture installs meaning in our lives from the very first moment we enter the social world. Our sexual orientation or sexual identity – or even the notion that there is such a thing – is defined by the symbolic order of that world through the use of verbal as well as non-verbal language and images. Heterosexuality as a *social* category is much more than the fact of one's sexual or affectional attractions. What we think of when we talk about heterosexuality or refer to ourselves as heterosexual is a product of a society's meaning-making processes. In reality, heterosexuality operates as a highly organized social institution that varies across nations, social groups, culture, history, region, religion, ethnicity, nationality, race, lifespan, social class, and ability. In America and elsewhere, the wedding ritual represents a major site for the installation and maintenance of the institution of heterosexuality.

The title of this chapter pays homage to French feminist Monique Wittig whose classic and provocative essay "One is Not Born a Woman" examines what she calls the political regime of heterosexuality and its requisite categories of man and woman. She argues that the category of woman and all of the meaning attached to that category would not exist were it not necessary for the political regime of (patriarchal) heterosexuality. For the purpose of this chapter, the same holds true for the taken-for-granted category of bride. While it may seem obvious to most that one is not born a bride, in reality many women see themselves as following a naturalized path toward heterosexual womanhood.

But how did this contrived and constructed social practice become naturalized? The task of examining this taken-for-granted social arrangement requires a conceptual framework capable of revealing how heterosexuality has become institutionalized, naturalized, and normalized. Any attempt to examine the institution of heterosexuality requires a theory capable of understanding how this institution with all its social practices such as dating, proms, and Valentine's Day, is often viewed by many of us as natural.

The heterosexual imaginary

French psychoanalyst Jacques Lacan's concept of the "imaginary" is especially useful for this purpose. According to Lacan, the imaginary is the unmediated contact an infant has to its own image and its connection with its mother. Instead of facing a complicated, conflictual, and contradictory world, the infant experiences the illusion of tranquility, plenitude, and fullness. In other words, infants experience a sense of oneness with their primary caretaker. Louis Althusser, the French philosopher, borrowed Lacan's notion of the imaginary for his neo-marxist theory of ideology, defining ideology as "the imaginary relationship of individuals to their real conditions of existence." The "imaginary" here does not mean "false" or "pretend" but, rather, an imagined or illusory relationship between an individual and their social world. Applied to a social theory of heterosexuality the *heterosexual imaginary* is that way of thinking that relies on romantic and sacred notions of heterosexuality in order to create and maintain the illusion of well-being and oneness. This romantic view prevents us from seeing how institutionalized heterosexuality actually works to organize gender while preserving racial, class, and sexual hierarchies. The effect of this illusory depiction of reality is that heterosexuality is taken for granted and unquestioned, while gender is understood as something people are socialized into or learn. The heterosexual imaginary naturalizes male to female social relations, rituals, and organized practices and conceals the operation of heterosexuality in structuring gender across race, class, and sexuality. This way of seeing closes off any critical analysis of heterosexuality as an organizing institution and for the ends it serves (Ingraham 1994, 1999). By leaving heterosexuality unexamined as an institution we do not explore how it is learned, how it may control us and contribute to social inequalities. Through the use of the heterosexual imaginary, we hold up the institution of heterosexuality as fixed in time as though it has always operated the same as it does today. This imaginary presents a view of heterosexuality as "just the way it is" while creating obligatory social practices that reinforce the illusion that, as long as one complies with this naturalized structure, all will be right in the world. This illusion is commonly known as romance. Romancing heterosexuality is creating an illusory heterosexuality for which wedding culture plays a central role.

The lived reality of institutionalized heterosexuality is, however, not typically tranquil or safe. The consequences the heterosexual imaginary produces include, for example, marital rape, domestic violence, pay inequities, racism, gay-bashing, femicide, and sexual harassment. Institutionalized heterosexuality and its organizing ideology – the heterosexual imaginary – establishes those behaviors we ascribe to men and women – gender – while keeping in place or producing a history of contradictory and unequal social relations. The production of a division of labor that results in unpaid domestic work, inequalities of pay and opportunity, or the privileging of married couples in the dissemination of insurance benefits, are examples of this.

Above all, the heterosexual imaginary naturalizes the regulation of sexuality through the institution of marriage, ritual practices such as weddings, and state domestic relations laws. These laws, among others, set the terms for taxation, healthcare, and housing benefits on the basis of marital status. Rarely challenged – except by nineteenth-century marriage reformers and early second-wave feminists – laws and public- and private-sector policies use marriage as the primary requirement for social and economic benefits and access rather than distributing resources on some other basis such as citizenship or ability to breathe, for example. Heterosexuality is much more than a biological given or whether or not someone is attracted to someone of another sex. Rules on everything from who pays for the date or wedding rehearsal dinner to who leads while dancing, drives the car, cooks dinner or initiates sex, all serve to regulate heterosexual practice. What circulates as a given in Western societies is, in fact, a highly structured arrangement. As is the case with most institutions, people who participate in these practices must be socialized to do so. In other words, women were not born with a wedding gown gene or a neo-natal craving for a diamond engagement ring! They were taught to want these things. Women didn't enter the world with a desire to practice something called dating or a desire to play with a "My Size Bride Barbie," they were rewarded for desiring these things. Likewise, men did not exit the womb knowing they would one day buy a date a bunch of flowers or spend two months' income to buy an engagement ring. These are all products that have been sold to consumers interested in taking part in a culturally established ritual that works to organize and institutionalize heterosexuality and reward those who participate.

Heteronormativity

A related concept useful for the study of the heterosexual imaginary and of institutionalized heterosexuality is heteronormativity. This is the view that institutionalized heterosexuality constitutes the standard for legitimate and expected social and sexual relations. Heteronormativity represents one of the main premises underlying the heterosexual imaginary, again ensuring that the organization of heterosexuality in everything from gender to weddings to marital status is held up both as a model and as "normal." Consider, for instance, the ways many surveys or intake questionnaires ask respondents to check off their marital status as either married, divorced, separated, widowed, single, or, in some cases, never married. Not only are these categories presented as significant indices of social identity, they are offered as the only options, implying that the organization of identity in relation to marriage is universal and not in need of explanation. Or try to imagine entering a committed relationship without the benefit of legalized marriage. We find it difficult to think that we can share commitment with someone without a state-sponsored license. People will frequently comment that someone is afraid to "make a commitment" if they choose not to get married even when they have been in a relationship with someone for years! Our ability to imagine possibilities or to understand what counts as commitment is itself impaired by heteronormative assumptions. We even find ourselves challenged to consider how to marry without an elaborate white wedding. Gays and lesbians have maintained long-term committed relationships yet find themselves desiring state sanctioning of their union in order to feel legitimate. Heteronormativity works in all of these instances to naturalize the institution of heterosexuality while rendering real people's relationships and commitments irrelevant and illegitimate.

For those who view questions concerning marital status as benign, one need only consider the social and economic consequences for those who do not participate in these arrangements or the cross-cultural variations that are at odds with some of the Anglocentric or Eurocentric assumptions regarding marriage. All people are required to situate themselves in relation to marriage or heterosexuality, including those who *regardless of sexual (or asexual) affiliation* do not consider themselves "single," heterosexual, or who do not participate in normative heterosexuality and its structures.

One is not born a bride, and yet to imagine oneself outside of this category is to live a life outside of the boundaries of normality and social convention. To live outside this contrived and constructed social practice is to live on the margins of society, excluded from the social, legal, and economic rewards and benefits participation brings. To resist membership in the heteronormative social order – as bride or as groom – is to live with the penalties and challenges to all those who resist. It means living a life where you have to defend your sexual loyalties on a daily basis – are you straight or are you gay?

Weddings

To demonstrate the degree to which the heteronormative wedding ritual regulates sexuality we must begin with an investigation into the ways various practices, arrangements, relations, and rituals standardize and conceal the operation of institutionalized heterosexuality. It means to ask how practices such as weddings become naturalized and prevent us from seeing what is at stake, what is kept in place, and what consequences are produced. To employ this approach is to seek out those instances when the illusion of tranquility is created and at what cost. Weddings, like many other rituals of heterosexual celebration such as anniversaries, showers, and Valentine's Day, become synonymous with heterosexuality and provide illusions of reality that conceal the operation of heterosexuality both historically and materially. When used in professional settings, for example, weddings work as a form of ideological control to signal membership in relations of ruling as well as to signify that the couple is normal, moral, productive, family-centered, upstanding citizens and, most importantly, appropriately gendered and sexual.

To study weddings means to interrupt the ways the heterosexual imaginary naturalizes heterosexuality and prevents us from seeing how its organization depends on the production of the belief or ideology that heterosexuality is normative and the same for everyone – that the fairytale romance is universal. It is this assumption that allows for the developmert and growth in America of a $35 billion-per-year wedding industry. This multibillion dollar industry includes the sale of a diverse range of products, many of which are produced outside of the USA – wedding gowns, diamonds, honeymoon travel and apparel, and household equipment. Ironically, the production of these goods frequently occurs under dismal labor conditions where manufacturers rely on a non-traditional female workforce, indirectly altering cultural norms in relation to heterosexuality and family. In Mexico, Guatemala, and China, for example, the effect has been to shift the job opportunities away from men with the consequence of significant levels of domestic violence and femicide. Sexual regulation in these locations is directly related to the gendered division of labor working to produce goods that support the American heterosexual imaginary. Veiled in the guise of romance and the sacred, these social relations conceal from view the troublesome conditions underlying the production of the white wedding.

When you think of weddings as "only natural," think again! This process of naturalization begins with children. By targeting girls and young women, toy manufacturers have seized on the wedding market and the opportunity to develop future consumers by producing a whole variety of wedding toys, featuring the "classic" white wedding, and sold during Saturday morning children's television shows. Toy companies, generally part of large multinational conglomerates that also own related commodities such as travel or cosmetics, work to secure future markets for all their products through the selling of wedding toys. Mattel, the world's largest toymaker and a major multinational corporation, has offices and facilities in thirty-six countries and sells products in 150 nations. Their major toy brand, accounting for 40 percent of their sales, is the Barbie doll – all 120 different versions of her. Mattel's primary manufacturing facilities are located in China, Indonesia, Italy, Malaysia, and Mexico, employing mostly women of color and at substandard wages. Annually, Mattel makes about 100 million Barbie dolls and earns revenues of $1.9 billion for the California-based company. The average young Chinese female worker whose job it is to assemble Barbie dolls lives in a dormitory, sometimes works with dangerous chemicals, works long hours and earns $1.81 a day. Since 2013, Mattel's profits on Barbie dolls have been declining in relation to their other lines, such as their vampire-based *Monster High* dolls (Anderson, 2013).

The staging of weddings in television shows, weekly reporting on weddings in the press, magazine reports on celebrity weddings, advertising, and popular adult and children's movies with wedding themes or weddings inserted, all work together to teach us how to think about weddings, marriage, heterosexuality, race, gender, and labor. Through the application of the heterosexual imaginary, the media cloak most representations of weddings in signifiers of romance, purity, morality, promise, affluence or accumulation, and whiteness. Many newlyweds today experience their weddings as the stars of a fairy-tale movie in which they are scripted, videotaped, and photographed by paparazzi wedding-goers, not as an event that regulates their sexual lives and identities along with those of the laborers who make their wedding possible.

The contemporary white wedding under multinational capitalism is, in effect, a mass-marketed, homogeneous, assembly-line production with little resemblance to the utopian vision many participants hold. The engine driving the wedding market has mostly to do with the romancing of heterosexuality in the interests of capitalism. The social relations at stake – love, community, commitment, and family – come to be viewed as secondary to the production of the wedding spectacle.

The heterosexual imaginary circulating throughout the wedding industry masks the ways it secures racial, class, and sexual hierarchies. Women are taught from early childhood to plan for the "happiest day of their lives." (Everything after that day pales by comparison!) Men are taught, by the absence of these socializing mechanisms, that their work is "other" than that. If they are interested in the wedding it is for reasons other than what women have learned. The possibilities children learn to imagine are only as broad as their culture allows. They are socialized to understand the importance of appropriate coupling, what counts as beauty, as appropriate sexuality, what counts as women's work and men's work, and how to become "good" consumers by participating in those heterosexual practices and rituals that stimulate their interests and emotions and reap the most rewards.

One is not born a bride. One learns to comply with the social and cultural messages that flow to and through the wedding ritual. It is the rite of passage for appropriate heterosexual identity and membership. It is everything but natural.

References

Anderson, Mae. 2013. "Barbie sales slide as Mattel profit falls." *USA Today.* Online at www.usatoday.com/story/money/business/2013/07/17/mattel-2q-profit-falls-barbie-sales-slide-again/2523879/. Last accessed April 16, 2016.

Ingraham, Chrys. 1994. "The heterosexual imaginary", *Sociological Theory* 12(2): 203–19.

——.1999. *White Weddings: Romancing Heterosexuality in Popular Culture.* New York: Routledge.

21

Promoting marriage for America

The intimate relationship between the state and heterosexuality

Melanie Heath

> Our position is that we're a marriage initiative designed to encourage activities that lead to marriage, and our state has defined marriage as an act between a man and a woman and until the state defines it differently, we . . . it's really all defined for us. We don't get into the debate about it.
>
> *(Mary Myrick, Oklahoma Marriage Initiative)*

Mary Myrick, the founder and president of Public Strategies, a public relations/public affairs firm which managed the Oklahoma Marriage Initiative, offered the above quote in response to my question about how the initiative dealt with the debate over same-sex marriage. It was 2004, the year in which a state constitutional amendment to define marriage as the union between a man and a woman passed in Oklahoma with 76 percent of voters in favor. Several years before in 1999, the governor had created the marriage initiative as a statewide, multi-sector effort "to strengthen marriage" (Dion et al. 2008, p. xi). The words of Mary Myrick made explicit what is implicit in state efforts to promote and strengthen a marriage culture: until forced to define it differently, the state saw it as a heterosexual institution (Heath 2012, 2013). In 2015, Oklahoma was forced to change its definition following the US Supreme Court decision in *Obergefell* v. *Hodges* that struck down all state bans on same-sex marriage and made it legal in all fifty states. In light of the legalization of same-sex marriage, this chapter looks back on my research on the intimate relationship between heterosexuality and the state.

My *Gender & Society* article on marriage promotion and the contested power of heterosexuality (Heath 2009) asked how does the gendered and sexualized state respond to crisis tendencies in the institution of heterosexuality? I drew on Raewyn Connell's (1987, 2005) theorization of "crisis tendencies" in the gender order of capitalist societies, which include the weakening of patriarchal family structures where state policies have unsettled the legitimacy of men's domination over women (e.g., through laws and policies such as those criminalizing domestic violence and rape within marriage). Connell specifically identified a crisis of sexuality, where forms of heterosexuality that have historically privileged men over women are troubled by women's more assertive sexuality and by social movements for LGBTQ rights. She (1996) situated these crisis tendencies in the complex interplay of gender and state. Her approach reflects the goals of feminist state theory to shine light on the ways that the state has shaped gender relations and how gender relations shape the state (Haney 2000). Feminist sociologists studying the state, however, have often taken for granted normative ideas about heterosexuality, including the presumption of heterosexual coupledom when conceptualizing the relationship between the state and social institutions like marriage and family. While Connell recognized the importance of sexuality in conceptualizing the power of the state to shape social institutions like the family, heterosexuality is still theorized as one element in the relationship between gender and the state, and not in relationship to the state on its own terms.

My research on marriage promotion politics specifically addressed the crisis tendencies in the relationship between the state and sexuality by illuminating governmental policies and practices that seek to stabilize the norm of white, middle-class, heterosexual marriage. I argued that policies to strengthen and promote marriage point to how heterosexual marriage is seen as an increasingly fragile institution in need of defense. This objective fit into a broader theoretical focus on the critical study of heterosexuality (Ingraham 1994; Jackson 1996, 1999, 2006; Katz 1995; Rich 1980; Richardson 1996). Ingraham (2008), for example, theorized heterosexuality as an "imaginary," which appears timeless, outside of history, and beyond question (p. 13). She argued for the need to study the hierarchies and power relationships involved in maintaining its invisibility. The "wedding industrial complex" is one such structure, where heterosexuality sits at the nexus of the state, marriage, religion, media, and popular culture. Canaday (2009) examined how the state has shaped homosexual identities and how sexual identity has shaped the state. Her theorization of the "straight state" pointed to the way that the state not only intervenes in but is also intervened by sexuality (in that the state is a contested sexual site), illuminating tensions between the state and norms of sexuality (p. 6). Puri (2016) further elaborated the relationship between the state and sexuality in conceptualizing "sexual states" (p. 6). For her, institutions like marriage that regulate sexuality are crucial mechanisms in the creation of states. These more recent theorizations of the contested and constitutive connection between sexuality and state are important for thinking about how the power of heterosexuality is instituted through governmental policies that seek to re-institutionalize heterosexual marriage, and what this means for American society today after it has legalized same-sex marriage.

Studying state efforts to re-institutionalize marriage

Oklahoma was my home for ten months. I began conducting my ethnographic research early in 2004 in this state whose marriage initiative began in 1999, after the governor announced that he would designate $10 million of the state's Temporary Assistance to Needy Families (TANF) Federal Block Grant for the purpose of promoting marriage and fighting against divorce. The 1996 federal law, called the Personal Responsibility and Work Opportunity Reconciliation Act, ended more than sixty years of federal welfare benefits to poor families. In the place of federal funding, the law created discretionary state block grants under the rubric of TANF and specifically designated marriage promotion as a sanctioned use of federal funds. Oklahoma is known for having the longest-running marriage initiative in the nation and has provided an example to other states and programs that proliferated in the 2000s. In 2016, the state ceased to provide funding to the initiative due to budget cuts (Brown 2016).

At its inception, the state contracted with Public Strategies, Inc. (a private, for-profit firm) to develop and manage the initiative. Public Strategies trained state employees, community leaders, and other volunteers to offer marriage education workshops throughout the state. The workshops used the Prevention and Relationship Enhancement Program (PREP), a research-based curriculum created by Howard Markman and Scott Stanley that teaches communication skills, conflict management, and problem solving. The initiative also trained volunteers to offer a Christian version of PREP in settings that were not state funded. Recipients of the free training pledged to provide at least four free workshops in their own communities. Workshops for the general public were free of charge, and engaged couples received a $45 discount on their $50 marriage license for attending. At the time, the workshops included large Sweethearts Weekends that occurred every few months on a Friday evening and all-day Saturday with an average of fifty couples. Smaller workshops met weekly for six to eight weeks and tended to draw a much smaller number of participants. In addition to the workshops for the general population, the statewide marriage initiative targeted specific populations, including welfare recipients, low-income parents, high school students, the prison population, the military, and Native Americans. I conducted fieldwork on the workshops for both the general and target populations and found that the more sustained efforts were the workshops for the general population.

I conducted participant observation of thirty workshops for the general public that were advertised on the marriage initiative's website, including three Sweetheart Weekends (six classes), three six-week workshops (fifteen classes), and twenty-four weekend workshops (twenty-four classes). At the beginning of each class, I introduced myself and my research and took detailed field notes. In addition, I attended a state-sponsored PREP training weekend to discover the method for training volunteers. Finally, I conducted twenty in-depth, semi-structured interviews with volunteer participants and leaders from workshops and fifteen with marriage initiative leadership and department of human services staff, which lasted between one and two hours. All participants were given pseudonyms, except in cases where the respondent agreed to use her or his actual name. The transcribed interviews and field notes were coded using a qualitative software program, Atlas.ti.

Ultimately, I discovered that the marriage initiative taught about the importance of what I call "marital heterosexuality," based on an ideology of polarized gender roles and the ideal of the white, middle-class family. The state sought to deal with crisis tendencies in the heterosexual family by rehearsing ideas about marital heterosexuality in thousands of workshops held across the state. The following sections examine the three ways that the state maintained the unitary nature of institutionalized heterosexuality through its marriage initiative. First, it sought to define the problem of marital heterosexuality by providing classes that drew white, middle-class couples and focused on the breakdown of these types of families. Second, it taught about gender as the visible problem for couples to reinforce the importance of marital heterosexuality. Finally, while the state policy did not formally exclude lesbians and gay men from attending the classes, the focus on marital heterosexuality was fundamentally an exclusionary practice.

Reinforcing white, middle-class marital heterosexuality

The marriage initiative had a goal of strengthening relationships and marriage. These efforts focused on fortifying marital heterosexuality by providing workshops to the public that implicitly rehearsed notions of the ideal family—white, middle-class and heterosexual. The concept of "marital heterosexuality" points to the center of the "charmed circle" in the sex hierarchy that Rubin (1999) theorized, where "good," "normal," and "natural" sexuality occurs (p. 151). It occupies the mostly invisible core of natural and desirable sexuality, and homosexuality the periphery as perverse and unnatural (Roseneil 2002). Legal marriage has consequently been a central mechanism the state has used to regulate institutionalized heterosexuality and the construct of the "natural" (white, middle-class) family.

Leaders of the marriage initiative that I interviewed spoke of the need to focus on marriage as a special kind of family form. One program manager stated: "We believe that marriage is a different kind of relationship with different kinds of outcomes, and so we are not in any way, shape, or form going to do anything that sells that goal short." By "outcomes," this marriage initiative leader referred to the social scientific statistical debate about childhood outcomes showing that, on average, children growing up in a one-parent family experience some disadvantage compared to those growing up with two parents. Although scholars are divided about the causes of these disadvantages (e.g., Blankenhorn 2007; Cherlin 2003), marriage promotion advocates often spoke of this body of research to justify the importance of promoting marriage so that every child might grow up with her or his biological, married parents.

A central feature of the social scientific debate over marriage relates to the racialized ways that family breakup has historically occurred in society. Marriage initiative leaders expressed consternation over the declining significance of marriage, and the fact that this was occurring among white families was an often implicit, sometimes explicit, source of apprehension. As one report put it, the strategy of the marriage initiative is to provide marriage workshops to all Oklahomans to effect "specific behavior change at the individual level" and to "restore support for the institution of marriage as a valued social good" (Dion 2006). Leaders referred to two texts that argued for the negative societal effects of marriage decline. The first was by Barbara Dafoe Whitehead (1993), titled "Dan Quayle was right," which contended that the breakup of black families had reproduced behaviors that "damage the social ecology, threaten the public order, and impose new burdens on core institutions" (p. 84). According to Whitehead, there is general reason for concern as chaotic family breakup is now spreading to white families. Thirteen years later, Kay Hymowitz (2006) wrote a popular book on *Marriage and Caste in America*, noting that "The Mission" of white, middle-class families is to educate the young to be self-reliant members of a society. Similar to Whitehead, Hymowitz expressed concern that the "dysfunctional" breakup of black families is now becoming widespread. For her, poor black parents are not "simply middle-class parents manqué; they have their own culture of child-rearing, and—not to mince words—that culture is a recipe for more poverty" (p. 76).

These two texts draw from the "culture of poverty" thesis that was first theorized by Oscar Lewis (1966) and conceptualized in a report on the black family by Daniel Patrick Moynihan (1965). For Lewis, persistent poverty engendered a set of beliefs, values, and practices that shape a culture to perpetuate itself over time, even when structural conditions change. Moynihan focused specifically on the black family and the tangle of pathologies that resulted from the cumulative effects of slavery that led to structural poverty among many African Americans. Critiques of this approach to understanding poverty argued that it blames the victims for their problems, suggesting that "people might cease to be poor if they changed their culture" (Small, Harding, and Lamont 2010, p. 7).

The focus on the family as *the* key mechanism to creating societal dysfunction is at the heart of the debate over the importance of promoting the institution of heterosexual marriage to sustain a strong social order. As policy focused on family breakdown, the mostly unspoken concern of marriage promotion leaders was the norm of the white, middle-class family and the harm caused to this norm. The director of the Oklahoma Department of Human Services (DHS) characterized what he saw as the cost of "fractured families":

> Another piece of this, when you sit back and think about it, we spend $40 million in this state to run our child support enforcement division. Every one of those faces is a fractured relationship. So, we are spending $40 million in the state to do nothing but administer the transfer of cash from noncustodial parents to custodial parents who have experienced fractured relationships. You can see the high cost of having fractured relationships. It's worth the investment.

The director's words suggested that the "deviancy" of fractured families hurts middle-class families that consist of good citizens who pay taxes and embrace Hymowitz's (2006) "Mission."

Marriage promotion follows a long history in the United States of protecting the ideal gendered, heteronormative family against "deviant" others, with attendant social consequences of race and class inequalities. While positioning fractured families as the social problem that the state needed to address, the marriage initiative's workshops and classes predominantly attracted white, middle-class couples who gathered together in a bounded heterosexual space to learn about how to create strong marriages. Issues of race and class would disappear as the focus turned to the problematic of gender relations for heterosexual couples. Heterosexuality became the unexamined backdrop to teach about the "opposite sexes" within the ideal family.

Lessons on marital heterosexuality

Crisis tendencies, spurred on by growing marriage activism of lesbians and gay men, ran beneath the surface of state efforts to strengthen heterosexual marriage. For example, I asked the director of the Oklahoma DHS to explain to me the goal of the marriage initiative. His answer confirmed the ideal of promoting marital heterosexuality: "In terms of the marriage initiative, it's relationships between men and women which are committed preferably for life." His emphasis on "relationships between men and women" points to a need to define the kinds of relationships that are important to the initiative, specifically between men and women. This kind of precision would have been unnecessary thirty years ago, and suggests state efforts to prohibit the recognition of non-heterosexual coupledom.

Marriage workshops, offered free of charge to the general population, attracted largely white, middle-class, heterosexual couples. These workshops encouraged self-discipline and motivation to do gender according to the ideals of marital heterosexuality. The curriculum engaged communication and problem-solving skills, and facilitators of the thirty workshops that I attended taught about the importance of sustaining marital heterosexuality through mastering skills to manage difficult gender dynamics in the context of marriage. The conceptualization of marital heterosexuality was prevalent in the three-day, state-sponsored leadership training, taught by the creators of the PREP curriculum—Howard Markman and Scott Stanley—and Vice President Natalie Jenkins. Participants attending the training were predominantly white, many of them counselors and educators receiving continuing education units.

Crisis tendencies in the dominance of marital heterosexuality were prevalent in the training, as facilitators noted the impact of the decline of marriage on men and women. For example, Stanley argued that in today's society, young people think that cohabiting can serve as a trial run before marriage. In reality, he argued, practicing serial non-monogamy harms women because marriage is the only means to ensure a man's commitment. Citing research, Stanley explained that, for young men, living with a girlfriend often means that she is not the "one." He clarified: "We have talked young people out of thinking that marriage matters, particularly young women. Women get the worse deal if men don't marry them." A dominant script of marital heterosexuality is that marriage is key to helping men settle down and control their sexual urges. For marriage advocates, the decline in the marriage culture also harms men who no longer marry as a way to begin an adult life where sexual drives are contained.

Throughout the training, the presenters performed gender based on conservative gender norms and made jokes that drew on the innate differences between men and women to underscore the challenges of understanding the "opposite" gender (Butler 1999; West and Zimmerman 1987). For example, Scott Stanley explained how researchers have found a pattern that involves women's pursuing an issue and men's withdrawing. From this, he surmised the biological foundation of gender for men to be more physiologically reactive and women to be more emotionally aroused. While acknowledging that these patterns of behavior are complex, Stanley argued that these patterns point to the need to understand and manage fundamental gender differences within marriage, acknowledging the implied importance of promoting marital heterosexuality as a key aspect of the marriage initiative.

The doing of gender in the presentations subtly suggested a gender hierarchy that compels women to put up with men's idiosyncrasies, portraying men as leaders in society. At one point, Howard Markman asked the audience jokingly how many men it takes to change the toilet paper. The punch line: "There is no scientific answer because it has not happened." The implied message is that changing toilet paper is women's work, not men's. When it came time for Natalie Jenkins's presentation, Markman began flipping the remote as if he were surfing television channels. She commanded him to sit, addressing the audience that she should have remembered to take the batteries out of the men's toy; however, she did need these guys because she is not the most technologically advanced. After watching a video of a couple arguing over the way the husband put the laundry soap in the washing machine, Jenkins remarked that the wife was "missing the miracle. He's doing the laundry!" Later, in discussing the need to clarify expectations, Jenkins told a story about how when she was first married, she wanted flowers because all her friends were getting them. The family budget was tight, so she found a 99-cent coupon for a dozen carnations. She provided her husband with four quarters, the coupon, and a note saying, "Honey, if this coupon expires so will you."

This gender work solidified the importance of the essential differences between men and women. Men's stature placed them above tedious tasks like changing the toilet paper and made them naturally able to deal with technology. Women's more frivolous nature made them want flowers and it also meant a predisposition to doing household chores like doing the laundry. State-sponsored trainings made clear the goals of the marriage initiative to help men and women recognize their roles and manage their gender-based conflicts to strengthen marital heterosexuality. At heart was a lesson about gender difference as the glue that keeps two people of the opposite sex together. The ideal for white, middle-class families was configured as a gender hierarchy as a way to solidify marital heterosexuality.

Fortifying marital heterosexuality

Thus far, I have examined the crisis tendencies in state control of the structured ordering of marital heterosexuality, arguing that these tendencies motivated efforts to shore up marriage's boundary around gender and heterosexuality for white, middle-class couples. The thirty workshops I attended mirrored the state-sponsored training by focusing on gender differences within marriage. Generally left unarticulated was the need to guard against the impinging visibility of non-heterosexual relationships. The idea of banning same-sex couples from the free workshops did emerge during my interviews. Deidre, an employee of the Oklahoma Department of Human Services, told me about a memo sent to the initiative by the federal government announcing that government-funded marriage workshops should not be afforded to lesbian and gay couples because they are not recognized as legally married. As a supporter of LGBT rights, this memo infuriated Deirdre who had sought to provide services to same-sex couples. The marriage initiative ultimately did not overtly discriminate or ban lesbians and gay men from attending workshops, but neither did it do anything to provide services to this population or encourage same-sex couples to attend.

It took courage to attend the workshops in Oklahoma as a same-sex couple. Two of the six-week workshops I attended included just such brave individuals, pushing the crisis tendencies of martial heterosexuality into sharp relief. Tammy and Chris, white lesbians in their fifties, had introduced themselves as "life partners" on the first day, surprising the other fifteen predominantly white heterosexual couples. This workshop was led by two volunteers: David, a white married professional, and Randy, a white married associate Baptist pastor. The next workshop brought Amanda and Jennifer into the mix of nineteen couples. They were a younger white lesbian couple in their late twenties. Randy and Susan, a white woman who attended Randy's church, were the facilitators. In both workshops, the focus on marital heterosexuality compelled each lesbian couple to participate in an intricate dance between visibility and invisibility that I describe below.

The focus on gender within the confines of marital heterosexuality worked to make invisible the presence of the same-sex couples. The two facilitators in the first workshop used numerous sports references to capture the attention of participants who were men. When describing how one person often withdraws in an argument, Randy said, "This is just what men do, withdraw." He drew on an analogy to baseball, where after you get hit a few times, you tend to give up. The same is true for the case of arguing, he observed; sometimes it just feels easier to give up or withdraw. Not withdrawing takes effort and practice. David joked, "Can you do the same analogy with knitting?" and Randy retorted, "I can't, but I'm sure there are those in the audience who can!" In the following six-week workshop, Randy told the men that having "crappy experiences in marriage is a man thing, not a God thing." It is a "big boy thing," he added. "God gives me a good picture of how I am supposed to be in a relationship." This repertoire reiterated the fundamental differences between men and women: men play sports and women knit, men withdraw and women persist, etc.

This kind of language did not fit well with teachings that could apply to relationships between two women. Tammy and Chris often spoke up to make their presence felt. In the final class, David asked participants about their feelings on sensuality and touch. Even though David conveniently ended the discussion before Tammy and Chris had a turn to participate, Tammy still spoke up: "We assume that what we like, the other person likes." Her words differed from other responses that focused on how men and women like different things, challenging the taken-for-granted assumption that sexuality is only about pleasure between "opposite" bodies.

The teachings on marital heterosexuality excluded the lesbian couples, and their presence made many of the heterosexual participants uncomfortable either because they disapproved of homosexuality or were inexperienced in dealing with same-sex relationships. Tom, a white man in his mid-twenties, recounted how he was caught off guard by "the two girls who were there together. They were like lesbians!" He went on to say that he didn't have a problem with the fact that they attended, but he was just surprised. Becky, a white woman in her thirties in an interracial marriage, answered my question about whether she ever felt uncomfortable in the workshop by discussing her disapproval of same-sex couples:

> Mmm. I did feel uncomfortable with the fact that there were couples in there of the same sex, just because I feel strongly about family values and what the traditional family is. But I know it is something that is happening in the United States, and there is really nothing I can do about it. And, I mean, they are human. They have needs too. It doesn't mean that I agree with them.

As a self-identified evangelical Christian, Becky recounted a certain resignation that many conservative Christians expressed with the fact that same-sex relationships were becoming more visible in society. She begrudgingly admitted that "they are human and have needs too."

Norm, a white man in his sixties, answered my question by expressing his fear of the unknown and moved seamlessly into discussing his disapproval of homosexuality. He said,

> At first, the unknown [was uncomfortable]. When you go around and there is more and more interaction, I felt like there was a quality of responses and information given by the men in that class that usually doesn't happen. [Pause] I do consider homosexuality a sin, but I'm not here to judge that. I have a lot of patients that are gay, and they have a lifestyle I do not approve of. But I thought even the gay couple had a lot of good information to toss out.

Norm's response reflects the condemnation that other participants discussed of homosexuality; however, he recognized that the same-sex couple brought good information to the table. While the workshops were taught in a way that made same-sex couples invisible and confirmed the power of heterosexuality to exclude, these couples still were able to the trouble dominant ideas about marital heterosexuality through their participation.

The lesbians in the class expressed their awareness that their attendance challenged the norms of marital heterosexuality and provided a different perspective for those who had no experience dealing with lesbians and gay men. Amanda, one of the younger lesbians, told me that taking a class with a lesbian was important to change people's perceptions. She said,

> I don't know the personal story of all these people in our class, but if they never met a lesbian before, and now they do, now they see, and hear what I say in class, and don't think we are the devil now, you know, that's a goal in itself. I mean, people are ignorant, and they don't know. So just being open and honest about stuff and talking to people or just being a good person around them and knowing you are gay, it has a positive influence.

Her words rang true. Even though most of the participants I interviewed expressed negative feelings about homosexuality, when faced with a same-sex couple, their stereotypic perceptions tended to soften.

Thus, the presence of same-sex couples in the workshops had the effect of both strengthening and disrupting the power of marital heterosexuality. Teaching the class as if the same-sex couples were invisible served to reinforce the dominant heterosexual norm that is perpetuated by the state: the kinds of relationships it wants to promote are heterosexual and married, implicitly and sometimes explicitly excluding same-sex relationships. In this way, the teachings on gender and marital heterosexuality inscribed a powerful conception of the heteronormative family. Still, the prevailing image of marital heterosexuality was disrupted by the increasing prominence of lesbian and gay couples as they made decisions to disrupt what might be seen as a "natural" heterosexual space. Even in the face of what appeared to be a monolithic achievement to promote gender and marital heterosexuality, instances of defused power created small opportunities for social change.

Conclusion

It has been fourteen years since I conducted my ethnographic research on the state initiative to promote marriage. Much has changed in the United States. In 2004, the 1996 federal Defense of Marriage Act (DOMA)—defining "marriage" as between one man and one woman and ensuring that no state was compelled to recognize the same-sex marriage contract of another state—was still in full force. Most individual states had passed their own DOMAs and some passed "super-DOMAs," laws that blocked recognition not only of same-sex marriage but also of civil unions and domestic partnerships. However, the crisis tendencies that I have described above were already evident in state policies in 2004. In 2003, public controversy over same-sex marriage followed the decision by the Massachusetts Supreme Judicial Court in *Goodridge* v. *Department of Public Health* that established a right to marry for same-sex couples in the state's constitution. Much more quickly than most people likely expected, legal and legislative victories led to the legalization of same-sex marriage in 2015.

What do these developments tell us about the promotion of marital heterosexuality? Does the legalization of same-sex marriage mean an end to the state regulation of sexuality in general? The answers to these questions are complicated and will require future research to understand the continuing relationship between the state and sexuality. Marriage promotion initiatives have been one of the most visible ways that the state has sought to shore up marital heterosexuality. While the marriage initiative in Oklahoma lost its funding in 2016, state initiatives and programs persist across the country to strengthen marriage. Jennifer Randles (2013) conducted ethnographic research in 2008 and 2009 on a federally funded relationship skills program for low-income, unmarried couples with children, which had a significant fatherhood component. She found that the program she studied promoted "marital masculinity," a concept that focused on the need to reinforce masculinity through ideologies of the breadwinner model. It is completely conceivable that these marriage programs will continue to promote a gendered ideal of marital heterosexuality despite fundamental societal changes that make legal marriage available to same-sex couples.

Social movement and sexuality scholars have debated whether the legalization of same-sex marriage will result in an assimilation of LGBT individuals into a conservative institution (marriage), or whether its legalization can facilitate transformative social change of that institution (Bernstein, Harvey, and Naples 2018). Bernstein and Taylor (2013) argue that many gay activists have been "motivated by a desire to build bridges toward the dominant group," while many also "maintain a sustained critique of heteronormativity (the social system of heterosexual privilege). In short, these positions are not always opposed" (p. 2). From the perspective of my research, a similar tension can be said to exist in the relationship between sexuality and the state. The state increasingly opened its door to making the institution of marriage legal for same-sex couples, with the attendant benefits and responsibilities. Regarding state regulation of sexuality, there has been a slight shift to include lesbians and gay men in the charmed circle of the ideal family. At the same time, it is likely that marital heterosexuality will continue to structure the way that the state deals with its problems of discrimination against LGBT populations, poverty, gender inequality in organizations, sex work, etc. Time and research will tell.

References

Bernstein, M. and Taylor. V. (eds.) (2013) *The marrying kind? Debating same-sex marriage within the lesbian and gay movement.* Minneapolis, University of Minnesota Press.

Bernstein, M., Harvey, B., and Naples, N. A. (2018) Marriage, the final frontier? Same-sex marriage and the future of the lesbian and gay movement. *Sociological Forum*, 33, 30–52.

Blankenhorn, D. (2007) *The future of marriage.* New York, Encounter Books.

Brown, T. (2016) State ends marriage initiative as part of budget cuts. *Oklahoma Watch.* Available from: https://oklahomawatch.org/2016/08/03/state-ends-marriage-initiative-citing-budget-cuts/ [Accessed September 24, 2018].

Butler, J. (1999) *Gender trouble.* New York, Routledge.

Canaday, M. (2009) *The straight state: sexuality and citizenship in twentieth-century America.* Princeton, Princeton University Press.

Cherlin, A. (2003) Should the government promote marriage? *Contexts*, 3, 22–29.

Connell, R. (1987) *Gender and power: society, the person and sexual politics.* Stanford, Stanford University Press.

Connell, R. (1996) New directions in gender theory, masculinity research, and gender politics. *Ethnos*, 61(3–4), 157–176.
Connell, R. (2005) *Masculinities.* Cambridge, Polity Press.
Dion, M.R., Avellar, S.A., Zaveri, H.H., Strong, D.A., Hershey, A.M., Silman, T.J., and Santos, B. (2008) *The Oklahoma Marriage Initiative: a process evaluation.* Washington, DC, Mathematica Policy Research.
Dion, R. (2006) The Oklahoma Marriage Initiative: an overview of the longest-running statewide marriage initiative in the U.S. ASPE Research Brief. Available from: https://aspe.hhs.gov/system/files/pdf/180016/rb.pdf.
Haney, L.A. (2000) Feminist state theory: applications to jurisprudence, criminology, and the welfare state. *Annual Review of Sociology*, 26, 641–666.
Heath, M. (2009) State of our unions: marriage promotion and the contested power of heterosexuality. *Gender & Society*, 23(1), 27–48.
Heath, M. (2012) *One marriage under God: the campaign to promote marriage in America.* New York, New York University Press.
Heath, M. (2013) Sexual misgivings: producing un/marked knowledge in neoliberal marriage promotion policies. *The Sociological Quarterly*, 54(4), 561–583.
Hymowitz, K. (2006) *Marriage and caste in America: separate and unequal families in a post-marital age.* Chicago, Ivan R. Dee.
Ingraham, C. (1994) The heterosexual imaginary: feminist sociology and theories of gender. *Sociological Theory*, 12, 203–219.
Ingraham, C. (2008) *White weddings: romancing heterosexuality in popular culture*, 2nd ed. New York, Routledge.
Jackson, S. (1996) Heterosexuality and feminist theory. In: D. Richardson (ed.) *Theorising heterosexuality: telling it straight.* Buckingham, Open University, pp. 21–39.
Jackson, S. (1999) *Heterosexuality in question.* London, Sage.
Jackson, S. (2006) Interchanges: gender, sexuality and heterosexuality: the complexity (and limits) of heteronormativity. *Feminist Theory*, 7, 105–121.
Katz, J.N. (1995) *The invention of heterosexuality.* New York, Plume.
Lewis, O. (1966) *La vida: a Puerto Rican family in the culture of poverty – San Juan and New York.* New York, Random House.
Moynihan, D.P. (1965) *The Negro family: the case for national action.* Washington, DC, Office of Policy Planning and Research, U.S. Department of Labor.
Puri, J. (2016) *Sexual states: governance and the struggle over the antisodomy law in India.* Durham, NC, Duke University Press.
Randles, J.M. (2013) Repackaging the "package deal": promoting marriage for low income families by targeting paternal identity and reframing marital masculinity. *Gender & Society*, 27(6), 864–888.
Rich, A. (1980) Compulsory heterosexuality and lesbian existence. *Signs*, 5(4), 631–660.
Richardson, D. (ed.) (1996) *Theorising heterosexuality.* Philadelphia, Open University Press.
Roseneil, S. (2002) The heterosexual/homosexual binary: past, present, and future. In: D. Richardson and S. Seidman (eds.) *Handbook of lesbian and gay studies.* London, Sage, pp. 27–44.
Rubin, G. (1999) Thinking sex: notes for a radical theory of the politics of sexuality. In: R. Parker and P. Aggleton (eds.) *Culture, society and sexuality: a reader.* London, UCL Press, pp. 143–178.
Small, M.L., Harding, D.J., and Lamont, M. (2010) Reconsidering culture and poverty. *ANNALS of the American Academy of Political and Social Science*, 629(1), 6–27.
West, C. and Zimmerman, D. (1987) Doing gender. *Gender & Society*, 1, 125–151.
Whitehead, B.D. (1993) Dan Quayle was right. *Atlantic Monthly*, April, 47–84.

Part V

Rethinking sexual fluidity, straight privilege, and allyship

22

Straight girls kissing

Heteroflexibility in the college party scene

Leila J. Rupp, Verta Taylor, and Janelle M. Pham

From Katy Perry's 2008 hit "I Kissed a Girl" to Rita Ora's controversial 2018 song "Girls," the phenomenon of presumably straight girls kissing and making out with other girls has staying power in contemporary popular culture. The dominant notion is that men, especially in the alcohol-fueled college party scene, egg women on for their own enjoyment, and women indulge them solely as a way to attract male attention. But increasingly we have come to recognize that there is more going on than meets the male gaze: that what the boys are watching might be experimentation, bi-curiosity, heteroflexibility, or some other aspect of sexual fluidity. And it might have little to do with the watchers.

We focus here on erotic interactions women engage in for their own purposes in the straight college party scene. Using the case of one progressive public research university, the University of California, Santa Barbara, we argue that heteronormative hookup culture can make room for at least some women's non-heterosexual experiences. Heterosexual men's erotic interest in girl-on-girl action—primarily between conventionally attractive feminine women—and the social acceptability of women's sexual fluidity create the conditions for women to engage in same-sex sexual interactions without necessarily challenging their heterosexual credentials.

Women's sexual fluidity, the hookup scene, and sexual markets

We know that sexual desire, behavior, and identity do not neatly match in contemporary US society, especially for women. Among women and men who identify as heterosexual, 13.6 percent of women and 4.6 percent of men report attraction to members of the same sex, and 12.6 percent of women and 2.8 percent of men have had some sexual contact with a same-sex partner (Hoy and London 2018). Even more striking, of all the same-sex desire and behavior reported in national surveys, the majority is accounted for by those who identify as heterosexual, and especially women: 61.9 percent of same-sex attraction and 65.2 percent of same-sex sexual behavior. For men, the comparable figures are 52 percent and 43.4 percent (Hoy and London 2018). This intriguing way of looking at heterosexual identity and same-sex desire and behavior supports the notion, advanced by scholars over the years, of women's greater sexual fluidity (Blumstein and Schwartz 1977; Budnick 2016; Diamond 2008; England, Mishel, and Caudillo 2016; Golden 2006; Moore 2011; Ott et al. 2011; Peplau and Garnets 2000; Rust 2000a, 2000b; Tabatabai 2015).

The hookup scene on college campuses is a profoundly gendered and heteronormative sexual field (Armstrong, England, and Fogarty 2012; Armstrong, Hamilton, and England 2010; Currier 2013; England, Shafer, and Fogarty 2007; Hamilton 2007; Pham 2017; Reid, Elliott, and Webber 2011). Yet the party scene that gives rise to hookups also fosters the practice of women making out with other women in public, generally to the enjoyment of male onlookers (Rupp and Taylor 2010; Rupp et al. 2014). In this context, race and class dynamics determine where, and which, women may engage in sexual acts with other women, particularly on selective elite college campuses (Budnick 2016). As previous research shows, women arriving on these campuses with the right forms of cultural, social, and economic capital are more apt to gravitate toward campus "party pathways" occupied by class-privileged others who emphasize partying as part and parcel of a standard college experience (Armstrong and Hamilton 2013; McCabe 2016; Stuber 2011). The campus party scene's location in particular campus spaces and its association with student populations marked by greater financial and social capital (e.g., Greeks, athletes), combined with the tendency for these environments to be controlled by white men (Armstrong, Hamilton, and Sweeney 2006), regulates who is likely to access these spaces. Finally, the campus party scene's emphasis on drug and alcohol consumption and casual sex informs women's behaviors when participating in the party scene, including their sexual interactions with other women.

The ubiquity of the party culture belies the racial, gendered, classed, and heteronormative dynamics inherent in its construction. Yet, visible or not, those dynamics affect who may transgress these dynamics through engaging in same-sex sexual behavior. Campus party scenes can be theorized as distinctive "sexual markets," or spatially and culturally distinctive environments facilitating the process of sexual partnership between similarly positioned others (Laumann et al. 2004; Pham 2018). As we argue, women's strategic use of the party market on college campuses is an expression of women's sexual fluidity and is facilitated by the norms of the male-dominated heteronormative hookup scene.

The study

The University of California, Santa Barbara, with an undergraduate population of just over 21,000 students, sits atop a picturesque coastal mesa on the edge of the Pacific Ocean, about 90 miles north of Los Angeles. Currently 62 percent of undergraduates are students of color, mostly Latinx (it has been designated a Hispanic Serving Institution) and Asian American, and 42 percent are first-generation college students. This has changed rather dramatically in the last decades as the university worked hard to recruit and retain students of color and students from low-income families. The campus ranks high as both a party school and as queer-friendly, with a rowdy party scene in the adjacent predominantly student community of Isla Vista and a large, visible, and diverse queer community on campus. Although sexual markets are shaped by the histories and institutional environments of universities (Pham 2018), so that UC Santa Barbara is by no means representative of all US campuses, there is also no reason to think that it is unique. Pham's research points to the similarities as well as differences between UC Santa Barbara and the University of Pennsylvania, both progressive research universities with party school reputations and strong queer communities.

Two different empirical studies of same-sex sexuality at the University of California, Santa Barbara, provide the evidence presented here. Rupp and Taylor, with coauthors, are studying the experiences of lesbian, bisexual, gay, queer, and other women with non-heterosexual identities on campus (Miller, Taylor, and Rupp 2016; Rupp 2019; Rupp and Taylor 2010; Rupp, Taylor, and Miller 2016; Rupp et al. 2014). Pham's project (2018) traces the development and experience of three different sexual markets—the party market, student of color market, and queer student market—at UC Santa Barbara and the University of Pennsylvania. We draw from 126 interviews from the Rupp/Taylor study conducted between 2006 and 2012, some by students in classes and the rest by undergraduate and graduate research assistants, and 27 UC Santa Barbara students interviewed by Pham in 2016–2017 for her dissertation.

For the Rupp/Taylor study, students in the courses located their own interviewees, and research assistants mobilized their personal contacts and snowball sampling to find students willing to be interviewed. In terms of race and ethnicity, the students interviewed are close to the current campus profile: 55 percent are students of color and 45 percent white. Sexual identities include bisexual, lesbian, queer, fluid, pansexual, gay, uncertain, and none. In addition to the 120 interviews for the main project, we make use of six interviews for a student project in one of Rupp's classes with heterosexual students specifically focused on kissing in the party scene.

Pham recruited participants through in-person advertising in undergraduate sociology courses, flyers in public campus spaces, print ads in student newspapers, and social media posts on Facebook. She deliberately oversampled for students of color, who represent 74 percent of her UC Santa Barbara sample, and for queer students, who make up 40 percent, with identities including bisexual, queer, pansexual, questioning, bi-curious, and heteroflexible. All of the names used here are pseudonyms. Although both sets of interviews covered a wide range of topics, we concentrate here on women's strategic use of the heterosexual party scene for the purposes of same-sex intimacies.

The party sexual market

What is most distinctive about UC Santa Barbara is the adjacent community of Isla Vista, a densely populated area where students live on the ocean's edge in crowded and overpriced housing. Isla Vista's party scene consists of fraternity parties (although Greek membership is relatively small, just 12 percent of the student population), large open house parties, and what the students call "kickbacks," or smaller gatherings with friends. Alcohol flows freely, drugs are available, women sport skimpy clothing, and students engage in a lot of hooking up. Zoe, a pansexual Chinese student, juxtaposed the large open house party, where "you know maybe two people," to kickbacks, "more of a group of friends . . . pretty much everybody there knows each other." The environment of these gatherings is more muted than the raucous, dance-filled "raves" found at fraternity or large house parties. "If I were to break down parties I would say there are 'DP' parties [located on Del Playa Drive, which borders the Pacific Ocean], which is just loud techno music and people in a backyard dancing and whatever," Ellen, a bisexual Asian American student explained, "And then there are house parties, which are more chill, a kickback kind of thing. People are playing beer pong or chilling on the couch or smoking."

While women of all races describe immersion in Isla Vista's party market, women of color were more apt to describe these party environments in racialized terms, to include reflecting on standards for entry that tended to privilege hegemonically feminine white women. This was particularly prevalent within the fraternity circuit. "I have noticed . . . the frats tend to favor, of course, the white girls more," shared Marie, a Latina senior who described herself as an avid partier. Jenn, an Asian American senior, also noted that girls who are "extremely hot" tend to be given priority getting into fraternity parties. The large "open" house party presents prime opportunities for fraternity members or athletes to fill their houses with desirable women, with the hosts of these parties determining who can gain entry.

At Isla Vista parties, the practice of presumably heterosexual women kissing and making out with other women is widespread. As Maria, a white bisexual student, reported, "It's just normal for most people now, friends make out with each other." The student newspaper sex columnist in

October 2008 began her column, "I kissed a girl and liked it," recommending "if you're a girl who hasn't quite warmed up to a little experimentation with one of your own, then I suggest you grab a gal and get to it." She posed the "burning question on every male spectator's mind . . . Is it real or is it for show?" (Perez 2008). Most of the time it is for show, but as it turns out, some students also take advantage of the scene to experiment with same-sex activity and to act on acknowledged desire, sometimes with women who consider themselves heterosexual.

Performing for the male gaze

We do not doubt that most of the kissing and making out in the party scene is a performance for men, as queer students well know. And, of course, the boys are interested only in what they consider attractive and feminine women they can imagine having themselves, a dynamic which, in a predominantly white party scene, may afford class-privileged, white women greater license to engage in same-sex kissing than women of color and/or those who present as less hegemonically feminine. Stacy, a white heterosexual student who admits to giving her friend what she calls "love pecks" and engaging in some "booby grabbing," says,

> I think it's mainly for attention definitely. It's usually girls that are super drunk that are trying to get attention from guys or are just really just having fun like when my roommate and I did it at our date party . . . It is alcohol and for show. Not experimentation at all.

Shana, a white heterosexual woman who was clear about her dislike for the party market, recalled the one party she attended as a student. "People flipped their shit when two girls started making out. So I saw that and thought 'okay, you are just doing that for attention, I am out of here.'" A straight Asian American student, Rachel, says "the majority of girls that hookup at parties are actually heterosexual, or identify as such . . . it's the attention that they get." Heterosexual women describe pressure from men to engage in sexual acts with each other. "It just seems like it's kind of something that is stereotypical," shared Roxy, a white bisexual. "Oh, you want to be cool, you want the guys to look at you make out with a girl."

Queer women students have different opinions about the "straight girls kissing" scene: some are annoyed, thinking it trivializes their desires, and some are convinced women are really experimenting or acting on real but unacknowledged desires. And some, if they can pass muster, are willing to take advantage if drunk straight women come on to them or otherwise signal availability. So, for at least some participants, there are more reasons than wanting guys to look at you for women making out with other women at campus parties.

Experimenting with desire

Sometimes performing for the boys turns into something else. Elena, a white student who identifies as straight, says "I have kissed girls on multiple occasions." One night she and a friend were "hammered, walking down the street, and we're getting really friendly and just started making out and taking pictures," which they then posted on Facebook. "And then the last time, this is a little bit more personal, but was when I actually had a threesome. Which was at a party and obviously didn't happen during the party." She mentions "bisexual tendencies" as an explanation, in addition to getting attention: "I would actually call it maybe more like experimentation." Another white student, Kira, who calls herself straight "with some bi-curious tendencies," says girls do it for attention, but also, "It's a good time for them, something they may not have the courage to express themselves otherwise, if they're in a room alone, it makes them more comfortable with it because other people are receiving pleasure from them." She told us about being drunk at a theme party ("Alice in Fuckland"), where she and her friend "Maria" "just started going at it in the kitchen. And this dude, he whispers in my ear, 'Everyone's watching. People can see you.' But me and 'Maria' just like to kiss. I don't think it was like really a spectacle thing, like we weren't teasing anybody. We just like to make out. So we might be an exception to the rule," she giggled.

In another interview, a white bisexual student, Jenny, described a friend as liking "boys and girls when she's drunk . . . But when she's sober she's starting to like girls." And another white student, Lynne, who called herself "technically" bisexual, explained that she hates that term because in Isla Vista "it basically means that you make out with girls at parties." Before her first relationship with a woman, she never thought about bisexuality: "The closest I ever came to thinking that was, hey, I'd probably make out with a girl if I was drinking." "I feel like being drunk, people use that as an excuse to lower their inhibitions and be like 'oh my God, I'm so drunk, kiss me!'" explained Ellen, an Asian bisexual and a former sorority member. "Because it is actually what they want, but then they kind of use that [excuse] and you kind of laugh about that and giggle." These stories make clear that experimentation in the heterosexual context of the hookup culture and college party scene provides a safe space for some women, especially white women, to explore non-heterosexual possibilities.

Using and being used in the party scene

Given that there are women willing to make out solely for male attention and others experimenting with potential desire, the party scene, with alcohol flowing freely, has some possibilities for queer women, although primarily for those who can pass as straight girls kissing. Viola, a bisexual and biracial (Native American/white) student, at first identified as "one of those girls" who makes out at parties.

> I may have fallen into that trap of like kissing a girl to impress a guy, but I can't really recollect doing that on purpose. It was more of just my own desire to be with, like to try that with a woman.

Jasmine, a queer Korean American student, kissed her best friend at a party and thought "it was pretty cool." She explains that it wasn't for male attention: "I wanted to kiss her so I did." An Asian American bisexual student, Madison, says she has made out with lots of straight women at parties. Lea, a white pansexual student, had a boyfriend who thought she might be bisexual or a lesbian and encouraged her to experiment sexually, so her first year in college she made out with girls, including her boyfriend's younger brother's ex-girlfriend. In these cases, students acted on their desires in the public party scene.

Sometimes straight women initiate the encounters. Roxy, a white bisexual student, in her first years on campus hooked up with women she met at fraternity and house parties.

> I've definitely made out with a lot of girls at frat parties who seem they might just be doing it because we're at a frat party. And I kind of feel like I'm almost taking advantage of people because they probably wouldn't be doing it normally.

Sometimes she would get their numbers and text them, but they weren't interested in anything more. Lea says she has some friends who are "I guess pretty slutty or whatever and they're fine with just being the experimental hookup." For at least some queer students looking for hookups, the straight women at parties can be fair game.

Although men might have little interest in watching masculine or genderqueer students kissing other women, some straight women come on to students who don't fit the mold of straight-looking and feminine. Kacy, a masculine black gay student, says she gets hit on by women a lot at straight parties. Dro, a black genderqueer pansexual student, tells of a straight woman coming on to her at a bar and enjoying the encounter. And Danny, a bisexual Asian American and genderqueer student, says straight friends sometimes want to make out with her when they're drunk. In such cases male attention would seem to have little to do with the encounters on either side.

But if there are opportunities to be found in the party market, queer women can also feel used by the whole scene, choosing not to kiss other women at parties to avoid drawing unwanted attention, particularly from heterosexual men. "I have friends who are bi or gay," shared Samantha, a white heterosexual senior. "They don't necessarily kiss people in public because they are either not fully out, or they are not comfortable with the fact that lesbians are used as something to ogle at here." These varied positions on kissing women at college parties juxtapose strategically "using" or taking advantage of straight women in drunken situations—a view voiced by Roxy above—with those women who do not want to "be used" as a form of entertainment for heterosexual men. For students like Roxy, not involved in the queer community, the party market works for hookups but not for anything more. Zoe prefers to seek women through online apps, given that "if I was going to a party to hit up a girl or something, it might be a little harder. At least to find somebody who wasn't trying to just experiment."

Other students agonize over whether a friend who tries to kiss them while drunk really means it. Alyssa, a Russian-born lesbian who worried about her high school friends thinking she was sexually attracted to them, went to a party at one of the co-op houses on campus known for being queer-friendly during the spring of her first year. She didn't drink but the friend she went with got really drunk and wanted to kiss her. "And I, like, freaked out and kinda stood there looking like I was having an anxiety attack because I like wanted to and I didn't know what was happening." Isabel, a queer Latina, describes her relationship with a good friend in college becoming "more than friendly." When they partied, "she would always push me to kiss her and I never agreed. I was scared to. One day she got me drunk enough to agree and I did." In this case, things worked out when they realized that they weren't drunk and were still making out and ended up together. But the uncertainty about what is going on when presumably straight women want to kiss and make out with women with acknowledged same-sex desires can make the party scene a fraught space.

Sometimes women both use and are used by the party scene when they engineer threesomes with a man and another woman when interested only in the woman. Kissing another woman often provokes offers of a threesome. Melissa, a white student who identifies as fluid, says if she kisses her girlfriend at a straight party, they "would get ten guys swarming on you, like, 'Hey, you wanna do a threesome?' or 'Let me get in on that,' or 'Let me watch.'" When Carey, also white and fluid, found herself attracted to a friend, she hesitated to come on directly so

> brought in this other third party male and so it was more of a threesome, but as soon as the threesome had kind of gotten underway I kind of realized I didn't want him there; I was, like, "You're superfluous, go away," you know, but it then was too late.

Kara, an Asian American student already identifying as bisexual, had a crush on a coworker, a swinger romantically involved with a man, so sought out sex with both of them. "I am too chicken-shit to make the first move, or I'm too shy to approach girls, or I never know if they are queer or not," she explains. Threesomes, whether prompted by men's or women's desire, can serve as an opportunity for women to experiment with or act on desire, but women can also end up in what may be at least a partly unwanted sexual encounter.

The difficulties some queer women experience meeting other queer women makes the party market a possible place to find partners, although there the difficulties are magnified since it is not always possible to tell if a woman is really interested in a sexual encounter. Alcohol and the interest of men in girl-on-girl action confuse the picture. As a result, queer women both use and feel used in the party market. But their participation shows that the dynamics are more complicated than drunken women making out for the pleasure of men.

Heteroflexibility

What does all of this tell us about heterosexualities? We know that sexual desire, sexual behavior, and sexual identity are not totally aligned for either women or men, and that women in particular exhibit a great deal of sexual fluidity. Certainly, the women who identify as heterosexual but are into kissing and making out with other women reveal the role of sexual fluidity in the hookup scene. Says Tessa, a Greek American straight-identified student, "It's not like they're way different from anyone else. They're just making out." About her own experience, she says, "It's just like it's okay because we're both drunk and we're friends. It's not like we identify as lesbian in any way."

As Tessa suggests, making out with another woman can have no impact on one's identity as heterosexual. Kira says, "And yeah, I imagine a lot of the girls that you know just casually make out with their girlfriends would consider themselves straight. I consider myself straight." Stacy would agree: "I would still think they're straight girls. Unless I saw some, like level of like emotional and like attraction there." That's where the line begins to blur. Viola thinks "they're definitely bi-curious at the least . . . I think that a woman who actually does it for enjoyment and like knows that she likes that and that she desires it again, I would say would be more leaning towards bisexual." Lynne describes kissing her girlfriend at a party "and some guy came up and poured beer on us and said something like 'stop kissing her you bitch,'" suggesting that any sign that women are kissing for their own pleasure puts them over the line.

So, although girls who kiss girls are not "different from anyone else," if they have an emotional reaction or *really* enjoy it or want to do it again, then they've apparently crossed the line of heterosexuality. Straight college students today can make out with women or engage in threesomes and call themselves "bi-curious" without challenge to their heterosexual identity, but the same kind of flexibility does not extend to lesbians. Kira explains that she doesn't think "the lesbian community would accept me right off because I like guys too much, you know." And she doesn't think she has "enough sexual experience with the women to be considered bisexual." Molly, a white lesbian, says her first girlfriend, who was straight when they met, says "she's bi but I'm really sure she's a lesbian, cuz she does not hook up with guys." A white bisexual, Michelle, is adamant that you cannot be a lesbian and sleep with men. Queer white Rachel, because she still finds men attractive, finds it "hard for me to call myself a lesbian." Hannah, an Asian American lesbian, identifies that way "because I am only attracted to females and I honestly know this because I am not physically, sexually, or emotionally attracted to guys." Students seem clear that lesbians are attracted only to women, even if they have had heterosexual experience prior to coming to call themselves lesbian. Identities such as queer, pansexual, and fluid, as well as, of course, bisexual, are less rigid, which may be why they are increasingly embraced by students at UC Santa Barbara.

Straight women, then, can be "heteroflexible" or "barsexual" or "bi-curious" or "mostly straight," but too much physical attraction or emotional investment crosses over the line of heterosexuality. What this suggests is that heterosexual women's options for physical intimacy are expanding, although still with limits. The experiences of women on campus help to make sense of the national data on the sexual desires and behavior of women who identify as straight. Straight girls kissing may be a turn on for men, but they are also a sign of the times.

References

Armstrong, E. A., and Hamilton, L. T. (2013) *Paying for the party: How college maintains inequality.* Cambridge, MA: Harvard University Press.

Armstrong, E. A., England, P., and Fogarty, A. (2012) Accounting for women's orgasm and sexual enjoyment in college hookups and relationships. *American Sociological Review*, 77 (3), 435–462.

Armstrong, E. A., Hamilton, L., and England, P. (2010) Is hooking up bad for young women? *Contexts*, 9, 22–27.

Armstrong, E. A., Hamilton, L., and Sweeney, B. (2006) Sexual assault on campus: A multilevel, integrative approach to party rape. *Social Problems*, 53 (4), 483–499.

Blumstein, P. W., and Schwartz, P. (1977) Bisexuality: Some social psychological issues. *Journal of Social Issues*, 33, 30–45.

Budnick, J. (2016) "Straight girls kissing?" Understanding same-gender sexuality beyond the elite college campus. *Gender and Society*, 30, 745–768.

Currier, D. M. (2013) Strategic ambiguity: Protecting emphasized femininity and hegemonic masculinity in the hookup culture. *Gender and Society*, 27, 704–727.

Diamond, L. M. (2008) Female bisexuality from adolescence to adulthood: Results from a 10-year longitudinal study. *Developmental Psychology*, 44, 5–14.

England, P., Mishel, E., and Caudillo, M. L. (2016) Increases in sex with same-sex partners and bisexual identity across cohorts of women (but not men). *Sociological Science*, 3, 951–970.

England, P., Shafer, E. F., and Fogarty, A. C. K. (2007) Hooking up and forming romantic relationships on today's college campuses. In: Kimmel, M. S. and Aronson, A. (eds.) *The gendered society reader* (3rd ed.). New York: Oxford University Press, pp. 531–547.

Golden, C. (2006) What's in a name? Sexual self-identification among women. In: Savin-Williams, R.C. and Cohen, K. M. (eds.) *The lives of lesbians, gays, and bisexuals: Children to adults.* Fort Worth: Harcourt Brace, pp. 229–249.

Hamilton, L. (2007) Trading on heterosexuality: College women's gender strategies and homophobia. *Gender and Society*, 21, 145–172.

Hoy, A., and London, A. S. (2018) The experience and meaning of same-sex sexuality among heterosexually identified men and women: An analytic review. *Sociology Compass*, 12 (7).

Laumann, E. O., Ellingson, S., Mahay, J., Paik, A., and Youm, Y. (eds.) (2004) *The sexual organization of the city.* Chicago: University of Chicago Press.

McCabe, Janice M. (2016) *Connecting in college: How friendship networks matter for academic and social success.* Chicago: University of Chicago Press.

Miller, S. D., Taylor, V., and Rupp, L. J. (2016) Social movements and the construction of queer identity. In: Stets, J. E. and Serpe, R. T. (eds.) *New directions in identity theory and research.* New York: Oxford University Press, pp. 443–469.

Moore, M. G. (2011) *Invisible families: Gay identities, relationships, and motherhood among black women.* Berkeley: University of California Press.

Ott, M. Q., Corliss, H. L., Wypij, D., Rosario, M., and Austin, S. B. (2011) Stability and change in self-reported sexual orientation identity in young people: Application of mobility metrics. *Archives of Sexual Behavior*, 40, 519–532.

Peplau, L. A., and Garnets, L. D. (2000) A new paradigm for understanding women's sexuality and sexual orientation. *Journal of Social Issues*, 56, 329–350.

Perez, J. (2008) Hope my BF don't mind. *Daily Nexus*, October 15, 10.

Pham, J. M. (2017) Beyond hookup culture: Current trends in the study of college student sex and where to next. *Sociology Compass.* 11: e12499. https://doi.org/10.1111/soc4.12499.

Pham, J. M. (2018) The sexual organization of the university: Women's experiences of sex and relationships on two American college campuses. PhD Thesis, University of California, Santa Barbara.

Reid, J. A., Elliott, S., and Webber, G. R. (2011) Casual hookups to formal dates: Refining the boundaries of the sexual double standard. *Gender and Society*, 25, 545–568.

Rupp, L. J. (2019) Queer dilemmas of desire. *Feminist Studies*, 45 (1), 67–93.

Rupp, L. J. and Taylor, V. (2010) Straight girls kissing. *Contexts*, 9, 28–32.

Rupp, L. J., Taylor, V., and Miller, S. D. (2016) Learning to be queer: College women's sexual fluidity. In: Fischer, N. and Seidman, S. (eds.) *Introducing the new sexuality studies* (3rd ed.). New York: Routledge, pp. 195–206.

Rupp, L. J., Taylor, V., Regev-Messalem, S., Fogarty, A., and England, P. (2014) Queer women in the hookup scene: Beyond the closet? *Gender and Society*, 28, 212–235.

Rust, P. C. R. (2000a) Bisexuality: A contemporary paradox for women. *Journal of Social Issues*, 56, 205–221.

Rust, P. C. R. (2000b) *Bisexuality in the United States.* New York: Columbia University Press.

Stuber, Jenny M. (2011) *Inside the college gates: How class and culture matter in higher education.* Lanham: Lexington Books.

Tabatabai, A. (2015) *Lesbian, queer and bisexual women in heterosexual relationships: Narratives of sexual identity.* Lanham: Lexington Books.

23

A mixed-method study of same-sex kissing among college-attending heterosexual men

Eric Anderson and Mark McCormack

Introduction

Research on men and masculinities has demonstrated the negative impact that homophobia has had on heterosexual men's gendered behaviors in the United States (Floyd 2000). Homophobia has been used to regulate how heterosexual men discuss emotions (Monroe, Baker and Roll 1997; Way 2011) and their physical intimacy with each other (Derlega et al. 1989). This is particularly true of behaviors that are coded as sexual, including same-sex kissing between men (Floyd 2000). As a result, many of the attitudes and behaviors that have been esteemed characteristics of masculinity in the United States have had damaging consequences for many heterosexual men.

However, recent research has documented the emergence of heterosexual men kissing each other in public settings while still maintaining social identities as heterosexual (Anderson, Adams and Rivers 2012). Occurring in the United Kingdom, this phenomenon has been attributed to the liberal attitudes toward gay people within the United Kingdom (Clements and Field 2014). This is because there is less social regulation of same-sex kissing when same-sex sexuality is not stigmatized (Anderson 2014). Further research has found same-sex kissing in Australia, but with much lower prevalence than in the United Kingdom (Drummond et al. 2015). There is no empirical examination of the extent to which heterosexual men in the United States are kissing, even though the liberalization of attitudes toward gay people found in the United Kingdom is present in the United States (Keleher and Smith 2012), albeit to a lesser extent. Given the new trend of heterosexual men kissing each other in other countries (Anderson et al. 2012; Drummond et al. 2015), we examined the prevalence of same-sex kissing among young adult males in the United States and their rationale for this behavior.

In this chapter, we assess the prevalence of same-sex kissing behavior among heterosexual young men in the United States. We utilize a mixed-method study of 442 quantitative surveys and 75 in-depth interviews among a racially diverse group of participants from 11 universities in order to understand the frequency, context and meanings of same-sex kissing. We found that 40% of participants had kissed another man on the cheek and 10% on the lips. Both types of kisses were generally described as non-sexual expressions of affection, occurred between friends in a range of contexts, and were predicted by positive attitudes toward gay men. Thus, we contend that same-sex kissing occurred in a greater range of contexts than previously found. We situate these findings within broader theoretical debates about masculinities and the meanings associated with heterosexual masculinity in US culture.

The censure of same-sex kissing between heterosexual men

Central to the study of men and masculinities is the recognition that many men gain social privilege from their gender. However, these benefits are unevenly distributed, with white, heterosexual, middle-class men gaining the most benefits as a group (Connell 1995). Fundamental to this framework of masculinities is the notion that even this group of men suffered both physically and psychologically from the social dynamics of masculinities (Courtenay 2000).

Social norms related to traditional forms of masculinities encourage men to put their health at risk, and also cause damage by stigmatizing behaviors that have been associated with positive mental and emotional health (Way 2011). Emotional expressionism, intellectual endeavor, physical tactility and exhibiting caring behaviors are all stigmatized due to their association with femininity (Plummer 1999).

However, the stigmatization of femininity is also a factor in the explicit rejection of same-sex desire from masculinity for heterosexual men. This is because sexuality and gender are conflated in US culture, with the presence of feminine behaviors in men deemed evidence of being gay and any same-sex desire thus questions masculinity. This stigmatization of gay people has been so extreme that any individual act socially coded as "gay" has traditionally been used to marginalize a person as having a stigmatized gay identity (McCreary 1994).

Anderson (2008) conceptualized this conflation of a socially coded "gay" behavior with a gay identity as the "one-time rule of homosexuality." The rule holds that any single act of same-sex intimacy may cause the participant to be labeled as gay by others. Highlighting that this only applies to same-sex interactions, Schwartz and Rutter (1998, p. 12) write, it is "as if one drop of homosexuality tells the truth of self while one drop of heterosexuality in a homosexual life means nothing." So intense was this rule in the homophobic 1980s that two heterosexual men participating in non-sexual same-sex kissing would normally result in their being socially perceived as gay (Derlega et al. 1989).

This stigmatization of same-sex kissing means that it has been erased from many arenas of men's public lives (Connell 1995). However, it also speaks to the historical and social context of masculinity. It has been possible, for example, for heterosexual men to kiss in particular contexts in the US, such as at sports events and when drunk (see Anderson et al. 2012), and between father and son. Similarly, certain kinds of same-sex kissing between men are neither stigmatized nor indicative of gay identity in homophobic countries like Iran (see Anderson 2009). In order to understand the operationalization of homophobia in policing gender in the US context, it is necessary to theorize the links between homophobia and masculinity.

Theorizing the intersection of homophobia and masculinity

Research in the twentieth century documented the centrality of homophobia to the social dynamics of masculinities (Floyd 2000). While this scholarship powerfully captured the ways in which homophobia was used to police and stratify masculinities, the cultural context of pervasive homophobia in the 1980s and early 1990s meant that there was little recognition that this homophobic version of masculinity was specific to that period. That is, there was not the conceptual apparatus to understand cultures in which homophobia was prevalent but did not police masculinities.

Anderson (2009) developed the concept homohysteria to understand the social conditions necessary for homophobia to regulate gendered behaviors. Defined as the fear of being socially perceived as gay, there are three factors that determine the level of homohysteria in a culture (McCormack and Anderson 2014). For a culture to be homohysteric, there must be: 1) recognition in that culture that same-sex desire exists as a static sexual orientation within a significant portion of the population; 2) high levels of attitudinal homophobia; 3) a conflation of gender and sexuality such that femininity in men is equated with maintaining a gay identity. When these conditions are met, homophobia serves as an effective mechanism to socially regulate masculinities. Homohysteria enables recognition of the different ways in which homophobia is operationalized in specific contexts, giving greater understanding of the dynamics of those cultures.

McCormack and Anderson (2014) developed a stage model of homohysteria rooted in research on masculinities in the US since the late 1800s. They argue that three stages exist: 1) homoerasure (1880s–1970s); b) homohysteria (1970s–1992); c) inclusivity (1993–). In the stage of homoerasure, gendered behaviors were not regulated by homophobia because it was not recognized that men could be gay. Here, there were homophobic laws and condemnation of same-sex sexuality, yet men exhibited physical and emotional intimacy (see Ibson 2002). These cultures were homophobic, but not homohysteric.

A combination of social factors led to an upsurge in homophobic attitudes in the 1980s. High levels of homophobia occurred for three reasons: 1) HIV/AIDS became synonymous with gay identity and was labelled the "gay plague" in a way that resulted in an upsurge of antigay violence and homophobia; 2) there was a growth in traditional religious beliefs, with fundamentalist Christianity gaining increasing political sway; and 3) the Republican Party used fear of AIDS to create a moral panic around gay people. It was in this homohysteric culture that hypermasculine gendered displays predominated (Connell 1995).

The third stage is one of inclusivity. McCormack and Anderson (2014, p. 154) define this as "a culture where people with positive attitudes toward homosexuality are in the majority, and where there is widespread recognition of homosexuality as a sexual identity" (see also Dean 2014). The key driver for the decline in homohysteria is the improving attitudes toward gay people (McCormack and Anderson 2014). There is evidence of a liberalization in attitudes toward gay people in the United States: General Social Survey (GSS) data show the proportion of the US population condemning same-sex sexuality has steadily declined since 1987. In a statistical analysis of these data, Keleher and Smith (2012) contend that "willingness to accept lesbians and gays has grown enormously since 1990" (p. 1232), arguing that "we are witnessing a sweeping change in attitudes toward lesbians and gay men" (p. 1324).

These changes have occurred alongside a softening of masculinity among heterosexual men (see Anderson and McCormack 2016). Barrett (2013) documents the importance of bodily touch in friendships between gay and heterosexual men, and hugging and limited forms of cuddling is present in US high schools (Anderson 2014; Morales and Caffyn-Parsons 2017). Young men increasingly value emotional support and tactility as integral components of close friendships (McCormack 2011), even labelling these friendships *bromances* (Robinson, Anderson and White 2018).

However, there has not been any research about the prevalence of heterosexual young men engaging in same-sex kissing in the United States. This is despite research showing same-sex kissing occurring between heterosexual male students in the United Kingdom and Australia. Indeed, short interviews conducted at two British universities found that 89% of heterosexual men reported kissing their heterosexual male friends on the lips, with half reporting that they would kiss a gay male friend in a similar fashion (Anderson et al. 2012). In a replication using interview data from 90 heterosexual Australian undergraduate men, 29% reported kissing their heterosexual male friends on the lips (Drummond et al. 2015). Given the absence of empirical research on this topic in the United States, the current study explores the prevalence and meanings associated with kissing between heterosexual men in the United States.

Methods

This research uses a mixed-methods design to investigate the frequency and meanings of heterosexual young men kissing in the United States. We surveyed university students located in the Southern, Eastern and Western regions of the United States, including those located in both liberal and conservative areas. We do not class these universities as liberal, and highlight that three universities had religious affiliations, although none had compulsory religious education. We utilized 442 surveys from undergraduate heterosexual men across 11 geographically diverse US universities during the 2011–2012 academic year: four universities were located in states in the West, four in the East, and three in the South. We undertook 40 surveys at 10 institutions, and 42 at one institution.

We then added 75 in-depth, semi-structured interviews. We interviewed seven participants at nine of the universities, and six at the remaining two. These universities were the same institutions as those where the surveys were collected. Participants ranged in age from 18 to 25 years old, fewer than half (43%) belonged to a sport team or fraternity, and 37% were white (39% Asian, 12% Hispanic/Latino, 4% black, 8% other). No other demographic information was collected.

Survey procedure

Two white male undergraduate research assistants recruited undergraduate participants from populated areas (e.g., near a food court) within eight universities (three from the West, two from the South and three from the East). The same two research assistants undertook this work at all universities. Every third male who passed the research assistants was asked to participate in a brief, anonymous study. Interested participants were verbally asked their age, sexual orientation (by how they identify), racial identity, and fraternal or sporting affiliation. Only those who identified as heterosexual, undergraduate students and between the ages of 18 and 25 were invited to continue the study. In addition to this, we recruited students from three general education courses at one Western, one Southern and one Eastern university, recruiting 40 participants at two universities and 42 at one. We did not recruit participants through the first method at these institutions. These surveys were completed during participants regularly scheduled class time. This approach enabled us to collect data from students who do not readily put themselves forward for research (i.e., those recruited using the first method). We gained access to these classrooms through professional contacts at each university.

From both recruitment methods, we totaled 40 surveys at each university (with the exception of one university where 42 surveys were collected). Eligible participants were briefly informed about research findings concerning heterosexual men kissing in the United Kingdom and Australia and were told that they would be asked questions to ascertain what was occurring in the United States. After hearing this information, participants were asked "what is your attitude to gay men," and given a four-point rating scale (*1 = entirely negative, 2 = somewhat negative, 3 = somewhat positive, 4 = entirely positive*). We determined that neutral would be a confusing response, so eliminated that as a choice. This is not intended as a nuanced tool for understanding attitudes toward gay men, but as a method of understanding a person's general disposition.

Next, participants responded to 13 short questions related to kissing men on the cheek and lips. "Kissing" was not defined for participants, who used their own definitions. We did not differentiate between kisses that were active (i.e., the person instigated the kiss) or passive (i.e., the person received the kiss). This open definition reflects the personal and contextualized nature of intimate behaviors.

Interview procedure

We augmented survey responses with 75 in-depth, semi-structured interviews lasting an average of 45 minutes each. These interviews reflected the same themes as the short survey but enabled further discussion. The participants were obtained by having two white male undergraduate research assistants standing in populated areas of each of the 11 universities. They asked passing male students if they wished to earn $20 by participating in a one-hour interview for academic research. Interested individuals received an information sheet about the study. In order to prevent repetition of findings, we only interviewed men who had not filled out the survey.

Analysis

We analyzed responses to the short surveys in several ways. First, we examined participants' self-reported attitudes toward gay men and the number of gay male friends they had to understand their pre-existing attitudes toward gay people. We then examined basic frequencies of same-sex kissing (i.e., kissing on the cheek, kissing on the lips). We noted that both indices of same-sex kissing were positively skewed, so we applied a Box-Cox transformation to normalize the data prior to significance testing. We then explored several predictors of same-sex kissing, including Attitudes Toward Gay Men (*1 = entirely negative* to *4 = entirely positive*), Membership in a Fraternal Organization (*0 = No, 1 = Yes*), and Number of Gay Friends (*continuous*). The data were nested hierarchically: multiple students participated from each university, so we tested our quantitative hypotheses using multilevel regression equations (GEEs; Zeger and Liang 1986) to account for within-subject dependencies. In all GEE models, continuous predictors were mean-centered and dichotomous predictors were effect-coded prior to testing. We report the results of these models in terms of unstandardized regression coefficients (*B*s) and Wald *z*s. Unstandardized regression coefficients represent measures of effect size, indicating that a one-unit increase in the predictor variable is associated with a *B*-unit increase in the outcome variable.

Then, using a constant-comparative method of open and axial coding, we examined the qualitative data gained from in-depth interviews. Following initial coding, we compared 10% of the transcriptions for inter-rater reliability discrepancies (IRR.85). We acknowledge that this coding was based on an interpretive framework; however, we contend that the rigor of our interpretive inquiry and the richness of our descriptions lend credibility to the analysis.

Limitations

Social desirability bias and researcher positionality may have affected participants' responses. Our findings are also restricted to college-attending heterosexual men. While we recruited participants from a diverse range of geographical and institutional settings, data does not reflect the true diversity of the United States. Similarly, while our population is diverse in terms of race, we have not provided detailed analysis of this variable in this chapter.

There were also differences in percentage across surveys and interviews. This could be attributed to several factors: the nature of random data collection; self-selection factor among men opting into a long interview; or that in-depth interviews permitted the researchers more clarity in expressing that they were not equating kissing behaviors with a closeted gay identity.

Results: attitudes toward gay men

Participants reported relatively favorable attitudes about gay men. We conducted a one-sample *t*-test on mean ratings of attitudes toward gay men, comparing the mean to the midpoint of the scale to determine whether participants' attitudes were generally positive or negative. The mean rating of attitudes toward gay men was significantly above the midpoint of the scale ($M = 3.11$, $SD = 0.88$, $t(409) = 13.66$, $p < 0.001$). Descriptively, 74% of participants reported "somewhat positive" or "entirely positive" attitudes toward gay men. Furthermore, participants in this sample had an average of more than four gay friends ($M = 4.25$, $SD = 11.31$), with 80% of the sample reporting at least one gay friend.

Data from in-depth interviews confirmed these findings. Of the 75 men interviewed, only one offered disparaging remarks about gay men, and two reported too little contact with gay men to draw strong conclusions. Conversely, unlike heterosexual men of the previous generation (Plummer 1999), most men maintained friendships with gay men. There was evidence that social contact with gay men promoted inclusivity toward gay men for these participants. Corey said, "I have lots of gay friends. In fact, the closest friend I have is Gabriel, and he's gay . . . I share everything with him." Rob even grew emotional when discussing his gay male friend:

> I was at a party my freshman year, sitting talking to one of my close gay guy friends and I told him my whole life story, including some bad stuff that happened in the past. After, I said to him "the support you show me is why I will always support gay rights. I want to stand up and be counted."

Six of the 75 men interviewed said that their best friend or a close friend was gay. This type of positive social interaction among gay and heterosexual men occurred even on conservative campuses.

Prevalence of heterosexual men who kiss other men

We explored our primary hypotheses regarding the number and amount of same-sex kissing among straight men in this US sample. Descriptive survey data revealed that 38% of the 442 heterosexual men reported having kissed another man on the cheek and 9% on the lips. There was substantial variability in the frequency of these behaviors, with the number of cheek kisses for each participant ranging from 0 to 30 and the number of lip kisses ranging from 0 to 5. We conducted one-sample *t*-tests comparing the average number of cheek and lip kisses to a null value of zero. As expected, mean levels of kissing were significantly greater than 0 for the cheek, $t(442) = 15.44$, $p < 0.001$, and marginally greater than 0 for the lips, $t(439) = 6.26$, $p < 0.001$.

We noted slight differences in rates of reported kissing between the surveys and the in-depth interviews. Nine percent of heterosexual men reported kissing or being kissed by another man on the lips in surveys, whereas 13% reported kissing in the interviews. A similar trend emerged for reports of kissing on the cheek: 38% of those surveyed indicated that they had kissed or been kissed on the cheek by a heterosexual male friend, compared to 53% of those undergoing in-depth interviews. Averaging across the two methodologies, 10% of self-identified heterosexual undergraduate men in our sample reported kissing or being kissed by another man on the lips, and 40% reported kissing or being kissed by another man on the cheek.

Contextualizing kissing

Previous work in the United Kingdom (Anderson et al. 2012) and Australia (Drummond et al. 2015) found that homosocial kissing occurred at higher rates among men who: 1) were involved with either a fraternity or an all-male competitive sport; 2) had more positive attitudes toward gay people; and 3) consumed alcohol. We sought to replicate and extend these findings to undergraduates in the United States.

To explore links between fraternal affiliations and same-sex kissing, we regressed both of the kissing variables (cheek and lips) individually onto Membership in a Fraternal Organization. Compared to men who were not in a fraternal organization, those who were in a fraternal organization reported significantly more kissing on the lips, $B = 0.007$, $SE = 0.003$, $z = 2.29$, $p = 0.022$, but not on the cheek, $B = 0.008$, $SE = 0.006$, $z = 1.35$, $p = 0.178$.

The increased rate of homosocial kissing among members of fraternal or sports organizations was something that participants also noted during interviews. Evidencing this, Jordan said, "I guess I see it [same-sex kissing] much more between men on the sports teams; I mean everyone knows that they do that kind of thing." Derek agreed, saying, "A few of the guys in the frat have been known to kiss each other when drunk, it's become pretty normal now. We all know who the kissers are! [laughs]."

We then tested whether participants' broader attitudes toward gay men were associated with reports of same-sex kissing by regressing both of the kissing variables (cheek and lips) individually onto Attitudes Toward Gay Men. Compared to participants with less favorable attitudes toward gay men, those with more favorable attitudes toward gay men reported significantly more kissing on the cheek, $B = 0.008$, $SE = 0.002$, $z = 5.21$, $p < 0.001$, and marginally more kissing on the lips, $B = 0.007$, $SE = 0.004$, $z = 1.82$, $p = 0.069$.

Interviews with men who kissed other men explained that this form of tactility was an expression of affection for a close friend. University men often kissed in public venues like dance clubs and house parties. Tom, a biology student at a university located in the American South, said, "Me and my friend were drinking and dancing in a bar and we kissed on the lips. It was just in the moment of ecstasy. It's not really an issue in these kinds of places." Exemplifying the possible influence of alcohol on cross-cultural rates of kissing, survey participants who reported having kissed another man on the lips indicated that this behavior occurred in the context of alcohol about 10% of the time ($M = 10.29$, $SD = 28.44$). While similar effects have not been quantified in other research, alcohol consumption emerged as a dominant theme in British men's kissing narratives (see Anderson et al. 2012).

Participants in our study stated that they did not consider their kissing a sexual act. Instead, participants likened these brief kisses to a strong embrace and described it as a demonstration of affection for a close friend in particular contexts. When asked about why he kisses his friend, one participant said, "I kiss him because I love him. I'm not attracted to him like that, but I do love him." And when another was asked about who is worthy of being kissed, he said, "I guess just my really close friends, the guys I'm closest to."

Kisses occurred in various locations, but most often in public spaces like bars, dance clubs, and fraternity parties. Alcohol was frequently involved but not always. A few of the participants suggested that they kissed a friend in a private space, such as a dorm room, but this was exceptionally rare. Still, when asked if the kisses were performed any different in private, no participant indicated that they were. James said, "It doesn't matter where you kiss him, the point is you're doing it to show your love."

Thus, our US sample contextualized same-sex kissing as associated with membership in a fraternal organization, having positive attitudes toward gay men in general, and alcohol consumption away from campus. These acts were not described as sexual or romantic in nature, framed instead as expressions of friendly affection. These findings provide a framework for understanding how, when, and why heterosexual men choose to engage in tactile behaviors with one another.

Men who do not kiss other men

In addition to examining prevalence and context of same-sex kissing among young men in the United States, we also investigated the reasons why men did not kiss other men. Analysis of interview data highlighted three themes: 1) kissing is reserved for romantic relationships only; 2) heterosexual men do not kiss other men; and 3) kissing another man is associated with being gay.

The predominant reason that men gave for not kissing another man is that they view kissing as something that should be reserved only for romantic relationships. One participant from the Midwest said,

> I consider it to be an intimate thing, something I'd only do with a significant other. That crosses boundaries that aren't anything to do with gay. I wouldn't even do it with a female friend because that'd just be weird.

Another participant said, "The lips is a little weird. It's too personal for me, something saved for a girlfriend. Most of my friends would be the same. It wouldn't start a fight but it wouldn't be acceptable." For these participants, kissing remained a sexual endeavor.

Five of the undergraduates associated kissing with a gay identity. One student said, "Kissing [guys] on the lips is more towards homosexual or the gay place, and I'm not gay so I don't like doing that. I don't enjoy that." Three other men said that they feared that being kissed or kissing another guy might compromise their heterosexual identity. These men espoused a more aggressive disposition, one said, "I'm not gay. That shit isn't for me." Nonetheless, 89% of the men we interviewed did not provide strong evidence of homohysteria. This suggests, at least indirectly, that homohysteria was not a particularly strong reason for heterosexual men to avoid same-sex kissing contact with one another.

Discussion

This study examined the prevalence and rationales for same-sex kissing among university-attending young men across the United States. Overall, 40% of the self-identified heterosexual undergraduate men in our sample reported kissing or being kissed by a male friend on the cheek, while 10% reported kissing or being kissed by a male friend on the lips. Despite kissing rates varying across universities, our statistical models accounted for the fact that observations were nested within universities. Thus, our estimates refer to the sample at large, demonstrating that this form of kissing occurs across these 11 universities that are located in different areas of the country and hold diverse student populations.

While same-sex kisses could be viewed as sexual exploration, the narratives of participants suggest that kissing does not have sexual connotations for these men. They described it as a form of social bonding, and a way of demonstrating close friendship. Corroborating international scholarship on men's kissing behaviors (Anderson et al. 2012; Drummond et al. 2015), same-sex kissing among heterosexual undergraduate men appears to be an act of emotional expression, and not sexual fluidity. Only five of the men said that same-sex kissing would connote a gay identity. Thus, while heterosexual men kissing one another may not be as widespread as in the United Kingdom or Australia, it is not entirely stigmatized for participants in this study.

The emergence of heterosexual men kissing documented in this study has important implications for theoretical understandings of masculinity in the United States. While limited in prevalence, these behaviors provide a challenge to orthodox forms of masculinity that marginalize behaviors associated with femininity or gay identity (Connell 1995). Whereas traditional articulations of masculinity do not permit heterosexual men to engage in intimate behaviors with other men (Anderson 2008; Plummer 1999), a great deal more flexibility is afforded to participants in this study who do not see kissing another man as a threat to a social identity as heterosexual. With participants espousing positive attitudes toward gay people and kissing without censure, this study supports the growing body of literature that discusses the emergence of inclusive masculinities (Anderson and McCormack 2016). With research showing that some men engage in same-sex sex while maintaining heterosexual identities (see McCormack 2018), kissing is not necessarily sexual and can be coded as an emotional, bonding experience.

This study develops the growing body of research on inclusive masculinities in several ways. First, by providing quantitative evidence of the emergence of same-sex kissing among undergraduate heterosexual men, it demonstrates the extent to which a once-censured form of tactility is present among men in the United States. Second, it enables comparison of levels of kissing with the United Kingdom (Anderson et al. 2012) and Australia (Drummond et al. 2015). We contend the differences in attitudes toward gay people in these cultures are the primary reason for the cross-cultural differences in kissing. Structural variance in access to alcohol is likely a contributing factor. Given that alcohol acts as a disinhibitor that escalates emotional expression, the more liberal drinking laws in the United Kingdom and Australia (where drinking is permitted at 18) and on university campuses, may result in more tactile gendered behaviors in these contexts.

Age and social context are likely to be important factors in this research. In contemporary research, kissing has only been demonstrated among younger men, and it is argued that youth is an important context in which these behaviors occur (Anderson 2014). College-attending young men have the space to explore same-sex kissing with heterosexual friends, while the social context of decreased homophobia means men are less likely to be regulated if they engage in such behaviors (Anderson et al. 2012).

In conclusion, this research provides a significant addition to empirical understanding of contemporary masculinities, showing that same-sex kissing between men is a behavior that can be engaged in while maintaining a heterosexual identity at these universities. We demonstrate that these attitudes are correlated with same-sex kissing behaviors. While occurrence is less than found in other countries (Anderson et al. 2012; Drummond et al. 2015), we demonstrate that a proportion of men at these universities are able to engage in same-sex kissing without being regulated by their peers.

References

Anderson, Eric. 2008. "'Being masculine is not about who you sleep with . . .:' Heterosexual athletes contesting masculinity and the one-time rule of homosexuality." *Sex Roles*, 58: 104–115.

Anderson, Eric. 2009. *Inclusive masculinity: The changing nature of masculinities*. London: Routledge.

Anderson, Eric. 2014. *21st century jocks: Sporting men and contemporary heterosexuality*. Basingstoke: Palgrave Macmillan.

Anderson, Eric and McCormack, Mark. 2016. "Inclusive masculinity theory: Overview, reflection and refinement." *Journal of Gender Studies*, 27(5): 547–561.
Anderson, Eric, Adams, Adi and Rivers, Ian. 2012. "'I kiss them because I love them': The emergence of heterosexual men kissing in British institutes of education." *Archives of Sexual Behavior*, 41: 421–430.
Barrett, Tim. 2013. "Friendships between men across sexual orientation." *The Journal of Men's Studies*, 21: 62–77.
Clements, Ben and Field, Clive D. 2014. "Public opinion toward homosexuality and gay rights in Great Britain." *Public Opinion Quarterly*, 78: 523–547.
Connell, Raewyn. 1995. *Masculinities*. Berkeley: University of California Press.
Courtenay, Will H. 2000. "Constructions of masculinity and their influence on men's well-being." *Social Science and Medicine*, 50: 1385–1401. http://dx.doi.org/10.1016/S0277-9536(99)00390-1
Dean, James J. 2014. *Straights*. New York: New York University Press.
Derlega, Valerian J., Lewis, Robin J., Harrison, Scott, Winstead, Barbara A. and Costanza, Robert. 1989. "Gender differences in the initiation and attribution of tactile intimacy." *Journal of Nonverbal Behavior*, 13: 83–96.
Drummond, Murray J., Filiault, Shaun M., Anderson, Eric and Jeffries, David. 2015. "Homosocial intimacy among Australian undergraduate men." *Journal of Sociology*, 51: 643–656.
Floyd, Keith. 2000. "Affectionate same-sex touch: The influence of homophobia on observers' perceptions." *The Journal of Social Psychology*, 140: 774–788.
Ibson, John. 2002. *Picturing men: A century of male relationships in everyday life*. Washington, DC: Smithsonian Books.
Keleher, Alison and Smith, Eric R.A.N. 2012. "Growing support for gay and lesbian equality since 1990." *Journal of Homosexuality*, 59: 1307–1326.
McCormack, Mark. 2011. "Hierarchy without hegemony: Locating boys in an inclusive school setting." *Sociological Perspectives*, 54: 83–101.
McCormack, Mark. 2018. "Mostly straights and the study of sexualities: An introduction to the special issue." *Sexualities*, 21(1–2): 3–15.
McCormack, Mark and Anderson, Eric. 2014. "The influence of declining homophobia on men's gender in the United States: An argument for the study of homohysteria." *Sex Roles*, 71: 109–120.
McCreary, Donald R. 1994. "The male role and avoiding femininity." *Sex Roles*, 31: 517–531.
Monroe, Michael, Baker, Richard C. and Roll, Samuel. 1997. "The relationship of homophobia to intimacy in heterosexual men." *Journal of Homosexuality*, 33: 23–37.
Morales, Luis and Caffyn-Parsons, Edward. 2017. "'I love you, guys': A study of inclusive masculinities among high school cross-country runners." *Boyhood Studies*, 10(1): 66–87.
Plummer, David. 1999. *One of the boys: Masculinity, homophobia, and modern manhood*. New York: Routledge.
Robinson, S., Anderson, E. and White, A. 2018. "The bromance: Undergraduate male friendships and the expansion of contemporary homosocial boundaries." *Sex Roles*, 78(1–2): 94–106.
Schwartz, Pepper and Rutter, Virginia. 1998. *The gender of sexuality*. Walnut Creek: AltaMira Press.
Way, Niobe. 2011. *Deep secrets*. New York: New York University Press.
Zeger, Scott L. and Liang, Kung-Yee. 1986. "Longitudinal data analysis for discrete and continuous outcomes." *Biometrics*, 42: 121–130.

24

Bud-sex

Constructing normative masculinity among rural straight men that have sex with men*

Tony Silva†

Mainstream understandings of heterosexuality emphasize that straight men's attractions, behaviors, and desires should be oriented exclusively toward women, and yet research indicates that some straight-identified men have sex with other men. There are multiple reasons why some men who have sex with men (MSM) identify as straight, including internalized heterosexism, participation in other-sex marriage and childrearing, and enjoyment of straight privilege and culture (Ward 2015). Few interview-based studies of straight MSM exist, and previous studies focus on urban, military, or prison contexts. Most are part of a sexual health literature that problematizes straight MSM as a vector for HIV transmission (e.g., Barnshaw and Letukas 2010). Others use content analyses of Craigslist ads or other materials to theorize about this population (Robinson and Vidal-Ortiz 2013; Reynolds 2015; Ward 2015).[1] Counterintuitively, straight-identified men who post ads looking for same-sex sex may be distinct from those who engage in it: as Robinson and Moskowitz (2013, 562) found, straight-identified men often viewed Internet cruising, posting, and emailing as "self-contained erotic acts" that did not transition into offline behavior. Given that online ad representations may inaccurately reflect the narratives of straight MSM—and will at best capture only snippets of their lives—researchers need to conduct interviews for fuller insight. Additionally, there is a widespread urban focus in sexualities and gender literatures (Halberstam 2005), which obscures the role of geography in the construction, maintenance, perception, and experience of gender and sexuality. As Connell and Messerschmidt (2005) explain, researchers should examine masculinities that differ by place; few have done so with rurality (exceptions include Morris 2008). By using interviews, this study is one of the first to examine how straight MSM themselves understand their own genders and sexualities, and how rurality affects these perceptions.

* The editors would like to thank The Sexualities Project at Northwestern University for a generous grant to pay permissions costs for this chapter.

† AUTHOR'S NOTE: I would like to thank C. J. Pascoe, Sarah Diefendorf, Connor Gilroy, Kristen Barber, Matt Norton, and members of the University of Washington Gender Group for their detailed and helpful suggestions, which greatly improved the article. I would also like to thank editors Jo Reger and Amy Stone, as well as the anonymous reviewers of this article, all of whom provided feedback that greatly strengthened the manuscript.

How do rural, white, straight MSM understand their gender? Through complex interpretive processes, participants reworked non-normative sexual practices usually antithetical to rural masculinities to actually construct normative masculinity. Participants selected male sexual partners on the basis of masculinity, race, and sexual identity. Most chose other masculine, white, and straight or secretly bisexual men for secretive sex without romantic involvement. By choosing these partners and having this type of sex, the participants normalized and authenticated their sexual encounters as straight and normatively masculine. The married men framed sex with men as less threatening to their marriages than extramarital sex with women, helping to preserve a part of their lives that most described as central to their straightness.

Rather than referring to participants as MSM, a public health term, I describe them as guys who engage in *bud-sex*. I use "bud-sex" when referring to the participants' sexual activities and "MSM" when referring to broader populations of straight men that have sex with men.[2] Similar sexual practices carry different meanings across populations and contexts, including among different groups of MSM. Ward (2015) examines *dude-sex*, a type of male–male sex that white, masculine, straight men in urban or military contexts frame as a way to bond and build masculinity with other, similar "bros." Carrillo and Hoffman (2016) refer to their primarily urban participants as *heteroflexible*, given that they were exclusively or primarily attracted to women. While the participants in this study share overlap with those groups, they also frame their same-sex sex in subtly different ways: not as an opportunity to bond with urban "bros," and only sometimes—but not always—as a novel sexual pursuit, given that they had sexual attractions all across the spectrum. Instead, as Silva (forthcoming) explores, the participants reinforced their straightness through unconventional interpretations of same-sex sex: as "helpin' a buddy out," relieving "urges," acting on sexual desires for men without sexual attractions to them, relieving general sexual needs, and/or a way to act on sexual attractions. "Bud-sex" captures these interpretations, as well as how the participants had sex and with whom they partnered. The specific type of sex the participants had with other men—bud-sex—cemented their rural masculinity and heterosexuality, and distinguishes them from other MSM.

The results demonstrate the flexibility of male heterosexuality and the centrality of heterosexuality to normative rural masculinity. First, the participants interpret same-sex sex as compatible with heterosexuality. It is not the sexual practices themselves but individuals' interpretations of them that are central to sexual identity and gender. These findings complement previous research, which reveals the extent to which heterosexual masculine homosociality structures and gives meaning to other-sex sexual encounters (Flood 2008). While there is a framework to describe women's sexual flexibility—"sexual fluidity" (Diamond 2009)—there is no such framework for men. Straight men's sexual flexibility is often described as indicative of lessening homophobia (e.g., Anderson's 2008 study of young men), when it also demonstrates that *male heterosexuality is fundamentally flexible across the life course*. Second, heterosexual identification is key to constructing normative rural masculinity. While the participants' sexual practices did not align with mainstream definitions of heterosexuality, their identification with straightness—and their interpretations of their sexual practices that reinforced it—bolstered their normative rural masculinity. Given that normative masculinity is critical for social acceptance in rural areas, identification with heterosexuality to bolster normative masculinity was especially important. The findings reinforce the centrality of place for how individuals identify and express their sexuality and gender.

The social construction of sexuality

How individuals understand and experience sexuality is profoundly social: scripts (Simon and Gagnon 1986), discourses (Foucault 1978), and interactions between individuals (Plummer 1996) and between structures, agency, and practice (Stein 1989) all inform perceptions of sexuality and the forms sexualities take. Cultural norms about what sexual practices are acceptable, their significance, their relation to identity, and even what practices are considered sexual are all socially constructed (Foucault 1978). Identification based on sexual behavior emerged only in the late nineteenth century (Chauncey 1994; Foucault 1978). As Sedgwick (1990) explains, defining individuals in this way is only one of many ways sexual identities could potentially operate. Sexual identities are socially constructed and differ by culture and time period (Katz 1995), and often these identities cannot fully describe complex combinations of sexual practices, attractions, and desires. Relatedly, the relationship between sexual identity and gender practices differs between cultures and time periods. Current ways of identifying individuals reflect new ways of defining acceptable gender practices in response to changing gender dynamics in workplaces and education in the late nineteenth and early twentieth centuries (Chauncey 1994), as well as late nineteenth-century medical discourse (Foucault 1978). Gender performance and sexual practice, rather than biological sex or attractions, were key for understanding sexuality in the late nineteenth and early twentieth centuries. At that time, many conventionally masculine men who penetrated men, before heterosexuality was introduced as an identity, were considered "normal" (Chauncey 1994). This continued in some rural areas into the mid-1900s, where same-sex sex involving "normal" men was common, albeit often intentionally ignored (Boag 2003; Howard 1999; Johnson 2013). Understandings of sexual identities and practices also differ between and within cultures. Among some MSM in Mexico, men who are penetrated are considered gay, while those who penetrate are perceived as straight (Cantú Jr. 2009). Within the United States, individuals with similar sexual attractions may adopt different sexual identities because of a differing emphasis placed on sexual attractions and current sexual behaviors (Rust 1992) or the presence—or lack thereof—of emotional attractions (Adam 2000). In addition, stereotypical views of sexual identities (e.g., lesbian women are butch) may affect the one that individuals adopt (Kitzinger and Wilkinson 1995). Sexual identities reflect culture, time period, social structures, and personal interpretations.

Despite increasing acceptance of same-sex sexuality, hegemonic masculinity remains distinctly heterosexual (Connell 1987). Homophobia is often a key aspect of normative masculinity (Kimmel 1994), and from a young age: Pascoe (2011) explores how boys utilize a "fag discourse" to regulate the masculinity and heterosexuality of peers. Similarly, many measures of normative masculinity—such as support for all-male institutions—are related to homophobia (Britton 1990). The relationship between heterosexuality and normative masculinity remains, even as overt homophobia has lessened in many contexts (Anderson 2008; Bridges 2014; Connell 2005; Dean 2014; McCormack 2013). Heteronormativity is entrenched within U.S. institutions and is strongly related to normative masculinity, which affects men's sexual identification, practices, and interpretations. This article draws on Connell's (1987, 2005) framework explaining gender as a social structure, composed of hierarchically organized masculinities that together legitimate inequalities between men and women and among men. It also reflects that masculinity is an ongoing interpersonal process through which actions inconsistent with hegemonic masculinity are policed by others, and often suppressed in homosocial spaces (Bird 1996). Incorporating these theoretical elements, "normative masculinity" in this article refers to gender practices that eschew femininity and reinforce white, straight, male, and masculine (i.e., nonfeminine) dominance. Because rural spaces in different regions (e.g., rural Alabama vs. rural Québec) are distinct and will consequently develop unique masculinities in those spaces, this article specifically examines normative masculinity in U.S.-based rural regions in the Midwest and Pacific Northwest—areas that share social conservatism and demographic white majorities (Bump 2014; United States Census Bureau 2016).

Intersections of rural masculinities and sexualities

Research about the intersections between rural masculinities and sexualities points to the importance of normative rural masculinity for social tolerance, normality, and safety, though historically this may have varied (Johnson 2013). Bridges (2014) finds that some young, straight, white men expand socially acceptable masculine performances by drawing upon "sexual aesthetics" relating to tastes, behaviors, or ideologies appropriated from gay cultures, albeit in ways that reinforce inequalities related to sexualities and gender. Although seemingly more sensitive expressions of masculinity are available to some privileged men in or near urban areas, this is not something most rural men do. Nor do most change the "style" of masculinity (Messner 1993), for example by investing an increasing amount of time and money into personal appearance (Barber 2016). Most rural men do not have socially viable alternatives to conventional expressions of masculinity, and the masculinity they construct reflects the rigid expectations of many rural men today (Courtenay 2006). Thus, due to differing social contexts, masculinities in rural areas are distinct from those in urban locations.

"Rural masculinity" refers to masculinity as it is "constructed within what rural social scientists would recognize as rural spaces and sites" (Campbell and Bell 2000, 540). Rural masculinities differ based on local context as well as intersections of social identities, and central to many of them are physical labor and toughness (Morris 2008; Kazyak 2012). The strong link between heterosexuality and masculinity is especially evident in rural areas, which are often more conservative than urban locales (Bump 2014). Rural men are likelier than urban men to engage in unsafe behaviors, and intersections with non-normative sexualities can exacerbate these dangers (Courtenay 2006). For rural men with marginalized sexualities, normative rural masculinity is particularly important because it provides them a degree of social acceptance (Boulden 2001; Fellows 2001). Many rural gay men even distance themselves from feminine gay men and point out their similarities with (purportedly masculine) straight men (Annes and Redlin 2012). Relatedly, in her interview study of rural Midwestern gays and lesbians, Kazyak (2012) found that gay men had little flexibility in gender practices; they either performed conventional rural masculinities or were rejected by their community. Research on rural queer youth (Gray 2009) and rural trans men (Abelson 2014) indicates that challenging gender norms often leads to fear of physical harm, encouraging gender normativity.

This study expands on Ward (2015) and Carrillo and Hoffman (2016). Departing from Ward's (2015) analysis of urban and military men through content analysis, I examine rural men through their own narratives. Further, while Ward (2015, 4) examines white heterosexual masculinity more broadly, arguing "that homosexuality is an often invisible, but nonetheless vital ingredient—a constitutive element—of heterosexual masculinity," my study focuses *only* on the normative masculinity constructed by rural straight men who regularly or semiregularly have sex with men. Carrillo and Hoffman's (2016) online interview study emphasizes how "heteroflexible" men perceive their identities; most participants viewed heterosexuality as compatible with same-sex sexuality by emphasizing attractions to women and framing same-sex sex as emotionless. However, they do not analyze how straight MSM construct normative masculinity, which is this article's focus.

Methods

I posted advertisements in several men-for-men casual encounters sections of Craigslist, which is organized regionally. Unlike most other apps/websites, Craigslist is widely used, anonymous, free, and frequented by individuals with a variety of sexual identities. I also included project information on Grindr, an app catering to gay and bisexual men, which recruited two participants. Of the approximately 100 men that inquired about participation, 19 agreed to participate: 15 over the phone and four in person. This study utilizes phone/in-person semistructured interviews. During each interview, I used an interview guide. Inquiries included the following: Describe yourself in terms of masculinity and femininity. How has [growing up/living in] a rural area affected how you see yourself in terms of [masculinity/femininity]? Describe the kind of guy you prefer to meet up with. Do you view sex with men outside of your [marriage/partnership] as cheating, and why or why not? Walk me through the last time you met up with another guy for action. In what ways was this encounter typical or not typical of other encounters you've had? I reordered and rephrased questions to make the interview less formal, which allowed me to follow-up on leads. Interviews lasted approximately one-and-a-half hours. I uploaded all transcripts to the qualitative data analysis software NVivo to apply codes and repeated this as I coded additional transcripts and created new codes. I created all codes during analysis rather than at the beginning of the study; as the sole researcher, I created and applied all codes.

All the participants live in Missouri, Illinois, Oregon, Washington, or Idaho; these rural spaces share similarities by virtue of their social conservatism and predominant white populations (Bump 2014; United States Census Bureau 2016). All but two participants currently live in, or were raised in, a rural area. Thirteen currently live in a rural area, and 15 were raised in rural areas. By rural, I refer to an area with fewer than 25,000 residents. The only two exceptions were participants who were raised in urban areas but currently live in what I term semirural areas: cities with 25,000–60,000 residents in isolated areas of the Pacific Northwest. All the participants are white, challenging the perception of straight MSM as urban blacks on the "down low" (Ward 2015). They are skewed toward older ages with the majority over 50: 20s (1), 30s (3), 40s (1), 50s (6), 60s (6), and 70s (2). The participants have a variety of educational and occupational backgrounds, but most are middle class. One reported a doctorate as his highest degree, five a master's, three a bachelor's, five an associate's, two some college, and three high school. As shown in Table 24.1, the sample has considerable diversity in sexual attraction. Further, although all tell others they identify as straight, 17 actually identify as straight or some variation thereof, one as gay, and one as bisexual. Thus, while all are secretive about their same-sex sex, only two are "closeted" in terms of sexual identity, as only two identify as gay or bisexual but tell others they identify as straight.

Constructing bud-sex

"Strictly masculine": average, rural, masculine guys

All 19 participants described themselves as masculine, much like Robinson and Vidal-Ortiz's (2013) analysis of Craigslist ads, and they did so in terms of their actions: mannerisms, behaviors, communication styles, hobbies, and skills. Through these descriptions, all framed themselves as normal, masculine men. Given the association of femininity with same-sex sexuality, subcultures of gay men may embrace or reject femininity (Hennen 2008). The men in this study, however, uniformly described themselves as masculine, thus distancing themselves from the purported relationship between same-sex sexuality and femininity.

The men's gender self-descriptions largely conform to conventional understandings of masculinity. Brad (48) is a "T-shirt and Levi kind of guy" who is "straight-acting [and] masculine." Jon (39) is "pretty much masculine" because "I'm a . . . straight guy that likes to hunt, fish, camp, and I raise cattle for a living." Jack (52) shared similar sentiments: "The things I do, interests, all masculine. I like to shoot, I like to hunt. . . . " Cain (50) explained, "My demeanor may be more gentleman-like than . . . the rugged cowboy type," but described himself as having "a type A

Table 24.1 Participant Characteristics

Pseudonym	*Age*	*Private Sexual Identity*	*Reported Sexual Attractions*	*Reported Changes to Attractions?*	*Relationship Status with Women Partners*
Mike	50	Straight	Only men	Yes	Married
Brad	48	Gay	Only men	Yes	Single, divorced
Cain	50	Straight	Almost equally men/ women	Yes	Married
Will	52	"Straight-leaning bisexual"	Almost equally men/ women; leaning toward men	Yes	Single, divorced
Marcus	38	Straight	Only women	No	Married
Pat	69	Straight	Only women	No	Married
Richard	75	Straight	Only women	No	Single, divorced
Reuben	28	Bisexual	Almost equally men/ women	No	Single, never married
Kevin	69	Straight/mostly straight, with "a percentage towards bi"	About 75% women, 25% men	No	Married
Ryan	60	Straight/mostly straight	About 75% men, 25% women	Yes	Married
Jon	39	Straight	50% men, 50% women	No	Married
Mark	61	Straight and bisexual	95% men, 5% women	Yes	Married
David	74	Straight	80% women, 20% men	Yes	Married
Matt	60	"Straight but bi, but more straight"	80% men, 20% women	Yes	Married
Tom	59	Straight	90% women, 10% men	Yes	Married
Joe	63	Straight and bisexual	Only women	No	Married
Jeff	38	Straight	80% women, 20% men	Yes	Married
Billy	59	Straight and bisexual	80% women, 20% men	Yes	Married
Jack	52	Straight	80% men, 20% women	Yes	Single, divorced

personality" with the potential to "be kind of aggressive." Similarly, David (74) is an "alpha male" who enjoys shooting and fishing. Richard (75) described himself "as masculine as John Wayne; I'm definitely not feminine in any way, shape, or form." Kevin (69) noted, "I've always done blue-collar type work, I live in a rural area, I'm a farmer." Will (52) leans "a lot toward masculine," because "I can clean a deer. . . . I can catch some fish. . . . and I'm a very good handyman," while Billy (59) enjoys "trudgin' in the wilderness, cuttin' firewood and throwin' logs." Will and Billy both conflated masculinity with heterosexuality, describing themselves as individuals no one would suspect to be attracted to men. Pat (69) similarly blurred the lines between masculinity and heterosexuality, and used rural tropes to describe himself:

> [V]ery masculine. 15 year collection of Playboy magazines, I don't think gay people subscribe to Playboy. Fantasize about women, oh yes. . . . Drive a pickup . . . I like guns, I'm not good at hunting, but I like to go up in the woods and sit there and drink my half pint of Jack Daniels and act like I am hunting. I'd say very masculine. I like baseball.

Marcus (38) similarly noted, "I portray myself as very masculine. I wear jeans and boots and camouflage hats and sleeveless T-shirts, drive a truck, and like to shoot stuff." Reuben (28) also noted rural hobbies: "I exercise, I play sports, I take part [in] what you'd call stereotypical masculine activities. I go hunting every now and then . . . things that a quote unquote manly-man would do."

The participants' rural locations played a large role in their self-descriptions as masculine. Eleven described themselves using elements of rurality, such as hobbies (hunting, fishing, shooting, cutting firewood), occupations (farming, ranching), ways of dressing (camo, T-shirts, and Levi jeans), or images of rugged rurality (John Wayne). Another used rural tropes (rugged cowboys) as a comparison to his own masculinity. Central to the men's self-understanding is their rural background; they perform a rural masculinity, which they seek to reaffirm through their same-sex sexual encounters. They embody a country-masculine *habitus* (Desmond 2006, 393), which guides their "thoughts, tastes, and practices. It provides them with their fundamental sense of self; it structures how they understand the world around them; and it influences how they codify sameness and difference." The participants' rural masculinity structured their experiences and perceptions, including their sexual ones.

"Guys like me": partnering with other masculine, white, non-gay men

The participants overwhelmingly preferred to have sex with men like themselves: masculine, white, and not gay—straight or secretly bisexual. This is a key element of bud-sex. Partnering with other men similarly privileged on several intersecting axes—gender, race, and sexual identity—allowed the participants to normalize and authenticate their sexual experiences as normatively masculine, as Ward (2015) also describes. Desires for types of sexual partners reflect culture rather than biological drives (Ward 2015). The socially constructed (and problematic) relationship between normativity and male masculinity, whiteness, and straightness shapes sexual desires such that individuals with these characteristics are often perceived as desirable sexual partners. By having sex with these *types of men*, the participants were able to construct and reinforce normative masculinity—*despite having sex with men*. Alignment with normative masculinity is especially important for men in rural areas, where it is a virtual prerequisite for social acceptance (Abelson 2014; Annes and Redlin 2012; Boulden 2001; Fellows 1998; Kazyak 2012). Other studies suggest that straight MSM prefer to hook up with men privileged on several dimensions, especially men that are masculine and straight or DL ("down low") (Robinson and Vidal-Ortiz 2013; Reynolds 2015; Ward 2015), though no other interview study explores this.

Seventeen participants—all of those who identify as straight—stated that they prefer masculine male sexual partners, and each explained that the majority of their male sexual partners are masculine. Masculinity in sexual partners helped construct and validate their own normative masculinity. The straight participants often equated masculinity with non-gayness (heterosexuality or secretive bisexuality) or normality. As Cain said, "I'm really not drawn to what I would consider really effeminate faggot type[s]," but he does "like the masculine looking guy who maybe is more bi." Similarly, Matt (60) explained, "If they're too flamboyant they just turn me off," and Jack noted, "Femininity in a man is a turn off." Ryan (60) explained, "I'm not comfortable around femme" and "masculinity is what attracts me," while David shared that "Femme guys don't do anything for me at all, in fact actually I don't care for 'em." Jon shared, "I don't really like flamin' queers." Mike (50) similarly said, "I don't want the effeminate ones, I want the manly guys. . . . If I wanted someone that acts girlish, I got a wife at home." Jeff (38) prefers masculinity because "I guess I perceive men who are feminine want to hang out . . . have companionship, and make it last two or three hours."

The four participants who reported exclusive sexual attractions to women also stated a preference for normatively masculine male sexual partners, revealing the social origins of their attractions. As Marcus explained,

> A guy that I would consider more like me, that gets blowjobs from guys every once in a while, doesn't do it every day. I know that there are a lot of guys out there that are like me . . . they're manly guys, and doing manly stuff, and just happen to have oral sex with men every once in a while [chuckles]. So, that's why I kinda prefer those types of guys. . . . It [also] seems that . . . more masculine guys wouldn't harass me, I guess, hound me all the time, send me 1000 emails, "Hey, you want to get together today . . . hey, what about now." And there's a thought in my head that a more feminine or gay guy would want me to come around more.

Like Jeff, Marcus finds normative straight, masculine men like himself better sex partners than feminine and/or gay men. Echoing Mike, Richard stated, "Given a choice I prefer masculine; I don't want a substitute woman," and Joe (63) shared, "Feminine guys don't interest me at all." Preferences for masculine men both validate the participants' own normative masculinity and reveal the socially constructed nature of sexual desires.

Similarly, the vast majority of the past and present male sexual partners of 16 participants—all except Reuben, Tom (59), and Mark—are white. Unlike many urban straight MSM who fetishize interracial sex, as Robinson and Vidal-Ortiz (2013) found with the largest proportion of their sample and Ward (2015) found with a sizable minority, the participants in this study fetishized whiteness. For most of the straight participants, racial sameness was a strategy to align themselves with normativity and, in so doing, to construct normative masculinity. Thus, whiteness is central to bud-sex, which reinforces the participants' straightness and normative rural masculinity. Twelve participants stated that they prefer white male sexual partners, and four others explained their mostly white sexual history as happenstance. When explaining why he prefers white men, Kevin noted, "I guess because I'm white and, I guess you'd say more normal for me to be with white guys." Marcus and Richard reported exclusive sexual attractions to women, and yet they too noted preferences for white men, indicating that attractions are not the only determinant of sexual partnering and reinforcing the social influence of sexual desires. Although Richard reported, "It's not about the person, I'm only interested in the dick," he also stated, "White would be my choice." Joe shared, "The closer to white you get, Hispanic's OK, but the further from me you get, if you get to the black side, I'm just not in." Jeff also explained racial preferences as stemming from desiring men like himself: "Probably because I am sexually attracted to myself. . . ." David echoed, "I would lean primarily towards white guys that are more or less like me." By choosing men like themselves—other white men—the participants normalized their encounters as straight and normatively masculine.

Of the 17 straight participants, nine reported preferences for straight or bisexual men and 13 noted that a majority of their sexual partners are straight, bisexual, and/or married to a woman. Their partners' not-gay sexual identities—straight or secretly bisexual—are an important component of the men's normative masculinity. The narratives of the four men with predominately straight or bisexual sexual partners who did not state a preference reveal numerous reasons: (1) They did not want to sound prejudicial; (2) rurality makes it difficult to find sexual partners, so they are at times open to gay men; (3) mostly engaging with straight or bisexual men makes meeting with gay men less threatening; and (4) their partners' masculinity and the discreet, nonromantic nature of the encounter makes them comfortable enough to occasionally hook up with gay men. Many of the straight participants who noted preferences for straight or bisexual men did so because of perceived greater compatibility and greater confidence in discreetness. As Jeff stated, he is "basically seeking the same" kind of guy as himself. Marcus explained his preferences as a cultural fit:

> Straight guys, I think I identify with them more because that's kinda, like [how] I feel myself. And bi guys, the same way. We can talk about women, there [have] been times where we've watched hetero porn, before we got started or whatever, so I kinda prefer that. [And] because I'm not attracted, it's very off-putting when somebody acts gay, and I feel like a lot of gay guys, just kinda put off that gay vibe, I'll call it, I guess, and that's very off-putting to me.

Marcus feels more comfortable with straight or bisexual men because he dislikes a "gay vibe," reinforcing how social factors such as culture affect sexual desires. Similarly, Tom noted choosing a bisexual man as his ideal male sexual partner because he would "kinda be closer in tune to what I am." Joe would also choose a bisexual man "because he would be of the same mind that I am. He would understand what I'm feeling, and would respond probably similarly. So we could engage with common knowledge." Jack noted, "He would be in the same boat as me. He would be straight, preferably married or definitely partnered up with a female, with one thing on his mind, getting his rocks off with me . . . they're not gonna out me." Similarly, Cain said he would not hook up with gay men, explaining, "No, I'm not out, and so, someone who is out, I'm sometimes a little bit hesitant about what they may say to others."

That a majority of 13 straight participants' male sexual partners are straight or secretly bisexual, despite bountiful opportunities for sex with gay and openly bisexual men on Craigslist, indicates that partnering with non-gay men is a strategy to reaffirm their own normatively masculine sense of self. It also reflects that the sexual meanings attributed to encounters are socially produced; while many gay men are also masculine and enjoy romance-free sex, most of the participants view straight or secretly bisexual partners as more desirable because of the link between normativity and non-gayness. Given the centrality of heterosexuality to normative rural masculinity, the participants were able to align themselves closer to both by selecting straight and secretly bisexual male sexual partners. While most expressed frustration about the difficulty of finding sexual partners in rural areas, they nonetheless mostly chose men who are masculine, white, and straight or secretly bisexual, underscoring the importance of these characteristics for their normative masculinity and bud-sex.

Secretive and nonromantic: ingredients for bud-sex

Consistent with other research about straight MSM (Humphreys 1970; Reynolds 2015; Ward 2015), the participants preferred secretive, nonromantic same-sex sex, key ingredients of bud-sex. They did not necessarily prefer one-time meet-ups, however; their histories with "regular" male sexual partners indicate they appreciate the benefits of a sexual friendship. Departing from content analyses, data indicate that relationships with sexual partners are not necessarily *emotionless*, but are rather *nonromantic*. Further, like Robinson and Vidal-Ortiz's (2013) findings, the participants had a wide range of sexual preferences—all had either oral or anal sex (or both). Few, however, tied specific sex acts with masculinity or straightness. For these men, what was paramount to their masculinity was not *what* they did sexually, but *how* they did it. All 19 participants described the need for sexual encounters to be secretive, and this secrecy was tied to rurality. Rurality had both its advantages and drawbacks. On one hand, vast expanses of unpopulated land meant participants could easily find places to have secretive sex. On the other, community interconnectedness necessitated increased caution. As Pat said, "[I]n a small town everyone knows more about your business than you do. . . . I suppose in the city you don't have to be discreet. But here in [a] small rural area, yes, you've gotta be discreet." By meeting men who understood the need for secrecy—most of them straight or secretly bisexual—the participants were able to maintain their public identities. All but one participant described their same-sex sex similarly to Cain: "no strings attached."[3] The absence of romance reframed encounters as normatively masculine and compatible with straightness. Even while avoiding romantic attachments, 13 participants currently have regulars, three others had regulars in the past, and two others would like one or are open to it. While most are open to one-time hookups, most also prefer regulars. By doing so, they reinforce their masculinity by seeking consistent partners on the same page about what sex between straight guys should constitute. This is especially important in rural areas, given that each attempt to find a new sexual partner opens the participants to potential discovery in a small pool of acquaintances.

While relationships with regulars were free of romance and deep emotional ties, they were not necessarily devoid of feeling; participants enjoyed regulars for multiple reasons: convenience, comfort, sexual compatibility, or even friendship. Pat described a typical meetup with his regular: "We talk for an hour or so, over coffee . . . then we'll go get a blowjob and then, part our ways." Similarly, Richard noted, "Sex is a very small part of our relationship. It's more friends, we discuss politics . . . all sorts of shit." Likewise, with several of his regulars Billy noted, "I go on road trips, drink beer, go down to the city [to] look at chicks, go out and eat, shoot pool, I got one friend I hike with. It normally leads to sex, but we go out and do activities other than we meet and suck." While Kevin noted that his regular relationship "has no emotional connection at all," it also has a friendship-like quality, as evidenced by occasional visits and sleepovers despite almost 100 miles of distance. Similarly, David noted, "If my wife's gone for a weekend . . . I'll go to his place and spend a night or two with him . . . we obviously do things other than sex, so yeah we go to dinner, go out and go shopping, stuff like that." Jack explained that with his regular "we connected on Craigslist . . . [and] became good friends, in addition to havin' sex . . . we just made a connection. . . . But there was no love at all." Thus, bud-sex is predicated on rejecting romantic attachment and deep emotional ties, but not all emotion.

The participants enjoyed a wide range of sex acts, but few framed penetrating/being penetrated as tied to masculinity or straightness; these interpretations reaffirmed their own straightness and normative masculinity, regardless of sexual practices. Eleven both penetrated others and were penetrated in oral and/or anal sex, often with the same person, while eight either mostly penetrated or were penetrated. Of those who had anal sex more than a handful of times, five were mostly tops, four mostly bottoms, and two versatile.[4] Only three of the straight participants, plus Reuben (who identified as bisexual), tied sex positions to masculinity or straightness, yet none questioned their own masculinity or straightness, and none of the straight participants viewed the men they penetrated (if any) as not masculine because of that penetration. As Mark (61) noted, "I see it [being penetrated] as a very masculine thing. No one knows how to please a man better than another man." Likewise, David shared, "It's a mutual sexual satisfaction, however you get it. I don't feel any less of a man if I'm bent over and he's in me, at all. I just don't." Sex acts were overwhelmingly driven by personal preferences and physical abilities (e.g., erectile dysfunction). This indicates cultural differences in the meanings given to sexual acts, as some Mexican MSM attribute certain practices with masculinity or straightness (Cantú Jr. 2009; Carrillo and Fontdevila 2014). By rejecting stereotypical associations between masculinity and straightness, on the one hand, and sex acts involving penetrating or being penetrated, on the other, the participants reaffirmed both their straightness and normative rural masculinity.

It was not *what* the participants did sexually, but *how* they did it, that affected their perceptions of their masculinity. By maintaining secretive and romance-free same-sex sex, and interpreting sexual acts as unrelated to masculinity or straightness, they were able to act on desires in a normatively masculine way and reaffirm their normatively masculine sense of self. Collectively, these interpretations and preferences help define the type of sex they had: bud-sex. Unlike many of the Craigslist ads examined by Reynolds (2015) and Ward (2015), only three participants reported using women through pornography or conversation to secure a straight masculine sexual dynamic. Thus, men's online posts may not always reflect what they do when they actually meet men.

No big deal: extramarital same-sex sex

For the 17 straight participants, a key aspect of their straightness was marriage and/or child rearing. Each currently married man indicated a desire to stay married. As they explained, sex with men either does not constitute cheating or is less threatening to their marriage than extramarital sex with women, because it is devoid of deep emotional ties. Sex with women is far more threatening to marriage, as this breaks vows and/or has the potential to involve emotional attachment. As Tom explained, "Being romantic and emotional is more cheating than just havin' sex." Similarly, Cain shared, "I'm not cheating on my wife. I don't have the intention of leaving her." Kevin echoed this: "Meetin' up with women would be cheating on my wife. And when I meet up with guys, I justify it by sayin' 'well it's only fun between me and the other guy, it's not like I have another woman . . .' I'm sure she or other people would argue [with] that, but that's just the way I feel."

For the currently married straight men, their perceptions of their extramarital same-sex sex bolster their normative masculinity: sex with men is simply a way for them to fulfill sexual desires without affecting any other part of their lives. Four framed sex with men as not cheating in part because they no longer had sex with their wives. As Pat said, sex with men is not cheating "because part of marriage is sex, and my marriage has no sex." Perceptions of extramarital same-sex sex as insignificant are tied to rurality: rural areas have a stronger focus on other-sex marriages than urban locales, where cohabitation and nonmonogamous relationships are often more visible (Chetty and Hendren 2015; Leonhardt and Quealy 2015). Thus, by framing same-sex extramarital sex as insignificant, the men interpret their sexual practices in ways that make them compatible with the marriages that are central to their heterosexuality and normative rural masculinity.

Aging: not ready to give up sex

Age affected the participants' interpretations of their sexuality and gender, both because of generational dynamics and aging itself. Fourteen participants are 50 or older and internalized heteronormativity and strict masculine norms during some of the most difficult decades to express sexual or gender non-normativity (Seidman 2002). This, combined with the lack of visibility of non-normative sexualities and gender expressions in most rural areas in the 1950s–1980s, shaped the participants' relationship with masculinity and straightness. As Kevin shared, "I grew up in an area where that [being gay/bisexual] wasn't an option, in a time and area both," and Jack noted, "Back in the day when I was growing up, it was absolutely not accepted."

Additionally, sex with men helped nine participants bolster their masculinity, despite the fact that they or their wives were experiencing age-related bodily changes that made sex more difficult. Seven explained that sex became uncomfortable or undesirable for their wives, and sex with men helped relieve sexual desires. As Ryan shared, "As physically there's been changes to our bodies and it's even painful for my wife to have sex, I have no problem taking care of myself with another guy." Similarly, David explained, "I'm not getting sex at home, and I want sex," and "older men are a lot more receptive to sex, they're more enthusiastic," because "senior women have kinda lost their desire to do much of anything." Two others began having sex with men because of erectile dysfunction, which limited their ability to penetrate. As Tom described, "I'm a straight guy that has ED and doesn't want to give up havin' sex." Turning to sex with men or increasing the relative frequency of sex with men was a way for each to maintain their sex lives and masculinity despite bodily changes related to aging. The centrality of sex to masculinity has been noted in other contexts, as well (e.g., Loe 2001). Lastly, 12 participants experienced profound and long-lasting changes to their sexual attractions in their 20s, 30s, 40s, 50s, or 60s, catalyzing desires for male–male sex years or decades after their other-sex marriage. Combined, these results indicate the need for life-course research on sexualities and masculinities (Diefendorf 2015) and reinforce that men as well as women have the capacity to experience sexual flexibility.

Conclusion

The results demonstrate that some rural straight men who have same-sex sex construct normative masculinity through their choice of sexual partners on the axes of masculinity, race, and sexual identity, as well as through the type of sex they prefer. By having sex mostly with other privileged men—conventionally masculine, white, and not gay—and by enjoying secretive and romance-free same-sex sex, the participants framed their encounters as straight and normatively masculine. Through complex interpretive processes, they reframed same-sex sex, usually antithetical to rural masculinities, such that it actually helped them construct normative rural masculinity. The type of same-sex sex they have is distinguishable from that of other groups of MSM: *bud-sex* captures their unique sexual interpretations (Silva, forthcoming), as well as their partnering preferences and the type of sex they have, and it helps construct their normative masculinity and straightness. The concept of bud-sex helps clarify that similar sex practices have different meanings across contexts and populations. Non-normative sexual practices—same-sex sex—can actually be used to reinforce normative masculinity and straightness. The results also demonstrate the flexibility of male heterosexuality over the life course, and the importance of heterosexuality to rural masculinity. Given the centrality of heterosexuality to normative masculinity in rural areas, the participants' identification with straightness—bolstered by their interpretations of their sexual practices—reinforced their normative rural masculinity. Because normative masculinity is critical for social acceptance in rural areas, identification with heterosexuality to bolster normative masculinity was especially important. This study is one of the first to use the narratives of straight MSM themselves to explore how they understand their masculinity. It is also the first to examine this population in rural areas, reinforcing the centrality of place for how individuals perceive and experience gender and sexuality. More broadly, this study is part of a growing scholarship that points to masculinities that differ by time period, race, class, and location (Pascoe and Bridges 2016).

The participants' narratives illustrate historical shifts to the relationship between gender and sexuality. In the late nineteenth and early twentieth centuries, many masculine men penetrated feminine men without feeling as though their masculinity or sexual identity was threatened; this is because gender and sexual practice (i.e., penetrating or being penetrated) was an organizing element for how sexuality was understood, and the concept of sexual identity was not yet widely used (Chauncey 1994). Today, the biological sex of sexual partners is the organizing element for sexuality, and for men there is a widespread perception that femininity is tied to same-sex sexuality. Thus, today, men that engage in bud-sex distance themselves from femininity and normalize their sexual encounters as masculine by partnering with other normatively masculine men.

Future research could expand on this study. Because of the difficulty of finding participants, researchers should extend the time devoted to recruitment. Additionally, urban and suburban straight men should be interviewed, as should rural men from locations outside the Midwest and Pacific Northwest, given that there are vastly different rural spaces across the United States. Further, men of other races should be interviewed to understand how their construction of their normative masculinity differs from—or is similar to—the white men in this study, especially with regards to racial partnering.

The social implications of straight masculinities open to same-sex sex are complex. On one hand, diversity within expressions of heterosexuality and masculinities demonstrate that normativity can be unintentionally challenged from within dominant identities. On the other, the participants' masculinity reinforces inequality. All 19 participants in this study maintain straight privilege by publicly identifying as straight and keeping secret their same-sex encounters. All of the straight men avoid effeminate men, and several disparaged male effeminacy, contributing to the widespread devaluation of femininities. Moreover, 13 were married and had extramarital sex without their wife's knowledge, underscoring their male entitlement and unwillingness to consider ethical nonmonogamy.[5] The participants enjoy marginalized sexual practices, but they are unwilling to challenge heterosexism or other forms of domination, maintaining numerous systems of inequality.

Notes

1 Reback and Larkins's (2010) interview study is an exception; because half of their sample had sex with men out of economic necessity and most were substance users, their study represents a specific, highly marginalized group of MSM.
2 The participants did not use any particular phrasing to describe their sex, necessitating a new term. I use "MSM" to refer to broader populations of men that have sex with men, given that there are few other terms that can describe them.
3 While most of Mark's encounters were nonromantic, he did report several semiromantic relationships with regulars; his narrative indicates that while he currently identifies as straight, he is open to transitioning to an openly nonheterosexual identity and a male partnership if his wife divorces him.
4 "Top" means penetrating in anal sex, whereas "bottom" refers to being penetrated; "versatile" means both topping and bottoming.
5 Only Joe was in an open relationship with his wife; as he said, "I like big dicks, she likes big tits."

References

Abelson, Miriam J. 2014. *Men in context: Transmasculinities and transgender experiences in three US regions.* Ph.D. diss., University of Oregon, Eugene, OR.

Adam, Barry. 2000. Love and sex in constructing identity among men who have sex with men. *International Journal of Sexuality and Gender Studies* 5 (4): 325–39.

Anderson, Eric. 2008. "Being masculine is not about who you sleep with . . . ": Heterosexual athletes contesting masculinity and the one-time rule of homosexuality. *Sex Roles* 58 (1–2): 104–15.

Annes, Alexis, and Meredith Redlin. 2012. The careful balance of gender and sexuality: Rural gay men, the heterosexual matrix, and "effeminophobia." *Journal of Homosexuality* 59 (2): 256–88.

Barber, Kristen. 2016. *Styling masculinity: Gender, class, and inequality in the men's grooming industry.* New Brunswick, NJ: Rutgers University Press.

Barnshaw, John, and Lynn Letukas. 2010. The low down on the down low: Origins, risk identification and intervention. *Health Sociology Review* 19 (4): 478–90.

Bird, Sharon. 1996. Welcome to the men's club: Homosociality and the maintenance of hegemonic masculinity. *Gender & Society* 10 (2): 120–32.

Boag, Peter. 2003. *Same-sex affairs: Constructing and controlling homosexuality in the Pacific Northwest.* Berkeley: University of California Press.

Boulden, Walter. 2001. Gay men living in a rural environment. *Journal of Gay and Lesbian Social Services* 12 (3/4): 63–75.

Bridges, Tristan. 2014. A very "gay" straight? Hybrid masculinities, sexual aesthetics, and the changing relationship between masculinity and homophobia. *Gender & Society* 28 (1): 58–82.

Britton, Dana. 1990. Homophobia and homosociality: An analysis of boundary maintenance. *Sociological Quarterly* 31 (3): 423–39.

Bump, Philip. 2014. There really are two Americas. An urban one and a rural one. *The Washington Post*, 21 April.

Campbell, Hugh, and Michael Bell. 2000. The question of rural masculinities. *Rural Sociology* 65 (4): 532–46.

Cantú, Lionel, Jr. 2009. *The sexuality of migration: Border crossings and Mexican immigrant men.* New York: NYU Press.

Carrillo, Héctor, and Jorge Fontdevila. 2014. Border crossings and shifting sexualities among Mexican gay immigrant men: Beyond monolithic conceptions. *Sexualities* 17 (8): 919–38.

Carrillo, Héctor, and Amanda Hoffman. 2016. From MSM to heteroflexibilities: Non-exclusive straight male identities and their implications for HIV prevention and health promotion. *Global Public Health* 11 (7–8): 923–36.

Chauncey, George. 1994. *Gay New York: Gender, urban culture, and the making of the gay male world 1890–1940.* New York: Basic Books.

Chetty, Raj, and Nathaniel Hendren. 2015. *The impacts of neighborhoods on intergenerational mobility: Childhood exposure effects and county-level estimates.* Cambridge, MA: The Equality of Opportunity Project.

Connell, R. W. 1987. *Gender and power: Society, the person, and sexual politics.* Palo Alto, CA: Stanford University Press.

Connell, R. W. 2005. *Masculinities*, 2nd ed. Berkeley: University of California Press.

Connell, R. W., and James Messerschmidt. 2005. Hegemonic masculinity: Rethinking the concept. *Gender & Society* 19 (6): 829–59.

Courtenay, Will. 2006. Rural men's health: Situating risk in the negotiation of masculinity. In *Country boys: Masculinity and rural life*, edited by Hugh Campbell, Michael M. Bell, and Margaret Finney. University Park, PA: Pennsylvania State University Press.

Dean, James. 2014. *Straights: Heterosexuality in post-closeted culture.* New York: New York University Press.

Desmond, Matthew. 2006. Becoming a firefighter. *Ethnography* 7 (4): 387–421.

Diamond, Lisa. 2009. *Sexual fluidity: Understanding women's love and desire.* Cambridge, MA: Harvard University Press.

Diefendorf, Sarah. 2015. After the wedding night: Sexual abstinence and masculinities over the life course. *Gender & Society* 29 (5): 647–69.

Fellows, Will. 2001. *Farm boys: Lives of gay men from the rural Midwest.* Madison: University of Wisconsin Press.

Flood, Michael. 2008. Men, sex, and homosociality: How bonds between men shape their sexual relations with women. *Men and Masculinities* 10 (3): 339–59.

Foucault, Michel. 1978. *The history of sexuality: An introduction*, volume 1. New York: Vintage Books.

Gray, Mary. 2009. *Out in the country: Youth, media, and queer visibility in rural America.* New York: New York University Press.

Halberstam, Judith. 2005. *In a queer time and place: Transgender bodies, subcultural lives.* New York: New York University Press.

Hennen, Peter. 2008. *Fairies, bears, and leathermen: Men in community queering the masculine.* Chicago: University of Chicago Press.

Leonhardt, David, and Kevin Quealy. 2015. How your hometown affects your chances of marriage. *The New York Times*, May 15.

Howard, John. 1999. *Men like that: A Southern queer history*. Chicago: University of Chicago Press.

Humphreys, Laud. 1970. Tearoom trade: Impersonal sex in public places. *Transaction* 7 (3): 10–25.

Johnson, Colin. 2013. *Just queer folks: Gender and sexuality in rural America*. Philadelphia, PA: Temple University Press.

Kazyak, Emily. 2012. Midwest or lesbian? Gender, rurality, and sexuality. *Gender & Society* 26 (6): 825–48.

Katz, Jonathan. 1995. *The invention of heterosexuality*. New York: Dutton.

Kimmel, Michael. 1994. Masculinity as homophobia. In *Theorizing masculinities*, edited by Harry Brod and Michael Kaufman. Thousand Oaks, CA: Sage.

Kitzinger, Celia, and Sue Wilkinson. 1995. Transitions from heterosexuality to lesbianism: The discursive production of lesbian identities. *Developmental Psychology* 31 (1): 95–104.

Loe, Meika. 2001. Fixing broken masculinity: Viagra as a technology for the production of gender and sexuality. *Sexuality and Culture* 5 (3): 97–125.

McCormack, Mark. 2013. *The declining significance of homophobia*. Oxford: Oxford University Press.

Messner, Michael. 1993. "Changing men" and feminist politics in the United States. *Theory and Society* 22 (5): 723–37.

Morris, Edward. 2008. "Rednecks," "rutters," and 'rithmetic: Social class, masculinity, and schooling in a rural context. *Gender & Society* 22 (6): 728–51.

Pascoe, C. J. 2011. *Dude, you're a fag: Masculinity and sexuality in high school*, 2nd ed. Berkeley: University of California Press.

Pascoe, C. J., and Tristan Bridges, eds. 2016. *Exploring masculinities: Identity, inequality, continuity, and change*. New York: Oxford University Press.

Plummer, Ken. 1996. Symbolic interactionism and the forms of homosexuality. In *Queer theory/sociology*, edited by Steven Seidman. Cambridge, MA: Blackwell.

Reback, Cathy, and Sherry Larkins. 2010. Maintaining a heterosexual identity: Sexual meanings among a sample of heterosexually identified men who have sex with men. *Archives of Sexual Behavior* 39 (3): 766–73.

Reynolds, Chelsea. 2015. "I am super straight and I prefer you be too": Constructions of heterosexual masculinity in online personal ads for "straight" men seeking sex with men. *Journal of Communication Inquiry* 39 (3): 213–31.

Robinson, Brandon, and David Moskowitz. 2013. The eroticism of Internet cruising as a self-contained behavior: A multivariate analysis of men seeking men demographics and getting off online. *Culture, Health & Sexuality* 15 (5): 555–69.

Robinson, Brandon, and Salvador Vidal-Ortiz. 2013. Displacing the dominant "down low" discourse: Deviance, same-sex desire, and Craigslist.org. *Deviant Behavior* 34 (3): 224–41.

Rust, Paula. 1992. The politics of sexual identity: Sexual attraction and behavior among lesbian and bisexual women. *Social Problems* 39 (4): 366–86.

Sedgwick, Eve. 1990. *Epistemology of the closet*. Berkeley: University of California Press.

Seidman, Steven. 2002. *Beyond the closet: The transformation of gay and lesbian life*. London: Routledge.

Silva, Tony. Forthcoming. "Helpin' a buddy out": Perceptions of identity and behavior among rural straight men that have sex with each other. *Sexualities*.

Simon, William, and John Gagnon. 1986. Sexual scripts: Permanence and change. *Archives of Sexual Behavior* 15 (2): 97–120.

Stein, Arlene. 1989. Three models of sexuality: Drives, identities, and practices. *Sociological Theory* 7 (1): 1–13.

United States Census Bureau. 2016. Annual estimates of the resident population by sex, age, race alone or in combination, and Hispanic origin for the United States and states: April 1, 2010 to July 1, 2015. Washington, DC: United States Census Bureau, Population Division. http://factfinder.census.gov/faces/table-services/jsf/pages/productview.xhtml?src=bkmk#.

Ward, Jane. 2015. *Not gay: Sex between straight white men*. New York: New York University Press.

25

'Straight with a pinch of bi'

The contours of male heteroflexibility*

Héctor Carrillo and Amanda Hoffman†

> I think I'm straight. From time to time I might get the urge to have sex with a guy, but I'm not attracted to them. (Blaise,[1] age 39, white)
>
> I would say [I'm] straight. I love women. But when they are not available I get head from guys. (Freddie, age 25, Latino/white)
>
> I'm straight but a pervert. A bi guy is just attracted to either or. (Charlie, age 38, white)

In these passages, Blaise, Freddie, and Charlie succinctly explained why they self-identify as straight men in spite of the fact that they engage in sex with men. Within a strict classificatory system that divides people into three groups according to their sexual orientation – heterosexuals, bisexuals, and homosexuals – these men would be classified as bisexual based on their sexual behaviours with women and men. Men such as these ones, however, often find that the label bisexual does not adequately represent them – that being straight is crucial for their sense of who they are as individuals and as men. In this article, we examine the logics that allow adult US men such as Blaise, Freddie, and Charlie to make sense of their same-sex desires and behaviours and make them consistent with a straight sexual orientation. We argue that in the process of interpreting their sexualities, these men change the definition of heterosexuality, in effect turning it into a considerably elastic category.

Our analysis is based on in-depth interviews conducted with 100 men who self-identified as straight, but who were recruited while they were pursuing sexual encounters with men online. Our data show that, contrary to many beliefs and stereotypes about such men, many of them have engaged in considerable reflection about their sexualities and sexual lives, and their reflections

* The editors would like to thank The Sexualities Project at Northwestern University for a generous grant to pay permissions costs for this chapter.

† Carrillo, H., Hoffman, A. 'Straight with a pinch of bi': The construction of heterosexuality as an elastic category among adult US men. *Sexualities* 21(1–2), pp. 90–108. Copyright © 2017 by the Authors. Reprinted by permission of SAGE Publications, Ltd. www.sagepub.co.uk

have led them to conclude that their self-identification as straight is warranted. In particular, we focus on these men's interpretations of their sexual self-identification and sexual attractions, the meanings that they assign to their same-sex behaviours, their sense that same-sex behaviours provide them a respite from the everyday pressures of being a man, and the perception that their same-sex behaviours relate to specific sexual fantasies and a desire for experiencing sexual transgression.

Our study is somewhat unique in two significant ways. First, most of the recent studies of men whose sexual identities could be described as 'mostly heterosexual' have focused on young, college-age men, leaving the question of whether their experiences and interpretations can be generalized beyond their generation and their particular moment in the life course. By contrast, the men in our sample ranged in age from 18 to 70.

Second, studies of straight-identified MSM (men who have sex with men) that have included older participants have tended to focus on men who are 'on the down low', a colloquial term that refers to African American and Latino men's secretive involvement in sex with men, as well as to those men's perceived cultural reluctance to adopt bisexual or gay identities. The focus on men of colour, and the perception that the down low is an exclusively African American and Latino phenomenon, has often led to reproducing racial stereotypes (Ford et al., 2007; González, 2007; Malebranche, 2008; Phillips, 2005). By contrast, a majority of the straight-identified men in our study are white, and many are also secretive about their same-sex desires and behaviours, which challenges the notion that the so-called down low is prevalent exclusively among African Americans or Latinos. We begin by providing some background that will help us frame our analysis and findings, followed by a more detailed description of our methods and sample.

Making heterosexuality more elastic

Around the turn of the 21st-century, various labels began to appear in popular and academic discourse to suggest changing contours of heterosexuality. One of the first such terms to surface was 'heteroflexible'. In an early blog posting entitled 'Heteroflexibility: The latest semantic ploy to keep sexual options open really pisses me off', sociologist Laurie Essig (2000) commented that 'heteroflexible' generally indicated that a 'person has or intends to have a primarily heterosexual lifestyle' but 'remains open to sexual encounters and even relationships with persons of the same sex'. Essig elaborated: 'It is a rejection of bisexuality since the inevitable question that comes up in bisexuality is one of preference, and the preference of the heteroflexible is quite clear.' Such a preference involves retaining a self-identification as heterosexual by thinking of heterosexuality as a flexible sexual orientation category. To be heteroflexible is therefore perceived as the opposite of being heterorigid. It compels a redefinition of heterosexuality, expanding the category to allow some degree of same-sex desires so that individuals who are not exclusively sexually interested in members of the 'opposite sex'[2] can continue thinking of themselves as straight or heterosexual.

Around the same time, other similar terms and phrases emerged that were meant to indicate slight departures from heterosexuality that are not significant enough to permanently transfer an individual to the sexual orientation category of bisexuality, including 'bi-curious' and, later, 'mostly straight' and 'mostly heterosexual'.[3] Behaviourally speaking, however, the sexual desires and behaviours that these terms are meant to describe are not new. The fact that some straight-identified men – or, previously, men who thought of themselves as 'normal' or 'regular' – engage in sexual interactions with men has been well documented, for example, by the historical research on the sexual cultures of early 20th-century USA. The well-known work by historian George Chauncey described sexual interactions between men who thought of themselves as 'normal/straight' and 'queer/fairies' during the early decades of the 20th century (Chauncey, 1993, 1994).

Empirical sexuality studies conducted since the 1940s have also documented the participation of straight-identified men in same-sex behaviours. Perhaps most famously, Kinsey et al. (1948) found that more than one in three of the men in their sample had engaged in homosexual behaviours at some point in their lifetime. The degree of behavioural variation that they detected led them to propose the idea of a sexual continuum – which took the form of the well-known Kinsey scale – that classified men into seven categories, ranging from those who had exclusive heterosexual behaviours (a zero in the scale) to those who exclusively engaged in homosexual behaviours (a six on the scale).[4] Other scholars later identified and described situational male homosexuality: the occurrence of sex between men who are confined in all-male spaces, such as prisons and all-male schools (Kunzel, 2002). Still others have studied the sexualities of men who lived heterosexual lives but pursued sex with men in public sex venues (including public restrooms or 'tea rooms'; Humphreys, 1970), or have described how straight-identified men use economic considerations to justify their participation in male-male pornography (Escoffier, 2003).

The emergence of terms such as heteroflexible and bi-curious at the beginning of the 21st century possibly signalled a shift in sexual attitudes in a younger generation of Americans (in her piece, Essig (2000) was reacting to the ease with which her college students publicly used the term heteroflexible in describing their own sexualities; see also Kelleher and Smith, 2012; Savin-Williams, 2005). These new terms and labels of sexual identity seemed to represent a renewed sense of sexual identity among straight people who have same-sex desires, and possibly also their search for public recognition and social acceptance of their non-normative heterosexual lifestyles. At the same time, by not adopting the label 'bisexual' those youths also signalled that their sexual interest in both women and men need not transfer them out of the heterosexual category; they sought to indicate that same-sex desires and behaviours are not altogether incompatible with heterosexuality.

For instance, in a study of young American college male soccer players Anderson and Adams (2011) reported that although their participants accepted bisexuality as a legitimate category and an alternative for some people (although few actually knew any bisexually-identified people), they also believed that having some degree of same-sex attraction did not automatically transfer a person to the bisexual or gay categories.[5] This was occurring in a context of what these scholars describe as decreasing 'homohysteria' among American youth, which may explain why some increasingly believed that it would be fine for a straight man to acknowledge having sexual interest in men. Finally, this study's participants saw bisexuality as a slightly problematic category because they perceived it as devoid of emotional attachment (compared to being straight or gay), and a category that overly emphasizes the physicality of sexual interactions. Such emphasis, they felt, makes bisexuality less attractive as an identity than the more encompassing identities gay and straight.

Around the same time scholars began to report evidence of yet another emerging notion, represented by the terms 'mostly straight' and 'mostly heterosexual' (Cohen and Savin-Williams, 2010; Savin-Williams et al., 2012; Savin-Williams and Vrangalova, 2013; Thompson and Morgan, 2008; Vrangalova and Savin-Williams, 2012). These terms are increasingly being conceived in scholarly work as an additional category of sexual orientation that is distinct from both heterosexuality and bisexuality.

This idea is well illustrated by Savin-Williams and Vrangalova (2013) in a review article entitled 'Mostly heterosexual as a distinct sexual orientation group: A systematic review of the empirical evidence'. As this title suggests, these scholars emphasized the notion of mostly heterosexual as a category that is altogether separate from heterosexuality. In their analysis, they 'found support for the claim that mostly heterosexuals form a unique sexual orientation group from four separate sources of evidence: sexual orientation profiles, prevalence, stability, and subjective relevance'. Their analysis led Savin-Williams and Vrangalova to conclude that:

> Specifically, mostly heterosexuals of both sexes and across developmental ages revealed a distinctive sexual orientation profile – they were more same-sex oriented than heterosexuals, but less so than bisexuals, in their sexual/romantic attraction, fantasy, behaviour, and physiological arousal.
>
> *(Savin-Williams and Vrangalova, 2013: 76)*

These scholars also assessed that mostly heterosexuals are the 'most numerous nonheterosexual group, often larger than all other nonheterosexual groups combined' (p. 76). Furthermore, they also found that 'qualitative accounts of those who identified as mostly heterosexual portrayed individuals with a sexual identity that felt authentic, genuine, and accurate', stressing that 'assessments that failed to include a mostly heterosexual option were criticized by youth as inappropriate to capture an understanding of their sexual self' (Savin-Williams and Vrangalova, 2013: 76–7).

As noted in this last quotation, a majority of participants in the research that Savin-Williams and Vrangalova reviewed were youths. Moreover, based on what they saw as limited data on older groups they assessed that identifying as mostly heterosexual may be 'significantly less common in later adulthood' (Savin-Williams and Vrangalova, 2013: 81). Also noteworthy is the fact that several of the studies referenced 'found individuals who, even when given the opportunity to select a mostly heterosexual identity, classified themselves as heterosexual and then reported some non-zero same-sex sexuality' (Savin-Williams and Vrangalova, 2013: 78).

In fact, Ward (2015) has demonstrated that the idea that white men can be strictly heterosexual while having and enacting same-sex desires has considerable cultural salience in mainstream American society. Based on analysis of a range of practices and cultural expressions in the USA throughout the 20th century, including online ads posted by straight white men in the Craigslist Casual Encounters website, Ward argued that the enactment of same-sex physicality plays an important role in fostering the sense of what being a heterosexual man is all about. Ward (2015: 4) concluded that homosexuality is a 'vital ingredient' and a 'constitutive element' of heterosexual masculinity, even when heterosexual men who engage in same-sex behaviours must carefully manage those behaviours – using 'pretense, disidentification, and heteronormative investments' as strategies to make same-sex behaviours consistent with a heterosexual identity.

Ward's analysis is particularly helpful for our purposes, both in its focus on a broader age range, and in its rejection of the idea of the down low as something specific to racial and ethnic minority cultures. What Ward did not do, however, is interact with straight-identified men one-on-one in order to learn directly from them how they make their sexual identities consistent with their same-sex desires, behaviours, and attractions. That is where the present work comes in. As our own findings will show, even when adult men such as Blaise, Freddie, and Charlie, quoted at the beginning of the article, have begun to (sometimes reluctantly) adopt secondary terms and descriptors as part of their self-identification, the logics of their sexual interpretations still strongly align them with the idea that they are essentially and primarily heterosexual. Moreover, they see themselves as being in many ways no different than other heterosexual men, in spite of their same-sex desires, and behaviours.

Methods

During the first phase of a two-phase study, we interviewed 100 US men recruited in the 'Men-4Men (relationships)' and 'Men4Men (casual encounters)' sections of Craigslist.org, a popular online personals website where people seek friendships, relationships, or sex. We chose this recruitment method because for many straight-identified men the internet has become the preferred venue for hooking up with other men (Ross et al., 2005; Ward, 2008). Men who expressed interest were directed to our study website and asked to fill out a short screener to determine eligibility. We sought men who self-identified as straight, had experienced same-sex desires after the age of 13, and were 18 or older.

The interviews were conducted by three female interviewers, primarily using an online chat function. Before the interview, participants were asked to provide informed consent and also filled out a short demographic survey. Online interviews lasted between 120 and 210 minutes, often including long pauses during which participants attended to other personal matters.[6] Among other topics, we asked participants about their sexual identities; sex lives, partners, and relationships; sexual desires, practices, and fantasies; and how they manage their same-sex desires. As indicated in Table 25.1, these men's ages ranged from 18 to 70 and were well distributed within that span. Seventy-eight were white, 11 Latino, five African American, three Native American, two Asian American, and one Middle Eastern/white. Fifty-nine were or had been in relationships with women, including 38 who were married to a woman.

During a second phase we recruited and interviewed 19 gay men and 21 women who had sexual or romantic relations with straight-identified men who have same-sex desires. For the purposes of this article, however, we focus almost exclusively on the interviews with straight-identified men. We only draw a few selected quotations from our interviews with gay male partners.

Data analysis

We analysed patterns of lived experience and interpretation using Atlas.ti, a software package for qualitative analysis that helped us organize and code our data. Based on an initial reading of our

Table 25.1 Demographics (N = 100)

Age	
18–29	26
30–49	46
50–70	28
Race/ethnicity	
White	78
Latino	11
African American	5
Native American	3
Asian American	2
Middle Eastern/white	1
Relationship status with women	
Single	38
Stable relationship	18
Married	38
Divorced	2
Widowed	1
Declined to answer	3

interviews, we created approximately 20 codes for each set of interviews. Three coders independently coded a sample of transcripts, achieving an average rate of 82% inter-coder reliability. This was calculated based on the number of times that all coders assigned the same codes to specific text passages (Miles and Huberman, 1994). We then proceeded to code all interviews and conducted thematic searches to identify patterns in the data, as well as disconfirming cases. We also re-contextualized selected quotations in relation to the individual cases from which they were drawn.

The contours of male heteroflexibilities

Self-identification

The 100 men in phase one self-identified as straight at the time that we recruited them. However, more nuanced patterns emerged over the course of their interviews. Fifty confirmed that they exclusively self-identify as straight. The rest also described themselves using secondary labels. Among them, 23 used a range of terms and descriptors that indicate a sense of heterosexuality as a flexible category, 27 indicated that they might privately call themselves bisexual, and one described himself as gay. These patterns suggest that, beyond a primary and public self-identification as straight, these men often also hold a more specific and private sense of their location across an imagined spectrum of sexual orientation that includes heterosexuality on one end, homosexuality on the other, and bisexuality in the middle.

Many participants, however, perceived that in spite of increasing acceptance of sexual diversity, these three categories do not have equal social status. Thus, they generally saw no social advantages to abandoning the identities as straight into which they were socialized, and their narratives made clear that they perceived a very strong social pull toward the heterosexual side. As Frank (24, white) put it, 'Who wouldn't prefer a hetero lifestyle? It is what is expected of us by the society at large.' They also felt that being straight is the only way of being that they know how to perform. Bradley (21, white), for instance, explained that he has identified as straight all his life, 'since I was born, or rather, since I knew what being straight was', and Devon (39, white) indicated that 'society teaches people to be straight and it messes a lot of people up in the process . . . you could say I was bi . . . but often times I tell people that and five minutes later they are telling someone I am GAY'. Implicitly, these men felt that adopting a label other than 'straight' would result in a loss of the privileges associated with heterosexuality. Moreover, as we will see later, they believed that their identifying as straight is legitimate because they are primarily attracted to women.

Some were willing to depart from a strict identification as straight as long as 'straight' or 'heterosexual' was still part of the equation. They used a range of labels and descriptors (summarized in Table 25.2), including 'heteroflexible' (Miles, 30, white; and Corey, 24, white), 'mostly heterosexual' (Sterling, 34, white), 'bi-curious, but mostly straight' (Sean, 34, white), 'straight with bi tendencies' (Travis, 20, white), 'straight with a pinch of bi' (Peter, 40, white), and 'straight with a little weirdness from time to time' (Lawrence, 57, white). Asked if he thought his sexual behaviours are in fact weird, Lawrence responded that he sees them as 'off the common path. I don't think of any of it as harmful; but private, yes'. Rather than seeing their sex with men as just a behaviour, as some of the men who think of themselves as strictly straight do, men who adopted secondary descriptors aimed to somehow incorporate their same-sex desires into their identities.

Others went further and saw their same-sex desires as significant enough for them to privately think of themselves as bisexual. As Simon (27, white) put it:

> I think everybody is a little bi. Isn't that what this research is about? There's the Kinsey scale . . . It's not like Bush saying you're either with us or with the terrorists. I think I'm probably bi but what I present to the world is a heterosexual man. Internally I'm bi, but that's not something most people know. I'm not ashamed, but the majority of people are ignorant and close-minded.

Such men believed that bisexuality is common, and they did not struggle with the idea of being bisexual, but they also believed that the outside world would not understand them if they publicly called themselves bisexual. They imagined identifying as bisexual only in certain situations, most often in the context of their sexual interactions with men. Dustin (28, white) said, 'I am not openly bisexual to society except in sexual situations . . . I don't have relationships with men; I am in a relationship with my wife and only love her. [I'm bisexual] only with men behind closed doors.'

Only a few claimed that, given the right situation, they might be willing to publicly self-identify as bisexual, disclosing also to female partners. For instance, Ethan (38, white) participated in a threesome involving his wife and another man, which made it possible for him to tell his wife that he is bisexual. She concurred with this belief, and Ethan felt that she liked the idea of his being bisexual, since 'she brings it up when [she] gets aroused'. Peter, who self-described as 'straight with a pinch of bi', also said that he would say that he is bisexual 'if asked by someone I'm comfortable with'.

In our analysis of self-identification (as well as in our analyses of sexual attraction and behaviour), we looked for differences within our sample according to age. Interestingly, we did not identify any noteworthy differences that depended on the age of our participants.

Table 25.2 Sexual identity (N = 100)[a]

Exclusive self-identification as straight or heterosexual		50
Self-identification as straight or heterosexual plus secondary descriptors [b]		50
Bisexual/privately bisexual	27	
Bi-curious	9	
Mostly heterosexual/straight	3	
With bi tendencies	2	
75–80% straight	1	
Curious	1	
Experimenting	1	
Gay	1	
Hetero-curious	1	
Heteroflexible	1	
Leaning toward bi	1	
Maybe bi	1	
Queer	1	
Somewhat bi	1	
Straight-curious	1	

[a] All 100 participants were initially recruited as being straight or heterosexual

[b] Although 50 individuals used secondary descriptors, two of them used two (bi-curious/mostly straight, and bisexual/queer), with the result that the total frequency of secondary descriptors in this table is 52.

Linking self-identification to sexual attraction

As part of their self-identification as straight, for many of our participants it is of utmost importance to assert that they are primarily attracted to women and not to men. Sean (34, white) justified his identification as 'bi-curious but also straight' in these terms:

> If I'm out in a social situation, I'm almost 100% looking at women, and not at men . . . Bisexual is closer to 50/50 in terms of attraction to both sexes . . . Bi-curious, to me, tends to be more attracted to the opposite sex and more likely not openly identifying as interested in homosexual sex.

Sean also stressed that his primary attraction to women is permanent, and distanced himself from 'people who identify as bi-curious who are on their way to being openly bisexual or even openly gay or exclusively homosexual'.

Others argued that they have no attraction to men at all, in spite of the fact that they engage in sex with men. As Reggie (28, African American) put it:

> I know what I like. I like pussy. I like women . . . the more the merrier . . . I would kiss a woman. ANYWHERE. I can barely hug a man . . . I do have a healthy sexual imagination and wonder about other things in the sexual realm I've never done . . . Sometimes I get naughty and explore . . . That's how I see it.

By interpreting his same-sex desires as the result of naughtiness and sexual exploration, Reggie rationalized that he is not attracted to men and that his sexual activity with men is not self-defining. Similarly Charlie (32, white) stated:

> Women are hot . . . I can see a beautiful woman walk down the street and I instantly can become hard and get horny. I don't think I've ever seen a guy walking by and got a boner. Also, I would not want to kiss or make out with them or love them. They would be more like a sexual experience.

As Charlie's comment suggests, for some of these men, whether they feel that they are sexually attracted to someone or not depends not only on a sense of physical attraction, but also emotional attraction. Indeed, a measure of their lack of sexual attraction to men was the frequent perception that they could fall in love with a woman but not with a man (on this issue see also Reback and Larkins, 2010). For instance, Ajay (22, Asian American) stated: 'I can't see myself with a guy in anything more than sex, and lately it's with me getting head. With a girl I can see myself [spending] the rest of my life.' Similarly, Gus (27, white) felt 'no craving for anything long term' involving a man, 'there's no wanting to be emotionally intimate', and Freddie (25, Latino/white) went further by saying: 'I don't enjoy [being with] men. I use them, I guess you would say. I would describe a bisexual as someone who likes guys and girls, not just one, and I only really like women.' For men such as Freddie, men are purely sexual objects.

Paradoxically, although sex with men can be arousing and exciting, for some of these men it does not involve a sexual attraction toward male bodies. In Josh's words (21, white), 'I could never really be attracted to a male body, well most of the time I would say. Just everything that makes up the human body, face, legs, etc.' And Rodolfo (22, Latino) likewise stated: 'I never feel attracted to men physically, never have I looked at a guy and say, "wow, good looking guy." It is more about the sex part.'

To be sure, a few acknowledged having some level of physical attraction toward men, but they saw such attraction as highly conditional and bounded to very specific 'types' (compared to women, for whom their attraction is automatic and generalized). Joseph (64, white), in a manner reminiscent of the research by Ward (2008, 2015), strictly preferred 'boy-next-door, jock types. No beards, goatees, moustaches, piercings, etc. Tattoos are ok if they are small.' He also rejected effeminate men. Others were equally specific: 'Tall, fit to average; a little hair on the chest and crotch; very well hung; uncut; big balls. Ethnicity is white or black usually; all of them very hygienic and clean' (Matt, 41, white) or 'masc men that are younger (25–40), [and] that are not overweight' (Alexander, 52, white).

Some men distinguished between attraction to men and attraction to penises, which they believed are two very different things. They felt that male bodies do not arouse them, but penises do. Ajay (22, Asian American) was motivated to have sex with men 'mostly [because of] their cock. Every time I did anything with a guy it mostly depended on their cocks. I didn't really care what they looked like.' And Josh (21, white) saw a penis as an improvement over a dildo. 'There's just something about the living male penis that is much hotter than a toy made out of some material made to look or slightly feel like the male penis', said Josh. In a similar vein, Sam (42, white) said, 'these playmates are only living and breathing dildos'. This emphasis on the attractiveness of penises also made pre-op transgender women perfect partners for some of these men. For instance, Josh (21, white) liked trans women who have 'the features of a girl's body . . . and the most "exciting" part of a guy'.

That men were able to recognize being attracted to the penis as the only salient feature of the male body, as something better than a sex toy ('a living dildo'), or even as an exciting part of a non-male body, but at the same time denied being attracted to men, suggests the intricate interpretations that these men must make to convince themselves that they are indeed straight. Bisexuals and gays are attracted to men, and could fall in love with a man, but not them. This idea was further confirmed by the less typical case of Byron (43, white), who said that he started thinking of himself as possibly bisexual 'when I realized I could have romantic feelings for a guy . . . the difference for me [was] when being with a man was no longer merely about sex with a man'. Finally, our participants' sense of their primary attraction to women is also indirectly reflected in their estimates of the lifetime number of sexual partners, which appear in Table 25.3.

Table 25.3 Reported number of sexual partners (N = 100)

Estimated # of lifetime female sexual partners	
0	4
1	5
2–10	26
11–50	47
>50	18
Estimated # of lifetime male sexual partners	
0	9
1	8
2–10	48
11–50	22
>50	12
Declined to answer	1

Same-sex behaviours and their meanings

In terms of their sexual behaviours with men, our straight-identified participants most commonly reported receiving or giving oral sex (see Table 25.4). A smaller number reported engaging in anal intercourse, which suggests the possibility that some carefully limit their same-sex sexual repertoire as an identity-management strategy. This idea was expressed by some gay male partners interviewed during the second phase of our study, who explained the reluctance of their straight partners to engage in anal intercourse in terms of the practice's symbolic association with gayness. For instance, Stewart (46, white), discussing a straight partner who refused to have anal sex, observed: 'He always said that that didn't interest him at all. But I honestly think it was that he considered [it] to be "too" gay for him.' Similarly, Graham (27, white) stated that:

> . . . some guys want to try everything, but I'd say 95% of the guys I've been with I knew identified as straight absolutely refuse receiving anal sex. I'm just speculating here, but I think that's the line between gay behaviour and straight behaviour for them.

Interestingly, among those straight participants who engaged in anal intercourse with men, more reported being penetrated than penetrating, which raises questions about the perceived association between being penetrated and gayness that Graham noted.

Several straight-identified participants felt compelled, nonetheless, to minimize the significance of their sex with men and highlight the satisfaction they received in their sex with women (and this works as a corollary to their sense of their exclusive sexual attraction to women). For instance, Shaun (30, white) described receiving oral sex from a male partner, but clarified, 'odd . . . it wasn't the same afterglow that I would have with a woman . . . the feel good feeling after sex'. This male partner made him 'cum harder, [but] afterward it was odd shifting back to guy talk'. And, when this man made a move toward initiating anal intercourse, Shaun stopped him. 'He situated me to put his cock into my ass, and I couldn't do it'. Similarly, Miles (30, white) described enjoying 'anal play [with men] . . . both giving and receiving, toys and also participating

Table 25.4 Reported sexual behaviours with men[a]

Oral sex (mouth/penis)	
Receiving	59
Giving	53
Fantasies only	3
Anal intercourse	
Receiving	34
Giving	20
Fantasies only	5
Other sexual practices	
Mutual masturbation (including group masturbation)	22
Cybersex and masturbating to male sexual imagery	3
Receiving erotic massage	2
Anal play and rimming	5

[a] Participants could report more than one behaviour, so the frequencies do not add to 100.

in anal sex'. Yet he added: 'I've given oral-anal sex, though I don't have the same enthusiasm for it as I do giving women oral-genital contact'.

Finally, some straight men who fantasized about being anally penetrated by a man acknowledged having been anally penetrated by women using dildos. Matt (41, white), for instance, had asked his wife to use a dildo on him, and after they divorced, he began to use dildos on himself. 'I imagine that must be similar to what it really feels like', he added, suggesting that he had reflected on the possibility of experiencing being penetrated by a live penis.

Masculinity, fantasy, secrecy, and transgression

Beyond the various issues that we have discussed so far, our participants sometimes expressed enjoying sex with men because of the secrecy, transgressions, and sexual fantasies involved. Those aspects of their sexual interactions with men explained for them why they are drawn to seeking sex with men even when they are not attracted to them. Josh (21, white), for instance, mentioned that 'the thought of having sex with a guy is a big turn on, maybe 'cause it's so taboo'. Gerard (57, white) emphasized that none of his friends, including his girlfriend of 14 years, 'know that I sometimes like to stroke with a guy. I think that's part of the attraction . . . that's it's a secret'. And Jonathan (26, white) emphasized the pleasure of fantasizing about the forbidden: 'I think it's just [in] the fantasy world . . . basically like you can think about stealing all day long, but you aren't a thief until you do it'.

Some straight men also reported enjoying sex with men because it allows them to suspend social expectations about masculinity. Twenty-seven mentioned a desire to be dominated, and most among them thought that can be most thoroughly achieved in sexual interactions with men. Matt (41, white) described himself as 'an alpha male in a male dominated profession . . . I am aggressive, a decision maker. Masculine means the ability to do guy stuff and be strong . . . fix things, be brave, provide'. He often fantasized about sex with men who are more masculine than he is, 'maybe because I am always in charge in my real life'. In a similar vein, Russell (54, white) poignantly said:

> For most of my sex life I'm in control of things. I'm not a boss at work anymore but I've been in situations where I've managed a hundred people at a time. I take care of my family. I take care of my kids. I'm a good father. I'm a good husband in providing material things for my wife . . . I'm in charge in a lot of places . . . There's times when I don't want to be in charge and I want someone to be in charge of me . . . that's what brings me over [to] the bisexuals . . . it's kind of submitting to another guy or being used by another guy.

In these and other cases, sex with men provided a respite from the pressures of being a man, a much desired space where men felt they could suspend social expectations about being in charge, as well as enjoy the pleasures of being dominated. Interestingly, being dominated by a man seemed to them less threatening than being dominated by a steady female partner, perhaps because it could be construed as a temporary fantasy, instead of meaning a permanent change in the gender balance.

Discussion and conclusion

For most of the men in our primary study, being straight is a crucial aspect of their identities. Our findings show that they are motivated to maintain identities as straight in part because they see no real personal or social advantages that would stem from publicly adopting an identity as bisexual or gay. So, within what they imagine to be a continuum of sexual orientation, they believe that they fit best at the heterosexual end, or very close to it. Moreover, they are able to sustain their straight identities by relying on multiple indicators that tell them that their choice is fully justified.

Those indicators include the following: They interpret that they are exclusively or primarily attracted to women, and many also conclude that they have no sexual attraction to men in spite of their desire to have sex with men. They define sexual attraction as a combination of physical and emotional attraction, and they assess that their interest in women includes both, while their interest in men is purely or mainly sexual, not romantic or emotional. Moreover, some perceive that they are not drawn toward male bodies in the same way as they are drawn to female bodies, and some observe that the only physical part of a man that interests them is his penis. Men in the latter group do not find men handsome or attractive, but they do find penises attractive, and they thus see penises as 'living dildos' or, in other words, disembodied objects of desire that provide a source of sexual pleasure. Finally, as a management strategy for judging that their sexual interest in women is greater and more intense than their interest in men, they sometimes limit their repertoires of same-sex sexual practices or interpret them as less important than their sexual practices with women. That way, they can tell themselves that their sexual interest in women is unbounded, while their sexual interest in men is not.

All this contributes to their sense that they qualify as being called straight or heterosexual, even when some also recognize that their sexualities do indeed differ from exclusive heterosexuality, which in turn leads them to adopt secondary descriptors of their sexual identities. As indicated by the variety of terms that they used, those descriptors often reinforce a perception that, as a sexual orientation category, heterosexuality is elastic instead of rigid – that some degree of same-sex desire and behaviour need not automatically push an individual out of the heterosexual category. And while some men are willing to recognize that their sexual behaviours might qualify their being called bisexual – and they may privately identify with that label – they feel that there is no contradiction between holding a private awareness of being bisexual and a public persona as straight or heterosexual. Again, this conclusion is strengthened by a lack of social incentives to adopt bisexual identities.

Ultimately, a majority of the straight-identified men in our study do not see their sexualities as distinct from those of other straight men, and for many of them any suggestion that their same-sex desires would transfer them to an altogether different category of sexual orientation would be unlikely to be received as an attractive proposition. Our findings thus raise questions about whether the construction of a category of 'mostly heterosexual' as a distinct and separate sexual orientation would be welcomed by these men and seen as adequately representing their sexualities. Our sense is that many would probably reject the idea of being reclassified and transferred to a separate category, which is in part why they have rejected a public identification as bisexual in the first place.

In studies that revealed greater willingness to adopt the term 'mostly heterosexual', prevalence of the term was higher among young adults and college students (Savin-Williams and Vrangalova, 2013: 74). Their willingness to openly and publicly identify as mostly heterosexual may possibly reflect generational shifts in sexual attitudes and what Anderson has called 'the fall of Western homohysteria' (Anderson, 2011; see also McCormack and Anderson, 2014), and may also tell us something about the situational context of colleges and universities. As we noted, we did not find important differences by age in our sample with regard to self-identification. In our study, men across all ages self-identified primarily as straight. Even among those who also used a secondary descriptor, only three also called themselves 'mostly heterosexual' or 'mostly straight'.

This brings us to some observations about the construction of mostly heterosexual as a distinct sexual orientation category. Scholars who propose that idea see it primarily as a research tool – as a way to ensure that future sexuality studies can count on having better analytical tools to assess sexual orientation – and clearly they are not motivated by a desire to impose a new identity category that would merely push everyone who has same-sex desires out of the category of heterosexuality (Savin-Williams and Vrangalova, 2013; Vrangalova and Savin-Williams, 2012). Furthermore, they also recognize that specific categories of sexual orientation represent discrete points along a continuum that may not adequately classify or encapsulate all individuals who have particular sexual desires or behaviours.

We worry, however, that if mostly heterosexual becomes deployed as a distinct category of sexual orientation, it could easily become normative in the public realm and come to be seen as the depository for anyone who is not strictly heterosexual or who self-identifies as bisexual. In other words, the category could potentially be used to reinforce what Anderson (2008) has called a 'one-time rule' that would automatically exclude any and all individuals who enact same-sex desires from the realm of heterosexuality, regardless of their own self-identification. Our concern is that, if this were to happen, it could alienate individuals who believe that their same-sex desires do not make them sufficiently different from other straight-identified people to warrant being transferred to a different category. In other words, we fear that mostly heterosexual could end up becoming as controversial a category as bisexuality.

We concur with Ward (2015) that a productive alternative would be to view same-sex desires as a constitutive part of heterosexuality. Her analysis supports our finding that it would be beneficial to view heterosexuality as a more elastic category than has been typically assumed. This in turn raises new questions about the broader implications of such elasticity. In particular, it remains unclear whether more flexible interpretations of heterosexuality end up reinforcing heteronormativity (and hegemonic masculinity) or challenging it, and it could be that different enactments have divergent outcomes in this regard.[7] Our data indicate that both reinforcement and challenge may be occurring simultaneously. For example, some of our participants expressed that they see no advantage to abandoning the privileges of being seen as heterosexual at the same time as they view the idea of adopting secondary labels of identity (though sometimes only privately) as sexually enlightening.

In relation to race, our findings challenge the notion that the phenomenon of the down low, and the secrecy that is associated with it, is prevalent exclusively among men of colour. Most of the straight-identified men in our study are white, many are married to or in stable relationships with women, and many carefully manage to whom they disclose their same-sex desires and behaviours. This pattern is consistent with the wave of white religious figures and politicians in the United States who in recent years have been found to secretly engage in same-sex behaviours, many of whom were publicly antigay. Indeed, our white participants rely on interpretations that may reflect a mainstream sexual culture that still devalues non-heterosexual identities and behaviours (see Ward, 2015).

Finally, our findings confirm how important it is to consider sociocultural meanings, contextual and situational factors, and historical contingencies in analyses of sexual orientation and sexualities more generally. Our hope is that as popular interpretations and scientific analyses of sexual diversity move forward, the effects of social, cultural, and historical contingencies, such as the ones that are highlighted by our findings, can be given the full attention that they deserve.

Acknowledgements

Our special thanks go to our study participants. We are grateful to our research team, especially to Christine Wood and Pavithra Prasad for conducting and coding interviews. Our thanks also go to Steven Epstein for commenting on drafts of this article, to Mark McCormack for shepherding this special issue, and to the journal's reviewers for their insightful comments.

Funding

The author(s) disclosed receipt of the following financial support for the research, authorship, and/or publication of this article: This work was supported by the American Institute of Bisexuality (AIB) and the Sexualities Project at Northwestern (SPAN).

Notes

1 All participant names are pseudonyms. Quotations are taken from participants' online typed comments. We have slightly edited the quotations for clarity, correcting misspellings, typos, and grammar, but being careful not to change the participants' intended meanings.
2 It is important to acknowledge that the gender binary that divides people into men and women and, relatedly, the use of the phrase 'opposite sex sexuality' in association to heterosexuality, have been problematized, particularly with wider recognition of non-normative and liminal gender identities.
3 Researchers have reported additional terms and phrases used by their participants to describe sexualities that are not exclusively heterosexual, including 'sexually bi with a lifestyle as straight' (Escoffier, 2003), 'bending a little' and 'straight but not narrow' (Cohen and Savin-Williams, 2010), and 'straight until the right guy comes along' (Vrangalova and Savin-Williams, 2012).
4 Contrary to what is often assumed, Kinsey et al. (1948: 639) did not think of the seven points in the scale as descriptors of discrete sexual orientation categories. In fact, they were opposed to the notion of sexual identity as a defining characteristic, emphasizing instead behavioural variation.
5 On the changing attachments to sexual identity labels among youths, see also McCormack et al. (2015) and Savin-Williams (2005).
6 In addition to the 100 initial interviews, we conducted follow-up interviews with 24 men, during which we asked them further details about their lives and experiences.
7 On the issues of heteronormativity and shifting masculinities, see Dean (2014), Anderson (2012), and McCormack and Anderson (2014).

References

Anderson E (2008) 'Being masculine is not about who you sleep with . . . ': Heterosexual athletes contesting masculinity and the one-time rule of homosexuality. *Sex Roles* 58: 104–115.
Anderson E (2011) The rise and fall of Western homohysteria. *Journal of Feminist Scholarship* 1: 80–94.
Anderson E (2012) Shifting masculinities in Anglo-American countries. *Masculinity and Social Change* 1(1): 40–60.
Anderson E and Adams A (2011) 'Aren't we all a little bisexual?': The recognition of bisexuality in an unlikely place. *Journal of Bisexuality* 11(1): 3–22.
Chauncey G (1994) *Gay New York: Gender, Urban Culture, and the Making of the Gay Male World.* New York: Basic Books.
Chauncey G (1993 [1985]) Christian brotherhood or sexual perversion? Homosexual identities and the construction of sexual boundaries in the World War I era. In: Melosh B (ed) *Gender and American History since 1890.* New York: Routledge, pp. 72–105.
Cohen KM and RC Savin-Williams (2010) Can men have sex with men and still call themselves straight? Available at: http://www.alternet.org/story/148876/can_men_have_sex_with_men_and_still_call_themselves_straight (accessed 28 February 2015).
Dean JJ (2014) *Straights: Heterosexuality in Post-Closeted Culture.* New York: New York University Press.
Escoffier J (2003) Gay-for-pay: Straight men and the making of gay pornography. *Qualitative Sociology* 26(4): 531–555.
Essig L (2000) Heteroflexibility: The latest semantic ploy to keep sexual options open really pisses me off. Available at: http://www.salon.com/2000/11/15/heteroflexibility (accessed 28 February 2015).
Ford CL, Whetten KD, Hall SA, Kaufman JS and Thrasher AD (2007) Black sexuality, social construction, and research targeting 'the down low' ('the DL'). *Annals of Epidemiology* 17: 209–216.

González MA (2007) Latinos on 'da down low': The limitations of sexual identity in public health. *Latino Studies* 5: 25–52.

Humphreys L (1970) *Tearoom Trade: Impersonal Sex in Public Places.* Chicago, IL: Aldine Publications.

Kelleher A and Smith E (2012) Growing support for gay and lesbian equality since 1990. *Journal of Homosexuality* 59(9): 1307–1326.

Kinsey AC, Pomeroy WB and Martin CE (1948) *Sexual Behaviour in the Human Male.* Philadelphia, PA: W.B. Saunders Company.

Kunzel R (2002) Situating sex: Prison sexual culture in the mid-twentieth-century United States. *GLQ: A Journal of Lesbian and Gay Studies* 8: 253–270.

Malebranche D (2008) Bisexually active black men in the United States and HIV: Acknowledging more than the 'down low'. *Archives of Sexual Behaviour* 37: 810–816.

McCormack M and Anderson E (2014) The influence of declining homophobia on men's gender in the United States: An argument for the study of homohysteria. *Sex Roles* 71: 109–120.

McCormack M, Wignall L and Anderson E (2015) Identities and identifications: Changes in metropolitan bisexual men's attitudes and experiences. *Journal of Homosexuality* 15(1): 3–20.

Miles MB and Huberman AM (1994) *Qualitative Data Analysis: An Expanded Sourcebook.* Thousand Oaks, CA: Sage.

Phillips L (2005) Deconstructing 'down low' discourse: The politics of sexuality, gender, race, AIDS, and anxiety. *Journal of African American Studies* 9(2): 3–15.

Reback CJ and Larkins S (2010) Maintaining a heterosexual identity: Sexual meanings among a sample of heterosexually identified men who have sex with men. *Archives of Sexual Behaviour* 39: 766–773.

Ross MW, Månsson S-A, Daneback C and Tikkanen R (2005) Characteristics of men who have sex with men on the internet but identify as heterosexual, compared with heterosexually identified men who have sex with women. *Cyberpsychology & Behaviour* 8(2): 131–139.

Savin-Williams RC (2005) *The New Gay Teenager.* Cambridge, MA: Harvard University Press.

Savin-Williams RC and Vrangalova Z (2013) Mostly heterosexual as a distinct sexual orientation group: A systematic review of the empirical evidence. *Developmental Review* 33: 58–88.

Savin-Williams RC, Joyner K and Rieger G (2012) Prevalence and stability of self-reported sexual orientation identity during young adulthood. *Archives of Sexual Behaviour* 41: 103–110.

Thompson EM and Morgan EM (2008) 'Mostly straight' young women: Variations in sexual behaviour and identity development. *Developmental Psychology* 44(1): 15–21.

Vrangalova Z and Savin-Williams RC (2012) Mostly heterosexual and mostly gay/lesbian: Evidence for new sexual orientation identities. *Archives of Sexual Behaviour* 41: 85–101.

Ward J (2008) Dude-sex: White masculinities and 'authentic' heterosexuality among dudes who have sex with dudes. *Sexualities* 11(4): 414–434.

Ward J (2015) *Not Gay: Sex between Straight White Men.* New York: New York University Press.

26

No homo*

Joshua R. Brown

Parents, instructors, and anyone else in relatively constant contact with young adults and children can easily attest to the prevalence of "that's so gay," meaning "that's so stupid."[1] However, I was struck in the fall semester of 2008 by a new phrase, at least to my ears. A male student, speaking loudly with his neighboring classmate before the start of class, was making plans to study with him for the upcoming exam: "Are we meeting up tonight? No homo." The casual laugh and grin from his interlocutor and the muffled giggling from other classmates piqued my interest. It seemed that they were familiar with, although not necessarily surprised by, what sounded to me like derogatory homophobic slang. I did some investigating and found instances of this term in a variety of sources:

(1) How do u whistle with your fingers? I will attempt all methods (no homo). . . . (Celtic (imflashy.com, 2008)
(2) Hey man, pass the nuts. No homo. (Anonymous, 2003)
(3) I imagine that if Belle and Sebastian front man Stuart Murdoch and I ever met we'd instantly become soul mates and while away lazy Sundays prancing through meadows, picking wildflowers, reciting poetry to each other, and sharing intimate secrets under the moonlight. But not in a gay way. No homo. (Rabin, 2009, p. 216)
(4) "Shut up, Devon, or I'll give you tights to wear for the fashion show," Annarese exclaimed. "No homo," he said, shaking his head no. We all laughed. Devon was the comedian in our club. (Inside, 2007, p. 306)

Aside from the above examples, further investigation showed that "no homo" has origins in a much different venue. The phrase arose in the 1990s as a discourse interjection in the hip-hop

* I am indebted to the valuable and insightful comments and suggestions provided by three anonymous reviewers, as well as Atia Sattar and Rebecca Zajdowicz on earlier drafts. All errors that remain are my own.

music scene, predominately in lyrics by members of The Diplomats, Juelz Santana, and Cam'ron (Weiner, 2009). These artists have continued to include the phrase in recent lyrics:

(5) I'm lo-lo from the block again/Po-po and the cops again,/No homo but they cocking them. (Hanson, Giles, & James 2003)
(6) See the problem is I ain't goin nowhere/Can shoot at me, can stab at me/Take your best shot (this is the remix)/Suck a dick no homo/DipSet, remix, let's go! (Cam'ron, 2005)

Additionally, it is used by other hip-hop artists including Jay-Z (2009) and Lil Wayne (2007):

(7) It's crazy how you can go from being Joe Blow/To everybody on your dick, no homo.
(8) Listen ma, I don't know karate, but after the brain, I kick you out,/You niggas suck like Tony Romo, no homo,

The meaning of "no homo" is relatively clear from these eight examples. In both volumes of the *Urban Dictionary*, it is defined as a "phrase used after one inadvertently says something gay. His ass is mine. No homo" (Peckham, 2007, p. 176). As discourse interjection, "no homo" functions to negate a supposed misconception or misconstrued reading of a previous utterance or it may preface such an utterance (as in example 5 above). In saying something that the speaker might think will be understood as "homosexual," the added "no homo" disqualifies such a misunderstanding for the audience. In the anecdotal student exchange example, the male speaker chose to disassociate himself from an implied (at least in his mind) sexual encounter that evening with his male interlocutor. Appending "no homo," he qualified his question as purely platonic.

I argue that "no homo" serves as a defense to an interlocutor's presumed attack on one's masculinity. By using "no homo," one is preempting the verbal strike. Popular discussions on "no homo" call for its censorship and claim it is blatant homophobia. I maintain here that these counts egregiously overlook the greater implications that such a term has.

The function of "no homo" in discourse seems to be equivalent to that of an earlier term, "pause," which achieved the same result. In his 2007 Madison Square Garden Network interview, director Spike Lee comments on the NBA draft:

(7) Spike Lee: I like [Dan] Dick[au].
Gus Johnson: Pause (dreparker, 2007)

Here, Gus Johnson's use of "pause" is intended most likely for comedic effect on the double entendre spoken by Spike Lee. By adding the word "pause," the interlocutor hopes to achieve a moment of reflection, a pausing, in the discourse to note the seemingly covert sexual innuendo. For Johnson, reflection is required immediately after a man says: "I like Dick." In this example, it is the interlocutor who suggests the sexual connotation of the utterance, similar to "no homo" as used above in example 4.

I assume that "no homo" derives from larger phrases like "I ain't 'no homo,' I'm 'no homo,' I'm not 'no homo,'" and others, potentially mirrored on negated nominal discourse interjections like "no lie," "no joke," "no kidding," and "no way." Comparatively, "no homo" achieves much the same discourse function as these, negating a supposed misconception or misconstrued reading of a previous utterance. Given the frequency of the phrase, it has become ritualized as a sort of incantation, protecting the speaker from interpretations of their own words. Much like the superstitious "knock on wood," which arises when the speaker believes that they have jinxed their luck with their words, the effect of the impending bad luck is reversed. Because of consonant ritualized incantations for linguistic protection, the absorption of "no homo" into colloquial American English is relatively easy. Phonetically, it has both assonance and staccato-like syllabic patterning; "no homo" is, thus, unobtrusive.

Although "no homo" began with African-American male musicians in The Diplomats, the diversity of users has grown considerably. Nathan Rabin, who uses the term in his memoirs (example 3, above), is a 33-year-old White male. Parodies of the term on youtube.com by two younger White males for King Melvin Productions also exist. These parodies view "no homo" as a hyperbolic saving grace:

(8) Maybe my D got a little too tight, cuz I touched his ass/And that aint right He dropped the ball, looked at me and said, "Whoa Bro!"/It's all good man, I called 'No Homo.' (KingMelvinProductions, 2009)

The absurdity of the parody lies in the fact that the two men in the video are convinced that "no homo" magically "cures" their sexual transgressions. Women can and do use "no homo," although the instances are markedly less in frequency. In fact, several Internet forums openly ask if women can use the phrase. Female commentators claim that they use the phrase with their female friends in complimenting appearance, especially:

(9) i am a gurl so like ok i be like nicki minaj is sexy.i say no homo so ppl wont b/confused of mhy sexuality. (Nikki, 2010)

And yet, others, in this instance someone who identifies as male on the same Internet forum, disagree:

(10) i think girls dat say no homo are mad corny and dat shyt is annoying when they/say it. (Guest5309, 2010)

Interestingly enough, Nikki in example 9 writes about female hip-hop artist Nicki Minaj (2010), who used "no homo" in her song "Baddest Bitch":

(11) And if he want some pussy that's a no-no/I only fuck with bad bitches no homo/Flow sicker than LL.

From its origins, "no homo" cuts across gender and racial boundaries, but its use among members of the lesbian, gay, transgender, and queer (LGBTQ) community is more nebulous. Although it certainly is not improbable that a gay man might use "no homo," its function in discourse must be entirely different if intended for something other than ironic effect. I could imagine a gay man using "no homo" when complimenting a straight man on his appearance, for example—distancing the compliment from a sexual advance, when a gay man feels threatened or seeks to protect himself from a misunderstanding. Of course belying this use is the assumption that gay men only want to engage in sexual activity with any other man with heightened awareness of homosocial tensions.

Although "no homo" remains intact morphologically, semantically, and pragmatically, its scope has increased. In returning to the *Urban Dictionary*'s (Peckham, 2007) definition, I ask: What is "inadvertently gay"? Obviously, an utterance needs some negotiation of meaning either between the interlocutors or in the mind of the sole speaker. Utterances that are seen to be transgressions of sexuality, gender, or even homosociality on the part of the speaker or audience will vary across time, space, and context. As such, "no homo" can represent a large spectrum of uses. In several online parodies and remarks, the term is used rhetorically or for an intended comedic effect. In these instances, "no homo" has begun to lose its homosexual context. Returning to the hip-hop lyrics of Cam'ron's (2009), the following line is in his song "Curve":

(11) and I chop, blo-blo, no homo.

This seems to be a simple rhyming scheme, despite the presence of "blo-blo," which could potentially be interpreted as fellatio. On the surface, however, there seems to be nothing either covertly or overtly homosexual about it. Even if "blo" is interpreted as fellatio, the coparticipant is not mentioned, and we are left to guess at their gendered identity. Similar instances exist with little to no homosexual message, as in this line from "Weezy Ambitions" by DJ Drama and Lil Wayne (2006):

(12) got money out the ass no homo.

Perhaps by simply mentioning a man's posterior, the rapper must include a qualifier of non-homosexuality. By extension, it is possible that anal intercourse is an automatic association that one makes when a man mentions his "ass." Lil Wayne's (2008) song "Lollipop" starts out with no homo, even though the subsequent lines address a male-female interaction:

(13) Uh huh, no homo./She said "he so sweet, make me wanna lick the wrapper"/So I let her lick the wrapper.

Additionally, Cam'ron's (2009) album *Crime Pays* contained a song "Silky (No homo)," though the lyrics do not contain the phrase and the title does not necessarily hint at its use. These uses seem restricted only to hip-hop music lyrics, but they reflect a morphing of the term's scope within its original context. Griffin (2007) writing for the *Daily Princetonian* notes that he has heard both: "I just finished that hot dog. No homo" and "Pass me the mayonnaise. No homo." These examples implicate that the term may have taken on a simple jocular meaning, devoid of its sexual connotations. The adoption of the term outside of hip-hop also reflects an interesting, although not necessarily unexpected, shift in the scope of the phrase. Its integration into mainstream discourse and its continued unmarked use in hip-hop invoke larger ideas of accepted sexual boundaries and, of course, gender boundaries.

Critics protest that at the core of the term "no homo" is a sense of homosexual panic. Dr. Marc Lamont Hill of Fox News called the phrase a "slur" ("Roundup," 2009). Similarly, Andrew Matson (2009) of *The Seattle Times* refers to the use of "no homo" in hip-hop lyrics to show its "unhealthy relationship with homosexuality, a relationship based in fear." Nick Catucci (2009) of *New York Magazine* maintains that "no homo is just a more evolved way of calling someone a 'faggot.' " In the fall of 2009, the Black Caucus of Penn State University (2009) hosted a discussion entitled "No Homo: Homophobia in the Community," where members of both the Black Caucus and the LGBT community could comment. These sentiments express a marked reversal of former popular opinion about hip-hop lyrics. Dyson (1996, p. 184) formerly critiqued the mainstream media for overshadowing the problem of homophobia in hip-hop language with greater concern over lyrics about violence. He maintained that such subjugation, the focus on violence over homophobia, insists on the "inferiority" of gays and lesbians in mainstream society.

It seems, though, more than a decade after Dyson's remarks, that mainstream op-eds are noticing homophobic language in lyrics. With an increase in LGBT sympathies comes an increased sensitivity to disparaging remarks in popular culture.

However, opposite Hill ("Roundup," 2009), Matson (2009), and Catucci (2009), stands Jonah Weiner (2009) of *Slate Magazine*, who turns the discussion away from homophobia: "No homo tweaks this dynamic because it allows, implicitly, that rap is a place where gayness can in fact be expressed by the guy on the mic, not just scorned in others." He goes on to admit that the most "homoerotic MCs in rap" [Cam'ron and the Diplomats] use the term most frequently and claims that they are "smuggling in a fuller, less hamstrung notion of masculinity" (Weiner, 2009). For Weiner, the context and the identities of these musicians stand at such an obvious disconnect with homophobia that the phrase challenges the idea of masculinity within the hip-hop music scene. For him, the existence of the phrase is itself admittance that homosexuality is a topic that can be expressed frankly within hip-hop culture. This is an interesting spin on the trend to denounce "no homo". However, I am not content with these critiques.

I believe and hope to explain in the remainder of this article that mention of "no homo" in hip-hop creates a consciousness of language and action that was formerly missing in discussions. By simply casting off "no homo" as part of rampant homophobia in hip-hop, as critics do, I believe that we overlook the intricate negotiation of masculinity in hip-hop and fail to realize the beneficial analyses that "no homo" may offer. Further, by focusing solely on its function in hip-hop, we ignore the increased frequency of the term beyond those venues. While Weiner points out the disconnect between the term and rappers, I believe that we can take his assertions further. Forthcoming, I hope to discuss the possible functions of the phrase in its speech community of origin, hip-hop music culture, and then explore its existence beyond that speech community.

Although we can speculate the viability of "no homo" within youth parlance and beyond, we would be remiss to exclude a discussion of the macrosociological undercurrents present in the invocation of the term. As mentioned above, "no homo" originated in hip-hop music lyrics of the 1990s. Several studies of the hip-hop lexicon exist (Major, 1994; Smitherman, 1997, 1998), and it is beyond the scope of this article to offer a review of the sociolinguistics of hip-hop. One aspect is clear from the growing bed of research on hip-hop language, namely, that language is central to expressions and negotiations of hip-hop identity. Alim (2009) comments specifically on the language of musical aspects of hip-hop:

> Rappin, one aspect of hip hop culture, consists of the aesthetic placement of verbal rhymes over musical beats, and it is this element that has predominated in hip hop cultural activity in recent years. Thus, language is perhaps the most useful means with which to read the various cultural activities of the Hip Hop Nation.
>
> *(p. 272)*

Language is one of a number of cultural identifiers used by groups and individuals to identify themselves or be identified as members of a particular speech community, sociocultural group, or movement. It should come as no surprise, then, that one's sexual identity and gender identity may be expressed through language (and silence) to both identify oneself with the group and also to disassociate oneself from other groups or even other members within the ingroup. This ability of language is perhaps nowhere more viable than in hip-hop, where verbal dexterity is the cornerstone of cultural tradition, as the work of sociolinguists Remes (1991) and Smitherman (1997) pointedly exhibit what Alim (2009) calls the "creativity, ingenuity, and verbal virtuosity of Africans in America" (p. 273). This verbal dexterity has created characteristics such as bustin' and signifyin', which attack the interlocutor with words and exploit cultural awareness, intertexuality, and performance. Words become piercing and exacting instruments in a verbal duel; these instruments best exemplify the fascinating ability of humans to play with their language. A prolific hip-hop blogger Jay Smooth (2008) has compiled a "Beginner's Guide to No homo" video, where he discusses its origins and uses, noting particularly the verbal dexterity aspect of the phrase.

By couching hip-hop language in terms of verbal dexterity, it becomes readily apparent what the function of "no homo" was in its hip-hop origins. "No homo" is not necessarily addressing homosexuality, but creating a verbal defensive in the musical battlefield that is wrought with signifyin' and bustin'. They realize that a lyric, which is "inadvertently gay," is fodder for another's verbal attack on their masculinity within hip-hop culture. In an attempt to divert their own demasculinization, musicians presuppose those attacks at their masculinity.

This use of "no homo" is similar to findings on the term "fag" in high schools by Pascoe (2007). "Fag" is used by heterosexual men in a variety of contexts and at different times. It is a fluid description of one's identity from others—calling another man a fag connotes feminine actions in speech and manner as well as homosexual actions in sexual intercourse. Both compromise the individual's expressions of masculinity. The problem is not necessarily that you commit a sexual transgression, but that you have committed a gender transgression. The sexuality of the musicians is not what is at stake; everyone is aware of their sexuality. The greater attack is at their gendered identity, which is often a theme in hip-hop language. Even female rappers use similar phrases to demasculinate male rappers in the male-dominated music scene (cf. Haugen, 2003; Diner 2006; Morgan, 2005). Rose (1994) importantly notes the occurrence of "fruity" in female hip-hop lyrics in reference to male rappers as a way of attacking their masculinity. In so doing, the masculinity of hip-hop is challenged. And, of course, from example 11 above, we know that at least one female rapper uses "no homo" in her lyrics.

I echo the assertions of Whitehead and Barrett (2001) that men "do" masculinity rather than possess it intrinsically, and, moreover, that this doing of masculinity is achieved through self-regulation. As such, the performance of gender is through negotiation of individual context. For those in hip-hop who use "no homo," and for the many outside of hip-hop who have adopted it, the phrase functions successfully as a self-regulating method for the continued construction of their masculinity. The construction of heterosexuality often begins with the bifurcation of gender (Kiesling, 2001, 2002). In other words, the power struggle in idealized expressions of masculinity is for one to be dominant and subjugate the "feminine," "gay," or "non-masculine." The linguistic play here is one of maintaining dominance in a situation and not allowing oneself to be subordinated via a homosexual tendency. Moreover, the idea, particularly in sociology, that attacks on homosexuals are often fueled by the equation of male homosexuality with femininity (Connell, 2001; Messner, 2001) indicates that any "homosexually" couched utterance is, thus, seen as not masculine enough.

As such, uttering "no homo" can be viewed as regulating oneself to maintain social dominance, to remain "masculine," and to mask any alleged gender transgressions. In light of this, "no homo" came to life simply as a thread in hip-hop language to preserve masculinity. Dyson (2001) has termed this phenomenon "femiphobia":

> Femiphobia has become a crucial aspect of the culture of signification in rap that influences the lyrics of hip-hop artists, measure authentic rap—and hence, male—identity, specifies a pervasive machismo, and forges masculine bonds within the culture.
>
> *(p. 182)*

For Dyson, the "culture of signification" breeds these demeaning verbal cues. Yet, this "culture of signification" importantly draws from larger societal norms and expectations. This is certainly not a hip-hop problem, nor do I suggest that hip-hop is somehow more homophobic than the rest of American culture. At play here is identity construction in discourse via societal legitimization. In short, a heterosexual man cannot be intimate with or complimentary to another man without societal intervention—an intervention that would potentially posit both as homosexual. I note, however, that this is not just something that heterosexuals do: Gays and lesbians also "self-protect" themselves linguistically (Liang, 1999) with, for example, gender ambiguous pronouns and terms like "the one" and "anyone" when talking about their partners with heterosexual interlocutors. Ironically, those identifying as homosexual use linguistic conventions for reasons similar to those used by straight-identifying men and women, who use them to protect themselves from a gay identity.

For me, then, a much more fruitful discussion about "no homo" includes the struggles of hip-hop music in producing masculinity. I have already addressed those struggles within hip-hop and among rappers in negotiating their identity through verbal dexterity. Word duels are an excellent way of constructing rapper identity. However, external struggles must also be addressed for a more holistic approach to understanding the existence of "no homo." Rose (1994) recounts the duality of hip-hop:

> On the one hand, music and cultural critics praise rap's role as an educational tool, point out that [B]lack women rappers are rare examples of aggressive pro-women lyricists in popular music, and defend rap's ghetto stories as real-life reflections that should draw attention to the burning problems of racism and economic oppression, rather than to questions of obscenity. On the other hand, new media attention on rap seems fixated on instances of violence at rap concerts, rap producers' illegal use of musical samples, gangsta raps' lurid fantasies of cop killing and female dismemberment, and [B]lack nationalist rappers' suggestions that [W]hite people are the devil's disciples.
>
> *(p. 1)*

As a society, we are in a constant struggle with hip-hop. The good, the bad, and everything between and beyond are perhaps the reasons that we scratch our heads in thinking about terms like "no homo." Critics are appalled that such a phrase originated in hip-hop music, but, at the same time, they are not surprised, given its homophobic and misogynistic lyrics. The term may have been created by African-American rappers into the hip-hop scene, which struggles with and inevitably often subjugates femininity (Adams & Fuller, 2006; Armstrong, 2001), but renouncing it outright overlooks the possibility of future discussions.[3] I resoundingly echo sentiments of Perry (2004):

> I argue that masculinity in hip hop reflects the desire to assert [B]lack male subjectivity, and that it sometimes does so at the expense of [B]lack female subjectivity and by subjugating women's bodies, while at other times it simply reveals the complexity of [B]lack male identity.
>
> *(p. 118)*

I believe that the same is true for "no homo." While the speakers subjugate homosexual and feminine identity, we are nonetheless confronted with their own struggles of identity expression. I remain steadfast in the belief that simply damning these lyrics for their homophobia, homosexual panic, or misogyny escapes a genuine discussion of other aspects contained therein. A more thorough discussion of these lyrics (and by extension the proliferation of "no homo" into the mainstream) should offer what Ogbar (1999, p.181) calls a "more substantive criticism of the social, economic, and political apparatus that create the pathology described by rappers." The pronounced occurrence of homosexual distancing in the hip-hop lexicon speaks to the struggles for gay African Americans within their ingroup. They have been described as having a "double burden" (Harris, 2003), being both gay and Black, caught between the pressures of two "intersecting oppressions" (Collins, 2001). As such, femininity for some is seen as strengthening societal defeat (Collins, 2004; Lemelle & Battle, 2004), perhaps even aligning oneself with Whiteness.[2] This problematic social frame, compounded with weak programs geared toward African-American gays and lesbians, have been blamed for the prevalence of AIDS and HIV in those communities, surpassing both Whites and heterosexuals (Lemelle 2004). The stakes are very high for claiming membership in a Black gay and lesbian community. Hip-hop exposes Black male subjectivity at the expense of female and homosexual subjectivity. At the same time, however, it exposes Black male identity. With any identity, aspects are both negative and positive. Dyson (1996) explains frankly:

> But [B]lack culture is too broad and intricate—its artistic manifestations too unpredictable and challenging—for us to be *obsessed* with how [W]hite folk view our culture through the lens of our art. And [B]lack life is too differentiated by class, sexual identity, gender, region, and nationality to fixate on "negative" or "positive" representations of [B]lack culture. Black culture is good and bad, uplifting and depressing, edifying and stifling. All of these features should be represented in our art, should find resonant voicing in the diverse tongues of [B]lack cultural expressions.
>
> *(p. 181)*

Why should Black culture and hip-hop culture be held to a higher moral code? Art has both positive and negative sides, and it is both of those aspects which Rose explained in unpacking the duality of the performance in society: attention to racism and economic oppression and fixations on violence. Often times, as Dyson (1996) recalls, hip-hop, in embracing both the positive and negative parts of that culture, points out the major (often unsaid) contentions in society. Would it still not be socially unacceptable to have sexual advances made by a homosexual man to a straight man? Perhaps hip-hop is underscoring the idea that although diversity in sexuality is embraced, the "sexual" aspects of that sexuality are still uncomfortable for most to deal with.

The usefulness of "no homo" in dissecting these social constructs surrounding word usage cannot be ignored, nor treated lightly. Yes, we can view "no homo" as simply reinforcing socio-historical and sociopolitical notions of power, dominance, and "normative" gendered identities. Yet, perhaps its continued discussion, in light of other gendering terms in both hip-hop discourse and elsewhere, will bring to the fore those areas of contention for the individual which threaten one's identity in society. Perhaps then we can engage theories on more agentive notions of identity negotiation in discourse, as well as engage clearer perceptions on discourse socialization into belonging to a particular gendered identity. I believe that rather than censoring lyrics and censuring musicians, perhaps we need to focus on the consciousness that such a term has brought. Perry (2004) explains the reasoning for such insentivities:

> Social marginalization often leads to an insensitivity to the concerns of other groups and even other members of one's own group. Understanding this, our witness of [B]lack violence and misogyny should provoke analysis and alarm more than offense.
>
> *(p. 125)*

Beyond hip-hop, such insensitivity is rampant. My work on chat room expressions of sexual identity among gay men has found similar insensitivities and marginalizations within the *gay community* regarding gender transgressions. Although in an interview with CNN, Joe Solomonese, president of the Human Rights Campaign, deplored the use of "fag" and declared that "there is no question that [the word *fag*] is just as offensive to members of the gay and lesbian community as the n-word is," these data show otherwise (gayrightswatch, 2007). The following excerpts from online chat data (Brown, 2008) show how men identifying as gay use the term "fag" as a marginalizing linguistic tool within their own community:

(13) John: i call gays fags all the time
Dave: yeah its ok
John: i sometime call myself a fag
Ron: yeah he has a lot to learn
Charles: omg fag where lol
Ty: but the n wordis worse than fag.

(14) Gus: isnt it usually the ones whom say that theyre real butch
Greg: come on with the muscle shirts on and there faggy ass voice
Ray: yes
Tim: lol
Greg: And they insist there masculine
Gus: [shrug]
Tim: haha . . . well i've seen those too
Gus: i just smile and nod
Tim: i just bust out laughing.

From these two excerpts it appears that gay men have "femiphobia" as well. A "faggy ass voice" is enough to prompt ridicule from these gay-identifying men. In so doing, they sacrifice other identities to place masculine subjectivity at the forefront of the desired. Calling "no homo" homophobic is far too facile. Placing the blame on hip-hop musicians not only ignores the many uses of the term beyond their lyrics, but also ignores the prevalence of similar marginalization techniques within other minority communities of practice.

Although terms like "fag" and "gay" are rampant in American adolescent and young adult circles as terms of derision toward effeminacy or non-masculinity, the purpose of each term is one of positioning another as an "other" and, thereby, subordinating the other. "No homo" is different. "No homo" disassociates; in effect, it rejects that subordination head on and places the speaker outside of that community. "No homo" achieves agency. It is not an attack from another, like one boy calling another boy a "fag." With "no homo," the speaker determines his expression of masculinity. Moreover, "no homo" comes close to sexual innuendo and has the added option of being interpreted as desire. One reviewer of this article cast this in light of a similar interaction between a man and a woman, where the man would say: "Are we meeting up tonight? And not for sex." The inclusion of "and not for sex" functions similarly to "no homo," but here we can see just how close "no homo" comes to sexual desire.

We cannot ignore that hip-hop is performed and consumed not only by Black men, but outside of the Black culture as well. After all, Kitwana (2005) has written an entire manuscript on the White consumption of hip-hop, and many of the "no homo" examples in this article were composed by Whites. Although the origin of the term "no homo" most definitely arose from Black, male hip-hop musicians, its scope and diversity of users has increased and broadened. Given the prevalence and acceptance of hip-hop lexical items like "dope" to mean cool, "whack" for stupid, and "off the chain," for really great (Cutler, 2007, p. 524), we cannot discount the viable future of "no homo" in American English. Its function is to provide linguistic protection from sociosexual and gender transgressions. With an increase in use beyond Black male rappers to White men and women, the phrase comments on societal norms. It forces out into the open what people believe are sexual connotations and, I believe, presents an important area of further scrutiny. We have a linguistic marker in discourse to systematically describe the perceptions of gender transgressions. "No homo" is a tool to examine discourse to see exactly what people think is too intimate, too homosocial. If nothing else, hip-hop musicians have brought these issues to consciousness. While "no homo" may be offensive, its use as an analytic tool is undisputable. What is "inadvertently gay"? What is "inadvertently non-masculine"? What is "inadvertently non-normative"? From it, we can learn what triggers homophobia and femiphobia, and better understand the struggles of identity within marginalized communities.

Notes

1 "That's so gay" and other homophobic terms in middle and high schools are reviewed in Wessler and DeAndrade (2006).
2 Both Bucholtz (1999) and Fordham and Ogbu (1986) relate sounding White (i.e., the use of standard speech) with homosexuality.
3 Some authors encourage the use of hip-hop songs particularly in the classroom to show what feminism is; cf. Springer (2002) and Stovall (2006).

References

Adams, T. M., & Fuller, D. B. (2006). The words have changed but the ideology remains the same: Misogynistic lyrics in rap music. *Journal of Black Studies*, *36*(6), 938–957.
Alim, H. A. (2009). Hip hop nation language. In A. Duranti (Ed.), *Linguistic anthropology: A reader, 2nd ed* (pp. 272–289). Malden, MA: Wiley-Blackwell.
Anonymous. (2003, October 21). Re: No homo. [Online forum comment]. Retrieved from http://www.urbandictionary.com/define.php?term=no%20homo
Armstrong, E. G. (2001). Gangsta misogyny: A content analysis of the portrayals of violence against women in rap music 1987–1993. *Journal of Criminal Justice and Popular Culture*, *8*(2), 96–126.
Black Caucus of Penn State University. (2009). "No homo": *Homophobia in the community*. [Poster]. University Park, PA: The Pennsylvania State University.
Brown, J. R. (2008). *Negotiation of sexual identity in gay men's discourse*. Unpublished manuscript.
Bucholtz, M. (1999). "You da man": Narrating the racial other in the linguistic production of White masculinity. *Journal of Sociolinguistics*, *3*(4), 443–460.
Cam'ron. (2005). Get'em daddy. On *Killa season* [CD]. New York, NY: Diplomat Records.
Cam'ron. (2009). Curve. On *Crime pays* [CD]. New York, NY: Diplomat Records.
Cam'ron. (2009). Silky (no homo). On *Crime pays* [CD]. New York, NY: Diplomat Records.
Catucci, N. (2009, August 7). "No homo": Cause for hope in hip-hop? Retrieved from http://nymag.com/daily/entertainment/2009/08/no_homo_cause_for_hope_in_hip.html
Celtic (imflashy.com. (2008). How do u whistle with your fingers? I will attempt all methods (no homo) and the one that works wins? Retrieved from http://answers.yahoo.com/question/index;_ylt=ApPG8.kmRphCllNqqYaoojYjzKIX;_ylv=3?qid=20080523185154AAC4RuB
Collins, P. H. (2001). *Black feminist thought: Knowledge, consciousness and the politics of empowerment*. New York, NY: Routledge.
Collins, P. H. (2004). *Black sexual politics: African Americans, gender, and the new racism*. New York, NY: Routledge.
Connell, R. W. (2001). The social organization of masculinity. In S. M. Whitehead & F. J. Barrett (eds.), *The Masculinities Reader* (pp. 30–50). Malden, MA: Blackwell.
Cutler, C. (2007). Hip-hop language in sociolinguistics and beyond. *Language and Linguistics Compass*, *1*(5), 519–538.
Diner, R. (2006). 'The other White meat': Princess superstar, irony, sexuality, and Whiteness in hip hop. *Canadian Review of American Studies*, *36*, 195–209.
DJ Drama, & Lil Wayne. (2006). Weezy ambitionz. On *Dedication 2* [Download]. Phoenix AZ: 101 Distribution.
dreparker. (2007, July 16). pause (spike lee). Retrieved from http://www.youtube.com/watch?v=zBLrSz0oNvs

Dyson, M. E. (1996). *Between God and gangsta rap: Bearing witness to Black culture.* New York, NY: Oxford University Press.

Dyson, M. E. (2001). *Holler if you hear me: Searching for Tupac Shakur.* New York, NY: Basic Civitas Books.

Fordham, S., & Ogbu, J. U. (1986). Black students' school success: Coping with the "burden of acting White." *The Urban Review, 18*(3), 176–206. Retrieved from http://www.dailyprincetonian.com/2007/11/16/19386/

gayrightswatch. (2007, January 30). *Joe Solomonese from HRC on the word "faggot."* Retrieved from http://www.youtube.com/watch?v=IA7JagvzmPI

Griffin, W. (2007, November 16). Nice article, no homo. *The Daily Princetonian.*

Guest5309. (2010). Re: Can girls say No homo? [Online forum comment]. Retrieved from http://www.maybenow.com/Can-girls-say-No-Homo-q8570664

Hanson, E., Giles, C., & James, L. (2003). Dipset (Santana's Town) [Recorded by Juelz Santana featuring Cam'ron.] On *From me to u* [Download]. Phoenix, AZ: Diplomat Records.

Harris, W. G. (2003). African American homosexual males on predominately White college and university campuses. *Journal of African American Studies*, 7(1), 47–56.

Haugen, J. D. (2003). "Unladylike divas": Language, gender, and female gangsta rappers. *Popular Music and Society*, *26*, 429–444.

Inside, I. (2007). *Being one: No one is like no other. High school the next frontier.* Morrisville, NC: Lulu Press.

Jay Smooth. (2008, August 16). A beginner's guide to no homo. Retrieved from http://www.illdoctrine.com/2008/08/a_beginners_guide_to_no_homo.html

Jay-Z. (2009). Run this town. On *The Blueprint 3* [Download]. New York, NY: Roc Nation.

Kiesling, S. F. (2001). "Now I gotta watch what I say": Shifting constructions of masculinity in discourse. *Journal of Linguistic Anthropology*, *11*(2), 250–273.

Kiesling, S. F. (2002). Playing the straight man: Displaying and maintaining male heterosexuality in discourse. In K. Campbell-Kibler, R. J. Podesva, S. J. Roberts, & A. Wong (Eds.), *Language and sexuality: Contesting meaning in theory and practice* (pp. 249–266). Stanford, CA: CSLI.

KingMelvinProduction. (2009, April 13). The "no homo" song. Retrieved from http://www.youtube.com/watch?v=CfrqjYxzxFQ

Kitwana, B. (2005). *Why White kids love hip hop: wankstas, wiggers, wannabes, and the reality of race in America.* New York, NY: Basic Civitas Books.

Lemell, A. J., Jr. (2004). African American attitudes toward gay males: Faith based initiatives and implications for HIV/AIDS services. *Journal of African American Studies*, 7(4), 59–74.

Lemelle, A. J., Jr., & Battle, J. (2004). Black masculinity matters in attitudes towards gay males. *Journal of Homosexuality*, *47*(1), 39–51.

Liang, A. C. (1999). Conversationally implicating gay and lesbian identity. In M. Bucholtz, A.C. Liang, & L. A. Sutton (Eds.), *Reinventing identities: The gendered self in discourse* (pp. 293–310). New York, NY: Oxford University Press.

Lil Wayne. (2007). Back on my grizzy. On *Da drought 3* [Download]. New Orleans, LA: Young Money.

Lil Wayne. (2008). Lollipop. On *The Carter III* [Download]. New Orleans, LA: Cash Money Records.

Major, C. (1994). *Juba to jive: A dictionary of African-American slang.* New York, NY: Penguin.

Matson, A. (2009, July 27). The continuing saga of KUBE morning host Eddie Francis and American English's current homophobic lexicography. Retrieved from http://seattletimes.nwsource.com/html/matsononmusic/2009546491_the_continuing_saga_of_kube_mo.html

Minaj, N. (2010). Baddest bitch. On *It's Barbie bitch* [Download]. Phoenix, AZ: 101 Distribution.

Messner, M. A. (2001). Friendship, intimacy, and sexuality. In S. M. Whitehead and F. J. Barrett (eds.), *The masculinities reader* (pp. 253–265). Malden, MA: Blackwell.

Morgan, M. (2005). Hip-hop women shredding the veil: Race and class in popular feminist identity. *The South Atlantic Quarterly*, *104*, 425–444.

Nikki. (2010, October 26). Can girls say No homo? [Online forum comment]. Retrieved from http://www.maybenow.com/Can-girls-say-No-Homo-q8570664

Ogbar, J. O. G. (1999). Slouching toward Bork: The culture wars of self-criticism in hip-hop music. *Journal of Black Studies*, *30*(2), 164–183.

Pascoe, C. J. (2007). *Dude, you're a fag: Masculinity and sexuality in high school.* Berkeley: University of California Press.

Peckham, A. (2007). *Mo' urban dictionary: Ridonkulous street slang defined.* Kansas City, MO: Andrews McMeel.

Perry, I. (2004). *Prophets of the hood: Politics and poetics in hip hop.* Durham, NC: Duke University Press.

Rabin, N. (2009). *The big rewind: A memoir brought to you by pop culture.* New York, NY: Scribner.

Remes, P. (1991). Rapping: A sociolinguistic study of oral tradition in Black urban communities in the United States. *Journal of the Anthropological Society of Oxford, 22*(2), 129–149.

Rose, T. (1994). *Black noise: Rap music and Black culture in contemporary America.* Hanover, NH: Wesleyan University Press.

Roundup: Kiss-ins spread, "no homo" must go. (2009, August 1). Retrieved from http://www.advocate.com/News/Daily_News/2009/07/21/Roundup__Kiss-ins_Spread,%C2%A0_No_Homo__Must_Go/

Smitherman, G. (1997). The chain remain the same: Communicative practices in the hip hop nation. *Journal of Black Studies, 28*, 3–25.

Smitherman, G. (1998). Word from the hood: The lexicon of African-American vernacular English. In S. Mufwene, J. Rickford, G. Bailey, & J. Baugh (Eds.), *African American English: Structure, history, and use* (pp. 203–225). New York, NY: Routledge.

Springer, K. (2002). Third wave Black feminism? *Signs: Journal of Women in Culture and Society, 27*(4), 1059–1082.

Stovall, D. (2006). We can relate: Hip hop culture, critical pedagogy, and the secondary classroom. *Urban Education, 41*(6), 585–602.

Weiner, J. (2009, August 6). Does this purple mink make me look gay?: The rise of "no homo" and the changing face of hip-hop homophobia. Retrieved from http://www.slate.com/id/2224348/

Wessler, S. L., & DeAndrade, L. L. (2006). Slurs, stereotypes, and student interventions: Examining the dynamics, impact, and prevention of harrassment in middle and high school. *Journal of Social Issues, 62*(3), 511–532.

Whitehead, S. M., & Barrett, F. J. (2001). The sociology of masculinity. In S. M. Whitehead & F. J. Barrett (Eds.), *The masculinities reader* (pp. 1–26). Malden, MA: Blackwell.

27

"With allies like these . . ."

Toward a sociology of straight allies

Patrick R. Grzanka

I was straight when I first started seeing Human Rights Campaign (HRC) equality logo stickers around my suburban Washington, DC college campus. I did not understand what they were or signified then, in the early 2000s. And though I quickly became familiar with the HRC and their version of equality politics—what Lisa Duggan (2003) termed "Equality, Inc."—as I became queer, this knowledge did not clarify for me exactly what the increasingly ubiquitous blue and yellow equal sign actually meant. Sometimes it signaled sexual orientation identity, but certainly not always. Indeed, if the equality stickers had actually meant "I'm queer and/or trans," then I would guess that approximately half of the University of Maryland's student body was LGBT+[1] identified. Much of the time, maybe even *most* of the time, the stickers were used by straight and cisgender people to indicate something about their view of LGBT+ people, including their support for marriage equality or civil rights. On car windshields, laptops, water bottles, and office doors, the stickers did the work of saying "I'm with you, but not one of you." Goffman (1956) might have called the stickers props in the performance of liberal cis-heterosexuality. When straight and cisgender people display them, the stickers manifest a well-intentioned, interactive gesture that functions as a kind of impression management and identity work: I want you to know that I support you. I didn't have the word for it then, but 20 years later, the word that comes to mind is "ally."

Along with Safe Zone stickers, which indicate that whoever occupies that space (i.e., office, dormitory room) has completed a few hours of training on LGBT+ issues, the HRC stickers strike me as a fairly integral part of the emergence of contemporary "straight allies" in the United States. While heterosexual- and cisgender-identified individuals have been involved in social movements for LGBT+ equality since the creation of the modern social category of "homosexual" (Sullivan 2003), the identity of straight allies is a more recent, culturally emergent social identity and label (Grzanka et al. 2015). And while there has been sustained academic interest in straight allies, particularly among psychologists, less attention has been paid in the literature to the structural and cultural conditions that (do not) engender straight allies, as well as the actual *social practices and formations* of allyship. Moreover, like much of the academic work on White allies, the scholarship on straight allies generally takes a psychological frame that emphasizes the role of pro-LGBT attitudes (i.e., less homonegativity than other straight people) and behavior (i.e., voting), as opposed to power, history, and the structural dynamics that co-produce, modify, and sustain the meaning of straight allyship. Yet myriad questions remain about the spaces that allies inhabit, the consequences of their behaviors and political organizing, and ways that straight ally practices may change the meanings and matterings of heterosexualities *and* queer sexualities in the twenty-first century.

In order to advance empirical and critical inquiry into straight allyship, I argue that we need a strong research program in the sociology of straight allies. In this chapter, I offer a critical survey of the extant empirical and theoretical work on straight allies in the social sciences—a state of the field, so to speak—and then pivot to a proposal for a critical sociology of straight allies. Drawing on Pascoe's (2013) parallel critique of psychological and *psychologizing* research on bullying, I suggest that a critical sociology of straight allies might attend (1) to the historical and structural dimensions of ally identity emergence, rather than (merely) attitudinal and behavioral antecedents; (2) the dynamic and contested nature of ally *and* heterosexual or straight identities in the twenty-first century but also across historical and transnational inquiry; and (3) intersectionality, particularly the co-constitution of racism, sexism, cissexism, classism, and heterosexism, and the diverse ways that straight allies are situated at the nexus of various social forces. While I do not imply that sociology offers the exclusive or even most valuable disciplinary perspective through which to investigate allyship (cf. Russell and Bohan 2016), I do contend that a sociological lens could sensitize scholarly inquiry on allies to contextual, political, and structural factors without which straight allyship can be reduced to attitudes and behaviors, rather than a particular, historical social formation entailing its own meaning-making practices for allies themselves.

What allies are

Social scientific research on straight allies draws upon theories specific to allyship that might be conceptualized as applied social research, as well as broader theories of social processes that posit ally behavior as exemplifying more universal or "basic" processes of collective action. In the vein of applied social research, Broido's (2000) model of allyship is among the most influential. Derived from in-depth interviews with six straight, White, cisgender, students who first engaged in ally practices during college, Broido's framework is strongly influenced by the higher education and student affairs discourse in which her work is situated. Though Broido's schema certainly has a developmental component that offers insight into how allies come into their allyship, her work also sketches what allies are. She defines allies as individuals who first have encountered people and ideas who are different from them and who have become motivated through this contact to do social justice work on behalf of members of a stigmatized group, typically—in the context of undergraduate education in the United States—people of color, women, and sexual and gender minorities. Her theory suggests that members of dominant groups may encounter difference in identity, experience, and thought during college and, if these experiences are nurtured and sustained, may result in a lifetime commitment to social justice work. Though based on limited data, Broido's work suggests a kind of analytic generalizability (Luker 2008) by offering an explanatory framework of what catalyzes allyship. Nonetheless, as a result of her developmentally focused research questions, Broido's (2000) model offers less about what allies actually are and more about how they become committed to social justice work. The vagueness of the actual content of allyship in Broido's model may indeed contribute to some of its popularity.

The circumstances that Broido (2000) describes—encountering perspectives that challenge your own, engaging in perspective taking, and changing attitudes—has, of course, long been the target of psychological research on intergroup contact, attitude transformation, and collective action. Various social psychology paradigms suggest underlying mechanisms of intergroup processes, social cognition, and identity work that catalyze and buttress allyship. Wilkinson and Sagarin (2010) used the theory of planned behavior to examine predictors of ally behavior. Swank and Fahs (2012, 2013) have used collective action frames and identity work and management as guiding theoretical principles to understand (predictors of) allyship, notably drawing upon explanatory frameworks that are not limited to the study of allyship. Nonetheless, much of the ally research that draws upon existing social psychological theory seeks to understand how individuals become allies; less work has investigated what happens once people become allies, including the subjective meaning-making straight allies practice to determine what constitutes allyship.

Psychologists have offered some insight into the consequences of allyship for straight people. For example, Rostosky and colleagues (2015) surveyed nearly 300 straight allies via LGBT+ social media and used thematic analysis to generate the positive, prosocial results of allyship for allies themselves. Their participants elaborated a range of benefits including increased knowledge of gender and sexuality issues, reward for speaking out against injustice, heightened awareness of their own privilege, and belonging in the LGBT community. Notably, a minority of respondents articulated a sexuality- and gender-"blind" perspective (à la color-blind racial ideology) by stressing how LGBT people are just like straight people. Rostosky et al. position their work as unique for their focus on the positive dimensions of allyship in contrast with the majority of work on straight people that focuses on changing their negative, homophobic attitudes. However, among the straight allies scholarship, their work exemplifies two common themes: (1) focusing on positive dimensions of allyship for allies, as opposed to for LGBT people, and (2) collapsing or conflating allyship to sexual and gender minorities whereby straight ("heterosexual") allies are automatically or implicitly framed as (cisgender) allies to transgender people.

From a quantitative psychological perspective, Jones and Brewster (2014) created a psychometric tool to measure ally identities organized around three interrelated concepts: knowledge and skills, openness and support, and oppression awareness. Sample items included "I am comfortable being openly identified as an ally to LGBT individuals" and "I am aware of the sexual minority rights movement in the United States, and its role in increasing equality for sexual minority groups." In a follow-up study, Jones and Brewster (2017) defined an ally as "a cisgender heterosexual person who recognizes the impact of discrimination on LGBT groups, aligns themselves with political and social groups that challenge systematic oppression, and serves the needs of sexual and gender diverse populations through social action and activism," expressly noting this kind of ally is cisgender and engages in activism (p. 680). Using similar quantitative survey methods, Goldstein and Davis (2010) reported that undergraduate gay-straight alliance members (N = 46) had prior intergroup contact, exposure to sexual prejudice, endorsed of positive stereotypes, and believed sexual orientation is immutable, i.e., "born this way"-type ideology. Notably, a third of their respondents, most of whom were non-religious liberal White women, were unsure of whether gay men and lesbian women experience workplace discrimination, and less than half had ever attended an "LGBT event" off campus; however, those who did engage in activism to reduce sexual prejudice were also likely to engage in efforts to reduce sexism and racism, suggesting a kind of global if not necessarily intersectional understanding of social inequality.

In an interview study with straight allies recruited from social media—in particular, those who had made "It Gets Better" videos, a video campaign started by sex columnist Dan Savage to promote hope that life improves for LGBT+ youth in adulthood (Grzanka and Mann 2014)—my colleagues and I found that allies did not share a common definition of their ally identities (Grzanka et al. 2015). Instead, in the context of our interviews, they engaged in a practice we termed "identity choreography," the functional construction of an identity category based on their own subjective life histories, emotions, and political activities (or lack thereof). Participants distinguished between "active" and "passive" allies by suggesting that passive allies merely signal political affinity with LGBT+ people, whereby active allies engage in behaviors and activities that seek to affirm LGBT+ people and fight sexual prejudice. Our participants articulated a range of emotions associated with allyship, including negative affect, such as feeling uncomfortable in their roles as allies, and a diversity of experiences that led them to allyship and to their personal understanding of what motivates heterosexist and homophobic attitudes. We did not find, however, that privilege was a theme in our interviews, because participants spoke more about roles as supporters of LGBT+ people than as unfairly privileged straight and cisgender people. We used identity choreography to describe the practices through which our self-identified allies "made up" the meaning of allyship, rather than strictly inheriting the qualifications and responsibilities of allyship from broader cultural norms or scripts. In other words, the concept of "straight allies" was a deeply emergent and contested construct. In light of the diverse and divergent understandings expressed by respondents across various studies of allyship, it seems that we ought to think of the plural "allies" as denoting not only multiple people, but also multiple forms of allyship.

Where allies come from

A distinctive element of social science research on straight allies is a focus on the antecedents of allyship (see Toomey and McGeorge [2018] for a helpful overview). I suggest this focus reveals at least two underlying assumptions: first, that straight allies are good for LGBT+ people and society at-large, therefore we should want more of them; and, second, that creating more allies is more important than what they actually do or do not do. This work has neither generally determined a relationship between allies' attitudes and beliefs nor explored the meaning-making practices of allies' behaviors and identities. In other words, research has produced insufficient evidence to claim that attitudes toward sexual minorities come to serve as the basis of allyship, or whether participation in ally behavior, groups, or trainings produces positive attitudes toward sexual and gender minorities. Further, intersectional perspectives suggest an even more complex nexus of attitudes, behavior, and identities, whereby activism and allyship are influenced by membership in one or more socially marginalized or stigmatized groups (Curtin et al. 2016; LeMaire and Oswald 2016).

Generally cross-sectional, the data on straight allies illuminate correlations between experiences, attitudes, beliefs about sexual and gender minorities, and a range of behaviors associated with allyship. This is not necessarily a "limitation" insomuch as these relationships need not be conceptualized as linear or sequential. For example, Swank and Fahs (2013) asked what motivated straight social work students (N = 159) to engage in electoral activism and protest behaviors. They found that key predictors of such behavior were educational attainment, interaction with other activists, recognizing heterosexism, and a commitment to social justice. Scheer and Poteat (2016) similarly examined why straight high school students (N = 156) across multiple high schools became involved in GSAs; they found that the strongest predictors of GSA involvement were current LGBT friends, as well as positive feelings at initial GSA meetings.

In addition to positive feelings, gender and negative emotions appear to play some role in the production of allies for LGBT people. Calcagno (2016) explored how gender, collective guilt, and close friendships with LGBs may prompt collective action among straight people. She found an indirect effect of gender whereby straight women with close LGB friendships were significantly more likely to engage in collective action in response to straight guilt than were straight men (see also Russell 2011). Likewise, Fingerhut (2011) found that gender predicted ally behavior, which he operationalized as behaviors including donating money for LGBT causes. He also found that those with more education and more gay and lesbian friends were more likely to be allies. However, empathy did not predict alliance in Fingerhut's sample, though prejudice did negatively predict alliance. Similarly, in an experimental study, Perrin and colleagues (2014) did not find an effect across conditions but did observe a strong relationship between social justice attitudes of LGBT prejudice, which was qualified by a gendered interaction: women were more likely to possess social justice attitudes and exhibit less prejudice than men. Affect played a substantial role in the lives of the 12 straight individuals who participated in Duhigg et al.'s (2010) interview study. Emotional reactions to recognizing their own privilege were a typical theme in their analysis and included feelings of sorrow, anger, and guilt. In contrast to the participants we interviewed (Grzanka et al. 2015), these allies found that recognizing oppression and privilege as straight people was essential to their ally development and was deeply emotional (see also Eichler 2010). Empathy was a recurring theme in Stotzer's (2009) interviews with a large sample of 68 undergraduate students, most of whom were White women. Indeed, Stotzer posited "an encounter with a peer that elicited an empathetic response" as the most common event that shaped her respondents' attitudes toward LGB people (p. 74). But Stotzer also expressly studied the development of *attitudes* toward LGB people—not ally identities or behaviors. On the other hand, Asta and Vacha-Haase's (2013) interviews with straight psychologists and trainees ($N = 12$; 10 women) did not find empathy played a role in the development of their participants' ally identities (cf. Gonzalez et al. 2015). However, their participants did report the influence of positive reinforcement from others in sustaining their ally work.

Other research theorizes ally identity development as an emotional journey undergirded by political convictions. Beginning with an introspective analysis of his own ally identity development (Ji 2007), Ji and colleagues explored dimensions of ally development in the context of a structured institutional setting designed to promote pro-LGBT+ attitudes and behavior, such as an actual academic course on ally development (Ji et al. 2009). Their findings suggest that (predictably) students were initially hesitant but grew more confident in their allyship through exposure and interaction with LGBT people and issues. Ji and Fujimoto (2013) developed an ally identity measure (the "Ally Identity Development" scale) based on their earlier work (Ji et al. 2009), which specified an ally identity development journey through the cultivation of knowledge about and positive attitudes toward LGBT people, development of ally skills, identification as an LGBT ally, and ultimately positive interpersonal feedback for ally work. Their 53-item instrument encompasses both intrapsychic/interpersonal dimensions (e.g., "Others think of me as an ally to the LGBT community") and actual behavior (e.g., "I am a part of a group where I have a role as LGBT ally"). Their findings are at least partially supported by Jones and Brewster's (2017) investigation of antecedents of LGBT activism, in which they found (using their own scale, the Ally Identity Measure [Jones and Brewster 2014]) that a mixture of perceived self-efficacy, identification as an ally, education level, and expectation of outcomes predicted activism (as opposed to simply awareness of LGBT social issues). Meanwhile, empathetic perspective taking was not related to LGBT activism among Jones and Brewster's respondents ($N = 207$), nor was positive marginality, which they operationalized as experiencing other forms of identity-based discrimination, such as sexism or racism. Further, they found environmental factors accounted for a relatively small amount of variance among predictors of LGBT activism in contrast to other work that emphasized the role of institutional settings in engendering allyship (e.g., Toomey and McGeorge 2018). For example, Swank and Fahs (2012) reported that among both sexual minority and straight college students ($N = 820$), environmental and interpersonal factors were equally predictive of LGBT activism, including peers' political orientations and personal connections with activists, as were personal dimensions, such as the ability to recognize heterosexism and maintaining an activist identity (see also Swank et al. 2013).

Consistent with the theory of planned behavior (TPB), Wilkinson and Sagarin (2010) found intentions and others' perceptions of allyship predicted allies' behaviors. That is, the straight, cisgender undergraduate students (N = 237) were motivated to support the LGB resource center if they thought it mattered, that others would think such support was a good thing, and if they imagined their allyship to be an important part of their identity. Although Wilkinson and Sagarin focus on psychological precursors to supportive behavior, these constructs are deeply interactional (Poteat 2015) and stress the degree to which pro-LGB behavior may be situationally contingent and constituted by self-construal and imagined others—consistent not only with the TPB but with sociological perspectives, such as symbolic interactionism, which I return to below. Their results are similar to those of Swank et al. (2013), who found heterosexuals' electoral activism (i.e., support for a petition for LGBT employment protection) was strongly influenced by "framing variables," including attitudes toward LGBT issues, political identity, comfort disclosing sexual identity, and a sense of personal efficacy. Indeed, the effects of these variables on support for protections from employment discrimination for LGBT people were twice as strong for straight, cisgender respondents (n = 1,707) than for LGBT respondents (n = 367); even the consistently observed gender differences in straight allyship disappeared when accounting for these framing variables, further highlighting the importance of these interactional, social psychological factors.

In a similar vein, Wilkinson and Sagarin (2010) and Swank et al. (2013) measured ally behavior via a relatively low-risk behavior, i.e., supporting a petition. Their work leaves unanswered questions about the degree to which the TPB may explain more active, high-risk behaviors, such as bystander interventions or sustained activism for LGB people. Meanwhile, Russell's (2011) widely cited paper presents grounded theory-based findings from 127 interviews with visible straight activists conducted over 17 years and concludes that convictions and life histories are key self-reported motives. Among Russell's highly engaged activists, fundamental principles, such as social justice and morals, paired with personal life experiences, such as relationships and the transformation of guilt, were the foundation for their collective action in the interest of LGBT rights. Notably, Russell's empirically impressive work is one of the few I found that examined allies who were engaged in extensive activism (as opposed to ally attitudes) and stressed the role of social movements and collective action, rather than individual convictions or voting behavior.

What allies do

In contrast to research that catalogues what motivates individuals to become allies as well as their distinguishing features, some popular and academic writing examines and critiques what allies actually do. In particular, popular and social media, including activist- and social justice-oriented websites and blogs, have offered far more critical accounts of allyship than the bulk of academic literature on allies. For example, author Mia McKenzie's (2013) well-circulated treatise on White allies, aptly titled "No more 'allies,'" is an argument against the notion that ally-status is a category to be inhabited much less celebrated:

> It's not supposed to be about you. It's not supposed to be about your feelings . . . It's not supposed to be a *performance*. It's supposed to be a way of living your life that *doesn't* reinforce the same oppressive behaviors you're claiming to be against.

McKenzie suggests "currently in solidarity with," as opposed to the term "ally," to describe actions in the present, rather than past or imagined future behavior. She rejects the linguistic construction of ally as a label or identity. "It's a practice," she writes. "It's an active thing that must be done over and over again, in the largest and smallest ways, *every day*" [emphasis in original]. If fighting intersectional oppression daily sounds exhausting to readers, she suggests "Maybe how exhausted you are is a good measure of how well you're doing the work."

While writers such as McKenzie criticize the self-importance of those who take on ally identities, sociologists Brodyn and Ghaziani (2018) likewise investigate how liberal-identified straight people, in integrating (i.e., gentrifying) historically gay neighborhoods or "gayborhoods," deploy strategies to manage interactions with their sexual minority neighbors. In one of the more critical assessments of straight allies or ally-adjacent straight people in the academic literature, Brodyn and Ghaziani elaborate Ghaziani's (2014) multidimensional concept of "performative progressiveness." Their qualitative investigation, based in Chicago's Boystown and Andersonville neighborhoods, suggests a disjuncture between well-rehearsed scripts echoing pro-equality sensibilities and conservative and homonegative behaviors "on the ground" (p. 309). Highlighting the social psychological adages that attitudes are (often) a poor predictor of behaviors and that quantitative assessment of such attitudes therefore indicate less about behavior than one might suspect, they document affective and behavioral strategies liberal-identified straight people use to reproduce heteronormativity in previously gay-dominant spaces.

In detailing the "spatial expressions of community life," Brodyn and Ghaziani (2018) posit a four-part typology. First, they document expressions of spatial entitlements, in which straight people subtly reiterate their assumed control of urban space, for example, once gay and lesbian developers have proverbially "cleaned up" the neighborhood. Second, they offer evidence of rhetorical moves, in which straight people accept certain kinds of homonormative gay and lesbian expression and embrace *sexual*, but not racial, ethnic, or class, "diversity." By moving into spaces dominated by (middle class and wealthy, White) sexual minorities, (White) straight people use linguistic maneuvers to suggest that they (i.e., straight people) are the victims of marginalization. These rhetorical practices elide the materiality of power dynamics and open the door for claims of "reverse discrimination" by sexual minorities against straight people. Brodyn and Ghaziani note that claims of reverse discrimination work to undermine the ability of queer people to claim queer cultural spaces as their neighborhoods.

Consonant with other research on diversity and gentrification (Maher 2015), Brodyn and Ghaziani also elaborate the political indifference and inaction of straight residents who suggest that living in gay neighborhoods constitutes efficacious allyship in and of itself (see Grzanka et al. [2015] re: "passive allies"). Finally, like Grzanka et al. (2015), Brodyn and Ghaziani identify the affective dimensions of performative progressiveness, underscoring the logic straight residents used to demand emotional labor from gay and lesbian residents. Straight people in their sample want gay people to (a) be "happy" about straight people's perception of political progress for sexual equality, and (b) stop being "angry" about queer objections to straight people's presence in queer spaces (e.g., bachelorette parties in gay bars).

I suggest that a central element of performative progressiveness is sexual neoliberalism (Grzanka et al. 2016), in which any structural imagination that might explain complex and conflictual neighborhood dynamics is effaced by individuating narratives of choice-making *except when* straight people wish to make broad claims about gay and lesbian people. In other words, Brodyn and Ghaziani's (2018) performative progressiveness (see also Ghaziani [2014]) is ironically bidirectional: their straight participants interpret examples of gay and lesbian disadvantage as evidence of individuals' poor decision-making but also attribute conflict in gayborhoods to sociological forces, including queer people's occasional unwillingness to acquiesce to straight people's demands for a post-identity urban landscape. Brodyn and Ghaziani's critique sits across an epistemic chasm from the psychological research I have surveyed, which documents pro-LGBT+ attitudes and explicitly advocates the production of these attitudes as the key to social justice for sexual and gender minorities.

Research in applied psychology and related fields (i.e., higher education, student affairs and college student development) consistently advances an empirically based (both qualitative and quantitative) argument that (self-identified) straight allies do meaningful, consequential work on behalf of cisgender LGB and sometimes trans people. But these data are almost always self-reported and retrospective, as opposed to external or objective assessments of the consequences of straight people's actions on the lives of LGBT+ people. This means that much of what we know about straight allies is rooted in straight allies' subjective assessments of themselves, or even other straight people's perceptions of allies (Goldstein 2017; cf. Brown and Ostrove 2013). For example, in a study of student affairs professionals involved in an LGB-related professional network, DiStefano and colleagues (2000) used an open-ended survey to qualitatively document straight allies' experiences. Their respondents (N = 87) most frequently cited LGB-affirmative programming or training as their regular ally activities, which is unsurprising given the population (student affairs professionals); they also noted signage, such as stickers and books in their offices. They expressed positive emotions about their ally work, including feeling proud of themselves. But they also admitted to not always behaving as an ally, because ally work is "exhausting" and it is not always the "best times" to act (p. 137). The researchers do not investigate if and how these allies may have experienced constructive criticism, rejection, or negative feedback from LGB people for their ally work, nor did they report participants' articulation of how they have come to believe their ally work actually impacts LGB people or results in positive social transformation. Consonant with Grzanka et al.'s (2015) findings, straight allies were inclined to talk about the feelings of allyship, as opposed to its contexts and consequences.

Likewise, Gonzalez et al. (2013) surveyed a large group of parents (N = 142) with LGBTQ children and found parents generally reported positive outcomes, some of which are consistent with positive dimensions of virtually any close relationship, such as personal growth, social connection, and closeness. However, Gonzalez et al. did find many parents reported increased perspective taking, pride, and even activism. A substantial minority (one-third) said they engaged in activist behavior, including involvement in PFLAG, political advocacy, and providing social support for other parents. Consistent with other findings (i.e., DiStefano et al. 2000) and themes in the broader literature, these positive dimensions of allyship were articulated in terms of how they were positive *for allies,* as opposed to for LGBT+ people. Gonzalez et al.'s work is corroborated by Johnson and Best's (2012) ethnographic observations of PFLAG meetings and events, but their methods enable them to reveal a dynamic potentially obscured by retrospective self-report. Johnson and Best conclude from their participants that these parents reluctantly engage in LGBTQ activism (e.g., marching in Pride parades) and are motivated by traditional social norms. They conclude that their participants are "radical normals," who seek to embody idealized family dynamics—including the social role of supportive, loving parents—and so manifest activism as a way to produce this role. Notably sociological in their approach, they frame parents' development as activists in terms of the symbolic interactionist concept of "moral career," and they consider straight and cisgender parents' social activism around LGBT+ issues to be a form of functional identity work (see also Broad 2011; Broad et al. 2004; Fields 2001; Ryan et al. 2013).

A large and empirically ambitious body of research on gay-straight alliances (GSAs) has further substantiated notions of positive outcomes for straight allies in these kinds of groups, even as outcomes for LGBT+ youth are mixed (Toomey et al. 2011). A distinction of this work, however, is that GSAs are not ally-exclusive groups, so some research reports positive outcomes for both LGBTQ youth and their cisgender heterosexual allies. For example, Poteat et al. (2018) found, among 295 youth in 33 different GSAs, the relationships between GSA involvement and greater civic engagement, LGBTQ advocacy activities, and awareness raising did not differentiate according to sexual orientation or gender identity. Their work draws upon "positive youth development" models, which position GSAs as groups that help to promote civically engaged youth. Lapointe's (2015) qualitative interviews with five Canadian GSA members similarly positions GSA involvement as generally positive, but also uses her participants' experiences to argue that these groups alone are insufficient for transforming school climates. Lapointe's conclusions mirror Mayberry's (2013) earlier qualitative findings that GSA participants and school administrators perceive the groups to be psychologically empowering but constricted in their ability to catalyze systemic resistance of heteronormativity within education settings. Using an advanced statistical technique called latent profile analysis (Grzanka 2016), Toomey and McGeorge (2018) likewise observed that student athletes ($N = 159$) were more likely to be engaged (but not visible, per se) LGBTQ allies when they perceived that their coaches held more supportive attitudes. Intuitively, they also found that athletes were more likely to be highly engaged and visible allies when they possessed social justice beliefs, though their cross-sectional data did not allow them to determine whether allyship encouraged these beliefs or vice versa.

Ethnographic research on LGBTQ advocacy groups and organizations consistently unsettles the more uniformly positive conclusions drawn from interviews and self-report measures. Mathers et al. (2018) report findings from Mathers's year of ethnographic fieldwork in a Southeastern US LGBTQ advocacy group composed of straight, cisgender allies and LGBTQ members, nearly all of whom were White. Opening their work with a scene in which a lesbian-identified group leader proposed changes to the group's by-laws that would require a heterosexual-identified co-president, Mathers and colleagues explore the subtle and often well-intentioned ways in which heterosexuality (and, really, cis-heteronormativity) are reproduced and re-centered through everyday dynamics in the group, "Allied Pride." Though the group's stated agenda is LGBTQ advocacy, Mathers found the practical activities of the group focused on parents of LGBTQ children. Like the participants described in Grzanka et al. (2015) and Johnson and Best (2012), the allies in Mathers et al.'s (2018) Allied Pride group engaged in definitional work about allyship that "sanctified" allies and valorized heterosexuals' efforts to support LGBTQ people absent self-interest. For example, they describe how group members saw parents of LGTBQ people as having a "biased investment" in LGBTQ equality, as opposed to those heterosexuals who were involved sans a personal or "emotional" investment in LGBTQ people (p. 850). Because these straight allies would not want to intrude on LGBTQ spaces or organizations, Allied Pride was regularly positioned as a heterosexual group: the involvement of heterosexual people constituted the group's identity in terms of heterosexuality. And while straight allies were constantly being praised for what they did (or did not) do, Mathers and colleagues found that—like must of the research on straight allies—there was little specific evidence of what straight allies *do*:

> ze began asking group members what role allies played in the group or in the push for sexual equality. In so doing, ze discovered that both allies and other members typically stressed what allies "could do," but offered very few examples of things they actually did.
>
> *(p. 851)*

When questioned, straight allies cited kindness toward sexual and gender minorities, as well as displaying pro-LGBTQ stickers and buttons, as regular ally activities; conversely, they appeared to have well-rehearsed explanations for why they had *not* acted in certain contexts, such as telling LGBTQ friends to not express their identities around heterosexist and transphobic relatives. In sum, the allies in Mathers's study reflected academic research's failure to delineate much of what ally behavior is in exchange for extensive writing about ally identities and the benefits of allyship for straight people.

Analytic priorities for a sociology of straight allies

I have identified several key themes in the published literature on straight allies, much of which takes a psychological approach and prioritizes the antecedents of allyship, which are usually operationalized as ally identities or positive attitudes toward LGB(T) people. While there is nothing inherently problematic about psychological investigations into allyship *or* an emphasis on identities and attitudes, my review suggests several ways in which the existing archive of academic research on straight allies might be enhanced and extended by a more thoroughly sociological theoretical and methodological framework. As Russell and Bohan (2016) noted, discussions (academic and otherwise) of straight and cisgender ally activism "have been characterized by an unreservedly positive view of both the process by which such activism occurs and the change potential it embodies" (p. 335). However, some of the most promising, *critical* (i.e., especially sensitive to power) research in this area has already illustrated the potential dividends of a sociology of straight allies and allyship (e.g., Brodyn and Ghaziani 2018; Mathers et al. 2018). This work has exposed how what self-identified straight and cisgender allies *actually do* in institutional and community contexts may be at least as important and a potentially far more consequential question than how one comes to self-identify as an ally. À la Pascoe's (2013) itinerary for a sociology of bullying, I conclude by sketching three domains or analytic priorities that might animate the sociology of straight allies, proposing work in this area pivot from an identitarian orientation toward a structural conceptualization of how straight and cisgender individuals negotiate power when interacting with LGBT+ people and communities across all levels (micro, meso, and macro) of social life.

A sociology of straight allies would situate allyship within historically and locally constituted power relations. Beyond cursory gestures to major events or legal decisions, psychological and psychology-adjacent work on allies has deeply undertheorized how allyship emerges historically and contextually, as well as psychically and behaviorally. Though the culturally and historically contingent dimensions of allyship are evident (e.g., see my observation about HRC stickers that began this chapter), academic inquiry into allyship has typically jettisoned such concerns for a universal or generalizable framing of ally identities, behaviors, and attitudes. Again, generalizability in and of itself is not problematic, but sociological inquiry should illuminate dimensions of allyship that possess what Luker (2008) distinguished as "analytic generalizability," as opposed to statistical generalizability. Brodyn and Ghaziani (2018) exemplify such an approach to analytic generalizability in their study of gentrifying gay neighborhoods. Whereas their work stops short of claiming generalizability, their theory of performative progressiveness offers an analytic device with which to think about other manifestations of straight liberalism and self-proclaimed progressive politics in other sites. Constructs like performative progressiveness may be less valuable to psychologists than sociologists, but these critical concepts capture contextual power dynamics in ways that surveys often do not. For example, the participants in Brodyn and Ghaziani's study would likely have scored relatively low on measures of sexual prejudice—especially when compared with straight people who don't live in gayborhoods. But their normative levels of prejudice are less materially consequential, find Brodyn and Ghaziani, than their meaning-making practices in the actual gayborhood. Their specific manifestations of performative progressiveness are in fact certainly *not* universal, but they reveal power dynamics that certainly manifest elsewhere, such as the contradiction between stated values (i.e., belief in LGBT equality) and behaviors (i.e., microaggressions against LGBT people, supporting anti-LGBT policies and practices).

An investment in the historicity of allyship should also beget empirical attention to the interactional nature of allyship and the extent to which even the apparently prevalent identity of "ally" is fundamentally dynamic. In my own work, I have argued that ally identities are deeply emergent and that allies engage in identity choreography to "make up" the content and boundaries of allyship (Grzanka et al. 2015). Mathers et al. (2018) take a similar approach to their ethnographic, symbolic interactionist-informed observations in a mixed-sexuality and gender identity-diverse activist organization. They found that straight and cisgender members were actually able to reproduce cis-heteronormativity while doing purportedly pro-LGBT+ work (see also Johnson and Best 2012). In contrast to psychologizing approaches that seek a taxonomic profile of allies, the sociology of allies would consider how straight allyship is co-produced through interactions with sexual and gender minorities and is more broadly reflective of the co-constitutive nature of hetero- and homo-sexualities (Dean 2014; Ward 2015). I suggest that scholars move beyond intergroup contact dynamics, which focus on how dominant group members' attitudes change when they interact with minority or stigmatized group members, to investigate how the meanings and practices of allyship are created through interactions with LGBT+ people. Like popular criticism of actual allyship (McKenzie 2013), the scholarship on allyship centers straight and cisgender subjectivities to the detriment of understanding how allyship is dependent upon sustained interpersonal, affective, and deeply political interactions with sexual and gender minorities. As Johnson and Best (2012) observed straight parents of queer children transforming their identities and parenting behaviors according to pro-LGBT+ politics *and* heteronormativity, the sociology of straight allies would take seriously the centrality of non-heterosexual, non-cisgender identities in the production of allyship. Important questions remain about how straight and cisgender individuals sustain their status as heterosexuals while engaging in allyship, including prominent activist work. Ward's (2015) important assertion that heterosexuality is as much a position as a set of behaviors or an identity is acutely relevant to the study of allies, who take on allyship to the potential detriment to their status as cisgender and straight. Further, the slippages in the existing literature with regard to the inclusion or naming of transgender people in ally work (i.e., LGB versus LGBT, straight ally versus straight + cisgender ally) further underscores the necessity of considering how conflations of trans and LGB experiences are both reflective and productive of allyship that retains a conceptual and political investment in heteronormativity and cisnormativity.

Russell and Bohan's (2016) call for research on allies that focuses less on individuals and more on the institutional dimensions of ally work portends a shift toward both a more structural *and* intersectional approach. Like Ray's (2019) recent observations about the racial nature of *all* organizations and the need for a racial theory of organizations—rather than a theory of how (some) organizations are racial—the literature on straight allies needs a deeper engagement with the institutional dimensions of allyship (see also history, above). Critical sensitivity to how allies become allies and do allyship within organizations likewise necessitates an intersectional imagination that recognizes how no institution is solely sexual, racial, or gendered. Indeed, the literature I surveyed in this chapter is almost exclusively the study of *White* straight allies, and yet the discourse on race is virtually nonexistent in the straight allies literature. Virtually none of the literature I reviewed even mentions the term intersectionality, with a few notable exceptions (e.g., Montgomery and Stewart 2012); none considers the Americanness of the work. Rather than merely diversify samples—though we should certainly do that—researchers should consider the intersectional nature of allyship, including how multiple systems of domination inform how people come (or not) into ally identities. Further, intersectional analyses may also elucidate how some forms of allyship may not be legible to dominant (i.e., White, American, middle-class) assessments of ally work. Moreover, intersectional perspectives can bring other relevant constructs to bear on the study of allyship, such as homonormativity (Duggan 2003) and homonationalism

(Puar 2007), that may facilitate specifying diverse manifestations of allyship, as well as documenting the racial, national, and class dimensions of dominant versions of allyship. Useful models already exist (Ward 2008), and an explication of various approaches to intersectionality is beyond the scope of this chapter (see Grzanka 2019); nonetheless, I insist that a sociology of straight allies be fundamentally intersectional so as to account for the relevance of race, class, gender, nation, and other intersecting dimensions of inequality in allyship.

Allyship after allies

In the popular discourse on dominant group allyship, there is a lot of anger toward allies (Richardson 2018), though you would not know it from academic literature. The literature on straight and cisgender allies, specifically, assumes that allies are the best versions of straight and cisgender people. But as I have attempted to outline here, a sociology of straight allies might help us to render allyship in structural relief. Like Pascoe's (2013) proposal for a sociology of bullying to intervene in psychologizing research that fixates on *some* kids who get bullied and some kids who *bully*, a sociology of straight allies would explore the increasingly normal production of allies amid the persistence of heteronormativity, cisgenderism, and sexual prejudice. What sense do we make of queer and trans people's frustration with allies even as straight people pursue allyship in diverse institutional and interpersonal settings? How do we reconcile ubiquitous equality stickers with the election of Donald J. Trump? And what good is allyship if straight allies are simultaneously racist, xenophobic, and transphobic (Duggan 2003)? The extant academic literature on straight allies provides an empirical foundation for thinking about what makes allies into allies and what they do once they become allies. Our next step is to consider what lies *beyond* allies, so that we can imagine coalitions and intersectional configurations of social justice work outside and without the binary of dominant and subordinate groups. How might ally models ironically limit how we conceptualize social justice work? Asking these questions is important not because we will necessarily abandon straight, cisgender allyship as an integral part of LGBT+ equality, but rather it's important because we should consider what kinds of knowledge and justice might happen without unwavering loyalty to what we already think we know. I still don't know exactly what those HRC equality stickers mean when straight, cisgender people use them. But I want to figure it out.

Note

1 In this chapter, I use LGBT+ purposefully to signal the relevance of this identity-based typology to the literature on straight allies; the "+" symbol acknowledges the limits of those four letters to capture many other non-heterosexual sexualities and non-cisgender gender identities. While "sexual and gender minorities" may be a more inclusive term, that language emerged in academic literature, as opposed to the social movements that are the subject of this chapter.

References

Asta, E.L. and Vacha-Haase, T. (2013) Heterosexual ally development in counseling psychologists: Experiences, training, and advocacy. *The Counseling Psychologist*, 41, 493–529. Available from: doi:10.1177/0011000012453174.

Broad, K.L. (2011) Coming out for parents, families and friends of lesbians and gays: From support group grieving to love advocacy. *Sexualities*, 14(4), 399–415. Available from: doi:10.1177/1363460711406792.

Broad, K.L., Crawley, S.L., and Foley, L. (2004) Doing "real" family values: The interpretive practice of "families" in the GLBT movement. *The Sociological Quarterly*, 45(3), 509–527. Available from: doi:10.1525/tsq.2004.45.3.509.

Brodyn, A. and Ghaziani, A. (2018) Performative progressiveness: Accounting for new forms of inequality in the gayborhood. *City and Community*, 17(2), 307–329. Available from: doi:10.1111/cico.12298.

Broido, E.M. (2000) The development of social justice allies during college: A phenomenological investigation. *Journal of College Student Development*, 41(1), 3–18.

Brown, K.T. and Ostrove, J.M. (2013) What does it mean to be an ally? The perception of allies from the perspective of people of color. *Journal of Applied Social Psychology*, 43(11), 2211–2222.

Calcagno, J. (2016) Transforming straight guilt into collective action for LGBs via close cross-group friendships: A gender-moderated process. *Psychology of Women Quarterly*, 40(3), 451–463. Available from: doi:10.1177/0361684315627362.

Curtin, N., Kende, A., and Kende, J. (2016) Navigating multiple identities: The simultaneous influence of advantaged and disadvantaged identities on politicization and activism. *Journal of Social Issues*, 72(2), 264–285. Available from: doi:10.1111/josi.1216.

Dean, J.J. (2014) *Straights: Heterosexuality in Post-Closeted Culture.* New York: New York University Press.

DiStefano, T., Croteau, J., Anderson, M., Kampa-Kokesch, S., and Bullard, M. (2000) Experiences of being heterosexual allies to lesbian, gay, bisexual people: A qualitative exploration. *Journal of College Counseling*, 3(2), 131–141.

Duggan, L. (2003) *The Twilight of Equality? Neoliberalism, Cultural Politics, and the Attack on Democracy.* Boston: Beacon Press.

Duhigg, J., Rostosky, S., Gray, B., and Wimsatt, M. (2010) Development of heterosexuals into sexual-minority allies: A qualitative exploration. *Sexuality Research and Social Policy*, 7(1), 2–14. Available from: doi:10.1007/s13178-010-005-2.

Eichler, M. (2010) Joining the family: Experiences of being and becoming ally activists of LGBTQ people. *Journal of Transformative Education*, 8(2), 89–102. Available from: doi:10.1177/1541344611406904.

Fields, J. (2001) Normal queers: Straight parents respond to their children's "coming out." *Symbolic Interaction*, 24(2), 165–187. Available from: doi:10.1525/si.2001.24.2.165.

Fingerhut, A.W. (2011) Straight allies: What predicts heterosexuals' alliance with the LGBT community? *Journal of Applied Social Psychology*, 41(9), 2230–2248. Available from: doi:10.1111/j.1559-1816.2011.00807.x.

Ghaziani, A. (2014) *There Goes the Gayborhood?* Princeton: Princeton University Press.

Goffman, E. (1956) *The Presentation of Self in Everyday Life.* New York: Random House.

Goldstein, S. (2017) Stigma and stigma by association in perceptions of straight allies. *Journal of LGBT Youth*, 14(4), 245–358. Available from: doi:10.1080/19361653.2017.1326867.

Goldstein, S. and Davis, D. (2010) Heterosexual allies: A descriptive profile. *Equity and Excellence in Education*, 43(4), 478–494. Available from: doi:10.1080/10665684.2010.505464.

Gonzalez, K., Riggle, E., and Rostosky, S. (2015) Cultivating positive feelings and attitudes: A path to prejudice reduction and ally behavior. *Translational Issues in Psychological Science*, 1(4), 372–381. Available from: doi:10.1037/tps0000049.

Gonzalez, K., Rostosky, S., Odom, R., and Riggle, E. (2013) The positive aspects of being the parent of an LGBTQ child. *Family Process*, 52(2), 325–337. Available from: doi:10.1111/famp.12009.

Grzanka, P.R. (2016) Queer survey research and the ontological dimensions of heterosexism. *WSQ: Women's Studies Quarterly*, 44(3–4), 131–149. Available from: doi:10.1353/wsq.2016.0039.

Grzanka, P.R. (Ed.) (2019) *Intersectionality: Foundations and Frontiers.* New York: Routledge.

Grzanka, P.R. and Mann, E.S. (2014) Queer youth suicide and the psychopolitics of "It Gets Better." *Sexualities*, 17(4), 363–393. Available from: doi:10.1177/1363460713516785.

Grzanka, P.R., Adler, J., and Blazer, J. (2015) Making up allies: The identity choreography of straight LGBT activism. *Sexuality Research and Social Policy*, 12(3), 165–181. Available from: doi:10.1007/s13178-014-0179-0.

Grzanka, P.R., Mann, E.S., and Elliott, S. (2016) The neoliberalism wars, or notes on the persistence of neoliberalism. *Sexuality Research and Social Policy*, 13, 297–307. Available from: doi:10.1007/s13178-016-0255-8.

Ji, P. (2007) Being a heterosexual ally to the lesbian, gay, bisexual, and transgendered community: Reflections and development. *Journey of Gay and Lesbian Psychotherapy*, 11(3–4), 173–185. Available from: doi:10.1300/J236v11n0310.

Ji, P. and Fujimoto, K. (2013) Measuring heterosexual LGBT ally development: A rasch analysis. *Journal of Homosexuality*, 60(12), 1695–1725. Available from: doi:10.1080/00918369.2013.834211.

Ji, P., Du Bois, S.N., and Finnessy, P. (2009) An academic course that teaches heterosexual students to be allies to LGBT communities: A qualitative analysis. *Journal of Gay and Lesbian Social Services*, 21(4), 402–409. Available from: doi:10.1080/10538720802690001.

Johnson, J. and Best, A. (2012) Radical normals: The moral career of straight parents as public advocates for their gay children. *Symbolic Interaction*, 35(3), 321–339. Available from: doi:10.1002/SYMB.23.

Jones, N. and Brewster, M. (2014) The creation and validation of the LGBT ally identity measure. *Psychology of Sexual Orientation and Gender Diversity*, 1(2), 181–195. Available from: doi:10.1037/sgd0000033.

Jones, N. and Brewster, M. (2017) From awareness to action: Examining predictors of lesbian, gay, bisexual, and transgender (LGBT) activism for heterosexual people. *American Journal of Orthopsychiatry*, 87(6), 680–689. Available from: doi:10.1037/ort0000219.

Lapointe, A. (2015) Standing "straight" up to homophobia: Straight allies' involvement in GSAs. *Journal of LGBT Youth*, 12(2), 144–169. Available from: doi:10.1080/19361653.2014.969867.

LeMaire, K. and Oswald, D. (2016) How gender affects heterosexual allies' intentions of confronting sexual prejudice. *Psychology of Sexual Orientation and Gender Diversity*, 3(4), 453–464. Available from: doi:10.1037/sgd0000190.

Luker, K. (2008) *Salsa Dancing through the Social Sciences*. Cambridge, MA: Harvard University Press.

McKenzie, M. (2013) No more "allies." *Black Girl Dangerous*. Weblog. Available from: www.blackgirldangerous.com/2013/09/no-more-allies/ [Accessed May 26, 2019].

Maher, J.T. (2015) The capital of diversity: Neoliberal development and the discourse of difference in Washington, DC. *Antipode*, 47(4), 980–998. Available from: doi:10.1111/anti.12136.

Mathers, L.A.B., Sumerau, J.E., and Ueno, K. (2018) "This isn't just another gay group": Privileging heterosexuality in a mixed-sexuality LGBTQ advocacy group. *Journal of Contemporary Ethnography*, 47(6), 834–864. Available from: doi:10.1177/0891241615578905.

Mayberry, M. (2013) Gay-straight alliances, youth empowerment and working toward reducing stigma of LGBT youth. *Humanity & Society*, 37(1), 35–54. Available from: doi:10.1177/0160597612454358.

Montgomery, S.A. and Stewart, A.J. (2012) Privileged allies in lesbian and gay rights activism: Gender, generation, and resistance to heteronormativity. *Journal of Social Issues*, 68(1), 162–177. Available from: doi:10.1111/j.1540-4560.2012.01742.x.

Pascoe, C.J. (2013) Notes on a sociology of bullying: Young men's homophobia as gender socialization. *QED: A Journal of GLTBQ Worldmaking*, 1(1), 87–104.

Perrin, P.B., Bhattacharyya, S., Snipes, D.J., Calton, J.M., and Heesacker, M. (2014) Creating lesbian, gay, bisexual, and transgender allies: Testing a model of privilege investment. *Journal of Counseling and Development*, 92(2), 241–251. Available from: doi:0.1002/j.1556-6676.2014.00153.x.

Poteat, V.P. (2015) Individual psychological factors and complex interpersonal conditions that predict LGBT-affirming behavior. *Journal of Youth and Adolescence*, 44(8), 1494–1507. Available from: doi:10.1007/s10964-015-0257-5.

Poteat, V.P., Calzo, J., and Yoshikawa, H. (2018) Gay-straight alliance involvement and youths' participation in civic engagement, advocacy, and awareness-raising. *Journal of Applied Developmental Psychology*, 56, 13–20. Available from: doi:10.1016/j.appdev.2018.01.001.

Puar, J.K. (2007) *Terrorist Assemblages: Homonationalism in Queer Times*. Durham, NC: Duke University Press.

Ray, V. (2019) A theory of racialized organizations. *American Sociological Review*, 84(1), 26–53. Available from: doi:10.1177/0003122418822335.

Richardson, C. (2018) With allies like these we don't need enemies. *Very Smart Brothas*. Weblog. Available from: https://verysmartbrothas.theroot.com/with-allies-like-these-we-dont-need-enemies-1822385301 [Accessed February 25, 2019].

Rostosky, S.S., Black, W.W., Riggle, E.D.B., and Rosenkrantz, D. (2015) Positive aspects of being a heterosexual ally to lesbian, gay, bisexual and transgender (LGBT) people. *American Journal of Orthopsychiatry*, 85(4), 331–338. Available from: doi:10.1037/ort0000056.

Russell, G.M. (2011) Motives of heterosexual allies in collective action for equality. *Journal of Social Issues*, 67(2), 376–393. Available from: doi:10.1111/j.1540-4560.2011.01703.x.

Russell, G.M. and Bohan, J. (2016) Institutional allyship and LGBT equality: Underlying processes and potentials for change. *Journal of Social Issues*, 72(2), 335–354. Available from: doi:10.1111/josi.12169.

Ryan, M., Broad, K., Walsh, C., and Nutter, K. (2013) Professional allies: The storying of allies to LGBTQ students on a college campus. *Journal of Homosexuality*, 60(1), 83–104. Available from: doi:10.1080/00918369.2013.735942.

Scheer, J. and Poteat, V. (2016) Factors associated with straight allies' current engagement levels within gay-straight alliances. *Journal of Applied Developmental Psychology*, 43, 112–119. Available from: doi:10.1016/j.appdev.2016.01.007.

Stotzer, R.L. (2009) Straight allies: Supportive attitudes toward lesbians, gay men, and bisexuals in a college sample. *Sex Roles*, 60(1–2), 67–80. Available from: doi:10.1007/s11199-008-9508-1.

Sullivan, N. (2003) *A Critical Introduction to Queer Theory*. New York: New York University Press.

Swank, E. and Fahs, B. (2012) Resources, social networks, and collective action frames of college students who join the gay and lesbian rights movement. *Journal of Homosexuality*, 59(1), 67–89. Available from: doi:10.1080/00918369.2011.614908.

Swank, E. and Fahs, B. (2013) Why do social work students engage in lesbian and gay rights activism? *Journal of Human Behavior in the Social Environment*, 23(1), 91–106. Available from: doi:10.1080/10911359.2013.740336.

Swank, E., Woodford, M., and Lim, C. (2013) Antecedents of pro-LGBT advocacy among sexual minority and heterosexual college students. *Sexuality Research and Social Policy*, 10(4), 317–332. Available from: doi:10.1007/s13178-0136-3.

Toomey, R. and McGeorge, C. (2018) Profiles of LGBTQ ally engagement in college athletics. *Journal of LGBT Youth*, 15(3), 162–178. Available from: doi:10.1080/19361653.2018.1453428.

Toomey, R.B., Ryan, C., Diaz, R.M., and Russell, S.T. (2011) High school gay-straight alliances (GSAs) and young adult well-being: An examination of GDA presence, participation, and perceived effectiveness. *Applied Developmental Science*, 15(4), 175–185. Available from: doi:10.1080/10888691.2011.607378.

Ward, J. (2008) *Respectably Queer: Diversity Culture in LGBT Activist Organizations*. Nashville: Vanderbilt University Press.

Ward, J. (2015) *Not Gay: Sex Between Straight White Men*. New York: New York University Press.

Wilkinson, W. and Sagarin, B. (2010) Psychological antecedents of heterosexuals' pro-gay activism behavior. *Journal of Homosexuality*, 57(7), 878–894. Available from: doi:10.1080/00918369.2010.494908.

Index